The Writing of American History

THE WRITING OF AMERICAN HISTORY

Revised Edition

By
Michael Kraus
and
Davis D. Joyce

UNIVERSITY OF OKLAHOMA PRESS : NORMAN AND LONDON

By Michael Kraus

Intercolonial Aspects of American Culture on the Eve of the Revolution
(New York, 1928)
A History of American History (New York, 1937)
(Coauthor), *William Hickling Prescott* (New York, 1943)
The Atlantic Civilization: Eighteenth Century Origins (Ithaca, N.Y., 1949)
The North Atlantic Civilization (Princeton, N.J., 1957)
The United States to 1865 (Ann Arbor, 1959)
Immigration: The American Mosaic (Princeton, N.J., 1966)
The Writing of American History (Norman, 1953; Revised Edition with
Davis D. Joyce, 1985)

By Davis D. Joyce

Edward Channing and the Great Work (The Hague, 1974)
History and Historians (Washington, D.C., 1983)
(Coauthor with Michael Kraus), *The Writing of American History*, Re-
vised Edition (Norman, 1985)

Library of Congress Cataloging in Publication Data

Kraus, Michael, 1901–
    The writing of American history.

    Bibliography: p. 415.
    Includes index.
    1. United States—Historiography. I. Joyce, Davis D., 1940–
II. Title.
E175.K75   1985   973'.072   84–40689
ISBN 0–8061–1519–X (cloth)
ISBN 0–8061–2234–X (pbk.)

3   4   5   6   7   8   9   10   11   12

for Carole
with all my love

Contents

Preface to the Revised Edition

I HAVE CHOSEN to reproduce below the preface to Michael Kraus's *History of American History*, published in 1937, as well as the preface to the original edition of this book, published in 1953, which was really a revision of *A History of American History*. The two prefaces taken together clearly set forth the author's intent. To avoid duplication I have omitted from Kraus's second preface the material that he simply carried over from the first.

The claim that Kraus made in those pages for his work's primacy in American historiography was well founded. Oscar Handlin, reviewing the first edition for the *American Historical Review* in 1954, acknowledged the work of 1937 as "the first full-length study of the development of American history." It "supplied a helpful factual framework," said Handlin, "at a time when historians in the United States were beginning to be aware of the problems of their historiography."

Although Handlin was somewhat critical of the version of 1953, it has long been accepted as one of the few truly standard works in its field. Indeed, only Harvey Wish's considerably different book, *The American Historian: A Social-Intellectual History of the Writing of the American Past*, published in 1960, is comparable in its attempt to cover the entire span of American historiography.

However, 1953, not long ago in history, was a very long time ago in the history of American historical writing. In other words, as the years have passed and the field has become ever more massive and complex, the need for a revision of Kraus's work has become increasingly evident. This is my effort to do that.

Several of Kraus's early chapters have stood the test of time surprisingly well. The closer to the present, of course, the more changes have been required, until, near the end, some material has been entirely eliminated, and several new chapters dealing with the period since World War II have been added. Kraus did consider the Progressive historians, but in several different places; I have grouped them here into a single chapter. The chapter on biography has been omitted, in part because of space limitations, but mostly because it seemed marginal to the general story of American historical writing. For purposes of consistency and continuity I have followed Kraus's approach and style as closely as possible.

For this edition a bibliography has been added. It is intended as a reasonably comprehensive guide to the major books on American historical writing. The works of the historians dealt with in the text are not included.

Michael Kraus approved my plan to revise his book. It has been an honor, an exciting challenge, and an incredibly difficult task. Surely in these days of diversity, complexity, crisis yet growth, and specializations within specializations, there is something to be gained from looking once again at the impressive overall history of American historical writing.

There are many people to thank when one writes a book; without them it simply would not be possible. To begin with, my wife, Carole, provided me with the necessary moral support all the way through this project. She must have tired of hearing about "Kraus," but she never said so. She also helped with proofreading. My comments here and the dedication are token efforts to show my appreciation.

Several of my former colleagues in the University of Tulsa helped read various chapters: William A. Settle, Jr., Thomas H. Buckley, Michael W. Whalon, Arlen L. Fowler, and Patrick J. Blessing. John S. Ezell, of the University of Oklahoma, also helped with this chore; he too deserves a special note of thanks here for the continuing interest he has taken in me since I completed my Ph.D. under his able supervision all those years ago. Finally, J. G. A. Pocock, of Johns Hopkins University, read some chapters; the summer I spent working with him in a seminar on British and American historical thought in the eighteenth century, sponsored by the National Endowment for the Humanities, broadened my mind in ways which I hope are evident in the book. Thanks to all of these for their help; any weak portions of this work probably resulted from my insistence on following my own bent rather than their advice.

Edwin B. Strong, Jr., when he was the dean of my college, was always supportive of my work and helped secure some financial assistance.

John N. Drayton, editor-in-chief at the University of Oklahoma Press, deserves special thanks. I also wish to thank the assistant editor, V. S. Brown, for her copyediting work.

DeCora Fowler, one of my graduate assistants, made a significant contribution to developing the bibliography. Last but by no means least, Starr Arning ably and patiently typed most of this massive manuscript; Mary Lou Baker typed portions of it as well. Typists rarely get enough credit; perhaps it is enough to state, quite bluntly, that I could not have typed it myself.

Thank you all.

DAVIS D. JOYCE

Chicago, Illinois

Preface to the First Edition (1953)

S TUDIES IN AMERICAN HISTORIOGRAPHY were relatively few until recently. . . . My volume *A History of American History* appeared in 1937. Later that same year *The Marcus W. Jernegan Essays in American Historiography*, edited by William T. Hutchinson, was published. Since then the number of studies in this field has rapidly increased and gives every promise of continued growth.

This book, though based on my original work, has been rewritten and expanded to carry the study to date. Since the materials are so voluminous, it was necessary to be selective; I have given scant attention to specialized histories . . . in order to concentrate on the writings that deal with American history in a comprehensive manner. Obviously, it was impossible to include in a single volume all works worthy of consideration; arbitrary choices had to be made, but I hope writings of fundamental importance have not been overlooked.

I wish to thank my colleague Professor Oscar Zeichner for reading a portion of the manuscript and making valuable suggestions. To my wife, Vera Edelstadt, I express gratitude for her aid.

MICHAEL KRAUS

New York City

Preface to A *History of American History* (1937)

A T VARIOUS TIMES in the past the development of American historical writing has been treated in summary fashion in leading periodicals such as *The Monthly Anthology* and the *North American Review*. (George Bancroft wrote an article in the latter in 1838.) On later occasions critical essays on historians were printed in Henry B. Dawson's *Historical Magazine*. Moses Coit Tyler included historians in his study of American literature. It was not, however, until J. Franklin Jameson published his sketch of American historical writing in 1891 that any satisfactory treatment of the subject appeared. Dr. Jameson's short study stopped before reaching the developments that occurred in the 1880s after which time some of our most important contributions were made. John Spencer Bassett also turned his attention to the subject, and published in 1917 *The Middle Group of American Historians,* which deals mainly with Sparks, Bancroft, and the archivist, Peter Force. Professor Marcus W. Jernegan's students at the University of Chicago have published a number of articles on historians in the *Mississippi Valley Historical Review.* Professor Arthur M. Schlesinger, in his stimulating *New Viewpoints in American History* (1922), dealt with some contributions of contemporary scholars in rewriting our history. But no survey of the whole field of American historical writing was available.

The need for such a volume became apparent to me when I was pursuing my graduate studies, and for more than a decade I kept the project before me—reading and sifting a great mass of materials. Finally I decided to include only those individuals who were influential in the creation of a tradition of historical scholarship and who have contributed most to the writing of American history in a comprehensive manner. Prescott, Motley, Lea, and other Americans who did not write on our history have been omitted. On the other hand, a few Europeans, because of their influence on the writing of our history, are discussed, for they unquestionably belong in a study of American historiography. Military, naval, constitutional, diplomatic, and religious histories are barely mentioned. I have omitted Alfred T. Mahan, who influenced international relations more than he did the writing of our history. Other historians have also been omitted because they did not fall properly within the scope of this book, but I hope I have included all those who fit into my design.

I am indebted to many of my colleagues in the History Department at the College of the City of New York who have aided me with their suggestions. Professor Nelson P. Mead and Professor Holland Thompson read portions of the material, and the entire manuscript benefitted from the suggestions of Dr. Henry David. Professor Harry A. Carman, of Columbia University, also read a large section of the manuscript, and his encouragement is deeply appreciated. I am especially indebted to Professor Allan Nevins, of Columbia University, who, despite his own busy schedule, always finds time to aid other scholars. He has been most generous and has made many valuable suggestions throughout the manuscript. I cannot easily express my gratitude for the patience and helpfulness of my wife, Vera Edelstadt, in bringing this book to completion.

MICHAEL KRAUS

Stony Point, New York

The Writing of American History

Convention has assigned the writing of history and the writing of historiography to separate categories. The distinction has tended to become more rigid in modern times; the difference appears to be less an indication of labor divided than of substance discriminated. A study of the influence of French civilization upon Frederick the Great, for example, is viewed as history; a study of the literature dealing with Frederick is classed as historiography.

The distinction is misleading. Not only is the historiographer a historian, but the historian is almost always a historiographer. The meaning of both words was once the same. Unless the historiographer regards himself simply as a chronicler or as a bibliographer, his methods, problems, and functions are identical. His purposes are also identical. . . .

The historian is perforce a critic; the historian of history is a critic of critics. . . . History is always written because history is always made. Historiography is always revised because history is constantly remade.

—Bert James Loewenberg, *American History in American Thought: Christopher Columbus to Henry Adams,* pp. 11–23.

CHAPTER 1

The Historiography of Exploration and Discovery

THE WRITING OF AMERICAN HISTORY began before there were any white American settlers; it began in Europe long before John Smith wrote his first chronicle of events in the Jamestown colony. This historical writing depicted the exploration and settlement of a world that had outgrown its European limitations, and it envisioned limitless fields to conquer. Sometimes it had the blustering quality of the successful Elizabethan adventurer, sometimes the pathos of quest defeated. Not until William Bradford wrote the *History of Plimoth Plantation* do we have a full-bodied narrative reciting the pleasures and pains of a transplanted people. To the end of the seventeenth century American historians were European emigrants or the sons of emigrants, and they were so near to the days of colonial foundation that they could not easily take the backward glance of the historian without also taking the forward view of the prophet; to them God had let His countenance shine upon the New World.

With the appearance of Cotton Mather's work we have American history by an American. Mather himself was one of the first to use the word "American." His contemporary, the Virginian Robert Beverley, was also a historian with a definite native stamp. This period of American historiography was almost exclusively regional in scope, and it continued so down to the Revolution. Only a very few writers took a comprehensive view of all the colonies, and they were not provincial born. Some work of genuine merit, even when measured by later standards, was produced in this colonial period. Such writers as Thomas Prince, Thomas Hutchinson, and William Stith developed a method of historical research that was of great significance in establishing a scholarly tradition.

The War of Independence pervaded much of American historical writing in the last quarter of the eighteenth century and the first six decades of the nineteenth. Although the great struggle took shape as a glorious epic in the minds of citizens of the young Republic, its poetry was not evident in the many prosaic treatments accorded it. Provincialism was still the hallmark of most historians; the histories of colonies had become the histories of states. Some individuals, however, such as Abiel Holmes and Timothy Pitkin, were now taking the whole of the American nation for their theme. Jared Sparks contributed the largest addition to the growing library of Revolutionary literature, but it was left for George Bancroft to transcend all other names in the popular historiography of the day. Bancroft, like his contemporaries William Hickling Prescott and John Lothrop Motley, belonged to the school of romantic historians who flourished in America and Europe in the midnineteenth century. Bancroft's history, in its eagerness to celebrate the virtues of democracy, shed an unreal halo over early America, attributing to it ideals of which the colonists were unconscious. But Bancroft, a spokesman for Jackson, was not alone in allowing a political bias to guide his pen. It should be remembered that the struggles between the Federalists and the anti-Federalists—Hamiltonians and Jeffersonians—were reflected for generations in the books of their ideological descendants.

After the 1870s American historical writing ceased to consider itself a branch of literature and claimed the exalted position given to those subjects called "scientific." The influence of Leopold von Ranke became paramount, and the German seminar was transplanted to the University of Michigan, Harvard, and Johns Hopkins. As yet the teaching of history and the writing of history were, in the main, distinct crafts. Skilled amateurs with a broad humanistic culture continued to contribute the larger part of our historical narratives as they had done before the Civil War, but within a short time this was no longer true. There were only eleven professors of history in the United States in 1880. Within two decades, however, their number had greatly increased, and they wrote history as well as taught it. The year 1884 was the *annus mirabilis*, marking the birth of the American Historical Association and the copyright of the first volume of Justin Winsor's *Narrative and Critical History of America*, the open sesame to American historical materials. In this period, too, the dazzling generalizations of Auguste Comte and Henry Thomas Buckle on the unfolding of civilization stirred imaginative Americans to seek clues to their own country's development. Charles Darwin and Herbert Spencer stimulated the intellectual world in all its phases, and American historical scholars quickly seized on so fruitful an insight as the theory of evolution.

A swarm of specialists now scoured the field and in limited surveys charted their small portions of American history. Some were courageous enough (and sufficiently long-lived) to take extended periods of our history, covering the whole of American territory. The strong bias of earlier writing was moderated and the content of the volumes changed. The glamour of war and the intricacies of politics shared space with, or were even shunted aside by, details of institutional developments.

Americans, like their European colleagues, turned to the history of civilization (*Kulturgeschichte*), and in John Bach McMaster's *History of the People of the United States*, whose first volume appeared in 1883, we have the real precursor of the social-history school in America. The vastness of collected materials soon made it almost impossible for a single individual to cover the whole of American history, and comprehensiveness could be achieved only by cooperative enterprise.

It is an old adage that we should study the past to understand the present. But we should also study the present to understand why contemporary historians interpret the past as they do. Our conception of the past has been molded by historians whose personal tastes have chosen particular episodes around which to fashion their stories. Actually events do not live on because of their occurrence; they live on because writers have re-created them. Deeds themselves are short-lived, and the memory of them depends upon the skill of the narrator. Paul Revere's ride, for example, was quickly vanishing from the records in the first half of the nineteenth century when Henry Wadsworth Longfellow snatched it from approaching oblivion and gave it a dramatic place in our history. The writer of prose was quick to catch the impulse communicated by the poet, and Revere now rides on in spirited passages in our narratives. We may well consider the personalities as well as the works of those who have written our history, for it is often through our knowledge of the historian that we can understand the history he has written.

As Dixon Ryan Fox once reminded us in his biography of the historian Herbert L. Osgood:

The man of action, the statesman, the soldier, the interpretative artist whose achievement passes in a moment, the musician, the great actor—such men need biographers to set down what they have done. But an annotated history needs no history, double record, as it is, of past events and of the process by which the truth about them has been found. And an historian's biography is not likely to make interesting reading, for his external life is not dramatic and one who watched him at his desk turning yellowed sheets of manuscript and printed record and then scribbling notes, relieved from time to time by little journeys to the book-shelf, would soon grow tired of a spectacle so drearily monotonous. The excitement of discovery, the pride of well-considered judgement, the baffling search for logical connection in the evidence, the pain of composition, cannot easily be made the subjects of a narrative; fortunately the reader may surmise them as he follows through the history.

Yet this reader's curiosity may not all be slaked by inference; he is likely to desire that the picture of the author which he forms in his mind's eye be filled in by a few external facts, so that he may see more clearly the man with whom he has to deal. Such is the purpose of these pages.[1]

The Norse Voyages

In medieval lore there was mention of a lost continent in the West and of islands in the Atlantic that had disappeared beneath the sea, but the earliest authentic references to voyages of Europeans to America were found in two Icelandic sagas, the *Saga of Eric the Red*, considered the more dependable source for the Norse voyages, and the *Vinland History of the Flat Island Book*. These works, as written down, were later than Adam of Bremen's *Description of the Northerly Lands* (ca. 1070). Adam, a writer on ecclesiastical history, had lived for a while at the court of the Danish king Svend Estridson, from whom Adam learned about "Vinland," its grapevines, and its wheat fields.[2]

The voyage of Leif, son of Eric, from Norway, and the discoveries that he made in the year 1000 were told in the *Saga of Eric the Red*: "Leif put to sea. . . . and came upon lands of which he had previously had no knowledge. There were self-sown wheat fields and vines growing there. There were also those trees there which are called mansur [maple]. . . . Some of the timbers were so large that they were used in building." The *Flat Island Book* said of the return: "A cargo sufficient for the ship was cut and when the spring came, they made their ship ready, and sailed away; and from its products Leif gave the land a name, and called it Wineland."[3]

In the *Saga of Eric the Red* we are told that "there began to be much talk at Brattahlid [Greenland] to the effect that Wineland the Good should be explored. . . . And so it came to pass, that Karlsefni and Snorri fitted out their ship, for the purpose of going in search of that country." In all, 160 men and women sailed southwestward. The Norsemen saw many wild beasts and a heavily wooded region which they called "Markland" [forest land]. . . . "They remained there that winter."

The Norse engaged in trade with the natives, whom they called "Skrellings." "It so happened, that a bull, which belonged to Karlsefni and his people, ran out from the woods, bellowing loudly. This so terrified the Skrellings, that they sped out to their canoes." When they came back, they were in a belligerent mood, and a battle followed, whereupon Karlsefni and his people "forthwith prepared to leave, and determined to return to their own country."

Historians differ on whether it was New England or farther north where Leif Ericson and Thorfinn Karlsefni landed. The number of people who went with Thorfinn and their comparatively elaborate preparation indicated that they were planning to stay. Apparently the hostility of the natives was too much of a handicap. The unexpected bellowing of a Norse bull, it has been amusingly suggested, delayed the settlement of America for five hundred years.[4]

The narratives of the Norsemen's adventures bear little relationship to the beginnings of historical writing in America after Columbus. Probably the final word on the subject, or at least all we need to know, is to be found in Samuel Eliot Morison's excellent and encyclopedic volume *The European Discovery of America: The Northern Voyages, A.D. 500–1600* (1971).

Discovering the New World

The Norse sagas, the earliest historical narratives of settlement in America, remained in manuscript for hundreds of years and were known only to a handful of scholars; in fact, Columbus's story was in print before that of the Norsemen. Not until the works of Spanish historians appeared did a continuous chain of narration begin to link up with our own day. Memories of adventure were still fresh when narrators wrote of the discovery and settlement of new lands, and their publications contained subject matter of unending novelty.

It was fortunate for American history that printing had already been developed when Columbus announced his discovery. The printed accounts informed numerous readers of the voyages made in the great era of exploration. Peter Martyr and Richard Hakluyt knew that they were privileged observers at the birth of the Atlantic community, and with great care they recorded the New World beginnings.

Peter Martyr, who might well be considered the first historian of the New World, was living in Spain when Columbus made known his discovery. From the first, Martyr was alive to its meaning. He wrote to a friend on October 20, 1494: "I have begun to write a work concerning this great discovery. If I am suffered to live I shall omit nothing worthy of being recorded. . . . At all events I shall supply the learned world, in undertaking the history of great things, with a vast sea of new material."[5]

The letters that Martyr wrote to his friends about the discoveries were at length elaborated into the chapters that formed his history, *De Orbe Novo*, which did not appear in its complete form until 1530. In addition to the firsthand information he received from the discoverers themselves, Martyr had access to official documents which enabled him to fill out important details in his narrative. His inclusion of fantastic items was no reflection on Martyr's worth as a historian, because for centuries after his death almost anything was believed of this "Western Hemisphere"—a phrase he originated.[6]

Of great significance in the historiography of the New World was the work of Bartolomé de las Casas, "Apostle of the Indies." In 1502, Las Casas went to Española (Haiti), where he performed a valuable missionary service to the Indians. His *Short Relation of the Destruction of the Indies* was a highly colored disclosure of the brutalities to the natives by Spaniards and other Europeans.

The work that associated Las Casas more directly with historians of America was the *Historia general de las Indias*, begun in 1527 while he was still living in Española. The book remained in manuscript form for over three centuries, but many scholars made use of it before its publication, and his history has continued to have great value for the student. Personally acquainted with many of the early discoverers, Las Casas had in his possession Columbus's papers and other documents which have since disappeared,[7] a storehouse for subsequent historians. He lived to complete the narrative only to 1520, but many students agree with Morison's estimate of Las Casas's work, that it was "a great and noble history. . . the one book on the history of America that I should wish to preserve if all others were destroyed."

Antonio de Herrera was one of those who saw the work of Las Casas in manuscript. He made generous use of it, omitting the criticisms directed by Las Casas at colonists and explorers, in his *Historia general de los hechos de los castellanos en las islas y tierra firme del mar oceano* (1601-15). The *General History of the Indies*, as it is known, included the story of the discovery to the year 1554. The innumerable sources of information available to Herrera (many of which have since been lost) give his work a comprehensiveness of great importance. It opened with the opinions of ancient peoples on the world outside Europe and then proceeded to give the reasons why Columbus thought of finding a new world. A very large part of the work concerned the conquistadors; there was little on life in the New World, administration, or similar matters. This deficiency was to a degree compensated for by a short *Descripción de las indias occidentales*, which was published at the same time as the *General History*.

At the same time Las Casas was writing his history, another work was being written by Gonzalo Fernández e Oviedo y Valdés. As a young page at court, Oviedo had seen the reception accorded Columbus on his triumphant return in 1493, and his later career was largely associated with the New World. He was named chief chronicler of the Indies in 1532, but complete publication of his *Historia general y natural de las indias occidentales* awaited action by the Spanish Royal Academy of History in 1851, which issued it in four volumes with a biography and critical notes.

Oviedo wrote on the flora and fauna of the West Indies and the natural resources of the continent, but much political history was also included. In general he went about his task with good judgment. There was a lack of proportion in the narration of events, however, that sometimes made it difficult to follow him with interest. Oviedo's learning was encyclopedic, but Washington Irving thought that he was less to be depended upon for the history of Columbus's voyages than for those of lesser note.[8]

Other historians celebrated the achievements of the better-known conquerors. The conquest of Mexico by Cortés was recorded in the *Chronicle of New Spain* by Francisco López de Gómara, who also wrote a *History of the Indies*. An old companion in arms with Cortés, Bernal Díaz del Castillo, sought to correct Gómara's inaccuracies in his work, *A True History of the Conquest of New Spain*, issued in 1632. Pizarro's adventure was chronicled at his order by Francisco de Xérez in the *True Narrative of the Conquest of Peru* in 1534, and in 1605 de Soto's story was published in Garcilaso de la Vega's *La Florida del Inca*. . . .

Within a short time translations and collections of their reports were being made for European readers. The most famous of these collections in the sixteenth century was the work of the Italian Giovanni Battista Ramusio, perhaps the greatest geographer of his day. He devoted a volume to American voyages in his series *Delle Navigazioni e Viaggi*. The Italian geographer was the first man of mature judgment and wide scholarship to edit the narratives of the early voyages. The link between Ramusio and the English students of the history of discovery was direct and immediate.[9]

Richard Hakluyt

English interest in overseas expansion, both practical and literary, quickly mounted after a slow start. The demand for historical literature in Elizabethan England was so great that summaries and condensations of larger works were published for the popular taste. The greatness of England and the spread of her power overseas were celebrated in many histories written in Tudor and Stuart days. The English bourgeoisie experienced a very rapid development in the sixteenth century, and to the economic needs of a rising capitalist class was joined a swelling national confidence in England's imperial destiny.

Richard Eden was the first Englishman of importance to acquaint his countrymen with the new worlds in the East and West. In 1553 he published his *Treatise of the New India*, a translation of some material from Sebastian Muenster's *Cosmography*. A more elaborate work of Eden's appeared two years later, *The Decades of the Newe Worlde*, a partial translation of Martyr's, Oviedo's, and López de Cómara's works, as well as those of other historians. Eden's work acquainted the English with the most important historians of New World discoveries: "With this book," wrote George B. Parks, "England woke to the new day."[10] In 1588, Thomas Hariot, an Oxford professor and adviser to Raleigh, wrote from personal experience *A briefe and true report of the New found land of Virginia*. Hariot's informative work, illustrated by his fellow colonist John White, fixed in the minds of its readers a romantic image of the New World for many decades thereafter.

More important than all others in awakening England to the significance of expanding her overseas empire was Richard Hakluyt, the adviser of Gilbert and Raleigh. The history of Hakluyt's career is largely, in Parks's words, "the intellectual history of the beginnings of the British Empire."[11] In 1582, Hakluyt published his *Divers Voyages touching the discovery of America*. . . . Two years later Raleigh chose him to present his case to the queen, which he did in *The Discourse on the Western Planting*. Hakluyt had already become an organizer of geographical publishing, and he inspired a number of other publications.

The work which established Hakluyt's fame was *The principall Navigations, Voiages and Discoveries of the English nation*, published in 1589 and usually called *The English Voyages*. Hakluyt had planned to include in one volume the whole record of English maritime activity from Arthur's day to the Armada; most of the book, however, was on English enterprise in the sixteenth century. With the exception of the medieval travel reports, his narratives were based on eyewitness accounts, including the story of his own two-hundred-mile trip to consult the last survivor of an early voyage to Newfoundland. This book earned for Hakluyt a place with the Italian compiler Giambattista Ramusio, whose own work had influenced the Englishman's.

Between 1598 and 1600, Hakluyt's last great publication appeared, a three-volume enlargement of the *Voyages* entitled *The Principal Navigations, Voyages, Traffics, and Discoveries of the English Nation*. The greatly increased body of information in Hakluyt's masterpiece, especially on the regions westward, reflected the expansion of English maritime activity between 1589 and 1598. The Englishman, who in 1575 had access to a few scattered books of travel in his native tongue, had by 1600 a full library, which made him a sharer in spirit of English imperial enterprise. Because his volumes recorded the movements of English traders and discoverers overseas, his place was high among England's empire builders.

The Principal Navigations was unquestionably one of the most important works of the century, and the British historian James A. Froude called it the "prose epic of the modern English nation." Hakluyt,

however, was more than the historian of English expansion. The settlement of England's first colony in America owed much to his energy,
and he was listed among the directors of the Virginia Company.

On the death of Hakluyt many of his manuscripts passed into the
hands of a fellow clergyman, Samuel Purchas, who seized the opportunity to carry on the work of the illustrious editor. In 1625, Purchas
published a five-volume work entitled *Hakluytus Posthumus or Purchas
his Pilgrimes*. To Hakluyt's collection as a nucleus Purchas added
records of universal travel as well as of the latest English voyages.
Unlike Hakluyt, who was not only a historian but also a participant
in the process of English expansion, Purchas was essentially an antiquarian who fell far short of Hakluyt as an editor. Nevertheless, his
work, along with that of his master, was of inestimable service to later
historians. In the nineteenth century the distinguished historian Jared
Sparks remarked that to Purchas and Hakluyt his generation was "still
indebted as were our ancestors two hundred years ago, for almost all
the knowledge which we possess respecting the early discoveries in
America."[12]

CHAPTER 2

The First Settlements

THE MEN WHO LED THE COLONISTS in establishing the first settlements wrote their own story. The new settlers brought with them the keen Elizabethan appreciation for historical writing. As pioneers in a new land, however, they were less concerned with past events than with history in the making, and their chronicles have the flavor of freshness that comes from first discovery. Hidden away in a corner of the universe, as so many of the early settlers felt themselves to be, they were often apologetic for detailing events that were highly significant for them but might be thought trivial by the world outside. Cotton Mather once expressed this thought in his characteristic manner: "If a war between us and a handful of Indians do appear no more than a Batrachomyomachie [battle of frogs and mice] to the world abroad, yet unto us at home it hath been considerable enough to make a history."[1]

The first settlers were conscious of the importance of their work for posterity, and they were fearful lest the record vanish. Their children's children must know of the dangers met and overcome in settling a new world so that they might be proud of their forebears and draw courage from their courage. The Puritan saw the need to render unto God a statement of actions done in His name and to thank Him for beneficent guidance. The task of the historian was not to entertain the reader but to discover his people's place in God's plan for the universe. To the Puritan all history displayed divine wisdom, and the past had been merely the prologue to the settlement of New England.

The monastic chroniclers of medieval Europe had their successors in New England's long line of minister-historians, but religion was less significant in the settlement of the South. Virginia's historians, therefore, had closer ties with Hakluyt, who savored more freely this mundane world.

John Smith

John Smith was of the breed of Elizabethan adventurers whose exploits have been preserved by Hakluyt, and though he was a captain in pursuit of gain, so glamourous an air of adventure surrounded his chase that he seemed rather a contemporary of Don Quixote than a man of business. Smith served in an executive capacity in the young Virginia colony, but his strong temper soon drew him into bitter controversy over the management of Jamestown. After leaving Virginia, Captain Smith was employed by the Plymouth Company, for whom he rendered distinguished services. From 1615 to his death in 1631, Smith lived in England, turning his restless hand to the composition of several works of literature.

His strictly historical works were two: a brief tract called *A True Relation . . . .* and a more extensive book, *The Generall Historie of Virginia, New-England and the Summer Isles.* The other works of Smith were descriptive; though not historical writings, they were important historical material.

A True Relation was written hurriedly in the Virginia wilderness in May, 1608, a year after the founding of the colony. In a racy, virile style Smith told of his personal experiences (the pronoun "I" was prominent in his writings), and the small space devoted to the events in Jamestown was colored with his strong bias against some fellow members on the council. With simple clarity he spoke of the uncertainties of settlement, of the dwindling food supply and how it was replenished:

Our provision being now within twentie dayes spent, the Indians brought us great store both of Corne and bread ready made; and also there came such aboundance of Fowles into the Rivers, as greatly refreshed our weake estates, whereuppon many of our weake men were presently able to goe abroad. As yet we had no houses to cover us, our Tents were rotten and our Cabbins worse then nought; our best commoditie was Yron which we made into little chissels. The president and Captaine Martins sicknes constrayned me to be Cape Marchant, and yet to spare no paines in making houses for the company; who notwithstanding our misery, little ceased their mallice, grudging and muttering.

Smith's encounters with the Indians filled most of his pages, and though he was sometimes worsted, it was only great odds that overcame him; he was always a match for his opponents if there were not too many of them. He closed his *True Relation* on a note of optimism: "We now remaining being in good health, all our men wel contented, free from mutinies, in love one with another and as we hope in a continual peace with the Indians: where we doubt not . . . in after times to see our Nation to enjoy a Country, not onely exceeding pleasant for habitation, but also a very profitable for comerce in general."

In 1612, at Oxford, another publication under Smith's name was

issued. It was *A Map of Virginia: with a Description of the Countrey* . . .
whereunto is annexed the proceedings of those Colonies. . . . Smith wrote
the "description" while his friends combined to write the "proceedings." The men who had been opposed to Captain Smith in the colony
received short shrift in the narrative.

Virginia, said Smith, was a country "that may have the prerogative
over the most pleasant places of Europe, Asia, Africa, or America, for
large and pleasant navigable rivers: heaven and earth never agreed
better to frame a place for mans habitation . . . were it fully manured
and inhabited by industrious people." After pointing out England's
dependence on other countries for various commodities, Smith struck
a true mercantilist note in his plea for the colonization of Virginia:
"Here is a place a nurse for souldiers, a practise for marriners, a trade
for marchants, a reward for the good, and that which is most of all
a businesse (most acceptable to God) to bring such poore infidels to the
true knowledge of God and his holy Gospell." This description of the
new colony revealed Smith as a careful observer of nature, topography,
and Indian customs, although like others he ignored the difficulties
of settlement.

While the *Generall Historie*, published in 1624, exhibited many of
the animosities that characterized the *True Relation*, it earned Smith a
place among American historians; only a small portion of the former,
however, was written by him. The work was divided into six books,
the fourth of which is the most interesting to the student of American
historical writing.

Smith gave a graphic description of the "starving time," when the
settlers were reduced to eating roots, nuts, and berries, some even re-
sorting to cannibalism. Here, too, Smith told rather simply the story
of his rescue by Pocahontas, which most students largely discredit.
"After some six weeks fatting amongst those Salvage Courtiers, at the
minute of my execution, she hazarded the beating out of her own
braines to save mine; and not onely that, but so prevailed with her
father, that I was safely conducted to Jamestowne." Smith further
embroidered this incident in various retellings. The introduction of
black slavery, so momentous for later America, was mentioned casually
under the date 1619: "About the last of August came in a dutch man
of warre that sold us twenty Negars." A number of pages vividly
described the terrible Indian massacre of 1622, which reduced the twelve
hundred settlers of the colony by more than three hundred.

As a kind of valedictory Smith penned these parting lines at the
close of the fourth book: ". . . here I must leave all to the triall of
time . . . : praying to that great God the protector of all goodness

to send them as good successe as the goodnesse of the action and country deserveth, and my heart desireth."

"If American historiography does not actually begin with Captain
John Smith," wrote Bert James Loewenberg, "it is not because of any
lack of effort on his part."[2] Smith was certainly intemperate, and he
had a very high opinion of himself, but his works have much reliable
information, and he was doubtless a man of real courage. A careful
study of the sources now available has in the main substantiated Smith's
judgment of conditions in the colony and the maladministration of the
Virginia Company. Another great Virginian's final assessment is appropriate; Thomas Jefferson wrote thus of Smith in his *Notes on Virginia:*
"He was honest, sensible, and well-informed; but his style is barbarous
and uncouth. His history, however, is almost the only source from
which we derive any knowledge of the infancy of our State." And in
1975 Alden T. Vaughan still could write of Smith as "the first and principal historian of Virginia."[3]

Edward Winslow

Somewhat similar in spirit and purpose to the *True Relation* from
Virginia was the small production from New England known as *Mourt's
Relation.* There was a continuing demand at home for publications on
the lands newfound beyond the horizon, and leaders among the first
settlers wrote their unfading narratives for eager English eyes. *Mourt's
Relation,* or *Journal of the English Plantations Settled at Plimouth,* was
first printed in 1622, in London. Edward Winslow was the author of
this slim volume, which recorded the daily happenings of the colony's
first year. Winslow served as governor of Plymouth, but his most valuable work was done in England as agent for the Bay Colony. "Mourt"
was George Morton, a fellow Pilgrim in London who published the
manuscript, against the will of Winslow, because he thought "it not
a misse to make them [the journals] more generall."

Written by a participant in the events described, *Mourt's Relation*
was of the highest authority. It referred to the famous Mayflower
Compact in these words: "It was thought good there shoud be an
association and agreement, that we should combine together in one
body, and to submit to such government and governours, as we shoud
by common consent agree to make and choose." The sense of wonder,
the contact with phenomena of nature new to him and the caution
of man in unusual surroundings were vividly present in Winslow's
Journal. With much delight the writer chronicled the recognition and

discovery of familiar and unfamiliar trees "and the best water that ever we drunke."

When the time came for a more permanent habitation, said the *Journal,* "we tooke notice how many Families they were . . . so Lots were cast where every man should lie [build his house] which was done, and staked out." Treaties and alliances with Indian neighbors were important steps in securing the safety of the colony. "Wee have found the Indians very faithfull in their Covenant of Peace with us. . . . We often goe to them and they come to us," said the *Journal.* Next to Myles Standish, Winslow was the Pilgrims' most important individual in dealing with the Indians; interestingly, his works are far friendlier to the Indians than those of Cotton Mather and other later writers.

A work by Winslow of 1624 entitled *Good News from New England* was a continuation of *Mourt's Relation.* Winslow's narratives constitute the only contemporary record of the settlement's earliest years, since Bradford seems not to have begun work on his *History* until 1630.

William Wood

Although Smith and Winslow wrote descriptions of the Indians and their environment, it was their histories of white settlement which mainly hold our attention. Other writers, however, had far less interest in history than in arousing enthusiasm among prospective settlers or in furnishing vicarious adventure to the fireside reader. They were eager to bring to the attention of Europeans a knowledge of conditions to be encountered in the New World, the novelties of nature, and, the most fascinating novelty of all, the Indians. An interesting example of this type of literature was *New England's Prospect,* which appeared in London in 1634. William Wood, its author, had been in America for four years. His small book answered questions that many prospective emigrants were asking.

The book was divided into two parts. The first treated of the topography of the region, the climate, the fauna and flora, and "what provision is to be made for a Journey at Sea, and what to carry with us for our use at hand." The second, a study of the Indians and their customs, included a section on "their Kings government, and Subjects obeddience." Here Wood struck a note that was to interest the critics of royalty in Europe: "For though hee [the king] hath no Kingly Robes, . . . nor dayly Guardes to secure his person, . . . yet doe they yeeld all submissive subjection to him, accounting him their Soveraigne." Wood was thinking of conditions in England when he wrote of the Indians: "For theft, as they have nothing to steale worth the life of a man, therefore they have no law to execute for trivialls; a Subject being precious in the eye of his Prince, where men are so scarce."

Wood's book was a sprightly composition. Within a few years it went through several editions; its compact size and logical organization must have appealed to the inquiring voyager. Unlike many other writers, who painted the colony all dark or all bright, depending on their prejudices, Wood included a few pages "of the evills, and such things as are hurtful in the Plantation." Wolves were mentioned, and particular attention was called to the rattlesnake. The "Musketoe" was acknowledged to be a nuisance, although Wood said that he had been troubled "as much with them or some like them, in the Fen country of England." He observed that many of the early difficulties of the settler were due to his own negligence: "The root of their want sprung up in England; for many hundreds hearing of the plenty of the Country, were so much their owne foes and Countries hindrance, as to come without provision; which made things both deare and scant." Wood assured the voyager freedom from want and a comfortable home if he carried provisions for a year and a half and if he was industrious.

America was a Utopia that could be won by the man willing to work, "for all New England must be workers in some kinde," wrote Wood, in a spirit peculiarly American. "So little is the poverty of the Country," he continued, "that I am perswaded if many in England which are constrained to begge their bread were there, they would live better than many doe here, that have money to buy it."

Wood's writing, then, was partly promotional but was more honest than most such works and was also better written. It was the best description of Massachusetts Bay which had appeared. Not really a history, for Wood covered nothing beyond his four-year sojourn in the colonies, *New England's Prospect* offers rich material for historians, and many have used it.

William Bradford

The most important of the founders' narratives was that by William Bradford. He knew firsthand the history of the Pilgrims; he had been among the earlier fugitives to Holland, and he was the foremost figure in Plymouth Colony. The history of Bradford's manuscript is itself of unusual interest. After various wanderings it found a home in the palace of the bishop of London. In 1896 the bishop presented it to Massachusetts, whose leading historical society published it in 1912 in an authoritative form under the direction of Worthington C. Ford (other editions had appeared before that date, the first in 1856).

Bradford's *History of Plimoth Plantation* was used in manuscript by later historians for over two hundred years before it was printed. It remains today the prime source for the story of the colony from the time just before the *Mayflower* sailed until 1646. Thomas Prince, William Hubbard, Cotton Mather, and Thomas Hutchinson all used Bradford's work when writing their own histories. It not only has permanent value for American history, but also possesses singular charm as literature.[4] The writing was unpretentious and earnest, as befit a Pilgrim. The rhythm of its language paid musical tribute to the memory of the deceased William Brewster: "He had this blesing added by the Lord to all the rest, to dye in his bed, in peace, amongst the mids of his friends, who mourned & wepte over him and ministered what help & comforte they could unto him, and he againe recomforted them whilst he could."

Bradford's narrative revealed as clearly as words might the ideal Pilgrim, who, though not a learned man, was a thoughtful one with a rare degree of intelligence. He would, he began, write "in a plaine stile, with singular regard unto the simple trueth in all things." Like his contemporaries Bradford was certain that it was God's intercession that kept Plymouth Colony alive, although he was grateful, too, for the aid offered by the natives Squanto and Samoset.

The forthright character of the historian and his unaffected simplicity shone in contrast to the frequent pomp and splendor of John Smith's self-created circumstance. There was vividness also in Bradford's writing. In the seventeenth-century atmosphere of bitter theological wrangling it was refreshing to read Bradford's tender judgment on Roger Williams: "But he is to be pitied, and prayed for, and so I shall leave the matter, and desire the Lord to shew him his errors, and reduse him into the way of truth, and give him a setled judgment and constancie in the same."

Bradford could write with anger, too, as in his description of the behavior of Thomas Morton. Bradford was incensed at Morton because of his traffic in arms with the Indians. "O the horriblenes of this vilaine!" exclaimed the historian, "how many both Dutch & English have been latly slaine by those Indeans, thus furnished." He went on to appeal to "princes & parlements ... to prevente this Mischeefe" before the Indians might overthrow the white settlements.

Bradford had cause to fear the collapse of his colony, which had been born in great travail. He clearly recalled the early days of settlements in the Dutch provinces and enumerated the reasons why the Pilgrims had become dissatisfied with conditions in Holland. They had intended moving "not out of any newfangledness," he carefully explained, "but for sundrie weighty & solid reasons." Among other motives was the desire for a home where the struggle of life would be less hard. The place that held greatest promise for his small group, said Bradford, "was some of those vast & unpeopled countries of America, which are fruitful & fitt for habitation" and which was "devoyd of all civill inhabitants." Objections had been raised against removal to the New World, where famine would be their portion, disease their companion, and the Indian their enemy. To these and further objections, the brave answer was made, "that all great & honourable actions are accompanied with great difficulties, and must be both enterprised and overcome with answerable courages. It was granted the dangers were great, but not desperate; the difficulties were many, but not invincible." Bradford explained that he wrote at length about all the plans and delays so that "their children may see with what difficulties their fathers wrastled in going through these things in their first beginnings."

Finally they got under way, and "after longe beating at sea they fell with that land which is called Cape Cod; the which being made & certainly knowne to be it, they were not a litle joyfull." After some deliberation the ship was turned southward "to finde some place aboute Hudsons river for their habitation. But after they had sailed that course aboute halfe the day, they fell amongst deangerous shoulds and roring breakers, . . . & the wind shrieking upon them withall, they resolved to bear up againe for the Cape [Cod]. . . . And the next day they gott into the Cape-harbor wher they ridd in saftie."

They had been delivered from ocean storms only to face the approaching winter in a hostile wilderness. The last days of November and the early days of December they spent in searching out a hospitable location and "the 25 day [of December] begane to erecte the first house for comone use to receive them and their goods."

The tragedy of the first winter Bradford revealed in all its horror, but he remembered also the courage that it called forth. "Ther dyed sometimes 2. or 3. of a day" during those cruel months; "that of 100. & odd persons scarce 50 remained." Sometimes only six or seven were sufficiently strong to be about and attend to the needs of the other survivors. The surprise of meeting with the Indians Samoset and Squanto, who could speak English and who were willing to help them gather the fruits of the new land, lighted up the gloom of the dark first winter.

Difficulties continued to beset the Pilgrims. Under the date 1622, Bradford wrote: "Now the wellcome time of harvest approached, in which all had their hungrie bellies filled." But the harvest was insufficient, and "also much was stolne both by night & day, before it became scarce eatable & much more afterward." Soon after, Bradford wrote, "God fedd them out of the sea for the most part," and thus early the cod became sacred in Massachusetts. An infrequent note of humor was struck in Bradford's answer to objections by prospective emigrants that mosquitoes were an annoyance: "They are too delicate and unfitte to begine new plantations and colonies, that cannot enduer the biting of a muskeeto; we would wish such to keepe at home till at least they be muskeeto proofe."

Slowly prospering despite hardships, the colony sent for another pastor, Charles Chansey, to assist John Reinor. Bradford then mentioned a minor controversy illustrative of the influence of environment upon religion: "Ther fell out some differance about baptising he [Chansey] holding it ought only to be by diping, and putting the whole body under water, and that sprinkling was unlawful. The church yeelded that immersion, or dipping, was lawful, but in this could countrie not so conveniente."

Bradford's work, in manuscript and in print, has been most effective in gaining for the Pilgrims and their settlement the distinctive place they hold in the history of America and in the folklore of her people. One of the finest legacies of the Plymouth settlement was the story told by Bradford, and his words have enriched the spirit of America. A grateful posterity endowed the Pilgrims with a wealth of virtue and accomplishment, but the myths that were created about them are less interesting than the facts of their history.

John Winthrop

Virginia had Smith, Plymouth had Bradford, and Massachusetts Bay had John Winthrop. Thus we have the story of the first settlements by those best equipped to tell it. All three had good judgment and sufficient literary skill to re-create for the reader the life of their day, which, but for their efforts, might have gone unrecorded.

John Winthrop, lord of the manor of Groton, was one of the most important creators of the Bay Colony, which he served as governor and deputy governor for nineteen years. With far more than the limited resources at the command of the Plymouth Colony, the Puritan group initiated one of the greatest mass migrations of modern times. A good part of the record of the early years of that settlement was preserved in Winthrop's *Journal*, known also as *The History of New England from 1630 to 1649*. It has been long recognized as the most valuable chronicle of the Bay Colony. Though it was not published in its entirety until the nineteenth century, New England historians had used it while it was still in manuscript.

The disconnected annals that are Winthrop's *Journal* are less interesting than is Bradford's history, whose greater unity and narrative charm made it a more distinguished performance. In justice to Winthrop it should be noted that his writing was done in the press of a very active life, more so than was Bradford's, and it is suggested that his *Journal* was to be the basis of a more carefully written account.

The work began on board the *Arbella*, "riding at the Cowes, near the Isle of Wight," on Easter Monday, 1630. The day before, Winthrop had written to his wife: "We are preparinge (by Gods assistance) to sett sayle in the morninge . . . and now (my sweet soule) I must once againe take my last farewell of thee in old England. It goeth verye neere to my heart to leave thee." After a stormy voyage the Puritans finally made port, and after the monotonous fare on board ship they were glad to go ashore and gather "a store of fine strawberries." The frequent references to the entrance and departure of ships, some with needed corn from Virginia, others with passengers from England; the transfer of livestock to the new community; and the toll that wolves levied on the cattle—all these were part of the narrative of the beginnings of settlement. Sometimes there appeared items of greater moment, as when Winthrop remarked, under the date 1632, that "this government was . . . in the nature of a parliament." The process of expansion was briefly referred to in March, 1633: "The governor's son, John Winthrop, went with twelve more, to begin a plantation at Agawam, after called Ipswich."

Under the date 1635 the annalist wrote: "The deputies having conceived great danger to our state, in regard that our magistrates, for want of positive laws, in many cases, might proceed according to their discretions, it was agreed that some men should be appointed to frame a body of grounds of law, in resemblance to a Magna Charta." Along with political information, Winthrop wrote about the costs of cattle and corn and about wages paid to workmen. "The scarcity of workmen had caused them to raise their wages to an excessive rate," he said in 1633, and because this resulted in inflation, the court ordered that carpenters, masons, and the like should receive only two shillings a day and laborers eighteen pence. No commodity was to cost more than fourpence in the shilling above what it would sell for in England.

Roger Williams and Anne Hutchinson often appeared in the pages of Winthrop, who was more lenient in his judgments upon them than were many of his contemporaries. Mrs. Hutchinson was "a woman of a ready wit and bold spirit" who had "brought over with her . . . dangerous [theological] errors." In justification of his own share in the controversy, Winthrop wrote that they "were so divided from the rest of the country in their judgement and practice, as it could not stand with the public peace. . . . So, by the example of Lot in Abraham's family, and after Hagar and Ishmael, he saw they must be sent away."

Despite serious rifts the colony continued to grow: "There came over this summer [1638] twenty ships, and at least three thousand persons, as they were forced to look out new plantations." Winthrop made plain the constitutional problems of the youthful settlement. "The people," he wrote in 1639, "had long desired a body of laws, and thought their condition very unsafe, while so much power rested in the discretion of magistrates"; the "Body of Liberties" was the result of this agitation.

Events in far-off England had serious economic effects in the colony during the early 1640s and caused important changes in the distribution of population: "The sudden fall of land and cattle, and the scarcity of foreign commodities, and money, etc. with the thin access of people from England, put many into an unsettled frame of spirit, so as they concluded there would be no subsisting here, and accordingly they began to hasten away." Winthrop was very much concerned about the departure of so many settlers.

In the same year, 1642, he noted the first commencement in an English American college: "Nine bachelors commenced at Cambridge; they were young men of good hope." Three years later Winthrop wrote that "by agreement of the commissioners [of the New England Confederation] . . . every family in each colony gave one peck of corn or twelve pence to the college at Cambridge."

In 1646 an occasion arose, wrote Winthrop, to consider "in what relation we stood to the state of England." The remarks that followed are of great interest to the student of American political theory who would understand some of the ideas that appear so prominently in the Revolutionary era. Although owing "allegiance and subjection" to the mother country, some New Englanders maintained that they "might be still independent in respect of government, as Normandy, Gascoyne, etc. were. . . . In point of government they were not dependent upon France." The *Journal* ended in the early days of 1649, the year of Winthrop's death, with an entry characteristically referring to the "righteous hand of God" raised against a man for profaning the Sabbath.

Winthrop's work sometimes reads like a sensationalist newspaper story rather than a routine account: fires, shipwrecks, and sex scandals. On the other hand, he told much about the creation of a society that built itself homes, schools, ships, and taverns. Scattered through his account were the details, which, when grouped together, told of the construction of a social organization more enduring than houses or ships or taverns. In the *Journal,* too, are the materials to help us judge the author, wise beyond most of his colleagues, the aristocratic servant of his people. He was no friend of democracy, religious toleration, or the Indians, either in his career or in his history, but his work has been a treasure trove for historians of New England, particularly of Massachusetts Bay.

Edward Johnson

Edward Johnson came to New England in 1630 with Winthrop, but soon returned to England. In 1636, however, he came back to America to stay. He was the leading figure in the founding of Woburn, and until his death in 1672 he remained one of the important personalities in his town. He was town clerk and surveyor and served in the General Court of Massachusetts. In this legislative body he met representatives of other towns; information from those leaders, added to his own intimate knowledge, enabled him to reconstruct a large part of the history of the colony.

The Wonder-Working Providence of Sion's Savior in New England was Johnson's contribution to historical writing. The volume was printed in London in 1654, under another title and without the author's name, but the work has become known by the quaint title which savors so much of the seventeenth-century Johnsonian mind. "The author," wrote J. Franklin Jameson, his descendant and editor, "was convinced . . . that there had been set up in New England an ecclesiastical and civil polity more closely according with the Word of God than any other which the world has seen, and that the Lord had manifested His approval by doing marvelous things in the wilderness for these His chosen people."[5] Throughout, Johnson spoke the language described by French wit as the *patois de Canaan.*

Johnson's was the first published history of Massachusetts, but it does not rank with the works of Bradford and Winthrop. *The Wonder-Working Providence* is difficult reading. It is burdened by frequent rhetorical and poetic flights, is poorly arranged, and contains many errors. It has little of the gentleness of Bradford or the culture and comparative tolerance of Winthrop. Johnson wrote history from the standpoint of the rank and file, thoroughly orthodox and intensely partisan. Against the detractors of New England, like Merrymount Morton, Johnson spoke the language of a crusader. As one might expect from so orthodox a character, Johnson's words were bitter against Anne Hutchinson.

Johnson, a Puritan, was a militant Christian, and the references to the "Souldiers of Christ in New England" were plentiful; their cruel slaughter of the Pequot Indians was vividly depicted. In book 2, chapter 22, was the classic description "of the manner of planting Towns and Churches in N.E." with particular emphasis upon Johnson's own town, Woburn. After that Johnson went on "to declare how this people proceeded in religious matters . . . it being as unnatural for a right N.E. man to live without an able Ministery, as for a Smith to work his iron without a fire."

Johnson's work deserves most credit for the interesting material he provided for the economic and social history of Massachusetts. As his biographer for the *Dictionary of American Biography* wrote: "Johnson's work is not an authority to be wholly relied upon in controversial matters, or for the events of the years when he was absent. But he gives many homely facts . . . of the people, which were ignored by more intellectual chroniclers like Bradford and Winthrop."[6] In short, Johnson told us more about the average New England citizen than about the governing elite.

At the conclusion of his first book Johnson had written: "Yet let them [critics of New England] also know the Souldiers of Christ in N.E. are not of such a pusillanimous Spirit, but . . . resolved . . . to keepe the government our God hath given us, and for witnesse hee hath so done, let this History manifest." This history manifested the tenacity of the Puritan will and indicated, as one critic observed, that Johnson "handled the pen as he did the sword and the broad axe—to accomplish something with it." In *The Wonder-Working Providence* the virtues as well as the limitations of the middle-class Puritan mind were laid bare. The Puritan had great courage and daring, but his hostility to dissent was unrelenting.

Nathaniel Morton

Nathaniel Morton, a nephew of William Bradford, had unusual opportunities to write a history; in addition to his kinship with the leader of the Plymouth Colony he was himself a member of the official family by reason of long tenure as clerk of the colony court. He was one of Plymouth's most important men and was reputed to know more of the colony's history than anyone else.

The short title of Morton's history, issued in 1669, was *New England's Memorial.* His audience was larger than might be supposed, for the reading of history for recreation was general among the literate public. New Englanders had a strong civic sense, and many of them had comparatively rich intellectual backgrounds. The proportion of university men to the whole population was very high; the ministers in particular made every sacrifice to send their sons to Harvard. Almost all of New England's literary output before 1700—tracts, pamphlets, verse, and histories—was written by the Harvard-trained clergy. Because of them a continuous tradition of intellectual vitality was maintained.

Two ministers, John Higginson and Thomas Thacher, sponsored

Morton's volume, pointing out the need for a history. They hoped that it would stimulate similar compositions in other colonies and that ultimately a comprehensive history of New England would be written.

Morton acknowledged that most of his material came from his uncle Bradford, but other sources of information, including Winslow's *Journal,* were also available to him. His history was a chronology which took the record of Pilgrim annals through 1668. Up to 1646 the work was almost entirely an abridgment of Bradford's unpublished manuscript, and this part of Morton's volume was therefore extremely valuable. The rest of the book was largely concerned with elections, the deaths of prominent individuals, and the blights of nature on man, animals, and crops. With the publication of Bradford's own manuscript in the nineteenth century, Morton's work lost value, but his volume and Johnson's had long been New England's standard histories. Fortunately Morton did more than write history; his care in preserving historical materials was long remembered.

William Hubbard

William Hubbard was graduated with Harvard's first class in 1642 and later served as president of his alma mater. He was also active in politics, opposing the government of Sir Edmund Andros on the issue of tax collections. In 1677, while others were likewise at work on histories of the Indian wars, Hubbard published his *Narrative of the Troubles with the Indians in New England.* He wrote another, more important work, *A General History of New England from the Discovery to MDCLXXX,* which remained unpublished until 1815, though it was used in manuscript by Cotton Mather, Thomas Prince, and many others.

In 1682 the government of Massachusetts supported Hubbard with a grant of fifty pounds toward the completion of his history, and later scholars thought the money well spent. Ezra Stiles, a noted president of Yale in the eighteenth century, classed the works of Hubbard, Bradford, and Winthrop as "the three most considerable accounts of the first settlement of New England." Much of Hubbard's history was in the form of annals like Winthrop's *Journal;* in fact, he added little about the period before 1650 to the material he found in Winthrop and Bradford. His view of the founding of Massachusetts Bay was different, however, from that of Winthrop. It is worth noting, too, that Hubbard's work was more secular than the histories written by his contemporaries.

Although Hubbard was supposed to write a chronicle of some sixty years of New England's history, the major portion was devoted to the first half of the period, on which his authorities were more extensive.

He hurried over the following three decades to 1680. Though prized by students in the eighteenth century, Hubbard's history was neglected by most later writers. This was doubtless partly due to Hubbard's attitude toward the Indians. He once referred to them as "perfidious cruel and hellish Monsters," and his story in general was one of inoffensive colonists pitted against sadistic savages.[7]

Increase Mather

Increase Mather, who has been called the foremost Puritan, belonged to one of New England's first families. He took a very active part in the life of Massachusetts as an official and a minister as well as president of Harvard. In 1676 he wrote *A Brief History of the War with the Indians* (King Philip's War), a day-by-day chronicle of the events reported orally and by letters when the news was fresh. Mather had an eye for the dramatic, and his narrative vividly pictured the struggle. In this volume Mather wrote, "I earnestly wish that some effectual Course may be taken (before it be too late) that a first *History of New England* be written and published to the World" (Mather apparently had no high opinion of the works of Johnson and Morton). It was reserved for his son Cotton to make the attempt twenty years later.

In 1677, Increase Mather published his *Relation of the Troubles . . . in New England . . . .* In this volume Mather again revealed his capacity to narrate the picturesque and significant, but it has been pointed out that important materials reflecting unfavorably on Massachusetts were omitted. As a moral lesson Mather drew a distinction between those who, he said, had come to America for reasons of trade and those who had come for religious motives. The traders, said Mather, "have been attended with blasting ruining Providences," while the others "have been signally owned by the Lord Jesus, for the like hath been rarely known in the World, that a Plantation should be raised out of nothing," to which Mather's nineteenth-century editor, S. G. Drake, answered, "That any Settlement was, or could have been made independent of Trade is preposterous."[8]

In composing his history of King Philip's War, Increase Mather was conscious of a rivalry with other New England historians, particularly Hubbard. Mather believed his own work to be superior to Hubbard's. In point of view they were very similar; the Indians, Mather asserted, "fought to dispossess us of the land, which the Lord or God hath given to us." Mather's outlook was generally broad enough, however, to welcome other workers in a common cause—the composition of New England's history. He corresponded with them on the subject, and Nathaniel Morton wrote to Mather asking him "to sett on foot and put forward a Generall History of New England." By inspiring his son Cotton to write history, the father may be said to have initiated the project of that general history.

Histories of the Indian Wars

Hubbard and the Mathers, father and son, were not the only historians of the Indian wars. The struggles between the whites and Indians were of absorbing interest; the narrow escapes from Indian capture and the sudden raids on lonely farms were the very essence of chilling narrative. Few writers, however, were able to capture the drama of forest conflict.

Although several contemporaries left accounts of the Pequot War, Captain John Mason wrote the one best known. His *History of the Pequot War* (1677) was a callous account of the struggle.[9] The exploits of another noted Indian fighter, Colonel Benjamin Church, one of the best soldiers New England produced, were commemorated in the volume by his son Thomas, *Entertaining Passages Relating to Philip's War...* (1716). Full of the nervous tension of Indian warfare, it remained a great favorite with readers long after its original publication. Stories of cruelty and heroism similarly filled the pages of Samuel Penhallow's *History of the Wars of New England with the Eastern Indians, 1703-1725,* which was published in the year of the author's death, 1726. Penhallow, chief justice of New Hampshire, belonged in the tradition of Bradford, Winthrop, and Morton—community leaders who wrote the histories of their times.

Daniel Gookin also wrote of the Indians, but his was a gentler spirit that sought to understand them and promote a friendlier relation between them and the whites. With the exception of John Eliot he was perhaps the most distinguished friend the Indians had. He wrote two books: *Historical Collections of the Indians in New England* which remained unpublished until 1792, and *An Historical Account of the... Christian Indians* which was also published long after it was written (1836). In the second book Gookin sought to protect from the fury of the whites the Christian Indians who had not joined with King Philip. Gookin's position was, of course, opposed to popular opinion, and his protests were disregarded.

Similar in theme but different in narrative construction were the hair-raising accounts of men and women captured by the Indians and later restored to white civilization. Their stories, generally referred to as "Indian captivities," have held enthralled generations of readers, the first of whom marveled at the tale of Mrs. Mary Rowlandson, captured during King Philip's War. "Now away we must go with those Barbarous Creatures, with our bodies wounded and bleeding, and our hearts no less than our bodies. . . . Oh the roaring, and singing, and dancing, and yelling of those black creatures in the night, which made the place a lively resemblance of hell. . . . All was gone, my Husband gone . . . my Children gone, my relatives and Friends gone. . . . There remained nothing to me but one poor wounded Babe." This and other narratives of captivity were published again and again for an awed and insatiable audience.

Cotton Mather

Cotton Mather was colonial New England's "literary behemoth," wrote Moses Coit Tyler.[10] A bibliography of over four hundred titles justifies the description. A rich intellectual heritage had helped endow him with a capacious memory for knowledge of all fields; his pedantic mind later paraded those facts across the pages of his numerous works. On his death in 1728 an obituary said of him: "He was perhaps the principal ornament of this Country, the greatest scholar that ever was bred in it."

The influence of his father's historical interests served to spur on a pen that needed no urging. About 1693 the son determined to write a general church history of New England. It was finished four years later, sent to London to be published, and, after many delays that caused heartaches in the Mather household, appeared in 1702. On October 30 of that year Cotton Mather wrote in his diary, "Yesterday I first saw my Church-History since the Publication of it."[11] It was called *Magnalia Christi Americana; or the Ecclesiastical History of New England.*

In his general introduction the author said, "I write the Wonders of the Christian Religion, flying from the deprivations of Europe, to the American Strand; and . . . report the wonderful displays of His infinite Power, Wisdom, Goodness, and Faithfulness, wherewith His Divine Providence hath irradiated an Indian Wilderness." He wrote that he had endeavored, "with all good conscience, to decline this writing meerly for a party," but he asked readers to be lenient toward historians who were not expected to be infallible in everything.

The story of the Plymouth colonists was a well-written, straightforward account which evidently gained much from an acquaintance with Bradford's manuscript. New England was settled solely to plant the Gospel, said Mather. The historian agreed with his father, Increase Mather, that "of all historical narratives, those which give a faithful account of the lives of eminent saints, must needs be the most edifying." There was a note of beauty in the reference to John Eliot, the apostle to the Indians. "He was one who lived in heaven while he was on earth," said Mather, "and there is no more than pure justice in our endeavours that he should live on earth after he is in heaven. He that will write of Eliot, must write of charity, or say nothing."

Mather, however, did not have Eliot's humanity for the Indians. He revealed, rather, the usual contempt of the settler who thought that the natives—those "abject creatures"—were uselessly cluttering up the land. "Our shiftless Indians," he wrote, "were never owners of so much as a knife till we come among them; their name for an English man was a knife-man. They live in a country full of the best shiptimber under heaven; but never saw a ship till some came from Europe hither." European settlers were therefore justified in taking over so fair a portion of God's territory from infidels who knew not how to use it.

When Mather came to write of his college, he maintained that Harvard promoted a more critical intelligence than did schools in England. Harvard, he said, did not show "such a veneration for Aristotle as is express'd at Queen's Colledge in Oxford; where they read Aristotle on their knees, and those who take degrees are sworn to defend his philosophy." He proudly said of his college, "Europe, as well as America, has from this learned seminary been enriched with some worthy men."

In *Remarkable Providences*, his sixth book, Mather attempted to carry out a plan proposed by his father years before. His "Church History is [now] become able to entertain the world with a collection of remarkable providences that have occurr'd among the inhabitants of New England." They included unusual rescues from disaster at sea or from hostile Indians, as well as stories of criminals who paid for their capital crimes. It is partly because of his chapter entitled "Relating the Wonders of the Invisible World" that Cotton Mather's reputation has severely suffered. In this he did indicate that even he, an erudite man, was not above the superstitions of his day. "Molestations from evil spirits," he asserted, "have so abounded in this country, that I question whether any one town has been free from sad examples of them."

In his account of the Salem witchcraft episode Mather mentioned that the "increasing number and quality of the persons accus'd" of witchcraft so amazed the officials that "at last it was evidently seen that there must be a stop put. . . . Therefore, the juries generally acquitted such as were tried, fearing they had gone too far," and Governor Phips reprieved the condemned. Mather added that "it was thought safer to under-do, especially in matters capital, where what is once compleated cannot be retrieved."

The last book in the *Magnalia* was concerned with the "Wars of the Lord" against heretics and Indians. Mather was comparatively lenient toward Roger Williams, whom "many judicious persons judged . . . to have had the 'root of the matter' in him, during the long winter of [his] retirement." Mather added, "There was always a good correspondence held between him and many worthy and pious people in the colony from whence he had been banish'd." Mather was not so gentle toward Anne Hutchinson, "the prime seducer of the whole faction which now began to threaten the country."

The Quakers were the object of his bitter invective: "This I know, they have been the most venomous of all to the churches of America." However, he distinguished between "the old Foxian Quakerism, . . . the grossest collection of blasphemies and confusions that ever was heard of," and "the new turn that such ingenious men as Mr. Penn have given to it," so that it had "become quite a new thing." Mather argued that no magistrate should "take the life of an offender solely for the crime of heresy," but the state must nevertheless protect itself against sedition.

Mather's work ended on a doleful note: "It must, after all, be confessed, that we have had one enemy more pernicious to us than all the rest, and that is 'our own backsliding heart,' which has plunged the whole country into . . . degeneracy. . . . God knows what will be the End."

The great Progressive historian Vernon L. Parrington was devastatingly critical of Mather after reading his diary, which Parrington referred to as "a treasure-trove to the abnormal psychologist": "What a crooked and diseased mind lay back of those eyes that were forever spying out occasions to magnify self! He grovels in proud self-abasement. He distorts the most obvious reality. . . . He labors to acquire the possessions of a scholar, but he listens to old wives' tales with greedy avidity."[12]

Few have been that hard on Cotton Mather as a historian. Yet his *Magnalia*, generally regarded as one of the most important books in American colonial historiography, has been variously appraised. Barrett Wendell, in his biography *The Puritan Priest*, rated it among the great works of English literature in the seventeenth century, while bitter critics of Puritanism have execrated it. Samuel Eliot Morison, who made considerable use of it in his *Builders of the Bay Colony*, indicated that he had a higher opinion of it than have most historians. Despite Mather's pedantry and inaccuracy and the fact that he "was not above *suppressio veri*," said Morison, he "does succeed in giving a living picture of the persons he writes about, and he was near enough to the first generation to catch the spirit and flavor of the times."[13]

Regardless of one's final evaluation of Mather as a historian, there is no doubt about his influence. His reputation, particularly abroad, surpassed that of any other American of the colonial era except Benjamin Franklin and Jonathan Edwards. Peter Gay, in his excellent study of the Puritan historians, *A Loss of Mastery*, wrote: "For two centuries and even longer, Americans . . . have seen the great struggle for New England's soul through Cotton Mather's eyes. . . . Everyone, consciously or not, absorbed its views and employed its categories. For whatever the liberals and rebels in Massachusetts did, . . . they did not write history."[14]

Mather chose his style to suit his theme; it could be simple and direct, as in his *Essays to do Good,* or it could be heavily laden with classical allusions and rhetorical fancies, as in the *Magnalia.* His history has no form and seems to have been thrown together piecemeal. "All the time I have had for my Church-History," Mather said, "hath been . . . chiefly, that which I might have taken else for less profitable recreations; and it hath all been done by snatches." Jumbled together with much new material were reprints of many of his earlier writings, and the history was of such bulk as to make it the largest work which had been produced in the British colonies.

In another of his works, *Manuductio ad Ministerium* (1726), Mather laid down a plan for a scholar's preparation for the ministry. History was to be "read with constant reflection upon God's power as revealed in past events"; but in studying history the reader was always to "believe with Discretion." On another occasion, when referring to Indian folklore, Mather wrote: "There is very little in any Tradition of our Savages, to be rely'd upon." It is a pity that the skepticism he showed toward the tales of "red devils" was absent when he wrote of the devilish spirits in white society.

The problem with Cotton Mather, of course, was really the problem of Puritan historiography in general, indeed of Puritanism itself. To turn again to Peter Gay: Puritanism created an atmosphere in New England in which "religious prescriptions encouraged, directed, and constricted learning. . . . Far from being radical, the Puritans' historical writings looked to the past, not only for their subject matter—that, after all, is the proper business of history—but for their method, their style of thinking." In the writing of history, as in all other areas, piety came first. Gay quotes the Reverend William Brattle's deathbed advice to his son: "Acquaint thy Self with History; know something of the Mathematicks, and Physick; be able to keep Accompts Merchant like in some manner; but let Divinity be thy main Study." Then Gay concludes:

In these words we may read the ultimate failure of Puritan historiography, and . . . the ultimate failure of the Puritan experiment in the New World. Much as the American Puritans enjoyed their history, they experienced the revolutionary developments in seventeenth- and eighteenth-century historiography as victims. . . . In Europe, historians were inventing new techniques, broadening their conceptions, and rushing forward into secularism; in America, Puritans continued to write history as though nothing had changed. This was the tragedy of Puritan historiography: it had no history of its own.[15]

CHAPTER 3

The Era of Colonialism

I N THE EIGHTEENTH CENTURY American historians continued to speak of colonial beginnings with awe and wonder, grateful for divine guidance. Most of the later colonial historians, however, with their strong secular approach, tended to locate the causes of events in a mundane and not in a supernatural plane. John Higham has written of this as the transition from the Puritan to the patrician stage of American historiography.[1] Ministers did continue to write history, but even in New England they no longer monopolized the field as the secularization of life in the Western world began to include America in its sweep. European letters deeply influenced colonial life, which went through profound changes in its economic and intellectual phases during the half century following King Philip's War.[2] Doctors, lawyers, merchants, and planters became historians, and their broad interests were reflected in the volumes they wrote. A critical temper and a skepticism characteristic of later scholarship were revealed in their histories. The best of these historians, though greatly handicapped in gathering materials, turned out narratives which compared favorably with those of English contemporaries.

From annals of conflicts with nature and malignant spirits writers turned to narratives of conflicts with governors and imperial administrators; the Indians, however, still played a dominant part in the lives of the colonists and therefore merited the space given them in histories. Historians wrote with a consciousness of Anglo-French rivalry for interior America, and their volumes strengthened imperial sentiment. With the passing of a century a society had emerged fairly well stabilized, proud of its past and confident of the future. Historians were conscious of the need to correct English misconceptions of America, and their writing reveals a nascent pride in the evolution of a colonial society distinct from that of the homeland.

Robert Beverley

Robert Beverley was the kind of Virginia aristocrat who easily combined politics and literature. Like many other Virginians, Beverley spent much time in England; it was there that he determined to write the history of his colony. The publisher who had accepted John Oldmixon's *British Empire in America* had asked Beverley to read the portion of the still-unpublished manuscript on Virginia, and the many mistakes Beverley found therein prompted him to write his own version. "It would take a Book larger than his own to expose [Oldmixon's] errors," said Beverley, angry that his province had "been so misrepresented to the common People of England."

The *History of Virginia* appeared in 1705 and an enlarged edition in 1722.[3] The purely historical narrative was of less general interest than were other parts of the *History*. Beverley's dislike of most colonial governors was rather obvious. His dependence on John Smith was well advised, for Smith's interpretation of the dissolution of the Virginia Company was nearer the truth than were the accounts of many later historians. Beverley's material on the Indians must have proved very interesting to contemporary readers, who learned from the pictures and accompanying explanatory remarks a great deal about the Indians' child care, homes, dress, and social organization. The historian supplied ammunition for critics of society who idealized Indians as "noble savages." "They claim no Property in Lands," wrote Beverley, "but they are in Common to a whole Nation. . . . They seem as possessing nothing, and yet enjoying all Things . . . without toiling and perplexing their Minds for Riches."

The historian painted a picture of his colony that would attract the prospective emigrant who had been frightened by exaggerations of burdensome work. Slaves, he said, were "not worked near so hard nor so many Hours in a Day as the Husbandmen, and Day-Labourers in England." Pride in his colonial home, coupled with a promoter's zeal, led Beverley to write: "This may in Truth be term'd the best poor Man's Country in the World. But as they have no-body that is poor to beggary, so they have few that are rich; their Estates being regulated by the Merchants in England" (this resentment of Virginia planters against their London factors was to grow stronger in the next sixty years). Even Paradise had no more to offer than Virginia, at least in terms of climate, "since it is very near the same Latitude with the Land of Promise."

Beverley's writing was fresh, his comments often shrewd, and his appreciation of nature exceptional. His style had a noticeably lighter touch than that of most contemporary New England historical literature, which often appears labored by contrast. As Bert James Loewenberg has written:

Bradford's history, while majestic, is but rarely amusing. Winthrop's pages, filled with moral intensity, are seldom humorous. Mather is always learned but almost never urbane. All three, moreover, though they deal with universal issues, are frequently provincial. Beverley, on the other hand, is informative and witty, learned and humorous, and sufficiently cosmopolitan to be detached from petty affinities—qualities which scholars in all fields have ever striven to attain.[4]

John Oldmixon

John Oldmixon's history was familiar to American writers, who usually quoted it only to condemn it, as had Beverley. William Douglass, for example, said that Oldmixon "generally writes, as if copying from some ill-founded temporary news-paper," and he quoted Cotton Mather as having said that Oldmixon once had eighty-seven falsehoods within fifty-six pages.[5]

The *Dictionary of National Biography* lists Oldmixon as "historian and pamphleteer."[6] Certainly he was at least as much pamphleteer as historian, and like other pamphleteers he knew no restraint when speaking of his political opponents, either in his pamphlets or in his histories. Oldmixon is perhaps best known for his association with the short-lived weekly paper the *Medley*, which followed Addison's *Whig Examiner* in replying to the Tory *Examiner*. This and other publications eventually ran him afoul of such notables as Clarendon, Swift, Pope, and Addison. His best-known historical works were *The Secret History of Europe* (1712–15) and *History of England* (1729–39). In all his histories "the designs of papists and Stuarts against the protestant religion and the British constitution were exposed."[7]

Actually, Oldmixon's first venture into historical writing was the two-volume work published in 1708, *The British Empire in America*. He had never been to the colonies—indeed, he was never to go there—and he admitted the probability of inaccuracies in his history. His main interest in writing was to emphasize the value of the colonies to the mother country; again, the pamphleteer as historian. The first volume covered the prestige and defensive importance of the mainland colonies. In his contentious style he took issue with "the Enemies of our Colonies," especially in dealing with the sugar plantations of the West Indies, the subject of his second volume. He concluded that "our Colonies in America are so far from being a Loss to us, that there are no Hands in the British Empire more usefully employed for the Profit and Glory of the Commonwealth."

Oldmixon's histories of individual colonies are fairly brief and, not surprisingly, are at least as much informational as historical; for example, flora and fauna, native inhabitants, towns, and crops all receive attention. Oldmixon was definitely not a careful historical scholar, even by the best standards of his own day. He uncritically used any source available (such as every word of John Smith's Pocahontas story); at times he seemed to be improvising; and at times he contradicted himself, apparently without realizing it.

While Oldmixon's work was held in disrepute by Americans, who frequently had access to the original authorities from whom he drew, his history was better than his sharper critics asserted. While it may be true that his major importance to American historiography was negative (that is, in stimulating Americans to write their own history to offset or replace his), *The British Empire in America* is also important in at least one positive respect: it serves to remind the student that the English usually thought of the West Indies and the continental colonies as something of a unit. American historians, concentrating their attention on the mainland colonies, forgot England's more comprehensive point of view and thus largely missed the "imperial" perspective of colonial history. Not until the twentieth century, particularly in the work of Charles M. Andrews, did American writers recapture that perspective. The final verdict on Oldmixon in the *Dictionary of National Biography*—that "his historical work has little value now, as his main object in writing it was to promote the cause of his party"[8]— is correct as to motivation but excessive in its conclusion.

William Byrd

William Byrd II, author of the sprightly *History of the Dividing Line betwixt Virginia and North Carolina,* belonged to one of Virginia's leading families, rulers of a princely domain. A large part of his life was spent in England in his younger years as a student and later as a colonial politician. Although he enjoyed London's coffeehouses, where he was much at home with the local wits, he had a great love for his native Virginia and his hospitable Westover mansion. There he indulged his taste for letters among his four thousand volumes, the largest library in the colonies. He was a member of the Royal Society, a rare honor for a colonial.

Not until Byrd was nearly sixty did he attempt any comprehensive literary work; during the twelve years remaining until his death in 1744 he wrote *Progress to the Mines, Journey to the Land of Eden,* and the two "Dividing Line" histories. Byrd, along with other individuals, was appointed to settle the long-standing boundary controversy between the two provinces, and the two works told of his experiences on this survey in 1728. These histories were not published until long afterward; the second, known as *The Secret History of the Line,* which was the more dependable of the two, did not appear in print until the twentieth century. Generally speaking, *The History of the Dividing Line* was a fairly faithful picture of the frontier, but its selection of incidents produced in the reader misconceptions regarding life in North Carolina.

In his narrative Byrd included a short introduction on colonial history, a description of flora and wildlife in the surveyed region, and observations on Indian and pioneer society. Byrd had no illusions about the original Jamestown colony. It consisted, he said, of "about an Hundred men, most of them Reprobates of good Familys; . . . like true Englishmen, they built a Church that cost no more than Fifty Pounds, and a Tavern that cost Five hundred."

The North Carolinians, said Byrd, were an easygoing lot, paying tribute neither to God nor to Caesar: "They are not troubled with any Religious Fumes, and have the least Superstition of any People living. They do not know Sunday from any other day. . . . But they keep so many Sabbaths every week, that their disregard of the Seventh Day has no manner of cruelty in it, either to Servants or Cattle." There was no place in the world, said Byrd, "where the Inhabitants live with less Labour than in N. Carolina. It approaches nearer to the Description of Lubberland than any other, by the great felicity of the Climate, the easiness of raising Provisions, and the Slothfulness of the People."

The man who added extensively (over 150,000 acres) to the already large holding of the Byrd family could also think more generally in imperial terms: "Our country has not been inhabited more than 130 years by the English, and still we hardly know any thing of the Appalachian Mountains . . . whereas the French, who are later comers, have rang'd from Quebec Southward as far as the Mouth of the Mississippi . . . and to the West almost as far as California, which is either way above 2000 miles." The French knew the resources of the country because they had traversed it on foot. "So long as Woodsmen continue to range on Horseback," wrote Byrd, a lover of the forest, "we shall be strangers to our own Country, and a few or no valuable Discoveries will ever be made."

Though he was not a careful student of the psychology of the frontiersman (as was a writer of the next generation, Crèvecoeur, author of *Letters from an American Farmer*), Byrd was fond of the frontier. The Virginia historian was a broad-minded, cultured aristocrat, the most brilliant forerunner of the imaginative group from the Old Dominion that dominated American life in the Revolutionary era.

Cadwallader Colden

Indians were more than mere biological novelties to the colonists. They were aids to commerce and threats to peace. They were determining factors in the diplomatic game played by the English and French for the continent. As political makeweights and as subjects of scientific inquiry, Indians attracted the attention of the versatile Cadwallader Colden. Like William Byrd, Colden had something of the imperial vision lacking in many other officials in the colonies as well as in the mother country.

Colden was one of New York's most illustrious citizens. In his public life, during his many years in office, he made his impress on colonial policy; in his life as a doctor, student, and writer his achievements merited him high rank. The end of his life coincided with the passing of English rule in 1776, a rule he had done so much to uphold during his career as New York's lieutenant governor.

Colden wrote *The History of the Five Indian Nations*... largely because he wished to convince the public in America and England of the importance of the Iroquois to the colony as a bulwark against the French and as a means of holding the West (interestingly, many of his sources were French). He also wished to draw attention to the fur trade, and last, he wished to preserve the materials relating to Indian life. This first New York history was published in 1727 by William Bradford, the colony's pioneer printer, and it was later reprinted in England.

Colden denounced the English for viciously degrading the Iroquois; if that practice continued to be "winked at," he said, the Five Nations would "joyn with every Enemy that can give them the hopes of Plunder." Colden justified an English interpretation of the history of the Iroquois because up to the time of his publication the French alone had written on this subject. His many references to the military adventures of small groups were excused on the ground that the Indian art of war was generally conducted in that manner; Indian oratory was frequently quoted as proof of native genius. The author included lengthy accounts of treaties, believing them to be of great interest to contemporary readers.

With a regard for authenticity that was characteristic of other historians of his day, Colden remarked: "He that first writes the History of matters which are not generally known ought to avoid as much as possible, to make the Evidence of the Truth depend entirely on his own Veracity and Judgment; For this reason I have often related several Transactions in the Words of the Registers." The New Yorker disparaged insubstantial work: "Histories wrote with all the Delicacy of a fine Romance, are like French dishes, more agreeable to the Pallat than the Stomach, and less wholsom than more common and courser Dyet."

The historian introduced his subject with a short sketch of Indian government and then went on to discuss the relations of the Five Nations with the English colonies. He blamed the Jesuits for alienating the Iroquois, though he could not refrain from lauding the bravery of the missionaries who lived among the Indians "at War with their Nation." Colden's observations on Indian character are still worth reading. His work was well known in his own day, for it was one of the few books in English that gave significant details about the history and institutions of the native peoples who occupied so strategic a place in the life of the colonists.[9]

Colden left in manuscript a continuation of his history, which was not published until the twentieth century. It revealed again his preoccupation with the need to win the Iroquois to the English side. He also left a history of New York during the administrations of Governor Cosby and Lieutenant Governor Clark, which included a section on the famous John Peter Zenger trial defining freedom of the press. The author's friend James Alexander defended Zenger, the printer charged with libel, and Colden sided with the defendant.[10]

Colden, whose writing is at times dull and confusing, was always rather sensitive to criticism, but he held it a man's duty to his country to "patiently submit to Scoffs & Jests & revilings when he thinks he cannot avoid them by being usefull." He hoped that in writing his history he had been "in some degree usefull" to his country; "If it be so," he said, "I shall truely gain my end without any further view." The testimony of his contemporaries and of later generations is that Colden did write a "usefull" book; indeed, his work can well be regarded as one of the most significant histories of the colonial era, with its sidelights on ecology, sociology, anthropology, and cultural history.

Daniel Neal

Daniel Neal was a dissenting minister in England who was very much interested in the life of New England; like Oldmixon, however, he never went to the colonies. He corresponded with colonists who, in the pursuit of their own historical interests, made frequent reference to the contributions of their colleague in the mother country. Harvard recognized his work with the highest honor it could grant at that time, the degree of master of arts.

Neal's *History of New England . . . to . . . 1700* was published in two volumes in 1720. The New World was praised as a "Retreat for oppressed Protestants in all Parts of the World"; their sufferings in the Old World were pointed up to exhibit the advantages of the New. Neal's sources were the familiar names: Winslow, Morton, Wood, Increase Mather, Hubbard, and especially Cotton Mather. Neal as-

serted that he wrote with "Freedom and Impartiality, tho' I can't
help declaring myself sometimes on the Side of Liberty, and an Enemy
to Oppression in all its Forms and Colours."

The early chapters concerned the discovery of America, with a
description of native civilization and an account of the Puritans in
the Old World. Neal thought very highly of the clergy who went to
New England; though not all of them were learned, they had a better
share of learning than did "most of their neighboring Clergy at that
Time." The historian wrote profusely on missionary activities among
the Indians, using materials composed by John Eliot. He also devoted
much space to the Quakers, his treatment being something of an apologia for early New England's attitude toward this sect. He was himself,
however, opposed to depriving a man of his civil rights because of his
religious doctrines; such deprivation should be visited only on dis-
turbers of the public peace. Writing half a century after the events
he described, Neal was pleased that New England's attitude toward
the Quakers had changed.

The second volume, which continued the account after 1661,
devoted many of its pages to the wars with the Indians, especially
King Philip's War. The activities of Sir William Phips were chronicled at length, and so, of course, was the witchcraft episode. For
these incidents and characters in New England's history Neal had
fuller authorities than those available to him for the early period, but
in the main he transcribed much of what he found in Cotton Mather.
It is interesting that he went against the Mathers in his treatment of
the witchcraft hysteria. "All the Confessions that were made," said
Neal, "seem to me either the effects of a distemper'd Brain, or ex-
torted from Persons to save their Lives."

Neal was one of several writers who weighed the possibility of a
revolt against the mother country. He thought it remote, believing
New England disinclined to a revolution that would be against its
own interest. For, he maintained, in order to live, New Englanders
must trade with Europe, "so that if we could suppose them to rebel
against England," they would only fall into the hands of another power,
"who would protect them no longer than he could sell them to advantage."

Another large-scale undertaking by Neal was a four-volume history
of the Puritans (1732–38); this work had little material on the Puritans of New England, and most of that was interwoven with the history
of their coreligionists in England. Although Neal's history of New
England was harshly criticized by Thomas Hutchinson and others as
scarcely more than an adaptation of Mather's *Magnalia*, it continued
to be quoted by historians for many years. It contained the "medulla"

of the *Magnalia,* said one writer, but it was superior in style, "with such sentiments and observations as Mather had not language to describe nor a head and heart to conceive." It is not surprising that Neal's work was regarded highly by his fellow Puritans and criticized severely by others.

Thomas Prince

Neal was an observer living in the homeland who recorded New England's history with sympathy. Better known and more valuable in the establishment of a continuous historical tradition was the work of a native New Englander, Thomas Prince. Prince was born in Massachusetts in 1687. After study at Harvard he accepted the pastorate of the South Church, Boston, a position which he held to his death in 1758. He had traveled widely abroad, and conscientious study fitted him for a career of distinction. He enjoyed an intercolonial reputation as one of the leading scholars in America.

Prince's interest in history was aroused at an early date. When he was but a freshman, he began collecting books for his "New England library." After naming the authors whose acquaintance he had made when he was young—Morton, Johnson, Hubbard, the two Mathers (his friend Cotton Mather was a stimulus to his historical writing)—Prince confessed: "I longed to see all things disposed in the order of time wherein they happened, together with the rise and progress of the several towns, churches, counties, and provinces throughout this country. . . . In my foreign travels, I found the want of a regular history of this country everywhere complained of." While he was in England, Prince had gathered books on America's early history, and he thought that on his return home in 1717 he would have sufficient leisure to "attempt a brief account of facts at least in the form of annals." But the cares of his pastorate allowed him time only to collect materials, not to digest them.

In 1736, Prince brought out the first volume of his *Chronological History of New England.* His work showed him to be more New Englander than orthodox minister, more supportive of the claims of his region than of those of his religion. He spoke of the large mass of manuscripts at his disposal, and his work, he said, was in part an effort to preserve valuable materials, some of which had already been destroyed by fire. Prince wrote that Bradford's grandson, Major John Bradford, had given him permission to use the Plymouth history "& take out of it what [he] thought proper for [his] New England chronology." The inveterate collector added the old Bradford manuscript to his own library, where it remained until the time of the Revolution.

Prince's standard of scholarship was unusually high, guided as it was by a healthy skepticism. He had become thoroughly familiar with European historical scholarship, and he is sometimes credited with being one of the first American historians to follow European precedent: "I would not take the least iota upon trust; if possible, I examined the original authors I could meet with . . . I cite my vouchers to every passage; and I have done by utmost . . . to find out the truth, and . . . relate it in the clearest order." After paying his critical respects to writers who protest their own impartiality, Prince stated his credo: "I own I am on the side of pure Christianity; as also of civil and religious liberty. . . . I am for leaving everyone to the freedom of worshipping according to the light of his conscience. . . . And I hope my inclination to these great principles will not bias me to a misrecital of facts, but rather to state them as I really find them for the public benefit."

Like the medieval historians, Prince felt it necessary to start his work with man's beginning, from Adam, "Year one, first month, sixth day." His chronology went on to the birth of Christ, then to Columbus's discovery, the introduction closing with the "discovery of New England by Captain Gosnold." After this very long introduction Prince began with the chronology of New England. His history, which appeared in one volume, stopped with the events of 1630; the annals for the following three years, which were to be part of a second volume, were published separately, long after the first volume was issued; and publication then ceased. Nowhere in the American colonies of that period was there a demand for so detailed a history. In a letter referring to Prince's work, John Callender, a contemporary historian in Rhode Island, expressed sorrow that the *Chronology* was so ill received. "I look on it as an honor to the country, as well as to the author," he wrote, adding prophetically, "and doubt not but posterity will do him justice."[11]

With but few exceptions Prince adhered to his intention to give the unadorned facts. Some events, however, such as the settlement of New England, moved him to speak a more vibrant language than a dry chronology ordinarily used: "Divers attempts are made to settle this rough and northern country; first by the French . . . and then by the English, and both from mere secular views. But . . . a train of crosses accompany these designs of both nations . . . till a pious people of England, not there allowed to worship their Maker according to his institutions only . . . sailed from Plymouth in England . . . in search of some uncultivated region in North Virginia, where they might quietly enjoy their religious liberties, and transmit them to posterity."

For the most part Prince's work was aridly factual, and yet it was the orderly arrangement of those facts and the tests to which he submitted them before their inclusion in his catalog that have given Prince his reputation as an American pioneer in scientific historical writing. Probably as important as any other inheritance we possess from him is the extremely valuable collection of Americana he spent so many years gathering and which, though sadly diminished, rests now in the Boston Public Library.

The prophecy of Prince's contemporary that posterity would do him honor was abundantly fulfilled, and a long list of historians later paid their tributes to him. His *Chronology* inspired similar attempts, and as late as 1791 a keen student of history, John Pintard, of New York, when compiling an American chronology, wrote to Jeremy Belknap, "I shall do pretty well as long as Prince holds out. But shall be at a loss after I part with him." Many historians, it might be added, clung to Prince to avoid getting lost.[12] He set a precedent for careful, accurate scholarship and influenced such important later historians as Thomas Hutchinson and Jeremy Belknap.

William Stith

When Prince was writing his history of New England, an Anglican minister was writing with equal care the story of Virginia. William Stith, who had been educated at Oxford, was rector of the parish of Henrico and a governor of William and Mary College. In 1747 he published *The History of the First Discovery and Settlement of Virginia;* he thus became the first to produce a history of Virginia in the main current of English historical writing. Like his contemporaries, Stith was afraid that historical materials then available might be lost if they were not immediately used.

He began his history in a rather sophisticated tone: "Every Country," he wrote, "hath it's Fables concerning it's Original, which give great Scope to light and fanciful Historians, but are usually passed over with a slight Mention by the solid and judicious. . . . Even this new World hath been endowed with it's Fabulous Age." He expressed "Contempt and Aversion for all such learned Trumpery" and wrote that he would apply himself "to give a plain and exact history of our Country, ever regarding Truth as the first requisite and principal Virtue in an Historian, and relating nothing without a sufficient Warrant and Authority."[13]

Stith's narrative ended with the year 1624. The earlier part was mainly based upon John Smith; much of the later part treated in detail the squabbles within the London Company, for which the "Records" of the company (made available through William Byrd's assistance) were the important source. Stith characterized Smith as an honest and reliable writer about the events with which he was connected in America but considered him somewhat confused. As for the quarrels between the company and the king, Stith's sympathies lay with the former.

Although he wrote with the consciousness of America's growing strength and challenged English historians to take account of her history, his narrative was temperate and written with unusual regard for scholarly standards; thus he has sometimes been called the most modern of colonial historians. His errors of interpretation, which favored the company, were the result of excessive faith in the court records, which were partisan. It should be added that since Stith's day most historians who have also taken these records at their face value have misunderstood much of Virginia's early history.

Stith had promised that he would continue his work, but he never went on with it. It is supposed that so detailed a history was not to the taste of Virginia gentry, and the lack of support discouraged him. In point of scholarship Stith's contribution ranks with the very best produced in the colonial period and has long been one of the standard works in early Virginia history.[14]

William Smith

The most distinguished historical studies in the colonial period were being produced in New England and Virginia, but able historians were also at work in the middle colonies. Their volumes described contemporary society and reflected the bitter political controversies in these developing provinces. William Smith, the historian of New York, was born there in 1728. His father held several high offices in the province. The son was educated at Yale and then returned to his native city to study law. Very soon he gained a large practice, becoming a leading member of the bar, and entered actively into politics.[15] Named a member of the New York colonial council at the time when revolutionary discussions were alienating friends of long standing, Smith drew up a plan of colonial union that he hoped would prevent dismemberment of the British Empire. The historian became more conservative as the radical temper of the colonists increased, and when the war broke out, Smith became a Loyalist. He left for England when the British troops evacuated New York and remained abroad until 1786, when he was appointed chief justice of Canada, a post he held until his death in 1793.

Because of the stigma of Toryism, Smith's history was long in disrepute, but it scarcely deserved such a fate. *The History . . . of New York*, first published in 1757, closed with the year 1732; a continuation to

1762 was later added. Smith was reluctant to write on the period following 1732 because his father, during those years, had been engaged in bitter controversy with the governor. The history of those times, he said, "will be better received from a more disinterested pen. . . . Besides, a writer who exposed the conduct of the living will inevitably meet with their fury and resentment. The prudent historian of his own times will always be a coward, and never give fire till death protects him from the malice and stroke of his enemy."

Although Smith did not write with a disinterested pen, he usually managed to avoid extremes. He was one of the leading Presbyterian dissenters in the colony, engaging in a number of serious religious controversies, and it was hardly possible for him to avoid partisanship. Because of favored family associations the historian knew many of the actors in the later part of his story. His writing, though good, did not escape that moralizing which was then characteristic of most historians, and he often asked support for causes in which he was interested. Some sentences he neatly turned, as, when writing of missionary activities among the Iroquois, he remarked, "The French priests boast indeed of their converts, but they have made more proselytes to politics than religion."

The larger portion of Smith's work dealt with the eighteenth century, since he had no direct acquaintance with the Dutch documents and understood little of the early history of the colony. Though he told a strictly political story, he added substantial descriptions of geography, trade, religion, politics, and the law. Today these descriptions are probably the most interesting parts of his work. He wrote from the standpoint of an aristocrat, but he did supply some information about the life of "persons of inferior station," as he put it. He had nothing but contempt for such "demagogues" as Jacob Leisler, and he regarded Zenger as "a low printer, dandled upon the knee of popular applause." To Smith's credit, he did show something of the Enlightenment virtue of tolerance toward Jews and blacks. He was proud of his birthplace: "With respect to riches there is not so great an inequality amongst us as is common in Boston, and some other places." He could also see the flaws in his colony:

Our schools are in the lowest order—the instructors want instruction; and, through a long shameful neglect of all the arts and sciences, our common speech is extremely corrupt. . . . In matters of religion we are not so intelligent, in general, as the inhabitants of the New England colonies; but both in this respect and morals, we certainly have the advantage of the southern provinces.

Throughout Smith's work appeared his distaste for real and fancied Episcopal oppression, abetted by the government. The historian, provincial-born, disliked many of the governors sent over from England, though he was partial to William Burnet. Smith's history was scorned by Cadwallader Colden, who thought it unfit "to pass for a chronicle of the Province of New York." Later generations, removed from eighteenth-century partisan strife, have, however, found much to praise in Smith's history.[16] Unfortunately, what was arguably the most important part of Smith's work was never published; housed in the New York Public Library, this vital manuscript carries the story of New York from the eve of the Revolution to its conclusion in 1783 and is considered by many to be indispensable to an understanding of New York's role in the Revolution.

Samuel Smith

Samuel Smith, a contemporary of William Smith, was the author of *The History of the Colony . . . of New Jersey. . . .* It appeared in 1765 under the imprint of James Parker, one of the most famous of colonial printers; it was found sufficiently serviceable to be issued in a second edition more than a century later (1877). Smith came of a Quaker merchant family and held several important public offices in addition to practicing his trade of printer.

The writer said he was eager to present the "plain state of facts" of New Jersey's history, not only because so little had appeared abroad but also to unite the people of New Jersey in the knowledge of their colony and its past. Unlike Prince, who began with Adam, Smith went no further back than Columbus. Nearly half of his book described the events of seventeenth-century New Jersey. Materials on immigration were included, along with the text of many documents which were not easily accessible to the eighteenth-century reader and which today are the joy of the genealogist.

In the pages on the administration of Lord Cornbury, first royal governor of the colony, Smith wrote as a patriotic colonial: "Tho things were carried to arbitrary lengths, there was not wanting in the province, men of discernment to see and lament the unhappy situation of their country, and of spirit to oppose its greatest enemies." Cornbury, said Smith, ruled by "trick and design." He was, not surprisingly, even harder on the infamous Sir Edmund Andros: "He bore the unfavourable character of an arbitrary governor, who made the will of his despotic master [James II] and not the law, the chief rule of his conduct."

Like other historians Smith gave much attention to Indian customs and to the relations between the natives and the colonists. His observations on the Indians were free from rancor; his Quaker background led him rather to emphasize their peaceful qualities. He was also sympathetic to the plight of slaves in both his public life and his history.

Smith is perhaps more remembered as a preserver of historical materials than as a historian, since there was less of his own writing in his book than that of authors of various public and private papers whom he quoted at great length. His history, however, has great value, partly as a political tract of the times. Published at the peak of a crisis in imperial relations, it showed Smith an ardent defender of colonial rights. It deserves the praise it has received as the starting point for all later histories of New Jersey and should hold a place in the literature of the Revolution as well.

William Douglass

Historians in this period were mainly concerned with their respective colonies, but they were aware of a broader field of historical inquiry. The dawning sense of unity among the colonies was already apparent. At least one colonial historian, William Douglass, viewed the provinces as a whole, and although his work was inadequate, it showed the American mind in transition. Douglass's *Summary, Historical and Political . . . of the British Settlements in North America,* published in two volumes in 1752, attracted more attention than it deserved, partly because it received favorable mention in Adam Smith's *Wealth of Nations.*

Douglass was a physician by profession; indeed, for some years he was Boston's only duly licensed doctor. Having arrived in the colonies from Scotland in 1718, he first appeared in the public eye as an opponent of inoculation for smallpox (he later changed his mind on this issue). His chief claim to fame as a physician rests on his masterly account of Boston's epidemic of scarlet fever in 1736, the first adequate clinical description of the disease.

As a historian Douglass fell far short of the best standards of his day. He was extremely contentious and especially delighted in attacking the works of fellow historians; he referred to the work of Cotton Mather and other New England historians as "beyond all excuse intolerably erroneous" and to Neal's *History of New England* as "a tedious silly ridiculous conjectural account." He obviously wrote at odd times stolen from his professional work—his writing is badly organized and seems more like a mass of pungent, ill-digested notes than a finished history. Frequently he drifted into long digressions, some of medical importance, but others on irrelevant subjects which seemed to interest him at the moment. Finally, and most seriously, he was extremely careless about his sources. He denied the necessity of using original sources: "This is a laborious affair, being obliged to consult MSS records." And he gathered material to support his views from the reports of unreliable correspondents. "Historians, like sworn Evidences in Courts of Law, ought to declare the Whole Truth (so far as comes to their knowledge) and nothing but the Truth." So proclaimed Douglass at the beginning of his second volume, but his work fell far short of that ideal.

In many ways Douglass's work is comparable to Oldmixon's; both wrote of the colonies in general rather than of a particular colony, and both are sometimes regarded as early imperial historians. But Oldmixon's work, with all its flaws, is superior to Douglass's, even though Douglass called Oldmixon "an erroneous Scribbler." Certainly Oldmixon would have agreed with Douglass that "it is a common but mistaken notion, that sending abroad colonists weakens the mother-country.... The people sent from Great-Britain and their progeny made vastly more profitable returns, than they could possibly have done by their labour at home."

Douglass began his *Summary* with a short survey of ancient and modern colonization and then went on to the settlement of North America, including Canada. The materials on the colonies outside New England, however, were comparatively scanty. Clearly, despite the mass of misinformation Douglass supplied, his volumes did possess value. A section entitled "Loose Proposals Towards Regulating the British Colonies" contained interesting material on imperial reorganization and showed that, even though Douglass deplored such abuses of England's power as impressment of colonial seamen by the Royal Navy and the sending of colonial troops to fight outside the colonies, he was essentially a defender of the royal prerogative. Douglass's work included far more economic and social history than did the books of most of his contemporaries, and his strong dislike of anything tending toward inflation pleased some later economists. For the most part, however, posterity has been less impressed by Douglass's history than were his contemporaries, especially those in England; the *Monthly Review* praised it highly, saying that it contained a "fuller and more circumstantial account of North America, than is anywhere else to be met with." Perhaps that is more a commentary on the lack of information readily available on the colonies than justifiable praise for Douglass's history.[17]

CHAPTER 4

The Growing National Spirit: 1750–1800

AMERICANS' GROWING SELF-CONSCIOUSNESS in the Revolutionary era fostered the study and writing of historical narratives which in turn nurtured the new national identity. As historians began more frequently to transcend local boundaries, many histories of provinces and states appeared. The argument that state histories would "lay a good foundation for some future compiler in writing a general history of the country" encouraged Jeremy Belknap, for example, to write his history of New Hampshire.[1]

Ezra Stiles, president of Yale, was particularly conscious of America's strides toward maturity. For many years he corresponded with diverse individuals for his projected *Ecclesiastical History of New England and British America*. According to Stiles, one Englishman offered to secure five thousand subscriptions for his history.[2] In letters exchanged with Thomas Hutchinson, Stiles said that a European could not "do justice to the history of the American provinces." He was pleased that Hutchinson, who was then writing a history of Massachusetts, was of New England descent, and Stiles urged him to broaden his narrative to include all four New England colonies in his survey: "You would thus write a complete history of an intire people."[3] Stiles said that his own plan to write on "British American History" would begin with the history of New England "as of one intire emigration, people and settlement, to deduce it through the civil, military, commercial, moral and ecclesiastical changes and revolutions to the late . . . war" (the Seven Years' War). Although Stiles's work was never published, he left to his son-in-law, Abiel Holmes, many useful manuscripts for the latter's *American Annals*.[4]

Other historians, notably the Baptist Isaac Backus, searched all the colonies for materials. His three-volume *History of New England with Particular Reference to the . . . Baptists* (1777–96) enhanced his reputation as a champion of religious liberty in America. In accord with the best scholarship of his time, he sought out documentary sources and named "his principal vouchers on purpose to have his performance thoroughly examined." "So solid was his history despite his own obvious bias," wrote Backus's biographer William G. McLoughlin, "that no serious challenge to its accuracy was ever made. To this day it remains one of the great source books for Colonial history."[5]

Backus objected to most of the existing histories for their biased treatment of minority religious groups. When he reached the Revolution in his narrative, Backus did include a discussion of the war, but on the whole it remained an ecclesiastical history.[6]

After 1750 newspapers, magazines, and almanacs began to reflect the rising interest in history. One writer solicited subscriptions through the newspapers for a proposed work on the colonies.[7] Nathaniel Ames included in his almanac for 1756 "An Account of the Several Provinces in North America," which was copied and expanded by a New York almanac. Another editor, Samuel Nevill, published a history of North America in his *New American Magazine*. To prepare citizens for active participation in politics, Ames recommended the study of geography and history, adding the nationalistic note that "it is proper to begin with the history of your own nation."[8]

A friendly Englishman, Dr. John Fothergill, encouraged the study of America, hoping that one historian would describe her contemporary civilization, with a fresh description made every twenty years. "If the history of the actions of men in civil life are of any use to posterity," he wrote, "what advantages might not be gained by thus taking time by the forelock?"[9] Magazines devoted hundreds of pages to general and national history. In the 1780s there was a special interest in ancient history; it was hoped that study of the ancients would guide the young Republic.[10]

The American Revolution was certainly in part the result of the interest of the Founding Fathers in history and also the result of the particular view of history that they held. H. Trevor Colbourn has made this clear in *The Lamp of Experience: Whig History and the Intellectual Origins of the American Revolution:*

The history made by the American Revolutionaries was in part the product of the history they read, in part the product of their translation of a whiggish Clio into "an expression of the American mind" [Jefferson's phrase] of universal significance. The historical principals of whiggery relating to the right of resistance, royal prerogative, and civil liberty were basic ingredients in the colonial constitutional theory of the pre-Revolutionary period. Americans read history in a highly selective manner, shrewdly sorting out and altering to American requirements whiggish views in support of their doctrines on their rights as Englishmen.[11]

The Revolution, of course, was also a strong impetus to historical writing. A "History of the Late War in America," a serial copied from the *Annual Register*, published in London, appeared in the *Worces-*

ter Magazine (1786–88). The *Columbian Magazine* in 1789 also used information from the *Annual Register* to publish a historical digest of the war. The *Boston Magazine* in 1783 seemed to specialize in history; indeed, some of its original backers helped organize the Massachusetts Historical Society a few years later. The *American Magazine*, edited by the nationalist Noah Webster, awakened interest and lively discussion in American history. Jeremy Belknap published a series of biographical articles in the *Columbian Magazine* in 1788 under the title "The American Plutarch." Belknap's close friend Ebenezer Hazard, who had long been gathering materials, published his two-volume *Historical Collections* in 1792 and 1794 to "lay the Foundation of a good American History," as he put it. Belknap advised Hazard that people wanted to know why Hazard did not write history instead of publishing sources when "a regular history of the United States would be a more popular and profitable work than such a collection," but he warned that "it would cost you years of labor."[12] Belknap and Hazard were part of a circle of historians who assisted one another; other members included William Gordon, David Ramsay, and Jedidiah Morse.[13]

In the 1780s, in the exuberant glow of independence, plans were formulated for national education; naturally, history was assigned a special place. Benjamin Rush, who was prominent in this movement, advised the study of ancient history and of the "progress of liberty and tyranny" in Europe. The young student was also to learn American history, in particular the events of the years just ended. Webster believed that the principal textbook in the country should be a manual of American history.

Every phase of American life felt the impact of eighteenth-century nationalism. Nathaniel Chipman urged a more careful investigation into the laws of national development, since he felt that earlier historians had been too concerned with "battles and sieges only, the intrigues of statesmen, and the revolution of empires." For a deeper understanding of civilization Chipman advocated the study of the "history of man in society" and of the "development of the human mind."[14] Still another contemporary writer, Samuel H. Smith, speaking in the accents of the philosophes, stressed the educational value of history in liberating people from "fanaticism and superstition"; history would also teach students to regard war as the instrument "of vice and folly." Knowledge of the causes of mankind's progress or regression, said Smith, would enable man to view his own society more intelligently.[15] The New York lawyer and historian William Smith had long before urged the reading of history for prospective members of the bar. He also understood that history was distinguished from chronology and required the student to "take a larger scope."[16]

European observers were interested in the Revolution and sought information from leading Americans. To the Abbé Gabriel Bonnet de Mably, John Adams communicated his thoughts on writing the history of America's Revolution. Acknowledging that "it is yet too soon to undertake a complete history of that great event" and that no one had the necessary materials for writing it, Adams explained that a writer should divide the history of America into four periods: the first included the years up to 1761, when the disputes began; the second to 1775, spanning fourteen years of "a war of the quill"; the third ended with 1778, the period when the "war was exclusively between Great Britain and the United States"; and the last period led up to the peacemaking. "The whole of a long life, to begin at the age of twenty years," said Adams, "will be necessary to assemble from all nations . . . the documents proper to form a complete history of the American Revolution, because it is indeed the history of mankind during that epoch." Adams also suggested a study of four New England institutions—the towns, congregations, schools, and militia—to learn how the Revolutionary spirit was fostered.[17] Unfortunately, Mably never followed through on Adams's suggestions.

With peace did come histories of the war, and it was from a pro-American English publication, the *Annual Register*, that historians secured their material; in fact, so great was their debt to this work that several writers were later accused of plagiarizing from it. There were historians, however, whose work was original; among them was Benjamin Trumbull, who reflected the sentiment of his contemporaries. "After the revolutionary war," he said, "it was the desire of many pious men, that the remarkable deliverance, which the United States of America had experienced might be fully exhibited to the public, as a tribute of praise to their Great Deliverer, and for the instruction of posterity." Such writing would bring Americans "into a more general acquaintance with each other," he said, and would "awaken their mutual sympathies, promote their union and general welfare."[18]

Trumbull's phrases indicate that historians were still tracing the finger of God in history and that the past was to be studied for a guide to social behavior. With respect to the latter point, Trumbull and all the other proponents of national education were in accord with one of the greatest and most widely read historians of their century, Voltaire. The philosophe, like his fellow thinkers of the Enlightenment, looked upon the study of history as valuable training in creating a virtuous citizenry. The historian was to describe the progress of society up to his own day, presumably the highest goal yet achieved, and then he was to suggest the lines of future conduct. The alert Boston clergyman Jonathan Mayhew wrote to Harvard's benefactor Thomas Hollis in thanks for the gift of Voltaire's *Philosophy of History* and the *Philo-sophical Dictionary*. He disagreed with their author's religious ideas, but added: "I cannot but think, these, as compositions, to be very fine performances. I have read them with delight, as containing much useful learning . . . & written throughout in a most spirited, enter-taining & masterly way; so that I would not be long without them for twice their value."[19]

Where earlier historians had seen the working of God's will, later writers saw instead the working of natural laws. Even so, throughout the nineteenth century and up to our own day, despite the develop-ment of "scientific" history, there has been a strong tendency to make history a lay sermon instructing the reader to enlightened social con-duct. Although the lessons in modern histories may be somewhat dif-ferent and their didactic quality less obvious than those of colonial his-tories, in spirit they are less widely separated than may superficially appear.

Thomas Hutchinson

It is significant that some of the most valuable histories of the Revo-lutionary era were written by Loyalists: Hutchinson, Hewat, Proud, and Chalmers. The tone of their works was conservative, and their concern was generally to justify the established order. Fate placed them on the defeated side, but the loss of historians such as these had an adverse effect on the intellectual life of the young Republic for a whole generation.

"By far the best of the Loyalist histories was Thomas Hutchinson's," wrote Bernard Bailyn.[20] Thomas Hutchinson, historian, was but one aspect of a personality that devoted itself to a long life of public service, a career that was cut off by the War of Independence. Hutch-inson's forebears had been prominent in Massachusetts from its early days. As a young man he was interested in politics, and in 1737 he entered the legislature, where he became an expert on public finance. During his long career he held the offices of chief justice, lieutenant governor, and governor, gaining with each step the increasing confi-dence of a larger number of voters. The British government, too, had learned to place confidence in Hutchinson; thus it was he who tried to serve as moderator between the two antagonists when they had passed beyond the stage of reasoning. Radical Americans would not listen to his Loyalist words; British ministers scorned his provincial advice.

Hutchinson left Massachusetts in 1774, never to return, although his spirit, spent in futility in London, was still anchored in his native home. "I am not able to subdue a natural attachment to the very soil and air, as well as to the people of New England," he wrote in his exile. In these last bitter years the historian found solace in the completion of his history. In his diary for October, 1778, he wrote, "I finished the revisal of my History, to the end of my Administration, and laid it by." The last volume remained in manuscript until 1828—fifty years later—when it was published in London.

Even as a boy Hutchinson favored the study of history. From New England chronicles he went on to histories of Great Britain. "The history of Great Britain and of its dominions," he said, "was of all others the most delightful to me; and a thorough knowledge of the nature and constitution of the supreme and of the subordinate governments thereof, I considered as what would be peculiarly beneficial to me in the line of life upon which I was entering." Hutchinson was chiefly interested in institutional history, and his prestige gave him access to a great many manuscripts relating to New England. In the true spirit of the historian he explained that people were interested in the past because of the need to prolong their lives "to the utmost length."

In the last days of 1764 appeared the first volume of *The History of the Colony of Massachusetts Bay*, which brought the story to 1691. Following his political history, Hutchinson included chapters on religion, laws, Indians, and the geographical conditions of settlement. He could occasionally be critical of his native province, as he was in recording the persecution of the Quakers: "May the time never come again," he concluded firmly, "when the government shall think that by killing men for their religion they do God good service."

The welcome reception accorded this volume stimulated Hutchinson to continue his history, and he had made considerable progress on the second volume, carrying his story to 1730, when the political storm broke. In the summer of 1765, Stamp Act rioters broke into Lieutenant Governor Hutchinson's home and scattered his possessions in the muddy streets. A contemporary observer wrote:

But the loss to be most lamented is that . . . [of] a large and valuable collection of manuscripts and original papers which he had been gathering all his lifetime. . . . As these related to the history of the policy of the country, from the time of its settlement to the present, and was the only collection of its kind, the loss to the public is great and irretrievable.

With the help of a friend Hutchinson managed to recover the manuscript of the second volume of his *History*, and it bears to this day the mudstains of Boston's riotous streets in 1765. After bringing the story of the province up to 1750, he published it in 1767.[21]

The calm and moderate tone of the first volume was also characteristic of the second, despite the savage events that marked its progress. With much dignity Hutchinson wrote in the preface to volume 2: "We shall never all be of one mind in our political principles." The author rarely permitted his personal feelings to intrude, believing it the historian's function to remain impartial. Still, in his generally excellent account of the Salem witchcraft episode his words were sharp. It was, he wrote, "as strange an infatuation as any people were ever under. A considerable number of innocent persons were sacrificed to the distempered imagination, or perhaps wicked hearts, of such as pretended to be bewitched." Like many another rationalist, Hutchinson, though liberal in intellectual matters, was conservative in politics: "In a well constituted government it is of importance to the people that the share even of the popular part of the constitution should not be unduly raised to the suppression of the monarchical or aristocratical parts." This volume contained a long narrative of the controversy between the advocates of paper money and the defenders of "hard money"; Hutchinson clearly counted himself among the latter.

The third and last volume covered the period from 1750 to 1774, during which the author had been very active in Revolutionary controversies. Even in this final volume, finished abroad, when Hutchinson wrote about events that burned in his soul, surprisingly little bitterness was revealed; for example, there was a very straightforward account of the Stamp Act riots—in the third person. In the sadness of exile he knew the costs of war, and he wrote movingly of its evils. The judicial temper of Hutchinson's mind remained unruffled; his portraits of some political adversaries, though unflattering, were largely true. A few months before the first volume came off the press, Hutchinson told Stiles that he might write a book on his own period and remarked not ill-naturedly, "I threaten Mr. Otis sometimes that I will be revenged of him after I am dead."

Although Hutchinson was sincere in his aim to write the truth, he failed at various points. Despite his great industry, his public life exacted so much of his energy that he had not found sufficient time to examine many pamphlets, newspapers, and legislative documents that might have served to correct some of his judgments. As a stylist, too, he was deficient, and he knew it. He once explained that his work was unpolished because the constant calls of public business never gave him time "to write two sheets at a sitting."[22] He felt that he had "no talent at painting, or describing characters." Perhaps the historian was too modest, for his writing had the vigor of his personality, and his literary skill increased the more he wrote. The modern reader frequently finds the character sketches the most interesting portions of the *History*. As the number of his pages increased, the note of political conservatism strengthened — a natural consequence of the stand the author took in the Revolutionary controversies.

Hutchinson's book was the first general history of that province which produced so many historians. One authority, William F. Poole, said that Hutchinson's three-volume *History* and his one-volume *Collection of Original Papers relative to the History . . . of Massachusetts Bay*, published in 1769, were "the four most precious books" on that period of American history. Hutchinson intended to publish a volume of documents to go along with each volume of his history, but managed to complete only the first. The severest modern critic of Hutchinson, A. C. Goodell, charged that the historian did not make the best use of the materials at his command. The basis of his work, the legislative journals of governor and council, was inadequate, said Goodell, who further criticized Hutchinson for omitting a survey of the advances of civilization in New England in the eighteenth century.[23] While this criticism is in some respects justifiable, Hutchinson's work nevertheless ranks above all other colonial historians. His organization of materials and his historical sense were far beyond those of most of his contemporaries. His analysis of the Revolutionary controversy showed greater objectivity and was nearer the truth than that of any succeeding historian for almost a century.[24]

Robert Proud

Hutchinson was not the only Loyalist historian whose work, written during the war years, awaited quieter days for publication. Robert Proud's two-volume *History of Pennsylvania*, published between 1797 and 1798, was written from 1776 to 1780, "but the great change in this country, which ensued," prevented publication at that time. In the view of Proud, Pennsylvania's golden age lay in the past, before the Revolutionary years had tarnished its glory; thus he chose not to deal with the Revolutionary movement at all in his history.

Proud was in his early thirties when he arrived in Philadelphia from England in 1759. In his new home he became an instructor in a school conducted by fellow Quakers, where he remained until the outbreak of the Revolution. His Loyalist associations during the war soured him against his rebellious neighbors. During the war he wrote to his brother in England, "[I] . . . lived in a very private and retired Way, even like a Person dead amidst the Confusions, and conversing more with my Books than with Persons."

Proud's history opened with a long introduction containing the memoirs of William Penn, for whom he had the highest praise, and an account of the rise of the Quakers. The historian described Penn's effort to obtain the grant, including in his text complete versions of important documents and letters. In the manner of other contemporary histories, Proud's writing was often a mere thread connecting pages of documents. The second volume covered the years from 1709 to 1771, but after 1725 the narrative was very thin and the selections from documents much fewer. Proud concluded the history proper with some characteristic remarks: "Thus far appears the manner of the rise, colonization, increase and happy establishment of the flourishing province of Pennsylvania . . . . But all things have their time. And both kingdoms and empires, as well as smaller states and particular persons, must die."

Although the historical narrative was inadequate for the later years of the colony's history, the hundred pages or more on Pennsylvania in the ten years following 1760 offered some compensation. The historian took great pride in the number of humane institutions in his province. Proud justly made much of the religious tolerance that prevailed in Pennsylvania. As did other historians of the time, he included many details on the Indians, but his critical sense was much sharper than that of most writers on the subject.

In a long appendix Proud gathered documents that he could not fit into the text. At a time when these papers were scattered in various places, if they were in print at all, his diligence in grouping them was of real value. In general, though, Proud's history was not outstanding; certainly it was vastly inferior to Hutchinson's. As Joseph E. Illick III said in his recent comparison of Proud and Mather: "Like Cotton Mather, who, when his world was collapsing about him, wrote *Magnalia Christi Americana* to remind his contemporaries of the glory that was Puritan Massachusetts, Proud was attempting to restore the past. He enjoyed a success equal to Mather's."[25]

Alexander Hewat

Historians of the South in the colonial period were few compared with those in the North; except for Virginians they were very rare for many years. During the Revolutionary era, however, when the English were eager for information on all parts of the empire, there began to appear historical material on the lesser-known colonies. In 1779 a two-volume work was published in London by Alexander Hewat, *An Historical Account of. . . South Carolina and Georgia*; the major portion of the history dealt with South Carolina. Hewat had migrated from Scotland to Charleston, where, as a Presbyterian minister, he was in a position to learn much of the character of American society. He sided with the Loyalists when the war broke out and was exiled by South Carolina's

Revolutionary government, but he maintained his friendly relations with some of his neighbors in Charleston to the end of his life.

Hewat modestly referred to his work as "only a rough draught" intended to acquaint England with the commercial possibilities of the southern colonies. Like other historians of the South he could not resist criticism of New England: "We may challenge the annals of any nation," he said, "to produce a code of laws more intolerant than that of the first settlers in New England." Hewat firmly opposed slavery as well as religious intolerance.

The first volume ended with the change from the proprietary form of government in South Carolina to that of a royal province in 1728. A good deal of social history and some natural history were interspersed in his writing, but it was rarely related to the dominant theme, politics. Hewat spoke of a new era in the government of South Carolina when it became a royal province—an era of freedom, security, and happiness. He presented a good firsthand account of life in South Carolina, describing manners, the educational level of the people, and the like. The narrative went as far as the outbreak of the Revolution, and, although Hewat promised to write further on the subject, he published nothing more. In naming the causes for disputes with the mother country, he made some interesting observations on the development of the colonial consciousness of power and the gradual rise in disaffection toward the mother country among the second and third genrations of colonists.

Because Hewat's book was the first history of South Carolina, it deserves the praise accorded any other pioneering work. David Ramsay, a contemporary historian, in recommending it to Belknap, said that it was unreliable on the background of the war because of the author's Tory sentiments, but that on other matters "you may rely on his accounts."[26] Historians for years afterward, including Bancroft, turned to the pages of Hewat for material not readily available elsewhere. The first historians to be receptive to Hewat's analysis of the coming of the Revolution were naturally those of the imperial school, for his relatively dispassionate analysis foreshadowed theirs in many ways.

George Chalmers

George Chalmers was one of the ablest historians in eighteenth-century America. He left behind a greater body of writing than that of any other American loyalist, and it was better than most. In the early years of the troubled 1760's he had gone from Edinburgh to Maryland, where he practiced law. When the War of Independence broke out, he sailed for London and was appointed to a government post. There his official connection gave him access to state papers, which he used intelligently in discussing many historical problems.

Chalmers believed that an examination of the development of the relations between England and the colonies would show that the constitutional position maintained by the rebellious American was wrong. With this in mind he published his *Political Annals of the Present United Colonies . . .* in 1780, which narrated their history to the revolution of 1689. He observed that, although much attention had been given to the history of Great Britain and Ireland, neglect had too often been the portion of "that considerable part of the empire, the British colonies."

According to Chalmers, he was issuing his volume because he thought that "it might at this time possibly do some good." His sources included the acts of assemblies, the printed collections of state papers, and the journals of the Board of Trade and Plantations—materials which contained items generally unfamiliar to other historians. "He hath always cited minutely the various authorities on which he relied," wrote Chalmers of himself, "partly in order to authenticate his own assertions, but more to enable succeeding writers . . . to pursue his track with greater ease to themselves and advantage to the world."

Chalmers's examination of the legal status of the colonies left him critical of their demands. He was especially hostile to New England and to the whole North in general. He wrote that New England "has at all times found delight amid scenes of turbulence" and said:

In the colonists of the south, we see a just regard to their liberties as Englishmen, and to the laws of the state; but in the proceedings of those of the north, we behold their characteristic principles breaking out; and their expressions of "dependence upon England, and relationship to it," were at that time what they have always been, mere words. For the essence of subordination is obedience.

At the close of his volume Chalmers described the privileges that emigrants could claim as subjects of the crown in 1689: "The various plantations formed no more than the dependencies of a great kingdom which directed their affairs. And they enjoyed no portion of sovereignty." But the colonists, he added, "enjoyed perfect freedom" even though their legislatures were restrained. Colonists were not inferior to Englishmen because both were equally subject to the king; "Colonial legislatures were only subordinate because they were neither co-ordinate nor supreme." Where the colonies invoked doctrines of natural rights to establish their claims, Chalmers traced the historical development of the colonies to prove those claims to be unwarranted.

Chalmers later published his *Introduction to the History of the Revolt of the American Colonies*, in which he intended to prove, first, that from an early date the colonists had aimed at independence and, second, that the British government had exhibited tragic negligence in permitting the provincial assemblies to increase their authority. Although he failed to substantiate his first thesis, he was successful in proving the second. The correspondence of governors and other crown officers in the colonies formed the basis for much of Chalmers's work. Obviously this meant that only the official British point of view was presented. "Yet we are enabled to ascertain from these volumes, better than from any others," wrote the editor of the Boston edition of 1845, "the kind of intelligence which the ministers received from their agents in America, and to arrive at a clearer understanding of the grounds of their public acts."

Chalmers in his later work showed the same partiality to the southern colonies that he had exhibited in the *Political Annals*. "The original Virginians," he wrote, "transmitted habits of respect for the constitution of England, which long engaged their obedience to her rules. . . . The enthusiasts, who planted New England derided the authority of their native land." Chalmers further charged that the "contagion" of the New England spirit of independence, even before the end of the seventeenth century, "soon overspread the southern colonies."

Although Chalmers's books were thought to be unfair by many Americans, they did stimulate them to a fresh study of their own history. His work, said one, "has ever been quoted by American writers with entire confidence and respect." Chalmers's fault was the same fault of many of the most eminent Englishmen of his day in their attitude toward the rebellious colonies: he overemphasized the legalistic approach. In his later life the historian was reported as saying that the mother country should have yielded to expediency and not insisted on her legal rights in her relations with the colonies.[27] For many years American historians, even when they disagreed with details in Chalmers's work, looked to it as a standard by which to gauge the merit of their own achievements.

William Gordon

Historians who lived in the Revolutionary era, even when writing on earlier periods, reflected the heightened pulse of the public. The nearer the writers were to the Revolution, the faster the pulsebeat, although some authors maintained a fairly even temper in writing their narratives. Since these historians were familiar with many of the events and personalities they described, their volumes were credited with veracity. In the works of at least two, however, William Gordon and David Ramsay, that confidence seems to have been at least partly misplaced.

They are the two main historians who have been charged with plagiarism from the *Annual Register*. For a hundred years Gordon received respectful attention from students of American history because of the contribution he was supposed to have made to its records. And then an inquisitive scholar raised serious doubts.

Gordon, who had come to America from England in 1770 to become a minister in Roxbury, Massachusetts, was an ardent participant in colonial politics, though many American leaders were scarcely friendly to him. John Adams, for one, wrote in 1775: "I fear his indiscreet prate will do harm. . . . He is an eternal talker and somewhat vain, and not accurate nor judicious." Gordon appreciated the significance of current events, and he was determined to collect information from American leaders. He asked Adams for assistance, mentioning that others, including Washington, had given him access to their papers. He explained, "I am collecting materials for an history of the rise, progress, and successful issue of the American revolution."

When the war was over, Gordon thought that it would be safer to write his history in England, at which distance his intended impartial remarks on the colonies would prove less dangerous to his person. To Horatio Gates he wrote in 1782: "Should Great Britain mend its constitution by the shock it has rec'd . . . life liberty and character will be safer there than on this side the Atlantic; and an Historian may use the impartial pen there with less danger than here."[28] Unfortunately for Gordon, he found that England also objected to an impartial history. John Adams, then in London as American representative, gave his point of view on what had happened to Gordon's History: "His object was profit. He was told that his book would not sell if printed according to his manuscript. It was accordingly thrown into a new form of letters between a gentleman in England and one in America . . . The style and spirit was altered and accomodated more to the British taste and feelings. . . . Had the original manuscript been printed the work would have appeared very differently."

In the first part of his history Gordon built the case against Parliament's claim that it could tax the colonies without their consent. The Revolutionary movement, he insisted, began in 1761 with the writs-of-assistance controversy in Massachusetts; from this, he wrote, "may be dated, the fixed, uniform, and growing opposition which was made to the ministerial plans of encroaching upon the original rights and long established customs of the colonies." Gordon had no respect for the "party of aristocracy" led by John Hancock and others.

In February, 1789, Gordon wrote to Washington that he was sending him the four volumes of his recently published *History of the Rise, Progress and Establishment of the Independence of the United States of*

America . . . . In his letter Gordon revealed his standard of scholarship: "I apprehended it to be often necessary to introduce sentiments and information while I suppressed the names of the writers from whose letters they were taken, and at times inserted them as though they were originally my own."

In 1899 a student, Orin G. Libby, showed that Gordon inserted far more than he admitted.[29] Gordon had copied the *Annual Register* "wholesale," said Libby, accomplishing "one of the most complete plagiarisms on record." Nearly all the material available to him in America had been collected to no purpose; the *Annual Register* had evidently been a more convenient source. Gordon was also heavily indebted to Ramsay's *History of the Revolution in South Carolina.* Ramsay had been kind enough to send Gordon his manuscript, but the latter was sufficiently unkind to use it frequently with no acknowledgment. The volumes of Gordon, once prized by Edward Channing as "the most valuable history of the Revolution from a British pen," have now been entirely rejected by many as a source for this period.

Perhaps that is unfortunate, since Gordon's volumes certainly contain much of value. He did acknowledge that he drew from the *Annual Register.* Clearly it was a good source, and a logical one for an American (or pro-American) historian to draw from. The relevant sections of the *Register* were for many years written by its editor, Edmund Burke, the Whig leader of the pro-American faction in Parliament. It is difficult to pronounce the final verdict on the plagiarism issue. As Bert James Loewenberg has appropriately reminded us, "Quotation marks were not so essential a part of scholarly decorum in the eighteenth century as they have since become."[30] David D. Van Tassel, in *Recording America's Past: An Interpretation of the Development of Historical Studies in America, 1607–1884,* insists even more forcefully that the proof of what we would consider extensive plagiarism by such Revolutionary historians as Gordon and Ramsay need not make their work useless: "All that is necessary to render them valuable sources is a careful application of the ordinary rules of historical evidence which apply to any document."[31]

David Ramsay

For more than a century the work of David Ramsay, a physician and distinguished political figure in South Carolina, was regarded as historical literature of a high order. His reputation, however, fell like Gordon's, though perhaps not quite so severely, in part because he was a better historian and in part because he wrote more than just histories of the Revolution. His writings include a biography of Washington, a history of South Carolina, and a general history of the United States.

Ramsay published *The History of the Revolution in South Carolina* in 1785, and four years later he brought out *The History of the American Revolution*. Both works were republished in Europe, the second appearing in several English editions and in translations on the Continent. He said that he had been collecting materials for years while he was a member of Congress and had had "access to all the official papers of the United States." He claimed that "every letter written to Congress by General Washington was carefully perused and its contents noted."

Despite Ramsay's opportunities for gathering materials, his claims were empty. Libby proved beyond question that Ramsay plagiarized many of his pages from that ever-fertile source, the *Annual Register*, instead of utilizing the documents that were near at hand. He and Gordon often had copied identical passages from the *Register*, changing indirect discourse to direct discourse. "Each copied from the other," concluded Libby, "and the fault was shared mutually." The fault might also have been shared by publishers who wanted to profit from public interest in the American Revolution by encouraging the hasty preparation of books to meet the demand.

Still, Ramsay's work was extremely important, and its nationalistic interpretation set the tone for many later works. Also, Ramsay's career illustrated a painful reality for writers of American history—the Treaty of Paris had reduced considerably the British market for their work.

Jeremy Belknap

Jeremy Belknap belongs in the very first rank of historians who wrote in the Revolutionary period. So close to that of the modern historian was his approach that his work has been of lasting value. He was born in Boston in 1744 and was educated at Harvard. At twenty-two years of age he was ministering to the religious needs of the community of Dover, New Hampshire, and he remained there until 1786. After difficulties with his congregation he accepted a call to a Boston church the next year, and from then to the end of his life Belknap was satisfied with an arrangement that left him time for his literary activities.

Belknap had from his youth been interested in history, a pursuit which his teacher, Thomas Prince, had strongly fostered. He was still a college student when he indicated his awareness of the high standards demanded of historians: "There are required so many qualifications and accomplishments in an *Historian*, and so much care and niceness in writing an history that some have reckoned it *one of the most difficult labors human nature is capable of.*"[32]

In New Hampshire he gathered written and oral records, accepting hearsay with proper caution. To one of his correspondents, Ebenezer Hazard, he wrote of hunting in "garrets and ratholes of old houses" for private papers when not one paper in a hundred "would repay him for the trouble."[33] During the feverish days before military hostilities began, Belknap's enthusiasm for the patriot cause had been aroused, and in the pages of his history describing the Revolution his feeling was too strong to be bound by the canons of impartiality.

In 1784 the first volume of Belknap's *History of New Hampshire* was published; it was, said the author, the first comprehensive narrative of that state. From the height of a rationalist's stand Belknap looked back scornfully to Puritan intolerance and seventeenth-century superstition. Writing of King Philip's War, he said, "Our gravest historians have recorded many omens, predictions, and other alarming circumstances during this and the Pequot war, which in a more philosophical and less credulous age would not be worthy of notice." To his good friend Hazard he once expressed the wish that they could be together to laugh at Mather's *Wonders of the Invisible World.*[34] Belknap consistently opposed slavery and was also sympathetic to the plight of the Indians. "However fond we may have been of accusing the Indians of treachery and infidelity," he wrote, "it must be confessed that the example was first set them by the Europeans."

Undaunted by a discouraging public reception to his history, Belknap brought out a second volume in 1791, followed by a third the next year. When the first volume appeared, Hazard urged him to hurry along with the second, but Belknap replied that it would take a few years. The first took him, "off and on, nine or ten years," he said, and then he added: "I know that it might be run through in a much shorter time by a Grub Street Gazetteer, who would take everything on trust and had materials ready prepared."[35]

In writing his second volume (1715–90), Belknap took issue with Chalmers's description of the people of New Hampshire and also differed with that well-known authority on other matters. A sentence near the close of this volume illustrated Belknap's perspicacity—and Federalism: "By the funding of the Continental debt, and the assumption of the debts of the individual states, into one general mass, a foundation is laid for the support of public credit; by which means the American revolution appears to be completed."

The last volume included descriptions of the state's geography, its natural history, and its society with its manners, laws, and government. The list of subscribers indicated that many of the country's leading citizens had begun to show an interest in Belknap's work. The many technical difficulties in publishing the history made it impossible to produce a product as finished as Belknap would have wished; for example, it was never proofread.[36] Qualified critics, however, knew the virtues of his work. Alexis de Tocqueville in the 1830s said that Belknap had "more general ideas and more strength of thought, than are to be met with in other historians, even to the present day."

While he was working on his history, Belknap broached the idea of collecting the lives of noted Americans into an "American Biographical Dictionary."[37] Hazard and he worked together on the project, but it lagged for many years. Finally, in 1794, the first volume of the *American Biography* was published; the second appeared in 1798. Considering the limitations of time and of access to materials, the whole was a very creditable performance. Among the excellent biographical sketches were those of Columbus, John Smith, and William Penn (Belknap especially praised Penn because of the religious freedom that prevailed in Pennsylvania).

Belknap was chiefly responsible for the formation of the Massachusetts Historical Society and was its leading member in the early years.[38] The long and valuable series of the society's publications date from 1792, when, largely through Belknap's efforts, the first volume of its *Collections* was published.

Belknap's work as a historian was of the first importance, but perhaps equally significant was the enthusiasm for history that he evoked in others. He was the first, said William Cullen Bryant, "to make American history attractive."[39] The death in 1798 of so illustrious a scholar was a cruel blow to New England. Christoph D. Ebeling, the noted German historian of America, who knew Belknap's worth, wrote to an American acquaintance, "He died, alas, too early for your literature and history."[40] The small circle of people devoted to history with whom Belknap had associated in the 1790s widened steadily in the following years, and the standards of his scholarship became a guide to excellence. Jere Daniell, an excellent present-day student of Belknap's work, has written that "no early nineteenth-century American history has had a better press than Jeremy Belknap's three-volume *History of New Hampshire.*"[41]

George Minot

Historical writing has always been an instrument of political-party warfare, and its function in ideological conflicts was clearly recognized by Americans. Federalists were heirs to Loyalist conservatism; Jeffersonians established a democratic tradition. George Minot and John Marshall were strong Federalists; Mercy Otis Warren, of Massachusetts, and John Daly Burk, historian of Virginia, belonged to the school of Jefferson.

George Minot was one of the earliest historians to fashion a Federalist view of American history. Unlike students who sought political guidance from ancient history, he drew a lesson from the events of his own day to stress the value of strong government. Shays's Rebellion had caused shivers to run up and down the spines of conservatives like Minot. Published in 1788, Minot's *History of the Insurrections in the year 1786...* gave only the Federalist side of the controversy and failed to explain why the debt-burdened farmers flouted authority.

Minot belonged to the Boston group that recalled with mingled feelings the history that Hutchinson had left unfinished when he departed for England in 1774. Although Mercy Otis Warren expressed malice in her recollections of Hutchinson, other historians felt no strong enmity against the governor, who had died an exile in London. Rather, there seemed to be disappointment that the history of Massachusetts begun by Hutchinson remained incomplete. Minot set himself the task of picking up the narrative where Hutchinson had left off in his second volume. In 1798, Minot published his *Continuation of the History of... Massachusetts Bay*, which covered the eight years after 1748. He was at work on a second volume when he died in 1802, and it was brought out in unfinished form the next year. It ended with the Stamp Act riots of 1765, which were condemned by the historian, who had treated Daniel Shays in similar fashion; the mob that destroyed Hutchinson's home was referred to as a "triumphant demonocracy."

Minot, whose thorough legal training had won him a judicial position, gave a good account of the constitutional issues between Massachusetts and England. His sources were few, but among them were the manuscripts of Jasper Mauduit, the colony's agent in England. Hutchinson, it will be remembered, did add a third volume to his own history, and with its publication in 1828, Minot's work was entirely eclipsed. His volume on Shays's Rebellion, however, was widely used and helped perpetuate the conservative interpretation of those troubled times.

Hannah Adams

In the Revolutionary era proposals were made by various writers for histories of all the New England states and even for the whole United States. Benjamin Rush, for example, asked Belknap to write the history of the establishment of the federal government.[42] There was, however, more talk than action. A volume published in 1799 that attempted to fill the need for an inclusive survey was *A Summary History of New England...*, by Hannah Adams (a distant cousin of John Adams), who was reputed to be the first American woman to earn her livelihood by writing. "It was poverty," she said, "that first induced me to become an author, or rather a compiler."[43] Her life spanned the period of the Revolution and the first thirty years of the nineteenth century. Toward the end of her life her friends—and there were many among the literati—settled an annuity upon her, and the timid, absentminded old lady spent her last years poring over ancient tomes in the Boston Athenaeum.

Adams followed the procedure of other contemporary historians: she compiled her book on New England from the few volumes of history that had been written up to that time. She also quoted from Ezra Stile's manuscript lectures on ecclesiastical history, which supplied much of her material on the state of learning in New England. In keeping with the spirit of her day, Adams was critical of the early settlers' intolerance. When her narrative approached the Revolution, she mentioned the public opposition to the proposed establishment of the Anglican episcopacy. Almost half of her volume was on the Revolution, and she drew much from Ramsay and Gordon, who were then considered the leading historians of the war. The historian extracted from the pages of Minot a Federalist interpretation of Shays's Rebellion, and in Morse's *Geography* she found the materials for her section on literature. An abridgment of the *Summary History* for the use of schoolchildren was published in 1807; this, too, was accorded a friendly welcome in New England. While Adams's history was inadequate, there were few of its kind at the beginning of the nineteenth century.

Mercy Otis Warren

A lady with an illustrious name, Mercy Otis Warren, set down her own record of the Revolutionary era, and her relationship with many of its leading figures gave her a special insight into the events of these years. The sister of James Otis and the wife of James Warren, she shared their intensely patriotic view of the struggle. Ironically, it was in the home of Thomas Hutchinson, bought by the Warrens, that she wrote much of the history that singled out the exiled governor for bitter scorn. In 1805, Warren—her name appeared on the title page as "Mrs. Mercy Warren, of Plymouth, (Mass.)"—brought out her three-volume *History of the Rise, Progress, and Termination of the American Revolution.* Although her work was published more than a score of years after the peace treaty, Warren said that she had been collecting materials "many years antecedent to any history since published"; it is probable that much of her work was written contemporaneously with the events described.

During the Revolution, Abigail Adams, John Adams's wife, had written to Warren that "many very memorable events which ought to be handed down to posterity will be buried in oblivion merely for want of a proper hand to record them." Adams gave Warren firsthand information regarding his negotiations with the Dutch, and a few years later another noted figure in Massachusetts politics, Benjamin Lincoln, offered her the use of his papers.[44] It is the combination of her access to the relevant materials and her personal acquaintance with the people who helped shape the events that gives Warren's history much of its value. To read her history is to catch a vivid glimpse of the thoughts and feelings of many Revolutionary leaders. Almost uniquely radical in its perspective among the Revolutionary historians, Warren's work is also arguably the best; certainly it is far superior to Gordon's and Ramsay's, for example. Her style, too (once the modern reader adjusts), is beautiful. Flowery and flowing, it shows the influence of her poetry and drama; she was something of a laureate for the patriot cause. Despite her evident abilities, it is not surprising that she had virtually no formal education, given the status of women in her day. In fact, she was a pioneer feminist, convinced of the intellectual equality of the sexes and of women's right to full educational opportunities.

After some introductory remarks, Warren began her history with the Stamp Act. Character portraits were one of her great strengths. She could have been harder on King George III; he was, she thought, "more obstinate than cruel, rather weak than remarkably wicked." But she could hardly have dealt more severely with Thomas Hutchinson. She saw the governor as "dark, intriguing, insinuating, haughty and ambitious, while the extreme of avarice marked each feature of his character"; she labeled him a disciple of Machiavelli. Most of Warren's work dealt with military hostilities, and she broadened her study with references to discontent in Ireland and domestic politics in England, which she attempted to relate to the American Revolution. The widening of the area of conflict into Mediterranean and West Indian waters was reflected in the enlarged scope of Warren's history. In making her work more comprehensive, she was in accord with John Adams, who held that to write on the American Revolution one must write the history of mankind during that period.

After her description of the war, said the author, her mind was "now at leisure for more general observations on the subsequent consequences, without confining it to time or place." The remarks that followed on the later history of the United States were certainly not of the high caliber of the rest of her work; still, this section hardly deserved the comment John Adams made to Warren: "After the termination of the Revolutionary war your subject was completed."[45] The problem, of course, was simply that Warren's anti-Federalist orientation was inexcusable to Adams; she in turn made some none-too-flattering comments about him (and it is well known that Adams could not handle criticism—witness the correspondence between him and Jefferson). "History is not the Province of the Ladies," he concluded huffily. Ironically, Adams earlier had encouraged Warren to write her history, noting that "there are few Persons possessed of more Facts, or who can record them in a more agreeable manner." Another comment shows that even Adams understood the major problem with Warren's history after 1783 to be her partisan differences with him; it also probably tells us more about John Adams than about Mercy Otis Warren: "It is my opinion that your history has been written to the taste of the nineteenth century, and accommodated to gratify the passions, prejudices, and feelings of the party who are now predominant."[46] Surprisingly, rather friendly relations were maintained between the Adams and Warren families to the end.

William Raymond Smith, an excellent modern-day student of Warren's work, insists that she built her history on a "basis of seventeenth-century Puritanism slightly tempered by eighteenth-century Enlightenment thought." The support of Providence was the central theme running through Warren's history; according to Smith, it was "not so much that God was on the side of the Americans, but that their social and political ideas were on God's side." Smith concludes:

In the historiography of the American Revolution, Mercy Warren's place is unique. Her work does not fit easily into the Whig interpretation, although she saw the revolution as a struggle for liberty. She used her familiarity with British politics and with events on the continent to broaden her context, but her history does not fall into the imperial school. Economic and social considerations played a prominent role, but to other purposes than those of the progressives. For her, the revolution was not complete in the hearts and minds of men before the war began, nor could it begin once the war was over. The revolution was a result of a complex of forces acting continually upon mankind. Because of a special combination of ideas, circumstances, and environment, revolutionary activity first manifested itself in America. For success, such activity had to be constantly defended and asserted. Having begun, the revolution could end only with the Last Judgement.[47]

Benjamin Trumbull

Among the historians of the late eighteenth and early nineteenth centuries who labored to preserve the memorials of an earlier day, none worked harder than Benjamin Trumbull. Practically all his life was associated with his native province, Connecticut, whose history he narrated. For sixty years before his death in 1820 he had been pastor of the North Haven Congregational Church. Although his historical publications did not appear until late in his life, Trumbull had been collecting materials for many years.

In 1801 he published *A Century Sermon, or Sketches of the History of the Eighteenth Century*.... This was "a sketch of the works of God in the century past," he said, "and especially His dispensations towards America, the United States, New England, and this town" (North Haven). The publication was a preliminary survey for Trumbull's larger work on the United States.

That comprehensive work appeared in 1810: *A General History of the United States of America... to 1792.* Three volumes were promised; the first took the narrative to the year 1765, but the other two were never published. Trumbull's materials were given to Jedidiah Morse, who was busy on his own historical projects. Trumbull spoke of his work as his offering of gratitude for divine aid granted to America in the Revolutionary years; his history, he hoped, would promote national feeling. He explained that his difficulties in research were multiplied because of the interconnection of colonial and British history, "which rendered a constant study of the history of [England] as well as of America necessary to authenticate and elucidate the work." Following a familiar convention, he gave much space to Indian civilization. And, again in the conventional manner, Trumbull heavily stressed the beginnings of white settlements, but he skimmed over the period from 1700 to 1750. The wars from 1748 to 1763 were given strong emphasis, but Trumbull's volume was not badly proportioned, measured by the standards of his day.

The work for which Trumbull is best known is *A Complete History of Connecticut*.... The first volume appeared in 1797, and the two-volume edition in 1818. Trumbull had planned his history before the Revolution, but the war forced him to postpone publication for many years. "As this is the first history of the colony," said Trumbull, "the compiler judged it expedient to make it more full and particular, than otherwise might have been necessary or proper." He wished to assist future historians and wanted to ascertain that nothing of importance would be lost. He acknowledged his sources, and he followed a soundly established precedent when he wrote that "very little has been taken upon tradition." Given the experiences of Hazard and Belknap, it is easy to believe Trumbull's statement that "the labor of collecting materials ... has been almost incredible."

In accordance with his promise Trumbull gave a very detailed and plainly written text. It contained religious, economic, and social history, with much valuable material on the growth of various towns, including even regions outside Connecticut borders. Trumbull thought that New England was settled "purely for the purposes of Religion"; he believed also that New England treated the Indians unfairly after the Pequot War. The scope of his work was encyclopedic; he "got Connecticut by heart before he began writing its history," said Bancroft. "He could tell the name, birthplace, and career of every minister that had preached a good sermon, and every militiaman that had done a notable thing. Not a savage was overcome, not a backslider censured by the church, but he knew it all."[48] Not only did he know it all, but he felt the necessity to *tell* it all, and he spun out the details to tedious lengths. He was proud to be Connecticut's first historian and treasured every fact about her, observing conscientiously the New England injunction "Despise not the day of small things."

Jedidiah Morse

Trumbull's younger contemporary, Jedidiah Morse, grew up in the Revolutionary era, when the rising self-consciousness of Americans sought expression in every field. He was born in 1761, attended Yale, became a minister and a member of the Society for the Propagation of the Gospel, and was a leader of the conservative Calvinist movement to stop the infiltration of Unitarianism into Harvard and other Congregational strongholds. Best known as "the father of American geography"—and of Samuel F. B. Morse—he was also something of a historian.

When he was teaching in New Haven in 1783, Morse became seriously interested in geography. William Guthrie's *English Geography* was then generally used in American schools, but its materials on America were very thin. The next year Morse collected his lectures into *Geography made Easy,* the first book on the subject ever published in America. He was constantly gathering information from far and wide, and on his travels he noted additional facts to be included in an enlarged edition of his geography. Belknap told him that "to be a true geographer it is necessary to be a Traveller"; he urged Morse to see things for himself and not to get secondhand information from other authors.[49]

In March, 1789, Morse's *American Geography* was published; in addition to the geographical material, the book contained much history. Some of his friends thought Morse should have restricted the geography to America, but he designed it to compete with the English geographies then in use in American schools. In a later edition he gave even more space to foreign areas. The book was an immediate success and was adopted by Yale as a text. European editions were also published, but in that day of book piracy Morse received no foreign royalties. C. D. Ebeling, at that time the greatest European student of American history and geography, testified that Morse was "the first who has cut a road through a vast wilderness."[50] A second edition, entitled *The American Universal Geography,* was published in two volumes, the first of which was mainly on America.

Morse's books sold so widely that his financial success became a topic of good-natured gossip among his contemporaries. Hazard wrote to Belknap that Morse was the only successful author in their triumvirate and added with mild regret, "What a pity it is that *we* had not been geographers instead of *historians.*"[51]

Morse next brought out *The American Gazetteer* (1797), containing seven thousand separate articles. Much of the historical matter in this book was taken from Hazard's work, which Morse praised as the best collection of facts in American history.

Morse also wrote and compiled purely historical works. Written with the aid of the Reverend Elijah Parish, Morse's *Compendious History of New England* went through several editions. It was an interesting blend of Calvinist morality, nationalism, and New England provincialism. It is worth noting that the authors began their history with the Reformation, not with Columbus or some other early figure; the next step of the historians, who in this respect were approaching the modern viewpoint, was to continue the narrative with the Pilgrims in Holland. One hundred years before James Truslow Adams criticized New England's part in the Pequot War, Morse had written: "This is a dismal section of our history . . . when pious Christians had so lost sight of their Saviour's precepts." Probably Morse's positive experience as a missionary to the Indians helped shape his indictment of the unnecessary brutality. On the whole this cooperative volume was well written and adequately proportioned, though Hannah Adams indignantly charged the authors with plagiarizing her own work.

In 1824, Morse brought out his *Annals of the American Revolution . . . ,* which included biographies of the war heroes among its varied features. Morse was a tired man by this time and had little interest in the book, saying that it was "professedly a compilation," its issue timed to coincide with Lafayette's widely publicized return to America. The most interesting part of the volume was the section of letters by Franklin and Adams on the causes of the Revolution. John Adam's letters had been written some years earlier in answer to Morse's inquiries. The historian's Federalist bias is abundantly clear in this work. Though Morse was not proud of his poorly arranged work, many Americans regarded it highly for many years.

John Marshall

War heroes were beginning to be commemorated by grateful contemporaries, and among those heroes none so dominated the American consciousness as did Washington. Chief Justice Marshall's five-volume study was classified as a biography, but it was in reality a political history of America during the life of the first president. Indeed, the first volume of *The Life of George Washington* . . . (1804–1807) was complete in itself as a history of the colonies and mentioned Washington only twice. Marshall's public and private associations gained him special access to materials. Bushrod Washington, the president's nephew, urged him to write the biography, and Chief Justice Marshall's need for money at the time was one of his reasons for undertaking it.[52]

The volume on the colonies was compiled from the few standard authors used by most historians; a writer who was covering the years up to the reign of William and Mary, said Marshall, needed little in addition to George Chalmers. Marshall himself knew how inconclusive was his own work, but he believed that there was a place for it in the absence of any other. He was apparently justified, for a reviewer in Boston's *Monthly Anthology* noted that it was the "first attempt to give a connected history of the various states."[53]

Some of Marshall's observations anticipated by many years certain later studies of the colonial period. For example, he wrote thus about the resolutions of the New York Assembly in 1711 against taxation without consent: "This strong assertion of a principle, the controversy concerning which afterwards dismembered the British empire, passed away without notice. It was probably understood to be directed only against the assumption of that power by the governor."[54] In speaking of another legal problem, Marshall pointed out that no accurate definition had ever been made of the degree of authority that the mother country could exercise over the colonies: "In Britain, it had always been asserted, that Parliament possessed the power of binding them in all cases whatsoever. In America, at different times, and in different colonies, different opinions had been entertained on this subject." Marshall then went on to present a very good discussion of this question, and in somewhat the temper of the modern historian he wrote of the rise of animosity against new taxation. His sentiment on England's retention of the tax on tea has been echoed many times: "Never perhaps did a great and wise nation adopt a more ill-judged measure than this."

History to Marshall was primarily past politics, and, not surprisingly, he saw the Revolution as essentially a constitutional struggle. His tone throughout was restrained, and even when he came to write on the Declaration of Independence, he was much more moderate than was the later George Bancroft. Marshall's last volume contained an excellent chapter on the causes that led to a change in the United States government and the adoption of stronger central powers, with emphasis on the role of President Washington in promoting support for a vigorous national government. This whole critical period was, of course, presented from the Federalist standpoint. The biography became a history of national politics and of diplomatic relations, but at the conclusion of his work Marshall gave a sound estimate of Washington's character. The remark of one reviewer was just: his complaint was not that there was too much history but that there was too little biography.[55]

Marshall's political associations had an adverse effect on the sale of the work, and only eight thousand of the anticipated thirty thousand subscriptions materialized. The price was high, and Republicans spread the rumor that it was a Federalist history of the United States, written as propaganda for use in the election of 1804. Jefferson, in a letter urging Joel Barlow to write a history of the United States, referred to Marshall's biography as "that five-volumed libel."[56] Madison was not as hostile, but he did think that the last volume (1783–99) was inaccurate. He also suggested that Marshall "would write differently at the present day [1827] and with his present impressions."[57] That staunch Federalist Chancellor James Kent, however, thought the fifth volume was "worth all the rest," considering the work as a whole to be "an excellent History of the Government and Parties in this country."[58]

Unfortunately for Marshall's reputation as a biographer, he was guilty of extensive plagiarism throughout his work. For the Revolution he was content to copy from Gordon and from the plagiarist's paradise, the *Annual Register.*[59] At that time, however, this was not quite the serious charge some have made it out to be, and Marshall made a contribution of prime significance to American historical literature, especially in terms of the development of a truly national history. In the words of Daniel R. Gilbert: "Marshall's work was an example of a new kind of national history designed to promote national unity. It rejected the parochialism of eighteenth-century histories of separate colonies, and it emphasized the connection of the colonial past with the emerging United States."[60] Obviously, there is a close relationship between Marshall's role as historian and his role as chief justice of the United States between 1801 and 1835.

Mason Locke Weems

The Revolutionary era and its leading figures were memorialized in rather sober histories, creating for the serious reader a more or less realistic pattern of our past. A different design, aimed at a wider audience, was sketched by the famous Parson Mason Locke Weems. The books by Weems were a particularly colorful culmination of the literature of the Revolutionary period; from them countless Americans (in some ways unfortunately) received an indelible impression of those stirring years. The parson's publications were better known than those of any other American in the first half of the nineteenth century.

Weems was born in Maryland in 1795 and was brought up in an atmosphere conducive to the glorification of George Washington's name. Weems studied medicine abroad, but he was more interested in healing the soul than in healing the body, and in 1784 he became Parson Weems, Episcopal clergyman, one of the first candidates to receive Anglican ordination for service in the United States. He briefly served Pohick Church, in Virginia, but that hardly justifies his claim on the title page of his biography of Washington to being "Rector of Mt. Vernon Parish." Not long after, he became a writer and itinerant bookseller, serving in the South as agent for the famous Philadelphia publisher Mathew Carey. "For thirty years there was no more familiar figure on the roads of the Southern States than this book peddler and author who . . . travelled his long route year after year, sleeping in wayside inn, farmhouse or forest, fiddling, writing [and] selling books."[61]

With the publication of his *Life of Washington* in 1800, Weems came into his own as an author. It was written as an antidote to Marshall's marble figure, which was too austere even for those with conservative tastes. John Adams called Marshall's biography "a Mausoleum, 100 feet square at the base, and 200 feet high." Weems, a Jeffersonian Republican, was also eager to prevent Federalists from monopolizing Washington's fame; *his* Washington, he said, was no aristocrat, "but a pure Republican."[62]

For more than two decades after publication of his *Washington,* Weems reaped the rewards of being the foremost American writer of juvenile literature. Large numbers of adults as well as children by the tens of thousands read his books, which were designed to inculcate the prized virtues of industry, temperance, and frugality. The story of Washington and the cherry tree, which first appeared in the fifth edition of the biography, became part of the national folklore. Despite its many inaccuracies and outright fabrications, the Parson's simple writing was so warm with enthusiasm that it brought to life figures already grown austere and remote:

"George," said his father, "do you know who killed the beautiful little cherry-tree yonder in the garden?" This was a tough question and George staggered under it for a moment. . . .

"I can't tell a lie, Pa, you know I can't tell a lie. I did it with my hatchet."

"Run to my arms, you dearest boy," cried his father . . . "glad am I, George, that you killed my tree; for you have paid for it a thousand fold. Such an act of heroism in my son is more worth than a thousand trees, though blossomed with silver, and their fruits of purest gold."

The style of the biographer was the style of the preacher, and in an age which admired oratory, Weems waxed eloquent indeed. Still, one does not have to be very cynical to question the practice of instilling the importance of truthfulness into American youth by telling them a great lie; even in Weems's day good historians knew better.

In his *Life of General Francis Marion*, Weems produced a historical romance that later was praised by the gifted writer William Gilmore Simms. Weems's accounts of military events, though partisan, were fairly dependable. In other respects his biographies drew more from his imagination than from the actuality. The spontaneity of the biographies of Washington and Marion was absent, however, in Weems's life of Franklin. The author's fondness for the Franklinian virtues was not enough to color the work; it was not easy to write glowingly of industry, temperance, and frugality.

Weems crusaded against drunkenness and gambling and was a moralist consistently true to himself as a biographer or a writer of moral tracts. He was first and last an uplifter. And many listened: over a million copies of his books were sold. "As a 'Maker' of history," remarked Edward Channing, Weems "vies with the household poets." Long stretches of Longfellow's *The Courtship of Miles Standish* or Whittier's *Barbara Frietchie* were no nearer the facts of history than was the *Washington* of Weems, and the parson "has had equal or greater influence on succeeding generations of Americans than any of these [poems]." It may be safe to say that generations of historical scholars have been unable to modify seriously the popular pictures Weems created of our Revolutionary heroes.

CHAPTER 5

Gathering the Records:
Awaiting the National Historian

THE STIRRING EVENTS of the twoscore years that followed 1760 were a stimulus to historical composition and the collection of documentary materials. It is therefore surprising that so little was done on a comprehensive scale. The correspondence of John Adams is a useful source in which to trace the story of early Revolutionary historiography. He complained to his fellow revolutionary Thomas McKean: "Can you account for the apathy, the antipathy of this nation to their own history? . . . While thousands of frivolous novels are read with eagerness and got by heart, the history of our own native country is not only neglected, but despised and abhorred." To Elbridge Gerry the former president also complained of the "total ignorance and oblivion of the revolution" among the younger generation.[1]

Conditions were not quite as bad as Adams declared. He himself had written to Mercy Otis Warren during the war of his plan to retire; he would write a history of the Revolution and "draw the portrait of every character that has figured in the business. But when it is done, I will dig a vault, and bury the manuscript, . . . not to be opened till a hundred years after my death."[2] Alas, Adams never wrote the manuscript, but he carried on a correspondence for years with a number of individuals whose interest in the Revolution was whetted by his memories.

While the Revolution was still in progress, Gerry had moved in Congress that each state should designate an official to collect memorials of the period. Had the motion been adopted, said Adams in 1813, "we should now possess a Monument of more inestimable Value than all the Histories and Orations that have been written." Recalling old times, McKean told Adams that he had often been asked to write a history of the American Revolution, Benjamin Rush having been especially insistent.[3] Rush himself had contemplated writing such a history and had gathered materials for it during the war. Joel Barlow, too, had prepared documents to write a history of the Revolution, and in his collection were the papers of General Gates.[4]

When Jedidiah Morse was seeking original materials on the Revolution, he turned to Adams, who sent him long and revealing letters. "A history of military operations from April 19, 1775, to the 3d of

September, 1783, is not a history of the American Revolution," wrote Adams. "The revolution," he said, "was in the minds and hearts of the people, and in the union of the colonies; both of which were substantially effected before hostilities commenced." The Revolution began, said the aged correspondent, with the Writs of Assistance in 1761. Pamphlets, newspapers and handbills from 1761 to 1774; the letters of the committees of correspondence—a study of all these, in all the states, was necessary to understand the growth of the Union. The real American Revolution, Adams reiterated, was the "radical change in the principles, opinions, sentiments and affections of the people" toward Great Britain. To Hezekiah Niles, who later compiled a useful book of documents, Adams was writing in the same vein, although he was doubtful that "the true history of the American Revolution" could be recovered.[5]

"Who shall write the history of the American Revolution?" Adams asked McKean. How could anyone write it when "the most essential documents, the debates and deliberations in Congress, from 1774 to 1783, were all in secret, and are now lost forever." In reply McKean said that Major General James Wilkinson had already written the history of the Revolution, but Adams retorted in words he had already used—the history of the hostilities was very different from a real history of the American Revolution.[6]

Adams was discussing these issues with Jefferson at the same time, and the Virginian likewise questioned whether anyone could write the history of the Revolution, "all its councils, designs and discussions having been conducted by Congress with closed doors, and no members, as far as I know, having ever made notes of them. These, which are the life and soul of history, must forever be unknown." Jefferson thought the lively history of the American Revolution by the Italian Carlo Botta was the best that had yet been written, allowing for the writer's invented speeches and his "fancying motives of action which we never felt." Wiser than Adams, who insisted that the Revolution began with the Writs of Assistance, Jefferson said that it would be as difficult to identify the moment when the "embryo becomes an animal, or the act which gives him a beginning" as to say when the Revolution began "and what incident set it in motion."[7]

The elder statesmen were busy in their last years looking over old papers and answering all sorts of queries. Madison wrote to Edward Everett that he was putting together his notes on the Constitutional Convention.[8] "It has been the misfortune of history," wrote Madison, "that a personal knowledge and an impartial judgment of things rarely meet in the historian." If the materials of America's history should fall into proper hands, he added, "the American History may be expected to contain more truth, and lessons, certainly not less valuable, than those of any Country or Age."

To William Tudor, editor of the newly established *North American Review,* Adams wrote of various incidents in the Revolution, and in these and other retrospective letters he suggested so wide a scope of inquiry that historians a century later had not yet filled in his outline.[9] Although Adams was more than eighty, his energy never flagged, and he envisioned broad areas for research. To America's youth and to the expansive national spirit following the War of 1812, Jefferson, Adams, and Madison contributed their reminiscences of the founding of the nation.

Tudor came under their influence, and through the pages of the *Review* he stimulated historical research. His scholarly maturity was evident in his urbane attitude toward early Puritan historians, particularly Cotton Mather.[10] Tudor's historical interests were of long standing, for in the *Monthly Anthology,* a predecessor of the *Review,* he had included articles on colonial historians. More than any other force the *Review* quickened the slow stream of intellectual life into a swift current.

Biographies of Revolutionary heroes were read carefully by the old guard, who conserved jealously the reputations of their dead comrades. "American History," wrote Adams to a friend, Dr. Benjamin Waterhouse, "whether in Fable, Allegory, Painting, Sculpture, Architecture, Statuary, Poetry, Oratory, or Romance: which forgets to acknowledge James Otis to have been the Father of the American Revolution, will be nothing but a Lie."[11] Tudor published a biography of Otis in 1823; in recommending it highly to a friend, George Ticknor wrote: "There is nothing like it . . . among our materials for future history, nor could such a book be made twenty years hence, for then all the traditions will have perished with the old men from whose graves he has just rescued them."[12] William Wirt drew from Jefferson his memories of Patrick Henry, and when Wirt's biography of the famed orator appeared, letters either praising it or censuring it were exchanged among the Revolutionary leaders. Thomas Jefferson Randolph's *Memoirs, Correspondence and Private Papers of Thomas Jefferson,* published in 1829, provoked intense public discussion and helped fix in the American mind the liberal image of the great Virginian. The "age of commemoration" had been ushered in. "We are no longer the new men of the new world," said one New Englander. "We have a noble inheritance in the fame of our ancestors."[13]

The last survivors of the signers of the Declaration of Independence and of the Constitution were conscious of a certain unity among themselves; Jefferson once spoke of the "Declaration-men."[14] They were aware of their unique position in American life. A few months before he died, Jefferson wrote to Adams, introducing his grandson, T. J.

Randolph: "Like other young people, he wishes to be able in the winter nights of old age, to recount to those around him what he has heard and learnt of the heroic age preceding his birth, and which of the Argonauts individually he was in time to have seen."[15]

In the winter nights of their own old age these Argonauts spun tales of their heroic era and bemoaned its lack of a written history. The time was near at hand, however, when materials for it would be systematically gathered. McKean regretted that the United States possessed no Thucydides, Tacitus, Hume, Robertson, or Gibbon; yet, he said, "we have gentlemen of great talents, and capable of writing the history of our Revolution with at least as much regard to truth as any of them has exhibited."[16] Many years were yet to pass, however, before the task was seriously undertaken.

Gathering the Records

Before any large-scale history could be written, the materials had to be assembled. There was no lack of materials, for New Englanders, as George Bancroft pointed out, "have always been a documentary people."[17] In fact, an overwhelming number of authors who wrote history or biography or compiled annals came from New England. Jared Sparks remarked in 1826, however, that "no work approaching to the character of a complete history of America, of the United States or of the American Revolution, has yet appeared." Sparks, the pioneer of documentary research both here and abroad, said that "the colonial history of America is shut up in the office of the Board of Trade and Plantations in England."

Sparks, eager to improve every aid to historical research, was critical of America's poor library facilities; he could number but seven libraries "in which a whole stock of books relating to America may not be ranged in the corner of a single case."[18] George Ticknor measured the influence of his education in Europe by the different perspective it gave him upon the resources of the Harvard Library. "When I went away," he said, "I thought it was a large library; when I came back, it seemed a closetful of books."[19]

Just when Sparks was complaining about difficulties that beset the American historian, they were beginning to be overcome. Hezekiah Niles published his *Principles and Acts of the Revolution . . .* in 1822; he made it clear that he was presenting documentary evidence "to show the *feelings* that prevailed in the revolution, not to give a *history of events.*" Between 1827 and 1830 Jonathan Elliot brought out four volumes of *Debates . . . in Convention on the Adoption of the Federal Constitution* (a fifth volume was added later). Publication of *The American*

State Papers began in 1833, and the introductory note to the first volume said that "in this compilation the future historian may find a body of authentic materials ready prepared for his hand."

Founded by Sparks and others, the field of American historical literature promised greater rewards, financial and otherwise, than any other literary genre. With missionary zeal, the new generation fused memories of hallowed traditions with glowing expectations for the years ahead. Every kind of old record was diligently explored. Begun in 1838, *The Journals of each Provincial Congress of Massachusetts in 1774 and 1775, . . .* edited by William Lincoln, announced that its primary object was "to *perpetuate materials* for the history of a glorious era in our national existence." Francis L. Hawks, lawyer, clergyman, and historian, was commissioned by the Episcopal church to collect materials on its history in the colonial period. He went to England and brought back a mass of documents that he used for his *Ecclesiastical History of the United States: Virginia,* published in 1836, and for his volume on Maryland. Similar activity farther south was represented by Bartholomew R. Carroll's compilation, the two-volume *Historical Collections of South Carolina,* brought out in 1836.

A notable effort to collect sources on the Revolution was begun in 1822 by Peter Force, a journalist and printer, in partnership with Matthew St. Clair Clarke, clerk of the House of Representatives. As their plan developed, its scope became far more comprehensive, projecting the publication in many volumes of an enormous body of sources on the history of the colonies. After many delays the first volume was published in 1837, with the title *American Archives. . . .* "The undertaking in which we have embarked," said Force, "is emphatically, a National one; National in its scope and object, its end and aim." Their work, the compilers said, was in harmony with "the tendency of the present age [which] has been justly and philosophically designated as historick." Publication of national records in Europe had been supported by government aid, and Force called for similar assistance by the United States.

Between 1837 and 1853 nine volumes of *American Archives* (concentrating on the Revolutionary era) were published with $228,000 in government aid; publication then ceased. Force also brought out four volumes of *Tracts and other Papers relating to . . . North America.* Bancroft hailed the *American Archives:* "Here are the clay and the straw, everything necessary but the forming hand" for historical composition.[20]

In addition to preserving many materials for the use of historians, Force was a focal point for the historical interests of the country.[21] He found time to participate in the activities of a short-lived American Historical Society in Washington, D.C.; he was, in fact, its vital spirit.

Collectors and authors wrote to him seeking information and encouragement; when Bancroft wanted information on the attitude of American newspapers toward the Stamp Act, he sought it from Peter Force. A list of Force's correspondents would almost exhaust the names of Americans who were then interested in the writing of history. In 1867, Force's remarkable library of some fifty thousand titles, perhaps the best collection of Americana in existence, was bought for the Library of Congress.

Public and private libraries were being developed on a grand scale. A significant addition to the Harvard Library was the purchase of the Americana collected by the German historian Christoph D. Ebeling. The Library of Congress was founded in 1800 and, after a slow start, grew rapidly in importance, especially after the acquisition of such collections as the books and papers of Jefferson and Madison. As early as 1829, Sparks was urging that a "copy of every book and manuscript in existence relating to America" be secured for the library.[22] Booksellers John R. Bartlett, in New York; Obadiah Rich, a transplanted American in Europe; and especially Henry Stevens, Jr., performed valuable services for libraries and prosperous scholars in uncovering rare Americana. The British Museum, said Sparks, had become one of the best places in the world for American historical research, due largely to Stevens.[23] The collections of John Carter Brown, of Providence, Rhode Island, and James Lenox, of New York, were of surpassing excellence. Older historical societies were reinvigorated, and new ones were founded everywhere in the country. Unfortunately, few of them functioned actively.

Through the efforts of some of the earliest Americans who had studied in Germany—Joseph G. Cogswell, George Ticknor, and Edward Everett—historical scholarship was greatly advanced. It was Cogswell who helped Harvard acquire Ebeling's collection, and at a later date he became the adviser to John Jacob Astor when the latter was building his library in New York.[24] Ticknor, the historian of Spanish literature, was an inspiration to Prescott. Ticknor's famous Spanish collection— the best in the world, he thought—was enshrined in a palatial home that was a favorite meeting place for Boston's intellectual elite. Ticknor's friend Everett also was interested in the advancement of American scholarship, especially history. Herman E. Ludewig, a recent immigrant from Germany, was one of the most indefatigable bibliographers of the period. Among his publications was a book dedicated to Peter Force, *The Literature of American Local History: a Bibliographical Essay,* published in 1846.[25]

Through the efforts of a few enthusiasts several of the states eventually published vast quantities of materials. No single individual was responsible for it, but the movement had its distant origins in Hazard's work, in the correspondence of the Founding Fathers, and more immediately in the patriotic impulse to preserve the historical records of the nation. Several states made efforts to acquire copies of historical materials in British depositories.

New York was more successful than other states in gathering the sources of her history. Governor DeWitt Clinton spoke of the need to set the state's records in order and to copy relevant materials from European archives. In 1814, asking public support for these researches even in the midst of war, Clinton wrote with great dignity, "Genuine greatness never appears in a more resplendent light, or in a more sublime attitude, than in that buoyancy of character which rises superior to danger and difficulty; in that magnanimity of soul which cultivates the arts and sciences amidst the horrors of war."

The state legislature supported Clinton's plea, and in subsequent years many volumes of Dutch records in local archives were translated by Dr. Francis A. Van Der Kemp. This request, made in 1814, resulted in the organization and exploration of the New York State archives and was followed by another in 1839, asking legislative support for an investigation of documents in Europe. With the passage of an act defraying the expenses for the collection of materials from archives in England, Holland, and France, John Romeyn Brodhead was named agent. After spending three years in Europe, Brodhead returned in 1844 with eighty volumes of documents. Brodhead's homecoming was an event of the first importance to historical societies in New England and the Middle Atlantic states, who sent representatives to a dinner honoring him. Bancroft in his characteristic style said that Brodhead's ship "was more richly freighted with new materials for American history than any that ever crossed the Atlantic."[26]

Brodhead's collection, while it was still in manuscript, was immediately useful to historians, but its utility widened when it was published as *The Documentary History of the State of New York*, in four volumes, and as *Documents relative to the Colonial History of the State of New York*, in fifteen volumes. Other states increased publication of their own records, and some acknowledged the inspiration provided by New York. In 1850, Samuel Hazard, in his *Annals of Pennsylvania*, expressed his gratitude to New York for permission to see the recently collected manuscript materials. In his *Pennsylvania Archives*, brought out in 1852, the same compiler noted that "the States of New York, Massachusetts, New Jersey, Maryland, Virginia and other members of the Union have commenced the publication of their Colonial and Revolutionary history."

One writer, announcing "A Great Historical Enterprise," proposed that historical societies in the United States undertake the publication of a general index to all documents in English archives referring to the American colonies, thus anticipating by forty years the series issued by the Carnegie Institution of Washington.[27] Sparks had long been urging that transcripts be made of materials in European libraries for deposit in Washington, where they would be accessible to historians.[28]

Thus the amassing of materials went on apace, but the popular historian who would put it all together did not appear until 1834. It was then that George Bancroft published his first volume. Wholly apart from his mixture of rhetoric and fact, so necessary to the success of a historian in that day, the acclaim that greeted him was largely the result of the yearning of Americans for a national historian. Shortly before Bancroft's work appeared, in 1827, a writer in the *American Quarterly Review* had expressed the national longing: "A matured work of genius" on American history, he said, "would be of incalculable value." Prescott welcomed Bancroft's history as the first native work likely to supplant those written by Europeans. He reminded fellow Americans that they formerly had to go to the work of the Italian Botta for "the best history of the Revolution" and to the Scotsman James Grahame "for the best history of the Colonies. Happily the work before us bids fair, when completed, to supply this deficiency." Prescott insisted that the foreigners could not comprehend "all the minute feelings, prejudices, and peculiar ways of thinking which form the idiosyncrasy of the nation."[29]

On the eve of Bancroft's publication, William Ellery Channing discussed the quality of national literature: "We think that the history of the human race is to be rewritten. Men imbued with the prejudices which thrive under aristocracies and state religions, cannot understand it. . . . we believe that the true principles for studying and writing [history] are to be unfolded here, at least as rapidly as in other countries." With these sentiments Bancroft was in perfect harmony. After his first volume appeared, he wrote to Sparks that Americans had a history worth knowing and that "a vein of public feeling, of democratic independence, of popular liberty, ought to be infused into our literature."[30]

Bancroft lived so long that he became a tradition in his own day. For half a century he dominated historical scholarship. His patriotic spirit, celebrating the triumphs of democracy, touched a proud nation and was welcomed by the great majority. A small, more restrained minority established a countertradition of the critical approach, but not until a later generation did that view find firm support. Charles Francis Adams wrote in the *North American Review* in 1831: "In this country . . . we are fond of celebrating the virtues of our forefathers . . .

by festive anniversaries and eloquent panegyric. . . . Yet it is much to be feared, that this is not the right way to come at that real history, and those cool and rational conclusions which can alone be supposed likely to confer permanent benefit." He further observed that the "modern fashion of what is called philosophical history is attended with one great disadvantage, in the ease with which it admits of the perversion of facts, to suit the prejudices of each particular writer."

Despite the criticism of Adams, who was ahead of his time and against the tide of contemporary historical writing, "philosophical" history was to be written and read for some time to come. The *American Review* reported that "the great English historians are to be found in our huts and farmhouses, and editions of them are multiplied without number." Twenty thousand copies of Macaulay's history were reportedly sold in the United States in 1849.[31] An exultant reviewer acclaimed Bancroft as "our western Macaulay."[32] The volumes that Bancroft, Prescott, and J. L. Motley wrote were well suited to the romantic taste of the public; historians had not yet begun to write largely for one another.

Abiel Holmes

The transition from the historians of the colonial and Revolutionary years to the writers of the full-blown national period was effected by Abiel Holmes. His was the first important attempt to comprehend American history in its entirety. Ezra Stiles and others in the eighteenth century had talked of such a project, but its fulfillment was delayed until Holmes took up the task.

Abiel Holmes, the father of Oliver Wendell Holmes, belonged in the long line of New England ministers who wrote history; his noteworthy contribution was made in 1805 with the two volumes of *American Annals* . . . ; a second edition under a slightly different title appeared in 1829. Holmes, who was Stiles's son-in-law as well as his literary executor, had written a biography of the Yale president in 1798, and the study of the many papers left by the older man stimulated him to write his own history.

Holmes observed that although local histories of particular portions of America had been written "no attempt has been made to give even the outline of its entire history." He set himself that task: "It has been uniformly my aim to trace facts, as much as possible to their source. Original authorities, therefore, when they could be obtained, have always had preference." Although Holmes had wished that his book might be better than a chronology, it proved to be little more; it belonged to the school of Thomas Prince.

The dryly factual *Annals* was occasionally lightened by a personal observation. On the witchcraft episode, for example, Holmes took the critical stance of the Enlightenment: "This part of the history of our country furnished an affecting proof of the imbecility of the human mind, and of the potent influence of the passions." When Holmes came to write on the Revolution, he partly realized his aim to compose narrative history. Holmes's pride in his country's past was matched by his confidence in her future. Perhaps too much of Holmes's pride, however, was in his native New England. He found little to criticize about it, and little to praise about the South. He asserted, for example, that Virginia was settled for crass economic motives while New England's settlers were motivated by the "natural and pious desire of perpetuating a church."

The *Annals*, despite its many deficiencies, marked a significant advance in American historiography. In Bancroft's summary of American historical writing in the *North American Review* in 1838, he said that Holmes deserved the gratitude of all students of American history. Holmes was the link that connected "the men of an earlier generation, Belknap, Hutchinson, Stiles, Trumbull, and the rest with the scholars of our own." Sparks called the *Annals* the "best repository of history, chronology, and biographical knowledge respecting America that can be found embodied in one work."[33] Long years afterward careful students still turned to it with confidence.

Timothy Pitkin

In 1828, Timothy Pitkin brought out his two-volume *Political and Civil History of the United States of America . . . 1763 to . . . 1797*, five chapters of which summarized colonial history to 1763. More than a hundred pages of sources were appended to the volumes, and similar matter was frequently imbedded in the text. Pitkin drew heavily from Chalmers for his coverage of the colonial period.

Pitkin said that Americans were sufficiently acquainted with the military events of the Revolutionary period. He believed it desirable, therefore, to present a "connected view of the political and civil transactions of our country, unmixed with military events, except so far as the latter had an influence on the former." He specifically disclaimed any intention of writing "a philosophical history."

At the end of his introductory chapters Pitkin devoted a few lines, still worth reading, to the difference between the European character and the American:

Though the motives and views of those who settled in the different colonies, were different, yet their situation in their new places of abode, being, in many respects, similar, naturally produced in all an energy of character, and a spirit of independence, unknown, in the great mass of the people they had left in Europe.... Every man was a freeholder, and his freehold was at his own disposal.... This independent condition of the colonists ... combined with that equality which existed among them, arising from an equal distribution of property, a general diffusion of knowledge, and a share which all had in the government, naturally produced a love of liberty, an independence of character, and a jealousy of power, which ultimately led, under divine Providence, to that revolution, which placed them among the nations of the earth.

Pitkin, adhering to his promise to confine the annals of military events to the barest minimum, gave much space to the negotiations between the colonies and England and between the new states and France, the formation of the Confederation, and the internal difficulties of the fledgling American governments. Pitkin's strong interest in finance led him to stress the subject of public credit. Not surprisingly, since he had been for some time an anti-Jeffersonian congressman from Connecticut, Pitkin wrote as a Hamiltonian Federalist: "The general government ... was totally inefficient, and the authority of the state governments greatly weakened....the only remedy that promised relief, was an essential alteration in the national compact." Then followed the Constitutional Convention, which was called, said Pitkin, largely because of Shays's Rebellion: "This open and formidable opposition to the laws threatened not only the destruction of the government of that state, but of the union."

The chapter on the convention at Philadelphia, which discussed among other matters, the public reaction to the proposed new form of government, can still be read with profit. Pitkin applauded the policies of the Federalists, designed to strengthen the national government. His history ended with Washington's "Farewell Address," an "inestimable legacy which the father of his country" left to the Americans.

Pitkin's work ranked far above most of the histories published up to that time, showing a power of organization and discrimination in choice of material that few could match, except for his disproportionate emphasis on New England. Although his history contained no writing of an inspired character, it was not heavy reading, and its observations often showed the mark of a shrewd intelligence. There were many books written years later on the same period, but they added little to what Pitkin wrote.

Pitkin's concern with economic questions led him to publish *A Statistical View of the Commerce of the United States of America* ... in 1816. It was an admirable work, still useful, expressive of the growing spirit of commercial enterprise after the War of 1812. Its sentences reflected the characteristic national pride in material growth: "No nation, it is believed, had ever increased so rapidly in wealth as the United States." Pitkin's fame as a statistician has eclipsed his reputation as a historian, but his achievement in writing history deserved a better fate.

Some European Historians of America

The story told in these pages is basically that of Americans writing their own history, but occasionally foreign historians of America deserve mention as well. That American history interested Englishmen in the eighteenth century was not surprising, of course, for the colonies were part of the empire. Even after that link was broken, however, English interest continued, thanks to a common background, a similarity of institutions, and a curiosity about developments in the young Republic. Students of other lands, Germany and France particularly, were also drawn to a study of American history, for the new country was a powerful stimulus to the historical imagination. Probably the most important of the works published by Europeans were those of Ebeling, Grahame, and Botta, the last being the best known. Unfortunately, except for the interest of some able scholars, Ebeling and Grahame were generally ignored. They might have greatly benefitted American students.

Christoph D. Ebeling, professor of Greek and history in the University of Hamburg, labored for forty years on various works relating to the New World. To a friend he confided that he had spent a good part of his life, all his money, and even much of his health collecting materials on the United States. He was said to have the best collection of eighteenth-century American newspapers in existence. Ebeling, who referred to himself as a "Cosmopolite," had a wide circle of correspondents in the United States, including Ramsay, Belknap, Morse, Stiles, and Holmes.[34]

Ebeling's interest in America was not only to write a better history than any other in existence but also to furnish for the benefit of a reactionary Europe a "faithful picture of a truly free republic." Between 1793 and 1816 his *Erdbeschreibung und Geschichte von Amerika* (An account of the land and the history of America) appeared in seven bulky volumes. It was the most inclusive work done on America by anyone, European or American, up to that time. Unfortunately the great mass of materials it contained were largely inaccessible to Americans since few could read German, and those who could found his work bereft of literary charm. A small number of historians, including Bancroft, found Ebeling's work helpful in their research.

Ebeling was also associated with other literary ventures relating to America, such as the *Amerikanische Bibliothek* (the American library), which stressed geography, and the *Amerikanisches Magazin* (the American magazine), which acquainted Germans with American constitutional documents, books, and miscellaneous news of life overseas. Ebeling's great library and map collection, purchased by Harvard in 1818, made the college the foremost native repository of American history. His material proved of real value to Holmes, and others used it also. Thus through his writing and his collections this German scholar, working under a severe handicap thousands of miles from the scene of his intellectual interests, ultimately contributed to the development of American historical writing.[35]

Carlo Botta, born in 1766, was a Piedmontese whose medical practice was sidetracked by his interest in politics and history. To Americans he was best known as the author of *A History of the War of Independence of the United States of America*, originally published in Italian in four volumes in 1809. An Italian edition was reviewed in a Philadelphia magazine, which spoke of it as the best history of the Revolution ever written.[36] Translated in 1820, it immediately became the subject of extensive correspondence among Americans. In later life Botta explained that a discussion had arisen in a Parisian salon regarding the most suitable theme for an epic poem. All agreed that the only event worthy of such treatment was the American Revolution. If it was suitable for a poem, Botta thought, it was equally so for a history.

The Italian historian followed classical models, putting speeches into the mouths of characters who may or may not have uttered them. He had only secondary sources to draw from, and he often copied Marshall's work. Interestingly, then, among those Americans who praised Botta's work was Thomas Jefferson, who carefully noted that Botta "transfused into his narration his own holy enthusiasm for liberty, of which his icy original [Marshall] had not one spark." As was seemly for a European, Botta gave much space to the worldwide ramifications of the American Revolution. Irish discontent was related to the struggle, and other episodes attracted Botta to such lengths that at one point he interrupted himself by saying that "it is time to return upon the American continent."

Americans, of course, were delighted with Botta's enthusiastic republicanism; Jefferson thought that his work would become the "common manual of our Revolutionary History." Apparently it did, for ten American editions were printed in the following years. Jared Sparks, who met Botta in Paris in 1828, testified to the latter's careful workmanship.[37] Madison thought that Botta's work would lend a strong impetus to a more critical study of the Revolution, but he did note flaws, especially the failure to credit John Adams with a proper share in the debates on the proposal for independence.[38] Despite its obvious defects, not until Bancroft's volumes appeared was there an American narrative that could compete with the fame of Botta's history of the Revolution.

At the time when Americans were complaining to one another about the lack of interest in their history, a Scotsman, James Grahame, was writing a history of the colonies which, when published, was to be accepted by critical authority as the best in the field before Bancroft began writing. It has been pointed out by more than one critic that Bancroft never adequately recognized Grahame as his predecessor.[39] Grahame's love of the spirit of liberty had turned him to a study of American history. In his diary entry for June, 1824, he wrote: "The subject seems to me grand and noble. It was not a thirst of gold or of conquest, but piety and virtue, that laid the foundation of those settlements." The Revolution in America, Grahame went on to write, was not promoted by infidelity as was that in France; on the contrary, the American Revolution in large part was caused by religious men.

In 1824, Grahame began the composition of his history. "History is everything," he wrote to a correspondent. "Religion, science, literature, whatever men do or think, falls within the scope of history. I ardently desire to make it a religious work, and in writing, to keep the chief end of man mainly in view." Taking his task very seriously, he went to Göttingen, where, he said, books were available that he could not get in England. The first two volumes of *The History of the United States of North America*... were published in 1827; they carried the narrative to the Revolution of 1689. Although his work was neglected in England, Grahame went on with his history.

The first significant welcome accorded his history was that of Charles Francis Adams in 1831 in the *North American Review*. Grahame's book, Adams said, was the "best that has anywhere appeared upon the early history of the United States." John Quincy Adams spoke about Grahame with similar enthusiasm to Jared Sparks, but Sparks was not impressed by the Scotman's work.[40] In 1836 the remaining two volumes of Grahame's history appeared, to be met again with ill-merited neglect. Curiously, Grahame never visited the United States, and his friendships included but few Americans.

The historian wrote with intense devotion to American principles, adopting throughout a high moral tone. Grahame, however, was no blind admirer of all things American: "I am far from thinking . . . that every part of the conduct of the American states . . . was pure and blameless." He gave a fair description of the policy of the Navigation Acts, not unlike that given by American historians many years later.

English colonial policy, he said, "on the whole, was much less illiberal and oppressive than that which any other nation of Europe had ever been known to pursue." Grahame, who was trained as a lawyer, paid special attention to the laws when he came to write the social history of the colonies.

An interesting appendix to the second volume described the state of the North American provinces at the close of the seventeenth century and their future prospects. The appendix recorded opinions of colonists about the sovereignty and policy of Great Britain. Bancroft and Osgood later included similar surveys in their own volumes on the seventeenth century.

In the eighteenth century, wrote Grahame, "British oppression and intolerance, which had founded most of the North American colonies, still continued to augment the numbers and influence the sentiments of their inhabitants." He was particularly conscious of American discontent with the mother country's religious policies. Long before other historians, who seemed in afteryears to rediscover the fact, Grahame showed how the British intention to introduce the Episcopal establishment in the colonies aroused intense opposition in New England.

The historian's insights were sharp: "Even although no other subject of quarrel had presented itself, the commercial restrictions alone must in process of time have occasioned the disruption of the American provinces from the British empire." There was a careful examination of the constitutional aspects of the Stamp Act controversy along with a reference to an aspect of history in this period that attracted Carl Becker and Arthur M. Schlesinger many years later. "The supporters of colonial rights in the higher classes of society at New York," said Grahame, "were struck with alarm at the riotous outrage committed by their townsmen [in the Stamp Act riots], and perceived the expediency of constituting prudent leaders for the management and control of the multitude." Grahame saluted the Declaration of Independence with a fervor matching that of native Americans: "While European sovereigns were insulting and violating every sanction and safeguard of national right and human liberty by the infamous partition of Poland, a revolutionary principle of nobler nature and vindictive destiny was developed in the earnest and wondering eyes of the world, in America."

Grahame's work was praised by competent American critics, but some held that because it was the work of a foreigner it could not have penetrated to the heart of their history. Grahame vigorously replied that a foreigner might well be fitted to write a country's history more impartially than could a native. He died in 1842, three years before a second edition of his history appeared with an appreciative memoir by Josiah Quincy. There were some Americans who held it no bar to excellence in writing American history that the historian had been born in Scotland.

Indeed, another Scotsman, the great historian William Robertson (frequently mentioned in the same breath as Gibbon or Hume), also turned his attention to this side of the Atlantic. Robertson published a two-volume *History of America* in London in 1777; several editions eventually appeared in America. The work was especially notable for its vivid descriptions and philosophical disquisitions on aboriginal society. With the outbreak of the American Revolution Robertson's *America* became more popular than either of his now better-known works about the British Isles. However, Robertson also blamed the Revolution for keeping him from completing his projected history of the North American colonies: "I must wait for times of greater tranquility," he wrote. Unfortunately he never carried his idea to fruition.

CHAPTER 6

Patriots, Romantics—and Hildreth

AMERICANS' LONG WAIT for national historians ended when Jared Sparks and George Bancroft appeared. More than any others they established American historical writing on a firm footing. They told the American people what they wished to hear about their past. In their many volumes, Sparks and Bancroft, and later John Gorham Palfrey, narrated in great detail the settlement of a new land and the victories won by the colonists in behalf of political and religious freedom. Important factors in the nation's early history, however, including economic factors, were inadequately considered by these "filiopietistic" historians. In their writings the ideas of freedom that they praised flowered regardless of the soil from which they sprang. Richard Hildreth, more perceptive than his fellow writers, had a clearer understanding of the forces at work in American history.

Jared Sparks

Jared Sparks was born in 1789 in the poverty of a small Connecticut farm, but his early brilliance at school opened the way to a richer life. It was his reading of Franklin's autobiography, he said, that first inspired him. Friends made it possible for him to be educated at Phillips Academy, in Exeter, New Hampshire, and then at Harvard. His study of theology brought him into the Unitarian fold as a pastor in Baltimore; his chief interest, however, was literary, leading him to become an editor of the *North American Review*. During his stay in Baltimore he had served as chaplain of the House of Representatives, and his acquaintance with the leading public figures of the day was to serve him well in his later career as a historian.

Sparks became the owner of the *North American Review* in 1823, and he quickly sought to lift it out of its New England provincialism and to make it more representative of the country as a whole. He was not very successful, however, for it continued to reflect, in the main, Boston tastes. Among Sparks's innovations was the practice of paying for articles; the rate was one dollar a page. The *Review* long remained the leading magazine in the country, exercising great power over the fate of new authors. In his editing of the magazine, as in his later editing of the letters of famous men, Sparks revealed a fatal weakness — he was timid about offending those in high places.

In the summer of 1823, Sparks wrote in his diary: "Meditating on the importance of having a new history of America. . . . I would go to the foundation, and read everything on the subject." The next year Charles Folsom, who owned a press in Cambridge, asked Sparks to help him publish a complete edition of Washington's writings. Sparks sent a request to Supreme Court Justice Bushrod Washington, in whose care at Mount Vernon were thousands of historic letters. After a long wait Sparks was given the coveted permission to study the great collection. Because of the attention he drew to these papers, the government bought them and added them to the growing collections of the Library of Congress.

The letters of the first president launched Sparks into a number of historical enterprises, on all of which he worked while preparing the edition of Washington's writings. During these years he considered editing the papers of Hamilton, Lafayette, and John Jay, but meanwhile he had become interested in the whole field of the Revolution. For months in 1826 he traveled through the Atlantic states, inspecting archives for material bearing on his great theme. He was more than ever convinced of the need for a study of the Revolution: "I have got a passion for Revolutionary history, and . . . I am convinced that no complete history of the American Revolution has been written. The materials have never been collected."[1]

Sparks delved into European archives in his quest for documents bearing on the Revolution; his visit to England in 1828 made him one of the first Americans to examine the British side of the Revolutionary struggle. He also went to Paris, and under difficult conditions he unearthed from the archives the story of French participation in the American War of Independence. Lafayette was Sparks's host for a few weeks, and every morning, as the old general recounted his memories of Washington and the Revolution, the historian took notes.[2]

The following twelve years were the most productive in Sparks's life. He published *The Life and Travels of John Ledyard*, the famous Connecticut traveler, in 1828; in the next two years *The Diplomatic Correspondence of the American Revolution* appeared in twelve volumes. The latter work, done under a federal contract by which the government took a large number of copies, proved profitable to Sparks. Sparks regarded his three-volume *Life of Gouverneur Morris* (one of his lesser achievements) and other historical labors as contributions to his major interest — writing the history of the American Revolution, a task he never finished.

Between 1834 and 1837 the twelve volumes of *The Life and Writings of George Washington* were published. There was a note of relief in Sparks's journal for July 22, 1837: "Finished the 'Life of Washington' and sent the last sheet of the manuscript to the printer. The whole . . . is now completed."[3] One volume contained the biography; the others included Washington's letters and public papers. Sparks denied that he had written a "historical biography"; Marshall's work, he thought, made another such publication superfluous. He took a dig at some of his competing Washington biographers:

I have seen many particulars of [his life] which I knew not to be true, and others which I did not believe. These have been avoided; nor have I stated any fact for which I was not convinced there was credible authority. If this forbearance has been practised at the expense of the reader's entertainment, he must submit to the sacrifice as due to truth and the dignity of the subject.

Sparks wrote thoughtfully, yet his *Washington* failed to fathom truly the general's greatness. Nevertheless, some of his remarks on the character of Washington were to the point:

Wisdom, judgment, prudence, and firmness were his predominant traits. . . . He deliberated slowly, but decided surely; and when his decision was once formed, he seldom reversed it, and never relaxed from the execution of a measure till it was completed. . . . It is the happy combination of rare talents and qualities, the harmonious union of the intellectual and moral power, rather than the dazzling splendor of any one trait, which constitute the grandeur of his character.

Sparks's work, however, did not seem much different from Marshall's "Mausoleum," as John Adams called the biography by the chief justice. Artemus Ward said that Sparks's Washington still appeared to be "a human angil in a 3 kornered hat and knee britches."

Before the last book of the Washington series was off the press, the first volumes of *The Works of Benjamin Franklin* were in the process of publication. Between 1836 and 1840, ten volumes appeared; nine contained letters and papers, and one told Franklin's life story. From this biography, adjudged Sparks's best work after his *Washington*, a new characterization of the Philadelphia patriarch emerged. Formerly Franklin had been presented as cunning and insincere, whereas in Sparks's hands he became a wise, honorable and patient soul. The biography carried on where Franklin's autobiography had ended. Sparks wrote that Franklin

possessed a perfect mastery over the faculties of his understanding and over his passions . . . in every sphere of action through a long course of years his single aim was to promote the happiness of his fellow men by enlarging their knowledge, improving their condition, teaching them practical lessons of wisdom and prudence and inculcating the principles of rectitude and the habits of a virtuous life.

It waited, however, for later biographers to make both Washington and Franklin more understandable to the mass of mankind.

Edward Channing in afteryears praised the two biographies as monuments to Sparks's industry and "historical insight." Despite his energy, however, neither the edition of *Washington* nor that of *Franklin* was complete. In justice to Sparks it should be mentioned that he foresaw the possibility that more papers would be unearthed. Many years elapsed, however, before more inclusive editions of the writings of the Revolutionary leaders were published.

While Sparks was busy publishing the biographies and correspondence of the Founding Fathers, he was also engaged in editing a series of ten volumes in The Library of American Biography. He had written in his journal on July 28, 1832, "I have been thinking of a project for a new publication to be entitled 'A Library of American Biography.'" This was to be a series of prominent lives, serving as a limited yet connected history of the country. John Quincy Adams with his usual acerbity pointed out to Sparks that John Sanderson's *Lives of the Signers of the Declaration of Independence* was a collection of eulogies: "Is it intended that [yours] should be so?"[4]

Sparks was too good a historian to serve up the blatancy of Sanderson, but he catered sufficiently to patriotic taste to ensure success for his venture. He followed it with a second series of fifteen volumes that were likewise written for popular consumption. Sixty biographies, of which Sparks wrote eight, were included in these twenty-five volumes. In theory the editor had a high standard of the art of writing biography. The subject, he said, was to be kept before the reader at all times. This kind of writing, as distinguished from memoirs, was rather difficult, wrote Sparks, because it required "a clear and spirited style, discrimination in selecting facts, and judgment in arranging them so as to preserve just proportions."

Later, in 1853, Sparks issued another publication that he had planned years earlier, the *Correspondence of the American Revolution; being Letters of Eminent Men to George Washington*, in four volumes. It had been projected when the editor was looking over Washington's papers, and the book was easily readied for publication.

It was clear to his contemporaries (as well as to later students) that much of Sparks's editing was outdated. Progressive as he was in many ways, he clung to a vanishing editorial custom—dressing up the words of the eminent lest the public see their idols in dishabille. It is unfair to compare Sparks with Parson Weems, who wrote fiction in the guise of history, yet the two shared a common purpose. For both authors the lives of great men, particularly Washington, were sermons exhorting lesser mortals to nobler personal achievement. Not all aspects of Washington's life, nor all his words, were fit to be sermons, and rather than exhibit Washington's human frailties, Sparks edited his language to fit the image that America worshiped. A number of critics who were acquainted with the original Washington letters challenged Sparks's "embellishments" of the first president's language. Another accusation leveled against Sparks was that he deleted from Washington's letters all the expressions unfavorable to New Englanders.

Sparks's shortcomings as an editor were clearly seen in the *Diplomatic Correspondence of the Revolution*. When a new edition of this correspondence was proposed some twenty years after the death of Sparks, an omission was discovered: the letters mentioning a plan to substitute Count Charles Francis Broglie (a general who was the brother of the Duc de Broglie and Marshal of France) for Washington as commander-in-chief in 1776–77.[5]

Most of Sparks's work was editorial. He lacked the temperament for creative writing and clearly did not belong to the New England school of literary historians, which included Bancroft, Prescott, and Motley. Sparks's emphasis on original manuscript sources, however, drew praise from Prescott, who noted Bancroft's lesser dependence on such documents. Bancroft, said Prescott privately, was "sketchy, episodical, given to building castles in the air," while Sparks, he said, was "on *terra firma*."[6]

The volumes Sparks published were widely circulated; over 600,000 copies of his books were sold in his lifetime.[7] In public appeal history vied with fiction. Sparks was well rewarded when he picked the subject that would yield the most fertile returns—Revolutionary history. Here was a rich drama of the struggle for liberty and the conquest of new lands, a drama that also provided themes for Bancroft, Prescott, Motley, and Parkman. They wrote when sagas of liberty and conquest were not dimly remembered tales of half-forgotten ancestors but when these epics were part of the very fabric of their lives. In their own day America as winning vast new regions beyond the Mississippi, and Americans were welcoming liberty-loving revolutionaries fleeing European reaction.

Sparks's scholarly contributions won him the McLean professorship of history at Harvard, the first chair in America specifically devoted to history. He gave a course of lectures on the American Revolution; he had no real interest in college teaching, however, and preferred

research. In 1849 he became president of Harvard, but he was unhappy in this post and resigned after four years. He seemed to enjoy
not only writing but speaking to large audiences on historical topics;
his courses of public lectures on the Revolution could attract two
thousand people.[8]

In his later years (he died in 1866) Sparks frittered away his energies
answering minor inquiries. Not all of his correspondence, however, was
inconsequential; historians and public figures wrote to him for advice
and information, and younger authors sought the guidance that came
so willingly from the older man.

In the enthusiasm of his younger years Sparks had once written to
Bancroft, "My absorbing passion is for books, knowledge, and thought;
I would not exchange it for all the wealth of the Indies." His anti-
climactic last years of diverted energy make a sad commentary on the
impermanence of youthful fire. In his days of vigor, however, his work
in American history had been prodigious. The library of nearly seventy
volumes associated with his name accounts for his high station in
American historiography. The few books by Abiel Holmes, Timothy
Pitkin, David Ramsay, and William Gordon that were available before
Sparks began publication indicate the vast gaps that he filled. Though
his work was eventually superseded, he deserves the label "first great
editor of American history" assigned to him by Bert James Loewenberg.[9] His vast range of activity altered completely the character of
our historical literature and indicated the direction that much contemporary and later research was to take. His place as a noted pioneer
in American historical scholarship is secure.[10]

George Bancroft

"Together Jared Sparks and George Bancroft gave American historiography its first modern scope and direction," wrote Loewenberg.[11] The
life of George Bancroft (1800–91) encompassed most of the whole first
century of the American Republic, the spirit of which he faithfully
mirrored. His father, the Reverend Aaron Bancroft, was a well-known
liberal clergyman leaning to Unitarianism, who wrote one of the spate
of biographies of Washington that appeared soon after the president's
death. It was written, said the elder Bancroft, not "for men of erudition,
but for the unlettered portion of the community." The son succeeded
better than the father in reaching the public.

George Bancroft was a promising youngster; he completed his studies
at Harvard before he was seventeen. One of his instructors, Edward
Everett, who had studied at Göttingen, advised Bancroft to attend that
German university. Through the generosity of a few Harvard men

Bancroft was able to spend four years in Europe, earning his doctoral degree in 1820.

Soon after his return he accepted a teaching position in Greek at Harvard, but his unconventional character and newly acquired foreign manners antagonized influential persons. Ralph Waldo Emerson was more discriminating in his judgment; Bancroft, said Emerson, "needs a great deal of cutting and pruning, but we think him an infant Hercules."

Along with George Ticknor, who had also studied at Göttingen and who was a fellow member of the Harvard faculty, Bancroft began a campaign to reform Harvard's teaching methods. They rashly hoped that new German pedagogic ideas would supplant the uninspiring student recitations. Conservatism had its way, however, leaving Bancroft sick at heart: "Our hopes of a reform at college have pretty much blown over," he wrote to a friend; "I am heartily glad that the end of the year [1823] is coming so soon." In his own classes Bancroft did institute effective changes in the learning process, but it was evident that he and Harvard would soon be parted.

Joseph Green Cogswell, also a former student at Göttingen, worked in the Harvard Library. He and Bancroft formed a partnership to found a school based on the model of the German gymnasium, or secondary school. "It is our schools," they said, "which cry out most loudly for reformation." The aim of their new Round Hill School, at Northhampton, Massachusetts, wrote Bancroft, was to contribute to "the moral and intellectual maturity of the mind of each boy we take charge of; and the means are to be first and foremost instruction in the classics. . . . We might indeed assume a pompous name, speaking of instituting a gymnasium; but let the name be modest. I like the sound of the word Schoolmaster." For eleven years, from 1823 to 1834, the school attracted attention and support as a worthy educational experiment. Bancroft left the school in 1831, convinced of his own limitations as a teacher. In addition, he was in many ways quite different from the highly imaginative, excitable young Harvard tutor of nine years before. For one thing, he was already concerned with the practical yet grand game of politics, but literary interests took precedence.

As part of his work at the Round Hill School he had translated and adapted the better German textbooks for his English-speaking students. One of the texts was the work of his old Göttingen master, Arnold H. L. Heeren, *Reflections on the Politics of Ancient Greece*. During these years, and later in life as well, Bancroft was instrumental in spreading a knowledge of German culture in the United States.

In 1828, Bancroft wrote to President J. T. Kirkland of Harvard describing a projected history course. Heeren's books were recommended wherever appropriate, and for the portion dealing with the United States Bancroft offered to write the necessary "outlines" himself. In the same year Bancroft translated Heeren's *Geschichte des Europaischen Staatensystem*, altering the title to suit American taste: *History of the Political System of Europe and its Colonies, from the Discovery of America to the Independence of the American Continent.* It is not unlikely that here lay the genesis of the future *History of the United States.*

In this period Bancroft was writing articles and reviews for the *North American Review*, but he was sometimes deeply hurt because editor Sparks took unusual liberties with the blue pencil. When Sparks altered his article on Goethe, Bancroft wrote him: "If I mistake not the character of the American public, there is no need of keeping back any truth from it. The public is willing to be shocked." Despite much bickering, the two remained good friends, and the older man felt privileged to offer advice to Bancroft: "You must not work yourself to death, nor be too greedy after the treasures of this world. But you are doing great things, and the fruits of your labors are to appear not in the present time only, but in the future ages." His remarks were to the point, for Bancroft was already determined to earn wealth as well as fame through his literary career.

Writing was not divorced from politics in Bancroft's view; indeed, he made each support the other. He soon left behind his association with New England Federalism and embraced Jeffersonian principles. In a Fourth of July oration in 1826 he declared his credo: "We hold it best that the laws should favor the diffusion of property and its acquisition, not the concentration of it in the hands of a few to the impoverishment of the many. We give the power to the many in the hope and to the end, that they may use it for their own benefit." It was Bancroft's article on the Bank of the United States in the *North American Review* in 1831 that largely determined the course of his political life. He supported Jackson against the bank, and thenceforth he received high preferment among Democratic politicians, who knew well how to use his literary talents.

In 1834, Bancroft ran for a seat in the Massachusetts legislature on the workingmen's ticket. Though defeated and bitterly attacked by the Whigs, he attracted wide attention. That same year the first volume of his history brought him national distinction, and he was soon exchanging letters with such prominent political figures as William L. Marcy and Martin Van Buren. He was named collector of the port of Boston, an office that he retained until the Whigs ousted him four years later, in 1841. He was by now, however, an acknowledged member in the national councils of the Democratic party. Although active in politics, he did not neglect his history.

Bancroft announced the publication of his first volume with a flourish:

I have formed the design of writing a History of the United States from the Discovery of the American Continent to the present time. . . . I am impressed more strongly than ever with a sense of the grandeur and vastness of the subject. . . . I have applied, as I have proceeded, the principles of historical skepticism, and, not allowing myself to grow weary in comparing witnesses, or consulting codes of laws, I have endeavored to impart originality to my narrative, by deriving it from writings and sources which were the contemporaries of the events that are described.

He was critical of those American historians who, he said, had taken on faith statements of earlier writers, and had failed to personally consult the original sources. He did not forget the training he had received in Germany. Once, in discussing the credibility of various contradictory sources, Bancroft referred to memory as "an easy dupe" and tradition as "a careless story teller." He maintained that "an account, to be of highest value, must be written immediately at the time of the event. The eyewitness, the earwitness often persuade memory into a belief of inventions." His long note on the speech given by James Otis on the Writs of Assistance is an excellent example of Bancroft's critical evaluation of sources.

Bancroft lost no time stating his main theme: "The spirit of the colonies demanded freedom from the beginning." This theme and variations thereof echoed and reechoed throughout his work. He glorified the Republic: "The United States constitute an essential portion of a great political system, embracing all the civilized nations of the earth. At a period when the force of moral opinion is rapidly increasing, they have the precedence in the practice and the defence of the equal rights of man." To Bancroft, the United States was the leader among all nations; no spokesman for the young Republic ever wrote with greater assurance.

This first volume treated the expansion of Europe into America, carrying the history of the colonies up to the Stuart Restoration. Concerning the founding of Saint Augustine, the historian said that "it sprung from the unrelenting bigotry of the Spanish king. . . . In its transition from the bigoted policy of Philip II to the American principles of religious liberty" it was of striking interest to Americans. "Its origin should be carefully remembered," Bancroft opined, "for it is a fixed point, from which to measure the liberal influence of time; the progress of modern civilization; the victories of the American mind, in its contest for the interests of humanity."

Though Bancroft's history abounded in rhetorical excursions, he could sometimes write simply and impressively, as in his reference to Raleigh's failure to establish a colony: "If America had no English town, it soon had English graves." As might be expected, Roger Williams was assigned an especially distinguished place in the historian's list of worthies. So, too, were the Quakers, whose New England persecutors were taken to task by this descendant of Puritans: "The fears of one class of men are not the measure of the rights of another."

During the next thirty years more volumes appeared, making ten in all and, carrying the narrative through the Revolution. The title of the first volume had promised a history to the "present time," but for such a task even Bancroft's long life was too short, and the later volumes bore the title *History of the United States from the Discovery of the American Continent.*

Though the second volume brought the story only up to 1689, Bancroft was already preoccupied with the Revolution. Writing of the regicide Hugh Peter's hanging "for opposition to monarchy," Bancroft observed, "The blood of Massachusetts was destined to flow freely on the field of battle for the same cause; the streams were first opened beneath the gallows." At another point he paused to write in the same vein, "The Navigation Act contained a pledge of the ultimate independence of America"; at still another, "Bacon's rebellion . . . was the early harbinger of American independence and American nationality." Bancroft liked sweeping phrases, using them more skillfully than has generally been acknowledged: "Tyranny and injustice peopled America with men nurtured in suffering and adversity. The history of our colonization is the history of the crimes of Europe."[12]

Bancroft ended his second volume with a summary, "The Result thus Far." There was a note of pride in the concluding sentence: "Thus have we traced, almost exclusively from contemporary documents and records, the colonization of the twelve oldest states of our Union." In these pages Bancroft presented views strikingly similar to those of later scholars. He dimly anticipated Edward A. Freeman and the latter's disciples, Herbert Baxter Adams and John Fiske, who believed that the roots of American institutions were to be found in the communities of primitive Germany: "Of the nations of the European world," said Bancroft, "the chief emigration was from that Germanic race most famed for the love of personal independence." Like younger contemporaries Bancroft celebrated the glories of the Anglo-Saxon mind. Another sentence anticipated Thomas C. Hall, who stressed America's indebtedness to the Lollards. "When America traces the lineage of her intellectual freedom, " wrote Bancroft, "she acknowledges the benefactions of Wickliffe." The volume concluded thus: "We have written the origin of our country; we are now to pursue the history of its wardship. The period through which we have passed shows why we are a free people; the coming period will show why we are a united people."

The third volume professed to cover the period from 1689 to 1748, but there was very little material on the eighteenth century except an account of Indian civilization and colonial wars. The generous space assigned to the Indians partly reflected American interest during the 1840s in the life of the Indian. This portion of Bancroft's work was much inferior to the first two volumes. It had no central theme, and the author wandered from one subject to another. For many years to come this was the neglected period of our colonial history.

The next volume in the series, introducing the first epoch of the American Revolution, was subtitled *The Overthrow of the European Colonial System, 1748–1763*. There was a distinct acceleration of the tempo, with Bancroft's tendency to look toward the future more marked than ever: "The hour of revolution was at hand, promising freedom to conscience and dominion to intelligence. History, escaping from the dictates of authority and the jars of insulated interests, enters upon new and unthought-of domains of culture and equality." The author quoted John Adams's declaration that "the history of the American Revolution is indeed the history of mankind during that epoch." Scattered through Bancroft's pages were many observations that indicated how superior were his concepts of historical writing to those of Prince and Abiel Holmes. He insisted, for example, that it was continuity "which gives vitality to history. No period of time has a separate being; no public opinion can escape the influence of previous intelligence."

In writing the history of the American Revolution, Bancroft believed that he was "bound to keep faith with the ashes of its heroes." This conflict was, he said, "a civil war" in which men of the same ancestry were pitted against one another, "yet for the advancement of the principles of everlasting peace and universal brotherhood. A new plebian democracy took its place by the side of the proudest empires. Religion was disenthralled from civil institutions. . . . Industry was commissioned to follow the bent of its own genius."

With the fifth volume, *How Great Britain Estranged America*, the work was becoming far more detailed; it covered only the three years up to 1766. The first part depicted eighteenth-century European life, laying particular stress on the English aristocracy and its remoteness from American thought. Bancroft's emphasis on the difficulty of mutual understanding between England and the colonies was, ironically, not unlike that of the later Charles M. Andrews in his *Colonial Background of the American Revolution*. The volume covered the storm over the Stamp Act and the debates in Parliament on taxing America.

The succeeding volume, the sixth, completed the history of the causes of the American Revolution and carried the narrative to May, 1774. The acts of that year, said Bancroft, "dissolved the moral connection between the two countries, and began the civil war." From the papers of Samuel Adams, with their revelation of the network of Committees of Correspondence, Bancroft drew his most valuable material for this period: "They unfold the manner in which resistance to Great Britain grew into a system, and they perfectly represent the sentiments and the reasonings of the time." As the chief engineer of the Revolution, Samuel Adams was accorded a high place, while Hutchinson was scorned.

The seventh and eighth volumes, *America Declares Itself Independent*, were detailed narratives of the two years before July 4, 1776. The rising tide of patriotism and the spirit of the Revolution were described with skill and proportion; probably no other general historical work has ever done the task better. Contrary to the conventional opinion of Bancroft's work, the historian was by no means eager to offend England. Discussing this very subject of animus, he wrote: "The tone of our writers has often been deferentially forbearing; those of our countrymen who have written most fully of the war of our revolution, brought to their task no prejudices against England, and while they gladly recall the relations of kindred, no one of them has written a line with gall."

The last two volumes brought the story to the peace treaty. While these, as well as the other volumes on the Revolution, were mainly accounts of military hostilities, Bancroft did set aside chapters on the constitutions and internal histories of the various American states. His awareness of the international aspects of the struggle was reflected in his large-scale study of European intervention. The title of one chapter—"The King of Spain Baffled by the Backwoodsmen of Virginia 1778-1779"—revealed Bancroft's constant attempt to lift events out of their provincial setting and to give them international significance. When he wrote about the causes of the French alliance, Bancroft concluded that "the force which brought all influences harmoniously together was the movement of intellectual freedom. We are arrived at the largest generalization thus far in the history of America."

Bancroft's first volume created an immediate sensation. Edward Everett wrote to him with unrestrained enthusiasm:

You have written a work which will last while the memory of America lasts; and which will instantly take its place among the classics of our language. It is full of . . . life and power. You give us not wretched pasteboard men, not a sort of chronological table . . . after the manner of most historians; but you give us real, individual, living men and women with their passions, interests and peculiarities.[13]

Emerson declared: "It is noble matter, and I am heartily glad to have it nobly treated"; Prescott placed Bancroft with the "great historical writers of the age."[14]

European praise was tempered with reservations. Heeren wrote from Germany, praising Bancroft's regard for sources and expressing amazement at the mass of materials he had used. Carlyle liked the color of the history but added, "All things have light *and* shadow." F. P. G. Guizot qualified his praise by saying that the work was "très démocratique"—Bancroft doubtless considered that to be praise as well. Even some Americans, at least in private, were keenly critical of Bancroft's achievement; John Quincy Adams noted in his diary that the historian's treatment of the Navigation Act of 1651 was a "very lame account," and he disapproved also of his "florid panegyric." Bancroft's morality, said Adams, was "ostentatious" but "very defective"; yet his "transcendent talents" and "brilliant imagination" deserved acknowledgment.

The faults which Adams saw were transformed into virtues by Bancroft's idolatrous public; America hailed with delight this full-blown expression of Jacksonian democracy. Bancroft's history at once became the standard work on the United States; within ten years ten editions of the first volume had appeared. This and subsequent volumes ran through twenty editions or more before 1875. His history made him wealthy, even though his expenses had exceeded $100,000. Students today, however, know scarcely more of his history than the author's name. Careful scholars take issue with "his loud and uncritical Americanism" and with the gaps in his colonial history. Where he wrote on the internal development of the colonies or on their relationship to the mother country, his story was weak. His treatment of the early decades of the eighteenth century was also very sketchy, showing no real understanding of imperial administration. The colonists in their struggle with king and Parliament were always right and their opponents always wrong. Bancroft belonged to that school of historians which came to be called "prosecuting attorneys."

Much of Bancroft's material on the colonial period was invalidated by the thesis that was for him the clue to America's history: that even the early colonial years revealed a marked tendency to independence. Like most other students of his day, he was interested in colonial history mostly as a background for the Revolution. Critical opinion encouraged that view. "What Mr. Bancroft has done for the Colonial history," said Prescott, "is, after all, but preparation for a richer theme, the history of the War of Independence, a subject which finds its origin in the remote past, its results in the infinite future." Jared Sparks, the most erudite student of American history at the time, took a similar approach but went deeper:

The more we look into the history of the colonies, the more clearly we shall see that the Revolution was not the work of a few years only, but began with the first settlement of the country; the seeds of liberty, when first planted here, were the seeds of the Revolution; they sprang forth by degrees; they came to maturity gradually; and when the great crisis took place, the whole nation were prepared to govern themselves, because they always had in reality governed themselves.[15]

In reply to later "scientific" historians who were critical of Bancroft's lack of objectivity, it should be remembered that he wrote at a time when history was something more than an investigation into the past — it was supposed to give instruction. The philosophical historians of the eighteenth century, in whose tradition Bancroft was largely reared (he read Gibbon daily), were not interested in history for history's sake.[16] As J. B. Black remarked, they wanted history to "prove something," to "take us somewhere," to "provide us with a view of the world and human life." The idea of "progress" animated the thought of this school, and Bancroft was an apt pupil. He saw in the United States the goal toward which all civilization should progress: "The inference that there is progress in human affairs is . . . warranted. . . . The trust of our race has ever been in the coming of better times." Bancroft in other respects, too, was akin to these eighteenth-century spirits who fancied that the moral world was "swayed by general laws. . . . Event succeeds event according to their influence . . . they form the guiding principle of civilization," arranging "checkered groups in clear and harmonious order." One could not, however, know "the tendency of the ages" intuitively but must learn it by disinterested research.

Bancroft's kinship to earlier and to later writers (to Lord Acton, for example) was found in his notion that "as a consequence of the tendency of the race towards unity and universality, the organization of society must more and more conform to the principles of freedom."[17] In later years, when Bancroft was United States minister to Germany, L. von Ranke told the American that in Ranke's own classes he referred to Bancroft's history as "the best book ever written from the democratic point of view." In response Bancroft said, "If there is democracy in the history it is not subjective, but objective as they say here, and so has necessarily its place in history and gives its colour as it should."[18]

Bancroft's effort to make his history a work of art often was oppressing to the reader. The stately rhythm of his writing became monotonous; the grand manner, too long sustained, grew boring. Bancroft in later life took Carlyle's criticism to heart and rewrote his history. Although he subdued somewhat the brilliance of the "light," he was never able to see any "shadow" in the history of his native land. As volume followed volume, the history became more moderate in tone and improved, too, in craftsmanship, but it continued "to vote for Jackson." That "cutting and pruning" which Emerson had thought necessary when Bancroft was still young should have been urged upon him all his life. Indeed, in the 1870s, Bancroft did publish a revised "Centenary Edition" of his history. The ten volumes were reduced to six, mostly through the cutting of much exuberent rhetoric. The belligerent patriotism which had drawn criticism was also tempered somewhat, but the basic philosophy remained unchanged.

During the years when Bancroft was first writing his history, he was also active in politics and held several appointive positions. President James K. Polk named him secretary of the Navy, in which position his chief contribution was to establish the Naval Academy. His next post was as minister to England in 1846, where he took advantage of opportunities to collect historical materials. With the growing ascendancy of the southern Democrats within his party, Bancroft was shunted aside for his opposition to slavery. His reentry into active political life was in part a reward for having written the message which President Andrew Johnson sent to Congress in December, 1865. Bancroft was given the congenial post of United States Minister in Berlin, where he remained from 1867 to 1874.

In the German capital the friendship of Bismarck gave Bancroft added distinction. The Jacksonian of the 1830s became the Junker of the 1870s. There had always been a contradiction between his private life and his political philosophy: he liked the distinctions of the aristocracy while heatedly defending American democracy. As early as 1823 he had written: "I love to observe the bustle of the world, but I detest mixing in it. I like to watch the shouts of the multitude but had rather not scream with them." Literary men in the romantic era often sentimentalized over the aspirations of mankind, but the behavior of man in the mass could be as suspect to "democratic" historians as it was to the most critical of conservatives.[19]

After Bancroft's diplomatic career was over, he decided to continue his history down to the adoption of the federal Constitution. In 1882 he published in two volumes his *History of the Formation of the Constitution of the United States of America*. He studied carefully the work of his only major predecessor on the subject, George Ticknor Curtis, author of the *History of the Origin, Formation, and Adoption of the Constitution of the United States*, published in two volumes from 1854 to 1858. Bancroft, however, commanded resources available to no one else. Now past eighty, he continued to write very much in the spirit of the thirty-year-old author:

In America a new people had risen up without king, or princes, or nobles, knowing nothing of titles and little of landlords, the plough being for the most part in the hands of free holders of the soil. They were more sincerely religious, better educated, of serener minds, and of purer morals than the men of any former republic. . . . [Their constitution] excelled every one known before; and . . . secured itself against violence and revolution by providing a peaceful method for every needed reform.

It is noteworthy that Bancroft, having lived through the Civil War, evidently had no desire to remember its violence when he was writing history.

Many students, though recognizing merits in Bancroft's work on the Constitution, have marked its weaknesses. It was innocent of skepticism and omitted too much of importance, notably the economic factors influencing political events. Interestingly, Bancroft perpetuated the conventional conservative view that Daniel Shays's uprising endangered property rights; Bancroft failed to understand the reasons for agrarian discontent. Perhaps as valuable as the text itself were the appendices of hitherto unprinted materials that comprised half of the work.

Although Bancroft transcribed many papers in European collections, rigorous critics have pointed out that he did not always use them wisely in his history. Following the practice of his day, he joined disconnected reports into seemingly unified speeches, which he then put into the mouths of his leading characters. One excessively harsh critic, Sydney G. Fisher, said of Bancroft: "His researches for material both in this country and in Europe are described . . . as the most remarkable ever made. . . . But strange to say, we see no result of this in his published work. . . . Many of his opinions are difficult to support with the evidence which the investigators are able to find."[20] Certainly some of the British papers he used should have given Bancroft another side of the controversy that preceded the outbreak of the Revolution.

Until his death in 1891, Bancroft was everywhere considered to be the greatest historian of America, but younger historians had already established a newer standard of scholarship, outdating his volumes. The new generation of scholars, under the influence of the "scientific" school of history preeminently exemplified by Ranke, went to extremes both in ridiculing Bancroft and in making apologies for him. Bancroft's faults, however, should be measured, not merely counted. He was in many respects a characteristic spokesman of his age, which witnessed both in Europe and in America the publication of important nationalistic histories. His American detractors were surely inconsistent to criticize

Bancroft for the very fault which they often overlooked in the German historians who were their idols. Bismarck thought that "next to the Prussian army, it was the German professors of history who had done the most to create the new Germany."

Bancroft, with all his weaknesses, brought order out of the records of America's past and placed the history of his own country in some sort of definite relation to that of Europe. That nearly everything he wrote has been rewritten is no very serious indictment—each new generation rewrites the past. A biographer suggested that one permanent value of Bancroft's history "may well be found to be as much in its presentation of the American point of view in the period in which it took form as in its record of an earlier time." Bancroft has often been spoken of as the "Father of American History." It is to the credit of modern historians of America that even before the third generation they had learned to avoid the sins of the father. It is ungracious of them, however, to ignore his virtues.[21]

Besides, it should never be forgotten that to generations of Americans, Bancroft's version of American history *was* American history. Even today, though the average person has doubtless never heard of George Bancroft, his view of American history, if he has one, is partly Weemsian and partly Bancroftian. In the words of Gerald N. Grob and George Athan Billias, editors of the excellent collection *Interpretations of American History: Patterns and Perspectives*, Bancroft organized his history around these three themes:

the idea of progress—that the story of America was one of continuous progress onward and upward toward greatness; the idea of liberty—that American history, in essence, symbolized the trend toward greater liberty in world history; and the idea of mission—that the United States had a special destiny to serve as a model of a free people to the rest of mankind in leading the way to a more perfect life.[22]

John Gorham Palfrey

The last decade of the eighteenth century, which saw the birth of Sparks and Bancroft, produced a writer who was to become preeminently the historian of New England. That man was John Gorham Palfrey. Born in Boston in 1796, he graduated from Harvard together with his classmate Sparks. From his youth Palfrey was deeply devoted to the past of New England, and his commencement address dealt with American history.

The first three volumes of Palfrey's *History of New England*, subtitled *During the Stuart Dynasty*, appeared between 1858 and 1864. The historian had two main objectives: to trace in detail the interrelations among the New England colonies; and to write a narrative of the concurrent events in the homeland that affected the lives of the colonists.

An account of the emigration to New England and of the establishment of a social system in the new surroundings filled the first volume. The historian, writing two hundred years after the events he described, fought again the political and theological battles that had disturbed his ancestors; for example: "The name of Mrs. Ann Hutchinson is dismally conspicuous in the early history of New England." In relating the events of 1689, Palfrey exhibited the traditional provincial attitude: he constantly interpreted the relations between the colonists and the crown as a conflict between "patriots" and "tyrants." He wrote apologetically of the witchcraft episode, seeking to palliate it by comparison with similar conditions in Europe.

Palfrey brought out a fourth volume in 1875. In his history, he said, he was describing

the strenuous action of intelligent and honest men in building up a free, strong, enlightened and happy state. . . . Each generation trains the next in the lessons of liberty, and advances it to farther attainments; and when the time comes for the result of the modest process to be disclosed, behold the establishment of the political independence of America, and the boundless spread of principles which are working for good in the politics of the world.

Thus in his eightieth year the historian was expanding his commencement address, "Republican Institutions as Affecting Private Character."

Palfrey's desire to see indications of the later Revolution in the events of the period from 1689 to 1740 was a fault common to most of his contemporaries. Like others, too, he skimped the first half of the eighteenth century in his hurry to reach the Revolutionary era. The work stressed politics, largely ignoring social and economic history.

"The plan of my work," said a hopeful Palfrey, "would be accomplished by the completion of one more volume, bringing down the narrative to the opening of the War of Independence." Palfrey substantially finished the manuscript of his last volume, the fifth, before his death in 1881, but it was not published until 1890. It was apparent that the declining vigor of the historian, already evident in the fourth volume, barely enabled him to carry on the research necessary for his last effort. This fifth volume, covering the events from 1740 to 1775, was more like an old-fashioned chronology; it lacked the comparatively good organization and consecutive narrative of the earlier volumes.

In a tribute to Palfrey a fellow New Englander said, "His excellence as the historian of New England and of her people is largely due to the strong flavor that was in him of the soil and the race."

From his research in England, Palfrey was able to get much valuable information in state papers, reports, correspondence, and other documents, and yet what he had once said of Hutchinson and his history might be more appropriate for his own work: "All the details of his subject were vividly before him; [but] he did not understand his subject." Palfrey had once said in a historical discourse: "The founders of New England left a rich inheritance to their children, but in nothing so precious as in the memory of their wise and steady virtue. May there never be baseness to affront that memory!" It was his self-appointed task to exalt that memory by patient, scholarly investigation; but in the words of another New Englander, Charles Francis Adams, Palfrey was "a victim almost of that terrible New England conscience" that guided his pen. The leading representative of the filiopietistic school of historians, Palfrey had set up an evanescent monument as a token of his ancestor worship.[23] As David D. Van Tassel has said, Palfrey may have "considered himself one of the group of historians led by Sparks and Bancroft," but "in one way he could never be part of that group, for they were national historians and he was a sectional historian whose only interest in national history was to see that New England was credited with a lion's share of the development of the nation."[24]

Richard Hildreth

Bancroft so overshadowed other historians of America that their writings were almost completely eclipsed. The works of some of his contemporaries, however, fared better than his own at the hands of a critical posterity. One of these historians was Richard Hildreth, whose writing stood in sharp contrast to the prevailing temper of romantic nationalism. This Harvard graduate of 1826 had thought in his student days of writing a history of the United States; the work he eventually wrote was published in 1849. In the interim he had edited an influential Boston paper, the *Atlas,* and had written a successful antislavery novel in addition to a campaign biography for William Henry Harrison.

The History of the United States of America . . . 1497–1789 was published in three volumes. Hildreth's opening words stated his view in unambiguous language:

Of centennial sermons and Fourth-of-July orations, whether professedly such or in the guise of history, there are more than enough. It is due to our fathers and ourselves, it is due to truth and philosophy, to present for once, on the historic stage, the founders of our American nation unbedaubed with patriotic rouge, wrapped up in no fine-spun cloaks of excuses and apology . . . often rude, hard, narrow, superstitious, and mistaken, but always earnest, downright, manly and sincere. The result of their labors is eulogy enough; their best apology is to tell their story exactly as it was.

The proud author noted that, in 1849, "no other work on American history, except mere compends and abridgments, embraces the same extent of time" (Bancroft had as yet published but three volumes, which had brought him only to the middle of the eighteenth century). "Nowhere else," said Hildreth, "can be found in the same distinct completeness the curious and instructive story of New England theocracy, the financial, economical, and political history of the colonies and the Revolution . . . the progressive, social, and intellectual development of our people."

The latter claim, however, was not completely justified by the text of Hildreth's work. The narrative was mainly political history, though he did touch on education, immigration, religion, and social customs. His writing was often hardheaded and matter-of-fact. Unlike many other writers, he refused to be enthusiastic about the Quakers: "Their divine illumination superior to reason," he said, was "in fact, but a whimsical, superstitious, ill-informed, passionate, narrow, ill-regulated reason, right no doubt, upon many important points, but often exaggerated; unwilling or unable to justify itself by argument or fact."

Hildreth's remarks on the effects of the revolution of 1689 have gained interest in the light of subsequent research:

By strengthening the Parliament, and increasing the influence of the manufacturing class, it exposed the American plantations to increased danger of mercantile and parliamentary tyranny, of which, in the acts of trade, they already had a foretaste—a tyranny far more energetic, persevering, grasping, and more to be dreaded than any probable exercise of merely regal authority.

The historian did not like Cotton Mather, whose "application," he said, with an apparent dig at Bancroft, "was equal to that of a German professor." During the witchcraft affair, Mather's "eagerness to believe invited imposture. His excessive vanity and strong prejudices made him easy game." Hildreth cautiously, however, reminded his readers of contemporary belief in animal magnetism and the like, lest they "hurry too much to triumph over the past."

When he described the events of the 1760s, he did so without sensationalism and sometimes his viewpoint found later approbation. Writing of the Stamp Act, Bancroft's contemporary, Hildreth, said: "As commonly happens on such occasions, the immediate actors in these scenes were persons of no note, the dregs of the population." Their "revolutionary acts, designed to intimidate," were "melancholy forerunners of civil war." He spoke of the Boston Massacre, "for so it was called, exaggerated into a ferocious and unprovoked assault by brutal soldiers on a defenseless people." Hildreth had no love for the tales of war that so frequently were the staple of historical writing of the time. He thought that war checked "the intellectual development of the people, or rather, turned that development almost exclusively into military and political channels. Of statesmen and soldiers, men great in action, we shall presently find enough. Thinkers are the product of quieter times." In 1850 a contemporary in the *Christian Review* praised Hildreth for not catering "to the morbid relish for the disgusting details of battles."

The critical temperament of Hildreth was not spoiled by emotional excesses even when he reached the stirring events of 1775: "There were in all the colonies many wealthy and influential men, who had joined indeed, in protesting against the usurpations of the mother country, but who were greatly disinclined to any thing like a decided rupture." The historian harbored no animosity toward England. He noted, however, "the domineering spirit of the British ministry and nation," at the same time paying quiet tribute to the New England yeomanry, "full of the spirit and energy of freemen," who "fought for their farms and firesides."

Hildreth handled impartially the question of the Loyalists, but his interpretations of Shays's Rebellion and of the events leading up to 1787 were strongly Federalist. The Constitutional Convention, he wrote, "represented in a marked manner, the talent, intelligence, and especially the conservative sentiment of the country. . . . The public creditors, especially, demanded some authority able to make the people pay." Although Hildreth granted that some eminent men opposed the Constitution, he thought that most of its opponents were "the advocates of paper money, and of stop and tender laws," who "took the same side, as did all those whose ruined and desperate circumstances led them to prefer disturbance and revolution to the preservation of social order." Charles Beard greatly admired Hildreth; perhaps part of the reason lay in the similarity of their views on the Constitution.

In 1851, Hildreth brought out a second series of three volumes continuing the narrative to the Missouri Compromise. He wrote:

In dealing with our colonial and revolutionary annals, a great difficulty had to be encountered in the mythic and heroic character . . . with which in the popular idea, the fathers and founders of our American Republic have been invested. . . . To pass from these mythical and heroic times to those which form the subject of the present volumes is like suddenly dropping from the golden to the brazen and iron ages of the poets.

He noted that some conspicuous personages during the Revolution were described as possessed of "superhuman magnanimity and disinterestedness," who became later "mere ordinary mortals, objects of sharp, bitter, and often unmerited obloquy."

Though Hildreth again disavowed the use of "meretricious rhetoric" in writing his history and denied that his book was fashioned to fit "any partial political theory," his fondness for the Federalists, occasionally evident in the first three volumes, became overwhelming in the second three. Their leadership he thought superb: in Washington, Hamilton, and Jay, America had "a trio not to be matched, in fact, not to be approached, in our history, if indeed, in any other." Hamilton, "the real leader of the Federal party," was described as "a very sagacious observer of mankind, and possessed of practical talents of the highest order." He was wise in recognizing that the greater danger to the Union lay in the "resistance of the states to federal power than executive usurpation." Hildreth did, however, fault Hamilton for believing that a president and senate chosen for life would strengthen the government. Jefferson was painted unsympathetically: "To sail before the wind as a popular favorite [was] the great object of his ambition." John Adams, on the other hand, wished "rather to guide public opinion than merely to sail before it."

In a memorable examination of party divisions, Hildreth spoke of America's "natural aristocracy," comprised of the judiciary, lawyers, large landowners, merchants, and capitalists, as well as the "clergy and the leading members of the great religious sects"; these generally supported Hamilton's measures. The "natural democracy" consisted mainly of small landholders, "men who cultivated their own farms with their own hands." Political divisions in the United States, as elsewhere, Hildreth remarked, "have arisen not so much from any direct contest between the principles of aristocracy and democracy, as from the factions into which the natural aristocracy has split; the democracy chiefly making itself felt by the occasional unanimity with which it has thrown itself into the scale of one or other such contending factions." Usually, however, there is no such unanimity, but a majority of the "natural democracy," influenced by the "natural aristocracy," has been won to the side of the latter.

In a discussion of the international complexities of the late 1790s, Hildreth's sympathies were with the Federalists and England. He thought that French "insults and injuries which, coming from Great Britain, would have set the whole country on fire, were submitted to with all the patience and even pleasure with which an overfond lover sometimes allows himself to be trampled upon and plundered by an imperious and profligate mistress." Again, referring to events a few years later, he wrote: "The manly resistance made by the Federalists to the insults and aggressions of France seemed to give them a hold upon the public mind such as they had never possessed before."

When the Republicans came to power, said Hildreth, they dropped their earlier criticisms and immediately adopted most of the governmental machinery established by the Federalists. For Hildreth this was "testimony as irrefragable as it was reluctant, that however the so-called Republican leaders might excel the Federalists in the arts of popularity, the best thing they could do, in the constructive part of politics, was humbly to copy the models they had once calumniated." The New England historian referred to the "years of vexatious and ruinous commercial restrictions" in Jefferson's administrations, followed by the War of 1812, a "most disastrous and aimless war, ending in a near approach to national bankruptcy, and seriously threatening, had it not been unexpectedly brought to a close, the dismemberment of the Union." Hildreth said that the conflict was "an offensive war, voluntarily undertaken on the part of the United States to compel Great Britain, by the invasion and conquest of her Canadian territories, to respect our maritime rights."

On the question of Missouri's admission to the Union, Hildreth, a Whig and always bitterly hostile to slavery, gave a decidedly northern interpretation. The leaders of the Hartford Convention, he claimed, had a just provocation: "The provocation on the part of the South was their not being allowed to spread what they admitted to be a terrible evil over the whole territory west of the Mississippi." In the North that action was termed "moral treason," he said bitingly, but "in Southern representatives was but a manly refusal to submit to a domineering interference with constitutional rights." It was from the Missouri question, wrote Hildreth in 1851, that "recent American politics take their departure." During the last few years of his life, Hildreth, worn out from his failed attempts to win financial success as a writer, watched the American political scene from Trieste, where he had been sent as consul by President Lincoln. He died in Italy in 1865.

Hildreth's forthright statements, right or wrong, were always refreshing. Self-consciously he wrote of offending New England, the "region of set formality and hereditary grimace," by his "undress portraits of our colonial progenitors." He was proud of "bursting the thin, shining bubble . . . of a colonial golden age of fabulous purity and virtue." Harvard's refusal to name him professor of history sharpened his hostile pen. In another work, *Despotism in America*, he referred to the "moral oligarchy" in early New England, and he anticipated later students with his observation that "the history of the contest in

New England between Democracy on the one hand and the priestly and legal alliance on the other, has never been written." He noted that because of its apparent lack of dramatic episodes that conflict had not attracted the attention of historians, who supposed that the progress of American democracy had been "quiet, silent and almost unresisted," whereas it was in fact a "most violent and bitter struggle."[25] Theodore Parker, one of America's ablest critics, was on the whole favorably impressed by Hildreth's historical work, though he objected to its lack of philosophy.[26]

Hildreth's formal history indicated his acceptance of the Federalist party program, but his other works revealed his opposition to much of their social philosophy. In these writings he sought to probe the factors—intellectual, moral, political, and economic—that operated in society. In 1853 he brought out his thoughtful *Theory of Politics*, in which the economic interpretation of history was more clearly elaborated than in his large-scale narrative. He had wide knowledge of leading European thinkers, and his analysis of the causes of revolts and political alignments was very keen. Though he did not regard wealth as the sole element of political power, he did consider it to be the most important, enabling the rich to buy up all the needed props to perpetuate their own power. The rich few could easily combine "to act together with energy and effect," paralyzing the opposition by bribing the leaders of the mass of the people. The only hope for the latter, he said, was for a split among the aristocracy followed by mass alliance with one of the factions.

In a reference to the French Revolution of 1848, Hildreth spoke of the socialist demands for the full return to the workers the value of the products that they created. If labor were the sole source of wealth, he asked, "why should not the wealth thus produced go exclusively to those whose labor has called it into existence, instead of sticking to the fingers of capitalists and speculators?" He went on to point out that rather than fight the socialists, French property holders had preferred the establishment of the Second French Empire.

His concluding chapter, "Hopes and Hints as to the Future," was largely Marxist in its argument. "The clergy, the nobles, the kings, the burghers have all had their turn. Is there never to be an Age of the People—of the working classes?" asked Hildreth. He wondered whether the "middle of this current century . . . [was] destined to be that age?" He emphasized that the distribution of the annual returns of labor was much more important than the distribution of the actually accumulated wealth. "But no redistribution even of that—though it might sweep away the existing comfortable class," he continued, "would suffice, very materially to elevate the condition of the great body of the people." What was really needed was a "great increase in the amount both of accumulated wealth and of annual products."

Hildreth was, however, more of an Owenite than a Marxist; he believed that social change was evolutionary, not revolutionary. He warned the rulers of society that "this socialist question of the distribution of wealth once raised is not to be blinked out of sight" or "settled by declamations and denunciations, and mutual recriminations any more than by bayonets and artillery." Hildreth urged restraint upon the party of progress, advising it not to attempt actions "for which it is at present disqualified by internal dissensions." The student of radical thinking in America might well turn to this and other little-known writings of Hildreth; indeed, increased attention has recently been given to him for his stimulating essays based on the utilitarian philosophy of Jeremy Bentham. Most scholars, however, apparently remember him chiefly for his half-dozen volumes of history.

So critical a student as Edward Channing, writing as late as 1917, said that Hildreth's work "remains to this day the most satisfactory account of the administrations of Washington and John Adams. . . . it gives the facts accurately and in usable form." It is well to remember that in his last three volumes he viewed most of America's history from George Washington's own geographical vantage point; he rarely left the Atlantic Coast, and even then he went not west but east, to Paris and London.

The difference between Hildreth's first three volumes and his last three may not be quite as great as some critics have claimed; as Loewenberg notes, the former have been regarded as "scientific, temperate, and objective," the latter as "intemperate, partial, and colored by a political and social predisposition."[27] Certainly Hildreth saw the six volumes as a unit, but the differences were there. If the first three volumes offset Bancroft by their objectivity, the second three offset Bancroft by their opposite political viewpoint; if every page of Bancroft voted for Jackson, many pages of Hildreth's second series voted for the Whigs. Hildreth himself was aware of the difference, for he remarked in the introduction to the second series that the events related therein were too recent for entirely impartial treatment. Hildreth, then, deserves some of the credit he won as a pioneer of the scientific viewpoint in America; but, like all others, he was a product of his time and place. As one perceptive student, Alfred H. Kelly, wrote:

He knew, even though he could not achieve the goal, that the supreme objective of history is to tell the truth; and Hildreth's monotonous pages sometimes deal with a truth which he felt noble enough to stand alone. His style is a mere reflection of his ideal; and that ideal was a much-needed antidote for the American historiography of his own day, in danger of becoming the handmaiden of patriotic self-esteem and manifest destiny. In his dry, matter-of-fact attempts to tell the truth, in his emphatic rejection of the propagandistic quality of earlier and contemporary historians, he struck a healthy vein, which most subsequent scholars have ever since continued to develop.[28]

Many writers in later years owed a large debt to Hildreth for his organization of material and his grasp of philosophy. College students were familiar with his work, using it as a text in the last decades of the nineteenth century, but thereafter Hildreth's volumes, along with those of Bancroft, were allowed to gather dust upon the shelves. New viewpoints on American history, as well as changed ideas regarding the proper content of historical narratives, outmoded these distinguished historians.[29]

The Southern Viewpoint

Historical writing in the South never matched the continuous vigor apparent in New England. Southerners who might have been qualified historians sometimes claimed that they were so occupied with the tasks of governing that they had no time to pore over the records of the past — "They who are acting history themselves, care not to read the histories of other men."[30] The number of publications in the South was not small, however. The reawakening of interest in historical writing around 1830 was part of a general movement throughout the country at the time, but it was also an indication of the South's desire for independent intellectual expression.[31] This desire naturally grew stronger as the sectional division grew sharper in the next three decades.

All the southern states had historians who were particularly eager to celebrate the achievements of their communities in the Revolutionary struggle. Major General William Moultrie wrote his *Memoirs of the American Revolution* in 1802, describing the battles fought in the Carolinas and Georgia. In 1812 fellow Revolutionist, the famous "Light-Horse" Harry Lee, also gave to posterity his interesting *Memoirs of the War in the Southern Department of the United States*. These works contained more than the mere record of the authors' personal experiences, for they were fairly extensive historical narratives. Hugh McCall published his *History of Georgia* in 1811 and 1816; the versatile physician Hugh Williamson published a *History of North Carolina* in 1812, but it was not highly regarded. Maryland had a historian, John L. Bozman, who in 1837 recorded in great detail the story of the colony's first thirty years. Another history of South Carolina was written in 1840 by one of the South's most distinguished literary figures, William Gilmore Simms. Historians had already told the stories of the newer states toward the west—John Haywood, of Tennessee, did so in 1823, and Humphrey Marshall, of Kentucky, in 1824.[32] Some periodicals, including *Southern Literary Messenger, DeBow's Review,* and the *Southern Quarterly Review,* published much historical material. But the South did not have the zest for history found in New England and the Middle Atlantic states. No one had yet surveyed the South as a whole, nor had anyone there written the history of the nation.

George Tucker

It was a source of some dismay that no southern Bancroft had appeared, but finally, in 1856, George Tucker attempted to satisfy the need with his four-volume *History of the United States . . . .* Tucker was born in Bermuda and educated at the College of William and Mary. The versatility of his talents rank him with the brightest intellectuals in the Old South, especially because of his work as a political economist. He had already been a member of Congress, a professor of moral philosophy in the University of Virginia, and a biographer of Jefferson when at the age of seventy-five he turned to write the history of the United States. He had known many prominent figures in American life who helped enlighten him on the course of American history. In later life his Whig ideas and his belief in the ultimate extinction of slavery alienated him from the South, forcing him to move to the more congenial environment of Philadelphia.

Tucker's historical concepts were broad. The modern historian, he once said, unlike the earlier writers who told only of politics and war, "aims to make us acquainted with the progress of society and the arts of civilization . . . everything indeed, which is connected with the happiness or dignity of man."[33] When he himself finally came to write history, however, he did so in much the same manner as the historians whom he had considered to be outdated.

Tucker rapidly disposed of the colonial period to reach the Revolution. He furnished a useful corrective to the writing of his day by pointing to the similarities rather than the differences among the colonies on the eve of the Revolution. He praised the political parties to whose clashing tendencies, he said, the United States "owe the highest civil freedom which is compatible with the salutary restraints of law and order." In an analysis of Jefferson and Hamilton, Tucker claimed that the influence of Hamilton's political principles had almost disappeared, whereas the Virginian's had gained greatly in prestige.

Extended treatment was given to Jackson's administrations, on which

Tucker wrote shrewdly and well. The most striking feature of these administrations, he said, was that their "presiding officer was unceasingly engaged in a series of angry controversies, which, whatever was their origin, always assumed more or less of a personal character." It could hardly be doubted, said Tucker, that Jackson's popularity "was rather increased than diminished by his belligerent propensities."

Tucker's work terminated at 1841; thus he carried it twenty years beyond Hildreth's terminal date. Tucker is basically not worthy of comparison with Hildreth or Bancroft, though he used the works of both as sources, in addition to the annual messages of the presidents and the acts of Congress.

Although he aimed at impartiality, Tucker laid no claim to being free of party prejudices. In his interesting concluding chapter he defended the right of the South to deal with the slavery question without interference from the North. While affirming the South's intention to guard its institutions, he expressed a pathetic hope that the Union might continue. Depressed by fears of oncoming strife, he died in April, 1861. The guns of war were already firing at the moment of his burial on the grounds of the University of Virginia.

Tucker's history, written from the southern point of view, naturally emphasized sectional problems, but it was probably as dependable as contemporary works written by northerners, whose accent was on their own region. It is one of history's minor ironies that Tucker's work was largely ignored by the very audience he addressed, who continued to read their own history as northerners told it.[34]

Charles E. A. Gayarré

The finest historian the South produced before the Civil War was probably Charles E. A. Gayarré. Of Spanish and French descent, he was born in 1805 in New Orleans, where his family had played an important part in the affairs of the old colony. As a young man Gayarré was sent to Philadelphia to study law and was later admitted to the bar. He was active in public life, both as a judge and as a United States senator, but ill health forced his retirement.

In his own community, Louisiana, Gayarré had before him the example of Judge François Xavier Martin, who had compiled a *History of Louisiana*. Gayarré translated and adapted Martin's history, bringing it out in 1830 with the title *Essai historique sur la Louisiana*. This historical romance — for it was not conventional history — covered the period to 1815. It displayed a literary skill that was to be an outstanding characteristic of all Gayarrés work. While regaining his health in France, he prepared his *Histoire de la Louisiane*, which was published in two volumes in 1846 and 1847. Partly inspired by Sir Walter Scott, who was a great favorite in the South, Gayarré turned to the popularization of history. Fiction and history were closely interwoven in *The Poetry, or the Romance of the History of Louisiana*, written in 1848 in English to reach a larger audience. The book dealt with the region's earlier years, but Gayarré had already been preparing materials on the later period. Subsequent volumes in 1854 on the French and Spanish domination of Louisiana fixed his place more firmly as an accurate and gifted writer. A final volume, *History of Louisiana: The American Domination*, was published in 1866. Other productions from his pen include a suggestive study of Philip II of Spain and an autobiographical novel.

Gayarré's historical volumes, written to a large extent from original documents, were as good as any other work then being done in the United States. The volume on the Spanish domination, perhaps his best, treated a period that was congenial to him. He said that people enjoyed living in Louisiana under Spain; the colorful years from 1769 to 1805 contained material well suited to his literary powers. The *American Domination* described the introduction of American institutions to a Europeanized Louisiana. Gayarré devoted much care to this volume, which covered the period from 1803 to 1816, with a supplementary chapter briefly sketching the years to 1861. The historian had tied his personal fortunes to those of his beloved state during the Civil War, and it was with a deep sense of tragedy that he issued this volume on the American domination. "My task . . . is done," he wrote, "but my love, as thy son, shall cling to thee in poverty and sorrow."

George Bancroft said in a note to Gayarré that the latter had given his state "an authentic history such as scarce any other in the Union possesses. I have for years been making ms. and other collections, and the best that I have found appears in your volumes." In the long period from the Civil War to his death in 1895, Gayarré eked out a difficult living, a sad epilogue to a valuable, productive life. "It is my horrible fate," he wrote to a friend, "to be compelled, for the sake of picking vile pennies, to live in the turmoil of a world of which I am so sick that I would become a monk if I could." The work of his earlier days placed him with American writers of the first rank; not until the twentieth century was the South favored with other historians of similar distinction.[35]

Washington Irving

In the second quarter of the nineteenth century, American interest in biography as well as history was intensified. Washington Irving, the most famous literary personage of his day, felt that "one of the most salutary purposes of history [was] that of furnishing examples of what human genius and laudable enterprise may accomplish." The career of the first president inspired the pen of many a biographer including Irving himself. Before Irving had started on this project, however, he was drawn off in 1826 on an exciting biographical quest of another figure who held the perennial interest of Americans—Christopher Columbus.

Alexander H. Everett, minister to Spain and a student of history, suggested to Irving that an English version of Navarrete's collection of materials on Columbus "by one of our own country would be peculiarly desirable." Martín Fernández de Navarrete, perhaps the most learned student of the era of exploration, was in the midst of publishing a series of volumes on the Spanish voyages and discoveries. Irving seized the opportunity and prepared himself for his task by living in Spain in the home of the great bibliographer Obadiah Rich, who was serving as American consul to that country. Irving soon saw that the English-reading public would have less interest in a translation of Navarrete's documents than it would in a popular biography of Columbus. He worked industriously and seems to have enjoyed it. "And so ends the year 1826," he wrote in his diary, "which has been a year of the hardest application and toil of the pen I have ever passed. I . . . close this year of my life in better humor with myself than I have often done."[36] After two years he completed the work, and in 1828, *The History of the Life and Voyages of Christopher Columbus* was published. Later he brought out another book, a study of the companions of Columbus.

Irving claimed to have used a wide variety of sources in his *Columbus*, but in the main it was based on Navarrete. Its vigor and charm substantiated his statement that he enjoyed writing it. His admiration for the discoverer was obvious; the description of the great voyage was well done, while the narrative of the return and the reception at Palos was particularly moving. Irving's success was immediate and long-lasting.

He then returned to his biography of Washington, abandoning a plan for a history of the United States. A good book on the first president, he said, "must be a valuable and lasting property. I shall take my own time to execute it and will spare no pains. It must be my great and crowning labor."[37] For many years thereafter *Washington* kept Irving busy, but he did not work on it as conscientiously as he had on *Columbus*; not until 1855 did the first volume appear. It dealt with the life of the first president before the Revolution, but this, like succeeding volumes, was in reality a history of the times in which Washington lived. Although the work was not Irving's "crowning labor," it did on occasion reveal keen insight. The early popularity of Washington, he noted, "was not the result of brilliant achievements, nor signal success; on the contrary it rose among trials and reverses, and may almost be said to have been the fruit of defeats."

Despite the length of his five-volume biography, Irving added very little to the earlier studies by Marshall and Sparks; in fact, he did not even pretend to tap unused sources. Sparks found the volumes entertaining and instructive but did not think they should be passed off as a life of Washington. "Indeed," he said, the work "can scarcely be called history; it is rather a delineation of striking events, adorned with amusing incidents and anecdotes."[38] Although Irving's *Washington* was not greeted with much enthusiasm, his *Columbus* long remained a favorite with the general public and with scholars. Even after much new material had been unearthed over the years, Henry Harrisse and Edward G. Bourne, two of the leading students of the literature of discovery, had kind words for Irving's *Columbus*.[39]

Thomas Hart Benton

In the period before the Civil War few of the men making history also wrote it. On occasion they recorded the passing scene in letters or diaries, but rarely did they produce a consecutive narrative. One of the era's most important publications, a combination of autobiography and history, was Thomas Hart Benton's *Thirty Years' View; or, A History of the Working of the American Government . . . 1820 to 1850,* brought out in two volumes in 1854 and 1856. Benton, who had been a United States senator from Missouri, worked on these volumes in his retirement, and historians have recognized them as works of the first importance. He also completed another useful book, the *Abridgement of the Debates of Congress from 1789 to 1856,* published from 1857 to 1861.

Benton said that as an active member of the Senate he "had an inside view of transactions of which the public only saw the outside." He could see how measures were promoted or thwarted; the secrets of "wirepulling" were open to him. His *Thirty Years' View,* he said, was not a "regular history" but "a political work, to show the practical working of the government."

The modern historian who wishes to peer beneath the surface of events and discover clues worth pursuing can find no better guide than Benton. For example, he analyzed legislation relating to the disposition of public lands, a problem in which he was vitally interested. Benton said that many members of Congress who were then, in 1820, debating whether to grant relief from debts contracted in land speculation were themselves "among the public land debtors, and entitled to the relief to be granted." In discussing the tariff bill of 1828, he quoted the remarkable speech of Representative George McDuffie in opposition: "Do we not perceive at this very moment," said McDuffie, "the extraordinary and melancholy spectacle of less than one hundred thousand capitalists . . . exercising an absolute and despotic control over the opinions of eight millions of free citizens, and the fortunes and destinies of ten millions?" Benton went on to refer to the many allusions "coupling manufacturing capitalists and politicians in pressing this bill." He pointed out that the South, formerly very prosperous, later grew slowly, whereas the North grew rapidly until it became "a money lender to the South."

Benton had promised Andrew Jackson, his hero, that he would write a review of his administrations. Much of his narrative was devoted to the Bank of the United States and his own opposition to it. Regarding foreign affairs, he pointed out that in this sphere, where Jackson's impetuosity was most to be feared, the president was successful. In sketches of fellow members of Congress, Benton presented excellent characterizations; that of John Randolph, of Roanoke, was notable. Throughout his work he digressed to point out alleged flaws in Tocqueville's critique of American democracy.

Benton was deeply troubled by the southerners' discontent with their lagging prosperity, which they attributed to unfair federal legislation. It was this belief in "an incompatibility of interest," said Benton, "which constitutes the danger to the Union, and which statesmen should confront and grapple with"; he maintained that there was "no danger to slave property, which has continued to aggrandize in value." Dissatisfaction with the distribution of wealth as effected by the laws "was the point on which Southern discontent broke out—on which it openly rested until 1835, when it was shifted to the danger to slave property." His appeal to the North to preserve the Union was largely based on the pecuniary advantage to be derived from it.

There was a cry of exultation in the chapter entitled "Last Notice of the Bank of the United States." For ten long years, wrote Benton, "the name of this bank had resounded in the two Halls of Congress," and in 1841, for the first time, a session passed in which its name was not mentioned once. "Alas," said this bitter foe, "the great bank had run its career of audacity, crime, oppression and corruption." On the subject of the Oregon Territory, Benton quoted the prophetic remarks of John C. Calhoun, who spoke in 1843 of the advantages to be gained in trading with China and Japan. Markets would be opened for European and American trade, and, concluded Calhoun, "what has taken place in China, will, in a few years, be followed in Japan and all the eastern portions of that continent."

Because of Benton's Jacksonian bias he hardly did justice to the opposition. Nevertheless, his work fulfilled his original intention: to be a guide to the practical workings of the government. When checked today against other sources, it still retains great value.

CHAPTER 7

Francis Parkman

THE STANDARD OF HISTORICAL WRITING in midnineteenth-century America compared favorably with that of contemporary Europe. On both sides of the Atlantic the nationalistic "romantic" school of historians predominated. The next generation looked back upon it and, ignoring its virtues, scorned it for its limitations—its obvious national, regional, and racial bias; its devotion to "drum-and-trumpet" history; its tendency to concentrate on colorful episodes and glamorous leaders. What the scornful critics neglected to note were the literary power and narrative skill displayed by the best of the rejected historians. The "romantics," it should also be said, were usually as careful in the use of sources as were their self-styled "scientific" successors; they were, however, attracted to different kinds of materials. The "scientific" historians won out, only to lose the wide public devoted to the "romantics."

Several individuals dealt with to this point might be candidates for a list of truly great American historians, including William Bradford, Thomas Prince, Mercy Otis Warren, Jared Sparks, George Bancroft, and Richard Hildreth. There is no doubt, however, that Francis Parkman belongs on such a list.

Parkman, historian of the Anglo-French conflict for control of North America, was nurtured in the "romantic" tradition, but his books were not left to die of neglect as were those of Bancroft. Their faults were fewer and their virtues more numerous. Parkman's scrupulous care in using sources is still unsurpassed, while his literary gifts have been the envy of a host of historians.

Francis Parkman, born in Boston in 1823, was graduated from Harvard in 1844, but his education seems to have been largely self-directed. He loved fine writing and read widely in the established English classics; his favorite books, however, were those on American Indians—Cooper rivaled Scott and Byron on his list of preferred authors.

At an early age he indulged his love of the forest, the setting that provided a main theme for his lifework. In an autobiographical note, written late in life, he said, "Before the end of the sophomore year my various schemes had crystallized into a plan of writing a story of what

125

was then known as the 'Old French War'—that is, the war that ended in the conquest of Canada." Here was a stirring drama for his superb artistry to recreate. Later, he indicated, he enlarged his plan "to include the whole course of the American conflict between France and England, or in other words, the history of the American forest; for this was the light in which I regarded it. My theme fascinated me, and I was haunted with wilderness images day and night." Two ideas possessed him: "One was to paint the forest and its tenants in true and vivid colors; the other was to realize a certain ideal of manhood, a little medieval, but nevertheless good." He once explained to a fellow historian how he had come to write the history of the French in America; it had come, he said, from his dual fascination: for books and for the forest.

Parkman took long walks through his beloved woods, tracing the battle lines that still scarred the now-peaceful forest. The notes that he made in his student diaries were the historical materials of his riper years. On July 17, 1842, he wrote: "I went this morning to see William Henry. The old fort is much larger than I had thought; the earthen mounds cover many acres. . . . the lines of Montcalm can easily be traced." In the fall of 1843 his poor health, not very robust to begin with and injured "by numerous drenchings in the forest of Maine," made it seem more advisable to send him to Europe than back to Harvard. From his personal contacts in Italy he gained a deep respect for Roman Catholicism, traditionally opposed by his Puritan forebears; indeed, he once considered joining a Catholic order. It is interesting, however—and this is not the only note of irony with Parkman—that he had little but contempt for the Catholic nations of Europe when he came to write of their activities in America.

Briefly, under family pressure, Parkman turned to law, but he could not keep his mind away from the Indians. He confessed he had "Injuns on the brain." Stealing time from law studies, he wrote Indian tales for the *Knickerbocker* magazine, all the while planning his great project. "In the way of preparation and preliminary to my principal undertaking," he said, "I now resolved to write the history of the Indian war under Pontiac, as offering peculiar opportunities for exhibiting forest life and Indian character." In the summer of 1845 on a trip to the West he gathered much material that eventually went into *The Conspiracy of Pontiac*. He wormed information out of old settlers, talked with Indians, and studied the topography of the region near Detroit. His correspondence on historical subjects was already very extensive, for he had decided to devote himself almost entirely to history. His desire to see the Indians in their native condition unchanged by contact with white civilization "as a necessary part of training for my work," he said, took him farther west in 1846. Although the trip was in preparation for historical writing, it incidentally resulted in a notable autobiographical book of travel and adventure, perhaps Parkman's best-known work, *The Oregon Trail.*

Parkman's health was worse after his western trip, and from then on it was always precarious. Few people, however, were aware of his suffering. Only after his death did it become generally known that he began the volume on Pontiac when his health was particularly poor and when his eyesight was so affected that he used a frame constructed like a gridiron to guide his black crayon: "For the first half year the rate of composition averaged about six lines a day." As time passed, his improved health allowed him to work faster, and he completed the history in two and one-half years.

The Conspiracy of Pontiac appeared in 1851. The manuscript had been read by Jared Sparks, whose comments furnish some measure of the difference between the standards of the older and newer historians. The *Pontiac*, wrote Sparks, "affords a striking picture of the influence of war and religious bigotry." He wished, however, that Parkman would draw moral lessons in his history: "I am not sure but a word or two of indignation . . . at unnatural and inhuman developments of the inner man . . . would be expected of a historian, who enters deeply into the merits of his subjects."

Parkman requested criticism from his friend Theodore Parker, whose keen observations are worth noting because of the many misconceptions which persist about Parkman's understanding of the Indian. Parker wrote: "You evidently have a fondness for the Indian, not a romantic fondness, but one that has been tempered by sight of the fact. Yet I do not think you do the Indian quite justice . . . you bring out the vices of the Indians with more prominence than those of the European—which were yet less excusable." Parker went on to say, "It seems to me that the whites are not censured so much as they deserve for their conduct toward the Indians in these particulars"—rum, women, treachery, and cruelty. Parker was certainly right. One of Parkman's most disconcerting elements from the perspective of his modern admirers is his racism. In *Pastmasters,* a collection of essays on American historians published in 1969, William R. Taylor perceptively notes that Parkman accepted, with only minor qualifications, the nineteenth-century belief in progress, "especially the progress of Protestant, Anglo-Saxon civilization, which he saw as predestined to overrun the world. . . . He was an outspoken racist who looked upon the Indian and the Negro as inherently and irretrievably inferior." Although modern students of ethnology have shown that Parkman's knowledge of the Iroquois was spotty at best, he was considered so

highly qualified in that field that he was offered the presidency of
the American Ethnological Society when it was founded in 1878.[1]

To his credit, Parker made some helpful remarks on the technique
of writing:

It always enriches a special history to drop into it universal laws or any
general rules of conduct which distinguish one nation from another. The
facts of history which you set down seem generally well chosen. The historian cannot tell all; he must choose such as, to him, most clearly set forth
the Idea of the nation—or man—he describes. Bancroft chooses one set of
facts, Hildreth another, & how different the N[ew] E[ngland] of Bancroft
from H.'s N.E.

The Conspiracy of Pontiac, while only a section of Parkman's large
canvas, sketched its main outlines:

The conquest of Canada was an event of momentous consequences in American history. It changed the political aspect of the continent, prepared a way
for the independence of the British colonies, rescued the vast tracts of the
interior from the rule of military despotism, and gave them, eventually, to
the keeping of an ordered democracy. Yet to the red natives of the soil its
results were wholly disastrous.

To rescue from oblivion their struggle against the menace of the advancing colonists was the object of his work: "It aims to portray the American
forest and the American Indian at the period when both received
their final doom."

The difficulties that Parkman faced in writing this and the other
volumes of his series were clarified in language fitting his subject:
"The field of history was uncultured and unreclaimed, and the labor
that awaited me was like that of the border settler, who, before he
builds his rugged dwelling, must fell the forest-trees, burn the under-
growth, clear the ground, and hew the fallen trunks to due proportion."

The character of the Indian, as Parker had noted, received a less
than just appraisal at the hands of Parkman, who said, "Ambition,
revenge, envy, jealousy, are his ruling passions." It was a proud white
man who wrote that the Indian "will not learn the arts of civilization,
and he and his forest must perish together." After an examination of
Indian civilization, Parkman studied the English and French rivals:

Canada, the offspring of Church and state . . . languished, in spite of all [sup-
port] from the lack of vital sap and energy. The colonies of England, out-
cast and neglected, but strong in native vigor and self-confiding courage,
grew yet more strong with conflict and with striving, and developed the

rugged proportions and unwieldy strength of a youthful giant.... In every quality of efficiency and strength, the Canadian fell miserably below his rival; but in all that pleases the eye and interests the imagination, he far surpassed him.

Pontiac, the foremost chief of the Ottawas, was determined to make war upon the victorious English, who were now spilling over into the diminishing lands of the Indians. The Indian chief, "though capable of acts of magnanimity, ... was a thorough savage.... His faults were the faults of his race; and they cannot eclipse his nobler qualities." The modern reader, although farther removed in time from the Indian than was Parkman, will question the justice of the remark that Pontiac was "the Satan of this forest Paradise." The implication of innocent white Adams and Eves was scarcely warranted.

The cries of warriors, the attacks on frontier posts, and the sickening details of border warfare filled most of the pages of *Pontiac*. The chieftain's long but futile siege of Detroit meant disaster to the Indian leader. Gradually his allies fell away, leaving him to make his peace with the English.[2]

Although Parkman had planned to begin work immediately on his story of the Anglo-French struggle, ill health again intervened to delay him. Not until 1865 was *The Pioneers of France in the New World* published, but Parkman had already written large parts of other volumes in his projected series. "Each volume," he said, "will form a separate and independent work." Probably the uncertainty of his health caused him to arrange publication in this way; it was his ultimate intention to remold his monographs into a continuous narrative.

Parkman wrote that the earlier volumes of his proposed series would be devoted to

"France in the New World"—the attempt of Feudalism, monarchy and Rome to master a continent.... These banded powers, pushing into the wilderness their indomitable soldiers and devoted priests, unveiled the secrets of the barbarous continent ... and claimed all as their own. New France was all head. Under King, Noble, and Jesuit, the lank, lean body would not thrive. Even Commerce wore the sword, decked itself with badges of nobility, aspired to forest seignories and hordes of savage retainers.

Against this combination "an adverse power was strengthening and widening with slow, but steadfast growth, full of blood and muscle— a body without a head." It was a case of "Liberty and Absolutism, New England and New France." When writing of the Huguenots' failure to establish a colony in Florida, Parkman added: "To plant religious freedom on this Western soil was not the mission of France. It was for her to rear in Northern forests the banner of Absolutism and of Rome; while among the rocks of Massachusetts, England and Calvin fronted her in dogged opposition." The historian, New England born, could, however, see the faults in his ancestral home: "Politically, she was free; socially, she suffered from that subtle and searching oppression which the dominant opinion of a free community may exercise over the members who compose it . . . in defiance of the four Gospels, assiduity in pursuit of gain was promoted to the rank of a duty, and thrift and godliness were linked in equivocal wedlock."

The Pioneers of France in the New World was divided into two parts, the story of the Huguenots in Florida and that of Champlain in Canada. The bitter struggles between the Spaniards and the French for Florida were detailed in all the horror of their massacres and counter-massacres: "This pious butcher [Menéndez] wept with emotion as he recounted the favors which Heaven had showered upon [his] enterprise. . . . It was he who crushed French Protestantism in America." The vengeance that Dominique de Gourgues visited upon the Spaniards was described in milder language; in fact, his exploit was termed "romantic," but his courage, said Parkman, was sullied by "implacable cruelty."

The historian felt a deep kinship with all the chivalrous characters whose burning enthusiasm glowed in his pages. His view of history was close to Carlyle's belief that overshadowing personalities direct the course of events. Parkman spoke feelingly of Champlain, who "belonged rather to the Middle Ages than to the seventeenth century." Parkman believed that "the *preux chevalier,* the crusader, the romance-loving explorer, the curious knowledge-seeking traveller, the practical navigator, all claimed their share in him."

The high praise with which *The Pioneers* was received was repeated with even more enthusiasm when subsequent volumes appeared. Shorter intervals separated their publication: *The Jesuits in North America in the Seventeenth Century* appeared in 1867; *La Salle and the Discovery of the Great West* in 1869; *The Old Regime in Canada* in 1874; *Count Frontenac and New France under Louis XIV* in 1877; *Montcalm and Wolfe* in 1884. The last work indicated that Parkman had leaped over half a century to write the final act of his great drama, which he considered more important than the intervening period.

In *The Jesuits* the historian sought to "reproduce an image of the past with photographic clearness and truth." Sketches of individual Jesuits and the trials and tortures they endured for their faith made up the core of the narrative. Parkman singled out in particular Isaac Jogues, "one of the purest examples of Roman Catholic virtue which this Western continent has seen." In the chapter "Priest and Puritan"

Parkman returned to his frequent comparison of the two competing civilizations, with the usual advantage on the side of New England. The Jesuits eventually failed to extend French influence: "The guns and tomahawks of the Iroquois . . . were the ruin of their hopes." The defeat of the Jesuits meant that the West would not be settled under the auspices of the French, and hence "Liberty," typified in Parkman's mind by New England, would ultimately triumph.

La Salle was revised and rewritten after much new material on the explorer was published by Pierre Margry, director of the Archives of the Marine and Colonies in Paris. La Salle had a powerful attraction for Parkman, who admired his strong personality. The Frenchman "would not yield to the shaping hand [of the Jesuits] and . . . could obey no initiative but his own"; always he had an "intense longing for action and achievement." La Salle's aims were in conflict with the plans of the Jesuits, who set themselves implacably against him, regarding him as their most dangerous rival for control of the West. The Jesuits, in La Salle's scheme of things, were to restrict themselves to the Great Lakes region; the English were to be kept behind the Alleghenies; and "it was for him to call into light the latent riches of the great West."

Parkman's rich language painted the climatic voyage down the Mississippi: "Again they embarked; and with every stage of their adventurous progress the mystery of this vast New World was more and more unveiled. More and more they entered the realms of spring. The hazy sunlight, the warm and drowsy air, the tender foliage, the opening flowers, betokened the reviving life of Nature." The journey was ending in the second week of April, 1682. As La Salle "drifted down the turbid current, between the low and marshy shores, the brackish water changed to brine, and the breeze grew fresh with the salt breath of the sea. Then the broad bosom of the great Gulf opened on his sight, tossing its restless billows, limitless, voiceless, lonely as when born of chaos." Parkman laid to rest La Salle, slain by conspiring subordinates, with the epitaph: "He belonged not to the age of the knight-errant and the saint, but to the modern world of practical study and practical action. . . . America owes him an enduring memory; for in this masculine figure she sees the pioneer who guided her to the possession of her richest heritage."

Starting with *The Old Regime in Canada,* Parkman set out to reveal the French monarchy's attempt to tighten its grip on its American colony, its partial success, and its eventual failure: "In the present book we examine the political and social machine; in the next volume of the series we shall see this machine in action." Ordinarily, Parkman was less interested in the slow process of establishing a civilization than he was in its unusual, colorful incidents. In this volume, however, he came closest to the modern interest in social history with such chapters as "Paternal Government," "Marriage and Population," "The New Home," "Trade and Industry," and "Morals and Manners." Although the material was well organized, the writing in these sections necessarily had less of the glow that lit the pages describing frontier battles.

"One great fact stands out conspicuous in Canadian history," wrote Parkman in conclusion, "the Church of Rome. More even than the royal power, she shaped the character and the destinies of the colony.... The royal government was transient; the Church was permanent." The historian's pride in his Anglo-Saxon ancestry dictated the final words: "A happier calamity never befell a people than the conquest of Canada by British arms."

The next volume, *Count Frontenac*, celebrated the deeds of "the most remarkable man who ever represented the crown of France in the New World." The first important struggle between the rival powers came during his rule. He organized a "grand scheme of military occupation by which France strove to envelop and hold in check the industrial populations of the English colonies." Parkman aimed to "show how valiantly, and for a time how successfully, New France battled against a fate which her own organic fault made inevitable. Her history is a great and significant drama, enacted among untamed forests, with a distant gleam of courtly splendors and the regal pomp of Versailles."

Montcalm and Wolfe, which followed, was acclaimed by the public as the finest book in the series, a judgment in which Parkman himself concurred. "The names on the title page," said the author, "stand as representative of the two nations whose final contest for the control of North America is the subject of the book." The historian explained that "the subject has been studied as much from life in the open air as the library table," a statement that was true of most of his work.

Parkman again compared the combatants and found that "in making Canada a citadel of the state religion ... the clerical monitors of the Crown robbed their country of a trans-Atlantic empire. New France could not grow with a priest on guard at the gate to let in none but such as pleased him. ... France built its best colony on a principle of exclusion, and failed; England reversed the system, and succeeded." The English colonies, representing the future, fought against the past, which was typified by French Canada: "moral and intellectual life" against "moral and intellectual torpor." It was a fatal struggle of "barren absolutism against a liberty, crude, incoherent, and chaotic, yet full of prolific vitality."

Throughout his work Parkman kept an eye on the European aspects of the colonial conflict. The glitter of Versailles cast a remote light in the darkness of the American woods, and the figure of imperial-minded Pitt, "this British Roman," loomed large in the Anglo-French struggle. Parkman, as was his way with his favorites, described the character of Wolfe at some length. The historian's own fondness for the military attracted him to the young commander, who seemed "always to have been at his best in the thick of battle; most complete in his mastery over himself and over others. . . . Wherever there was need of a quick eye, a prompt decision, and a bold dash, there his lank figure was always in the front." The long siege of Quebec wasted his frame, but "through torment and languor and the heats of fever, the mind of Wolfe dwelt on [its] capture." No writing could be more dramatic and more filled with suspense than the description of the successful attempt to scale the heights of Abraham. On the Plains of Abraham two gallant soldiers, Montcalm and Wolfe, gave their lives for their rival sovereigns.

Toward the very end of his narrative, reviewing the broad scale of military operations, Parkman wrote a few lines that modern students wish he had elaborated further:

Now [1762] more than ever before the war appeared in its true character. It was a contest for maritime and colonial ascendency; and England saw herself confronted by both her great rivals at once. . . . With the Peace of Paris ended the checkered story of New France; a story which would have been a history if faults of constitution and the bigotry and folly of rulers had not dwarfed it to an episode.

Praise from those fitted to speak came in abundance when *Montcalm and Wolfe* was published. Henry Adams wrote:

The book puts you in the front rank of living English historians. Of its style and narrative the highest praise is that they are on a level with its thoroughness of study. Taken as a whole, your works are now dignified by proportions and completeness which can be hardly paralleled by the "literary baggage" of any other historical writer in the language known to me today.

E. L. Godkin, editor of the *Nation*, said he had never "been so much enchained by a historical book. . . . No one else does nearly as much for American literature." The aged George Bancroft paid a warm tribute, while Theodore Roosevelt asked Parkman's permission to dedicate to him his own work *The Winning of the West*.

In 1889, Parkman wrote to his friend the Abbé Casgrain, the Canadian historian, that, although his health was better, "it is still an open question whether I shall ever manage to supply the missing link between the *Montcalm and Wolfe* and its predecessor *Count Frontenac*." Fortunately he was able to return to his task; *A Half Century of Conflict* was published in 1892. "The long day's work was done."

Of his last work Parkman wrote: "The nature of the subject does not permit an unbroken thread of narrative, and the unity of the book lies in its being throughout, in one form or another, an illustration of the singularly contrasted characters and methods of the rival claimants to North America." This book had less of the vibrant writing of the other volumes, and one sensed the author's hurry to finish his task; he was now a tired man. Parkman always liked to spin his history around some central character, and because he had none in his last installment, he was probably not as much interested in it.

Although Parkman meant to be fair to the French, whose political and religious system he believed to be mistaken, his Anglo-Saxon view pervaded his writing. A French critic, whom Parkman thought unjust, said the latter saw "Canadian defects through a microscope, and merits through a diminishing glass." He did not mind sectarian criticisms of his work: "Some of the Catholics and some of the Puritans sputter at the book [*The Jesuits*]—others take it very kindly only regretting that the heretical author will be probably damned."[3]

Parkman's sympathy for his aristocratic heroes, who were cast in a medieval mold, stemmed from his own political convictions, the one area in which he differed greatly from Bancroft. "I do not object to a good constitutional monarchy," he once wrote to a correspondent, "but prefer a conservative republic [with restricted suffrage], where intelligence and character, and not numbers hold the reins of power." He thought the nineteenth century "too democratic and too much given to the pursuit of material interest at the expense of intellectual and moral greatness." To Pierre Margry he spoke with glee of the conservative victory in a municipal election: "Fortunately the low and socialistic elements—for we have them thanks to the emigration of 200,000 Irish to Boston—have suffered a defeat." Parkman's love of the pageantry of war came from deep within him; military instincts, he said, "are always strongest in the strongest and richest nature." Even as a youth on his first trip to Europe he wrote in his diary: "Here in this old world I seem, thank Heaven, to be carried about half a century backwards in time. . . . Above all, there is no canting of peace. A wholesome system of coercion is manifest in all directions."

Godkin correctly placed a high estimate on the value of Parkman's contribution to American literature: for historians the New Englander's inspiration has an undying quality. Parkman wrote:

Faithfulness to the truth of history involves far more than a research, however patient and scrupulous, into special facts. Such facts may be detailed with the most minute exactness, and yet the narrative, taken as a whole, may be unmeaning or untrue. The narrator must seek to imbue himself with the life and spirit of the time. He must study events in their bearings near and remote: in the character, habits, and manners of those who took part in them. He must himself be, as it were, a sharer or a spectator of the action he describes.

John Fiske was probably right when he said of Parkman: "Of all American historians he is the most deeply and peculiarly American, yet he is at the same time the broadest and most cosmopolitan." Later students argued that his volumes, written in the glow of Byronic romanticism, did not quite fulfill the highest ideal of historical writing. Surely one of Parkman's serious faults was neglect of social forces whose pressure in affecting the course of history may well have been as weighty as that of his dominant leaders. Nevertheless, although details of his narrative may be altered by supplemental studies, the main structure of his work seems built for permanence.[5] Boston, nature, his blindness and illness, and the Civil War were all profound influences upon Parkman and his history. Much of the early stages of the professionalization of history in America took place in Parkman's lifetime, but he was relatively untouched by it all. He did benefit from the surge of activity in the editing of historical documents; John G. Shea's twenty-six volumes of *Jesuit Relations* provided Parkman with his single most important source. William R. Taylor provides a fitting conclusion; reading Parkman today, he suggests,

is apt to leave the contemporary reader, if he is a historian, with an odd mixture of feelings. Parkman wrote at an innocent stage in the development of historical art, before history became freighted with the responsibilities of social science and before it became entirely distinct from imaginative literature. Not only did Parkman adhere to a conception of history as story; he also conceived of his larger task as the interweaving of countless stories of individuals and groups whose corporate biographies comprised the experience of the society. Abstract generalizations are rare in Parkman, and for the most part confined to his prefaces. Even generalizations about large bodies of people are sparse. Parkman seems most comfortable with groups no more numerous than might be handled in a single novel. His method, too, is novelistic. He tends to offer a telling anecdote where one would expect to be provided with a historical analysis—and to the same purpose. The points he seems most anxious to make are essentially dramatic and moral rather than sociological. The resources of the human spirit in the face of adversity evoke his most lyrical writing, for the same reason that expressions of achievement and satisfaction by his historical figures provoke his wryest instances of irony. Parkman seemed to think of himself as living in a time when all heroes were dead or about to pass forever from the scene. In this sense, for all his obsession with concreteness and veracity, he appears to have undertaken a task no less amorphous than depicting the decline and fall of the human Will.[6]

CHAPTER 8

The Rise of the "Scientific" School

B Y THE 1870s two profound changes were beginning to influence the writing of American history. First, there was a change in leadership: the patricians, who had replaced the Puritans as the dominant group writing history, were now themselves replaced by the professional historians, usually teachers of history in the colleges and universities. This had a broadening effect, because the professionals came from a much wider range of social classes than had the patricians, and they came from all parts of the country. Second, a new intellectual milieu emerged that, in the words of Gerald N. Grob and George Athan Billias, "reflected the growing dominance of novel scientific ideas and concepts. Influenced by Darwinian biology and its findings in the natural sciences, historians began to think of history as a science rather than as a branch of literature."[1]

Thus when George Bancroft died in 1891, he had outlived his own school of historical writing by more than a decade. In a survey of American historical teaching in the 1880s, Francis N. Thorpe wrote: "Bancroft and Hildreth are our historians, but our history is yet to be written. The revival of historical studies in our generation is a step toward that consummation—the production of a complete history of America." The changes in historical writing were obvious in the 1880s: restraint in expression, caution in statement, and a broader consideration of the social and economic background of American history. With the passing of the "romantic" school went a certain exuberance and spontaneity whose charm had made literature of history. More than one observer regretted the passing of our younger days, fearing that our "matured" writing of history might die of old age.

Historical studies began to enter deeply into the public consciousness. On the elementary level in the pre-Civil War era a hundred textbooks in American history had been published. In the heat of the nationalism after the Civil War, North, South, and West joined in prescribing American history instruction in the schools.[2] Compilers of children's books, following the example of Noah Webster, substituted materials on American history for the conventional biblical stories that had been staple reading matter. About this time Benson J. Lossing and Thomas

W. Higginson were satisfying popular historical tastes with many magazine articles. Lossing, in his *Pictorial Field Book of the Revolution,* sketched in pictures and in prose those wartime incidents and scenes dear to American memory.

The expansive growth of historical societies and the vitalizing of those that had existed virtually in name only were other distinctive marks of this generation of historiography. The collection and publication of documents by these societies were of great aid to scholars. When the vast collections of sources were being made in England, Germany, France and Spain, materials were also being gathered in the United States to illumine the early history of the Republic. The published volumes of Peter Force's unfinished enterprise *(American Annals...)* had revealed the wealth of materials that lay at hand for the historical craftsman. State publications of colonial records were better organized than Force's work and proved a blessing to historians. In 1868, *A Bibliography of the Various Historical Societies Throughout the United States* showed how much work had already been done in publishing documents and in writing local history.

Henry Harrisse

As the collection of documents flourished, those on the era of discovery and exploration—"the great subject," as the munificent collector John Carter Brown called it—were especially important. For the first time American scholars as a group dug to the foundations of a subject, uncovering original sources upon which they based their narratives. Abandoning the preconceptions of earlier writers and speaking with caution, these scholars marked a transition from the older to the newer historical school. The interest of Americans in the period of discovery and exploration was but the local manifestation of a similar scholarly activity then in progress in Europe and Latin America.[3]

Noted collectors like Brown, James Lenox, and Samuel L. M. Barlow were enthusiastic bibliophiles who made available to students their rare materials. A number of writers turned their attention to episodes in the early history of the New World. John G. Shea studied early French exploration; he edited the *Jesuit Relations* (1857-66) that Parkman used so extensively. James C. Brevoort brought out his *Verrazano* in 1874, and the following year the noted collector Henry C. Murphy discussed another phase of the same subject in *The Voyage of Verrazano.* The learned Harvard librarian and cartographer Justin Winsor wrote a biography of Columbus in 1891 and then brought out in rapid succession three volumes on the exploration and settlement of the Ohio and Mississippi valleys. Winsor's interests were not Parkman's; rather, he was concerned with maps and documents for their own sake. A valuable work whose publication was largely the result of Parkman's vigorous aid was the six-volume collection of sources on French colonial history edited by Pierre Margry.[4]

Even more important than these were the writings, extended over some forty years, of Henry Harrisse. Because of his work some have credited him with founding the modern school of historians of the era of exploration and discovery.

Harrisse, born in Paris in 1830, came to the United States as a child and received his college education in the South. He qualified for the bar and moved to Chicago, where he vainly tried to earn a living. Eventually he went to New York and became a close friend of Joel Barlow, who inspired in him a love for the study of the period of discovery. "Next to Christianity," thought Barlow, "the discovery of the New World was the greatest event of our era."[5] He was constantly emphasizing the need to consult the original sources. "Even if there is . . . only one of our fellow-beings who longs to know the truth regarding the discovery and historical commencement of the New World, the book should be written," said Barlow. Harrisse, referring to himself, responded that "Mr. Barlow made one proselyte, and . . . the task will be continued to the last."

Harrisse, who saw a magnificent theme for the pen of a historian in the rise, decline, and fall of the Spanish empire in America, recognized that bibliographical studies first had to be made. His *Notes on Columbus*, published in 1866, was a good beginning. Encouraged by collectors, he undertook a more ambitious project that same year, the *Bibliotheca Americana Vetustissima—A Description of Works Relating to America;* it made known to the student over three hundred items on the period from 1492 to 1551. Harrisse said that he had unearthed rarities in various parts of the country, sometimes finding them "in the dusty garret of a dilapidated church," where he pored over them "when the thermometer stood below zero." Although the great importance of his work was recognized by a small circle, the general reader was uninterested, and in disgust Harrisse moved to Paris. There, at last, financial success as an international lawyer made it possible for him to devote most of his time to his studies. Moreover, French scholars, among them Ernest Renan, heartened him with their warm welcome.

The fruits of Harrisse's labor were amassed in thirty volumes and many pamphlets, all throwing light on various phases of his chosen subject. In 1872, six years after his bibliography of Americana was published, he issued a volume of *Additions*, which revealed how eagerly he had combed the libraries of Europe for material. He found to his surprise that no library in Europe could compare with some private

American libraries in their collections of books on his favorite period.

Harrisse had said of Alexander von Humboldt's work, the *Examen Critique*, that it was "the greatest monument ever erected to the early history of [America]." A similar tribute by a distinguished scholar was later paid to Harrisse's own publication *The Discovery of North America*, which appeared in 1892. Edward G. Bourne, who was well qualified to pass judgment, said that Harrisse's work was "the greatest contribution to the history of American geography since Humboldt's *Examen*." Harrisse's lavish volume was a critical, documentary, and historical investigation, its careful analyses of conflicting evidence reflecting the author's legal turn of mind.[6]

The discoverers of America who claimed most of Harrisse's attention were Columbus, Cabot, and Vespucci. His *Christophe Colomb*, brought out in 1884, marked an advance over earlier studies because of the publication of new documents and the author's customarily sharp criticism of the sources. This, like his other works, was less a narrative than a study in historical criticism. In Harrisse's study published in 1896, *John Cabot: The Discoverer of North America and Sebastian His Son*, the son was held up to scorn: "Sebastian Cabot was a man capable of disguising the truth, whenever it was to his interest to do so." Harrisse gathered much material on Vespucci and worked up some of it; but he died in 1910, and thus he did not live to present it in a form comparable to that of his other publications. While subsequent students have not accepted all his conclusions, no one in his day was more familiar with the literature of discovery and exploration than the peppery lawyer and scholar Harrisse.[7]

The Civil War and the Centennial

The age of exploration aroused interest in historical writing in only a few persons. A more powerful incentive was the Civil War, which stimulated interest in the whole field of American history, especially in the national period. Some escaped from the passions of war by returning to study the foundations of the Union which had just been preserved. Even during the war, in 1862, the *Historical Magazine* wrote that it was closing publication of that year's volume "in the midst of a struggle which will for the next century be a matter of historic research and examination, and which in its overwhelming importance seems to banish for a season the study of the past"; yet, said the editor, "our past history, now more than ever, claims, and is receiving, the attention of thinking men."

In the same magazine, soon after the war, a contributor made some acute observations. "It is really only now," he said, "that we are beginning to know for certain what were the undoubted facts in our revolutionary history of 1776. It will require fifty years of painstaking and painful waiting—fifty years of a new conscience and the . . . disrobing of passion" before the true history of the Civil War will appear.[8] While the war was still in progress, William H. Trescot, the historian of American diplomacy, was thinking of preserving materials for the future student. "It is only by a rigid and impartial scrutiny of all the testimony," he said, "that the future historian can reach the positive truth." The manuscript that he wrote in 1861 was "only a contribution to the materials of that future history."[9]

Memoirs of leading participants in the Civil War intensified public interest in history. Colonel Alexander K. McClure published a series of articles by military personalities in the *Philadelphia Weekly Times;* editors of other journals did likewise. The most famous of all was the series in the *Century* from 1885 to 1888 under the editorship of Clarence C. Buel. These articles, later brought together in a book entitled *Battles and Leaders of the Civil War,* were immensely popular and aroused widespread discussion.[10]

The approach of the centennial in 1876 also inspired historical writing. Moses Coit Tyler was most annoyed that his volumes on the history of American literature would not be ready for that date. Carl Schurz told Samuel Bowles, the famous newspaper editor, that a publisher had asked him to prepare a political history of the United States in time for the Centennial year.[11]

New periodicals exclusively devoted to history reflected the rising interest of Americans in their past: the *Magazine of American History* appeared in 1877 and the *Pennsylvania Magazine of History and Biography* in 1877. These journals, stimulated by the Centennial, had been preceded by the *Historical Magazine* (1857-75), in whose editing Henry B. Dawson and John G. Shea had had a large share. This publication came nearest to satisfying the need later filled by the *American Historical Review.* Samuel G. Drake, the Boston bookseller, antiquarian, and editor, was another influence in stirring up interest in history; not least among his labors was his editorial supervision of the early volumes of the *New England Historical and Genealogical Register.* The self-consciousness of the West was reflected in the establishment of the *Magazine of Western History,* published from 1884 to 1895.

Bibliography and Specialized History

The bibliographical activity of these decades was of transcendent importance, the names Harrisse, Joseph Sabin, Paul L. Ford, and Justin Winsor standing to the fore. The prospectus of Sabin's *Dictionary of*

Books Relating to America was issued in 1866, and two years later the first volume of this classic bibliography appeared. "Should I wait to make this bibliography as full and exact on all points as I trust it will generally be found, I should never complete it," he said. Sabin did not live to complete it, but Wilberforce Eames, the dean of American bibliographers, and Robert Vail eventually finished it. Another great work in this field was the *American Bibliography*, compiled by Charles Evans; the twelve volumes that were published included events down through 1799.

Improved studies of the individual states began to multiply, while narratives and collections of documents in religious history shed much light on the whole area of America's development. Very important work along these lines was done by Francis L. Hawks and William S. Perry. The latter's five-volume *Historical Collections Relating to the American Colonial Church*, published between 1870 and 1878, brought to the attention of students many papers hitherto inaccessible. Charles W. Baird wrote on *The History of the Huguenot Emigration to America*, published in two volumes in 1885. John G. Shea dealt with the Catholic church in America, Abel Stevens published three volumes on Methodism between 1858 and 1861, and Henry M. Dexter compiled a valuable bibliography on the literature of Congregationalism. An extremely useful work on all Protestant sects was the ten-volume *Annals of the American Pulpit*, edited by William B. Sprague and published between 1856 and 1868.

A reexamination of certain aspects of the Revolutionary era had already begun. A friendlier interpretation of the Tories was presented by critical historians, notably by Lorenzo Sabine in 1847 in his *American Loyalists*.[12] An interesting preliminary essay in that work examined the classes in colonial society and their political allegiance. Sabine's book, which appeared in an enlarged and revised edition in 1864, had a significant influence on later writers who rescued the Tories from traditional obloquy. A century of America's history was better understood because of the publication between 1850 and 1856 of the *Works of John Adams* in ten volumes, and between 1874 and 1877 of the *Memoirs of John Quincy Adams* in twelve volumes. The indications are many that interest in the nation's past was at a high level and that new forces were influencing the writing of history in America.

The Teaching of History in the Colleges

More important than any of the factors mentioned above in promoting a newer historical writing was the change in the teaching of history in American colleges and universities. The influence of these institutions of higher learning was such that historians whose misfortune it was to live outside academic walls were looked down upon with condescension. Nevertheless, until nearly the end of the nineteenth century, many of the narratives read by the general public were written by nonacademic historians—Bancroft, Hildreth, Parkman, and others. Not until the last few years of the century did the academicians exert a preponderant influence on American historiography.

For some time, however, colleges and universities had been affecting the teaching and writing of history. In earlier years Sparks at Harvard, William Dew at William and Mary, and Francis Lieber at South Carolina (later at Columbia) had given historical lectures of high quality, but these were isolated instances. Because of their intellectual preeminence in history and constitutional law Sparks and Lieber acted as clearinghouses for the ideas of their contemporaries.[13] They realized also the need for better historical texts, and Lieber sought to fill that need. Little progress was made, however, and throughout America pedagogy was in a sorry plight. Even gifted professors taught history by having their pupils repeat from memory the dates in a manual or by having them recite its words.

The complaint which William Ellery Channing uttered in 1830 in his *Remarks on National Literature* had not lost its validity. He granted that Americans were generous in spreading elementary education but added that

we fall behind many in provision for the liberal training of the intellect, for forming great scholars . . . [who] can alone originate a commanding literature. The truth ought to be known. There is among us much superficial knowledge, but little severe, persevering research . . . little resolute devotion to a high intellectual culture. . . . Few among us can be said to have followed out any great subject of thought patiently, laboriously, so as to know thoroughly what others have discovered and taught, concerning it, and thus to occupy a ground from which new views may be gained.

It was from Europe that Americans drew their inspiration for a fuller intellectual life. American and European intellectual relations had always been close, but never more so than in this period. What Americans need, said Henry Adams, writing home from London to his brother Charles,

is a *school*. We want a national set of young men like ourselves or better, to start new influences, not only in politics, but in literature, in law, in society, and throughout the whole social organism of the country—a national school of our own generation. And that is what America has no power to create. In England the universities centralize ability and London gives a field.

So in France, Paris encourages and combines these influences. But with us, we should need at least six perfect geniuses placed, or rather, spotted over the country and all working together; whereas our generation as yet has not produced one nor the promise of one. . . . One man who has real ability may do a great deal, but we ought to have a more concentrated power of influence than any that now exists.[14]

The "geniuses" that Adams so ardently desired for America very soon appeared.

Andrew D. White and Daniel C. Gilman had gone abroad in 1853 to study European educational methods. White, after a three-year absence, during which he heard lectures under French and German masters, went to the University of Michigan to institute the first history courses in an American school that represented the modern trend. The path to change in Michigan had been eased by the higher standards already instituted by the university's progressive president, Henry P. Tappan. The young White read to his students the original sources from the rich library he had begun to collect. It interested them, he said, "far more than any question at second hand could do." History was placed at the forefront of studies at Michigan. When White accepted the presidency of the newly established Cornell University, he carried there his enthusiasm for his favorite subject. White said that "the historical works of Buckle, Lecky and Draper, which were then appearing, gave me a new and fruitful impulse; but most stimulating of all was the atmosphere coming from the great thought of Darwin and Spencer—an atmosphere in which history became less and less a matter of annals, and more and more a record of the unfolding of humanity."

W. E. H. Lecky's history of rationalism stirred progressive minds in America.[15] Henry C. Lea, the historian of the Inquisition and one of the greatest scholars the United States has ever produced, thought that Lecky's book would aid in developing a school "in which history may be taught as it should be. We have had enough annalists to chronicle political intrigues and military achievements," said Lea, "but that which constitutes the inner life of a people and from which there are to be drawn the lessons of the past that will guide us in the future, has hitherto been too much neglected."

Auguste Comte, the founder of sociology, thought it possible, by applying the methods of natural science to history, to discover the laws of historical development and thus direct social evolution. He criticized the earlier historians with their too-colorful political episodes and romantic attachment to great personalities. He advocated instead a study of society as a whole, believing that all peoples have a mass psyche which underlie the group mores.[16] The Englishman H. T. Buckle believed that Comte had done more than any other writer to raise the standard of history, and his support of the French scholar's point of view helped strengthen Comte's hold in English-speaking countries.[17] John Stuart Mill, whom the young Henry Adams considered "the ablest man in England," also deeply affected American thought. Mill and Tocqueville were "the two high priests of our faith," confessed Adams.[18]

The influence of Buckle was particularly great, and many distinguished intellectuals fell under his spell. Theodore Parker was one of his first American correspondents, while Moses Coit Tyler once wrote of having been "obsessed . . . for weeks together" by the English historian.[19] Americans, reflecting on their own national experience, were decidedly attracted to Buckle's thesis of the relationship between environment and the development of humanity; one of their own scientists, John William Draper, had been studying and working on this theme independently of Buckle. In 1863, Draper, a professor of chemistry in New York University, published his *History of the Intellectual Development of Europe*, which had a wide influence because of its evolutionary approach to history.

Buckle, Lecky, and Draper were not the only forces opening new perspectives to the young student.[20] Seminar study provided an exciting experience to Americans abroad, and this new delight in scholarship infused their teaching with unwonted zest. Herbert Baxter Adams, recalling student days in Berlin, spoke of the seminar with particular warmth: "Authorities are discussed; parallel sources of information are cited; old opinions are exploded; standard histories are riddled by criticism; and new values are established." He added, "This process of destruction and reconstruction requires considerable literary apparatus, and the professor's study-table is usually covered with many evidences of the battle of books."[21]

Charles K. Adams, a former student of White, introduced a seminar at Michigan in 1869, two years before Henry Adams initiated one at Harvard. Henry Adams disparaged his own stay of seven years at his alma mater, yet his work was of great value. Several of his students were awarded Harvard's first doctorates of philosophy, among them some whose names are well known in the literature of history and economics—J. Laurence Laughlin, Henry Osborn Taylor, and Edward Channing. Disclaimers aside, Adams was proud of "baking" his first "batch" of doctors of philosophy in 1876. To one of them, Henry Cabot Lodge, he wrote: "I believe that my scholars will compare favorably with any others, English, German, French or Italian. I look with more hope on the future of the world as I see how good our material is." *Essays in Anglo-Saxon Law,* issued in 1876 by Adams and his students, "was the first original historical work ever accomplished by American university students working in a systematic and thoroughly scientific way under proper direction"—this, at least, was the observation of a coworker, Herbert Baxter Adams, who was more familiar with academic activities in history than any other teacher of his day.[22]

Most of the younger men in the 1870s and 1880s were under the strong influence of John Richard Green and Edward A. Freeman. Green's *Short History of England,* in particular, was a great success in America. Green, said Henry Adams, "was the flower of [his] generation." James Ford Rhodes believed that Green had more readers in America than any other historian except Macaulay, adding that Green's power to shape the opinions of the reading public ranked him with England's greatest historians.[23]

The whole range of knowledge in those years felt the impact of Darwinism, and principles of relationship and continuity were being sought in every subject. Edward L. Youmans, a champion of the new thought in America, wrote to Spencer in 1871 (the same year in which *The Descent of Man* was published): "Things are going here furiously. I have never known anything like it. Ten thousand *Descent of Man* have been printed, and I guess they are nearly all gone. Five or six thousand of [Huxley's] *Lay Sermons* have been printed . . . the progress of liberal thought is remarkable. Everybody is asking for explanation."[24] Charles Francis Adams said that "a new epoch in the study of history" dated from the publication of *On the Origin of Species,* adding that "human history has become part of a comprehensible cosmogony, and its area vastly extended."[25] Historians dreamed of winning immortality by successfully applying Darwin's method to human history.

As a result of attending the lectures of leading scholars in France and Germany, American students of this period laid great stress on the history of institutions, constitutions, social organization, legal theory, public law, administration, and government. Adams, who introduced to Harvard the tendency to emphasize institutional history, was thus akin in spirit to his contemporaries, Henry Maine and William Stubbs, Georg Waitz and Fustel de Coulanges. In the Johns Hopkins University seminar of Herbert Baxter Adams, who probably did more than anyone else to "Germanize" American historical scholarship, students read on the wall before them Edward Freeman's statement, "History is past politics and politics present history." They were surrounded by portraits of men whose ideas spawned their own—G. H. Pertz, Freeman, and J. K. Bluntschli, the revered master of Adams at Heidelberg. Above all others it seemed to be Ranke who most deeply influenced European and American historical scholars, who thought the great

German historian had worked out a scientific method to arrive at objective truth and to free the writer from preconceived ideas. This was at least partly a misunderstanding of Ranke, as John Higham has made clear:

Americans consistently attributed to Ranke the happy severence of history from philosophy, and acclaimed the German historian as the founder of their own severely factual, realistic approach. Yet only a couple of Americans studied under Ranke, who retired in 1871; few read his work extensively; and no American translated any part of it. Ranke himself, as most German historians recognized by the end of the nineteenth century, was a romantic idealist, who always sought an intuitive apprehension of the universal within the particular. For Germans in the idealist tradition, history embraced and fulfilled the task of philosophy; for American empiricists the two were worlds apart.[26]

"Scientific" history, then, as it came to be practiced in America, was an American creation.

The discontent that George Ticknor had felt fifty years earlier when he compared his attainments with those of Europeans was still being experienced by Americans. "Every day I feel anew," wrote Ticknor in 1815, "what a mortifying distance there is between a European and an American scholar. We do not yet know what a Greek scholar is; we do not even know the process by which a man is to be made one." Then he added with prophetic insight, "I am sure, if there is any faith to be given to the sign of the times, two or three generations at least must pass away before we make the discovery and succeed in the experiment."[27] The generations had now passed, the discovery had been widely made, and the experiment had already met with some success. The wish that Christoph D. Ebeling had expressed in 1817 was now beginning to be realized.[28] Referring to the four Americans (Ticknor, Edward Everett, Joseph G. Cogswell, and Augustus Thorndike) then studying at Göttingen, Ebeling wrote, "I hope they will be the means of a learned intercourse between the worthies of the United States and Germany."

In his later years Ticknor revealed to his friend, the eminent geologist Sir Charles Lyell, something of the intellectual excitement then stirring in the academic world. He referred to the establishment of the Museum of Comparative Zoology in Cambridge, Massachusetts:

I think such an institution will tend ... to lay the foundation for a real university among us. ... I had a vision of such an establishment forty years ago, when I came fresh from ... Göttingen; but that was too soon. Nobody listened to me. Now, however, when we have the best law school in the country, one of the best observatories in the world, a good medical school, and a good botanical garden, I think the Lawrence Scientific School, with the Zoological and Paleontological Museum, may push through a true university and bring up the Greek, Latin, mathematics, history, philosophy, etc., to their proper level. At least I hope so, and mean to work for it.[29]

Flushed with confidence, young Americans came back from Europe to their colleges and universities and made an important place for history in the reorganization of curricula at that time. In a report to the trustees of Cornell University in 1872, President White had bemoaned that an American must attend the lectures of Édouard de Laboulaye at the Collège de France or of Karl Neumann in Berlin to learn the history of his own country.[30] But it was not long before American history in America came into its own. Chairs for history were created and new courses instituted. Tyler held the first professorship of American history, established in 1881 at Cornell. In those years, said Charles K. Adams, American universities were more advanced than Scottish universities and close behind Oxford and Cambridge in the teaching of history. Indeed, James Bryce thought that Harvard and Johns Hopkins were already superior to British universities in their teaching of history and political science. Herbert Baxter Adams also believed that Americans no longer needed to go abroad for instruction in history; it was available at Harvard, whose work in this field, he said in 1887, rivaled that of a German university.

As the faculties in American universities became more firmly established, many more students began to be trained in the United States, especially at Johns Hopkins under H. B. Adams and at Columbia under John W. Burgess. J. Franklin Jameson spoke of the "revelation" that Johns Hopkins offered in 1876. Entrance into its atmosphere, he said, was "like the opening of the Pacific before the eyes of Balboa and his men. Here were no dated classes, no campus, no sports, no dormitories, no gulf between teacher and student where all were students, no compulsion toward work where all were eager."[31] The long bibliography printed in the memorial volume to Herbert Baxter Adams revealed the scope of the Hopkins influence in the last quarter of the nineteenth century. In a tribute to his teacher, Frederick Jackson Turner said of Adams that his importance lay not in keenness of scholarship or in the critical character of his investigations but in the power to inspire students "with enthusiasm for serious historical work and in bringing out the best that was in them."[32]

The works of many scholars were published in the Johns Hopkins Studies in Historical and Political Science and in the Columbia Studies in History, Economics and Public Law. Charles K. Adams brought to the student a guide to historical literature with the publication in 1882 of his *Manual of Historical Literature*. The work of a librarian like Justin Winsor was a valuable supplement to the efforts of Edward Channing and A. B. Hart to establish the summit of American history at Harvard. Channing and Hart, in their *Guide to the Study of American History* and in their many publications of rare documents, mapped out huge fields of our history.

The editorial labors of Benjamin F. Stevens, Reuben Gold Thwaites, Worthington C. and Paul Leicester Ford, and Victor H. Paltsits were of great assistance to historical writing; their volumes also fixed more firmly a high standard of editing. Among the many services to scholarship of J. Franklin Jameson was his work with the historical division of the Carnegie Institution of Washington. His was the principal spirit in animating important projects, particularly the editing of valuable manuscripts and the publication of guides to materials on American history stored in European depositories. Other projects proposed by Jameson and his colleagues included an atlas of American geography and a dictionary of national biography comparable with England's; years passed, however, before these and other publications came from the press.

The invigoration of intellectual life in America after the Civil War inspired scholars in the social sciences to form a number of societies. The founding of the American Historical Association in 1884, the establishment of the *Political Science Quarterly* in 1886, and the publication of the *American Historical Review* a few years later were signs of the changes in America's historical writing. High standards of craftsmanship were promoted, and the vigorous criticism of recognized scholars was a healthy stimulus to their younger colleagues.

Books changed in content when John Bach McMaster brought the "people" into his narrative. The aspirations and defeats of the multitude became as much the legitimate theme of historians as the intricate developments of constitutional theory had been the theme of historians in an earlier day. "Our history is not in Congress alone," wrote a colleague of McMaster's in 1887; "that is, indeed, a very small part of it. Our discoveries, our inventions, our agrarian interests, our settlements westward, our educational affairs, the work of the church, the organization of charities, the growth of corporations . . . are all sources for research."[33] Henry Adams was writing to a friend in similar vein: "Society is getting new tastes, and history of the old school has not many years to live. I am willing enough to write history for a new school; but new men will doubtless do it better, or at least make it more to the public taste." He told Parkman that their school of history would soon be antiquated: "Democracy is the only subject for history."

Charles Adams, Henry's brother, also thought "that the day of the general historian of the old school" was over, and he prophesied the increasing importance of the monograph.[34]

New points of view were suggested by Frederick Jackson Turner, who stressed the influence of the frontier in American history. The near-monopoly of New Englanders in writing American history was broken; middle westerners and southerners refashioned the traditional interpretations of the American past. "General United States history," said Turner, "should be built upon the fact that the centre of gravity of the nation has passed across the mountains into this great region [the Mississippi Valley]. To give to our history the new proportions which this fact makes necessary, must be the work of the younger generation of students."

The economic interpretation of American history (not unknown to some early students) was reinforced by a reading of Karl Marx, although he had little direct influence on American historical writing. Economists, particularly Thorstein Veblen, were among the first of the American scholars to appreciate the significance of Marx. Published in 1902, E. R. A. Seligman's *Economic Interpretation of History* analyzed the economic approach and noted its previous applications in English, French, and American historical writing. Although critical of a rigid economic determinism, Seligman spoke of its great importance, observing that "the entire history of the United States to the Civil War was at the bottom a struggle between two economic principles." Wherever one turns in the writings of recent historical investigation, he said, "we are confronted by the overwhelming importance attached by the younger and abler scholars to the economic factor in political and social progress." Few writers went as far in their strictly Marxian interpretation as did A. M. Simons in his *Social Forces in American History*, Gustavus Myers in *The History of the Great American Fortunes*, Herman Schlüter in *Lincoln, Labor and Slavery*, or Lewis Corey in his suggestive studies of American capitalism.

No one did more to impress his fellow scholars with the value of this approach than did Charles A. Beard. One of Beard's teachers, Herbert L. Osgood, was aware of the difference between their two generations. "Men of my generation," said Osgood, "grew up in the midst of great constitutional and institutional debates, and our interest turned to institutional history. Profound economic questions have arisen and students of the younger generation, true to their age, will occupy themselves with economic aspects of history."[35]

Osgood's forecast was correct. Indeed, even such historians of his own generation as Andrews and Jameson swelled the volume of this historical literature, the former with a study of the Boston merchants and the Revolution, the latter with a fine short survey *The American Revolution Considered as a Social Movement,* published in 1926. The most important contribution to the economic interpretation of the Revolutionary era had been made in 1918 by Arthur M. Schlesinger in *The Colonial Merchants and the American Revolution.* Beard's *Economic Interpretation of the Constitution* and *Economic Origins of Jeffersonian Democracy* transformed the whole climate of subsequent investigation of the early years of the Republic. Beard's views had been anticipated by the publication in 1907 of J. Allen Smith's *Spirit of American Government,* but it was Beard's documentation that made his work so impressive. The Civil War, too, underwent reexamination, and new light was thrown on its background by students who saw in it more than a constitutional struggle.

The development of nineteenth-century science, whose facile general principles explained so much, stirred students of history to seek a like universal generalization in their own field. Most historians, said Henry Adams of his contemporaries, "have, in the course of their work, felt that they stood on the brink of a great generalization that would reduce all history under a law as clear as the laws which govern the material world.... The law was certainly there ... to be touched and handled, as though it were a law of chemistry or physics."

No one tackled the problem with greater virtuosity than Adams, who found the Second Law of Thermodynamics a blow to current social thinking. As he expressed it: "It was absurd for social science to teach progress while physical science was committed to destruction."[36] Such efforts to relate history and science, valuable as they were, ran afoul of the fact that scientific "truths," in light of newly found data, can change; thus historical theories resting on them have transitory bases. A recognition of the special character of the organism of human society made scholars wary of drawing analogies between it and other organisms in nature.[37]

A most significant approach to history was the "collective psychological," advanced by Karl Lamprecht. According to this school the historian can understand the historical development of any age only in the light of its collective psychology, and the burden rests upon him to uncover the factors "which create and shape the collective view of life and determine the nature of the group struggle for existence and improvement."[38] Lamprecht's influence turned scholars back to intellectual history, and, under the leadership of James Harvey Robinson, a number of valuable studies were published exploring the growth of man's reason. Carl Becker, in particular, greatly enriched American perception of the spirit of the eighteenth century by his study of the philosophes and his analysis *The Declaration of Independence,* which appeared in 1922.

The "scientific" history of the nineteenth century had tended to strengthen conservatism. Historians, said Becker, generally "studied the past as an inevitable process which must in any case be submitted to, but which, once rightly understood, might at least be submitted to intelligently. 'What is the use of rebelling against historical right?' asked Ranke." But the divinity of "historical right" was no more respected than was the divinity of kings, and the "new history" raised the banner of revolt. Intellectual historians, like their forerunners the philosophes, called for a "reinterpretation of the past in the service of social reform."[39]

Historians increased enormously the scope of their narratives and measurably deepened their understanding of the past through the contributions of their colleagues in archaeology, geography, anthropology, ethnography, economics, psychology, and, particularly, sociology. The line between the historian and the sociologist seemed to vanish; in fact, by the 1930s, the dominant group writing American history was sometimes spoken of as the "sociological" school of historians.[40]

The accumulation of vast quantities of monographs and source materials made it increasingly difficult for any one person to master the whole field of American history; Edward Channing's survey was the last major attempt by a single individual to do so. The trend has been steadily in the direction of cooperative enterprise, and we may expect a continuing series of comprehensive histories written by individuals treating separate periods. The result, however, is often little more than a group of monographs thrown together, and, in the view of many, serves to emphasize the periodic need for newly integrated syntheses of the whole of American history.

Thus the rise of the "scientific school" had basically what must be regarded as a positive impact on the writing of history in this country. But "scientific" history was soon to run into serious criticism. Many laymen claimed that it was unreadable, and it was, indeed, hardly light reading: the "scientific" historical monograph was supposed to be purely factual and often devoted more space to footnotes than to narrative. More significant, however, was the criticism that came from other social scientists: "scientific" history was not even really scientific. Finally, it is surely not inappropriate to lament that there are no more Parkmans, that indeed for a long time only a few historians even wrote well, that laymen stopped reading history as they once had, and that few historians were courageous enough to attempt a general synthesis of America's history.

CHAPTER 9

Henry Adams

M OST HISTORIANS of the "scientific" school were trained in the university seminars of Europe and America, and by the 1880s and 1890s their writings began to assume significance. Henry Adams may well be said to have inaugurated this period in American historiography. The fluency of his style places him with the literary historians, while his vigorous critical standards, comparative objectivity, and influence over academicians prompt his classification with the "scientific" group. His own career marked the transition from the literary historians, exemplified by Parkman, Prescott, Motley, and Bancroft, to the professional historians of the late nineteenth century. Adams was devoted to French masters such as Jules Michelet, Ernest Renan, and H. A. Taine, who contributed much to his style and to his view of historical development.

The romantic historians stressed narrative, appealed to the emotions, selected colorful episodes, and immersed their readers in the past. Adams concentrated on the sources, appealed to the intellect, brought the past to the reader, and emphasized the evolution of societal institutions. "My own conclusion," said Adams, "is that history is simply development along the lines of weakest resistance, and that in most cases the line of weakest resistance is found as unconsciously by society as by water."[1]

The Adams family has been lavish in its contributions to American political and literary life. The family's most important gift to historical literature was Henry Adams's *History of the United States during the Administrations of Jefferson and Madison.* The author, a fourth-generation Adams and one of the most interesting of them all, was born in 1838. After studying at Harvard and in Germany, he assisted his father, the minister to Great Britain during the Civil War, in London. When he returned to America, he wrote historical articles for journals and dabbled in reform politics before accepting a teaching position in history at Harvard.

In 1871, President C. W. Eliot invited Adams to give a course on the Middle Ages. In his masterly autobiographical work (written in the third person), *The Education of Henry Adams*, Adams writes, ". . . between Gurney's classical courses and Torrey's modern ones, lay a gap of a thousand years which Adams was expected to fill." Despite his own gloomy judgments of his work he filled the gap well, according to the testimony of some of his illustrious students. "He was the greatest teacher that I ever encountered," was Edward Channing's tribute. But Adams was not satisfied with his work and left Harvard after seven years. In retrospect he wrote to Jameson about his teaching: "I became over-poweringly conscious that any further pretence on my part of acting as instructor would be something worse than humbug unless I could clear my mind in regard to what I wanted to teach. As History stands, it is a sort of Chinese Play without end and without lesson."[2] As he looked back, these academic years "seemed to him lost," but at the time he was "baking" his batch of doctors of philosophy in 1876, Adams saw himself and the world in a rosier light.[3]

In his last year at Harvard, Adams gave a course in the history of the United States from 1789 to 1840, from which his later writings on this period may have come. Lindsay Swift, a student of Adams, recalled that his teacher would assign students to debate on selected subjects, asking the sons of Federalist ancestors to exchange sides with sons of Republican ancestors. "To this day," said Swift, "I do not know which side Henry Adams favored—Federalist or Republican."[4] Adams measured his views against Henry Cabot Lodge's conservatism and thought that his own teaching tended toward "democracy and radicalism."[5]

As an Adams, he quite naturally inherited an interest in the early national history of the United States. In 1877 he brought out the *Documents Relating to New England Federalism, 1800–1815,* and in 1879 he published a biography of Albert Gallatin, which was a happy augury for more important work to come. Adams had genuine enthusiasm for Gallatin: "He was the most fully and perfectly equipped statesman we can show. Other men, as I take hold of them, are soft in some spots and rough in others. Gallatin never gave way in my hand or seemed unfinished. That he made mistakes I can see, but even in his mistakes he was respectable."[6] Less beneficial to Adams's reputation was his biography of John Randolph, a bitter enemy of his grandfather John Quincy. The bitterness was inherited by the grandson: "I am bored to death," wrote Adams to John Hay, "by correcting the proofs of a very dull book about John Randolph, the fault of which is in the enforced obligation to take that lunatic monkey au sérieux."[7]

After devoting "ten or a dozen years to Jefferson and Madison," said Adams in his *Education,* he brought out between 1889 and 1891 his nine volumes covering their administrations. He had been gathering materials for the work in America and in Europe, and in May, 1880, he wrote to Lodge: "I foresee a good history if I have health and leisure the next five years, and if nothing happens to my collection of material. My belief is that I can make something permanent out of it, but, as time passes, I get into a habit of working only for the work's sake and disliking the idea of completing and publishing." At first he had planned six volumes for the sixteen years: "If it proves a dull story, I will condense, but it's wildly interesting, at least to me— which is not quite the same thing as interesting the public." Adams, depressed by his wife's suicide in 1885, neglected his history for some time, but by 1888 he was able to write with some relief to a friend, "Midsummer has come, the strawberries and roses have dropped and faded, my last half-dozen chapters are begun."[8]

Historical scholars immediately recognized this work as one of the most significant that America had produced. Adams, following Macaulay's pattern, introduced his history with several remarkable chapters on the social and cultural state of the Union in 1800. The presentation of materials on social history has never been done in a more interesting manner. "Among the numerous difficulties with which the Union was to struggle, and which were to form the interest of American history," said Adams, "the disproportion between the physical obstacles and the material means for overcoming them was one of the most striking." As for the intellectual climate, Adams stated that "the American mind, except in politics, seemed . . . in a condition of unnatural sluggishness." The Congregational clergy, while retaining their prestige, "had ceased to be leaders of thought." Though Adams's belief in democracy was not robust, he had no sympathy for the extreme conservatism of New England Federalism, which had led to a dead end: ". . . the future direction of the New England intellect seemed already suggested by the impossibility of going further in the line of President Dwight and Fisher Ames." New York, said Adams, was less hidebound: ". . . innovation was the most useful purpose it could serve in human interests, and never was a city better fitted for its work." Its society, "in spite of its aristocratic mixture, was democratic by instinct." Pennsylvania had gone beyond her sister states; she appeared to be "the model democratic society of the world."

Adams portrayed Jefferson in words that described himself as well: the Virginian's "true delight was in an intellectual life of science and art," and "he shrank from whatever was rough and coarse." His subtlety and contradictions fascinated Adams, who preferred Jefferson to Hamilton: "I dislike Hamilton because I always feel the adventurer in him," he once wrote to Lodge.[9] Yet Adams's praise for Jefferson was always balanced by criticism. Rather than trying to figure out which hero Adams most admired, it may be more appropriate to emphasize, as

Bert James Lowenberg has done, that Adams came very close to being a determinist. He saw individuals as being carried along by the uncontrollable forces of the physical universe, and there was thus little room for great men in his theory of history. "With hero-worship like Carlyle's, I have little patience," he once wrote to the philosopher William James. "In history heroes have neutralized each other, and the result is no more than would have been reached without them."[10]

Even more helpful in understanding Adams's approach is Richard Reinitz's *Irony and Consciousness: American Historiography and Reinhold Niebuhr's Vision*, published in 1980. Reinitz argues convincingly that Adams "made more use of irony than any American historian before the twentieth century" and that his analysis of Jefferson was especially filled with "Niebuhrian irony."[11] For example, in Adams's words, Jefferson

had undertaken to create a government which should interfere in no way with private action, and he had created one which interfered directly in the concerns of every private citizen in the land. He had come into power as the champion of State-rights, and had driven States to the verge of armed resistance. He had begun by claiming credit for stern economy, and ended by exceeding the expenditure of his predecessors. He had invented a policy of peace, and his invention resulted in the necessity of fighting at once the two greatest powers in the world.

No one has written better than Adams on "American ideals," and he posed questions which democracy has not yet answered. He wrote that in 1800 "American society might be both sober and sad, but except for negro slavery it was sound and healthy in every part." In winged prose Adams re-created the dream of every American to fashion humanity anew. When he was composing his manuscript, Adams said that he did not intend to give "interest to the society of America in itself, but to try for it by way of contrast with the artificial society of Europe, as one might contrast a stripped prize fighter with a lifeguardsman in helmet and breast-plate, jackboots and a big black horse."[12]

Very skillfully Adams assembled the important personages at Jefferson's inauguration, and then he went on to discuss the organization of the new government. In a short time, said the historian, "the energy of reform was exhausted . . . complications of a new and unexpected kind began, which henceforward caused the chief interest of politics to centre in foreign affairs. . . . The essence and genius of Jefferson's statesmanship lay in peace," and the tenacity of Jefferson's hold on this idea is the clue "to whatever seemed inconsistent, feeble, or deceptive in his administration."

Adams wound his way nimbly over the tortuous path of American,

Spanish, and French diplomacy. "Between the Americans and the Spaniards," said Adams, "no permanent friendship could exist . . . . Their systems were at war, even when the nations were at peace," and it was the Americans who were the "persistent aggressors." As for the French, Napoleon's failure to crush the Negro revolt in Haiti forced him to give up plans of a colonial empire in America and led him to sell Louisiana to the United States. Adams lingered delightedly over the theatricals with which Napoleon invested the sale of the territory; it was always the historian's pleasure to watch the play of mind upon mind. The constitutional difficulties into which the purchase of Louisiana plunged the Jeffersonians seemed to amuse him, but he felt sorry for Jefferson. Privately he thought Jefferson "a character of comedy," a victim of circumstances, helplessly swept along by the course of history.[13] With incisive strokes Adams reached the heart of the debate over Louisiana, whose acquisition "profoundly altered the relations of the States and the character of their nationality."

The historian remarked that Jefferson's "extraordinary success" in foreign affairs in his first administration was paralleled by domestic accomplishments. Blundering northern opposition aided him, especially the conspiracy of Massachusetts Federalists to detach New England from the Union. Adams traced the far-flung conspiratorial web with patient skill. The historian, after appraising Republican success in internal improvements, wrote generously that Jefferson "might reasonably ask what name recorded in history would stand higher than his own for qualities of the noblest order in statesmanship." But Adams could not easily shed his New England inheritance. The national government during Jefferson's and Madison's administrations, he said, "was in the main controlled by ideas and interests peculiar to the region south of the Potomac, and only to be understood from a Southern standpoint. Especially its foreign relations were guided by motives in which the Northern people felt little sympathy."

Jefferson's "overmastering passion," said Adams, "was to obtain West Florida." Abetting him were Monroe and Madison, who could not "resist the impulse to seize it." But negotiations with Spain over Florida were soon overshadowed by grave difficulties with England. "To the world at large nothing in the relations of the United States with England, France, or Spain seemed alarming," wrote Adams. "The world knew little of what was taking place." With his ever-present will to know, Adams found out what had gone on behind the scenes and described the drama vividly. The millions of lives affected by this diplomacy, however, did not appear on the stage Adams created, not even as extras. The entire scene appeared very remote as Adams viewed it with the detachment of a scientist watching insects.

It was characteristic that in writing on domestic affairs Adams was particularly concerned with the internal response to questions of foreign relationships. His emphasis on American concern with international affairs contrasts with his remark that the "United States moved steadily toward their separate objects, caring little for any politics except their own." He wrote brilliantly on diplomacy and politics in a patrician age, but he had no feeling for the life of the mass of people. Nowhere did Adams more clearly reveal the gulf that separates him from later historians than when he wrote, "Every day a million men went to their work, every evening they came home with some work accomplished; but the result was matter for a census rather than for history." Even in his own day some historians were inclined to think that the life and work of a people were as much the proper subjects of historical inquiry as were minute details of diplomacy.

Beginning with the incidents of the *Chesapeake* and the *Leopard*, Adams measured the increasing tension in Anglo-American relations leading to the imposition and eventual failure of the embargo. As a result of the attack on the *Chesapeake*, said Adams, "for the first time in their history the people of the United States learned, in June, 1807, the feeling of a true national emotion." A clue to the niggardly policy of the administration toward the navy was found in the fact that the president "did not love the deck of a man-of-war or enjoy the sound of a boatswain's whistle; the ocean was not his element."

Adams, who clung to the original meaning of the word *history*, "inquiry," restlessly sought to know the psychology of nations. England expected her opponents to fight, and if they would not, "she took them to be cowardly or mean." The American administration, he said, "had shown over and over again that no provocation would make [it] fight; and from the moment that this attitude was understood, America became fair prey." Mingled with English contempt, however, was a "vague alarm" aroused by American threats to British commercial and naval supremacy. One effect of the events of this period, said Adams, was to make the Federalists a "British faction in secret league with [the English minister] George Canning." Jefferson preferred the embargo to war, with its dangerous influence on government, but Adams noted that "personal liberties and rights of property were more directly curtailed in the United States by embargo than in Great Britain by centuries of almost continuous foreign war." The chapter entitled "The Cost of Embargo" was a splendid example of Adams's philosophic approach to history. He never forgot his own exacting standard for historical writing. The historian, he said, "must be an artist. He must know how to keep the thread of his narrative always in hand, how to subordinate details, and how to accentuate principles."[14]

Adams carried the reader at a rapid pace through the further ramifications of American diplomacy with England and France, finally leading to the War of 1812. John Hay, who was his closest friend (but not his severest critic), wrote that volumes five and six "take the cake. There is a gathering strength and interest in these later volumes that is nothing short of exciting. The style is perfect, if perfect is a proper word applied to anything so vivid, so flexible and so powerful." Adams touched briefly on the economic significance of the embargo and non-importation acts: "American manufacturers owed more to Jefferson and Virginians, who disliked them, than to Northern statesmen, who merely encouraged them after they were established." The shifting status of Anglo-American relations was thus summed up: "As Canning frowned or smiled, faction rose to frenzy or lay down to slumber throughout the United States." For Henry Adams, George Canning was the evil genius throughout these protracted maneuvers; the harm he did was "more than three generations could wholly repair."

Turning back to the domestic scene, Adams took note of Henry Clay's maiden speech as a senatorial "war hawk"; it "marked the appearance of a school which was for fifty years to express the national ideals of statesmanship." Thereafter, "the Union and the Fathers were rarely omitted from any popular harangue." Henry Adams, descendant of diplomats, moved with easy grace in congressional halls, Napoleon's court, and British council rooms. He well understood how impulses originating in one place were communicated to the others, and he carefully measured these forces. The narrative moved forward machine-like, effect following cause in precise progression.

The Olympian viewpoint in Adams's writing put to shame the scrib-blings of lesser historians. Here was his "overture" to 1812:

As in the year 1754 a petty fight between two French and English scouting parties on the banks of the Youghiogheny River, far in the American Wilder-ness, began a war that changed the balance of the world, so in 1811 an en-counter in the Indian country, on the banks of the Wabash, began a fresh convulsion which ended only with the fall of Napoleon. The battle of Tip-pecanoe was a premature outbreak of the great wars of 1812.

The young Republicans, said Adams, "were bent on war with England, they were willing to face debt and probably bankruptcy on the chance of creating a nation, of conquering Canada, and carrying the American flag to Mobile and Key West." This New England historian reflected his region's hostility toward the war; he said that probably four-fifths of the American people thought it could have been avoided. Madison's first term ended with "the country more than ever distracted, and as little able to negotiate as to conquer."

Adams closely followed the trail of war on land and sea; the parliamentary and diplomatic battles that accompanied martial events hovered in the background of his pages. Napoleon, whose enigmatic character strongly attracted the author, played almost as important a part in Adams's interpretation of American history as did the president. The historian, at home on the sea, described with keen delight American naval successes, which he attributed to the superiority of American naval architecture. He suggested also that the privateers which inflicted great damage on English commerce "contributed more than the regular navy to bring about a disposition for peace in the British classes most responsible for the war." The incompetence of American leadership on land filled Adams with disgust.

In New England, Adams wrote, opposition to the war was increasing. Adams estimated that by 1814 "nearly one half of the five New England states supported the war, but were paralyzed by the other half, which opposed it." The national government itself was approaching exhaustion because of the lack of money and men to carry on the struggle; the Massachusetts Federalists now felt they could stop it. In his treatment of the Hartford Convention Adams was moderately critical, but he took pains to show the contribution of Massachusetts to the war in a light more favorable than that of most other writers. It seemed that in England, too, the "war had lost public favor." The treaty which was finally reached actually left all the points in dispute "to be settled by time, the final negotiator, whose decision they [the Americans] could safely trust," wrote Adams.

"The long, exciting, and splendid panorama of revolution and war, which for twenty-five years absorbed the world's attention and dwarfed all other interests, vanished more quickly in America than in Europe, and left fewer elements of disturbance." Prosperity in America, he said, "put an end to faction," but New England did not share much in this wealth. In fact, the end of the war brought distress to Massachusetts, whose influence in politics suffered a sharp decline while the South and West gained rapidly in economic and political importance. The Americans of 1815 were far less interested in the rights of man, which had troubled them in 1801, than they were in the price of cotton. In 1800 there had been indifference to internal improvements; sixteen years later people everywhere were actively interested in them. While the population was doubling within twenty-three years, wealth was doubling within twenty. Americans "with almost the certainty of a mathematical formula, knowing the rate of increase of population and of wealth . . . could read in advance their economical history for at least a hundred years," Adams observed.

"The movement of thought," which interested Adams more than the

"movement of population or of wealth . . . was equally well defined."
In religion excitement tending to emotionalism was clearly in evidence
except in New England, where "the old intellectual pre-eminence . . .
developed a quality both new and distinctive" in Unitarianism. In religion society tended to fragment; in politics public opinion slowly moved
in a fixed direction of emphasis on national sovereignty. Harvard College was at this time stimulating intellectual activity in many directions; "the American mind, as far as it went, showed both freshness
and originality." Americans of the period, thought Adams, "had as a
people little instinct of beauty; but their intelligence in its higher as
in its lower forms was both quick and refined."

The historian found that "the difference between Europe and
America was decided," and politically the American "was a new variety
of man." Adams, along with James Bryce, noted that "the South and
West gave to society a character more aggressively American than had
been known before." Although "the traits of American character were
fixed," as was the rate of population growth, Adams observed that the
concern of history thereafter was "to know what kind of people these
millions were to be." His reply was that "history required another
century of experience." His own volumes, he said, were "merely an
Introduction to our history during the Nineteenth Century and were
intended only to serve the future historian with a fixed and documented starting-point."[15]

One of the things that prompted Adams to write American history
was his desire to establish his favorite subject as an exact science.
Throughout his volumes he used the terminology of the physicist,
often with striking effect. "By rights, he should have been a Marxist,"
Adams said of himself in his *Education*, "but some narrow trait of the
New England nature seemed to blight socialism, and he tried in vain
to make himself a convert. He did the next best thing, he became a
Comteist within the limits of evolution." Comte did indeed have a
profound influence on Adams's ideas for many years, but in the end
Adams reversed his beliefs completely. Where he had once agreed with
Comte that society's progress was steady and worthwhile, he ended by
believing in the social tendency to degradation. It was his prediction
that by 1950 "present society must break its damn neck."

A vast amount has been written about Henry Adams since 1937—
indeed, more has probably been written about him than about any other
American historian—but none of it has really supplanted the brilliant
essay of that year by Henry Steele Commager in the *Jernegan Essays*.
Commager considered Adams's *Gallatin* "the best political biography"
and his *Jefferson and Madison* "the finest piece of historical writing" in
American literature. He also credited Adams with being "the only

American historian who has ever seriously attempted to formulate a philosophy of history." According to Commager, "The problem was to bring human history in harmony with the organic laws of the universe, and the formula that Adams hit upon was the Law of the Dissipation of Energy."[16] Adams was, of course, ahead of his time here; only in recent years has the Second Law of Thermodynamics begun to receive more widespread attention (especially in regard to the energy shortage and the general environmental crisis), as evidenced by the popular attention to Jeremy Rifkin's *Entropy: A New World View*, published in 1980.

Commager convincingly insisted that "of Adams alone, among the major historians, can it be said that what he was is more significant than what he wrote." Adams asked questions that he could not answer, that might even be unanswerable; he was concerned with "urging the necessity of *some* philosophy of history, *some* science of society; he was concerned with asking questions and pointing to the consequences of all conceivable answers."[17]

What Adams did, Commager went so far as to suggest, was relatively unimportant; he was more important for what he signified:

Obviously, then, it is not as a teacher or as a historian, or even as a philosopher, that Adams is chiefly significant, but as a symbol. Adams himself regarded his teaching experience as a failure, his historical work as negligible, and his philosophical speculations as suggestive rather than final; and Adams's critical acumen was so sharp, his judgement so sound, and his sincerity so unimpeachable that it would be insolent to differ with him.[18]

Finally, Commager insisted that the life of Adams could even be seen as something of a microcosm of American history itself:

It is an exaggeration, of course, to suggest that we can interpret the whole of American history in the person of Henry Adams, but it is no very shocking exaggeration to insist that to the student of American history the contemplation of Adams is the beginning of wisdom. For whether we confine ourselves to the mere outward aspects of Adams' career or embrace the history of the entire family which he recapitulated, or penetrate to his own intellectual and psychological reactions to his generation, we will find that Adams illuminates, better than any of his contemporaries, the course of American history.[19]

Edward Channing, a vigorous critic, termed the work of Adams a "masterpiece" and paid it the tribute of abandoning his own plans to write on Jefferson after he saw advance sheets of the *History*. Most students have praised the handling of diplomatic questions by Adams, who had an excellent knowledge of domestic and foreign manuscript materials. Many students, however, have also found fault with his treatment of internal affairs, which generally ignored the West and showed only a slight perception of the economic motivation in politics. In fact, long stretches of the *History* were merely a series of political episodes set in executive chambers or in the legislative halls of Europe and America. In his almost exclusive devotion to congressional proceedings as an expression of American politics, Adams was not unlike James Schouler, but he was infinitely superior to the latter in skill of composition and analysis. His lightning penetration illuminated dark corners and instantly blasted reputations.

Adams has not gone unchallenged. Defenders of Burr and the Virginians have denied the validity of many of the historian's strictures. One of the sharpest criticisms of his work came from Irving Brant, the biographer of Madison, who believed that Adams (along with almost everyone else) minimized the Virginian's role in American history after 1789. Adams, Brant argued, "did not understand the policies of Jefferson and Madison at all. He saw weakness and national humiliation, in their failure to go to war over this or that outrage" (impressment, the *Chesapeake* affair, or the French decrees). Jefferson and Madison, Brant asserted, preferred to husband the nation's rapidly growing strength as they faced "three choices—war, submission, or economic pressure and negotiation." They chose the third, "well knowing that war was the ultimate and probable alternative. Adams and a host of other writers have construed this course as submission, and have treated the War of 1812 as evidence of its failure."[20]

Adams was at his best in treating individuals. Like most others of his family, however, he was uneasy and unsympathetic in handling the masses. He was no Whitman drawing a turbulent democracy to his breast. "Democracies in history," he once wrote, "always suffered from the necessity of uniting with much of the purest and best in human nature a mass of ignorance and brutality lying at the bottom of all societies." Like Comte, Adams believed in the intellectual elite exerting beneficent leadership in guiding the masses in society, with himself holding a dominant position in the select hierarchy. The reformist program of his own group of intellectual aristocrats—honesty in government, civil service reform, lower tariffs—was too tepid for a society seeking solutions to the vast problems created by the industrial revolution. The peace of Adams's aristocratic soul was troubled by the disquieting symptoms he observed in American life. In his reformist period he wrote to his brother Charles that he was preparing an article on political "rings": "I am going to make it monumental, a piece of history and a blow at democracy."[21]

The later volumes of the *History*, it may be noted, were more critical than the earlier ones. "They were written . . . in a very different frame of mind from that in which the work was begun," Adams admitted. The work as a whole, he said, "belongs to the *me* of 1870; a strangely different being from the *me* of 1890."[22] The generous idealism and the hope for reform of earlier years had given way to ennui, cynicism, and gloomy predictions of worthless humanity's impending doom; yet his habit of reducing everything to ashes was often a pose (he called himself a "moral dyspeptic"). To his intimates he was warm and compassionate; his self-conscious rationalism covered a never-vanquished romanticism. Adams, like many other Americans, retreated to inner exile to escape the repulsions of an uncongenial world. Inner exile was reinforced by fleeing elsewhere, usually to Europe. Adams used both escapes and added a third, fleeing in time—the return to the Middle Ages, the pilgrimage to piety. The mass economic, political, and physical pressures of the modern mechanized world, which affected society with a glacierlike determinism, were antipathetic to his artist's temperament. As he stated it, he preferred the Virgin, symbol of the unity of the Middle Ages, to the Dynamo, symbol of the fragmentation of the modern technological age.

Adams wrote in his *Education* that he had "published a dozen volumes of American history . . . to satisfy himself whether, by the severest process of stating, with the least possible comment, such facts as seemed sure, in such order as seemed rigorously consequent, he could fix for a familiar moment a necessary sequence of human movement"; but he complained that he "had toiled in vain." The historian of today, who also knows how difficult it is to follow clues through seeming chaos, can sympathize with Adams and be grateful for his writings, for they mark one of the highest achievements in American historiography.

Loewenberg, like Commager, saw Adams as something of a symbol, but in a slightly different way:

With Adams, though not because of him, the world shifted its course. Adams' life represents a cross-section of the American mind in transition. America had passed from the agricultural-rural stage to the urban-industrial stage, from relative simplicity to increasing complexity. Unity made for optimism, doubt was the companion of multiplicity. The dynamo had come to stay. Scholarship was obligated to face the questions that it was the duty of Henry Adams to ask.[23]

The Nationalist School

THE GENERATION THAT GREW UP just after the Civil War and succeeding generations up to the present have read insatiably about the great conflict. Historians looking for a fit theme turned away from the fields of colonial history (already harvested, they thought) and eagerly seized upon the middle period. Some went back to the Revolution for a running start, but James Ford Rhodes, seeking an "epic" period, began with the year 1850. A southerner had gloomily prophesied that to the South's overflowing cup would be added the bitter taste of having the history of the war written by northerners. The publications for many years afterward verified his dour prediction.

Although many of the historians who wrote on this period were trained in the use of documents and the weighing of evidence, they did not believe that their task was completed with the mere statement of facts. They donned the judicial role also, and despite prior professions of impartiality they passed sentence upon the offending South. These prosecuting historians, worshiping the newly deified national state and believing in the essential immorality of slaveholding, indicted the South on two counts: as the assailant of nationality and as the defender of a decadent civilization. When their narratives digressed to include social and economic history, they generally revealed a basic conservatism. They identified progress with prosperity and were cold to protests for social reform—except for abolition. Labor, when treated at all, was generally associated with "troubles," such as strikes and "agitators"; agrarian discontent was identified with malignant currency inflation. For the most part, however, histories written by the nationalists dealt with the conflicting constitutional interpretations expressed by the mingled shouts of slavery and antislavery forces and by the murmurs of compromisers seeking to stave off armed struggle.

Deification of the national state was closely related to glorification of the role of Anglo-Saxon peoples in furthering political progress. Darwinism appeared to sanction the spread of Anglo-Saxon civilization because it seemed to be the culture most fit to survive, and other peoples should either pattern themselves after this dominant group or succumb in the inevitable struggle between them.

164

Before Darwin and Spencer supplied scientific terminology to the literary world, American historians had already preached the superiority of certain groups over others. In the eyes of Bancroft, Parkman, and Motley, liberty (political and religious) and the orderly progress of modern civilization were largely due to the efforts of Anglo-Saxon Protestants. Social change among Anglo-Saxons, it was said, was orderly, and even their revolutions were relatively polite, unlike such murderous Celtic or Latin catastrophes as the French Revolution. Peoples other than Anglo-Saxons, it was asserted, were obviously of inferior stock. Immigrants from Ireland and from southern and eastern Europe were often spoken of as "hordes of ignorant foreigners." The English historian Freeman claimed American support for his flippant remark that the United States would be a grand land "if only every Irishman would kill a negro, and be hanged for it."[1] On Freeman's coat of arms, said William A. Dunning, "were emblazoned the Anglo-Saxon militant, the Teuton rampant, and the Aryan eternally triumphant."

John Fiske, an ardent disciple of Darwin, Spencer, and Freeman, was convinced that the most suitable practice of political organization—federalism—had been created by American Anglo-Saxons. John W. Burgess, too, was a strong believer in the racial superiority of Anglo-Saxons and in their surpassing political wisdom. In his work *Political Science and Comparative Constitutional Law* (1890), Burgess asserted that the Teutonic peoples, because of their preeminence in building national states, must "assume the leadership in the establishment and administration of states." They should lead not only backward or "barbaric" peoples but also any people who were politically incompetent. With less emphasis, Hermann von Holst and John Bach McMaster held the same ideas. Their histories gave coherence to nationalism, and in the books of Burgess and Alfred T. Mahan writers found an arsenal whose weapons, though literary, helped prepare the way in the 1890s for the real instruments of war.[2]

Hermann von Holst

Hermann von Holst, whose history of the United States expressed an intense American nationalism, was born in 1841 in Livonia (now Estonia), a Baltic province of Russia inhabited by many Germans. He was trained at Heidelberg, where he took his doctoral degree in 1865. Hostile to the Russian regime, he sought the freedom of America two years later. In the New World he projected a work on the evils of absolutism, meanwhile participating actively in Republican politics in New York. He had not been in America long when his friends the noted teacher Heinrich von Sybel and the well-known student of American life Friedrich Kapp commended von Holst to Bremen merchants, who commissioned him to write informative essays on the United States. From the small beginning of von Holst's newspaper and magazine articles eventually came *The Constitutional and Political History of the United States,* an eight-volume work published between 1877 and 1892. He returned to Europe and became a professor in the new University of Strasbourg, lecturing on American history and constitutional law. Other academic posts followed, ending with that in the University of Chicago, where he stayed from 1892 to his death in 1904. The history he wrote was used for some time as a text, but the English translation did not always reflect the original German. In addition to his history, von Holst wrote a study of constitutional law in the United States as well as biographies of John Brown and of John C. Calhoun. The latter was von Holst's only work written in English; therefore, it did not suffer from the translation problems of all his other works, and it is regarded by many as his best. A volume in the important American Statesmen series, it reveals that von Holst admired Calhoun's abilities but considered him as the personification of the wrong cause, just as Brown personified the right.

A close acquaintance of von Holst said that he "valued history chiefly for its practical bearing on current problems" and that a "stern morality" guided his judgments on the past and the present. He was no believer in the virtues of that "objective" history so much talked of in his day. He held it a distinct right of the historian to measure events and men according to his own political and moral beliefs.

With the same confidence that most authors have in their own impartiality, von Holst wrote, "I venture to assert that among all the works covering about as large a ground as mine, there is not one to be found which has been written with as much soberness of mind." Indeed, he believed that he had an advantage over American historians because of his foreign birth. Though he did his own research in the sources, he probably was strongly influenced in his constitutional ideas and in his attitude toward slavery by Richard Hildreth.[3]

A brief section of von Holst's *History* covered the years under the Confederation, written from his nationalist standpoint. The objections of the "particularists" to Federalism were dismissed as absurd. In unfolding his narrative, he based his argument on the debatable theses that the Union was older than the states and that state sovereignty was nonexistent at the nation's birth; Calhoun, of course, held just the reverse. The main thesis upon which von Holst's book rested was thus stated: slavery was "the rock on which the Union was broken to pieces." Upon the dual themes—slavery and national sovereignty versus states' rights—he constructed his work: "The slave holding interest knit mesh after mesh in the net in which it sought to entangle the Union, but men did not or would not see this." Like a true Bismarckian, von Holst was, of course, a partisan of Hamilton. Jefferson, on the other hand, "was always ready to sacrifice much of his favorite theories to his feverish thirst for power and distinction."

A discussion of "The Economic Contrast Between the Free and Slave States" (later drawn upon by McMaster) gave a doleful picture of southern life. "Everything was considered in reference to the 'peculiar institution,'" said von Holst, "and therefore hostile distrust of everything was felt, because this institution was in ever sharper contradiction with the spirit of the age." The different industrial systems in North and South drove them further and further apart. Turning to a long study of the nullification movement of 1832, von Holst, quoting Bismarck, wrote, "Conquered and conquerors brought punishment upon themselves because they did not understand one thing, or, if they understood it, would not live up to it: 'Sovereignty can only be a unit and it must remain a unit—the sovereignty of law.'"

Beginning with Jackson's administration the narrative became increasingly detailed. Von Holst's characterization of Jackson won wide acceptance: "Since Louis XIV, the maxim, *l'état, c'est moi*, has scarcely found a second time, so ingenuous and complete an expression as in Andrew Jackson. The only difference is that it was translated from the language of monarchy into the language of republicanism." Although the author gave considerable space to the Panic of 1837, he soon returned to the main interests of his study, slavery and the Constitution. In his treatment of the annexation of Texas, von Holst adopted the view, conventional among antislavery writers, that the expansionist movement was solely the result of southern desires for more slave territory. With forced imagery von Holst wrote of the congressional process of annexation: "The bridal dress in which Calhoun had led the beloved of the slavocracy to the Union was the torn and tattered constitution of the United States."

The caption "Polk Weaves the Warp of the Mexican War" indicated von Holst's approach. He suggested the effect of annexation on the growth of abolition sentiment:

The long struggle over annexation had opened many eyes which had hitherto been struck with blindness. The thorn of the political rule of the slave holding interest had been pressed deeper into the flesh of many, and a still greater number, by a louder and clearer condemnation of slavery "on principle" sought refuge from their own consciences for having allowed or helped the slavocracy again to win a victory.

The historian thus referred to the southern domination of American politics: "Questions which had hitherto been hotly debated, were now settled, in accordance with the views of the South, almost without a struggle."

Von Holst's interpretation was that a vast conspiracy had been hatched by American political leaders. In preparing for the war with Mexico, Congress and the president were "participants in the guilt of the dark work which had been so busily and cunningly carried on in the White House." Ethics and the writing of history were always closely allied for von Holst, who denounced the "bold immorality, with which the leading Democratic politicians . . . devised and carried to its conclusion the whole affair of the war." The narrative inevitably led up to the statement that Polk "purposely brought on the war," but the author added that Congress, too, was in accord "with his crooked policy."

In view of his whole approach it was strange to find von Holst defending Manifest Destiny and writing that "history cannot decide . . . questions by the code of private morals." This son of a Bismarckian generation could write bluntly of established laws of historic growth: that "decayed or decaying peoples must give way when they clash in a conflict of interests with peoples who are still on the ascending path of their historic mission, and that violence must often be the judge to decide such litigation between nations."[4]

Von Holst, returning to a comparison of the North and the South, found once more that the latter was at a great disadvantage in economic strength. Intellectual life in the North, he continued, was also superior to that in the South. Most significant for von Holst was not that in every respect the South was behind the North "but that the forces which had caused it to remain so far in the rear still continue to operate, and it would therefore necessarily fall still farther behind." The historian was always the strong protagonist of urban capitalism, and to the end of his life he believed in a thoroughgoing laissez-faire doctrine. The proletariat of great cities he accepted as a necessary evil that came with economic growth.

The six years that followed the Compromise of 1850, von Holst declared, were "the most important in the development of the irrepressible conflict, between the North and the South." Politicians were powerless in these years "in the presence of the progressive and sternly logical development of actual circumstances." Thus did American history move on toward the inevitable tragedy with the precision of Greek drama.

In great detail von Holst noted how deeply the disputes over the Compromise of 1850 had affected public sentiment nearly everywhere. He concluded that Franklin Pierce won the election of 1852 because "the great majority of the people had become possessed by the quietistic conservative spirit, and did not wish their repose to be disturbed by any further contention as to the price paid for it." Stephen Douglas, with his "moral hollowness," was the villain in the drama of the Kansas-Nebraska Bill, whose "ultimate consequences . . . brought the Union and slavery face to face with the question of existence."

In the 1850s the slavocracy, said von Holst, continued to stir up sentiment for expansion, this time to the Caribbean. Although unable to secure Cuba, "the progressive fraction of the slavocracy which grew from year to year in weight and numbers, awaited only a new opportunity to take up the frustrated annexation project again, and they were resolved to create the opportunity if it did not offer of itself."

The history of these years was described in phrases suggestive of military tactics. The South under all circumstances during this period was "certain that none of the positions it had won could be wrested from it, for no hostile resolution of the house of representatives would receive the assent of the senate or the sanction of the president." For the South to triumph it needed to be on the offensive and to show a confidence in victory, "and assurance of victory was best manifested by its coming forward with new and bold demands." The Kansas troubles were all due to the slavocracy, which "in the name of law and order, and behind the protecting shield of the president . . . carried on [the propagation of slavery] with blood and iron, in the territorial domain of the Union." Von Holst's partisan prose cast a lurid glow over "Bleeding Kansas."

Buchanan's election had been bought by a more binding pledge to the slavocracy, said von Holst, adding that the "declaration of the Republicans that the era of compromises was forever closed, was answered from the South by the declaration that the time when the continuance of the slave states in the Union could be purchased by concessions, was forever past."

After a brief treatment of the Dred Scott decision, which the author saw as "the greatest political atrocity of which a court had ever been guilty," the narrative moved on to the Lecompton Convention. The scorching words with which von Holst indignantly castigated the slavocracy in Kansas have today lost none of their burning quality. Through these pages Kansas stalks like Banquo's ghost. The historian heard the voices of unlaid ghosts of free-soilers threatening the slavocracy with an early grave. As the "irrepressible conflict" neared its climax, Lincoln "loomed up higher and firmer, while . . . fragments of Douglas's armor strewed the ground."

In his infrequent departures from congressional history, von Holst took stock of the country's economic position in 1857, and he reflected on the low standard of morality in railroad finance in that decade. He noted, too, the growing opposition to immigration and Catholicism fostered by the Know-Nothing party and, though unsympathetic to Catholics himself, von Holst pointed out the danger of Know-Nothingism to American institutions. He drew a distinction between Anglo-Saxon immigrants (in particular, the Germans, who surpassed all others) and the Irish, who belonged "to the lowest stage of culture." He suggested, too, that nativism, as typified by the Know-Nothing movement, was an attempt to divert attention from the slavery question.

When the Thirty-fifth Congress ended, said the historian, the "funeral bells of the democratic party were tolling and hence the history of the Thirty-sixth Congress could not but become the knell of the Union." The crowded months after Harper's Ferry were the subject of von Holst's last volume. The prose swung into poetic rhythm as it celebrated John Brown, with his "homely realism" and "great, ideal loftiness of soul." From the sublimity of John Brown the reader was dropped to the grossness of party politics in 1860. Four parties were in the field, "one with a national, single-faced head; two double faced ones with the same name, and one with no face at all."

James Buchanan, who did not have "the moral courage to do his duty" in suppressing the insurrection, was the object of von Holst's severe criticism; his policy of noncoercion was thoroughly ridiculed. "His dread of assuming any responsibility," said the historian, "was as great as his delusion with regard to his own infallibility." After the failure of compromise measures to preserve the already broken Union, its restoration, concluded von Holst in characteristic language, "could be effected only by blood and iron."

In the great struggle between good and evil the latter was vanquished when the Republicans won in 1860. With Lincoln's inauguration "the restoration of a Union incomparably stronger, more majestic and richer in promise for the future, was beyond a question, for the corner-stones of the new foundation were to be the burial mounds of the three dark powers which unbound the furies of civil war: the doctrine of noncoercion, the slavocratic interpretation of state sovereignty, and slavery."

Von Holst, German even during his American university years, glowering at his class, "always striking hard, always striving to emphasize the great things," performed a pioneer task and stimulated much research. He was among the first to appreciate the significance of the records of congressional debates, and he also made good use of newspapers in an age when this kind of material was rarely used as a source.

One soon discovers that von Holst's work was really only a history of the slavery contest with but few references to other phases of American life. As he saw it, slavery was the principal question standing before the American people after 1830. Even before the historian finished his last volume, his work had begun to lose its hold on the more critical generation of American historians. Charles R. Wilson stated the most basic criticism of von Holst in *The Jernegan Essays:* "He appears to have accepted at face value any document which furthered his thesis, but to have made short shrift of the materials which disproved it." More than any other large-scale enterprise von Holst's represented the fullest flowering of the Federalist-Whig-Republican school of history—nationalist, northern, antislavery. His work, however, has withstood the test of time and critical scholarship less successfully than has that of any of his major contemporaries; as a result, in the words of Wilson, it is now "generally regarded as historic rather than historical, . . . something to be explained rather than accepted."[5] That is true, of course, of all but the best histories—and somewhat true even of them.

James Schouler

When von Holst was preparing his history, James Schouler was also at work on the same period. He began publishing his *History of the United States Under the Constitution* in 1880, with the explanation that there was no comprehensive narrative "from which one may safely gather the later record of our country's career." Schouler excepted in part Hildreth's history, praising its accuracy but differing from Hildreth "in many particulars, and most widely as to estimates of our political leaders and their motives," as he put it. Schouler, a lawyer without advanced academic training who wrote legal textbooks before he wrote his history, said that he wanted to begin where Bancroft "had seemingly laid down his pen" and to "supply the connecting link between the American Revolution and the Civil War." It was his distinction to be the first historian to bridge the gap from the Constitution to the end of Reconstruction by a continuous narrative. He was also the author of biographies of Jefferson and Hamilton; an excellent study entitled *Americans of 1776*, his only real excursion into social and intellectual history; and several miscellaneous volumes, mostly essay collections, of which the best known is *Historical Briefs*, published in 1896.

Schouler's history began with some introductory remarks on the states under the Articles of Confederation. The Constitutional Convention, he said, was "the protest of liberty protected by law against liberty independent of it." The historian halted his narrative at various points to portray the Founding Fathers; he described Washington in a long passage imitative of a decadent classicism. Schouler was less sympathetic to Hamilton than was Hildreth; therefore, by the usual rules of American historical writing, he was more friendly to Jefferson.

In many respects Schouler's arrangement of materials seemed to be nothing more than an enlargement of the older method of writing historical chronicles as practiced by Thomas Prince and Abiel Holmes. History, he once said, is the "record of consecutive events,—of consecutive public events"; to his mind "the only clear law of history is that of motion incessantly onward."[6] His divisions were based upon the succession of presidential administrations. This made it difficult for him to pursue any one topic for very long and reduced him to the clumsy expedient of using such a transition as: "The slavery question deserves attention in connection with the angry debates of this [1790] session."

Schouler's attitude regarding slavery, which strongly colored his later narrative, was revealed early: "That an institution, both wasteful and unrighteous, should have been suffered by wise statesmen to fasten its poïsonous fangs so deeply into the vitals of a republic whose essential foundation was freedom, is one of those political facts which only the theory of human imperfection can well explain, so inevitable must have been the final catastrophe." The Federalists were severely criticized for their party tyranny in sponsoring the Alien and Sedition Acts, but the historian paid a generous tribute to John Adams, who "was in closer sympathy with the people than most leaders of the party to which he belonged, and a more genuine American."

Schouler's statement that "Jefferson proceeded moderately, and by no means maliciously, in the matter of removals from office" was supported by later scholars. In a resumé of Jefferson's administrations Schouler said that they "had fixed immutably the republican character of these institutions, and vindicated this American experiment as never before." The country at the close of Jefferson's term of office was said to be living in a "miniature golden age"; the phenomenon of his administration "was undoubtedly the development of a West" whose population in the Mississippi Valley in later years was "to assert a great, if not the greatest, influence in national affairs." These pages broke fresh ground but plowed neither deeply nor widely.

At this point in his account Schouler swung back with zest to his political narrative, now leading up to the War of 1812. He wrote, "'On to Canada' had been the cry of the war party for years." The author found that "the disaffection of the New England States is a sad episode of the war history to contemplate, nor can the impartial historian on that topic hope to escape controversy." In his discussion of changes in parties he revealed no deep understanding of political motivation; for him it was the old drama, perhaps melodrama, of bitter personal rivalries: "jostling ambitions, intrigues to overthrow one administration and bring in another."

Schouler attempted to seize Bancroft's mantle of literary style, but he wore it ungracefully: "Proud in our annals was the year 1818, when the whole nation felt itself soaring upward in a new atmosphere, exhilarated and bold, like an eagle loosened from confinement." Indeed, style was one of Schouler's weakest points, especially his tendency toward long sentences broken up by an incredible number of commas:

In its upper chambers [in the White House], both for home and office life, dwelt Lincoln, like most of his predecessors; and his only summer variation was in using, with his family, a modest cottage at the Soldiers' Home on the northern suburb, towards which, by the main road, he might be seen riding in a barouche from the White House, on a bright September afternoon, with a few mounted cavalry for his escort.

Through rose-colored glasses he viewed the end of Monroe's administration when "the whole mechanism of society moved in perfect order. The democracy ruled, but it was a democracy in which jealousies found no root, and the abler and more virtuous of the community took the lead." Soon, however, "fiercer passions ruled once more the hearts of men."

Jackson's victory four years later was a triumph "of popular principles, and in a sense of the military . . . spirit in politics"; John Quincy Adams, "out of all the infamous abuse, scandal, and vilification heaped upon him . . . emerged pure as refined gold." Tocqueville was drawn upon for a discussion of American social history in 1830. Although Schouler wrote that "we are now at the portal of an epoch full of eager progress and the crowding, trampling ranks of humanity," that humanity remained but an abstraction. The West, scarcely mentioned up to this time by general historians, was given brief notice: "The phenomenon of American development was the growth of the great West." Nevertheless, New England's influence in fashioning and ruling northern society was strongest; she "was a sort of education, a great generator of ideas for American society." It should be remarked, too, that Schouler was not unsympathetic to southern society.

The historian's thoughts on nullification were clothed in language reminiscent of medieval chivalry: "These were glorious days for the constitution's allied defenders; the one matchless in debate, the other terrible in action and clad in popular confidence like a coat of mail." His whole treatment of the nullification controversy was strongly warped by a nationalist bias. Similarly, his introduction to a discussion of the annexation of Texas was characteristic: "A dark chapter opens in our national history." This whole episode was interpreted from the view of southern desires for more slave territory. Over most of these pages, in fact, hung the heavy shadow of slavery.

From his usual position Schouler surveyed the struggle with Mexico: "The glory of the Mexican War was the glory of the South, like the Texas conquest before it . . . to add largely to the area of slavery by annexations from Mexico was regarded by slaveholders as a necessary means of strengthening their power against Northern encroachments." The conventional Whig disapproval of Webster's Seventh of March speech was thus expressed: "He . . . bargained away his moral conviction for the sake of national harmony." The military adventures in Central America and Cuba were to Schouler "that cormorant appetite for seizing weak sovereignties," a "misguided policy of robbery and subjugation which seeks to conceal its cruel features under the mask of manifest destiny." Franklin Pierce was excoriated for being "an abject devotee of the slave holders." John Brown was utterly "irrational," but his treatment revealed the slave master's "innate tyranny and cruelty towards an adversary."

Schouler was more temperate in his remarks about the Civil War. " 'Conspiracy,' 'treason,' were names at first applied, all too narrowly, to those who struggled to break from the Union. 'Rebellion' is a more enduring and appropriate word. . . . We must divest ourselves of the false impression [one that Schouler himself gives] that the crime of a few Southern leaders produced the real mischief."

His volume on the Civil War had the benefit of his personal impressions as a youth witnessing the events he described. Although he tried "to do full justice" to the motives of both sections, he admitted that he had "not suppressed [his] personal convictions as to the real merits of this sanguinary strife, nor amiably shifted the ground of discussion." Earlier he had discountenanced the use of the word "conspiracy" in connection with the war, but he forgot his own injunction when he wrote, "There was something of a conspiracy, however, in the present Southern movement for breaking up the Union."

At the age of seventy-four Schouler picked up his pen again to add a seventh volume, on Reconstruction. His main purpose, he said, was to vindicate the "much maligned" President Andrew Johnson. Like his contemporary James Ford Rhodes, Schouler severely condemned the military Reconstruction Act because it forcibly uprooted "State governments already advanced towards natural conditions of self-rule" and replanted them "on a new political basis utterly impracticable and ruinous." The volume itself was little concerned with the southern side of Reconstruction. Schouler was deeply interested in the election of 1876. Although a partisan of Samuel Tilden, he wrote, "Iniquitous as we must deem that electoral figuring which places Hayes instead of Tilden in the White House, it was probably better, under all the circumstances, for the peace of the country."

Throughout his history Schouler had set up conventional heroes and villains; Lincoln, naturally, was one of his greatest heroes, and opposed to him was the "gloomy despot," Jefferson Davis. Aside from a few references to passing events in other parts of the country Schouler's history might have been written from a spectator's seat in Congress; his interests were almost entirely in political and constitutional history. His sources, like his organization, revealed that orientation. Most of the footnotes in his earlier volumes were references to *U.S. Statutes at Large,* the *Annals of Congress,* and the works of outstanding political figures. Indeed, Schouler deserves credit as a pioneer in certain areas of source utilization; he was the first researcher to use the manuscripts of four presidents (Monroe, Jackson, Van Buren, and Polk). There were also problems with his sources, however. As he reached his closing volumes, he was relying far more extensively on secondary sources, especially Rhodes. More seriously, his citations were so imprecise that they fell far short of the best standards, even those of his own day. For example, it is not at all uncommon to find in Schouler's footnotes references to "John Adams's *Works," "Congressional Documents," "New York Tribune* and other newspapers of the day" or even "Newspapers," and finally, the ultimate in vagueness and uselessness in a footnote, "author's recollections." He was inclined to conservatism and was protective of the status quo, while he was critical of predatory and ostentatious wealth. A stern Scottish morality pervaded his writing, and he once pleaded: "Whatever may have been my imperfections as a narrator of events ... I trust it may be said of me that I have written with a constant purpose to be just and truthful." Schouler was in reality not as judicious as those of his contemporaries who had learned to look more dispassionately at American history.[7]

John W. Burgess

John W. Burgess is more likely to be remembered for his work in founding and building up the School of Political Science at Columbia University and his many years of teaching service than for his contributions to American history. He came from a family of Tennessee slaveowners who were Whig Unionists. The idea of American unity inspired him from his boyhood. America, he felt, "was a great creative and regenerative force for the welfare of mankind."[8]

After Young Burgess had served in the Union Army, he studied at Amherst College and later in Germany, where he attended classes under that country's greatest masters of history and public law. These included Theodor Mommsen, Theodor Curtius, Leopold von Ranke, Johann Gustav Droysen, and the leading scholar of English law and government, Rudolph von Gneist, who had the most profound influence in directing Burgess's career.[9] Burgess came back from Germany in 1873 to a newly established professorship of history and political science in Amherst College. Three years later, when he went to Columbia to teach constitutional history and international law, he began an academic association that lasted throughout his life.

Burgess was the author of a number of studies in political science, but his several volumes on nineteenth-century America were more important for the student of historical writing. The publishing house Charles Scribner's Sons, believing that the time was ripe for a fairer treatment of the struggle between North and South, turned to Burgess as the man best suited by birth and training for the task. He considered it his "sacred duty" and fulfilled the obligation.[10]

Burgess began his work with a volume published in 1897, *The Middle Period, 1817–1858*, in which he said that it was high time that the history of those years "should be undertaken in a thoroughly impartial spirit. The continued misunderstanding between the North and South is an ever present menace to the welfare of both sections and of the entire nation." Almost incredibly, he saw no incongruity between his professed impartiality and his statement that this history must be written by an American and a northerner "and from the Northern point of view," because it is, in the main, "the correct view." The stern moralist thus spoke, "The time has come when the men of the South should acknowledge that they were in error in their attempt to destroy the Union and it is unmanly in them not to do so." Although his early environment made him sympathetic to the South, Burgess wrote that "not one scintilla of justification for secession and rebellion must be expected." The main theme in *The Middle Period* was the struggle between the northerners, who wished to adapt the government to changing conditions, and the southerners, who claimed that they adhered to the beliefs of the framers of the Constitution.

The two-volume *Civil War and the Constitution 1859–1865*, which appeared in 1901, was largely a history of military events and some political questions raised by the struggle. The increasing tendency of constitutional law to favor nationalism in these years was of special interest to Burgess. Although the historian disliked extremists on both sides, especially John Brown, he continued to maintain that the cause of secession was "constitutionally and morally indefensible." The constitutional arguments of the secessionists, he said, were "from every point of view, a mere jugglery with words."

In *Reconstruction and the Constitution, 1866–1876,* published in 1902, Burgess was largely interested in examining the means used to reconstruct the defeated states. He had once asked the South to acknowledge secession as an error; he now asked the North to make amends for Reconstruction. The purpose of Reconstruction, "to secure the civil rights of the newly emancipated race," was praiseworthy, but "erroneous means were chosen." The South should have been placed under a territorial civil government, he said, until the whites could be "intrusted again with the powers" of government. Consistent with the racist element in the nationalist school, Burgess insisted that there was a "vast difference in political capacity between races." He believed that it was "the white man's mission, his duty and his right, to hold the reins of political power in his own hands for the civilization of the world and the welfare of mankind." An epilogue to his historical trilogy was the small book he brought out in 1916, *The Administration of President Hayes,* in which the executive was praised for reestablishing "constitutional normality."

Although Burgess was intensely nationalist in his writing, he saw the danger of excessive centralization in practice. In his volume on *The Reconciliation of Government with Liberty* (1915) he concluded, "It is high time for us to call a halt on our present course of increasing the sphere of government and decreasing that of liberty." Later historical investigation played havoc with Burgess's theses on the great sectional struggle. He had no conception of it as a conflict between two differing civilizations, and even in his own narrower view—that differences over constitutional interpretation lay at the base of the war— his work was surpassed by the more penetrating essays of his former student, William A. Dunning. Posterity's verdict has been that Burgess gave us better historians than history.

James Ford Rhodes

Schouler and Burgess wrote about the Civil War as they saw it from a northern judgment seat. James Ford Rhodes's stand was nearer Mason and Dixon's line, but his sight, too, was obscured by the traditional point of view. Rhodes had very unusual opportunities to write the history of the period he chose for his theme. Noted Democrats were frequent visitors at the Rhodes home in Cleveland; through such associations Rhodes was able to write much of his history at first hand. A conversation with Judge E. R. Hoar, for example, enabled Rhodes to account for President Grant's personal honesty "while keeping such bad company."[11] Rhodes's father was a delegate to the Democratic convention of 1860 in Charleston, and his influence helped make the son a "sturdy Democrat." Rhodes was also clearly influenced by the antislavery and probusiness elements in his environment.

Rhodes's interest in history was aroused, he said, when he entered New York University in 1865 and studied under Benjamin N. Martin. The latter suggested stimulating reading to the young scholar, who reveled in Buckle's *History of Civilization* and Draper's *Intellectual Development of Europe;* these two books, he said, marked an epoch in his intellectual life. As he read the last words of Buckle's famous volumes, the young student "resolved some day to write a history."

"One evening in 1877, while reading Hildreth's *History of the United States,*" Rhodes related in an autobiographical sketch, "I laid down my book and said to myself why should I not write a 'History of the United States'?" From then on, despite the cares of business, he kept elaborate notes of his reading. "I resolved that as soon as I should have gained a competence, I would retire from business and devote myself to history and literature." In 1885, Rhodes kept his resolution, retired from business, and then plunged into a heavy schedule of reading.

The two volumes which appeared in 1892 carried on their title pages *History of the United States from the Compromise of 1850.* Rhodes planned to carry his narrative to the inauguration of Grover Cleveland in 1885, which marked the return to power of the Democrats. This period, he said, "ranks next in importance to the formative period— to the declaration and conquest of independence and the adoption of the Constitution." For eleven years before the Civil War, Negro slavery "engrossed the whole attention of the country. . . . It will be my aim," said Rhodes, "to recount the causes of the triumph of the Republican party in the presidential election of 1860, and to make clear how the revolution in public opinion was brought about that led to this result." The election of Cleveland was thought to be a "fitting close of this historical inquiry, for by that time the great questions which had their origin in the war had been settled as far as they could be by legislation or executive direction."

The influence of slavery upon politics was a central theme in the work. Like von Holst, Rhodes adopted an antislavery view and confessed that he had been "profoundly influenced" by the German's work. For Rhodes, too, Douglas was a deep-dyed villain. A supporter of unionism against secessionist theory, Rhodes wrote from the nationalist standpoint, but the *Nation's* reviewer, referring to the historian's treatment of slavery, said, "We doubt whether a fairer view of the subject can be met with." Burgess, however, thought Rhodes too strongly prejudiced against slavery and severely criticized him for the perpetuation of the John Brown cult.

The publication of these two volumes won for Rhodes a well-merited distinction throughout the country, and his position as a man of letters was assured to the end of his life in 1927. He was always conscious of his style, studying to improve it, feeling the need to make up for his minimal formal education and the earlier years that he had spent in business instead of literature. But try as he would, his writing rarely achieved distinction; the skill of a Parkman was denied him. He was proud of his acceptance in the best literary circles, but sometimes the reader senses his lack of assurance: "Please the élite, the rest will follow," he wrote in 1898; "I am aspiring for culture and wish to be a scholar." Even in later years Rhodes rather self-consciously spoke of acquiring culture.

"My history has grown on me," he wrote to a friend, "and I shall close the third volume in the blaze of glory of our victories of the early part of '62."[12] Rhodes was sensitive about his treatment of southern leaders. "My estimate of Lee is wholly sincere," he wrote to Frederick Bancroft, "and I shall be sorry if it shocks many of my old friends who bore the brunt and burden of the war and to whom Lee's 'traitorous conduct' obliterated in their minds all his virtues."

Two more volumes carried the story another four years to 1866. It was a narrative largely of the military and naval events of the war, but Rhodes included chapters on both northern and southern society. He confided to Charles Francis Adams that he lacked sufficient knowledge to grapple with the question of sea power. When Adams wrote to him gently that "no well and philosophically considered narrative of the struggle has yet appeared," the answer came that "a purely narrative historian should, so far as he can, put all philosophical conditions aside. His aim is to tell a story and leave philosophy to others."

Rhodes changed the original terminal date of his work (Cleveland's inauguration) to 1877, when the South recovered "home rule." The historian believed that questions other than the southern issue must be treated after 1877 but said that he "had a lack of basic knowledge" to attack the social issues involved. He closed his history on an optimistic note: It has

covered twenty-seven years of pregnant events; the compromise on slavery devised by great statesmen; its upsetting by an ambitious Northern Senator; the formation of the Republican party; the agitation of slavery; Southern arrogance and aggression; the election of Lincoln; the refusal of the South to abide by the decision of the ballot-box; the Civil War; the great work of Lincoln; the abolition of slavery; the defeat of the South; Reconstruction based upon universal negro suffrage; the oppression of the South by the North; the final triumph of Southern intelligence and character over the ignorance and corruption that so long had thriven under Northern misconceptions. . . . The United States of 1877 was a better country than the United States of 1850. For slavery was abolished, the doctrine of secession was dead, and Lincoln's character and fame had become a possession of the nation.

William G. Brown, well qualified to speak on the subject, said that Rhodes's seventh volume was "the best history yet written of Reconstruction" but criticized it for its digressions. Some of the historian's omissions were very serious: he paid little attention to the westward movement after the war and, curiously enough, despite his early business career, displayed no interest in economic history or in the relationship between economics and politics. There was nothing, for example, on the interplay of politics and federal grants for railroads in the 1850s. As for Andrew Johnson, he seems today a more important personality than Rhodes was willing to concede. Rhodes might have devoted less space to the failures of the Reconstruction period and given more to such successes as the institution of a public school system. He magnified the virtues and minimized the faults of Democrats, whereas for Republicans, especially black ones, he did the reverse.[13]

Aside from its position as a standard treatment of a momentous era, the work of Rhodes had immense value as balm to bitter wounds. "It is a sign that our country . . . is really getting past the time when the differences of 1861-1865 serve as red rags," wrote William E. Dodd to Rhodes. "May I say I believe your masterly *History* has done more than any other historical agency—perhaps any other agency of any sort—to bring about this state of feeling?"

A southerner, however, would have treated the years from 1850 to 1877 differently. "It is a history written from the Northern point of view," remarked Lester B. Shippee in the *Mississippi Valley Historical Review*, "by one who was willing to acknowledge . . . the rights on the other side, but who saw in *slavery* a great moral evil which had corrupted the greater portion of a whole society."[14] Slavery, for Rhodes, explained "practically all the main currents of American national history down to the close of Reconstruction." It should be stated, however, that in the pages on Reconstruction, Rhodes approximated more nearly a truly nationalist viewpoint.[15]

Rhodes should have let his "lack of basic knowledge" on the post-1877 period keep him from including it in his history, but in 1911 he announced the continuation of his work. "I am now living in the period 1877-1897," he wrote to a friend, "and have more original material at hand than I have eyes to read or brains to assimilate." His interest in historical writing, however, was ebbing fast. To Charles

H. Firth, historian at Oxford, Rhodes said, "I published in 1917 a [one-volume] *History of the Civil War* which you will not care for, but I will send you . . . the continuation of my History telling the tale from 1877 to 1899. I shall go on with it if life and health be spared, but I am indifferent whether I publish any more or not." *The History of the United States from Hayes to McKinley, 1877-1896* was published in 1919 and was followed three years later by *The McKinley and Roosevelt Administrations, 1897-1909.*

It was unfortunate that he published these two volumes, for they were far below the standard set by his earlier work. Without a central theme, which had previously been slavery, the historian seemed to lose his way. He showed no understanding of the great economic and social changes that had come over the United States since 1877, and his strong property sense colored his view of the Populists and of labor. Even in his own chosen field of political history he exhibited no critical approach to the events and personalities that fell within the scope of the later volumes. He knew many of the leading characters in American life who were portrayed in these volumes, and his appraisal of their actions was warped by friendly indulgence.

Although Rhodes could not number his readers in the large figures accredited to Fiske and Bancroft, those who did read him were persons who contributed most to molding public opinion—teachers, editors, political leaders. He had a high conception of a historian's calling: "Natural ability being presupposed, the qualities necessary for an historian are diligence, accuracy, love of truth, impartiality, the thorough digestion of his materials by careful selection and long meditating, and the compression of his narrative into the smallest compass consistent with the life of his story." In his earlier years, at least, Rhodes tried to live up to his own expressed standards. He was in many ways a throwback to the patrician historians, but his position as an important American historian is secure.[16]

John Fiske

John Fiske, whom Bert James Loewenberg somewhat accurately dubbed "the Bancroft of his generation,"[17] ranged over the whole field of American history. His career as academician and public lecturer embraced elements of both the older and the newer schools of historians; he was essentially a literary, philosophical historian, but his work had some kinship with the "scientific" group. Fiske seems strangely outdated. The intellectual battles that he helped fight and win have been largely forgotten by generations who have taken their victorious heritage for granted.

Fiske was born in Hartford, Connecticut, in 1842, and as a child was deeply interested in history. In 1860 he went to Harvard, where he quickly earned a reputation as an intellectual radical. That year he accidentally discovered the work of Herbert Spencer in a Boston bookshop and immediately subscribed for his volumes. For the rest of his life he remained an ardent follower of Spencer and Darwin, becoming an active champion of the theory of evolution. The English leaders in the fight to win acceptance for evolution were heartened by the support of Fiske, the leading exponent of these new ideas in America. When Eliot became president of Harvard, Fiske was invited to give a course of lectures on "The Positive Philosophy," from which grew his work *The Outlines of Cosmic Philosophy*. To the end of his days Fiske was still trying to harmonize his religious beliefs and ideals with the latest doctrines of science.

Opposition to Fiske's unconventional ideas prevented his appointment to the history department at Harvard. After serving the college as librarian, he left in 1879 to launch a career as lecturer in history, a career that has no parallel in America. His successful series of lectures on "America's Place in History" in 1879, given in the Old South Church in Boston, determined the future course of his life.

Fiske saw in America's development an excellent illustration of the theory of evolution applied to the history of civilization, and he popularized his thesis in his widely attended lectures. He clearly perceived how timely were such lectures. "The centennial has started it," he wrote, "and I have started in at the right time." He thoroughly enjoyed his experiences as a lecturer, writing after one appearance: "The applause was great. I had a sort of sense that I was fascinating the people and it was delicious beyond expression." In the same year of his American debut he delivered the series in London with astonishing success. Two years later, in 1881, he was lecturing on "American Political Ideas" under the auspices of Washington University, in Saint Louis. These lectures appeared in book form in 1885.

In the winter of 1883–84, Fiske gave a course of lectures on "The American Revolution," followed shortly by a new series on the Confederation, which resulted in the publication in 1888 of *The Critical Period of American History*. He took account of the difficulties facing the new nation and sketched the leaders in the Constitutional Convention. The historian went on to discuss the motives that prompted the states to accept the Constitution, and he included a vivid description of Washington's inauguration. Although it lacked documentation, and specialists quickly recognized its shallow scholarship, contemporary readers received it with much favor. *The Critical Period*, indeed, was probably Fiske's best work from the standpoint of interpretation. The interpretation was suggested by the title; it was made explicit in Fiske's analysis of the three "critical" areas (finance, frontier, and foreign affairs); and, finally, it was an interpretation with a great deal of staying power. It was not until the work of Merrill Jensen began to appear in the 1950s that Fiske's views were seriously questioned. Loewenberg has written correctly of *The Critical Period*:

This volume stamped its interpretation of the movement for the Constitution on the American historical mind. Still widely prevalent as a causal analysis, the most careful subsequent research has been unable completely to dislodge it. Fiske gave the years 1783 to 1789 a name and a character. He made them so critical that a strong central government seemed the only logical solution to chaos.[18]

Fiske then planned to write a comprehensive history of the United States. Before long *The Beginnings of New England* and *The American Revolution* were ready for the press. A considerable portion of the former book went far afield to explain why the world's political center of gravity shifted from the Mediterranean and the Rhine to the Atlantic and the Mississippi, from the Latins to English-speaking peoples. Love of the dramatic made Fiske give disproportionate space to some subjects (King Philip's War, for example). The degree to which his point of view was outworn can be measured by the chapter entitled "The Tyranny of Andros." Later the Andros episode was more likely to be described as an incident in imperial reorganization.

The American Revolution was largely a military history, revealing little of the internal social, economic, and political developments in the colonies. In the traditional manner George III was burdened with the chief responsibility for bringing on the war. The much-reviled king was to Fiske a typical villain: "Scantily endowed with human sympathy, and almost boorishly stiff in his ordinary unstudied manner, he could be smooth as oil whenever he liked. . . . He had little faith in human honour or rectitude, and in pursuing an end he was seldom deterred by scruples."

In 1890 at the Lowell Institute of Boston, Fiske gave a course of lectures on "The Discovery, Conquest and Colonization of America," an outline of the two volumes that appeared in 1892. This was Fiske's most careful work, and some critics have regarded it as his best, particularly because of his use of source material. Its documentation, alone among that of his many books, approximated modern historical standards, but in his usual digressive manner Fiske included many details of small significance. Phillips Brooks thought that the chapter on Bartolomé de las Casas was "the finest piece of historical narrative in the English language," while Rhodes exclaimed with too much enthusiasm that "the *Discovery of America* is a great book; it is the greatest historical work that I have ever read by an American except the *Rise of the Dutch Republic*."

Fiske allotted a very large proportion of space to pre-Columbian civilization, reflecting the contemporary interest in "primitive" peoples. He said that it was his investigation of prehistoric Europe and of early Aryan institutions that led him to study American aborigines. He thought that he might thus shed further light on the conclusions of the Aryan school of anthropologists.

In Fiske's *Old Virginia and her Neighbors* (1897) and his volume *The Dutch and Quaker Colonies in America* (1899) it was evident that much of his research was uncritical. As Osgood said, when Fiske "crosses the threshold of the eighteenth century, his narrative becomes so sketchy as to lose nearly all its value. . . . He can only express the pious belief that such and such things are so; the proving of them requires activity of an order different from that of telling a pretty story or sketching the results of earlier investigations."

New France and New England (1901) had very little documentation and, like Fiske's work on the American Revolution, was largely a military history. *The Mississippi Valley in the Civil War* (1900), the result of another lecture series, was also a military history. Fiske obviously devoted much of his lecturing and writing to military history because that phase of the subject could be made most interesting to the widest number of people. Another work, *Civil Government in the United States*, was dominated by the outmoded evolutionary theory that traced the origins of the New England township to Greek and Roman institutions.

Fiske's fondness for playing with ideas sometimes led him to unwarranted speculation upon the motives of men. Theorizing too often substituted for research, and while he had a wide acquaintance with monographic literature, his familiarity with primary sources was limited. It is well known that he frequently borrowed and summarized the research of others without acknowledgment; his *Critical Period*, especially, suffered from these frailties.

It is scarcely surprising that Fiske showed little direct knowledge of the sources. His need for money led to hurried composition and prohibited the leisurely examination of large masses of materials; besides, his grandiose view of history precluded close observation of any particular period. Fiske, however, had something of value to say on this subject. His remarks on Freeman were probably intended also as a justification of his own wide range of historical writing: Freeman "was remarkably free from the common habit—common even among eminent historians—of concentrating his attention upon some exceptionally brilliant period or so-called 'classical age,' to the exclusion of other areas that went before and came after. Such a habit is fatal to all correct understanding of history, even that of the ages upon which attention is thus unwisely concentrated."

Fiske's political and economic views resembled those of many of his fellow historians: currency inflation was dishonest and even blasphemous; governmental paternalism (which included a protective tariff) was a great evil, as social Darwinism demanded a policy of laissez-faire; "backward races," including the Spanish, should give way to Englishmen and Americans, whose common mission it was to establish "throughout the . . . earth a higher civilization and more permanent political order than any that has gone before." In fact, as Fiske imagined the future, the world might yet see the consolidation of the "Teutonic race" ruling all mankind.

Fiske won high praise for his activities in bringing to Americans the products of advanced European thought. In his historical and scientific writing alike, however, he gave no indication of any great originality. Although he theorized about evolution applied to history, his writings were for the most part conventional political and military history. He was really an amateur in history as well as in philosophy, with a zest for life that was infectious. He stimulated youthful Americans to a study of their own history; his picturesque writing "could enlist a hundred readers where ten had read before," said Schouler in tribute.

Charles M. Andrews, as a young scholar, felt the popular reaction to Fiske, who brought into a period of dull historical writing, provincial in tone, the volumes that captivated the American public. Andrews wrote:

He vitalized it [American history], bringing it out of its isolation into touch with the forces of world history. He . . . accomplished a remarkable feat when he turned the American people from Prescott, Irving, et al., whose subjects lay chiefly outside the limits of the present United States, and caused them to read with enjoyment books that dealt with their own origin and growth. Nothing that Fiske wrote is great history, but much of it is good history, and his place in American historiography is one of great merit and dignity.[19]

Robert L. Schuyler summed up Fiske's contribution with precision: "Both in his philosophical and in his historical work he was rather the live wire that diffused knowledge than the dynamo that generates it."[20] Still, as Loewenberg has argued convincingly, if Fiske "did not write great history, he did history great service. Men still read Fiske, and much of what he wrote still deserves to be read."[21]

Woodrow Wilson

Woodrow Wilson, like Fiske, was a successful popular historian. He, too, sought some key to the nation's history, but Wilson thought he found it in spiritual forces. Wilson, one of only a few American presidents who wrote history, along with Theodore Roosevelt and John F. Kennedy, is hardly remembered today as a historian whose volumes were once widely read, but his own attitude toward his historical work sufficiently accounts for the modern student's disesteem. His main interests were primarily political; historical writing was always subordinate. He once wrote to Frederick Jackson Turner: "I love history and think there are few things so directly rewarding and worth while for their own sakes as to scan the history of one's own country with a careful eye and write of it with the all-absorbing desire to get its cream and spirit out. But, after all, I was born a politician." It is well to observe also that much of Wilson's historical work was written for magazines. "The editors of the popular monthlies offer me such prices nowadays that I am corrupted," he wrote in 1900 in a light vein to Jameson. He assured Jameson, however, that he would not alter the quality "to suit the medium."

Like others of his generation who were entranced by Green's *Short History of the English People*, Wilson sought to write a similar book on America. It was Green's glory, wrote Wilson in an article in *Century Magazine* in 1895, "to have broadened and diversified the whole scale of English history."[22] The Princeton University professor of political science said that he wrote the history of the United States "in order to learn it" and that his interest was less in knowing what had happened than in finding out "which way we were going." The history of nations appeared to him to possess a spiritual quality; it is a thing, he wrote once, "not of institutions, but of the heart."

Wilson was not convinced that facts in themselves constituted the truth. The truth, he said in the same *Century* article, "is evoked only by such arrangements and orderings of facts as suggest meanings." A colorless presentation of facts was not true to the picture, and it was the historian's task to use the facts dug up by original research workers to convey "an impression of the truth"; obviously not everything can be told. He added that the historian must also be an investigator, knowing "good ore from bad." It was Wilson's belief that the history of every nation had a plan which its historian had to divine, and in writing of past generations he should inject himself into their atmosphere, "rebuilding the very stage upon which they played their parts." The historian should know no more of the period of which he wrote than those who lived at that time. It was the duty of historians to judge the sincerity of men and the righteousness of their policies.

Wilson contended that picturesque writers of history have always been right in theory; they failed only in practice. Writing at a time when a reaction was beginning to set in against the dry doctoral dissertation, Wilson concluded that the historian needed imagination as much as scholarship. "Histories," said this professor, who had a very large general audience, "are written in order that the bulk of men may read and realize."[23] Wilson had studied under Herbert Baxter Adams at Johns Hopkins, and he resented concentration on facts to the exclusion of artistic interpretation; he was clearly not much of a believer in "scientific" objectivity.

Whatever the subject of his inquiry, Wilson sought to probe its inner spirit, always thinking of the practical bearing of his work. In his postgraduate years he was attracted to government, finding in the writings of Walter Bagehot on English politics a model to guide him in his study of American political institutions. He wanted to present them as living organisms and to write a work that would reform them. "I want to contribute to our literature, what no American has ever contributed," he said, "studies in the philosophy of our institutions." This was no abstract philosophy, he insisted, but something immediate in its applicability. The result was his justly famous *Congressional Government*. Published in 1885, it was, in the words of Loewenberg, "the greatest book Wilson ever wrote and one of the truly significant books in the literature of American democracy."[24]

Wilson's most important historical contribution, *A History of the American People*, was published in five volumes in 1902 after its popular reception as a magazine serial. The great number of illustrations, sometimes irrelevantly placed in the narrative, made it much bulkier than it needed to be. Something of that remoteness from reality which critics in afteryears found in Wilson as president was noticeable in the historian: "It was the spirit of liberty and of mastery," he wrote, "that made the English swarm to America." The stern morality noted by his colleagues at the Peace Conference in 1919 was also a characteristic of the professor.

Wilson's handling of political events leading up to the Revolution, especially the activities of Samuel Adams, was very good, but correspondingly poor was his treatment of economic factors. For example, there was no presentation of the colonies as parts of an imperial system. Wilson did not attempt to utilize the work that historians of the "imperial" school were already producing on this phase of the subject. It was interesting to observe the generous interpretation of the Loyalist point of view in this history written mainly for popular consumption.

The place of the West was given heavy emphasis in the chapters on the early national period: "The instant cry of hot protest that came out of the West [because of Jay's proposed surrender of the navigation of the lower Mississippi] apprised eastern politicians of the new world a-making there, the new frontiers of the nation." The second struggle

with England was referred to as a "clumsy, foolhardy haphazard war."
The nine volumes by Henry Adams on Jefferson's and Madison's administrations were compressed into swiftly moving sentences that filled
only a few pages in Wilson's history.

In the 1820s there was a new spirit in the land: "The new nation,
its quality subtly altered, its point of view insensibly shifted by the
movement into the West . . . for the first time chose after its own
kind and preferred General Jackson." With a note of exultation Wilson
wrote: "The people's day had come; the people's eyes were upon everything, and were used in a temper of criticism and mastery. . . . Half
the economic questions of that day of change took their magnitude and
significance from the westward expansion."

Wilson unreservedly acknowledged Turner's influence; the two
were close friends and talked at length about the significance of the
frontier: "All I ever wrote on the subject came from him," Wilson
said on one occasion. At another time he wrote that our historical
writing had suffered from having been done almost exclusively by
easterners. Historians from regions most shocked by Jackson's election
spoke of it "as a period of degeneration, the birth-time of a deep and
permanent demoralization in our politics. . . . But we see it differently
now," said Wilson; it was "regeneration," with a change once and for
all of the old order. It was the West that "set the pace," and in the
West was to be found the true national spirit; the East, he said, was
sectional.[25] Wilson's history was spiced with interesting generalizations
and suggestive insights, but unfortunately he too often left them unsupported.

There was gentleness in Wilson's treatment of his native South that
contrasted strangely with the sternness of contemporary historians. In
some respects his attitude antedated the approach of William E. Dodd
and Ulrich B. Phillips. In a separate volume published in 1893, *Division
and Reunion, 1829–1889*, Wilson redressed the usual apportionment of
space in historical writings by emphasizing the South and presenting
its society in a sympathetic light. His contention that there was no
American nation until after the Civil War profoundly affected historical
interpretation. His judgment on the radical leaders (Stevens, Wade, and
the rest) was severe. It is hard to acquit them, he wrote, "of the charge of
knowing and intending the ruinous consequences of what they had
planned." The voice of a southerner who as a boy had known the dark
days of Reconstruction spoke in these pages, which were a vigorous
indictment of the Republican party. Still, this volume, part of A. B.
Hart's Epochs of American History series, was the Wilson history least
criticized by specialists.

In the fifth and last volume of his major history Wilson discussed the changed character of American industrial and agricultural life after the Civil War. His treatment of labor, particularly in the Pullman strike, was conservative. In fact, his history, generally speaking, showed little of the Progressivism that marked his later career. Grover Cleveland was one of the author's heroes, and these two Democrats, temperamentally, had many things in common. In the 1890s "a new sectionalism began to show itself, not political, but economic," wrote Wilson, remembering his talks with Turner. The analysis of events leading up to the election of 1896 was very thin, however. In view of William Jennings Bryan's influence on Wilson's political career, it is notable that the latter was not particularly friendly to the Nebraskan's candidacy in 1896.

Throughout his work Wilson delighted in characterizing political leaders; he was not, however, very effective in accounting for social changes. His smooth-flowing language transformed his materials, gathered from authoritative sources, into an attractive piece of literary craftsmanship. No extended research was needed to write his history; yet it is significant to note, as did Turner in his review of the volumes, that Wilson was "the first Southern scholar of adequate training and power to deal with American history as a whole in a continental spirit." His work, however, is no longer read, and one may with certainty conclude that Wilson will be remembered not as one who wrote history but as one who made it. [26]

Two Historians of the People: McMaster and Oberholtzer

While a number of writers in the last decades of the nineteenth century were conventionally narrating the political and constitutional history of the period following the Revolution, another historian emerged whose volumes were to have a remarkable influence on his own and the next generation. His work was called *A History of the People of the United States, from the Revolution to the Civil War.* It won for its author, John Bach McMaster, immediate recognition both in and beyond the academic world.

McMaster was collecting historical materials in his undergraduate days at the College of the City of New York, from which he was graduated in 1872. He became an instructor in civil engineering in Princeton, but his interest in history persisted. It was while he was on a surveying trip to the West, he once related, that he was impressed "with the drama of the settlement of a new land, the creation of a new empire, and determined to write its history before the spirit of the period was gone."[27] When his first volume was published in 1883, the University of Pennsylvania invited him to occupy a specially created chair of American history.

McMaster's first volume, with its catholicity of subject matter, was a unique contribution to historical writing in America and was instantly recognized as such. Social history thus made a conspicuous and very successful debut. During the thirty years that followed, eight volumes were completed by McMaster; after a long interval another, on Lincoln's administration, was added.

The author fixed the attention of the reader instantly with his declaration that "the subject of my narrative is the history of the people." The people "shall be the chief theme," though much would need to be written of political and military history. "It shall be my purpose," wrote the historian, "to describe the dress, the occupations, the amusements, the literary canons of the time; to note the changes of manners and morals." His history was also to describe the discoveries and inventions of a mechanical nature; "to tell how, under the benign influence of liberty and peace, there sprang up, in the course of a single century, a prosperity unparalleled in the annals of human affairs; . . . how by a wise system of free education and a free press, knowledge was disseminated, and the arts and sciences advanced."[28]

In his early volumes McMaster largely fulfilled his promise. A cross section of American civilization in 1784 took up a large part of the first volume. "The Constitution Before the People" was an excellent description of public opinion expressing itself on a matter of great importance. McMaster's discussion of Hamiltonian policies was friendly to the Federalists, while his pages on Shays's Rebellion were hostile to the debtors. The difficulties of organizing materials for social history were made vividly clear when one observed that descriptions of Noah Webster's spelling reforms and of John Fitch's steamboat were inserted in the chapter "The Breaking up of the Confederation." The titles of chapters are in fact very slight indications of their contents. Wander as he might, however, McMaster usually found his way back to the main thought of his chapter.

The historian credited the Federalists with responsibility for American prosperity in the 1790s. He denounced them, however, for their opposition to the Louisiana Purchase, calling them "mere obstructionists, a sect of the political world which of all other sects is most to be despised." His attitude toward Jefferson might have been dictated by his reading of Hildreth; he wrote that Jefferson on his return from France "was saturated with democracy in its rankest form, and he remained to the last day of his life a servile worshipper of the people." Privately the historian spoke of Jefferson as a "demagogue, a 'straddler,' a false friend, . . . and I mean to show him up." In dealing with the Whiskey Rebellion, McMaster was friendlier to the insurgents than he had been to the rebels who followed Daniel Shays. The historian never showed much understanding of agrarian problems, though "the people" he was describing were mostly farmers. In his thinking and in his writing he generally identified "the people" with the middle class.

McMaster, in attempting to be impartial in his analysis of diplomatic questions, wrote that it "is perfectly true that the Federal party did show a singular affection for England, did submit with meekness while she held their posts, impressed their seamen, condemned their cargoes and their ships; but it is likewise true that the Republican party exhibited a most infatuated love for France," where, they believed, a revolution similar to their own had been effected. At this point McMaster revealed a racial bias characteristic of his contemporaries. He distinguished between Celtic revolutions (like the French), marked by violence, and Saxon revolutions (like the American), "conducted with sobriety, with the dignity, with the love of law and order that has ever marked the national uprisings of the Saxon race."

McMaster spoke of matters that were rarely included in general history before his time. In a description of town and country life at the end of the eighteenth century he suggested, "There is not, and there never was, a text-book so richly deserving a history as the [New England] Primer." Shortly thereafter Paul Leicester Ford wrote a history of that famous book. It should be mentioned, too, that McMaster was one of America's earliest historians to take note of the West, and his lines on the pioneers have done service for many authors. The disposal of public lands interested him, but of special concern throughout his work were internal improvements; he rightly saw that transportation was the key to much of American history.

"No person could, in 1803, look over our country," said McMaster, "without beholding on every hand the lingering remains of monarchy, of aristocracy, of class rule. But he must indeed have been a careless observer if he failed to notice the boldness with which those remains were attacked, and the rapidity with which they were being swept away." There was little of democracy in the seaboard states, "but the leaven of Revolution was quietly at work," and restrictions were gradually removed. The opening of a new century brought with it "a great reform in manners, in customs, in institutions, in laws." The adoption of Ohio's constitution at this time, said the historian, "was another triumph for the rights of man."

As McMaster went along, he sometimes forgot his "people" and returned to conventional political and military history. Occasionally he forgot the meaning of his own material. Thus, despite his own pages on internal improvements, westward migration, and economic and social growth, he wrote, ". . . from 1793 to 1815 the questions which occupied the public mind were our neutral rights, orders in council, French decrees, impressment, embargoes, treaties." He was more accurate, however, in describing the nature of American interests after 1815: "Henceforth, for many years to come, the questions of the day were to be the state of the currency, the national bank, manufactures, the tariff, internal improvements, interstate commerce, the public lands, the astonishing growth of the West, the rights of the States, extension of slavery, and the true place of the Supreme Court in our system of government."

Monroe, said McMaster, must have been convinced after his tour of the country that the questions facing him were "of home, not of foreign origin; and that in settling those questions the West would have a most decisive influence." There were illuminating pages on the westward rush in these years. Instead of looking toward Europe, the seaboard inhabitants "now on a sudden veered around and faced the Mississippi Valley," and "an era of internal improvements opened which did far more to cement the Union and join the East and West inseparably than did the Constitution and the laws." In a very important chapter, "Pauperism and Crime," those social ills were related to the economic distress of the postwar years. This was a period of active humanitarian movements to mitigate the harshness of laws against debtors, to promote temperance, and to reform prison conditions.

"The condition of the workingman," wrote McMaster, "stood in need of betterment. In the general advance made by society in fifty years he had shared but little. . . . Ten years of rapid industrial development had brought into prominence problems of urban life and municipal government . . . new and quite beyond solution in 1825." From a consideration of growing complexities in urban life McMaster moved on to frontier life: "Common hardships, common poverty, common ignorance, and the utter inability to get anything more out of life than coarse food, coarse clothes, and a rude shelter, reduced all to a level of absolute equality which existed nowhere else." The historian inclined to the belief that because religion had a firm hold on frontier regions, "nowhere else was the standard of morality higher or more fully attained."

McMaster concerned himself at length with the Industrial Revolution, the status of blacks, and the rise of a militant antislavery movement. While the North was vigorously cultivating "every art and science which could add to the wealth, increase the prosperity and comfort of the people, and develop the material resources of the country," the South was indifferent to these forces that were changing civilization.

McMaster's main interest in the Industrial Revolution was to show how it operated to cause a strong antagonism between North and South.

The culture of the masses was always an important theme for Mc-Master, and in a long chapter on literature he gathered together materials on magazines, popular fiction, and "moral books," whose effect, he said judgmentally, was "to inculcate a morality of the most unhealthy sort." His remarks on the charges of American literary subservience to England were sensible; the preference of American readers for English authors, he said, "was not subserviency, but sound literary judgment."

McMaster had hailed Jackson's election as "a great uprising of the people, a triumph of democracy, another political revolution the like of which the country had not seen since 1800, and no mere driving from office of a man or class of men." On the other hand, he was also critical of his turbulent "people." He wrote, "The era of mob rule had fairly opened and issues of every sort were met with force." The steady growth of the country continued, however, aided by the rapid increase in migration from Europe. "Had it not been for the presence of the imported laborer great works of internal improvement could not have been built," wrote McMaster, "and the early thirties were remarkable for the number of turnpikes, canals, and railroads constructed."

The sixth national census, taken in 1840, provided McMaster with another opportunity for a view of society in the East, South, and West. As before, special attention was given to improved means of communication and America's rapid urbanization. The Atlantic migration was well handled, but migration within the Union was disposed of too briefly. In the section on the South, which was largely given over to a description of plantation life and slavery, McMaster again drew a comparison between the North and South, with the former strongly favored. "Socially and industrially," he concluded, "the North and South were now two distinct peoples." A chapter entitled "Social and Political Betterment" rounded out his survey of the country. The vigorous humanitarian movement and the further extension of political democracy in the 1840s enlisted McMaster's enthusiasm, so that even though interpretations were missing from the author's vast accumulation of facts, the reader did enjoy the narrative.

As the historian told the story of the 1850s, his "people," who had formerly been engaged in varied social, economic, and cultural activities, were now mainly involved in great political debates. The core of his narrative dealt with the spirit of secession in 1850, "Bleeding Kansas," and the presidential elections. In his treatment of the Lincoln-Douglas debates, McMaster left no room for doubt regarding his own position; he referred to one of Douglas's speeches as "his usual biased and partisan review of the political situation." With unwonted haste McMaster hurried through the debates and maneuvers relating to secession to reach the election of 1860. Buchanan, of course, he strongly criticized for not meeting firmly the secessionist threat.

Politics did not entirely eclipse other activities, even in the seething 1850s. Once again McMaster referred to the problems created by the rapid growth of cities, and the more radical labor movement then arising was chronicled with special emphasis on the influence of recent immigrants. The distress that came with the Panic of 1857 was pictured realistically; no less interesting were the startling comments of Mayor Fernando Wood of New York on the crisis: "Those who produce everything get nothing," the mayor said, "and those who produce nothing get everything."

In 1927, at the age of seventy-five, McMaster brought out a volume on Lincoln's administration. It was for the most part a story of people at war, with only brief sections on the nonmilitary aspects of American life during those years. In his treatment of northern economy he wrote, "Two years and a half of war had brought no economic or industrial suffering to the North." After the hardships of the first year, "the people soon adjusted themselves to war conditions and went on with their daily occupations more prosperous than ever." Although sympathetic to the stricken South, he was critical of the Black Codes which, he believed, were drawn "with cruel harshness and a deliberate intention to reduce the freedman as far as possible to his old state of slavery."

The pen that spilled so many words—literally millions—was busy on other historical works. Biographies of Franklin, Webster, Grant, and Stephen Girard are among the titles in McMaster's bibliography. His texts included far more social history than did similar books, and their success was spectacular; over 2,500,000 copies of his texts were sold. Pedagogically they did for American history what James Harvey Robinson's texts were doing for the teaching of European history.

It is on McMaster's vast *History* that his reputation must ultimately rest. The historian glorified the common man. Personalities were rarely emphasized; they were subordinated to their environment. He had no heroes; indeed, he rather tended to belittle traditional figures. He spoke of Washington's "cold heart. . . . Time has dealt gently with his memory, yet his true biography is still to be prepared."

McMaster had a gargantuan appetite for historical facts and for him they were all created equal. His was not a critical spirit that could probe into American life with a nice discrimination and express its findings with an economy of phrase; he was content to pile page upon page of description. The ebullience of most of his own generation was reflected in his volumes, which were pervaded with uncritical national enthusiasm. In a speech in 1898 on "The Social Function of the History of the United States," he said, in words reminiscent of Bancroft: "Our national history should be presented to the student as the growth and development of a marvelous people. . . . We are a people animated by the highest and noblest ideals of humanity. . . . There is no land where the people are so prosperous, so happy, so intelligent, so bent on doing what is just and right, as the people of the United States." A biographer of the historian, Eric F. Goldman, rightly quipped that, if Bancroft's history voted for Jackson, McMaster's voted for McKinley.

In his early years McMaster had chosen Macaulay for his model, but the further he drifted from the influence of the English historian the more accurate his own work seemed to become. The first volumes, in particular, contained many inaccuracies in quotations and in citations of sources and made some sweeping generalizations. It is very probable that the less enduring parts of his work were the sections on political history. Yet as his work gained in accuracy, it seemed to lose something of its engaging, picturesque quality.

From first to last McMaster has had his admirers and detractors, but he lived to see a whole school of historians follow in his footsteps. Some of his sentences and paragraphs have been elaborated into monographs; McMaster himself, however, while a pioneer in exploiting newspapers intensively, made little use of monographic materials, even when he wrote his later volumes, by which time special studies were available. He was perhaps the first to emphasize the place of the West in American history, and in stressing economic factors he was a predecessor of Beard as well as of Turner. Theodore Roosevelt, whose *Winning of the West* owed much to McMaster, wrote of the latter's work to Henry Cabot Lodge: "If all of McMaster's chapters were changed round promiscuously it would not, I am confident, injure the thread of his narrative in the least. He has put much novel matter in a brilliant, attractive way; but his work is utterly disconnected. . . . In fact all he has done is to provide material for history." Students of both greater and lesser maturity ever since have not hesitated to make good use of McMaster's bountiful offerings, beginning with John Fiske and ending with the latest novice in a class in American history. Bancroft, who was omitting footnotes in a new edition of his work, once advised McMaster to do likewise, because writers were in the habit of using these notes without acknowledgment. McMaster's friend Frederick D. Stone used to say when a new volume of the history appeared, "Now we shall soon have something from John Fiske."[29]

Albert Bushnell Hart, who saw at first hand the changes in historical fashions over a longer period than that observed by any other American historian, said that McMaster was "the founder of the modern school of [social] historians of the United States." The disciples have not followed McMaster uncritically, but they have accepted his lead in broadening immensely the boundaries of historical inquiry.[30]

Among the many students who passed through McMaster's classes at the University of Pennsylvania in the late 1880s was Ellis Paxson Oberholtzer. Under his teacher's influence the younger man turned in time to historical writing, as editor, biographer, and historian. He edited the series of American Crisis biographies, wrote *The Literary History of Philadelphia* (1906), and completed useful biographies of two of the most important financiers in the history of the United States, *Robert Morris* (1903) and *Jay Cooke* (1907). Oberholtzer had already published the first volume of *A History of the United States Since the Civil War* when McMaster brought out the final volume in his own history, which covered the years of strife. Handing a copy of his book to Oberholtzer, McMaster said: "There, I have come up to you. It is for you to go on."[31]

Oberholtzer did go on, publishing four additional volumes which brought his narrative to the assassination of McKinley. Following in the footsteps of his predecessor, Oberholtzer wrote a social and political history of the years after the Civil War without attempting much in the way of interpretation. The same types of sources were used to depict the life of the people—newspapers, pamphlets, congressional documents, and manuscript collections.

The most interesting chapters in the first volume were those on social conditions in various parts of the country. "The South after the War" was a tragic picture of misery and degradation with but few signs of economic reconstruction. "The Triumphant North" described the influx of immigrants, the price levels, and the material wealth of the region, in striking contrast with the poverty of the South. In something of the spirit of the more modern student, Oberholtzer spoke of President Johnson laboring "with industry, tact and patriotism to heal the great sectional wound." From a study of the Johnson Papers the historian concluded that the president had wide popular support. As might have been inferred from his attitude to Johnson, when the author came to write of the impeachment proceedings, he was hostile to the congressional radicals. Economic and political despoilers—Jay Gould, James Fisk, Daniel Drew, "Boss" Tweed—were the objects of his wrath, for he wrote with strong moral indignation. He had in his youth high regard for E. L. Godkin, editor of the *Nation*, whose "moral force" still influenced the writing of Oberholtzer years later.

Oberholtzer piled his details mass upon mass, but despite this accumulation of facts the reader was not very enlightened with respect to the passing scene. For example, in a reference to California he said that the state "was in the control, economically and politically, of a small oligarchy of men enriched by mines, railroads and other enterprises." Another general statement was typical: "The entire nation came through the year 1876 with an enlargement of view in an economical, an industrial, an artistic and an ethnographic sense, as well as with a finer comprehension of American history, and the purpose and design of the government." Oberholtzer would have done better to develop these statements, instead of leaving them unsupported by detail.

Oberholtzer was considerably less impartial than McMaster; he once expressed preference for the method of James Schouler, which would not be "impartial as between right and wrong, honorable and dishonorable conduct." His treatment of labor in particular revealed marked prejudice. He confused socialism with anarchism, called the Molly Maguires "black-hearted men," and in his story of strikes was grossly unfair. Without revaluing the evidence in the Haymarket Affair, he was convinced that the anarchists "merited" their punishment. His bias was apparent, too, in his remarks on the Mormons, whom he called "polygamous fanatics." There was no attempt to present fairly the point of view of the cheap-money advocates of this period. His sense of proportion was poor; too much space, for example, was given to the Alabama Claims and to the complications arising from Chinese immigration.

The division of Oberholtzer's volumes followed the tradition of the old political chronology, presidential administrations and congressional elections being the dividing lines. Thus the first part ran to 1868, the next to 1872, then there was a skip to 1878, and the fourth ended with the presidential election year 1888. Though McMaster clearly deserves credit as a pioneer in social history, the style of historical writing he and especially Oberholtzer utilized has declined in favor, for the modern student prefers a synthesis of materials rather than a mere accumulation of facts.

Justin Winsor

The ferment in historical circles in the two decades following the Civil War indicated that the time was ripe for a comprehensive treatment of American history. "What a boom in American history just now," wrote Edward Eggleston to Justin Winsor in 1882.[32] Winsor, who had ably edited *The Memorial History of Boston*, organized a more ambitious work covering the entire field of American history. He was well equipped to head so vast a project, for his knowledge of American history, according to Edward Channing, was unrivaled.

Between 1884 and 1889 the eight-volume *Narrative and Critical History of America* was published under his editorship. There were thirty-nine contributors; Winsor himself wrote about half of the entire work, including chapters credited to others. Volumes 1 to 5 contained a history of North and South America to the eighteenth century; volumes 6 and 7 were on the United States from 1763 to 1850; the last volume continued with the later history of British, Spanish, and Portuguese America. It is worthy of note that Winsor did not think of America as exclusively the United States.

The first volume, *Aboriginal America*, reflected the particular interest in earliest America shown by students at that time. Winsor, whose specialty was geography and the early discoveries, gave full rein to his enthusiasm, writing on Louis Joliet, Père Jacques Marquette, Louis (Johannes) Hennepin, and Baron de Lahontan. The section on the American Revolution in volume six contained a chapter by Mellen Chamberlain which was a great advance over Bancroft's treatment of the causes of that crisis, for it laid particular stress on the Navigation Acts. The disinclination of nineteenth-century historians to treat recent history was notorious; the nearest Winsor's history got to mentioning the Civil War was the last line in the chapter "The Constitution of the United States and Its History," by George T. Curtis. The volumes on the United States were the poorest of the eight. One can get no clearer picture of the rapid advance of historical knowledge and changing points of view on American history than by comparing the sixth and seventh volumes of Winsor with Channing's third, fourth, and fifth volumes. In an appendix Winsor, who was a great librarian as well as a learned historian, brought together some of the notes of his vast collection on the manuscript sources of American history; he added, too, a list of printed authorities.

Winsor disclaimed any intention of offering "a model for the general writing of history, based on a co-operative and critical method. There is no substitute for the individuality of an historian," he remarked. He suggested that one great value of works like his was to make accessible to students a summary of scattered material and to furnish them with a guide to the sources; each chapter was accompanied by editorial notes and a critical essay on bibliography. To judge by the mass of notes, one might say that it was these that were accompanied by the narrative chapters. As a matter of fact, it is the notes that still earn Winsor's volumes a place on the student's shelf. They unearthed a great treasure for historians, and they are still the open sesame for many subjects in American history. Winsor, said Channing, himself a contributor to the volumes, "made the scientific study of American history possible by making available the rich mines of material."[33]

Later readers hesitated to acquaint themselves with the forbidding volumes of the *Narrative and Critical History*. Winsor's own writing bore the mark of hasty composition and lacked grace. The work reflected the interests of older scholars of the day and was not representative of the views of the younger group of historians. The latter pointed to the preponderance of material on the period of discovery and exploration and noted also that the narrative did not extend beyond 1850. Younger scholars, dissatisfied with the existing state of historical writing and feeling the need for a work that would summarize the latest findings, were brought together at the turn of the century to produce the American Nation series.

The American Nation

The American Nation: A History, a series edited by Albert Bushnell Hart, represented the work of the first generation of trained American historians. The previous generation which had cooperated to produce Winsor's *Narrative and Critical History* were mainly skilled amateurs to whom history was an avocation (only two of them were professors of history). Contributors to the American Nation were almost entirely academicians. The series was a brilliant editorial accomplishment and led one critic to refer to Hart as the "most useful historical worker of his generation."[34]

The twenty-seven volumes of the American Nation series were published between 1904 and 1908; a volume on the later period appeared some years afterward. Hart introduced the series by remarking that no one would deny that

a new history of the United States is needed, extending from the discovery down to the present time. . . . On the one side there is a necessity for an intelligent summarizing of the present knowledge of American history by trained specialists; on the other hand there is need of a complete work, written in untechnical style, which shall serve for the instruction and the entertainment of the general reader.

The cooperative method, it was said, was the only one that could meet the problems involved. Although several European historical enterprises had employed the division of labor, the American Nation, the editor asserted, was "the first attempt to carry out that system on a large scale for the whole of the United States." This series was to be something more than political or constitutional history. It must include, said Hart, "the social life of the people, their religion, their literature, and their schools . . . their economic life, occupations, labor systems, and organizations of capital." Wars and diplomacy were also to be given their due by the historians, whose volumes were to be written from original sources. Bibliographical apparatus, though not on as lavish a scale as in Winsor's series, was part of each volume.

The American Nation was divided into five groups of books. The first group, "Foundations of the Nation," included five volumes that carried the story to about the end of the seventeenth century. The second group, "Transformation into a Nation," began with *Provincial America*, by Evarts B. Greene, and concluded with *The Confederation and the Constitution*, by Andrew C. McLaughlin. The next group, the "Development of the Nation," reached down through *Jacksonian Democracy*, by William MacDonald, and included the important *Rise of the New West*, by Frederick Jackson Turner. On the whole these three groups of volumes presented a well-proportioned, continuous narrative and were generally superior to the two later groups. The fourth group, "Trial of Nationality," heavily emphasized the Civil War. The last group, "National Expansion," was scarcely adequate to meet its promise, although it did include the valuable *Reconstruction, Political and Economic*, by William A. Dunning.

In the first group Edward P. Cheyney's *European Background of American History* presented much fresh material; perhaps one of the most important of his chapters was "The System of Chartered Commercial Companies (1550–1700)." *Spain in America*, by Edward G. Bourne, one of the best volumes in the series, gave a more favorable picture of Spanish civilization in the New World than Americans were accustomed to finding in their books. *Colonial Self-Government, 1652–1689*, by Charles M. Andrews, represented the author's own findings on the Navigation Acts and the problem of imperial administration. Many of the ideas in this volume were novel to historians and general readers alike in the first years of the twentieth century. Two closing chapters insufficiently explored the "Social and Religious Life in the Colonies (1652–1689)" and "Commercial and Economic Conditions in the Colonies (1652–1689)"; however, the last chapter, for its time, was very good.

Before Greene wrote his volume, the period from 1689 to 1740 was known as the "forgotten half-century." Bancroft and Hildreth had not treated this era with as much detail as they had the earlier years; hence there was not even a general background account available for the student of the first half of the eighteenth century. "Scholars generally agree that the subject matter of this volume has never been adequately treated as a whole," wrote Greene. The interest of this period, he rightly asserted, "lies rather in the aggregate of small transactions, constituting what are called general tendencies, which gradually and obscurely prepare the way for the more striking but not necessarily more important periods of decisive conflict and revolution." Two outstanding features characterized the history of these years: the first was a great expansion in the area of settlement, as well as in industry and commerce; the second was "the interaction of imperial and provincial interests."

New perspectives and additional materials have outmoded the volumes on the Revolution even more than they have the rest of the series. Claude H. Van Tyne, the author of *The American Revolution*, turned to this subject again in later years, publishing two excellent books embodying the latest research. Van Tyne had an unrivaled knowledge of the manuscript and printed materials on the Revolution. McLaughlin, in his book on the Confederation, did a valuable service in pointing out that this government "was more creditable to the men of that time than posterity has been willing to allow . . . from its mistakes the framers of the Constitution learned wisdom." This was but one of the volumes on constitutional history that McLaughlin published after many years of close study. He summarized his views in 1935 in *A Constitutional History of the United States*.

John Spencer Bassett's *The Federalist System* described the successful establishment of the new government, the organization of the Republican party, and the difficult problems faced by the young Republic in adhering to neutrality during the French Revolution. Bassett fairly credited the Federalists with a great achievement in launching the new nation. While Edward Channing's *The Jeffersonian System* had the benefit of the prior publication of Henry Adams's work, some independent research, of course, also went into its composition. George P. Garrison's *Westward Extension* described the region beyond the Mississippi, the causes for its settlement, and the development of sectionalism. Garrison was one of the relatively few western scholars of this generation whose research had made important contributions to American historical knowledge. Dunning's *Reconstruction* set a high standard that was not maintained in the volumes on the Civil War or on the later period.

The American Nation series received on publication, and still receives, the gratitude of scholars for its services in coordinating the contributions of many different authors and in presenting the latest results of scholarship. A work of this magnitude, however, was expected to contain not only the summing-up of the results of one period of research but also a forecast of the interests of the coming generation of scholars. This it failed to do. In the main the volumes, except Turner's, followed conventional lines of political history, with a chapter or two of "social" history thrown in as a sort of concession to the younger element in historical circles. When Hart called for a general history, he pointed out that one of the most serious failings in scholarship was an insufficient knowledge of social history. The volumes he edited, however, did not go far to remedy that failing. In general, the facts were there, but little attempt at interpretation was made. And yet the American Nation was unquestionably a stimulus to historical writing, for it showed the many gaps that needed to be filled. It also improved the writing of textbooks, whose authors found shortcuts to knowledge in Hart's series. The series thus deserves credit as a great pioneering work, one of the finest products of the first generation of professional historians. In addition it was the harbinger of the trend toward multivolume histories with each volume written by a specialist and away from general works by one author. It has long since been superseded, however, in part by the New American Nation series, which began publication in the 1950s.

Edward Channing

Edward Channing was one of the earliest and finest products of the "scientific" school of historiography in America. In him were combined its best and worst features. He was a strong nationalist, though no blind patriot; he could be objectively critical in weighing events and deliberately personal in measuring men. He heeded his master, Henry Adams, in cultivating keen analysis in the study of sources and exercising skepticism in treating tradition. The pupil, however, lacked the master's hand in shaping historical material.

Channing, temperamentally, seemed to be closely attached to the colonial era and the early Republic, but his field of interest came in time to embrace the whole of American history. In 1905 he brought out the first volume of *A History of the United States*, which he intended to complete in eight volumes. He was working on the seventh when he died, in January, 1931, in his seventy-fifth year.

Channing was a descendant of New England's brightest intellectuals. An appropriate environment drew him to history soon after his graduation from Harvard in 1878, and five years later he was named instructor at his alma mater. He was a vigorous critic, and the training he gave to students in dealing carefully with historical evidence was invaluable.

Among Channing's earliest studies was *The Narragansett Planters, a Study of Causes;* it illustrated his skepticism of accepted traditions and his desire to go to the sources for his narrative. His *Town and County Government in the English Colonies of North America* opposed the theory of Teutonic origins of New England towns. The first careful summary of the English Acts of Trade and Navigation affecting the colonies was made by Channing in a paper before the American Antiquarian Society in 1889. While he was still an undergraduate, Channing was taking notes for the history he was later to write. He once said that he decided to write a history of the United States from the sources after he had listened to the dogmatic lectures of Henry Cabot Lodge and had read the biased history by Hildreth.[35]

In the preface to his principal work Channing wrote:

I have undertaken a new study of the history of the United States from the discovery of America to the close of the nineteenth century. . . . The growth of the nation will . . . be treated as one continuous development from the political, military, institutional, industrial, and social points of view. . . . I have considered the colonies as parts of the English empire, as having sprung from that political fabric, and as having simply pursued a course in institutional evolution unlike that of the branch of the English race which remained behind. . . . I have also thought that the most important single fact in our development has been the victory of the forces of union over those of particularism.

The institutions and forces making for union were worthy of especial emphasis, said Channing, "for it is the triumph of these which has determined the fate of the nation."

Channing's treatment of the colonies as part of the English imperial system was a novel and important feature for its time. It belonged to the school of colonial historians whose most distinguished representatives were Channing's contemporaries, Osgood and Andrews. Channing, a descendant of Puritans, was more sympathetic to his ancestors than were some of his fellow historians. After noting that first-generation New Englanders were very much like those who stayed behind in the mother country, the author wrote that as a result of new conditions "the Puritan creed only slowly assumed the sternness of aspect which made intellectual excitation save for religious purposes an impossibility." Of the Virginia settlers Channing said, "They were the first heroes of American history."

In the closing pages of his first volume Channing turned again to the statement in his preface: "The greatest fact in American history has been the union in one federal state of peoples living in widely separated regions under very different conditions of society and industry." This had been effected because "the institutions and the political ideals of these communities had in them so much that was akin." While noting similarities to English precedents, the historian also stressed colonial divergences from them. His conclusion, however, was that the colonists in the seventeenth century "were still Englishmen in their feelings and prejudices, in their virtues and in their vices. Contact with the wilderness and freedom from the constitutional restraints which held down Englishmen in England . . . had not yet resulted in making the colonists Americans."

Channing's likes and dislikes were rather obvious. "Had the governors been persons of force, independent means, and character," he wrote, "they would have exercised an important influence upon colonial life and constitutional development." He added, "Fortunately, they were usually persons of quite opposite qualities."[36] In the chapter "Beginnings of Constitutional Controversy" in volume 2, Channing paid particular attention to New York, whose assembly fought out some of the issues later handled in a larger sphere and in a more dramatic fashion by James Otis and Patrick Henry.

By 1760, the historian stated, "changed climatic conditions and environments had already begun to alter the racial characteristics of the descendants of the first comers from England." Colonial institutional ideas and commercial interests diverged from those of England. "In all that constitutes nationality, two nations now owed allegiance to the British crown," Channing wrote perceptively. Then he cast his usual caution to the winds: "The colonists were patient and long-suffering; only prolonged misgovernment on the part of the rulers of Britain compelled them to declare themselves independent of that empire from which they had sprung."

"Commercialism, the desire for advantage and profit in trade and industry," said Channing, "was at the bottom of the struggle between England and America; the immutable principles of human association were brought forward to justify colonial resistance to British selfishness. The governing classes of the old country wished to exploit the American colonies. . . . The Americans desired to work their lands and carry on their trade for themselves." The historian went on to show how the colonists had drifted away from English political and social ideas. In contrast to older writers, said Channing, "the modern student sees in the third George no mere tyrant, no misguided monarch, but an instrument of a benign providence bringing, through pain and misery, benefit to the human race." Although the historian presented valuable information showing the burdensome taxes under which the colonists were laboring, he judged that the Stamp Act "was eminently fair and well constructed, [and] the sole objection to it was in the mode of passage." By 1774, "America was united; not that all Americans thought alike or were opposed to England, but everywhere the radical party had come to the same conclusion." The leaders of that radical party, Samuel Adams and Joseph Warren, were classed "among the most astute politicians this country had ever seen."

Channing introduced the events of 1775 with a note of pride: "In

Europe, war was a profession; in America it was only waged for life and family." The writer paid high tribute to Jefferson's work in drafting the Declaration of Independence: "Never in the whole range of the writings of political theorists has the basis of government been stated so succinctly." Although the ideas and even the words were Locke's, "the reader will go to Locke in vain for so lucid a statement of his ideas." In his treatment of the post-Revolutionary years Channing differed from those who had painted a gloomy picture of economic life at the time the Constitution was adopted. Americans, he said, "had already regained their footing in the commercial world and were experimenting in many directions to effect a diversification of their means of livelihood."

Channing required three volumes to reach the establishment of the Union; three more carried him another seventy-five years, through the crisis which threatened that Union. The generation after the adoption of the Constitution, he said, was "distinctly a period of transition from the old order of things to the new, from the modes of thought and action of the seventeenth and eighteenth centuries to those of our own times."

Channing discussed at some length the problems that confronted Washington, particularly those created by office seekers. The author's comment was illuminating: "The 'spoils system,' . . . instead of being an invention of Jacksonian Democrats or Jeffersonian Republicans, was an inheritance from the Federalist Presidents and by them had been built up on colonial and English precedents." Channing inclined toward the Federalists, especially the few leaders who, he asserted, "acted with a sagacity that the world has seldom seen." The historian, however, attempted to hold the scales severely equal, for elsewhere the Federalist party was described as "reactionary from start to finish," becoming "more aristocratic with each successive year." Hamilton was judged fairly; although Channing noted that "he made some of the cruelest blunders in our history," the historian concluded that America's debt to him cannot be overstated: "He was the organizer of exploitation, the originator of monopoly; but he did his work at the precise moment that exploitation needed to be organized and human ingenuity required excitation by hope of monopoly."

In a chapter entitled "The Revolution of 1800," the historian took a fling at one of the many traditions he brushed aside in the course of his work: "A change of less than two hundred and fifty votes . . . would have given New York's vote to Adams and made him President with seventy-seven votes to sixty-one for Jefferson—of such was the Revolution of 1800." Channing was rather friendly to Jefferson, and he was generous in praise of Albert Gallatin's financial policy. Like

his teacher Henry Adams, Channing showed how the Louisiana Purchase played havoc with Jefferson's political theories. The international
difficulties that arose during Jefferson's second administration had a
strong fascination for Channing, who had always been attracted to
this period of history. The embargo, he pointed out, did not effect
nearly as much injury as had been conventionally supposed (except
in Virginia). In fact, said Channing, "the extension of manufacturing
in New England and in other States north of Maryland, went on
throughout the period of commercial warfare; and thereafter was greatly
stimulated by the conflict with England."

In Channing's treatment of the Hartford Convention he was more
lenient toward New England than were other writers. The war's end
was greeted with delight, he wrote, and the American people, with
their backs to Europe and their faces to the West, now "addressed
[themselves] to the solution of the problems of the Nineteenth Century."

"The American mind, which had concerned itself only with political organization," said the historian with some exaggeration, "suddenly
turned to other problems of human existence and became renowned
for fertility of invention, for greatness in the art of literary expression,
and for the keenest desire for the amelioration of the lot of humanity."
As for the West, Channing was not much impressed by Turner's ideas
on the significance of the frontier. "It is remarkable," he said, "how
evanescent has been the influence of these new conditions, for the
American people is now and has been for some years among the most
conservative of the nations of the earth."

The New England historian, heir to abolitionist traditions, looked
upon extremists with disdain. He spoke with some feeling of William
Ellery Channing, his great-uncle, who in the abolition controversy
"took the middle path that satisfies no one, but sometimes is the path
of wisdom." The later Channing, indeed, showed much sympathy for
the owners of plantations: "It is by no means improbable . . . that
the slaves were often happier than their masters."

The ferment in religion and education before the Civil War strongly
interested Channing, who recorded at length the significant developments in each field. Though he duly recorded important gains in education, he was not greatly impressed with statistics:

There were more colleges and more secondary schools in proportion to the
total population [in 1850] than there were in 1800 or in 1820, but so far
they do not seem to have greatly affected the average intelligence of the
American people, and it was the education of democracy and not the breeding of scholars that underlay the whole educational movement of that time.
Indeed, by 1860, the golden age of American scholarship was passed.

It was in literature "that the renaissance of the American mind is most noticeable." Unlike narrower New England students of literature, Channing wrote that "the geographical distribution of writers, readers, and students shows that all sections of the country were interested in literature, using that word in its widest meaning." The conclusion of his discussion of literature was as exuberant as that on education was depressing: "This half-century in the United States in poetry, in fiction, and in history stands apart—it is without an equal since the days of Shakespeare, Francis Bacon, and John Milton."

While Channing's judgments on America's intellectual life were sometimes eccentric, he had a sure grasp of her political history. Writing about the period following the War of 1812, an era formerly considered to be barren of significance, he said that it was a formative era in domestic history "and in our international history of the greatest interest and of the highest importance." Forces were then "taking shape that were to determine the history of the United States down to the year 1865."

The historian accepted the general judgment that "the Missouri Compromise marked the end of the first chapter in the history of nationalism. From that time for forty years, the whole spirit of our development was towards dualism—for the Missouri Compromise practically marked the division of the country into two groups, having distinctly different economic interests." The highest praise was bestowed upon Webster's "Reply to Hayne," which Channing called "probably the most famous speeches ever delivered in the national Senate." Unfortunately, Channing's treatment of the Mexican War was essentially a whitewash of President Polk and the United States; he was doubtless influenced by the tone of Justin H. Smith's work that appeared in 1919, two years before Channing's fifth volume was published. Channing closed his treatment of the period to 1848 with this question: "Would the Republic remain one united country, or would it be divided according to the social and economic desires of the inhabitants of the several sections into which it was geographically divided?"

The way in which the country answered that question was the theme of Channing's final published volume, *The War for Southern Independence*. The historian thus set the stage for the coming drama: "By the middle of the century, two distinct social organizations had developed within the United States, the one in the South and the other in the North." Had there been proper leadership, "peaceable secession might have been achieved in 1850." Few northerners have been fairer than Channing in his analysis of the Old South. He reminded his readers that "all treatments of Southern life by Northern writers gave an entirely false assessment of the weaknesses and the strengths of the slave system." Nevertheless he was forced to conclude, "Almost alone in the advancing modern world, the South stood still."

Channing's disagreement with Whig historiography was clear in his defense of Webster's "Seventh of March" speech against abolitionist censure. As for *Uncle Tom's Cabin*, Channing credited the book with enormous influence in America and Europe; it "did more than any other one thing to arouse the fears of the Southerners and impel them to fight for independence." The eleven years before 1859 were termed the "most significant in our history, for it was then that the Southerners determined to have their own way within the United States, or else to leave the Union . . . ; and the people of the Northern States determined in their own minds that the time for concessions had passed and that there should be no more compromise with slave power." In his closing lines Channing clearly indicated what his outlook on Reconstruction would have been had he lived to write the volume. "Well would it have been," he said, "had the reconstruction of Southern society been in the hands of these men [leading soldiers] and of others who respected one another and were guided by Abraham Lincoln."

It is difficult to find any philosophy of history in Channing's volumes, although like others of his generation he carried over into history the twin beliefs in evolution and the idea of progress. Providence, in Channing's view, also played its part in guiding the fortunes of the nation. He was, of course, aware of the writings of Karl Lamprecht and his school, as well as of economic determinists. Now, he wrote, instead of the trend to emphasize purely economic factors, "It is more often the case to emphasize the sociological or psychical change that is wrought by changed modes of living and by the general operation of economic factors. Possibly the best way to analyze the problems of progress or of changes in human outlook would be to combine all these various factors into one, for surely one's mode of living exercises a very important influence on one's mode of thinking." His own environment, he clearly understood, determined his point of observation on American history. "The time and place of one's birth and breeding," he acknowledged, "affect the judgment, and the opportunity for error is frequent."

It is not surprising that there has been very strong sectional criticism of what may well be the last of the important New England interpretations of our history. Critics have pointed out that, in his treatment of the background of the Revolution, Channing included nothing to suggest antagonistic views between the Atlantic Coast and the back country, nor did he take account of sectional alignments in the post-Revolutionary period. Van Tyne remarked that this "historical account rarely leaves the Atlantic coast"; to the New England historian the Mississippi Valley was "Transappalachia." Channing's narration of the conflict with France and Spain for the great valley shared the weakness of older histories in revealing an Anglo-Saxon bias.

When, in some of his volumes, he emphasized social factors, these were not always related to political developments; he failed, for example, to link up economic questions with the call for a constitutional convention. Like his contemporary McMaster, Channing occasionally ranged over so wide a variety of materials as to cloud the specific objective of his chapters. Charles A. Beard's remark on Channing's volume dealing with the Civil War—that it told what doctors of philosophy thought of this period—was appropriate for the other volumes as well. The "Great Work," as the history was known to Harvard students, often seemed to be a series of seminar reports strung together. In the main it was a history for historians, and many specialists have found in Channing's contribution materials hitherto unknown to them. His work has had and will continue to have great influence on teachers and careful writers of American history.

Channing had no illusions about the permanence of a particular interpretation. He once wrote that "no historian can hope to live as can a poet or an essayist, because new facts will constantly arise to invalidate his most careful conclusions." His keenness of observation unsettled many judgments that were long thought permanent, and he stimulated much new research in many fields of American history.

Channing and his work provide an interesting example of the difficulty involved and the caution that should be employed in placing historians in schools of thought or style. If the use of the new scientific methodology constituted a "scientific" school, clearly Channing was a member; on most aspects of colonial history he aligned himself with the imperial school; on the Civil War, he was one of the outstanding nationalists. In reality, his scientific methodology, his problem-solving technique, and the fact that he developed no all-encompassing interpretation of American history but hundreds of worthwhile interpretations—all these tie him to no particular school but rather help to illustrate his independence and aloofness from all schools as such.

Chapter 11

The Imperial School of Colonial History

W RITERS ON AMERICAN HISTORY have usually regarded the colonists as living a life somewhat apart from the rest of mankind," wrote Channing in the preface to his Great Work. "Moreover, they have been apt to treat the founding of each colony and state as if it had been unlike the founding of other colonies and states; and they have generally traced the story of each isolated political unit from the point of view of the antiquarian." His own outlook, Channing insisted, was different: "I have considered the colonies as parts of the English empire, as having simply pursued a course of institutional evolution unlike that of the branch of the English race which remained behind in the old homeland across the Atlantic."

Many elements of what Channing said were significant: isolation, uniqueness, antiquarianism, the political-institutional emphasis, the English "race," and so forth. The key to understanding the imperial school's approach to American history, however, is the consideration of "the colonies as parts of the English empire." The imperial approach, while it does not necessarily imply a pro-British view, does clearly involve looking at the *entire* British Empire and looking from the perspective of the *seat* of the empire.

Long before Bancroft died, students were beginning to question the value of his work on the colonial era. He had laid far too much emphasis, they said, on exploration, martial events, and the conflicts between personalities. Critics argued that Bancroft, Palfrey, and other earlier writers conveyed no understanding of colonial institutions or their development, or the relationship of the colonies to the rest of the empire. It was not surprising that when many Americans were going to Europe to finish their studies they adopted a broader perspective in the writing of their own history. Moreover, the American eagle had begun to spread its own imperial wings, and thus it may be coincidence that, in looking back over their past, American historians became conscious of broader horizons. They also could not fail to be influenced by the renewed interest of Englishmen in their own empire, as evidenced in the works of Sir Charles Dilke and Sir John Seeley.

Bancroft, we have seen, was not as provincial as his later critics thought him to be. Writers of the modern school, however, have altered so greatly our understanding of the past that American colonial history now appears as but an episode in the expansion of Europe. Osgood, Channing, George L. Beer, and Andrews contributed much to this revision of the American historical narrative; Andrews went furthest in reconstructing the view of the colonial era from the vantage point of the English homeland. "The years from 1607 to 1783," he said, "were colonial before they were American or national, and our Revolution is a colonial and not an American problem."

To some degree these American historians were anticipated by several British writers. The works of George Otto Trevelyan and John A. Doyle were quite provocative to their younger trans-Atlantic contemporaries, as were the chapters on the American Revolution in William E. H. Lecky's *History of England in the Eighteenth Century* (1878-90). Moses Coit Tyler recommended Lecky to his classes at Cornell because he considered the English historian's treatment "the very best means of getting the coming generation of American students out of the old manner of thinking upon and treating American history, which has led to so much Chauvinism among our people."[1]

Moses Coit Tyler

Moses Coit Tyler, though primarily a historian of literature, helped to change the cultural climate in which political historians could shape a new view of colonial and Revolutionary history. Tyler had been trained for the ministry, but in his late twenties he resigned, explaining to a confidant, "I was not built for a parson." He preferred literature, "my passion and I think my mission." In his commonplace book he jotted down the idea of writing the history of American literature.[2] Although he gave up the ministry for a university career, his conception of the academician was somewhat akin to that of the ardent missionary. He once maintained that "while history should be thoroughly scientific in its method, its object should be practical. To this extent I believe in history with a tendency. My interest in our own past is chiefly derived from my interest in our own present and future; and I teach American history, not so much to make historians as to make citizens and good leaders for the state and nation."[3] Like so many other students of his day, Tyler felt the impact of Buckle, and he hoped to find the law of America's development through her literature.[4]

During his career as professor of English literature in the University of Michigan and later as professor of American history and literature in Cornell, Tyler found time to do a vast amount of research for his four volumes on America's literary history, to publish a biography of

Patrick Henry, and to make contributions to professional periodicals. His essay on the American Loyalists in an early issue of the *American Historical Review* was one of the first to strike the new, modern note in the country's attitude toward the Revolution.

In 1879, Tyler published *A History of American Literature* in two volumes, covering the years up to 1765. The arrangement of the work was intended to show how from "several isolated colonial centers, where at first each had its peculiar literary accent," there developed a "tendency toward a common national accent; until finally, in 1765 . . . the scattered voices of the thirteen colonies were for the first time brought together and blended in one great and resolute utterance" of defiance against England.

In lively prose that showed a lusty pride in his Anglo-Saxon heritage, Tyler described various writers in Virginia and New England. Tyler could expound with assurance upon the characteristics of colonial historians, poets, and theologians because his careful study of every book or pamphlet mentioned had given him an intimate acquaintance with its writer. For example, although he could be severely critical of Puritanism, Tyler had a genuine affection for many of the writers who were nurtured in its faith. The prayers of the Puritan, he said, "were often a snuffle, his hymns a dolorous whine, his extemporized liturgy a bleak ritual of ungainly postures and of harsh monotonous howls, yet the idea that filled and thrilled his soul was one in every way sublime, immense, imaginative, poetic—the idea of the awful omnipotent Jehovah, his inexorable justice, his holiness, the inconceivable brightness of his majesty."

A number of individuals were rescued from oblivion by the tender mercies of Tyler, and some were revealed to be writers of genuine worth. He called John Wise "the first great American expounder of democracy in church and state," and he pointed out the value of Nathaniel Ames, whose almanacs were, he said, superior to those of Franklin. Tyler's two volumes were immensely important when they appeared because they brought a much-needed organization to the study of American literature, but they seem less valuable today. Tyler was often too lenient in criticizing poor writing and sometimes excessive in praising merely good writing.

No sooner was this history out of the way than he prepared for its successor. In his diary entry for August 7, 1879, he wrote, "Began work with reference to next volumes of American literature." Nearly a score of years were to pass, however, before they were published. The two volumes of *The Literary History of the American Revolution, 1763–1783*, published in 1897, were Tyler's most valuable bequest to historians. With justifiable pride he said: "For the first time in a systematic and a fairly complete way, is set forth the inward history of our Revolution—the history of its ideas . . . in the various writings of the two parties of Americans who promoted or resisted that great movement." His plan was to let both parties "tell their own story freely in their own way." Along with formal genres, lighter literary forms—ballads, songs, and squibs—that shed illumination on the revolutionary era were included by Tyler.

This work was markedly different from other treatments of the Revolution. Tyler did not fix his eyes exclusively upon political or military figures or King George III. His interest, he said, was in "essayists, pamphleteers, sermon writers, song writers, tale tellers, or satirists, the study of whose work . . . may open to us a view of the more delicate and elusive, but not less profound or less real, forces which made that period so great."

Tyler presented a careful analysis of the publications of such noted political figures as John Adams, Daniel Dulany, and Jonathan Mayhew, as well as John Dickinson, whose *Letters from a Farmer in Pennsylvania* were described as "the most brilliant event in the literary history of the Revolution." Tyler also brought to a larger public the story of the relationship between politics and religion in the pre-revolutionary era. As a student of literature he was, of course, interested in the art of writing, but he was also concerned with the political significance of such writers as Francis Hopkinson, Philip Freneau, and John Trumbull.

In his study of the literature of the Loyalists, Tyler dispelled some hardy misconceptions about that unpopular group. He denied that the Tories were "a party of mere negation and obstruction," pointing out that they "had positive political ideas, as well as precise measures in creative statesmanship." It is erroneous, he said, to think of the Tories as "opposed either to any reform in the relations of the colonists with the mother country, or to the extension of human rights and liberties here or elsewhere." In a tone that put to shame persistent provincialism in American historical writing, Tyler said that it was an "error to represent the Tories of our Revolution as composed of Americans lacking in love for their native country." The outstanding Loyalists, Jonathan Boucher, Joseph Galloway, and Daniel Leonard, received extended consideration at the hands of the historian.

Nothing surpassing Tyler's work was done on the literary history of the Revolution for a long time, despite his defects of omission. Tyler failed, for example, to consider sufficiently the place of the newspaper in the Revolution, nor did he include some writers in England who were of American birth or who had resided in America, notably George Chalmers. He might also have given more space to southern writers. The judgment of Paul Leicester Ford, however, that these volumes were "far and away the best treatment of the literature of those years of turmoil," was certainly true.

All writers on early America have had their labors considerably lightened because Moses Coit Tyler lived before them. In his youth he had written that he intended to cover the whole of American literary history in three or four volumes, but his fourth brought him only to the era of the Revolution. Ghosts of buried controversialists encounter their ancient adversaries in the lively pages of Tyler, and whatever of immortality has been granted to them came through the enthusiastic research of the historian. A splendid standard of historical scholarship was not the least part of the heritage Tyler left to posterity.[5]

George Otto Trevelyan

Histories of America written by Englishmen in the eighteenth century were well known on this side of the Atlantic. English historical studies of America, written in the nineteenth and twentieth centuries, continued to be read in the United States, but only a few aroused any enthusiasm. Scholarly English interest in America was uncommon; when it did exist, it was often vitiated by a bias for or against democracy. Despite a prejudice against studies of America written by Englishmen, Americans read with an almost morbid curiosity the innumerable books by British travelers who condemned or praised the United States. Most of the Englishmen who wrote on America were strongly attracted to the drama of the Civil War, but some displayed an interest in the earlier period when the American colonies had been part of the British Empire. Two of the most important among them were Trevelyan and Doyle.

George Otto Trevelyan's history of the American Revolution remains one of the best-known works on America written by a European. Trevelyan was a nephew of Macaulay, whose influence was important in directing the younger man to the study of history. His concern with the American Revolution came by way of his study of Charles James Fox. Family tradition and a personal sympathy with the customs of the late eighteenth century enabled Trevelyan to breathe life into his picture of that society, forming the background for *The Early History of Charles James Fox* (1880). This volume, which fascinated the literary and political world, gave "the reader the entree as an intimate member of a bygone aristocratic society," in the words of the author's son.

To the regret of his friends, who used to say that a parliamentary statute should be passed to force Trevelyan to finish his biography of Fox, the historian turned to write on the American Revolution. His justification was that Fox's life between 1774 and 1782 was "inextricably interwoven with the story of the American Revolution." The actions of British public figures in these years, said the historian, could be understood only in the light of events in the colonies. Over a period of fifteen years (1899–1914), six volumes of *The American Revolution* were published.

Trevelyan began his work with illuminating comparisons between English and American society in the eighteenth century, in which the latter came off very well. Commenting upon some temperamental differences, he said: "There could be no personal sympathy, and no identity of public views, between the governors in Downing Street and the governed in Pennsylvania and New England. . . . All who loved England wisely dealt with satisfaction upon the prosperity of America."

The spirit of the historian's approach to the Revolution was suggested in the lines he quoted from Tennyson:

> *O thou, that sendest out the man*
> *To rule by land and sea,*
> *Strong mother of a Lion-line*
> *Be proud of those strong sons of thine*
> *Who wrench'd their rights from thee!*

For Trevelyan the Revolution was a civil war, and the differences were not exclusively between peoples on opposite sides of the Atlantic; there were divisions among Englishmen and hostilities among Americans themselves.

Trevelyan brought to life the leading protagonists in portraits penned with rare artistry, while his description of military operations upheld his reputation as a vivid and picturesque writer. Fox and Burke were his heroes; George III, Lord North, and Lord Sandwich were among his villains. Trevelyan's history was obviously a Whig interpretation of English politics; also, it did not attempt to discuss many of the internal American problems that arose during the Revolutionary years. Unfortunately the English historian neglected to use monographic studies that would have been more valuable than were Fiske or Benson J. Lossing.

The English have generally thought Trevelyan's narrative too favorable to Americans; even some Americans have thought so as well. Theodore Roosevelt, a nationalist historian if ever there was one, praised Trevelyan's work, but even he said the historian "had painted us a little too favorably." Roosevelt liked especially the descriptions of battles and the characterizations of soldiers such as Washington and Morgan. In a typical burst of enthusiasm Roosevelt sent to Trevelyan a letter saying that he had "written the final history of our Revolution."

It was the opinion of the historian's son and biographer that Trevelyan depicted English civilization during the era of the Revolution "in a pleasanter and more intimate light than any to which American readers were accustomed." To learn that many Englishmen also had once despised George III soothed American tempers. Perhaps Trevelyan's work will be discussed in the future less as a contribution to historical literature than as a factor in improving Anglo-American relations in the early years of the twentieth century.[6]

John A. Doyle

John A. Doyle was an Oxonian whose interest in America apparently awakened early. He won the Arnold Prize in 1869 with an essay, "The American Colonies Previous to the Declaration of Independence," and a few years afterward wrote a textbook on United States history. In his essay Doyle wrote with vigor and insight, anticipating the views of Benjamin F. Wright, who maintained that the colonists brought democracy with them and did not get it from contact with the frontier, as Turner had thought. Speaking of the Anglo-American empire in the middle of the eighteenth century, Doyle thought that in it "there was apparently little of the material for national unity. Its inhabitants were not of one race or one speech, still less were their institutions of worship the same. One thread alone bound them together—the common spirit of independence and self-government." Doyle concluded that "the whole key to the American Revolution lies in two facts; it was a democratic and a conservative revolution. It was the work of the people, and its end was to preserve, not to destroy or to construct afresh."

In the years following, Doyle made the studies that eventually led to the publication in five volumes of his history of the colonies. In his first sentences he indicated his nonprovincial approach to his subject: "I have preferred to regard the history of the United States as the transplantation of English ideas and institutions to a distant soil, and the adaptation of them to new wants and altered modes of life." The process by which these institutions were developed was his main theme. In the spirit of the modern student, Doyle perceived the significance of the transition from the period of exploration to that of settlement in the seventeenth century: "We pass, as it were, from a dreamland of romance and adventure into the sober atmosphere of commercial and political records, amid which we faintly spell out the first germs of the constitutional life of British America."

While Doyle's treatment of New England was better and more detailed than his account of the southern colonies, his attitude toward New England was more detached than Palfrey's, free as it was of any necessity to defend the actions of the Puritans. Doyle wrote that at her trial, Mrs. Hutchinson revealed in herself "a conspicuous union of self-reliance with dignified sobriety and restraint." At least one of the Puritan leaders, Winthrop, earned Doyle's unstinted praise: "He is, on a narrower stage, the counterpart of Pym and Hampden, the forerunner of Washington and Madison."

Throughout, Doyle's work was informed by stimulating generalizations. He spoke, for example, of the need of the Puritans to modify in afteryears their

rigid system of public morality. . . . Fresh wants, material, intellectual, and spiritual, have to be satisfied; commerce brings with it gradations of wealth, intercourse with the outer world calls out new ideas and new tastes. . . . To bridge over the gulf which severed the new life from the old, to modify Puritanism and to adapt it to fresh requirements, to secure change without risking disruption of violent reaction, this was the problem which new England had now to solve.

In his examination of disputes with the governors the Englishman offered a valuable corrective to the conventional, patriotic interpretation made by American historians.

In the year that Doyle died, 1907, his last two volumes were published. One treated the middle colonies; the other, *The Colonies Under the House of Hanover*, treated the provinces as a unit down to the Revolutionary period. In his description of politics in the middle colonies he was naturally concerned with the disputes between New York's Governor Cornbury and the New York Assembly, and he took the opportunity to observe the similarity between executive attitudes then and sixty years later. "There is in Cornbury," he wrote, "the same dull obstinacy, the same narrowness of view that we see in Gage and Dunmore. Like George III, and too many of George's Ministers, Cornbury deals with the question as though it were a mere legal controversy. . . . He wholly fails to see that the very fact of their being dissatisfied and disaffected is in itself of importance."

The accession of the Hanoverians was a convenient vantage point from which the historian could take a comprehensive view of the colonies. As Doyle expressed it, it was the internal history of the colonies which was of prime interest in the seventeenth century; in the next century it was the external. "External pressure, exercised by the mother country, becomes the main factor in colonial history. . . . The result is an entire and important change in our point of view. Henceforth we can regard the colonies as an organic whole forming part of an administrative system."

In his treatment of the commercial relations between the colonies and England, Doyle took a position similar to that of George L. Beer, although Doyle may have pressed his point too far when he said there was "no desire to sacrifice the colonies to the mother country." His handling of the general problem of imperial administration was inadequate. He failed to use the sources that lay close at hand in British depositories, depending instead on less reliable printed materials. While Doyle's last volume was unsystematic, it contained a fairer interpretation of the Revolutionary period than historians were inclined to make at that time. Doyle said that it was "the blind reliance of English statesmen on administrative methods whose doom had been plainly foretold" which was largely responsible for the eventual conflict.[7]

Doyle's work was chiefly a political history, but on occasion he turned to other subjects. One of his best chapters was a general survey of the institutions, manners, and economic life of New England in 1650. The chapter on religion in his last volume was excellent and probably gave the contemporary reader the best short treatment of the subject available at the time. In his section on immigration Doyle revealed a very strong bias against the Irish, but on the whole he did not give weight to his prejudices.

Charles M. Andrews referred to Doyle's volumes on the seventeenth century as "unquestionably the best that we have."[8] But the work of Americans—Osgood, Beer, and Andrews himself—soon superseded that of Doyle, particularly in handling internal colonial problems and in unraveling the complexities of imperial policies. Doyle's allotment of four volumes to the seventeenth century and only one to the eighteenth was, of course, a serious distortion of the relative significance of each period for the whole development of colonial life. Although they were important when they first appeared, Doyle's writings are rarely consulted today.

Herbert Levi Osgood

Until Osgood turned his energy to a study of the American colonies, there was no dependable, comprehensive treatment of this formative period of American nationality. A new orientation was required, and Osgood was among the first to see that a large part of American colonial history must be told with reference to the British imperial system, of which the colonies were but a portion. American colonial history, he once wrote, needed to be taken out of isolation and made to "appear as a natural outgrowth of the history of Europe." This departure from the conventional point of view, so orthodox today as to be part of all textbooks on early American history, produced important conclusions, particularly in rendering more understandable Britain's policy toward her colonies.

Herbert Levi Osgood was a student at Amherst when Julius H. Seelye and John W. Burgess were on the faculty. Burgess, at that time newly returned from study with the leading German historical scholars, directed Osgood's attention to what was soon to be his lifework. Following the advice of Burgess, he left for the Mecca of most young American scholars of the day—Germany. There he was most deeply influenced by the aged master Ranke, to whom, he said, American scholars owed a debt of gratitude which could not easily be repaid. Within a few years of his return from Europe, Osgood was added to the already strong faculty of history in Columbia University.

In looking over the fields as yet untilled by the methods of the modern historian, Osgood believed the development of American colonial institutions a theme worthy of a scholar's lifetime. His article "England and the Colonies," published in the *Political Science Quarterly* in 1887, indicated the direction of his future study. Referring to the Revolution, he wrote that "the whole struggle was but an episode in the development of the English colonial system." He also specifically criticized Bancroft and others for their "national prejudice and partisanship."

In a critical review of Fiske's *American Revolution*, Osgood had pointed out that a new environment had wrought a new people, so that soon after the middle of the eighteenth century "two political societies of quite different type were thus brought into conflict." The duty of the historian, he said, was "to do justice to the character and aims of both." Fiske, in Osgood's opinion, had done no better on this score than had his predecessors. The reviewer then went on to say:

The truth is until American historians cease the attempt to defend a dogma, and begin in earnest the effort to understand the aristocratic society which existed in England and the democracy which was maturing here, and the causes of conflict between the two, we shall not have a satisfactory history either of the colonial period or of the revolution. The Englishman too, who carries his party prejudices into the work will reach no better results.

On another occasion Osgood complained that scholars were concentrating on the seventeenth century and on the Revolution to the neglect of the period from 1690 to 1760. Our historians, he said, "come up to that period with a fairly full and comprehensive narrative, and then they become scrappy, inconclusive, and largely worthless."

In the main Osgood's subject was the colonies as they were in themselves and their relation to the mother country. He thought that

the history of the colonies fell into two phases: the system of chartered colonies and the system of royal provinces; and the change from
one form to the other. This change, he wrote, "was the most important
and significant transition in American history previous to the colonial
revolt." From the beginning of the eighteenth century to the War for
Independence the royal province was the prevailing form of colonial
government. He insisted that to understand the Revolution the student
must know the precedents that had been slowly established in the
royal provinces.

The details of Osgood's history were presented in relation to the
functioning of the state. Materials of a social, economic, or religious
nature were used only insofar as they threw light on political growth.
As Osgood's biographer, Dixon Ryan Fox, phrased it, "Land interests
him not as something to till with spades and hoes, or to sell for profit,
but as something that engenders controversy as to distribution and taxation by the different governments."

In the first two volumes of *The American Colonies in the Seventeenth
Century* (1904), Osgood stated that he had written "an introduction to
American institutional history." His work had a double purpose: "To
exhibit in outline the early development of English colonization on its
political and administrative side" and also to study "the origin of En-
glish-American political institutions." This meant that his attention
was devoted to the continental colonies, and the plan of his work could
not include extensive reference to the commercial and economic aspects
of colonization.

For an understanding of American history, he wrote, it was necessary to know the varied forms English institutions took when reproduced
in America and how they were modified overseas. Osgood pointed out
that the origins of American institutions were to be found not wholly
in the Revolutionary period but in earlier forms that "had undergone
steady development for a century and a half before the date of independence." Not until the earlier years had been thoroughly investi-
gated, he said, could a satisfactory history of the Revolution be written.

In the first as well as the last of his volumes Osgood was at special
pains to note the intercolonial relations that were to weave close ties
among the scattered colonists and prepare them for the needed cooperative activity of the Revolutionary era. At the close of his second volume
Osgood added some interesting conclusions about American society at
the end of the seventeenth century. He found that the colonists by this
time "in their large relations . . . were [still] subordinate to Europe,"
but "their personal and local concerns were as distinct from those of
contemporary Europeans as time or space could well make them. In
their languages and in the type and traditions of their culture they

were Europeans; but they were transplanted upon a new and distant continent, and felt chiefly the pressure of its environment. They had already become colonials in the full sense of the word but had not yet reached a developed American type." The characteristics of equality and uniformity in American society were by now clearly marked, especially in the corporate colonies. In this first century of American history "in their main outlines American institutions, both local and colonial, were fashioned. . . . If at any time the acquired rights of self-government of the colonies at large should be imperiled, that type of political theory which had its home in New England could easily be extended to fit conditions in the provinces." Conditions in America predisposed the colonists in favor of self-government, and in this temper they "faced the home government and any plans of systematic control which it might devise and seek to enforce."

A third volume on the seventeenth century, published in 1907, was entitled "Imperial Control: Beginnings of the System of Royal Provinces." For the first time, the author noted with justifiable pride, an attempt was made to trace the imperial system of control "as a distinct and separate feature of colonization. . . . Attention has been directed to the organs through which it was exercised, to the objects and ideals which were pursued, and to the obstacles which prevented their attainment." Osgood's most competent reviewer, Charles M. Andrews, said that this third volume completed "the most important interpretation of our colonial history that has thus far been made."

After taking the reader through the complicated and sometimes exciting events that made the colonies royal provinces, the historian concluded with effective generalizations. The changes that came toward the end of the seventeenth century were "accomplished by a combination of executive and judicial action. It swept away assemblies and boundary lines, and aimed to undo the results of a half century of historic growth." The British crown and Parliament were responsible for bringing about these changes. "Prerogative government over the colonies reached its high-water mark" in the reign of James II, wrote the historian, who added, "Never again was so much attempted or accomplished by this method. When, in later times, imperial pressure was again brought to bear, Parliament was resorted to at every step."

At his death in 1918, Osgood left the manuscript of *The American Colonies in the Eighteenth Century* almost completed, carrying the narrative to 1763. After much delay it was published in 1924 through the bounty of Dwight Morrow, a grateful student and subsequently President Coolidge's ambassador to Mexico. Osgood had stated in 1898 that the two most important themes in our history during the eighteenth century were imperial policy and colonial resistance, and because of their constant interaction it was difficult for him to divide his material arbitrarily, as he had done for the seventeenth century. Although several chapters dealt with the working of the imperial system seen from a distant viewpoint in London, most of the book was concerned with the internal history of the various colonies, and especially with the struggles between governors and assemblies.

With the beginning of the eighteenth century, wrote Osgood, "the controlling fact of the situation was the gradual coalescing of the colonies into one system, under the control of the British government." The historian faced the difficult task of following the individual growth of each colony and making clear its specific position as part of the British Empire. The arrangement of the work turned upon the succession of colonial wars and the intervals of peace in the struggle between the French and the English. The author's problem in recording the history of the separate colonies was to "bring out their peculiarities and their uniformities." With pardonable pride Osgood wrote that "in scope and plan, as in much of its material, this is a pioneer work"; no longer would the decades it covered be called the "unknown period" of American history.

Because of the strategic position held by New York in the wars with the French, that colony's place in the history of those years tended to be especially emphasized. Osgood's interest was not so much in the military events themselves as in their effects upon governmental institutions. He was at pains to show, for example, that the need for military appropriations increased the power of the New York Assembly.

Among the significant pages in the second volume were those on the attitude of English officials toward commercial questions. Up to about 1730, said Osgood, "though the cabinet and parliament were much occupied with questions of trade no new principles were evolved, though the application of those already accepted was slightly extended. Of special importance is the fact that no wholesale changes in the administrative or fiscal policy of Great Britain toward the colonies were considered or probably even mentioned in those bodies which were really responsible for the conduct of the British government."

This work contained chapters of particular excellence on the English church and the Dissenters; "The Growth of the Spirit of Independence," covering the years from 1749 to 1763, was very valuable, for it included material on the Great Awakening. Osgood was unsympathetic to a religious movement which, he wrote, had caused "no appreciable improvement in the morals of communities." In a discussion of the planners of colonial union the historian assigned William Shirley a high place. The latter's services in this cause, he said, were paralleled only by those of Benjamin Franklin.

Osgood gave careful attention to the problems created by the frontier; he associated the Albany Congress with westward expansion. In his final volume he discussed the fourth intercolonial war, which finally settled the struggle for supremacy in favor of the English. His judgment on the capture of Quebec was restrained; he said that the death of both commanders "lifted the event out of the realm of mere military success and defeat or of political change into that of sentiment. Wolfe in particular has been taken out of the category of ordinary men and raised to the rank of a hero. . . . But what really happened was that, backed by superior force and aided by fortunate circumstances, to which he contributed by good management, Wolfe . . . hit upon a plan which led to success, and it was crowned with a timely death."

Andrews wrote that *The American Colonies in the Eighteenth Century* was "not British history, nor yet American history in any narrow and exclusive sense of that term, but something between, more American than British and growing more and more American with every decade that passes." Unfortunately Osgood was not able to add to his volumes on the eighteenth century those illuminating generalizations with which he had concluded his volumes on the previous century. These interpretative passages were excellent summaries and particularly well written. His style was never ornamental, nor was it easy reading for those who like romanticized history. He wrote history for historians and did not think it was his function to make history fine literature, yet he was never obscure. Although he kept abreast of the published monographic material (much of it the outgrowth of his own seminar), the larger part of the historian's sources were in manuscript, particularly for his volumes on the eighteenth century.

Interest in social and intellectual history has so broadened the scope of research that it is now clear that Osgood's contribution, great as it was, left a large part of the colonial story untold. It is fair to say that he paid insufficient attention to economic and social forces acting on the course of legislation. His work included no adequate study of the commercial policy of England toward the colonies, a theme left largely for other scholars, especially Beer and Andrews. A pioneer in the modern study of the political origins of the United States, Osgood lived to encourage other students to walk more easily over the path he had so laboriously carved out.[9]

George Louis Beer

George Louis Beer's work, said Robert L. Schuyler, "ranks as one of the major contributions to knowledge made by American historical scholarship in the present century." Beer was a student of Burgess,

Seligman, and Osgood at Columbia University, and under Osgood's direction the young scholar took up the study of colonial history. In 1893, when he was but twenty years old, he published his master's thesis, *The Commercial Policy of England Toward the American Colonies,* which foreshadowed his later historical writing. This little book on a subject hitherto largely ignored heralded a new point of view in American history. Written free from any patriotic bias, it gave a new slant to the relations of England with her colonies, whose inhabitants were no longer to be viewed as people subjected to tyranny but as participants in the mercantile system. "Thus we can see," wrote Beer in the course of his argument, "that the laying of restrictions on colonial manufactures was a necessary consequence of the mercantilist system." The score of years preceding 1776, he suggested, "must be regarded as transitional, as a period during which it was to be determined whether the colonies were sufficiently mature, not only to assert, but also to maintain their independence."

Beer looked forward to rewriting his essay on an extended scale at an early date, but teaching (which he did not like) and business postponed fulfillment of this intention for a decade. In 1903 he made his long-planned trip to London to study the needed documents. He returned the next year to begin his immense task: "to describe and explain the origins, establishment, and development of the British colonial system up to the outbreak of the disagreements that culminated in the American Revolution; to analyze the underlying principles of British colonial policy [in] . . . trade and navigation." The details of his plan concerned the English fiscal system and the role of the colonies in it, colonial economic legislation affecting relations with the mother country, the economic life in the colonies themselves, the British official system in America and the extent to which the laws were enforced, and the relations of economics to the political system. In that part of his plan that he lived to complete, Beer gave us only the side of American history that was seen from the mother country. Far more than Osgood, Beer "deliberately took the reader from the soil of America and set him down in the midst of those who were viewing the colonies from a position 3,000 miles away."

Beer wrote the last volume of his projected series first: *British Colonial Policy, 1754–1765* (1907), which remains the most widely known of his works. Its wealth of sources showed the impossibility of writing on this subject from the printed materials available in America; in fact, for all his volumes Beer drew largely from manuscripts.

The center of his interest, he said, was the British Empire, not the rise of the United States. Beer wrote that on the positive side his book was "a portrayal of British policy, a study in imperial history; on its negative side it is an account of the preliminaries of the American Revolution." The imperial administrative system at that time was tightened, he pointed out, because in these years the question of defense became paramount because of the struggle with France. In this volume Beer gave the first satisfactory treatment of the illegal trade carried on by the colonists. The distance that he had moved from the interpretation of nineteenth-century nationalist historians was revealed in his conclusion that the aim of the "purely commercial regulations of the years 1764–1765 . . . was to encourage and not to restrict colonial industry." This book, in which the author leaned over backward in trying to be fair to England, played a large part in the later revision of the history of the America Revolution.

Beer then turned back to the sixteenth and seventeenth centuries to seek the beginnings of the colonial system. His investigation resulted in the publication in 1908 of *The Origin of the British Colonial System, 1578–1660.* Far in advance of theorists who evolved the doctrines of mercantilism, he showed that mercantilist principles were firmly established in practice. Two more volumes appeared later, in 1912, as the first part of *The Old Colonial System*, covering the years 1660–88. Beer had planned an additional six volumes to carry the narrative to 1754, but he had not yet found time to write on the early eighteenth century when World War I broke out in 1914, and he abandoned the past for the present. Anglo-American relations, once of intellectual interest to the historian, became an absorbing passion to this publicist who labored in effecting the peace settlement.

Beer defined a "colonial system" as "that complex system of regulations whose fundamental aim was to create a self-sufficient commercial empire of mutually complementary economic parts." One of his chief aims, he said, was to learn "precisely what the statesmen of the day sought to accomplish, what means they employed for their purposes, to what extent these instruments were adapted to the actual situation, and how the various parts of the Empire developed under these regulations." To Americans who still nursed a grievance against the English, Beer brought the salutary reminder that the colonial system was not a one-sided one and that it was recognized as mutually advantageous by the ancestors, both English and American, of aggrieved descendants in the twentieth century. To compensate for colonial trade restrictions, England protected the colonies "and gave such of their products as were needed and wanted a monopoly of the home market."

Although Beer was much interested in economic history, he generally ignored the machinery of commerce and industrial organization; only incidentally were freight charges, insurance, prices, and the like included in his discussion. He underestimated the place of the colonies as markets and emphasized rather their role as sources of supply.[10] He tended to exaggerate the role of the "sea dogs" in colonization, whereas the English merchants were far more important. These were, however, minor flaws in a pioneer work. Beer's volumes did not entertain the general reader who preferred his history with a dash of the dramatic. They have rather instructed both English and American students of colonial history in rereading their common past. The version of that past as expounded by Osgood, Beer, and Andrews has, with some revisions, come to be the one accepted by the careful student of today.[11]

Charles McLean Andrews

Charles M. Andrews had a long and distinguished academic career, most of it as a professor in Yale. In his youth he, like so many others who were to make valuable contributions to American culture, was drawn to the Johns Hopkins of the 1880s, aglow with the freshness of intellectual discovery. The favoring circumstances of birth and nurture—he was born and bred in New England—gave him the ideal background for a historian of the American colonies. "I am a Puritan of the Puritans," he once said in describing his ancestry.

The earliest publications of Andrews indicated the bent of his later major interests, especially his study *The River Towns of Connecticut* (1889). Since the emphasis in the 1880s and 1890s was on institutional history, it was not surprising that he should have been strongly attracted to the field of colonial institutions. The young scholar was critical of the behavior of the early settlers. "In all their relations with their brethren and neighbors in the Connecticut valley" he said, "the Puritans showed little of that austere honorableness for which they are famed." Andrews's intellectual independence also prompted him to dissent from the theses of Freeman and Herbert Baxter Adams, who had held that American political institutions had their origin in the ancient German village community.

Andrews, along with Osgood, made a plea for the study of American colonial history from 1690 to 1750. He asserted that an understanding of the later years rested not on the era of settlement but on the "middle period of conflict and experience."[12] This period, said Andrews, was

marked at its beginning by a strengthening of the old British colonial administration all along the line; an administration destined from this time forward to come more and more under the control of parliament and to pass from the hands of Crown and council who had hitherto directed colonial affairs. No writer has, however, made any proper attempt to emphasize this fact or tell us, by careful attention to details, how the experiment worked. Yet, so far as it concerned all the colonies together, it is the most important phase in their history after 1689.

Much of his scholarly labor was devoted to exploring archives in America and England, which gave him an unrivaled knowledge of the sources of American colonial history. In 1908, in conjunction with Frances G. Davenport, he brought out *A Guide to the Manuscript Materials for the History of the United States to 1783 in the British Museum* (and other depositories). "Notwithstanding the fact that for a hundred and fifty years our colonies were a part of the British empire," Andrews remarked, "no systematic attempt has ever been made by British or American historians to discover the extent and value of the material contained in British archives relating to American history."[13] Andrews subsequently published another guide to materials for American history in the Public Record Office of Great Britain. Osgood hailed the work of Andrews as "one among many signs that we have entered upon a new epoch in the study of American history. . . . It implies and will be followed by a more comprehensive and scientific treatment . . . than has been possible or even imagined. The era of partial views, and isolated efforts, whether in the collection of materials or the writing of history, is passing away."

While Andrews performed an immensely valuable service in providing these and other tools for research, he managed also on various occasions to give illuminating surveys of parts of the colonial period and, once, the whole of it. He contributed a volume to the American Nation series and two volumes to the Yale Chronicles: *Fathers of New England* and *Colonial Folkways*. These latter books, written for a more general audience, contained the distillation of his deep knowledge of colonial life. For the Home University Library, Andrews wrote an excellent volume, *The Colonial Period* (1912). He observed that earlier writers on this theme had emphasized the colonies to the exclusion of the mother country and had also neglected the relations between the two. It was his belief "that the balance should be restored." Thus he gave almost as much space to England as he did to the colonies, and in another departure from tradition he included in his survey Canada and the West Indies as well as the original thirteen colonies: "No distinction existed between them in colonial times and none should be made now by the writer on colonial history."

In 1924, Andrews published a volume of essays, *The Colonial Background of the American Revolution*. It still holds up well today and is probably as good an introduction as any other single volume to the approach of the imperial school. It restated his earlier thesis on the interdependence of mother country and colonies, which "determined to no small extent the attitude and policy" each bore to the other. Again he reminded his readers that historians writing of the events from 1763 to 1775 generally "failed to see that primarily they were but a part of the history of British colonization and should be interpreted in the light, not of the democracy that was to come years later, but of the ideas and practices regarding colonization that were in vogue in Great Britain at the time." Andrews contrasted the settled and smug ruling classes in England with the society in the making at the same time in the colonies and found that a conflict was almost inevitable. The colonies, he concluded, were too far advanced to "be held in leading strings; . . . such constitutional concessions as would have satisfied the demands of the colonists, these British statesmen could not make, because they were barred by the mental limitations of their own time and class."

On another occasion the Yale historian said that immobility was the characteristic of the English official mind in the half century before 1775.[14] Americans, meanwhile, were forming a new society:

The story of how this was done—how that which was English slowly and imperceptibly merged into that which was American—has never been adequately told, but it is a fascinating phase of history. . . . It is the story of the gradual elimination of those elements, feudal and proprietary, that were foreign to the normal life of a frontier land, and of the gradual adjustment of the colonies to the restraints and restrictions that were imposed upon them by the commercial policy of the mother country. . . . It is . . . the story of the gradual transformation of [colonial] assemblies from provincial councils that the home government intended them to be into miniature parliaments. At the end of a long struggle . . . they emerged powerful legislative bodies, as self-conscious in their way as the House of Commons in England was becoming during the same eventful years.

In 1934 and 1936, Andrews published the first two volumes of the long-awaited work *The Colonial Period of American History: The Settlements.* The point of view adopted years earlier was again affirmed: "I have approached the subject from the English end, and have broadened the scope of my inquiry to include all England's colonial possessions in the west" during the seventeenth century. It was necessary to do so, he maintained, because "final conclusions must always rest upon the experiences England had with all, not a part of her colonies." The reader was warned to keep in mind the fundamental difference between the seventeenth and eighteenth centuries; the former "shows us an English world in America, with but little in it that can be strictly called American: the eighteenth everywhere presents to the view an Anglo-American conflict. . . . The colonial period of our history is not American only but Anglo-American."

Andrews gave an excellent picture of the temper of English life in the sixteenth century and the emergence of an ambitious middle class whose aspirations were intimately linked with settlements in far-flung places. In the first forty years of the seventeenth century rapidly accumulating capital sought areas for operation other than those in the older region of European trade. The energetic men who founded companies to make settlements in the New World were members of an interlocking directorate whose aim was the creation of an empire. While Andrews seemed to stress more the material than the religious motive for colonization, he did speak of the latter as an important factor in overseas migration. As in his younger days he was not too kindly disposed to the Puritan settlers. Andrews skimmed lightly over social and economic history; his main interest was institutional history, and his range of knowledge here was unsurpassed.

Through the complexities of conflicting materials on the early years of Rhode Island, Andrews picked his sure way, giving on the whole a friendly yet dispassionately critical estimate of Roger Williams. He demolished many timeworn traditions, proving, for example, that no question of a search for religious freedom entered into the founding of Connecticut but rather "the allurement of a fertile valley." He also provided the reader with a badly needed corrective to the persistent misunderstanding of Puritan "democracy," observing that "the ideas of the Connecticut Puritans regarding the political and religious organization of society [were] far removed from the democratic ideas of later times." Andrews continually warned the student against accepting the older interpretations of Bancroft and his school, who saw in the seventeenth century the foreshadowings of the later American Revolution. Whatever rights and privileges the colonists claimed were the same that Englishmen everywhere were then claiming.

The historian's third volume, which appeared in 1937, closed his study of the founding of the colonies. The great work of settlement was now ended, and a new period in colonial history was at hand. The fourth and last volume in the series, published in 1938, subtitled *England's Commercial and Colonial Policy,* was a study of England's efforts to administer the colonies in the interest of trade and revenue and her attempt to work out more satisfactory commercial and constitutional relations with her overseas possessions.

Developments between 1660 and 1696 came to constitute a code which for over a century guided executive policy respecting the economic organization of the empire. The English found that it was a never-ending task to clarify the system to themselves, for the policy was fluid, "never reaching the stage of exact definition." Four decades, marked largely by failure, elapsed before any degree of "smoothness of operation" was achieved. The description Andrews gave of the operations of the agencies named to carry out the mercantile acts and effect a closer supervision of the colonies was a major contribution.

In his characteristic manner he modified or opposed conventional judgments, writing that the first Navigation Act of 1651, for example, "injured England's commerce more than it did the commerce of Holland." A study of vice-admiralty proceedings led to the conclusion that smuggling as a colonial pastime had been overemphasized by historians. Mercantile regulations were ineffective, and the colonist's freedom of action was only slightly hampered. An irrepressible conflict was in the making, for "just at the moment when the executive authorities were drawing together the bonds of control more tightly than ever before and becoming more insistent on enforcing their policy at any cost, the colonies themselves were feeling the urge for greater freedom and an overmastering determination to govern themselves."

In general Andrews evinced a tendency to present a conservative view of problems and people, denying, for instance, the existence of a proletariat in the colonies. Also, after marshaling the material supporting his thesis of economic conflict between the colonies and the mother country, he minimized it as a factor in bringing on the Revolution. The Revolution, he asserted, was primarily "a political and constitutional movement and only secondarily one that was either financial, commercial, or social. At bottom the fundamental issue was the political independence of the colonies, and in the last analysis the conflict lay between the British Parliament and the colonial assemblies."

The four volumes that Andrews lived to complete amassed an abundance of detail dealing with counting rooms and council rooms. The uncompleted portion of his work was intended to present other facets of colonial life, which the historian knew much about, and in it he wished to show how a more distinctively American civilization gradually emerged. When death intervened, the loss to historians was great. What Andrews did complete must rank as among America's ablest contributions to historical scholarship.[15]

New Light on the Navigation Acts:
Lawrence A. Harper
and Oliver M. Dickerson

A chief concern of the imperial school of colonial history was the study of the manner in which the economic life of the colonies was regulated by the mother country in accordance with the principles of mercantilism.

Although Beer and Andrews did much to shed new light on imperial regulations, there was still much that lay in shadow. Two scholars, Lawrence A. Harper and Oliver M. Dickerson, explained how the Navigation Acts really worked and what their effect was on imperial economy. Harper's book, *The English Navigation Laws: A Seventeenth Century Experiment in Social Engineering,* was published in 1939; it told historians clearly for the first time what these laws were, how they functioned, and what were their beneficial effects on English shipping. In other writings Harper carried his studies of the imperial economic regulations' impact upon the colonies up to the eve of the Revolution. In opposition to Beer, who did not believe these regulations weighed heavily upon the colonies, Harper concluded that in the 1760s they were burdensome and discriminatory.[16]

Dickerson's book *The Navigation Acts and the American Revolution,* published in 1951, is the most revealing study of this important theme. It followed several lines of investigation: the attitude of Americans and British toward the trade and navigation acts, how the acts worked in the colonies, the changed policy after 1764, and how that policy operated to destroy imperial unity. Dickerson found that because the Navigation Acts were not oppressive smuggling was not generally excessive, and most merchants preferred to operate within the existing structure of legislation. The trade and navigation system was in fact the "most important cement of empire" for one hundred years. Certainly, as the commercial system functioned, it did not seem to inhibit American prosperity. On the contrary, to British visitors America was wealthy and growing rapidly more prosperous. According to Dickerson it was Britain's envy and fear of this prosperity that led her merchants to back a change in commercial policy and thus help bring on the Revolution.

The colonists said that in the 1760s, the mother country changed the rules of the imperial game, transforming the regulations formerly designed to protect and encourage trade into laws for raising revenue. It was then that Americans began opposition. In 1767 a new regulatory body was set up: the American Board of Customs Commissioners with headquarters in Boston, designed to administer the trade and revenue laws. This body, said Dickerson, waged war "upon ships, seamen, merchants, and commerce in the interests of revenue." John Hancock was no smuggler but rather one of the board's victims; his was clearly a case of political "persecution." The establishment of this board, with authority practically independent of both the crown and the colonies (the members' salaries were paid out of what they collected) was a disaster for imperial unity, for it divided the colonial empire administratively. The mistakes of the customs commissioners led to one crisis after another—the seizure of Hancock's sloop, the Gaspee Affair, the Tea Party, the call for troops—until finally the empire was embroiled in civil war. The inevitable question which Dickerson's work raises is this: Would the Revolution have occurred if the old system of trade and navigation, minus the revenue-producing factors, had been permitted to continue after 1763?

Clarence Walworth Alvord

The concentration of eastern historians on the role of their area (to the exclusion of the West) in the Revolutionary era seemed mistaken to westerners, especially to students of Turner. Many sought to reinterpret American history with Turner's "frontier" thesis as a key, but none did better work than Clarence W. Alvord. Early in his career he established his claim to scholarly notice by discovering the records of the old French settlements in Illinois. He edited the *Kaskaskia Records, 1778-1790* (published in 1909) and, with Clarence C. Carter, later published *The New Regime, 1765-1767*, which appeared in 1916. With Lee Bidgood, Alvord issued in 1912 an important publication entitled *The First Explorations of the Transallegheny Region by the Virginians, 1650-1674*. The latter was the first attempt to tell the story of the discovery of this region by the Virginians, whose achievements had been unknown to Parkman and Winsor. Under Alvord's editorship, fourteen volumes of the Illinois Historical Collections appeared. He also edited one of the best state histories ever written, the Centennial History of Illinois, a series for which he wrote the first volume.

Alvord's most noteworthy historical narrative, published in two volumes in 1917, was *The Mississippi Valley in British Politics*, subtitled *A Study of the Trade, Land Speculation and Experiments in Imperialism Culminating in the American Revolution*. Alvord warned his readers not to expect in his pages the conventional narrative of the events leading up to the Revolution. "Whenever the British ministers soberly and seriously discussed the American problem," said Alvord, "the vital phase to them was not the disturbances of . . . Boston and New York, but the development of that vast transmontane region that was acquired in 1763 by the Treaty of Paris." Although his point of observation lay on the western prairies, his work, he said, was not a history of the West. Rather, his eyes were fixed on the British ministry "in the hope of discovering the obscure development of a western policy," for he thought it impossible to fathom the British-American policy unless contemporary British politics were thoroughly understood. The problems of Indians, land companies, fur traders, the rights of the various colonies in the West—all these issues had to be dealt with, and Alvord described the attempts made to solve them.

Like his fellow writers of the imperial school of colonial history, Alvord was hostile to political patriotic zeal. Indeed, like Beer, he seemed to lean over backward in his attempt to be fair to Britain. Although he made mistakes in his description of British politics, Alvord's general interpretation did much to narrate more accurately the real scope of conflicting interests in the Revolutionary era.[17] Some of his material was especially good, particularly his chapter "The Beginning of Western Speculation." By the 1770s, said Alvord, "British muddling in the West was doomed. By 1774 the colonists of the eastern seacoast . . . were already preparing to assert themselves. Thus there culminated at the same time two series of events, one eastern and one western, which had for years run parallel, so closely interwoven that any attempt to understand the one without a knowledge of the other must inevitably fail."

In his eagerness to restore the balance of emphasis Alvord minimized English public interest in the region of the Atlantic seaboard. Publications of all sorts, especially newspapers and magazines, reflected that concern, which he underestimated; but given this qualification, it should be granted that Alvord's volumes marked an important development in the historiography of the Revolution, an interesting combination of the frontier and imperial schools.[18]

Lawrence Henry Gipson

As earlier noted, the imperial interpretation of colonial history, though it is not always called that, managed to become essentially the accepted view among historians. The old patriotic, Bancroftian view, however (also not usually called that), showed amazing staying power in the popular mind. In the words of William W. Abbot in the 1973 yearbook of the National Council for the Social Studies, *The Reinterpretation of American History and Culture*, although the imperial approach may have become the predominant one on mother country-colonial relations, "imperial history has hardly been the primary concern of colonial historians since the Second World War. Most have in fact been searching for patterns within colonial society itself." Abbot continued, "[The latter historians] have generally been less interested than imperial historians in the evolution of political institutions and more interested in the formation of American society, in the creation of an 'American' character and an 'American' mind."[19] One scholar, however, Lawrence H. Gipson, worked on through the 1960s to become the major modern proponent of the imperial interpretation. Indeed, he produced what Ray Allen Billington called "a monumental work of scholarship that more than any other demonstrates the validity of the imperial approach to the study of colonial America."[20]

Neither Osgood nor Andrews lived to carry his detailed narrative beyond the first half of the eighteenth century, and the same kind of revision they had made of colonial history up to that point was obviously needed for the subsequent period. Many scholars have since attempted to refashion an interpretation of the quarter century preceding the Revolution. No one else, however, attempted it on a scale comparable to that of Osgood and Andrews until Gipson set himself the enormous task. An enthusiastic disciple of Andrews, Gipson carried over into his own studies views he learned from the master. A thorough grounding in colonial and imperial history prepared him to initiate the plan for his vast work, entitled *The British Empire Before the American Revolution.* The first volume appeared in 1936; the fifteenth and final one appeared in 1970. Gipson's dedication in taking on such a task is indeed impressive. Actually, the narrative of the years from 1748 to 1776 ended early in volume 12; the rest of that volume consisted of an excellent fifty-page summary of the series and a generally balanced and sometimes brilliant assessment by Gipson of virtually all the historians whose work preceded him on his subject. Thus, volume 14 was *A Bibliographical Guide* and volume 15 *A Guide to Manuscripts.*

The first three volumes surveyed the empire in the middle of the eighteenth century. Going a step further than Andrews, Gipson broadened his investigation to include not only the North American colonies but also the mother country and Africa, arguing that "Guinea carried the empire." Gipson called the British Empire of this period, with its tremendous vitality, "undoubtedly the most imposing politico-economic structure that the world had ever known." In Gipson's view it was mainly private enterprise, not state planning, which had expanded the bounds of empire. The British Empire, he said, was a "world of literate people devoted to freedom and opposed to governmental regulation."

Gipson's canvas continued to be large in his succeeding volumes; his intention was to trace the history of the empire by "beating its bounds." The fourth and fifth volumes, *Zones of International Friction, 1748–1754,* described the imperial conflict in all quarters of the globe, but the heart of the narrative was the rivalry for America. The historian tried to keep his eye not only on the center of the empire, London, but simultaneously on the colonies, in order "to view the operation of British imperial dynamism at its various sources of manifestation." That dynamism, as expressed in the Albany Plan of Union, was described in great detail in some of Gipson's best chapters.

The sixth, seventh, and eighth volumes narrated the years of defeat and victory in the Seven Years' War, which Gipson preferred to call "The Great War for the Empire," believing that the title could lift the conflict out of the narrower setting established by other historians. Contrary to earlier interpreters, he argued that traditional European techniques of warfare were more important than the practices of frontiersmen in winning the struggle in America. It was really, he said, "a European conflict in a New World setting." It was British superiority in several categories—her navy, her heavy industry, and colonial agriculture ("turned to warlike purposes")—which ultimately beat the French.

Volumes 9 through 13 carried the interesting title *The Triumphant Empire.* A major theme of those volumes, of course, was the "Triumphant Empire" coming apart. It is noteworthy that Gipson told the story of those crucial years of controversy and turmoil in the relationship between England and her North American colonies far more briefly in the contribution he made in 1954 to the New American Nation series, *The Coming of the Revolution, 1763–1775.* An excellent summary, the latter was praised by Clinton Rossiter as "pure Gipson," by which he meant "documented with severity, written with clarity, and marked by a measured, one might almost say Franklinian, affection of the old Empire."[21] Henry Steele Commager and Richard Brandon Morris, the editors of the series, suggested in their introduction to his volume that "to Dr. Gipson the Revolution marks the culmination in America of the twin forces of federalism and rationalism." Gipson, they continued, saw "no basic clash between England and her colonies over commerce or church policy or westward expansion. To him the forces of federalism and nationalism were irreconcilable with the outmoded system of imperial relationships upon which the old British Empire had been founded."

In his own preface Gipson succinctly summarized his view of the causes of the Revolution. The first cause was

the effort of the British Government, faced with vast territorial acquisitions in North America at the end of the Great War for the Empire, along with an unprecedented war debt, to organize a more efficient administration on that continent and to make the colonies contribute directly to the support of the enlarged Empire amounts over and beyond the indefinite and indirect contributions already provided through the operation of the old colonial system of controls.

The second cause was

the radically altered situation of the colonies after 1760, by which date they were at long last relieved of the intense pressure previously exerted along their borders by hostile nations. Thus, at the very time when their dependence upon the mother country had largely disappeared and they felt impelled to demand greater autonomy than ever, the colonials found, instead, that their sphere of freedom of political action was seriously circumscribed by the government at home.

Inevitably, he concluded, all this led,

first of all, to a re-examination by colonial leaders of the implications of the complicated British imperial system; then to challenging the doctrine of the supremacy of Parliament throughout the Empire; finally, to setting forth the counter-doctrine that the assemblies of the colonies were alone the ultimate judges of the extent of authority that the Crown and Parliament of Great Britain would be permitted to exercise within their borders.

This progression in American political ideas was indeed revolutionary, Gipson insisted.

Gipson concluded *The Coming of the Revolution* on the kind of cautious yet insightful note of which the imperial school was capable at its best. "The rupture of the old British Empire," he said, "did not come about as the result of the actions of wicked men—neither of the King or Lord North, on the one hand, nor of American radicals, on the other." Both sides were firmly convinced that they were right, and both were supported by an ardent minority on the other side of the Atlantic. Finally, "one is faced with the anomaly that in our own day the fundamental positions taken by Great Britain and America in the year 1775 are reversed." While Great Britain has repudiated its earlier position that sovereignty was indivisible within its empire, the United States,

as a result of the outcome of the Civil War, has just as firmly repudiated the Revolutionary War idea that each state is a sovereign entity within the federal system, in favor of the unitary concept of sovereignty as resting in the whole American nation—carrying with it the utter denial that the government of a particular state, despite its reserved powers, can determine the constitutionality of acts of Congress and as a consequence decide whether or not these acts shall be enforced within its borders or secede from the Union.

Even on the emotional Revolutionary issue of taxation without representation, noted Gipson, the American position has been disregarded, for "with . . . the establishment of territories, and the acquisition of overseas possessions, the federal government . . . assumes the right to tax people who are not and may never be represented in Congress."

In 1965, Gipson contributed an excellent essay on "imperial" history to Billington's *Reinterpretation of Early American History.*[22] He began by contrasting the imperial approach to the nationalist approach of most earlier historians. Whereas the nationalist approach "assumes the existence of the United States of America and then probes into the past in order to uncover the beginnings and the development of a group of thirteen English colonies destined to become the nucleus of a new nation," the imperial approach "views English colonization of the New World simply as part of the history of the rise and decline of the British Empire. In this approach London, the capital of the Empire, is always the nerve center." While Gipson insisted that each approach had "its merits and its disadvantages," it was clear where his sympathies lay. Bancroft, he said, was the "extreme example" of the nationalist approach; Gipson even said that Bancroft was the "antithesis" of Ranke as a historian, failing completely to live up to the great German's "intellectual detachment." The decline in the popularity of Bancroft's work, insisted Gipson, did not necessarily mean that his viewpoint had disappeared; somewhat incorrectly, Gipson suggested that Channing's work was among those continuing Bancroft's approach.

Gipson appropriately emphasized that the imperial approach was really nothing new, having begun in the early national period with the works of such Loyalist historians as Jonathan Boucher, Thomas Hutchinson, and Peter Oliver. Imperial history, however, "was neither desired nor needed by the American people engaged throughout the nineteenth century in the arduous task of consolidating the nation and adding to its prestige abroad," Gipson realized. "Only when the nation had become powerful and confident about its great future, only when intolerance of views that did not harmonize with traditional interpretations of the past had given place to a large measure of tolerance," was the nation ready for the imperial approach of Beer, Osgood, and Andrews. Gipson, of course, praised all these men, his precursors in the imperial school, especially Andrews, whom he considered "perhaps the greatest American colonial historian." It is in his assessment of Andrews that Gipson makes this important cautionary point about a common tendency to misunderstand imperial history: "To think that because he adopted the British imperial approach he was pro-British in his interpretation of early American history would be a serious mistake."

Gipson offered no challenge to Parkman's artistry, but he succeeded in reminding scholars of some problems and policies of the empire which the great nineteenth-century historian never considered. While he enlarged the scope of historical inquiry—attempting to spin a web of empire such as others had not done before—he did not always succeed in keeping his various strands in touch with one another. As he told the story, the American colonies were less weighty in the scheme of empire than has usually been believed. Possibly reacting too strongly to the old excessive patriotism, he minimized the role of the American colonists in the struggle with France. Then, too, like Andrews before him, it may be that in an effort to look at colonial conditions through English official eyes, the subtleties of American political expression in the direction of democracy may have escaped him. Still, his work stands as an outstanding accomplishment, the most comprehensive and in many ways the finest expression of the vital imperial school of colonial history.

CHAPTER 12

The Progressive Historians

I T HAS BEEN SUGGESTED that the average American accepts much of George Bancroft's view of American history, perhaps without ever having heard of Bancroft. The same is true of Frederick Jackson Turner and his frontier thesis. What American does not believe that rugged individualism, optimism, and democracy are American characteristics—perhaps uniquely American—and that these resulted from our frontier experience? Richard L. Rapson wrote in *Major Interpretations of the American Past:*

As a people, Americans cannot be called historically-minded. Turner recognized this and he probably would not be surprised, were he still alive, to discover that his name does not inspire instant recognition from all Americans. But if these same citizens were asked to explain how Americans differ from other peoples of the world, and why they differ, they would no doubt come up with an explanation very closely akin to that promulgated by Turner in his famous essay in 1895. The frontier thesis is America's most popular explanation of herself and it has held this place from 1893 through John F. Kennedy's call for a New Frontier and on to our explorations into space. Turner is America's historian.[1]

Turner also offers, like Edward Channing, an excellent example of the difficulty of placing historians in comfortable "schools." Gerald N. Grob and George Athan Billias write appropriately of Turner as "perhaps the most famous and influential representative of the scientific school of historians in the first generation of professional historians."[2] Clearly, however, he also belongs to the "frontier" school—indeed, one can argue that there would have been no such school without him. Finally, one may categorize Turner, as will be done here, by the term in the title of Richard Hofstadter's important study that appeared in 1968, *The Progressive Historians: Turner, Beard, Parrington.*

What is implied by the label "Progressive"? Gene Wise, in his extremely difficult but valuable *American Historical Explanations: A Strategy for Grounded Inquiry* (published in 1973 and revised in 1980), suggested that Progressivism has been "the dominant explanation form in twentieth-century American historical scholarship." Hofstadter's

book, he said correctly, is the finest study of the Progressive historians.[3] Charles Crowe, however, provided an excellent brief introduction in an article that appeared in the *Journal of the History of
Ideas* in 1966. In the article Crowe insisted that Progressive history was
neither a philosophy of history nor a consistent interpretation of American history but rather "a set of related impressions, a framework of
Pragmatic and Progressive assumptions and attitudes, which inspired
the great flowering of professional American scholarship in history."
According to Crowe, Progressive history had eight characteristics: (1) a
vivid sense of social, economic, and intellectual process which placed
man firmly in the stream of evolution; (2) a pragmatic determination
to deal only with concrete situations; (3) a sort of anti-intellectualism
which regarded ideas as secondary and as derived from such truly important historical forces as economics and geography; (4) an episte-
mological relativism which generally denied "scientific" history, and
sometimes even scholarly objectivity; (5) a "presentism" which stressed
the continuity of past, present, and future and which clearly subordinated the past to the present; (6) an emphasis on the moral and social
utility of history; (7) a tendency to see politics as a conspiratorial
process in which dominant abstractions masked the play of the real
historical forces; and (8) an interpretation of American history which
stressed economic and/or geographical forces and found a central theme
in the conflict of agrarianism with commercialism and capitalism.[4]

Grob and Billias equate the Progressive historians with the "second
generation of professional scholars" and suggest that they dominated
American historical writing from 1910 to 1945. Hofstadter extends
that dominance even a bit further by suggesting that "somewhere
around 1950 the tide began to run out for this [Progressive] view of
our history, and conflict as a vitalizing idea began to be contested by
the notion of a pervasive American consensus." Hofstadter believed
that "probably the last distinguished historical studies to be written
squarely in the Progressive tradition" were Arthur M. Schlesinger,
Jr.'s *The Age of Jackson,* published in 1945, and Merrill Jensen's *The
New Nation: A History of the United States during the Confederation,
1781–1789,* published in 1950.[5]

Obviously, if Progressive history really dominated American historical writing for so long, many historians wrote Progressive history.
Wise lists five Progressives who shaped the field: Turner, Beard, Parrington, Robinson, and Becker. James Harvey Robinson, however,
influential though he was, did most of his important work in European history. And Carl Becker, while he was surely important and
has deserved mention on several occasions in these pages, does not
quite stand up to the others in terms of influence. Hofstadter, while

acknowledging that Becker "had a subtler mind and wrote better prose" than any of the others, still felt that "no single book of Becker's compared in its effects" to theirs. His criterion was, above all, influence—"and among writers on American history it was Turner, Beard, and Parrington who gave us the pivotal ideas of the first half of the twentieth century."[6]

Frederick Jackson Turner

When Frederick Jackson Turner was growing to manhood, historical interests in the United States were still centered for the most part in a few communities close to the East Coast. Even when historians did enlarge their narratives to survey more of the country than the East Coast, they tended to skip over western sections hurriedly or to write of them without much understanding of their relationship to the East; for the most part they described a kind of enlarged New England.

A few students, however, watching the growth of the West in the midnineteenth century, were aware of the place of the frontier in American development: E. L. Godkin, editor of the *Nation*, McMaster, and James Bryce, to name three. Bryce, in his chapter "The Temper of the West" in *The American Commonwealth*, spoke of the West as "the most American part of America; that is to say, the part where those features which distinguish America from Europe come out in the strongest relief. What Europe is to Asia, what England is to the rest of Europe, what America is to England, that the Western States and Territories are to the Atlantic States, the heat and pressure and hurry of life always growing as we follow the path of the sun." Not until Turner began writing, however, was a clearly formulated expression of the place of the frontier in American life presented to students of American history.[7]

Turner was born in 1861 in Portage, Wisconsin, a region not yet out of the frontier stage of development. In an autobiographical note he said that he hunted and fished among Indian neighbors who came to town "to buy paints and trinkets and sell furs," and he asks, "Is it strange that I saw the frontier as a real thing and experienced its changes?" On his mother's side he was descended from preachers; he asks again, "Is it strange that I preached of the frontier?"[8]

Turner studied at the University of Wisconsin and then went to Johns Hopkins, where he took his doctoral degree in 1890. At Wisconsin he studied with William F. Allen, who had an important influence upon him, directing his attention to economic and cultural factors in history and to the role of western expansion in American development. More generally, Turner clearly remembered Allen's dictum "No historical fact is of any value except so far as it helps us to understand human nature or the working of historic forces." At Johns Hopkins he was influenced by Richard T. Ely, Albion W. Small, and Woodrow Wilson; the latter helped stir Turner's resentment against the predominant New England historians for their flagrant neglect of the South and West. Also, he clearly read the work of Italian political economist Achille Loria, because Turner's idea that "free" (unoccupied) land was the key to a nation's economic growth was originally Loria's.

Back at Wisconsin, where Turner was a member of the faculty until 1910, he did his most effective teaching. When Carl Becker, a freshman at the time, saw Turner in 1893, the young professor was so zestful and buoyant that he lifted students to new realms of the intellectual life. From no other man, said Becker, did he "ever get in quite the same measure that sense of watching a first-class mind at work on its own account . . . the most delightful sense in the world of sitting there waiting for ideas to be born; expectantly waiting for secret meanings, convenient explanatory hypotheses to be discovered, lurking as like as not under the dullest mass of drab facts ever seen." As a teacher Turner was not given to passing on to his students final judgments, and he was equally reluctant to do so in his writing. Born with a truly intellectual curiosity, he had a mind that was ever alert, fresh, and independent and which sought its own answers to the many problems that face a historian. "I have had a lot of fun exploring, getting lost and getting back, and telling my companions about it," he once wrote to Becker.[9]

In his earliest, little-known writings and in his teaching Turner suggested such broad areas of research and looked at American history with such wide-angled vision that it scarcely does him justice to regard him only as a sectional or frontier historian; in fact, he had strong objections to being labeled "primarily a Western historian." He certainly thought of himself as a truly nationalist historian, and, indeed, he believed that even for international organizations (such as the League of Nations) his knowledge of American frontier and sectional experience enabled him to contribute suggestions of significance. And yet because of his major writings and through the distorted emphasis of overzealous students, his name has been associated with a narrower, western view of American history.

Dissatisfied with the overemphasis on Herbert Baxter Adams's "germ theory of politics," which traced American political institutions back to primitive German customs, Turner sought an explanation in terms of the American environment. Thus in his earliest published work, *The Character and Influence of the Indian Trade in Wisconsin* (actually his doctoral dissertation and based on his master's thesis), he posed the question which in one way or another he tried to answer ever afterward. "The exploitation of the Indian is generally dismissed," he observed, "with the convenient explanatory phrase, 'the march of civilization.'" Then came his troubling question: "But how did it march?" Confining his research to America to illustrate this social process (though Adams had said that American institutions had already been sufficiently studied), Turner foreshadowed his own later approach when he wrote of the effects of the trading post upon the white man: "In every country the exploitation of the wild beasts, and of the raw-products generally, causes the entry of the disintegrating and transforming influences of a higher civilization."[10] And in studying American civilization Turner was especially interested in finding out what gave it the particular stamp that served to differentiate it from an older European civilization.

The West appealed to him as a factor in the creation of American life. While Rhodes and von Holst were immersed in the slavery struggle and other historians—Roosevelt, Winsor, and Thwaites—were attracted to the epic period of the West, Turner was "trying to see it as a whole . . . on its institutional, social, economic and political side." He saw that "there was a persistent persuasive influence in American life which did not get its full attention from those who thought in terms of North and South, as well as from those who approached the West as fighting ground, or ground for exploration history." He was less interested in the West as a region in itself than as an illustration of the process of American development.[11]

Turner's ideas gradually matured, and he presented them in 1893 before the annual meeting of the American Historical Association in an essay entitled "The Significance of the Frontier in American History." Word for word, probably no piece of American historical writing ever had such impact. In his first sentences he referred to the closing of the frontier and then added: "Up to our own day American history has been in a large degree the history of the colonization of the Great West. The existence of an area of free land, its continuous recession, and the advance of American settlement westward, explain American development."[12] Because of contact with each new frontier in its movement westward, American social development was in a constant process of being reborn, and it was this "continuous touch with the simplicity of primitive society" that furnished "the forces dominating American character. . . . The true point of view in the history of this nation is not the Atlantic Coast," said the professor from Wisconsin, "it is the Great West."

In transforming the wilderness, the pioneer was at first barbarized, but slowly he and the wilderness changed, and in that change a new personality was created that was distinctly American. The advance of the frontier, said Turner, "has meant a steady movement away from the influence of Europe, a steady growth of independence on American lines. And to study this advance, the men who grew up under these conditions, and the political, economic, and social results of it, is to study the really American part of our history." Unlike the Atlantic seaboard, where the population was predominantly English, the frontier was a region where immigrants became "Americanized, liberated, and fused into a mixed race English in neither nationality nor characteristics." It was the frontier with its vast public domain that conditioned "the growth of nationalism and the evolution of American political institutions," but most importantly the frontier profoundly affected the growth of individualism and democracy. Frontier life determined the type of religious organization built up in the United States and also had a marked effect in shaping intellectual characteristics—the inventive mind, often coarse and strong, with a comprehensive grasp of material things and exhibiting an unquiet, nervous energy. The disappearance of the frontier in 1890, said Turner, marked the closing of the first period of American history.

Turner realized that if we study the past, at least in part, to help us understand the present we must also utilize the insights of the present to help us understand the past. He wrote as insightfully as anyone ever has of the relationship between past and present: "A comprehension of the United States today, an understanding of the rise and progress of the forces which have made it what it is, demands that we should rework our history from the new points of view afforded by the present."

With the passing of the frontier came a gradual approach to social uniformity in the United States, and, as Turner watched this change, he endeavored to comprehend the play of forces in the country. Again, to understand the contemporary scene he sought light in the past, and in several essays he expounded the idea that the United States was a federation of sections whose rival interests created tensions which were eased by compromise in Congress.[13] Turner noted again and again the analogy between American sections and the nations of Europe; America, he believed, should be thought of in continental terms, not only in national terms. Unlike European countries, however, which must compose their clashing interests either peacefully by conferences or violently by war, the sections of the United States may compose theirs by parliamentary procedure. He was certain that sectionalism was not likely to disappear. Turner was careful to note that neither physical geography nor economic interests were the only factors in sectionalism; the habits of thought peculiar to various stocks were likewise of great importance. "We must shape our national action," he said, "to the fact of a vast and varied Union of unlike sections."

Over a period of forty years Turner continued to study his great theme, and occasionally he published essays and monographs illustrating his ideas. Once, by dint of A. B. Hart's persistent editorial persuasion, Turner was inveigled into writing a volume, the *Rise of the New West, 1819–1829,* for the American Nation series (1906). The rise of the new West, said the author, was "the most significant fact in American history in the years immediately following the War of 1812." Turner referred to the strongly national and democratic character of the West: "By the march of the westerners away from their native states to the public domain of the nation, and by their organization as territories of the United States, they lost that state particularism which distinguished many of the old commonwealths of the coast. . . . It was a self-confident section, believing in its right to share in government, and troubled by no doubts of its capacity to rule."

In several places in his writing, but especially in the *Rise of the New West,* Turner waxed eloquent about the man he considered in many ways the ultimate frontiersman. "If Henry Clay was one of the favorites of the west, Andrew Jackson was the west itself," wrote Turner. Jackson was "the very personification of the contentious, nationalistic democracy of the interior"; he was "the national hero, the self-made man, the incarnation of the popular ideal of democracy." Appropriately, the book was dedicated to Turner's father, Andrew Jackson Turner. Explaining what was happening as Jackson rose to power and frontier democracy spread back to the East, Turner continued: "Around this unique personality there began to gather all those democratic forces . . . characteristic of the interior of the country, reinforced by the democracy of the cities, growing into self-consciousness and power." A "new force," Turner continued, was making its presence felt in American life. "This fiery Tennesseean was becoming the political idol of a popular movement which swept across all sections, with but slight regard to their separate economic interests. The rude, strong, turbulent democracy of the west and of the country found in him its natural leader."

Turner's writing did not often take the form of a continuous narrative; in fact, he rarely concerned himself with history in the conventional sense of a narrative of events chronologically arranged. As Becker expressed it, Turner's writing is "all essentially descriptive, explicative, expository." Students of history waited in vain for the comprehensive work that was never written, for the illuminating generalizations that Turner worked out compressed much material into few pages. In his last years he was a research associate at the Huntington Library in California, and while there he almost brought to completion *The United States, 1830–1850: The Nation and Its Sections;* it was published posthumously in 1935.[14] Sadly, both of Turner's volumes to win the Pulitzer Prize (this one and a collection of essays published in 1932 entitled *The Significance of Sections in American History*) did so after his death in 1932.

Turner had long believed that the period from 1830 to 1850 offered "the best opportunity for a new work," the West in particular needing special study, "which as yet it hasn't received." His book on that period progressed slowly, however. "I find it very hard to write," he told a friend, "and suspect that I need to break for the wilderness and freshen up—rather than tie myself to the chair."

In many ways the most satisfying chapters of *The United States, 1830–1850* were those describing the various sections of the country. Although Turner's bias was always in favor of the West, he constantly referred to the great influence that native and transplanted New Englanders, as well as New Yorkers, had had in the life of this period. The generalizations that enriched his other writings were scattered in this volume also, and now, more than before, Turner inclined to an interpretation in terms of a class struggle. In speaking of the New York Locofoco party, for example, he said that

the movement was a landmark in the rise of organized demands of the common people for the control of government in the interests of their own economic and spiritual welfare. It presaged a succession of later movements (strongest in the western sections to which New England and New York sent settlers) that included the organization of Anti-Monopolists, Grangers, Populists, and the whole group of later progressive parties.

In a discussion of the U.S. Bank and the failure to renew its charter, Turner said: "The severance of official connection between the national government and the capitalist was one of the most important steps in American history. Thenceforth the industrial interests were obliged to act by underground methods and by the lobby."

This score of years appeared to Turner as one of fundamental importance in the history of the country, for the very character of its population was then changing because of increased immigration. In its economic, political, and intellectual life it was striking out in new directions: "Between 1830 and 1850 there was . . . a cycle of change in American ideals and in the composition of the people."

The search for the meaning of American life was ever in Turner's heart, and there was a warm pride that ran through much of his writing—the pride of frontier birth. In his later years he was deeply troubled by the question of the reconciliation and application to civilization in the twentieth century of frontier ideals of individualism and democracy. The exuberance and vitality of his writing and teaching, however, reflected for the most part a natural optimism.

In the process of developing his frontier thesis Turner more than once halted to ask himself, and his friends as well, whether he had overemphasized it. Scarcely any well-formulated criticism was directed at the thesis during his lifetime, although Channing, his Harvard colleague, voiced skepticism of its value. Then, in a sudden rush, a flood of vigorous statements were made against the Turner doctrine.

If it is true that Henry Adams has had more written *about* him than any other American historian, Frederick Jackson Turner has probably *stimulated* more writing than any other—about him, surely, both praise and criticism, but he also inspired fresh pursuits in every direction, all born from Turner's plethora of pregnant ideas. Four writers are crucial to an effort at a final evaluation of Turner the historian: Wilbur R. Jacobs, Howard R. Lamar, Ray Allen Billington, and Richard Hofstadter.

Jacobs contributed the essay on Turner to a volume entitled *Turner, Bolton and Webb: Three Historians of the American Frontier*, published in 1965. Jacobs insists in the preface to a reprinting of the volume in 1979 that "in the late 1970's Turner's historical interpretations continue to appear in numerous studies, including urban frontier histories, where his ideas are re-examined with the aid of masses of quantitative data not easily obtained in his day." Jacobs is also insistent that Turner should not be thought of as just a frontier historian, and he quotes Turner himself on this subject: "Although my work has laid stress upon two aspects of American history—the frontier and the sections (in the sense of geographical regions, or provinces . . .), I do not think of myself as primarily either a western historian, or a human geographer." Rather, he said, he had stressed these factors because they had been neglected, "but fundamentally I have been interested in the inter-relations of economics, politics, sociology, culture in general, with the geographic factors, in explaining the United States of today by means of its history thus broadly taken. Perhaps this is one of the many reasons why I have not been more voluminous!"[15]

The last comment necessitates further consideration of why Turner never wrote more than one book; his others were either incomplete or collections of essays; he signed contracts for at least nine books that were never written. Surely no other historian who wrote so little has come to be considered as important as Turner has, and all studies of him try to account for it. Jacobs quotes Avery O. Craven, a Turner student: "The trouble was that his conception of 'what is history,' was so complex that neither he nor anyone else could or can do much with it beyond the essay form." Jacobs concludes that Turner's "publications were held in check by precisely those qualities which made him a historian of such enduring value," namely, "his awareness of the enormous scope and complexity of history which precluded rash and casual judgments, and his strong sense of responsibility to his profession which caused him to busy himself so magnificently with its future practitioners, his students." Turner had, in short, all the difficulties of any other writer, magnified, in addition to some others. Hofstadter has the final word: "It is perhaps fairest to think of him not as a rich productive force full of primal energy who perversely failed to realize his talents, but rather as a constitutional non-writer whose work was wrung out of himself at immense psychic cost."[16]

In 1969, Howard R. Lamar contributed the selection on Turner to the *Pastmasters* volume edited by Marcus Cunliffe and Robin Winks. Though one of Lamar's contributions was to "test" the Turner thesis in relation to his own studies of the Dakotas and New Mexico and to find it inapplicable in several ways, he still had great praise for Turner, "a pioneer social historian and the father of a 'multiple hypothesis' theory of history." Turner was also, in Lamar's view, a good economist; he anticipated the ideas and methods of James Harvey Robinson's *New History* by twenty years and "formulated a theory concerning the role of sections in American history, which still shapes the framework of most college history courses that treat the coming of the Civil War." Lamar wrote, "Turner's concepts also anticipated some of the approaches used in the behavioral sciences today, and he is a respectable collateral, if not direct, ancestor of today's quantifying historians."

Lamar understood well why Turner's view of history had come to be so commonly accepted by the people: "Turner's greatest practical achievement may well be that he made every community feel it had contributed to the shaping of American democracy, for the thesis brilliantly related the average man and his past to national history and the national character." Turner's greatest overall contribution, however, at least for Lamar, was "his appreciation of the part free land played in the thoughts, plans, and economy of eighteenth- and nineteenth-century Americans." Finally, while Turner "may not have been a great historian in the orthodox sense," he was an "intuitive genius." Lamar concluded: "Somewhat like Thomas Jefferson he felt that he had the 'sense of America'; and just as Jefferson can be called democracy's spokesman, Turner deserves the title 'democracy's historian.' Until the words 'frontier,' 'free land,' and 'democracy' disappear from the American historians' vocabulary, the name of Turner remains secure."

The person who proved to be the greatest—at least most persistent—disciple of Frederick Jackson Turner was Ray Allen Billington. Indeed, it is hardly an overstatement that Billington (who became after a teaching career senior research associate in the Henry E. Huntington Library, thus following in his mentor's footsteps) made his entire life as a historian an extension of Turner's. In 1940, when he first published the widely used textbook *Westward Expansion: A History of the American Frontier*, he dedicated it to Frederick Merk, Turner's successor in frontier history at Harvard, "whose inspirational teaching and meticulous scholarship perpetuate the traditions of Frederick Jackson Turner." Billington, too, boldly stated in his preface that "this book attempts to follow the pattern that Frederick Jackson Turner might have used had he ever compressed his voluminous researches on the American frontier within one volume." In 1956, Billington was given the opportunity to contribute a volume on *The Far Western Frontier, 1830–1860* to the New American Nation series, and he made it clear that he had a "dual objective" in the book: "to describe, as thoroughly as space limitations permitted, both the movement of settlers into the Far West and the national or world events which directly influenced their migration" and "to advance evidence pertaining to the generations-old conflict over the so-called 'frontier hypothesis.'" Another volume on the frontier in that series, *The Rise of the West, 1754–1830*, by Francis S. Philbrick, published in 1965, took issue with Turner strongly but, most readers felt, ineffectively.

In 1973, Billington published a massive and generally excellent scholarly biography of Turner entitled *Frederick Jackson Turner: Historian, Scholar, Teacher*. His last work before his death was *Land of Savagery, Land of Promise: The European Image of the American Frontier*, a selection of the History Book Club in 1981 and praised by Lamar as possibly "the most important book about the frontier image since Henry Nash Smith's classic *Virgin Land: The American West as Symbol and Myth* appeared in 1950."[17]

Billington's major contribution was in editing, both the works of Turner and those of his critics and defenders. *Frontier and Section: Selected Essays of Frederick Jackson Turner* (1961) is the best example of the former; *The Frontier Thesis: Valid Interpretation of American History?* (1966), of the latter. Billington obviously admired Turner greatly; the tone of his introduction to the *Frontier and Section* volume is revealed by its title, "Frederick Jackson Turner—Universal Historian." Turner, claimed Billington, "pioneered most of the concepts and methods currently employed by historians." Yet Billington was willing to admit the validity of some of the criticisms of the frontier thesis, writing in 1965 in a pamphlet published by the American Historical Association:

Turner did pen unsubstantiated generalizations; Turner did allow his poetic instincts to lead him along metaphorical bypaths that obscured rather than defined his exact meanings. He did overemphasize geographic forces . . . . He did generalize too widely on the basis of limited observation. He did minimize the continuing influence of Europe's civilization on that of the United States, just as he minimized the impact of industrialization, urbanization, and immigration.[18]

Billington edited a multivolume series entitled Histories of the American Frontier. His own contribution, *America's Frontier Heritage*, published in 1966, was a reexamination of the Turner thesis, its critics, and its defenders in the light of modern findings in both history and the social sciences. Billington was somewhat critical of both opponents and defenders of Turner: both "squandered their energies on an academic trifle, for the validity of the frontier hypothesis had nothing whatever to do with Turner's *statement* of that hypothesis. If biologists had followed the same path," Billington suggested, "they would still be quarreling over the meaning of semantic mysteries in Darwin's *Origin of Species.*" What emerges at the end of Billington's book is a moderate, revised, modernized, intelligent restatement of Turner's thesis. Relics of the pioneer heritage do indeed remain to distinguish Americans from their contemporaries beyond the seas, wrote Billington:

Their faith in democratic institutions, their belief in equality, their insistence that class lines shall never hinder social mobility, their wasteful economy, their unwillingness to admit that automation has lessened the need for hard work, their lack of attachment to place, their eagerness to experiment and to favor the new over the old, all mark the people of the United States as unique. To say that these characteristics and attitudes were solely the result of a pioneering past is to ignore many other forces that have helped shape the American character. But to deny that three centuries of frontiering endowed the people with some of their most distinctive traits is to neglect a basic molding force that has been the source of the nation's greatest strength — and some of its most regrettable weaknesses.[19]

In *The Frontier Thesis,* Billington wrote that "no summary of the arguments against the frontier thesis is more comprehensive than that prepared by Richard Hofstadter,"[20] whose essay of 1949 in the *American Scholar,* "Turner and the Frontier Myth," is included in the summary section under the heading "The Thesis Disputed." That is true yet at the same time deceptive, for Hofstadter has also given us one of the most balanced and finest assessments of Turner available in his *Progressive Historians.*

Certainly Hofstadter could be devastating—for example, when he referred to the "blandness" of Turner's mind and again when he listed the aspects of western development which he felt should have shamed Turner and offset his pride: "riotous land speculation, vigilantism, and ruthless despoiling of the continent, the arrogance of American expansionism, the pathetic tale of the Indians, anti-Mexican and anti-Chinese nativism, the crudeness, even the near-savagery, to which men were reduced on some portions of the frontier." Concluded Hofstadter:

He did not fail to acknowledge now and then the existence of such things, but he did neglect to write about them with specificity or emphasis: it was not just that they did not arouse his indignation but that they seem not to have deeply engaged his interest and that he saw no imperative reason why Americans should be encouraged to confront these aspects of their frontier heritage. He saw history partly as science, partly as art, partly as a fountain-head of national and sectional pride, but he used it very sparingly as an instrument of intellectual or social criticism.[21]

That is strong criticism, indeed, the last charge seeming almost to disqualify Turner as a Progressive historian, for one of the major tenets of that creed, of course, was to use history as a tool for bringing about needed reform.

Yet Hofstadter certainly also recognized Turner's contribution. He quoted with apparent approval Beard's claim that Turner's essay of 1893 had "a more profound influence on thought about American history than any other essay or volume ever written on the subject." And he considered Turner "the first of the great professionals," not only because he "charted out a very large part of the course that American historiography was to run for the next generation" but also, especially, because he forged "a new historical genre, the analytical essay." Hofstadter concluded, "In certain ways, all modern American historical writing follows Turner in his emphasis on posing and defining historical problems, and in his belief that new methods were needed to solve them."[22]

Finally, Hofstadter understood better than most the real significance of the vast amount of Turner criticism. Turner's thesis "came under fire above all because its premises seemed incongruous with the realities of the Great Depression and the Second World War." In the end, however, the "mountain of Turner criticism is his most certain monument. Among all the historians of the United States it was Turner alone of whom we can now say with certainty that he opened a controversy that was large enough to command the attention of his peers for four generations."[23]

Charles A. Beard

When Beard said of Turner's "Significance" essay that it had "a more profound influence on thought about American history than any other essay or volume ever written on the subject," he made a claim that many would make for his own book *An Economic Interpretation of the Constitution of the United States*, published in 1913. Possibly no other American historian in the twentieth century had a wider influence than did Charles Austin Beard, who had a large audience among scholars and an even larger one among the general public. His skepticism, his inspired teaching, his literary skill, and his insistence that scholars should actively participate in public life endeared him to a host of people in and out of the groves of academe. Beard's youthful mind was stirred to question the status quo, influenced by Colonel James Riley Weaver, his teacher at DePauw University, and stimulated by his experiences at Oxford and his reading of John Ruskin. Beard, in turn, during his years of teaching in Columbia became a freshening breeze that swept away academic staleness.

In association with James Harvey Robinson, Beard produced textbooks of European history that immensely improved the standards of such publications. "The present has hitherto been the willing victim of the past; the time has now come when it should turn on the past and exploit it in the interests of advance," Robinson wrote in *The New History* in 1912. In one of the texts that he and Beard wrote together, this approach was very much in evidence. It had been "a common defect of our historical manuals," said the preface to *The Development of Modern Europe* in 1907, that they "have ordinarily failed to connect the past with the present." To offset that, they "consistently subordinated the past to the present," with the "ever-conscious aim to enable the reader to catch up with his own times." They also devoted "much less space to purely political and military events" and much more to "the more fundamental economic matters." Also with Robinson, Beard published sources, making it possible for young students to become acquainted with the primary materials of history, and he was in addition the sole author of texts on American history and politics.

Hofstadter helpfully suggested that Beard's massive body of work could be divided into three major areas: the economic interpretation of history, historical relativism, and continental isolationism. Beard made at least two significant contributions of original research with his *Economic Interpretation of the Constitution* in 1913 and his *Economic Origins of Jeffersonian Democracy* in 1915. The former was something of a bombshell in historical circles, although other writers had anticipated Beard in pointing to the economic factors that played a part in the adoption of the Constitution. Beard, however, dug up forgotten records showing that holders of the government debt ardently wished to create a strong government which would pay it off.

At the end of his long, complex *Economic Interpretation*—Beard himself called it a "long and arid survey"—Beard drew thirteen conclusions. They are brief enough and important enough to be quoted in their entirety:

The movement for the Constitution of the United States was originated and carried through principally by four groups of personalty interests which had been adversely affected under the Articles of Confederation: money, public securities, manufactures, and trade and shipping.

The first firm steps toward the formation of the Constitution were taken by a small and active group of men immediately interested through their personal possessions in the outcome of their labors.

No popular vote was taken directly or indirectly on the proposition to call the Convention which drafted the Constitution.

A large propertyless mass was, under the prevailing suffrage qualifications, excluded at the outset from participation (through representatives) in the work of framing the Constitution.

The members of the Philadelphia Convention which drafted the Constitution were, with a few exceptions, immediately, directly, and personally interested in, and derived economic advantages from, the establishment of the new system.

The Constitution was essentially an economic document based upon the concept that the fundamental private rights of property are anterior to government and morally beyond the reach of popular majorities.

The major portion of the members of the Convention are on record as recognizing the claim of property to a special and defensive position in the Constitution.

In the ratification of the Constitution, about three-fourths of the adult males failed to vote on the question, having abstained from the elections at which delegates to the state conventions were chosen, either on account of their indifference or their disfranchisement by property qualifications.

The Constitution was ratified by a vote of probably not more than one-sixth of the adult males.

It is questionable whether a majority of the voters participating in the elections for the state conventions in New York, Massachusetts, New Hampshire, Virginia, and South Carolina, actually approved the ratification of the Constitution.

The leaders who supported the Constitution in the ratifying conventions represented the same economic groups as the members of the Philadelphia Convention; and in a large number of instances they were also directly and personally interested in the outcome of their efforts.

In the ratification, it became manifest that the line of cleavage for and against the Constitution was between substantial personalty interests on the one hand and the small farming and debtor interests on the other.

The Constitution was not created by "the whole people" as the jurists have said; neither was it created by "the states" as Southern nullifiers long contended; but it was the work of a consolidated group whose interests knew no state boundaries and were truly national in their scope.

Beard's *Economic Interpretation* became an important document in the literature of Progressivism, many hailing it as a weapon against conservatism. "The time has come," said one Wisconsin Populist, "when all of us, who are looking toward a wider national life, must realize that the Constitution, which has ever been the retreat of privilege, must be changed. When we once realize that this was a human document, written by men acting in many cases under human impulse, we shall have achieved the initial attitude necessary to change it. Professor Beard's book, scholarly and incisive, will do more than any other volume to set us right."

"Filthy lies and rotten perversions . . . libelous, vicious, and damnable in its influence," was the verdict of Warren G. Harding's Marion, Ohio, newspaper on Beard's work; said the headline: "Scavengers, Hyena-Like, Desecrate the Graves of the Dead Patriots We Revere." That was not an uncommon reaction outside the academy, but inside its reception was on the whole quite favorable. Soon it had become the generally accepted view and had worked its way into all the textbooks. Though Beard himself began to back off a bit from his views in later works, it was not until the era of "consensus" history in the 1950s that two book-length criticisms of his work appeared.

In 1956, Robert E. Brown chose to publish his head-on confrontation with Beard, entitled *Charles Beard and the Constitution: A Critical Analysis of "An Economic Interpretation of the Constitution."* Brown's chapter titles were Beard's chapter titles, in quotation marks; he even offered a conclusion to answer each of Beard's. Essentially, Brown considered the Constitution a political document rather than an economic one. His central thrust, however, was to attack Beard's historical method; certainly it must be conceded that he found Beard guilty of some mistakes, perhaps even manipulations, in that area. He suggested that his own conclusions really added up to two major propositions: "The Constitution was adopted in a society which was fundamentally democratic, not undemocratic; and it was adopted by a people who were primarily middle-class property owners, especially farmers who owned realty, not just by the owners of personalty."[24] In a "review" of Beard's book in the *Social Science Quarterly* in 1976, Brown argued that "Beard failed to use easily-available evidence and often his evidence refuted his thesis. Instead of being an economic document put over on the people by upper-class capitalists in an undemocratic society, as Beard had said, Brown thought that "the Constitution was the product of a middle-class, agrarian, democratic society, the people were well-informed of the issues, and far from being a close fight, the 65 percent vote for the Constitution represented a landslide."[25] Hofstadter was right that Brown's was "a strange work." "One puts it down," Hofstadter wrote, "with the feeling of having lived through an obsessive pursuit, but it is a telling and important book whose appearance guaranteed that the Beardian view could never again enjoy an unchallenged position."[26]

The other book opposing Beard, published in 1958 by Forrest McDonald, was an entirely different matter. Again, the title is revealing: *We the People: The Economic Origins of the Constitution*, implying no attack and at least acknowledging that there could be economic origins of the Constitution. McDonald also wrote an essay on Beard for Cunliffe and Winks's *Pastmasters*, in which he described his own work as "an effort to compile economic biographies of the 1,805 men directly involved in the writing and ratification of the Constitution, and otherwise to fill in the details and do the research that Beard did not do."[27] McDonald's economic interpretation thus differed from Beard's in several particulars. In many ways the most helpful portion of McDonald's work was his "test" of Beard's thesis through a state-by-state analysis of the ratification process. In some states Beard held up fairly well, but in most he did not. As Hofstadter noted, McDonald showed himself to be "on one count closer to Beard than he cares to admit: he apparently agrees that the making of the Constitution will conform to a severely economic interpretation, once we have got our economics right."[28]

The critics of Beard—Brown, McDonald, and others—did not damage Beard's thesis as much as they and some of their admirers thought. Certainly to say that they "shattered" Beard or that his view was thereafter "discarded" by most American historians constitutes a gross exaggeration. "Beard somehow stays alive," said consensus historian Louis Hartz, because "as in the case of Marx, you merely demonstrate your subservience to a thinker when you spend your time trying to disprove him." As Hofstader concluded, "This is Beard's most enduring triumph: he no longer persuades, but he still sets the terms of the debate, even for those who are least persuaded."[29] Perhaps in the final analysis the suggestion of New Left historian Staughton Lynd that it is time to move "Beyond Beard" is most meaningful at this point.[30] That is to say, it is time to take the brilliant insight that Beard's book of 1913 obviously gave us, work into it the valuable modifications of his critics, and move ahead, rather than forever setting Beard up or knocking him down.

Beard continued his economic interpretation of American history in *The Economic Origins of Jeffersonian Democracy*. Hofstadter called it "a readable, shrewd, often highly illuminating book, . . . the most solid of his early works."[31] "Jeffersonian democracy did not imply any abandonment of the property, and particularly the landed, qualifications on the suffrage or office-holding," summarized Beard at the end of the book, nor did it involve "any fundamental alterations in the national Constitution which the Federalists had designed as a foil to the levelling propensities of the masses" or "propose any new devices for a more immediate and direct control of the voters over the instrumentalities of government." What, then, was Jeffersonian democracy? It "simply meant the possession of the federal government by the agrarian masses led by an aristocracy of slave-owning planters, and the theoretical repudiation of the right to use the Government for the benefit of any capitalistic groups, fiscal, banking, or manufacturing."

Beard's wife, Mary, was the coauthor of *The Rise of American Civilization*, published in 1927. It marked a significant departure for Beard in other ways, too: the economic interpretation was still very much present, though a bit toned down at times and placed in perspective with other factors; and the style was in marked contrast to his earlier works: more expansive, rhetorical, colorful, and, in short, more popular. According to Hofstadter, Beard "reached the peak of his public influence as a historian" with this two-volume general history, which "did more than any other such book of the twentieth century to define American history for the reading public."[32]

The work opened with a sentence showing clearly the Beards' belief in the utilitarian value of history: "The history of a civilization, if intelligently conceived, may be an instrument of civilization." They added, "The history of a civilization is essentially dynamic, suggesting capacities yet unexplored and hinting of emancipation from outward necessities." Their conception of history, like Voltaire's, was that it should stimulate self-criticism and aid in producing a richer intellectual climate. A more important place was given to women than was customarily done in the works of most other historians; this doubtless reflected Mary Beard's influence, for she was a pioneer in women's history. The distance that Beard had traveled since the time when a strict economic determinism had appeared of overwhelming significance to him may be measured by this statement: "The heritage, economics, politics, culture, and international filiations of any civilization are so closely woven by fate into one fabric that no human eye can discern the beginnings of its warp or woof. And any economic interpretation, any political theory, and literary criticism, any aesthetic appreciation, which ignores this perplexing fact, is of necessity superficial."

The work was divided into two sections, one on the era of agriculture and one on the era of industry, and the authors were concerned to show the influence of these respective ways of life on the psychology of people living them. With a grasp of the literature that astonished even specialists, the Beards managed to convey most vividly the interrelationship of various phases of American civilization and its dynamic quality. In certain passages, which were perhaps overwritten, that dynamism appears self-conscious, though admittedly the American people were indeed hurrying forward.

The revolt of the colonies against England, the authors asserted, was an "economic, social and intellectual transformation of prime significance—the first of those modern world-shaking reconstructions in which mankind has sought to cut and fashion the tough and stubborn web of fact to fit the pattern of its dreams." The writers showed, too, a better understanding of the middle period than that which has been expressed by most others. In the long perspective, they believed, this period will "appear as the most changeful, most creative, most spirited epoch between the founding of the colonies and the end of the nineteenth century." The Civil War, they pointed out, "was merely the culmination of the deep-running transformation that shifted the center of gravity in American society between the inauguration of Jackson and Lincoln"; that shift resulted in the triumph of industry over agriculture. The fundamental question at issue was whether the political revolution, which was anticipated by the economic change, was to be peaceful or violent.

The programs of northern industrialists and southern planters indicated the width of the cleavage between them. The American currency system was in disrepair by 1860—dangerous for business enterprise but relatively beneficial to agrarians. The courts, too, had let down safeguards for property rights. These were the weaknesses that business enterprise meant to remedy as a result of the war. As for slavery, in the questionable view of the Beards', abolition "was a minor element in bringing on the irrepressible conflict" and of far less importance than economics.

Thus the authors reached the period of the Civil War, which they termed the "Second American Revolution." The program of the planter aristocracy in 1860 demanded the surrender of the northern and western majority

to the minority stockholders under the Constitution. It offered nothing to capitalism but capitulation. . . . Finally—and this as its revolutionary phase—it called upon the farmers and mechanics who had formed the bulk of Jacksonian Democracy in the North to acknowledge the absolute sovereignty of the planting interest. Besides driving a wedge into the nation the conditions laid down by the planters also split the Democratic party itself into two factions.

The results of the war were shown to be of far-reaching significance: a new power, that of the industrialists, was placed in the government; great changes were made in class relationships, in the acquisition and distribution of wealth, in industrial development, and in the Constitution as well, in order to safeguard these changes:

Viewed in the large, the supreme outcome of the civil strife was the destruction of the planting aristocracy which, with the aid of northern farmers and mechanics, had practically ruled the United States for a generation. A corollary to that result was the undisputed triumph of a new combination of power; northern capitalists and free farmers who emerged from the conflict richer and more numerous than ever. It was these . . . facts . . . that made the Civil War a social revolution.

Four billion dollars' worth of property—slaves—was destroyed without compensation in "the most stupendous act of sequestration in the history of Anglo-Saxon jurisprudence."

The remaining treatment of American history followed lines more familiar to the general student. The presentation of the material, here as elsewhere in the Beards' history, was masterly. The authors may have erred in minimizing the place of abolition in bringing on the war; they may have overestimated the economic factor as a cause of the war with Spain, missing the full significance of the weight of public opinion manufactured by the newspapers;[33] but even with its defects *The Rise of American Civilization* is likely to stand for some time as one of the most brilliant interpretations offered by historical scholarship.

The Rise of American Civilization was followed by *America in Midpassage* in 1939, carrying the narrative through the "golden glow" of the 1920s to 1939, again with Mary Beard as coauthor. It was a good survey of those years; the biting quality of the chapters on the panic of 1929 and its aftermath was in the Beards' best vein, but it lacked the interpretative power of the earlier publication. The Beards' earlier dislike of the course of much in American foreign policy was again manifest; particularly objectionable was the alleged use "of the power of the United States to force any scheme of politics or economy on other peoples." They held that foreign policy "could easily be made the instrument to stifle domestic wrongs under a blanket of militarist chauvinism, perhaps disguised by the high-sounding title of world peace." The interpretation of Franklin Delano Roosevelt's foreign policy was generally hostile—though not nearly as hostile as it was to become—for the government was represented as deliberately wishing to intervene in the European crisis of 1938–39.

The first half of *America in Midpassage* was a study of politics and business; the second half was concerned with labor organization and the various manifestations of culture in the United States. While the authors were skeptical and even scornful of certain phases of New Deal politics, they had nothing but praise for the Federal Art Project; for the first time Americans were made aware "of the extent and nature of their esthetic resources." Though Roosevelt came off poorly in various other writings by Beard, in this work the concluding estimate was generous: "In his numerous discourses [Roosevelt] discussed the basic human and economic problems of American society with a courage and range displayed by no predecessor in his office; . . . he carried on the tradition of humanistic democracy which from colonial times had been a powerful dynamic in the whole movement of American civilization and culture— economic, political, literary, scientific, and artistic."

Toward the end of *America in Midpassage* the Beards spoke of the intensification of the love for democracy in the United States, producing "a tumult of praise for the idea and its institutional embodiments." In their subsequent work *The American Spirit*, published in 1942, the whole complex of ideas which were expressed in American civilization was analyzed at considerable length. The meaning that was given to the word "civilization" itself and the transformations it had experienced since the end of the eighteenth century were the main subjects of the volume. It represented, said the authors, an "effort to grasp . . . the intellectual and moral qualities that Americans have deemed necessary to civilization in the United States." The Beards, stressing the unique character of American civilization, colored their study with a faint antiforeign bias, which became more marked in their *Basic History of the United States*.

Charles Beard left Columbia in 1917 in protest against the dismissal of some colleagues for their failure to support the war adequately in the eyes of the trustees. Typically, he blasted the trustees as having "no standing in the world of education" and being "reactionary and visionless in politics, narrow and medieval in religion." When Beard, by all accounts a great teacher, announced his departure to a large lecture class, he received a standing ovation which left him speechless, tears running down his face. He continued to publish prolifically and was a consistent activist for causes he believed in. In 1925, when Count Michael Károlyi, the former socialist premier of Hungary, was temporarily admitted to the United States by the State Department— on the condition that he would not discuss politics—Beard gave a speech in his honor at a meeting of the American Civil Liberties Union in New York. Beard lambasted the State Department and then launched into a tirade against the official follies that had become commonplace after the war: "During the past decade officers of the Government of the United States have bullied and beaten citizens and aliens beyond the limits of decency." In 1935, before a meeting of the National Education Association, Beard took on William Randolph Hearst and his newspaper empire. Hearst "has pandered to depraved tastes and has been an enemy of everything that is best in the American tradition" said Beard.[34]

Most important for our purposes, Beard in the 1930s began to recognize the reality of historical relativism. Showing the breadth of his interests in a manner rare today, Beard was elected president of both the American Political Science Association and the American Historical Association. His presidential address before the latter in 1933 was the kind of bombshell which Beard was so adept at dropping. He called it, significantly, "Written History as an Act of Faith."

Beard insistently called attention to the manner in which the historians' milieu affected his judgment, repudiating the "conception dominant among schoolmen during the latter part of the nineteenth century and the opening years of the twentieth century—the conception that it is possible to describe the past as it actually was, somewhat as the engineer describes a single machine." In the selection and ordering of materials the personal bias of historians, in addition to their social and economic experience, plays a determining part. In the very act of writing history, the historian performs an "act of faith":

He is thus in the position of a statesman dealing with public affairs; in writing he acts and in acting he makes choices . . . with respect to some conception of the nature of things. And the degree of his influence and immortality will depend upon the length and correctness of his forecast—upon the verdict of history yet to come. His faith is at bottom a conviction that something true can be known about the movement of history and his conviction is a subjective decision, not a purely objective discovery.

While the historian must continue to use the scientific method, its limitations must be recognized, for a science of history cannot be established which will re-create the past in all its fullness. The historian's task is to define his own relationship to contemporary thought, and it is his function to read the trend of the times. Beard's own conjecture was that the world was moving in the direction of collectivist democracy.

No one has ever stated the "climate of opinion" or "frame of reference" phenomenon better than Beard. "Has it not been said for a century or more that each historian who writes history is a product of his age and that his work reflects the spirit of the times, of a nation, race, group class, or section?" asked Beard. He then supplied the answer: "Every student of history knows that his colleagues have been influenced in their selection and ordering of materials by their biases, prejudices, beliefs, affections, general upbringing and experience, particularly social and economic; and if he has a sense of propriety, to say nothing of humor, he applies the canon to himself, leaving no exception to the rule."[35]

Not surprisingly, Beard's comments led to attack from mainstream historians. Theodore Clark Smith led it off in the *American Historical Review* the next year. Even Hofstadter, however, who acknowledges that Beard's thinking on the problem of historical knowledge was "not only derivative but fragmentary, obscure, and sometimes contradictory," notes correctly that "Beard's openness to heresy and his humility about what the historian can do contrast strikingly with Smith's smug dogmatism about the impartiality of existing historical science."[36]

A more interesting attack on the "frame of reference" idea took place seventeen years later—significantly, in the opening year of the decade of consensus in American historical writing, the same decade that saw the two major attacks on Beard's economic interpretation. Samuel Eliot Morison tellingly entitled his 1950 American Historical Association presidential address "Faith of a Historian," and he openly announced his intention to "pay my disrespects to what Robinson called 'The New History,' and what Beard called 'Written History as an Act of Faith.'" Said Morison, "Contrary to Beard, who urges you to adopt a conscious 'frame of reference' or form of Utopia as a basis for the selection and arrangement of facts, I say that every historian should be wary of his preconceptions, and be just as critical of them, skeptical of them, as of the writings of his predecessors." Morison stood firm on the oft-quoted Rankean sentence that the aim of history should be to "simply explain the event exactly as it happened." Beard's writings, especially *An Economic Interpretation of the Constitution*, "probably contributed more than [those of] any other writer, except Henry L. Mencken, to the scornful attitude of intellectuals toward American institutions, that followed after World War I." What we need, Morison concluded—some might say contradictorily—is a history of the United States "written from a sanely conservative point of view."[37]

With the passage of still more time, it can now be seen that Beard's comments on historical relativism (as did his earlier economic interpretations) told a fundamental truth, something that could hold up despite all detractors, something that needed to be heard, whether or not it was welcomed.

Even some of Beard's more ardent defenders are uncomfortable with the third and last stage of his work, that body of writing dealing with isolationism—or, as Beard preferred to call it, American continentalism. Morison was right when he claimed that Beard, in a sense, went full circle: "His 1913 book was received with greatest acclaim in the camp of Eugene Debs; his 1948 book evoked the wild enthusiasm of the Hearst press and the Chicago *Tribune*."[38]

The latter book was *President Roosevelt and the Coming of the War, 1941*; it had been preceded in 1946 by *American Foreign Policy in the Making, 1932-1940*, which was in the same vein. Morison referred to Beard's "evolution from left to right."[39] Hofstadter saw, more perceptively, that Beard still "displayed much the same style of mind that had characterized his earlier works." In these two books he was still "given to an excessive preoccupation with the motives and methods of those in power, still disposed to draw a somewhat conspiratorial interpretation of their acts, still trespassing now and then over the border between a sound feeling for economic realism and a crude variety of economic reductionism." The problem was simply that "a style of thought which gave heart to Progressivism when he was exposing the machinations of the Founding Fathers had become congenial to postwar ultraconservatives and Roosevelt-haters, now that he was exposing the machinations of F.D.R."[40]

What, exactly, did Beard say in these two books? There is an element of truth to Morison's claim that *Roosevelt and the Coming of the War* provides "an example of what happens when a historian consciously writes to shape the future instead of to illuminate the past; of a man becoming the victim or the prisoner of his 'frame of reference.'"[41] Hofstadter managed to summarize the two volumes together more succinctly than Beard ever did; Beard, said Hofstadter,

devoted over nine hundred pages to a detailed historical polemic intended to prove that, from an early date, F.D.R. practiced deceit on the American people, promising them peace while leading them gratuitously into war, and that finally, having failed in his other moves toward war, he provoked the Japanese into an attack on Pearl Harbor. Roosevelt's motives—to save Britain at whatever cost to the American people and to their constitutional forms, and in so doing to aggrandize his own power—had been abominable; his methods had been deceitful; the results of his policies had been disastrous.

Finally, Hofsadter noted that Beard's later writings on foreign policy came back repeatedly to a central theme: "The United States never goes to war because of anything that is happening outside its borders, but because politicians want to evade a domestic crisis or bankers and munitions makers want outlets for their capital and products."[42]

The wide-ranging mind of Charles A. Beard grasped the significance of Lord Acton's precept "Study problems, not periods." In R. G. Collingwood's language, "Scissors-and-paste historians study periods; they collect all the extant testimony about a certain limited group of events, and hope in vain that something will come of it. Scientific historians study problems; they ask questions, and if they are good historians they ask questions which they see their way to answering."[43] Beard was forever asking questions, and, following in the train of European scholars (notably Croce) who were more than a generation in advance of Americans in this matter, he and Carl Becker asked their fellow historians to consider the meaning of their research and their writing. Beard reminded them that in every era partisans had used the writing of history to capture the human mind. Roman Catholics and Protestants had done so, and Voltaire had made history "a dynamic force for the French Revolution"; at a later time, "under the guise of romanticism, history had served the reaction." Every history, it was maintained, was "a selection of facts made by some person or persons and is ordered or organized under the influence of some scheme of reference, interest or emphasis—avowed or unavowed—in the thought of the author or the authors."

Modern historians, said Beard, "working in the scientific spirit, seeking emancipation from the tyranny of old assumptions," should legitimately use their discipline to illuminate "all divisions of contemporary thought and all formulations of public policy." Historical writing, Beard believed, should be an instrument for the advancement of social reform. More than anyone else, Beard stimulated scholars to recognize frankly this functional nature of historical knowledge. He asked, "For what reason . . . are particular aspects of history chosen for emphasis and other aspects excluded?"

The "relativist" school of historical writing came under attack from various quarters. One criticism was that history would be made vulnerable to the activities of pressure groups who would dictate what interpretations historians would have to employ.[44] The accent on presentism by the relativist school, it was said, tended to distort the significance of earlier periods of history. As Robert L. Schuyler observed, the presentist will "omit or play down those past events and developments that do not seem to him to account for the present, no matter how important they may have seemed to men at the time, and conversely, he will throw his spotlight on those that do appear to him to explain the present, no matter how unimportant they may have seemed at the time." Genuine historical-mindedness evaluates institutions in the light of the needs they serve, and not in relation to a later set of conditions. Schuyler warned that out of presentism may come a kind of partisan history whose real intent is not so much to discover the truth about the past as it is to reveal the historian's emotions toward it.[45]

While presentism may be deplored, it is a fact that, in general, historians have consciously or unconsciously been guided by it, though not always in an obvious manner. Even historians such as Channing and McLaughlin, who are considered objective and free of the compulsion to see the past by the light of their own day, were clearly conscious of the effect of their own cultural experience in dictating their view of American history. In a vigorous defense of the relativists Merle Curti maintained that historians of that persuasion were no less likely to be "objective" and accurate in their narratives than their critics. Howard K. Beale, indeed, argued that "writers with a determined philosophy of life of which they are fully conscious and which they make clear to the reader stand a better chance of approaching 'objectivity' than did the older writers who, if they used 'scientific tools,' thought themselves completely 'objective.'"

It is difficult to make a final assessment of a historian such as Charles A. Beard. Because of the staying power of so many of his views and the universal chords that he struck, the final word on his historical work will doubtless never be pronounced. Even his most ardent enemies in terms of interpretation have nearly always shown respect and admiration for Beard, and certainly none have denied his impact. Indeed, Beard was clearly one of the truly great historians this country has ever produced, and he has arguably had more impact than any other of that elite group.

Hofstadter's final evaluation of Beard is brilliant:

Today Beard's reputation stands like an imposing ruin in the landscape of American historiography. What was once the grandest house in the province is now a ravaged survival, afflicted, in Beard's own words, by "the pallor of waning time." As an admirer of Charles A. Beard approaches the house that Beard built—a pile of formidable proportions and a testament to the vaulting ambitions of its architect—he can hardly fail to feel a twinge of melancholy. True, its lofty central portion, constructed in the days when the economic interpretation of history was flourishing, remains in a state of partial repair, and one suspects that several of the rooms, with a little ingenious improvisation, might still be habitable; but it has become shabby and suggests none of its former solidity and elegance. The east wing, inspired by historical relativism and showing a little sadly the traces of a wholly derivative design, is entirely neglected. The west wing, dedicated to continental isolationism, looks like a late and relatively hasty addition; a jerry-built affair, now a tattered shambles, it is nonetheless occupied from time to time by transient and raucous tenants, of whom, one is sure, the original owner would have disapproved.[46]

Hofstadter may be a bit harsh here, especially on Beard's contribution in the area of historical relativism. Hofstadter himself may realize this when he insists that Beard was "foremost among the American historians of his or any other generation in the search for a usable past."[47]

Vernon L. Parrington

In 1927, two volumes of a proposed three-volume work, *Main Currents in American Thought*, were published by Vernon Louis Parrington, professor of English in the University of Washington. Parrington died in 1929, while he was writing his third volume. Even though most of the final portion was only in sketch form, his publishers paid him the tribute of presenting it to the public in 1930.

Alfred Kazin believed that Parrington's work represented "the most ambitious single effort of the Progressive mind to understand itself"; Gene Wise called it the "single work which crystallizes what Progressive historical writing was generally up to"; and, most dramatically, Charles Crowe pronounced it "the Summa Theologica of Progressive history."[48] Such statements abound. Hofstader also praised Parrington, adding that he had only two predecessors of note in his field, Edward Eggleston and Moses Coit Tyler, and that *Main Currents* won a more prompt and enthusiastic acceptance than the first major works of Turner and Beard. Yet Hofstadter also noted that "the most striking thing about the reputation of V. L. Parrington, as we think of it today, is its abrupt decline."[49] That may be somewhat exaggerated. As late as the 1960s some universities still had courses in English or history departments called "Main Currents in American Thought," with Parrington as the text. Even Hofstadter acknowledged that Parrington was "still [in 1968] widely read, . . . in fact more widely read in the paperback era than he was at the peak of his influence." The intellectual historian Ralph H. Gabriel provides the important corrective: "If it is true that *Main Currents* is a ruin in the landscape of scholarship, then it is the Melrose Abbey of American historiography. It will long be visited."[50] Certainly most modern students of history are likely to find Parrington far more enjoyable to read than the other progressive historians, especially because of his colorful portraits of individual American thinkers, which either damned or glorified their subjects.

Until the eve of publication, when he made a change at the insistence of his publisher, Parrington intended to call his work "The

Democratic Spirit in American Literature" and to use as an epigraph Carl Becker's words, "The business of history is to arouse an intelligent discontent, to foster a fruitful radicalism." Although he did neither, both show something important about his approach. "Officially I am a teacher of English literature, but in reality my business in life is to wage war on the crude and selfish materialism that is biting so deeply into our national life and character," Parrington once wrote to a friend.[51]

Through the influence of Taine's *Histoire de la Littérature* and the work of a close friend and colleague, J. Allen Smith (who wrote on the economic basis of politics), Parrington was stimulated to a reexamination of American literature. He "envisaged American literature as American thought; . . . economic forces imprint their mark upon political, social, and religious institutions; literature expresses the result in its thought content." Parrington wished to relate the literature of a people to its whole civilization; to do so meant the selection of material on other than belletristic grounds. Hofstadter aptly characterized Parrington's work as "a history of the literary aspect of American politics and of the most overtly political aspects of American letters."[52]

Parrington's youth in Kansas was clouded by events that caused many of his generation to become Populists, and those experiences helped shape his own interpretation of American life and letters. Memories of low prices for crops and mortgaged farms left lifelong scars. Corn was used for fuel, he remembered, "and if while we sat around such a fire, watching the year's crop go up the chimney, the talk sometimes became bitter . . . who will wonder?"

Parrington, making little pretense to objectivity, announced that his point of view was "liberal rather than conservative, Jeffersonian rather than Federalistic." Through the personalities of Roger Williams, Franklin, and Jefferson, he traced the line of liberalism in colonial America: Williams "first transported to the new world the plentiful liberalism of a great movement and a great century"; Franklin "gathered up the sum of native liberalisms that had emerged spontaneously from a decentralized society"; Jefferson "strengthened these native liberalisms with borrowings from the late seventeenth-century natural-rights school and from French romantic theory, engrafting them upon the vigorous American stock." Against these individuals, whose liberalism lay near Parrington's heart, he placed "the complementary figures of John Cotton, Jonathan Edwards, and Alexander Hamilton, men whose grandiose dreams envisaged different ends for America and who followed different paths."

The awakening of the American mind came in the Revolutionary era: "The liberalism that before had been vaguely instructive quickly became eager and militant [and] out of this primary revolution were to come other revolutions, social and economic, made possible by the new republican freedom." In Parrington's judgment, "The most important consequence of the Revolution was the striking down of this mounting aristocratic spirit that was making rapid headway with the increase of wealth." The passing of the Loyalists left the middle class "free to create a civilization after its own ideals." It did so through the agency of the centralized state: "This marked the turning point in American development; the checking of the long movement of decentralization and the beginning of a counter-movement of centralization — the most revolutionary change in three hundred years of American experience." Parrington's material on the Revolution owed a good deal to the works of Arthur M. Schlesinger, Claude H. Van Tyne, and particularly to Moses Coit Tyler's *Literary History of the American Revolution*. In fact, throughout his work Parrington was heavily indebted to contemporary historians whose critical scholarship, he believed, had much to offer students of literature.

The Federalists, under Hamilton's leadership, were victorious over the agrarian democracy. Shortly, however, because of the influence of French revolutionary ideas, opposition "to the aristocratic arrogance of Federalism, and disgust at its coercive measures," mounted quickly. The organizer and director of that discontent was Jefferson, who "far more completely than any other of his generation . . . embodied the idealism of the great revolution."

The Hartford Wits and the group represented by Philip Freneau were examined mainly in the light of their political affiliations. Parrington's own liberal sympathies helped determine his judgment that Freneau, Joel Barlow, and Hugh Henry Breckenridge represented the "best intelligence then being devoted to literature in America." Although "the new liberalism was in the saddle" with the Republican victory of 1800, its seat was precarious because the forces of capitalism and industrialism "were already at work preparing a different pattern of life for America . . . wholly unlike that of the simpler agrarianism with its domestic economy, which Jefferson represents. A new romanticism of the middle class was eventually to shoulder aside the aspirations of gentleman and farmer alike, and refashion America after its own ideal."

The theme of Parrington's second volume, *The Romantic Revolution in America, 1800–1860*, was the growth of an acquisitive society whose way of life, he thought, had less to commend it than did the ideals of the colonial farmer. The philosophy of this middle-class society, expressed by Adam Smith, came into conflict with French revolutionary equalitarianism, which had found a ready response in America in the

Mississippi Valley at the close of the eighteenth century. In the South was developed "the conception of a Greek democracy" with slave labor, which rejected "alike French equalitarianism and English individualism." Because it took no account of the aspirations of the middle class, the latter destroyed the dream of the South, and "with the overthrow of the aristocratic principle in its final refuge the ground was cleared of the last vestiges of the eighteenth century."

The scanty treatment of the South in the first volume was somewhat compensated for in the second. The seed centers of southern culture were Virginia and South Carolina. From the former came the intellectual offspring Kentucky and Tennessee; from the latter, Alabama and Mississippi. The intellectual leaders of these respective groups were Jefferson and Calhoun. Calhoun, who rejected equalitarian idealism and substituted for it economic realism, was also the victim of one of Parrington's excellent but nasty little characterizations—Calhoun, said Parrington, was "a potential intellectual whose mind was unfertilized by contact with a generous social culture." Through opposing representative figures like the agrarian democrat John Taylor and John Marshall, Parrington traced a chart of the Virginia mind "with its liberalisms and conservatisms running at cross purposes." By the late 1820s southern leadership had passed from Virginia to the more aggressive South Carolina. High praise was lavished upon William Gilmore Simms; he was, said Parrington, "the most richly endowed of any son" South Carolina "ever gave birth to . . . by far the most virile and interesting figure of the Old South."

Parrington frequently shocked and angered traditional students of American letters with his opinions—and with his choice of whom to include and exclude. For example, although he praised Edgar Allan Poe as "the first of our artists and the first of our critics," basically he did not treat Poe at all. "The problem of Poe," wrote Parrington in explanation, "fascinating as it is, lies quite outside the main current of American thought, and it may be left with the psychologist and the belletrist with whom it belongs." Parrington also gave short shrift to Longfellow.

In the mind of the "Middle East," New York and Philadelphia, there was more diversity of thought than in the intellectual centers of New England or the South. A friendliness, not so marked in his estimate of Washington Irving, was apparent in Parrington's appraisal of James Fenimore Cooper: "The more intimately one comes to know him, the more one comes to respect his honest, manly nature that loved justice and decency more than popularity." New York's world of literature was greatly indebted to New England, wrote Parrington, who set up against Irving, J. K. Paulding, and Cooper the contributions to idealism made by William Cullen Bryant, Horace Greeley, and Herman Melville.

The New England renaissance of these years, whose stimulus to American life was unusually strong, was, in Parrington's view, "the last flowering of a tree that was dying at the roots; . . . it was the last and in certain respects the most brilliant of the several attempts to domesticate in America the romantic thought of revolutionary Europe; and with its passing, civilization in this western world fell into the hands of another breed of men to fashion as they saw fit."

In Ralph Waldo Emerson and Daniel Webster, Parrington found the "diverse New England tendencies that derived from the Puritan and the Yankee; the idealistic and the practical . . . the intellectual revolutionary . . . and the soberly conservative." Webster "was a great man, built on a great pattern, who never achieved a great life." Along with Emerson, Henry Thoreau and Theodore Parker best typified the ferment in the mind and heart of New England. A sense of kinship quickened the language of Parrington when he wrote of them; Emerson was "a free soul . . . the flowering of two centuries of spiritual aspiration—Roger Williams and Jonathan Edwards come to more perfect fruition. . . . In Thoreau the eighteenth-century philosophy of individualism . . . came to fullest expression in New England." Parker was an unsparing critic of his contemporaries, and he was "one of the greatest, if not the last, of the excellent line of Puritan preachers."

Among the many reviews of Parrington's first two volumes, most of them positive, one of the most interesting was written by Beard. Richard L. Rapson, in *Major Interpretations of the American Past*, suggested an interesting relationship between Beard's work and Parrington's; he said that "it was not until the appearance of Parrington's *Main Currents in American Thought* that Beard's view was enlarged to a comprehensive picture of American society over a long period of time." Beard did not suggest that in his review, but he did say that Parrington had "yanked Miss Beautiful Letters out of the sphere of the higher verbal hokum and fairly set her in the way that leads to contact with pulsating reality—that source and inspiration of all magnificent literature."

The Civil War, said Parrington, hurried the nation "forward along the path of an unquestioning and uncritical consolidation, that was to throw the coercive powers of a centralizing state into the hands of the new industrialism"; this revolution engulfed "the older romantic America, its dignified literary ideals as well as its democratic political theory." From the vague romanticism of these years, however, was born at length "a spirit of realistic criticism, seeking to evaluate the worth of this new America" and to evolve, if possible, new ways of life. The expressions of this critical spirit were the theme of Parrington's incomplete third volume.

Parrington intended to trace the decline of "romantic optimism" after 1860, which resulted from three forces: "the stratifying of economics under the pressure of centralization; the rise of a mechanistic science; and the emergence of a spirit of skepticism which . . . is resulting in the questioning of the ideal of democracy as it has been commonly held hitherto, and the spread of a spirit of pessimism." America's intellectual history, thought Parrington, fell into three broad phases: Calvinistic pessimism, romantic optimism, and mechanistic pessimism.

Although the fragmentary and incomplete form of Parrington's third volume, *The Beginnings of Critical Realism an America, 1860–1920*, is a serious problem to the reader and certainly precludes comparing it with the first two, it still has much excellent material. His characterization of the Gilded Age as "The Great Barbecue" was a particularly revealing label, one of which he was very proud and one that stuck for some time. "A huge barbecue was spread to which all presumably were invited," he wrote. "Not quite all, to be sure; inconspicuous persons, those who were at home on the farm, or at work in the mills and offices, were overlooked; a good many indeed out of the total number of the American people. But all the important persons, leading bankers and promoters and business men, received invitations." It was from all this "that was fashioned the America we know today with its standardized life, its machine culture, its mass psychology — an America to which Jefferson and Jackson and Lincoln would be strangers."

Although much of his material on this last period was deeply gloomy, Parrington never failed to strike the courageous note that raised the spirits of a drooping liberalism. No longer were the theologians, political philosophers, industrial masters, or bankers "the spokesmen of this vibrant life of a continent, but the intellectuals, the dreamers, the critics, the historians, the men of letters, in short; and to them one may turn hopefully for a revelation of American life." To the end, Parrington held out Jeffersonian democracy as a hopeful ideal.

There was thrilling writing in these volumes that called a wayward America back from the drab reality of a business civilization to the daydream of an agrarian democracy. Parrington never escaped the influence of that arch foe of industrialism, William Morris. "In lovely prose," the American said, Morris "laid bare the evils of industrialism. . . . It was a message that stirred me to the quick and convinced me . . . that the business man's society, symbolized by the cash register and existing solely for profit, must be destroyed to make way for another and better ideal."

In Parrington's history there were serious omissions of whole fields of activity without which an observer cannot really understand the main currents of American thought, and there were also mistakes in judgment. For example, he was too harsh to the Puritans, whose virtues he neglected while emphasizing their limitations. He exaggerated French ideological influences in American politics. Historians complained that Parrington did not know enough history, while students of literature often disagreed with his estimates of literary figures. And yet, after everything unfavorable was said, there remained an important achievement. Many students of American society have used his work as a point of departure for further research, and the stimulating quality of its fruitful generalizations will continue to inspire additional study. This study may bear fruit of a kind different from that fancied by Parrington, but, whether in agreement or in disagreement with his main theses, no student of America should forgo the joy of reading him.[53] Indeed, all the Progressive historians deserve to continue to be read, and not just for pleasure; Turner, Beard, and Parrington all made lasting contributions to our understanding of American history.

As Hofstadter suggested:

The Progressives opened up arguments in areas where there had been too much agreement and too much complacency. They took the writing of American history out of the hands of the Brahmins and the satisfied classes, where it had too exclusively rested, and made it responsive to the intellectual needs of new types of Americans who were beginning to constitute a productive, insurgent intelligentsia. They were in the vanguard of a new generation of Midwestern scholars who were deeply involved in the critical ferment that was felt at the beginning of the century, rebellious about the neglect of their own region, eager to make up for the past failure of historians to deal with the interests of the common man and with the historic merits of movements of reform. They attempted to find a usable past related to the broadest needs of a nation fully launched upon its own industrialization, and to make history an active instrument of self-recognition and self-improvement. Something important we do indeed owe them.[54]

CHAPTER 13

Sectional Historians

H ISTORIANS HAVE WRITTEN WORKS of major importance dealing with sections of the United States, and frequently in so doing they have cast new light on the history of the country as a whole. Because of the vastness of the country, with its distinctive geographical divisions equal in size (and in economic significance) to entire European nations, careful sectional historians must spend the better part of a lifetime mastering the material pertaining to that section alone. Histories of New England have a tradition reaching back to the colonial period; in the South the histories dealt mainly with single states. George Tucker and Lyman Draper were interested in the history of the West, but in their day that region was still in the making; not until the West was well settled did scholars begin a comprehensive survey of its history, and, as a result of the efforts of Frederick Jackson Turner (see Chapter 12) and his co-workers, our national history has been recast.

The West

Hubert Howe Bancroft

"I cannot imagine anyone's writing about the history of the West without constantly referring to Bancroft," said Bernard De Voto.[1] Hubert Howe Bancroft's massive contribution to the history of the Far West developed in an unusual manner. Early in life he worked for a bookseller, and in 1858, after having moved from the East to San Francisco, he founded his own publishing and mercantile firm there. It was about this time, the garrulous Bancroft tells us in his *Retrospection, Political and Personal,* that he began to bring together all the books on California in his stock. He extended his field gradually to include the western half of North America from Alaska to Panama, including Mexico and Central America. He collected every scrap of material he could on this vast territory, traversed the entire terrain, employed copyists for years to build up the collections, took down the stories of elderly surviving pioneers, and bought libraries in Europe and America. After a decade of extensive and intensive collecting—he gathered some sixty thousand volumes in all—Bancroft set to work to write the history of the Pacific

Coast.[2] Because his training had been exclusively in business, Bancroft remarked, he could apply only business methods to the task of historical composition. "I became satisfied," he said, "that in no other way could anything have been made out of the situation."[3] About a dozen writers worked in Bancroft's library under his managerial direction, and it is not always an easy matter to assign credit for the composition of the various volumes. Bancroft's own writings made up some four volumes of the history.[4]

It was Bancroft's original intention to start with Central America, inasmuch as the earliest continental discoveries were made there. He had to give much space, however, to the Indians who occupied the territory before the discoveries, because they had played so large a part in the early story of the whole region. Thus in 1875 the first group of volumes in the long series appeared: *The Native Races of the Pacific States of North America* in five volumes, which anthropologists still find useful. Over a period of fifteen years came others: *Central America* (three volumes); followed by the *History of Mexico* (six volumes); the *History of the North Mexican States and Texas* (two volumes); the *History of California* (seven volumes); *Arizona and New Mexico;* the *Northwest Coast* (two volumes); *Oregon* (two volumes); *Washington, Idaho, and Montana; British Columbia; Alaska; Utah;* and *Nevada, Wyoming and Colorado.*

To the reader who wondered at the need for such bulk, Bancroft retorted that his major problem was how to condense without injuring the work. Although not many have written as extensively as Bancroft, the broad descriptive and narrative approach he utilized has tended to dominate western historiography. Six subsequent volumes, largely written by him, of *Popular Tribunals* and miscellaneous essays, nearly completed the catalog of this group of publications appearing under Bancroft's name. Later he published additional works; he died in 1918. His success in marketing his vast and expensive series was remarkable—six thousand sets were sold at a gross return of one million dollars.

The imprint of factory-style production on Bancroft's work should not make the student insensitive to his real achievement. In the first place, he did amass a great collection of material (it eventually went to the University of California at Berkeley), and he also had a vision of a broad historical approach rarely realized before or since. In an essay entitled "History Writing" he remarked that great men deserve their place in history but not in the foreground.[5] He urged historians to see how nations originate and develop, to study ecclesiastical as well as civil government, family relationships, "the affinities and antagonisms of class, occupation, and every species of social phenomena," including labor, industry, the arts, the intellect—"in short the progress of man's domination over nature." Bancroft, perhaps in self-defense, went on to say that a writer of history need not be a genius—"indeed, genius is ordinarily too erratic for faithful plodding"—but he must have good judgment, common sense, broad experience, and a wide range of knowledge. Bancroft rendered a great service to historical literature, and his histories, though flawed, were generally dependable. Later students corrected various details, but his biographer John W. Caughey asserted that the series still remains "the largest and the basic [contribution] to the history of Spanish North America."[6]

Reuben Gold Thwaites

One of those who made possible the writing of a fuller history of the region beyond the Appalachians was Reuben Gold Thwaites, who went west from Massachusetts to Wisconsin, where he became a colleague and friend of Turner. Thwaites was associated with the Wisconsin Historical Society and, following in the footsteps of Lyman Draper, became editor of its publications, making them models for those of other societies.

Thwaites was tremendously productive. In a period of some 25 years he wrote 15 books and edited and published over 160 volumes, besides writing articles and making addresses. His historical writing was occasionally good, but of far greater value was his work as an editor. He may have understood wherein lay his superior accomplishments, for he once wrote, "An editor of historical sources cannot with propriety comment upon the character or the motives of the actors in the drama outlined upon his pages; sufficient that ... he presents materials from which philosophical historians may construct their edifices."[7] Thwaites's weak critical ability marred his writing as well as his editing, but the many volumes issued under his name made it possible for others to study various phases of western history. His most important edited publications were the *Jesuit Relations*, the eight-volume *Original Journals of Lewis and Clark* (1904–1905), and the reprints of *Early Western Travels, 1748–1846*, the thirty-two volumes of which appeared between 1904 and 1907.

The *Jesuit Relations* was a monumental series of seventy-three volumes, mostly documents that were either rare printings or were still in manuscript. Thwaites had great admiration for the Jesuit missionaries, whose work he termed "one of the most thrilling chapters in human history." Some of the explorers, notably Champlain, left their own narratives, but it was the Jesuits who provided most of the extant information concerning the frontiers of New France in the seventeenth century. The missionaries' annual reports written between 1632 and 1673, which eventually reached France, comprised a series of volumes issued under the title *Jesuit Relations*. They have proved to be as useful to geographers and anthropologists as to historians.

Early Western Travels, collected in one vast publication, presented through the eyes of many travelers a panorama of the steady flow of settlers into the American wilderness, the quick formation of societies, and their evolution into urban settlements. Because of Thwaites's efforts documents and rare books which had been in the possession of a few individuals or libraries were now made available to a large number of students, and his own writings gave a definite impetus to the study and writing of western history.[8] Thwaites wrote the volume *France in America* for the American Nation series and was instrumental in the organization in 1907 of the Mississippi Valley Historical Association, later to become the Organization of American Historians.

Theodore Roosevelt

It is not surprising that Theodore Roosevelt, one of the men most influential in promoting expansionist sentiment in the United States in the late nineteenth century, became interested in the early westward movement. Roosevelt had lived on the far-western frontier for some time before writing his books on the pioneers. "The men who have shared in the fast-vanishing frontier life of the present," he wrote in his preface to *The Winning of the West*, "feel a peculiar sympathy with the already long-vanished frontier life of the past."

Roosevelt's interest in history was aroused very early. He said in his autobiography that as an undergraduate "I was already writing one or two chapters of a book I afterwards published on the Naval War of 1812." He found this subject far more to his liking than the topics assigned to him by his professors at Harvard. His methods would not always be considered orthodox by professionals. For example, he once wrote to Henry Cabot Lodge (perhaps half in jest): "I have pretty nearly finished Benton [a biography in the American Statesman series] mainly evolving him from my inner consciousness."[9]

To his friend Lodge, Roosevelt wrote in August, 1888: "I continue greatly absorbed in my new work [*The Winning of the West*], but it goes very slowly. . . . I shall try my best not to hurry it, nor make it scamp work." He consciously patterned his history after Parkman, weaving his narrative around prominent leaders and dramatic episodes. As he had promised his publishers, Roosevelt had the first two volumes ready the following year. He first sketched in the groups who contended for possession of the region between the Alleghenies and the Mississippi—the English-speaking peoples, the French, and the Indians. He had the frontiersman's view of the Indians as a people whose cunning, stealth, and "merciless cruelty" made them "the tigers of the human race." The historian, however, was also critical of many whites, who committed "deeds of the foulest and most wanton aggression." Although most of Roosevelt's work was concerned with the spectacular events of territorial expansion (he was at his best in narratives of frontier fighting), he could also compose descriptions of the backwoodsmen in their more peaceful moments. The Americans had gained a firm foothold in Kentucky by 1775, he wrote, for "cabins had been built and clearings made; there were women and children in the wooden forts, cattle grazed on the range, and two or three hundred acres of corn had been sown and reaped."

By 1783, with the coming of peace, a large immigrant tide flowed into Kentucky. "The days of the first game hunters and Indian fighters were over," Roosevelt observed, and the buffalo herds in this region were nearly gone. Churches, schools, mills, stores, racetracks, and markets told of the planting of a new civilization. In Tennessee also a new civilization was in the making, but Roosevelt paid scant attention to the frontier of the Southwest. The backwoodsmen were spread now almost to the Mississippi, and they had increased to some twenty-five thousand. "Beyond the Alleghenies," wrote Roosevelt, "the Revolution was fundamentally a struggle between England, bent on restricting the growth of the English race, and the Americans, triumphantly determined to acquire the right to conquer the continent."

Within a few years after the Revolution, said Roosevelt, "the rifle-bearing freemen who founded their little republics on the western waters gradually solved the question of combining personal liberty with national union." Separatist movements were nullified, and by 1790 the commonwealths beyond the Alleghenies "had become parts of the Federal Union." The pages on the struggle between the Spaniards and the Americans for the navigation of the Mississippi revealed Roosevelt's ardent nationalism. He convicted the Spaniards of "systematic and deliberate duplicity and treachery" in opposing "their stalwart and masterful foes." The spirit of Elizabethan buccaneers blustered through his writing, especially in his remarks on the ethics of territorial conquest. Here was the Bismarckian philosophy of "blood and iron" and the Machiavellian ethic that "the end justifies the means."

In late December, 1895, Roosevelt wrote to Lodge, "The 4th volume of my *Winning of the West* is done." It covered the period beginning in the 1790s with the wars against the northwestern Indians and closed with the acquisition and exploration of the Louisiana Purchase. The graphic pages on the rout of General Arthur St. Clair's army were followed by the story of Mad Anthony Wayne's victory over the

Indians. There was more to Roosevelt's story, however, than the sound and fury of frontier warfare. In his chapter "Tennessee Becomes a State, 1791-1796" he included some important items on land speculation, a subject at that time generally neglected by historians. The section entitled "Men of the Western Waters, 1798-1802" contained Roosevelt's best pages on economic and social history. "The pioneers stood for an extreme Americanism, in social, political, and religious matters alike," he concluded. "The trend of American thought was toward them, not away from them. More than ever before, the Westerners were able to make their demands felt at home, and to make their force felt in the event of a struggle with a foreign power."

It seemed that Roosevelt had been reading Turner, who said that Roosevelt's history "rescued a whole movement in American development from the hands of unskillful annalists." Turner added that Roosevelt's emphasis on American controversies with England and Spain over the frontier contributed to a fuller understanding of the "truly national history of the United States—a work that remains to be accomplished." The dramatic and the picturesque, rather than the institutional, usually interested Roosevelt, and because of that his work had much to offer the general reader. The special student who requires more careful research, especially in foreign materials bearing on the settlement of the Mississippi Valley, must look elsewhere.

Roosevelt was always scornful of scholars ("day laborers," he called them) who allegedly concerned themselves with minor matters, slowly accumulating carefully ascertained facts but presenting them without literary skill. Just before the annual meeting of the American Historical Association in 1912, he wrote to Lodge in his characteristic manner: "I am to deliver a beastly lecture—'History as Literature'" (it was the presidential address). None of the members of the association, he added, "believe that history is literature. I have spent much care on the lecture, and as far as I know it won't even be printed anywhere." Roosevelt's desire to make history literature was commendable. His tendency to make it the vehicle of American imperialism, however, marred the value of an otherwise signal achievement.[10] Like Woodrow Wilson, another president who wrote history, Theodore Roosevelt is remembered more as one who made history than as one who wrote about it.

Herbert Eugene Bolton

Most of the work of Bancroft, Thwaites, and Roosevelt was done before Turner's. The two men who are frequently considered along with Turner as the "big three" of American frontier historians, Herbert Eugene Bolton and Walter Prescott Webb, did most of their work later.

It is interesting that none of these three major frontier historians of America thought of themselves as merely "frontier" historians. Turner himself resented narrow characterizations of his work as "frontier history." Webb's work mostly fit into the West, but he used it to generalize about the entire world. Also, while the great bulk of Bolton's writing is pertinent to the history of the American West, he was essentially a specialist on Latin America. In addition, all three conceived of the West and the frontier in different ways. To Turner, the frontier was part of a historical process best exemplified by the late colonial and early national West east of the Mississippi. For Webb, on the other hand, the West centered in the plains of the trans-Mississippi West. For Bolton, the American West might better have been called the North.

The advance of the frontier, Bolton pointed out, had not always been from east to west; in the very earliest days of our history it was from south to north. In the study of New Spain's contribution to American history no one did more important work than Bolton. Beginning with the exploration of Mexican archives, he enlarged the field of investigation to include materials of the homeland in Spain to round out his story of the Spanish Borderlands in North America. Going beyond his preceptors, McMaster and Turner, Bolton proclaimed the epic of a greater America in which the essential unity of American history, North and South, was stressed; his was literally a history of the Americas, not merely the story of the expansion of the thirteen colonies into a nation. His research in anthropology, cartography, and history took him over all the lands once part of Spain's empire in North America. His long list of publications included *The Spanish Borderlands* (1921), *Rim of Christendom: A Biography of Father Kino* (1936), *Coronado On The Turquoise Trail* (1949), and many volumes of edited writings. A disciple of Bolton, Lawrence Kinnaird, expressed in this way the spirit of the historical school centered in California: "Many of the best-known students of the American frontier have failed to see that the proximity of the Spanish territory to the United States had any bearing upon their subjects. Documents of vital importance to the understanding of American expansion have remained unused in Spanish and Mexican archives while old-school historians, apparently oblivious of their existence, have attempted to write and rewrite early United States history."

In a textbook written with Thomas M. Marshall, *The Colonization of North America, 1492–1783*, published in 1920, Bolton gave the key to his point of view. More emphasis was placed on non-English colonies and on those English colonies which were not among the original thirteen: "By following the larger story of European expansion it becomes plain that there was an Anglo-Spanish and a Franco-Spanish as well as a Franco-English struggle for the continent, not to mention the ambitions and efforts of Dutch, Swedes, Russians, and Danes."

The works of two students of Bolton at the University of California are helpful in achieving an understanding of the man and his work today. John W. Caughey contributed the essay on Bolton to the little volume *Turner, Bolton, and Webb: Three Historians of the American Frontier,* a collection of essays, originally given as lectures before the Western History Association, which appeared in condensed form in the 1964 inaugural issue of its journal, the *American West.* John Francis Bannon edited the excellent anthology *Bolton and the Spanish Borderlands.*

Bolton was director of the Bancroft Library and chairman of the Department of History in Berkeley when Caughey first met him. Like most of Bolton's many other students—he trained more specialists on the West than did any other historian—Caughey was impressed by his energy, dedication, accessibility, and "simple yet demanding" methods. Bolton was a pioneer in the discovery and opening of foreign archival materials on American history. "I am an American historian," he once said, "and therefore I do my research in foreign archives," such as those in Mexico, Spain, the Vatican, France, the Netherlands, and the Jesuit Archives. Also, Bolton "took to the trails," as Caughey put it: "He was not content merely to pore over the manuscripts and old maps. He preferred to revisit the scene, to confirm or correct the locations, and to let the geography contribute directly to his understanding of the history he was studying."[11] One is reminded of Francis Parkman; indeed, Bolton often said that his aim was to "Parkmanize" the history of the Spaniards in North America. He made a great contribution, but he did not write nearly well enough or cover his subject consistently enough to compare with Parkman.

Caughey suggests that Bolton hit upon two "majestic ideas." One was his concept of the "Spanish Borderlands," the title of his 1921 contribution to the Yale Chronicles of America series. By "Spanish Borderlands" Bolton meant the northern advance of New Spain into the vast area from Florida and Georgia to California. Bolton's other idea, as Caughey states it, was that "history is best observed and best understood by reaching beyond the confines of a single nation." Bolton was thus a pioneer in comparative history, broadening the colonial period of American history to include the history of the Americas, not merely United States history, as his subject, thus challenging the usual concept. Caughey praises Bolton for his "cardinal belief . . . that people of all races and nationalities are very much alike" and suggests that a major virtue of Bolton's graduate seminar was that "his Latin American specialists received broad exposure to the history of the West and his Western Americanists got a grounding in the history of Latin

America." Much of this found its way into *The Colonization of North America* and into Bolton's presidential address in 1932 to the American Historical Association, "The Epic of Greater America." Unfortunately the broad "history of the Americas" that Bolton intended to write was never completed.

Caughey is somewhat ambivalent in his final assessment of Bolton. The following passage from *Turner, Bolton, and Webb* sounds quite negative:

Since Bolton concentrated on colonial studies—America's ancient history— it was inevitable that, as time went on, his subject matter and his findings would seem to have less bearing on the present and its problems.

His dream for hemisphere history has not come true.

His borderlands history struck many historians as "way out"—a fringe area to Spanish America, and a fringe area to the United States and thus to the American West. . . . His Spanish borderlands are rejected by Latin Americanists and neglected by historians of the West.

Caughey concludes, however, that "Bolton's ideas may have been rebuffed, but his writings have not been supplanted" and, surely carried away, suggests that Bolton "is ripe for legend as the Paul Bunyan of western historians."

Although John Francis Bannon strains at times to establish his particular view of Bolton and at other times is almost worshipful of his master, he provides a needed corrective to Caughey on some points and has made a significant contribution to our understanding of Bolton and his place in American historiography. Just as Ray Allen Billington wrote the textbook *(Westward Expansion)* that Frederick Jackson Turner never did, so Bannon wrote a *History of the Americas* and an updated overview of the borderlands, *The Spanish Borderlands Frontier, 1513–1821*, published in Billington's Histories of the American Frontier series in 1963. Bannon also published a biography of Bolton in 1978 entitled *Herbert Eugene Bolton: The Historian and the Man*. To his anthology of some of Bolton's more important writings, *Bolton and the Spanish Borderlands*, Bannon added helpful notes on each selection and a general introduction.

Bannon was concerned lest the controversy over whether the Americas had a "common history"—a term which was not coined by Bolton but which became the catchphrase for critics of his broad approach— might cause neglect of Bolton's "correct" place in the history of American historical writing. Bannon wrote succinctly of Bolton's place:

He was first and foremost the historian of the Borderlands. He may not have succeeded in his oft-professed aim to "Parkmanize" the story of the

Spaniards in North America; but he certainly laid the groundwork for the Parkman of the future if ever he appears and undertakes the gigantic task. Bolton's Borderlands studies have helped us to see and understand the totality of the American story much better. In this lies his greatest contribution to American historiography. The American story need no longer be an unrelieved, and in that measure, an unhistorical, Anglo epic.[12]

Bannon, in the last sentence quoted above, seems to hint at an important insight about the relationship between Bolton's Borderlands studies and his Greater America concept. Yet one weakness of Bannon's analysis is his insistence on separating the two. His book on Bolton includes the phrase "Spanish Borderlands," with no mention of the "Greater America" theme. Indeed, Bannon seems almost reluctant to reprint Bolton's presidential address to the American History Association; he does so only in a separate section at the end of the book, under the significant heading "The 'Other' Bolton." While he acknowledges that "there is a relationship, for from his extensive Borderlands studies came some of the inspiration out of which his broad approach to American history developed," Bannon stresses that the two are separate. Complaining that Bolton is sometimes regarded almost exclusively as "the Americas man," Bannon seems to make him almost exclusively "the Borderlands man." The last sentence of Bannon's introductory note to "The Epic of Greater America" says, "here is the 'other' Bolton, the 'Americas' Bolton, to match the more fundamental, the more enduring, the unimpeachable scholar, Bolton of the Borderlands." One can legitimately question whether the Greater America concept is really less central to Bolton's work than the Borderlands; certainly Bolton did not seem to think so—after all, he devoted his presidential address to the former. Even more fundamentally than that, separating the two seems unnecessary. Bolton's specialized interest was in the advance northward of the frontier of New Spain; clearly that interest could result only from a view of American history considerably broader than the traditional one which focused only on England's activities in the colonial period.

In short, Herbert E. Bolton was a frontier historian, and an outstanding one at that, but he was also far more than that. He stimulated innumerable students to follow paths he trod himself, and the historian who would gain more than an Anglo-American viewpoint on our history must read the works of Bolton and his disciples.

Walter Prescott Webb

It is true of Walter P. Webb even more than of Turner and Bolton that he was more than a frontier historian, for although Webb began with the Great Plains, he eventually generalized about the entire world. Joe B. Frantz, a former student of Webb who wrote extensively about him, suggested that "Webb was a man first, a writer second, a historian third, and an academic last and incidentally."[13] Certainly Webb was unorthodox, his views were always controversial, and he did not at all fit the mold for academic historians. He failed the preliminary examinations for his doctoral degree at the University of Chicago largely because he insisted on following his own interests rather than preparing for the examinations (he was, however, awarded the degree later by the University of Texas, where his major work, *The Great Plains*, was accepted as his dissertation after it had already been published as a book in 1931).

One of the many memorials to honor Webb after his tragic death in an automobile accident in 1963 was the establishment of a lecture series named after him at the University of Texas at Arlington. In 1975, the tenth year of the series, the lectures were devoted to Webb himself. They were published as a book, *Essays on Walter Prescott Webb*, not only to honor him and provide much information on him and his work but also to extend some of his ideas. Ray Allen Billington supplied the introduction, in which he praised Webb for seeing history "not solely as an academic exercise, but also as a panacea for the ills of society. History to him was not only an essential ingredient in cultured men; it was also—and more importantly—an instrument for social change that could, when properly used, better mankind's lot." In a sense, then, Webb was a Progressive historian; yet his optimism, in general and about what history could do, was to diminish considerably with time. Billington suggested that the *Essays* are a fitting tribute to Webb because they "explore unfamiliar terrain, are based on solid research, disdain petty pedantry in favor of sound speculation, apply interdisciplinary tools to the problems they seek to solve, and reach conclusions that are usable in bettering the world in which we live." In short, they are "the sort of history that Walter Prescott Webb himself wrote."[14] Frantz wrote on the important theme of Webb's relationship to the South; W. Turrentine Jackson heeded Webb's call for more comparative frontier studies, in particular studies including Australia; W. Eugene Hollon hailed Webb as a prophet because of his work on the aridity of the West; George Wolfskill extended Webb's Great Frontier hypothesis into the realm of international law; and Walter Rundell, Jr., who examined in detail Webb's early days as a small-town Texas schoolteacher, effectively showed the origin of many of the traits—imagination, creativity, independence of mind, confidence—that later served Webb so well as a mature historian.

The foreword to *Turner, Bolton, and Webb* summarized Webb's contribution as a historian perhaps as succinctly as possible:

Webb was a four-time revisionist. In *The Great Plains* he insisted that the force of the environment was of transcendent importance. In *Divided We Stand* he cried out against the economic colonialism pressed down on the South and the West. In *The Great Frontier* he reappraised what used to be called the expansion of Europe. 'Perpetual Mirage' came as a tract telling the West it was desert at the core.[15]

Frantz's essay in that volume is the best available brief evaluation of Webb and his work.

Webb wrote not primarily for other academics but rather for a broader audience; with the exception of his Mississippi Valley Historical Association and American Historical Association presidential addresses, he seldom published in the scholarly journals and was more inclined to favor *Harper's Magazine* or *Saturday Review.* Webb approached a historical problem much like a lawyer preparing a brief; in a sense he was not a good historian, for he was somewhat inclined to ignore contrary evidence—J. Frank Dobie once quipped, "Webb never lets facts stand in the way of truth." The relationship of Webb's major works to each other may not be immediately evident to the casual reader, but Webb acknowledged one overriding theme in them all: "In my work in history I have found it impossible to separate a civilization or culture from the physical foundation on which it rests," he said. "With this inclination toward physical geography . . . I was fortunate in choosing the American West as a field of study." Webb explained that he was "fortunate because in the American West, the environment is an overwhelming force which has made man and his institutions bend to its imperious influence."[16]

Webb, then, was among other things a pioneer environmental historian. The major work that illustrates this—and, in the usual view, his most important work—was *The Great Plains.* The basic concept was simple: the West, said Webb, was simply not like the East, and those who moved there responded by altering their institutions as they went. The ninety-eighth meridian was the crucial dividing line; it was "a sort of institutional fault line separating two physical environments, two animal kingdoms, and finally two human cultures, ancient and modern, i.e., Indian and European."

He stated the same point somewhat differently in his famous "three legs of civilization" thesis, but this time the Mississippi was the dividing line. East of the Mississippi, wrote Webb, "civilization stood on three legs—land, water, and timber; west of the Mississippi not one but two of these legs were withdrawn—water and timber—and civilization was left on one leg—land." Webb gave many examples of specific innovations required by the environment, but perhaps the three most effective were the windmill, barbed wire, and the six-shooter. Fred A. Shannon, a western historian perhaps best known for his *The Farmer's Last Frontier: Agriculture, 1860–1897,* produced a rather devastating critique of *The Great Plains* in 1940,[17] but Webb's work has otherwise stood the test of time very well. Seldom has history been written which portrays more effectively the interaction between man and his physical environment.

Although it was not one of his "idea" books, *The Texas Rangers* was Webb's next major publication, in 1935. Subtitled *A Century of Frontier Defense,* it was a very good book, frequently considered definitive on its subject, yet it was marred by Webb's racist treatment of Mexicans. Webb sold movie rights to it and later prepared a version for young readers, which he liked better because he "left out all those deadening facts."[18] *The Texas Rangers,* however, was not central to Webb's work as a historian.

Perhaps Webb saw the critical role of the environment in history because it had such a formative influence on his own life. In his presidential address before the American Historical Association in 1958, he said that he had begun his preparation for writing *The Great Plains* "at the age of four when my father left the humid East and set his family down in West Texas, in the very edge of the open, arid country which stretched north and west farther than a boy could imagine... The whole Great Plains was there in microcosm, and the book I wrote was but an extension and explanation of what I had known firsthand in miniature, in a sense an autobiography with scholarly trimmings."[19] Webb also spent time in the South—Texas itself, of course, had southern influences—and in some ways was very much affected by that experience. He was also capable of getting an idea for a book from a specific event—in at least one case, an event which angered him.

To Webb, Franklin D. Roosevelt and the New Deal constituted a modern version of William Jennings Bryan and Populism. Thus, when the Supreme Court began to rule against such New Deal measures as the National Recovery Act and the Agricultural Adjustment Act, Webb was very concerned. It was particularly the latter decision that set him off on a veritable crusade leading to his next book, *Divided We Stand.* Viewed superficially this work seems something of an aberration from Webb's usual work. He pitted the West and South, the nation's two "have-not" sections, against the avaricious and wealthy North; he particularly focused on the economic vassalage of the South. Actually, however, as Joe B. Frantz perceived, *Divided We Stand* "lies directly along the intellectual route from *The Great Plains* to *The Great Frontier.*" The subtitle was *The Crisis of a Frontierless Democracy.* "The closing frontier and the growing corporations—both synonomous with decreasing common opportunity—are offered as mated keys to the domestic crisis of the modern world's first great democracy," wrote Webb.

Divided We Stand was Webb's most personal book—and his most partisan. "The most obvious fact is that the South and the West cannot hope to find a solution for their problem through the Republican party as now constituted," he wrote. Webb believed that the South and West more nearly represented traditional principles of American democracy than the North, but he also thought that the two sections relied too much on their past and covered their inferiority "by proclaiming that they possess ancient virtues. They emphasize too much for practical purposes their civility or bluster, and yet nothing pleases them so much as to achieve recognition from the North."

Again, the most helpful final word on one of his own books comes from Webb himself. *"Divided We Stand* guaranteed that I would never be called to a Northern university," he said in his presidential address to the American History Association. "The book has been called a pamphlet, a philippic, and a good many other things. Because the people could read it and did, it was not objective." Webb concluded with his own summary of the book's thesis: "It explained how, after the Civil War, the North, directed by the Republican party, seized economic control of the nation and maintained it through corporate monopoly. The result was that by 1930 the North, with 21 per cent of the territory and 57 per cent of the people, owned and controlled approximately 85 per cent of the nation's wealth, although about 90 per cent of the natural resources were located in the South and West."

After *Divided We Stand,* Webb did not produce another major work for fifteen years. *The Great Frontier,* published in 1952, was perhaps his greatest work; certainly it was his broadest, most provocative, and most controversial. David M. Potter wrote in the *American Political Science Review* that it was "the most striking and effective reaffirmation of the frontier doctrine since Turner," and Henry Nash Smith in the *New York Herald Tribune Book Review* commented that Webb had "performed an indispensable service to scholarship in demonstrating that the frontier hypothesis need not confine historians to the parochial outlook characterizing far too much of the research carried on under Turner's influence." Oscar Handlin, however, reacted differently; *The Great Frontier,* he wrote in the *Nation,* "reduces the frontier conception to its ultimate absurdity."[20]

What was in this book that led such noted scholars to respond so differently? Basically, *The Great Frontier* showed that Webb not only accepted Turner's frontier hypothesis but, more than anyone else, widened and extended it to apply to the whole world. Europe he called "The Metropolis," the Western Hemisphere "The Great Frontier." The former's discovery of the latter led to a "400-year Boom," a time during which Europe was dominated by frontier forces and the emergence of such new institutions as modern democracy, capitalism, and the idea of progress. This "big boom," wrote Webb, "lasted so long that it was considered normal and its institutions permanent," but it could not, of course, go on forever. If "the boom rested on a four-century excess of land over population," suggested Webb, "the land base of the boom disappeared in 1930. . . . By 1940 the enlarged Western world was more crowded than the small world of Europe was in 1500."

Just as the disappearance of the American frontier raised questions about America's future, so the disappearance of the Great Frontier raised questions about the future of Western man. "There is an unpleasant logic inherent in the frontier boom hypothesis of modern history," Webb acknowledged. He insisted that there was no new frontier and that we must face this reality. Our halting efforts to do so were leading to reduction of individual freedoms at the hands of giant corporations and to democracy being threatened by totalitarianism—the list goes on. We cannot know if Gerard K. O'Neill's "High Frontier" (space) provides an answer for Webb, who did not live to see the first landing on the moon. It was doubtless the gloomy note of Webb's conclusion to *The Great Frontier* that accounted for much of its negative reception, especially in a period like the 1950s. That did not disturb Webb; he died in 1963, confidently predicting that it was his most enduring work and would not be truly appreciated until 1990. He may have been right; that remains to be seen. Says Frantz: "With the way the world economy has been changing lately, *The Great Frontier* is being re-examined for its somewhat gloomy prophecies that the boom days are past, and Webb may stand on the threshold of being hailed as a major prophet."[21]

According to the view that Webb was a "four-time revisionist," his fourth major contribution came not in a book but in one of his articles for *Harper's*. It appeared in May of 1957 with the title "The American West, Perpetual Mirage"; its central contention was that the American West was a desert. This article stimulated more controversy in the popular field than did *The Great Frontier* in the scholarly. The *Denver Post*, for example, called on Webb to "pull off your glasses and lay down your Ph.D. because you have picked yourself a fight."[22] Webb was, of course, basically correct. The idea of the Great American Desert was nothing new but had been conveniently forgotten as the region was developed. The chambers of commerce of western cities might not want to hear that their existence is precarious because they have located themselves in a desert environment, but a brief check of western newspapers for items on water problems in the area will reveal that Webb was once again something of a prophet. W. Eugene Hollon, another of Webb's students, published a thoughtful volume in 1966 entitled *The Great American Desert: Then and Now,* which is essentially a history of the American West based on the acceptance of Webb's perspective.

In the 1970s each of the big-three frontier historians had major biographies published: Billington's on Turner, Bannon's on Bolton, and Necah Stewart Furman's *Walter Prescott Webb: His Life and Impact* (1976). Wilbur R. Jacob's comments in the preface to the 1979 reprinting of *Turner, Bolton, and Webb* would seem to suggest that reports from some quarters of the demise of frontier history are somewhat premature:

In the late 1970's Turner's historical interpretations continue to appear in numerous studies, including urban frontier histories, where his ideas are re-examined with the aid of masses of quantitative data not easily obtained in his day. Bolton's borderland thesis has gained new respect because of the enormous impact of Spanish-speaking peoples in America, particularly in California, which, according to demographic projections, will have a more than 50 percent Chicano population by 1985. And Webb's attention to environmental concepts, especially the problem of water scarcity in the Southwest, makes him one of the best historical prophets of his time.[23]

Bannon in the same book summarizes appropriately: "The Midwest of Turner, the Great Plains of Webb, the Borderlands of Bolton are all integral parts of the great epic that is American History."

New England

Ever since the days when Increase and Cotton Mather urged the writing of a history of New England, a number of writers have attempted the task. Nearly all writers of New England history have confined themselves almost exclusively to Massachusetts, devoting comparatively little space to other states. Charles Francis Adams wrote expressly on Massachusetts, but James Truslow Adams gave more attention than others have done to the Bay Colony's neighbors. A nineteenth-century historian, William B. Weeden, was a successful manufacturer before he turned to history. He was keenly aware of the social problems created by the Industrial Revolution, and although he had something of the Christian Socialist outlook of the 1880s, he was in the main a strong economic individualist.[24] In 1890 he published his *Economic and Social*

History of New England, 1670–1789, one of the first attempts to do for a section what McMaster was doing for the nation as a whole. Weeden consulted sources rarely used before by historical scholars, and his chapters on money, lands, agriculture, fisheries, commerce, prices, and manners included materials that are still useful to the student. When he touched on political matters, such as the Navigation Acts, he gave an outmoded interpretation, but his volumes remain among the best of their kind. A later, excellent investigation of the relationship between communications and communal growth was that of E. C. Kirkland, the two-volume *Men, Cities, and Transportation: A Study in New England History, 1820–1900,* published in 1948.

Writers on New England have gone through cycles of pietism and of pitiless criticism. Seventeenth-century historians left untarnished the glories of that region's early days. With the growth of skepticism came a more detached view of ancestors, notably in the works of Hutchinson and Belknap. Palfrey's filial piety echoed the devotional spirit of Cotton Mather. A sharp reaction against the ancestor worship of Palfrey was revealed by Brooks Adams in the *Emancipation of Massachusetts* (1887), by Charles Francis Adams, and by James Truslow Adams. The latter, in particular, in his zealous attempt to restore the balance, erred seriously in his estimate of the Puritans. A sounder interpretation of the civilization of early New England was presented in the works of Kenneth B. Murdock, Perry Miller, Clifford K. Shipton, and Samuel Eliot Morison. Murdock's literary studies and his biography of Increase Mather showed a richness of Puritan culture apparently unknown to earlier students. Similarly the works of Miller, along with Shipton's essays and biographical sketches of Harvard graduates, revealed a depth and variety in Puritan thought largely ignored before then. Morison headed what was sometimes known as the "revisionist" school of New England historiography, whose organ was the *New England Quarterly.*[25]

Charles Francis Adams

The Adams family was in many ways America's "royal" family because of the regal gifts they made to their native land in public service, in scholarship, and in the creation of a critical tradition. A prince of the blood was Charles Francis, son of the Charles Francis Adams who served his country brilliantly as minister to England during the Civil War. While his brother Henry was acting as secretary to their father in London, Charles joined the Union army, convinced that at least one member of the family should offer deeds as well as words in behalf of his country. "For years our family has talked of slavery and of the South, and been most prominent in the contest of words," he wrote to his father, "and now that it has come to blows does it become us to stand aloof from the conflict?"[26]

Unlike Henry, Charles entered rather vigorously into the currents of American political and business life; for a long time his historical interests were little more than an avocation. Yet in the twenty-five years that followed his retirement from association with the Union Pacific Railroad in 1890, he delivered many addresses on history and published several works, including *The Life of Richard Henry Dana, The Three Episodes of Massachusetts History*, a critical appraisal of New England historians in *Massachusetts: Its Historians and History*, and *Studies: Military and Diplomatic*.

In his autobiography Adams spoke of two epoch-marking events in his life: the discovery of a book and an invitation to deliver an address. The former occurred when he was in England in 1865. "I one day chanced upon a copy of John Stuart Mill's essay on Auguste Comte," he wrote. "That essay of Mill's revolutionized in a single morning my whole attitude. I emerged from the theological stage, in which I had been nurtured, and passed into the scientific." It was the second event, the invitation to deliver an address some eight years later, that fixed more certainly the direction of Adams's intellectual life. He was asked by the citizens of the town of Weymouth to speak on the 250th anniversary of its settlement; out of so small a beginning he was led for many years thereafter "through pastures green and pleasant places."

Of the harvests he reaped, none has been of greater value than the sheaf of papers gathered together in *The Three Episodes of Massachusetts History*, published in two volumes in 1892. These episodes were the settlement of Boston Bay at Weymouth in 1623, the Antinomian controversy, and a study of church and town government. Seventy years before Charles Adams published his history, his great-grandfather John Adams had written to Jefferson about his own reading: "Controversies between Calvinists and Arminians, Trinitarians and Unitarians, Deists and Christians, Atheists and both, have attracted my attention. . . . The history of this little village of Quincy, if it were worth recording, would explain to you how this happened."[27] The great-grandson decided that its history was worth recording.

The first episode was enlivened by the figure of Thomas Morton, whose enigmatic, un-Puritan personality attracted Adams. The historian's examination of the treatment of Anne Hutchinson in the Antinomian controversy led him to write that her "so-called trial was, in fact, no trial at all, but a mockery of justice rather—a bare-faced inquisitorial proceeding." An Adams of the fourth generation was not likely to look at provincial events narrowly. The Antinomian controversy, wrote Adams, was much more than a religious dispute: "It was the first of the many New England quickenings in the direction of social, intellectual and political development—New England's earliest protest against formulas."

Members of the Adams family were not accustomed to mince words when their minds were made up. Charles Francis Adams could not drop this subject without some caustic references to New England historians who had sought to palliate or even to justify their ancestors' actions. "In the treatment of doubtful historical points," he said, "there are few things which need to be more carefully guarded against than patriotism or filial piety." In his third episode, which is probably the most interesting today, Adams told of the mores of Quincy. The American unit, he said, was to be sought in the towns and their records; "the political philosopher can there study the slow development of a system as it grew from the germ up." Chapters entitled "Population and Wealth," "Social Life," "Town Meetings," and "Intemperance and Immorality," were pioneer efforts, and still remain very useful.

In the opinion of Osgood, the work of Adams was "the most original and suggestive town history ever written in this country," and it set a precedent for critical treatment that James Truslow Adams and others remembered when they began to write on New England. Charles Francis Adams enjoyed a quiet satisfaction when contemplating in retrospect his *Three Episodes*. "It may not be great, and certainly has not nor will it obtain a recognized place in general literature," he said, "but locally, it is a classic." Posterity is not likely to quarrel with his own judgment of his book.[28]

James Truslow Adams

Writers outside academic halls were once responsible for some of our finest historical writings. That tradition has thinned since Henry Charles Lea, Parkman, and Prescott wrote their notable volumes, but it has been reinforced in more recent years by the work of Douglas Southall Freeman, James Truslow Adams, Bruce Catton, Barbara Tuchman, and others. James Truslow Adams did not regret his lack of academic experience; indeed, he thought "too long an academic training and career" was "rather a detriment than a benefit to a historian."[29] Turning away from a business career, he brought out a succession of volumes that made it possible once again for a historian to make a living by his writing. Adams fulfilled for himself the ambition of Macaulay—that his volumes would replace the latest novel on the drawing-room table. No name was better known than his among readers of history in America at that time.

Adams achieved prominence among the historical guildsmen with his *Founding of New England,* published in 1921. It was acclaimed by Morison as the "best short history of early New England that has appeared for a generation," but the justice of Adams's severe criticism of Puritan religious intolerance was widely questioned. It seems to have been generally overlooked that only three years before, in his history of Southampton, Adams had been very sympathetic to the Puritans; he wrote, "We should not sneer, as historians have sometimes done, at those who came to secure religious freedom and in turn denied it to some extent in others." He went on to a further defense: "Those engaged in the work of laying the foundations of a new civil and religious polity should not be blamed for refusing to passively watch others sap those very foundations which they were attempting to build up at the expense of so much they had held dear. Nor was their attitude either hypocritical or disingenuous." The work of the earliest settlers of Southampton, wrote Adams, "was stern and their theology as well, but their lives, like ours, were filled with the satisfaction of honest work and with the sweetness of love for their wives, tenderness for their children, and the joys of friendship."

For some unknown reason, when he came to write on the New England Puritans, in 1921, he seemed not to see their sweetness or tenderness or their joys. Instead, he concentrated on their shortcomings; perhaps he thought it necessary to overcome the influence of the "filiopietistic" school of historians as typified by Palfrey. Apart from this particular bias of Adams and the limitation of his volume (it was almost exclusively a political history), *The Founding of New England* merited high praise. It made excellent use of the work of Osgood, Beer, and Andrews in presenting the colonies as cogs in an imperial machine; the chapter called "The Theory of Empire" was especially good in this respect. Whereas Fiske in his *Beginnings of New England* entitled a chapter "The Tyranny of Andros," Adams called his own chapter on Sir Edmund Andros "An Experiment in Administration." He emphasized the economic rather than the religious factors behind the mass migration in the 1630s. In examining the workings of the theocracy, he said that "the domestic struggle against the tyranny exercised by the more bigoted members of the theocratic party was of greater importance in the history of liberty than the more dramatic contest with the mother country." His iconoclasm was refreshing, even if his brand of orthodoxy set up a new cult of anti-Puritanism.[30]

The second volume in the series, published in 1923, was *Revolu-*

tionary New England, 1690–1776. Adams traced the beginnings of colonial grievances, the gradual development of Revolutionary sentiment, and the rise of a radical party. From 1713 to about 1750, "we can see at work forces tending to develop democratic ideals in certain elements of the community, and foreshadowing the alignments and parties of a later time"; the ten years preceding 1750, he said, were "marked by an intense quickening of thought and action."

Adams studied the internal struggle for political and economic power between the mercantile aristocracy and the lower classes in the colonies, and he noted the growth in self-consciousness of these lower classes. The modern attitude toward the Loyalists was given full expression by Adams, who referred to the Revolution as a "Civil War." In these two volumes Adams possibly exaggerated the isolation of New England from the rest of the colonies. Leonard W. Labaree, in *Royal Government in America,* stressed many of the features of this period more lightly touched upon by Adams, and Labree believed that Adams did not adequately explain the Revolutionary movement.

The last of the trilogy was *New England in the Republic, 1776–1850.* Its main theme, said the author, "may be considered to be the continued struggle of the common man to realize the doctrines of the Revolution in the life of the community." In keeping with his awareness of the aspirations of the lower class, he gave a sympathetic review of Shays's Rebellion. In the conflict over the adoption of the federal Constitution, Adams was especially interested in the struggle between the conservative element and the opposition, which was seeking to preserve and extend the liberal doctrines preached in 1776.

In keeping with studies like those of Beard, *New England in the Republic* maintained that, having achieved their object in gaining their independence from England, the conservative leaders in America strove to prevent the Revolutionary movement from going further and thus altering the essential structure of American society. Once begun, however, the process of revolution was not easily stayed; the mass of the people had come to expect radical changes, "and for many decades after 1783," said Adams, "this struggle between these two groups constitutes the main interest of our history." He observed the conflict as it revealed itself in its various aspects—in business, politics, education, relations between capital and labor, religion, and the debate over slavery. A subordinate subject was the gradual growth of sectionalism and its decline after the ties of union proved stronger. After 1850 the nationalist forces "swept the New England states into the swift movement of what had by then become a genuinely national life."

Hostility to the Puritans was somewhat diminished in this later study, and in his closing lines Adams did mild penance: "We thus end the story as we began, with the leaders of the New England people wrestling with a transcendent moral problem [in 1850 it was slavery]. . . . Perhaps, at times, in a reaction against the old point of view which regarded all Puritans and all Revolutionary soldiers and agitators as saints and patriots, we may have been tempted to stress the shadows rather than the lights."

Adams wrote, "A small part of the public, God bless it, does want to know something about the past of our race, but it wants to be able to stay awake while it reads."[31] In his volumes on New England and in his very readable *Epic of America*, Adams kept many thousands awake while they enjoyed a stimulating interpretation of the American past.

Samuel Eliot Morison

The tradition of historical scholarship in New England is the strongest in American literature, and its contemporary representatives are worthy heirs. Foremost among them was Samuel Eliot Morison, who combined the precise scholarship of his master, Edward Channing, with the literary skill of Henry Adams. Morison's love of the sea led to a brilliant two-volume reconstruction of Columbus's voyage, *Admiral of the Ocean Sea*, published in 1942. Later Rear Admiral Morison was assigned the congenial task of writing the history of the Navy's role during World War II. He also produced a prizewinning biography of John Paul Jones; the superb, encyclopedic work *The European Discovery of America* (in two volumes: *The Northern Voyages, A.D. 500–1600*, published in 1971, and *The Southern Voyages, 1492–1616*, published in 1974); the classic textbook *The Growth of the American Republic*, written with Henry Steele Commager as coauthor and first published in 1942; and many other works of such diversity that it is not entirely accurate to label him a New England historian, perhaps not even primarily so. Naval history was in many ways his first love; of course, it was not unrelated to the history of New England.

In his reexamination of the earlier years of New England, Morison shed much new light on a familiar subject. He began with a two-volume study of Harrison Gray Otis, published in 1913. Otis was a distinguished Federalist who lived on long after his party had died. Morison subsequently wrote on a subject fancied by many New England historians in *The Maritime History of Massachusetts, 1783–1860* (1921). The contents were much broader than the title indicates, for in the period before the Civil War a large portion of American commerce was handled by ships from Massachusetts. The volume thus covered more than a provincial area; in fact, like the ships that sailed from New England's ports, it covered the world. In addition, for the lover of the sea, as well as for the student of history, there was real gusto in his enthusiastic, lively descriptions of the days of New England's glory.

After this volume Morison turned back to the years of the founders. In his *Builders of the Bay Colony*, published in 1930, he wrote about the first-generation historical figures who interested him most—men (and one woman, Anne Bradstreet) who typified the varied aspects of the first fifty years of Massachusetts history. Morison said that his "attitude toward seventeenth-century puritanism has passed through scorn and boredom to a warm interest and respect." In the sketches of Puritans that make up this volume, the historian pictured a people endowed with a broad humanity rarely seen by previous scholars, who also found them too little concerned with aesthetics. The Puritans who emerged from Morison's pages were real individuals whose characteristics belied the stereotype fashioned by superficial historians and cartoonists. Morison strongly supported the thesis that the motive for the Puritan migration was religious, not economic. He may have pushed this view too far, for while the leaders may have been largely motivated by religion, the evidence is not convincing with respect to the mass of their followers.

The Puritan Pronaos (1936), studies in seventeenth-century intellectual history, again revealed Morison's broad knowledge of the Puritan mind. As in the earlier *Builders of the Bay Colony*, Morison showed the Puritans' awareness of the world of their own day, and the clergy in particular were credited with being not merely the religious leaders of the community but the political and intellectual guides as well. Morison modified or discarded many timeworn traditions about New England's "reactionary clergy" who lagged behind and slowed the progress of the colonies. Unlike other scholars, who maintained that New England led a life apart from Europe, he showed that in many ways intellectual activity in the New World closely paralleled that in the Old. *The Puritan Pronaos* was released again twenty years later as *The Intellectual Life of Colonial New England*.

Morison's history of Harvard is of the first importance for an understanding of the development of American education. The first volume, *The Founding of Harvard College*, examined in detail the European background and the first fifteen years of the college. Emmanuel College, Cambridge, a training ground for many Puritans, greatly influenced the creation of Harvard. The broad purposes of the charter providing for a general education were properly emphasized by Morison, who stands in contrast to those who so often pointed to the narrowly ecclesiastical objectives of Harvard's training.

The sacrifices of the Puritans, who intended to make their school a worthy institution, and the returns that Harvard gave to the community in intellectual and spiritual guidance were clearly set forth by

Morison, a justly proud alumnus. A splendid composite "portrait" of the Harvard alumni concluded the third volume. With the completion of this four-volume work, published in 1936 as *The Tercentennial History of Harvard University,* Morison bestowed upon Harvard a written history unmatched as yet by that of any other educational institution, and at the same time he made a contribution of the first order to the intellectual history of New England and indeed, of America.

Perry Miller

Since the publication of Perry Miller's major works—*Orthodoxy in Massachusetts* in 1933, *The New England Mind: the Seventeenth Century* in 1939, *The New England Mind: From Colony to Province* in 1953, and *Errand into the Wilderness* in 1956—he has been regarded by most as the preeminent historian of Puritan New England. Indeed, his contributions in this area led many to regard him as one of the truly great American historians to write intellectual history after World War II.

Like Morison, Miller was a product of Harvard, and his career was centered there. Yet the differences between the two are frequently more striking than the similarities. Morison, for example, is usually commended for his beautifully readable style. Miller, on the other hand, has seldom been accused of being readable. Even Robert Middlekauff, who has high praise for Miller in general, acknowledges that his work "is written in a style that puzzles and even angers some readers."[32] This results, Middlekauff suggests, from a feeling that Miller "is making history too difficult for understanding." Furthermore, he agrees that Miller's style is complex: "Neither his sentence structure nor his choice of words make[s] for quick comprehension," Middlekauf says, "yet his writing is almost always clear and often graceful." Beginning to come to Miller's defense, he adds that the historian "possessed a sense of literary structure that lent his books coherence and power." What Middlekauff likes best about Miller's style is "its range of sounds and its success in transmitting a sense of the moods of men and eras."[33]

Miller began his career after Morrison and such other writers as Kenneth Murdock and Clifford K. Shipton had already begun laboring to destroy the persistent negative stereotype of the Puritans (for example, in the 1920s, H. L. Mencken had defined Puritanism as "the haunting fear that somewhere, someone might be happy"). Morison had clearly established that the Puritans were neither prohibitionists nor prudes, that they wore bright clothing and lived in colorfully painted houses, and that most of their sermons were not hellfire harangues but rather systematic theology. Miller departed from this pattern in both his method and his concern with ideas. Morison and the others had worked largely through biography; the nearest Miller approached that genre was in his brilliant intellectual biography of Jonathan Edwards in 1949. Miller was also no apologist for the Puritans—as Middlekauff said, he "never concealed his distaste for the Mathers and almost delighted in describing the irony of faithful adherence to creed—he did not call it fanaticism—leading to corruption. The way to an understanding of Puritans and of America, Miller believed, lay through ideas, and it was a way he traveled exuberantly."[34]

Middlekauff's mention of irony raises an interesting and somewhat controversial point in recent efforts to assess Miller's work. Richard Reinitz, in discussing Niebuhr's irony, saw Miller as "one of the important American historical ironists";[35] Gene Wise, in *American Historical Explanations*, used Miller extensively to illustrate his own development of Niebuhr's ironic approach to history into a new "counter-Progressive" explanation of American history. Middlekauff, however, deals with Miller and irony in this convincing manner:

Miller seems deliberately to have avoided treating some men and events with irony; he exposes, for example, the irony of Solomon Stoddard, whose authoritarianism earned him the title of "Pope," reforming the sacraments in order that the democracy might enter the church. But he did not treat Stoddard with irony. Nor was he ironic at the expense of the Puritans, though he presents them as a people who failed in part because they succeeded beyond their wildest dreams. He saw the incongruities in their ideals and conduct and he described them with relish, but he also felt the Puritans' joy and agony so deeply that he could not detach himself from them. Nor could he reject the Puritans, or their experience. The complexity of his attitude prevented either light or savage irony, and the depth of his feeling found other kinds of expression: admiration for their courage, anger at their self-righteousness, and an undecipherable passion at the glory of their attempt to know God and live according to His wishes.[36]

"Puritanism was not only a religious creed," wrote Miller; "it was a philosophy and a metaphysic; it was an organization of man's whole life, emotional and intellectual." Miller saw at the center of the Puritan mind a tension between piety and intellect. Ideas, he insisted, are autonomous; they have a life of their own, and thus a historian can treat them apart from experience. Miller did exactly that in *The Seventeenth Century*, the first volume of *The New England Mind*. He dealt with the Puritan mind as if it were static. "The first three generations in New England paid almost unbroken allegiance to a unified body of thought," he wrote. Many critics refused to accept this logic. In the second volume of *The New England Mind*, entitled *From Colony to Province*, he did describe changes over time, of course, and carried the narrative to 1730.

After Miller's death in 1965, Edmund S. Morgan, considered by many to be the ablest contemporary scholar of New England Puritanism, lamented that Miller had completed only two volumes but insisted:

What he did write must stand, with Morison's volumes on Harvard, as the outstanding achievement of the present century in early American history. In exhaustiveness of research, in subtlety of analysis, and in literary craftsmanship the writings of these two men have set standards for the entire profession. As far as New England history is concerned, they have defined the terms of discussion and established the norms by which every subsequent author knows that his work must be measured. Miller and Morison have not only made it necessary to take Puritanism seriously but have compelled discussion of the subject to begin at a level that has scarcely been approached in other areas of intellectual history.[37]

Significant contributions to New England history have been made by Alan Heimert, Sacvan Bercovitch, David D. Hall, Middlekauff, and, of course, Morgan himself. The tribute to Miller quoted above, however, still rings true. Perry Miller's historiographical relationship to New England Puritanism resembles Charles Beard's to the Constitution and Frederick Jackson Turner's to the frontier.

The South

Historical studies received a marked impetus in the North and Middle West soon after the Civil War, but they lagged in the South. Problems far more pressing than the study and writing of history occupied the southern states in the Reconstruction period, but the publication of many war memoirs maintained continuity with an earlier tradition of historical writing. Charles E. A. Gayarré was still alive and influential among students of history, and a couple of historical societies showed some signs of vigor. At the bar of history, the only tribunal left for the South, southerners pleaded their cause. To Alfred T. Bledsoe, editor of the *Southern Review*, General Robert E. Lee remarked: "Doctor, you ... have a great work to do; we all look to you for our vindication." The Southern Historical Society was founded in 1869, mainly to preserve materials bearing on the Civil War. The society's journal, the *Southern Historical Society Papers*, brought to light many documents. The *Southern Bivouac* (1882–87) was one of the most important contributions to historical periodical literature in the post–Civil War era. Later, in 1896, the Southern History Association was formed; its interests were wider than those of the Southern Historical Society. Johns Hopkins, the new university, provided an even greater vitalizing force. Yet as late as 1890 there was no great activity in history in the

South.[38] At that very time, however, young scholars were publishing their first studies; it must also be remembered that students in other parts of the country were occasionally drawn to southern topics, even though southerners at home might be negligent of them.

Herbert Baxter Adams and others were aware of the value of research in southern history. A writer in the *Nation* of May 26, 1881, for instance, pointed out that the history of local institutions of the South remained to be written: "It is a good field of investigation for the rising generation of students in that section of the country." William A. Dunning subsequently began a teaching career that created a body of excellent scholars devoted to southern history; William E. Dodd and John Spencer Bassett performed similar services. Woodrow Wilson studied his native region with an eye that looked askance at the conventional northern approach to southern history, [39] while William G. Brown, cut off too early in his career, published in 1902 a provocative new interpretation, *The Lower South in American History.*

Cooperative works were being published with more attention than was usually given to southern points of view. The History of North America series, in twenty volumes (1903–1907), edited by Guy C. Lee and Francis N. Thorpe, gave more space to the South than had the American Nation series. For example, a whole volume was devoted to the Civil War from a southern standpoint.

A cooperative series that more specifically expressed the southern consciousness and reflected the widening interest in its history was the thirteen-volume series The South in the Building of the Nation (1909). The scholarship of some of the writers ensured the high quality of their contributions. Philip A. Bruce wrote on Virginia; Bernard C. Steiner, on Maryland; William K. Boyd and J. G. de Roulhac Hamilton, on North Carolina; Ulrich B. Phillips, on Georgia; and Walter L. Fleming, on Alabama. The authors looked upon the South as a more or less distinct political and economic unit, "with an interrelated and separate history." The eleven states that organized the Confederacy; the border states Kentucky, Maryland, and Missouri; and the state of West Virginia fell within the scope of this southern history, the publication of which was justified on the ground that "no true history of the South has been written."

One volume of the series was on the South as a whole; a section entitled "The South in Federal Politics," made a valuable contribution. Another volume, on economic history from 1607 to 1865, was the first comprehensive attempt to compile such information in the South since De Bow's work in 1852. This volume, and a companion work which carried the treatment to 1909, broke new ground in research. In a useful section called "The Economic Causes of the Civil

War," John H. Latané redirected the attention that for too long had focused on the constitutional and moral aspects of the struggle. The series was broad enough to include volumes on the intellectual life of the South as well as social activities. For many years students seeking quick access to materials on the South found this series extremely useful.

Philip Alexander Bruce, Alexander Brown, and Edward McCrady

One of the most prolific of southern historical writers, and one of the most important, was Philip Alexander Bruce. In 1896 he brought out his exceedingly valuable two-volume *Economic History of Virginia in the Seventeenth Century*, in which he made use of previously unexplored manuscript collections. His was the first attempt, he said, "to describe the purely economic condition of the Virginia people in detail," and his volumes were filled with meticulous descriptions of manufactures and of the conditions of agriculture and labor. As a historian Bruce was, of course, too knowledgeable to accept the cavalier tradition of Virginia history, but he did say that "there are many evidences that a large number of the immigrants were sprung from English families of substance," and in another connection he said that "the moral influence of the large plantation was ... extraordinary." Throughout Bruce's work the reader sensed his nostalgia for the spacious days of the old landed aristocracy.

In 1907, Bruce published another study, *Social Life of Virginia in the Seventeenth Century*, an inquiry into the origin of the aristocratic planters and a description of the manners and diversions of the people. Except for its slaves, he said, the population of Virginia was socially a duplication of the smaller rural communities in England, although the physical surroundings of the New World had required some modifications. In a subsequent work, called *The Virginia Plutarch*, published in two volumes in 1929, Bruce honored the great Virginians, paying them the homage that is rightfully theirs.

In opposition to Bruce, Thomas Jefferson Wertenbaker minimized the influence of the aristocracy in Virginia's early history. In his *Planters of Colonial Virginia* (1922), Wertenbaker explained that the colony was filled with comparatively small farms "owned and worked by a sturdy class of English farmers." These white yeomen, Wertenbaker contended, were the most important element in the life of early Virginia until the spread of slavery in the eighteenth century transformed the colony "from a land of hard-working independent peasants, to a land of slaves and slave holders."

At the same time that Bruce was initiating his investigations into Virginia's early history, Alexander Brown was unearthing the important historical sources of the Old Dominion and publishing them. In 1890 he published *The Genesis of the United States* in two volumes, covering the years from 1605 to 1616, "the period of the first foundation." A continuation of *The Genesis*, with some changed opinions on men and events, was *The First Republic in America* (1898), in which Brown criticized severely the writings of John Smith. Brown wrote about the enemies of the Virginia Company almost as if they were his personal opponents. His thesis was that James I frustrated the growth of democracy in Virginia, thus beginning the long history of royal tyranny that ended with George III.[40] Basically, Brown's ability lay in collecting rather than in interpretation.

Interesting as the history of colonial Virginia has been to the student, equally rich in charm and incident is the history of colonial South Carolina. Edward McCrady, a lawyer by profession and a historian by avocation, wrote a *History of South Carolina* in four volumes, published between 1897 and 1902. He covered the entire period up to the close of the Revolutionary War; of special interest were several chapters on the decade just preceding the Revolution. These chapters gave an excellent picture of the professions and the economic and social life of the colony on the eve of the war. Although he treated rather fully the social conditions in the eighteenth century, McCrady did not consider the interaction between social and political events. He also failed to make clear South Carolina's position in relation to the rest of the empire. The remaining two volumes covered the war period, and McCrady carried out his task so well that his work has been recognized as one of the best state histories ever written.

William Archibald Dunning

William Archibald Dunning, a very sympathetic student of southern history, was one of the many young historians trained by John W. Burgess in Columbia University. He later joined his teacher on the faculty of that school, where he developed a whole group of scholars devoted to southern history. Dunning's initial effort after earning his doctorate was *The Constitution of the United States in Civil War and Reconstruction, 1860–1867*, published in 1885, in which he showed an independence of judgment that always remained a distinctive characteristic. When writing of the plans of Thaddeus Stevens and others to confiscate southern property, Dunning said that "all such propositions were the passionate fancies of fanatics more extreme than the Southern fire-eaters who had precipitated the war." In his closing lines he stated his thesis: In the revolution which had occurred "the written Constitution had been pronounced finished. It had held the fragments of the nation together till they should be welded inseparably in the white heat of war, but it had not itself escaped the blaze."

Dunning's concern with constitutional and institutional history was further manifested in his *Essays on the Civil War and Reconstruction* (1897). Unlike some later students who have seen in the acts of Reconstruction much evidence of powerful northern economic forces, Dunning wrote that their chief end was "purely political." He had high regard for the political and administrative capacity shown in the reconstruction of the southern states, judging it to be "one of the most remarkable achievements in the history of government"; his condemnation of the purpose of Reconstruction was equally straightforward. In his essay on the impeachment and trial of President Johnson, Dunning wrote, "The single vote by which Andrew Johnson escaped conviction marks the narrow margin by which the presidential element in our system escaped destruction."

To Dunning was assigned the task of writing the volume in the American Nation series covering the years immediately following the Civil War. *Reconstruction: Political and Economic, 1865-1877* instantly took its place as the foremost treatment of those troubled years. Instead of fixing his attention exclusively on the South during Reconstruction, as so many before him had done, the historian looked at the period as "a step in the progress of the American nation." In the record of the North in these years, he said, "there is less that is spectacular, less that is pathetic, and more that seems inexcusably sordid than in the record of the South." He did not depict those years as all white or all black, as many others have done, but he did try to help the reader understand more clearly the motives of the southerners in undoing the plans of Reconstruction.

In 1914 a number of Dunning's former students dedicated to him a volume entitled *Studies in Southern History and Politics*. Some of the authors of this testimonial, which was a fitting commentary on Dunning's influence in the promotion of study of the South, were among the leading students of this section: Ulrich B. Phillips, Charles W. Ramsdell, J. G. de Roulhac Hamilton, William K. Boyd, and Holland Thompson. The writings of his many students of Reconstruction in the several states supplemented Dunning's own investigations, but the "Old Chief," as this stimulating lecturer was affectionately called, did more than anyone else to rewrite the history of the years following the Civil War. "He was the first," said Hamilton, "to make a scientific and scholarly investigation of the period of Reconstruction." Of course, the Dunning interpretation has long since been significantly revised by the work of scholars W. E. B. Du Bois, Kenneth Stampp, John Hope Franklin, and many others.

Ulrich Bonnell Phillips

Ulrich B. Phillips was one of the many students who had been advised to study with Dunning. In 1902 he published *Georgia and State Rights*, which owed part of its inspiration to Turner. The latter had helped Phillips see that local political divisions rested on economic differences stemming from variations in soil fertility. Phillips had originally intended to study the effect of nullification upon Georgia politics, but his work expanded to become a complete survey of the state's history before the Civil War. Phillips, born in Troup County, Georgia, was a native of the cotton belt and, in picturing the region, endeavored to correct historical misconceptions concerning it. "The contrast between the extremes of wealth and poverty in the South," he said, "has been exaggerated; . . . the social system was by no means rigid in the cotton belt."

Other works followed in due course: *The History of Transportation in the Eastern Cotton Belt* in 1908 and *The Life of Robert Toombs* in 1913. Phillips edited two volumes of *Plantation and Frontier, 1649–1863* in the Documentary History of American Industrial Society, to which he prefixed valuable introductions. These volumes contained little-known materials on the South at work; his attempt, said Phillips, was to give a "reasonably full view of Southern industrial society." No one had a better knowledge of sources for the history of the South than Phillips, and his own library was practically unrivaled. He was also the author of *American Negro Slavery* (1918) and wrote articles on politics and economics. In his later years he was coeditor of *Florida Plantation Records*, which appeared in 1927, but the most important publication of his last days was *Life and Labor in the Old South* (1929), one of the most important books ever published on the South as a whole. This volume was the result of his own familiarity with conditions in the South and the distillation of the extremely detailed knowledge he had gained from old manuscript collections.

Phillips's concentration on his own region was, however, so exclusive that he missed important factors that impinged on the South. For example, concurrent northern developments such as the antislavery movement were never integrated into his work. Even within his own region his material was usually drawn from the records of large planters. He paints, therefore, an unsatisfactory picture of the smaller planters who owned few slaves, planters who were more typical of the South's economic structure. This segment of southern society was the theme of an informative study by Frank L. Owsley, *Plain Folk of the Old South* (1949). Owsley and others who have written on the yeomanry seem to have exaggerated its significance in the economy of a slave-holding society. As for the Negroes' view of southern life, it was beyond Phillips's comprehension. His understanding was that blacks were innately inferior to whites, and because they were accustomed to a lower status, slavery did not weigh heavily upon them. The blacks' smoldering and sometimes overt hostility to slavery was something that Phillips appears to have known nothing about. The militant aspect of slave society, though exaggerated by Herbert Aptheker in *American Negro Slave Revolts* (New York, 1943), had been neglected by earlier historians. In these and other matters Phillips's interpretation of the Old South has undergone important revision at the hands of Eugene Genovese, George P. Rawick, John W. Blassingame, and many others. Nevertheless, the work that he completed in his comparatively short career (he died at the age of fifty-six) bulks large in the intensified study of the South undertaken by the later generation of scholars. Even Genovese, the most noted Marxist historian of America, has insisted that, except for the element of racism—obviously a major exception—Phillips's work is still the best we have on the South.

William E. Dodd

Another scholar and teacher who contributed much to this field of research was William E. Dodd. Although he published few books, through them and various articles and addresses he instilled in his many students a better understanding of the Old South. A man of wide interests, he examined the characteristics of political leadership in his *Statesmen of the Old South* (1911), as well as in other biographies, and ranged at length over the territory covered in *The Cotton Kingdom*, a compact little volume published in 1921 in the Yale Chronicles of America series, a work that contained enough ideas for a shelfful of books. *Expansion and Conflict* (1915) anticipated other writers in pointing to the economic causes of the Civil War.

Dodd had as clear an understanding of the need for research in southern history as any other scholar in the field. In an article in the *American Historical Review* in 1913, "Profitable Fields of Investigation in American History, 1815-1860," he suggested political, economic, and biographical studies, a study of the Illinois Central Railroad, a survey of the attitude of the churches to slavery, and many other themes.[41] Taking to task McMaster and Henry Adams for confining their histories to a restricted area, Dodd said that a comprehensive work would include the debtor regions, the West and the South. On the theme of the Civil War he maintained, contrary to the conventional impression, that the abolitionists "were in no sense one of the great forces which shaped the national destiny"; they would have brought about a northern secession, said Dodd, had it not been for stronger economic and social forces opposing them. Powerful economic groups fought for mastery in the period from 1815 to 1860, and for a time the plantation owners dominated; but at the end the victory went to the northern industrialists, the protagonists of nationalism—a nationalism that protected their own economic interests. Throughout his work in scholarship and in public life (he was named ambassador to Germany in 1933) Dodd avowed himself a disciple of Jefferson.

David M. Potter and C. Vann Woodward

Of the many historians since World War II who have made important contributions to the history of the South—David M. Potter, C. Vann Woodward, T. Harry Williams, Bell I. Wiley, Francis B. Simkins, William B. Hesseltine, Clement Eaton, Emory Thomas, and Frank Vandiver—Potter and Woodward are, perhaps, preeminent. Neither, however, can be accurately labeled as exclusively southern historians.

Potter's first book, *Lincoln and His Party in the Secession Crisis,* published in 1942, was a revision of his doctoral dissertation at Yale. It immediately established him as a major figure in his chosen field. As Sir Denis Brogan wrote in *Pastmasters,* "the fact that the dissertation has been continually reprinted and was issued in 1962 in a new paperback edition with an important revisionary preface shows that the impression made by Potter's first work was durable."[42] *Lincoln and His Party* was a brilliant study of the period from Lincoln's election to the fall of Fort Sumter.

In a sense Potter's first book was to be his last. He shared the problem of another great American historian, Frederick Jackson Turner: he was such a perfectionist that he had great difficulty finishing a book. This is ironic, too, for the book considered by many as Potter's other major work (in addition to *Lincoln*) was *People of Plenty: Economic Abundance and the American Character,* published in 1954. It can be considered a criticism of Turner's frontier thesis or, perhaps more accurately, an alternate, broader explanation of the American past. Boyd C. Shafer brilliantly summarized *People of Plenty* in the *American Historical Review:*

American mobility and lack of status are characteristic. Abundance explains. Americans are democratic. Abundance permits. Americans believe they have a peculiar mission. Abundance explains both the mission and its peculiar nature. American historians have often followed Turner's frontier hypothesis. The frontier was part of abundance.[43]

Turner and Potter even had problems completing a similar project—

Turner his assigned volume *The Rise of the New West* for the American Nation series, Potter his book on the coming of the Civil War in the New American Nation series. In fact, Potter was awarded a contract for that volume in 1954, largely on the basis of his *Lincoln,* and had still not finished it at his death in 1971. His long-term Stanford associate Don E. Fehrenbacher completed it, and it was published in 1976 as *The Impending Crisis, 1848–1861.* It is a massive and brilliant synthesis of that complex, important era.

Two additional sets of Potter's lectures were edited by Fehrenbacher and published as books: *The South and the Concurrent Majority* (published in 1972) and *Freedom and Its Limitations in American Life* (published in 1976). More important were the two collections of essays published as books: *The South and the Sectional Conflict* in 1968, and *History and American Society: Essays of David M. Potter* in 1973. Fehrenbacher edited the latter collection, and in his preface he noted that these two volumes together "designate rather accurately the three principal categories of David Potter's unique contribution to historical knowledge and human understanding"—the South and the sectional conflict, the functional thought of American historians, and the distinguishing characteristics of American society.[44]

It must not be thought, Sir Denis Brogan argues convincingly, that "Potter has cast himself in the role of Civil War historian, still less in the role of Southern historian." Rather, "he is an *American* historian who has concentrated mainly on the problems of the middle period of American nineteenth-century history, and that of course involves concentration, but not an exclusive concentration, on the history of 'the South.'" Finally, Brogan makes an important point when he writes that "Potter, although never denying his Southern origins or his Southern interests, and writing about them with great penetration, is not . . . so burdened with the *damnosa hereditas* of the South as is the historian with whom one most naturally compares him, C. Vann Woodward."[45]

Woodward was born and reared in the South, and despite an academic career spent mostly at Yale he is usually identified as a southerner—his own preference. His first book, *Tom Watson, Agrarian Rebel,* published in 1938, was a revised version of his doctoral dissertation at the University of North Carolina. Essentially, the biography explained the foundering of popular leadership in the post–Civil War South on the rock of racial intolerance. Watson symbolized the 1890s in the South just as Henry Grady had the 1880s, Woodward suggested. Watson's creed, however, was essentially the reverse of Grady's. Watson stood for "agrarianism for the South; a glorification of the farmer and his way of life; war upon the industrial East and alliance with the agrarian West; open and relentless class conflict with the enemy classes both without and within the South; and the enlistment of the Negro in the battle for the farmer equipped with as many political weapons as Watson dared give him." Potter (in *Pastmasters*) praised Woodward's study of Watson as "the best and most revealing biography that has been written of any Southerner living in the period since the Civil War" and "one of the foremost psychological studies in American historical literature." Potter's praise was strongly worded but probably not excessive.[46]

There was a long interval before the publication of Woodward's next major work, *The Battle for Leyte Gulf*, in 1947. It seemed an aberration in the list of his publications; World War II accounted for this, of course. Woodward served from 1943 to 1946 as a lieutenant in the Office of Naval Intelligence and the Naval Office of Public Information. Although *Leyte Gulf* was generally praised by critics — Potter called it "a tour de force which showed what a wide range of things Woodward could do when he put his hand to them" — the book obviously had little to do with Woodward's major areas of study: southern history and historical philosophy.

Two major contributions appeared in 1951: *Reunion and Reaction: The Compromise of 1877 and the End of Reconstruction* and *Origins of the New South, 1877–1913*. *Reunion and Reaction* was a thoughtful and important book in which Woodward acknowledged the influence of Charles Beard's concept of the Civil War as a Second American Revolution. His own book, Woodward said, was based on that concept: "I merely attempt to add a description of the final phase of the revolution, the phase that the French speak of as *Thermidor* in writing of their great revolution."

Woodward supported with a wealth of detail the position of previous authors who described the alliance between northern and southern conservatives to end the "cold war" that developed after 1865. Part of the agreement ensured southern votes for Rutherford B. Hayes over Samuel J. Tilden and congressional support for building western railroads. The compromise, said Woodward, "revealed the party of Radical Reconstruction in alliance with ex-Rebels and ex-slaveholders; the party of emancipation and freedmen's rights abandoning the Negro to his former master." It assured the "dominant white's political autonomy and nonintervention in matters of race policy and promised them a share in the blessings of the new economic order."

Unlike Paul Buck's important book *The Road to Reunion* (1937), which emphasized social and cultural forces at work to reunite the nation, Woodward emphasized the political and economic forces. He concluded:

The Compromise of 1877 marked the abandonment of principles and of force and a return to the traditional ways of expediency and concession. The compromise laid the political foundation for reunion. It established a new sectional truce that proved more enduring than any previous one and provided a settlement for an issue that had troubled American politics for more than a generation. It wrote an end to Reconstruction and recognized a new regime in the South. More profoundly than Constitutional amendments and wordy statutes it shaped the future of four million freedmen and their progeny for generations to come.

Origins of the New South, a volume in the important series History of the South, was a logical continuation of *Reunion and Reaction;* indeed, the two books were essentially one. They grew out of the same research effort, and one chapter of *Origins* ("The Forked Road to Reunion") was a summary of *Reunion and Reaction. Origins* provided an important new interpretation of the years from 1877 to 1913 in southern history. It explained, as no other work had, the impact of a changing economy on the mind and map of the South. "Those who have undertaken to write of the New South have not always been careful to dissociate themselves from the implication of the phrase as a popular slogan," said Woodward. William B. Hesseltine, reviewing *Origins* for the *American Historical Review,* praised it for clearing away "the rubbish that has been said about the South by partisan attackers, vigorous apologists, and ill-informed historians."

Woodward dealt at length with the so-called industrial revolution of the South in the 1880s but insisted that the region remained fundamentally rural. Tracing the origins of southern Populism (Tom Watson, of course, appears prominently in these pages), Woodward made an outstanding contribution to the history of southern race relations both in this movement and in the South's "for whites only" progressivism. Education, literature, and other aspects of the southern mind were not excluded. Finally, Woodward concluded with treatment of the southern aspects of Wilsonianism. The South was back to a prominent position in the Union in 1913, he believed: "The change in the atmosphere at Washington represented a revolution in the geographical distribution of power," wrote Woodward. "For the contrast between the South's position in 1913 and the humble place it had occupied during the previous half century was almost as marked as the contrast between the South of the ante-bellum period and the South of the era that followed." To some, Woodward noted, the change recalled "the resurgence of the South upon the inauguration of Jefferson and Jackson. Whether the comparison had any validity beyond the matter of accents remained to be seen."

Race relations, always a major topic in southern history, were cer-

tainly important to Woodward. Indeed, the issue became so central
to his work that two major books were devoted to it: *The Strange
Career of Jim Crow*, published in 1955 and revised in 1957, 1966, and
1974; and *American Counterpoint: Slavery and Racism in the North-South
Dialogue*, published in 1971. *The Strange Career of Jim Crow* was Woodward's most controversial book, if not his most significant.

The origins of the book *Jim Crow* (as opposed to the origins of
the South's Jim Crow system itself) are not difficult to trace. True,
Woodward was a southerner, but he was also a liberal. While he was
a student at Emory University in Atlanta he came under the influence
of Will W. Alexander's Commission on Interracial Cooperation and the
noted debate coach Glenn Rainey, a liberal on racial matters. At North
Carolina, though Woodward worked in history under Howard K.
Beale, he was also influenced by Rupert B. Vance and Howard W.
Odum, who, in Potter's words, "conceived of the South in terms of a
regionalism which would no longer isolate Dixie from the national
scene, but would enable it to share in the prosperity and the constructive activities of the nation, while preserving its own distinctive qualities and values." Potter emphasized that to Woodward there were two
major values: the southern heritage and liberalism. In the fall of 1954,
just months after the Supreme Court's *Brown v. The Board of Education of Topeka* decision, Woodward delivered a series of lectures at the
University of Virginia which were published the following year as
The Strange Career of Jim Crow. Potter maintained that Woodward's
"greatest significance to historical studies may be in the fact that he
has made himself the foremost practitioner of a concept of history which
holds that the experience of the past can find its highest relevance in
the guidance which it offers in living with the problems of the present."[47] *Jim Crow* was his effort to make that contribution in the area
of race relations in the South.

In the first chapter, significantly entitled "Forgotten Alternatives,"
Woodward insisted that the legalized structure of segregation, which
in the minds of most southerners had always existed, in reality was not
formally instituted until years after the end of Reconstruction. Certainly
Woodward recognized that separation began soon after the Civil War
in the churches, and in the schools as soon as the former slaves began
going to school. He claimed, however, that there was scarcely any
"evidence of a movement to make segregation universal" until later:
"More than a decade was to pass after Redemption [the end of Recon-
struction] before the first Jim Crow law was to appear upon the law
books of a Southern state, and more than two decades before the older
states of Virginia, North Carolina, and South Carolina were to adopt
such laws." As Woodward carefully pointed out, he was not suggest-

ing that there had ever been a "golden age of race relations" in the South, and he acknowledged that "the evidence of race conflict and violence, brutality and exploitation in this very period is overwhelming." Many readers missed that crucial point and, perhaps engaging in wishful thinking, read into Woodward an entirely fallacious notion of a South in which racial antagonism did not appear until the early years of the twentieth century. It is, then, perhaps unfortunate that Woodward's least substantial book in a strict scholarly sense was the one that made his public, as opposed to his professional, reputation.

"My only purpose has been to indicate that things have not always been the same in the South," Woodward stated clearly, and explained: "In a time when the Negroes formed a much larger proportion of the population than they did later, when slavery was a live memory in the minds of both races, and when the memory of the hardships and bitterness of Reconstruction was still fresh, the race policies accepted and pursued in the South were sometimes milder than they became later." The policies of "proscription, segregation, and disfranchisement that are often described as the immutable 'folkways' of the South, impervious alike to legislative reform and armed intervention," were, Woodward insisted, of more recent origin. Therefore, "the effort to justify them as a consequence of Reconstruction and a necessity of the times is embarrassed by the fact that they did not originate in those times." Finally Woodward delivered his liberal punch line: "And the belief that they are immutable and unchangeable is not supported by history."

The Strange Career of Jim Crow was comprised of a series of lectures; two other books by Woodward, *The Burden of Southern History* (published in 1960) and *American Counterpoint*, were collections of essays. Woodward was at his best in such a format rather than in a broad narrative history. One essay, "The Age of Reinterpretation," was originally a paper delivered at the 1959 meeting of the American Historical Association. Potter said that it is "widely regarded as his most significant single piece of work and as one of the major contributions to the interpretation of American history."[48] In the essay Woodward spoke of the modern challenges to the task of the historian, such as the rapidity of change and our passage into the nuclear age. He warned that historians should avoid the assumption of a continuity linking the past to the present; the historian's job is equally to expose any discontinuity. The acceleration of historical change merely intensifies the job of the historian, who must go beyond understanding the past and interpret it appropriately for the present generation. "If historians evade such questions," Woodward warned, "people will turn elsewhere for the answers, and modern historians will qualify for the definition that Tolstoi once formulated for academic historians of his own day. . . . [He called them] deaf men replying to the questions that nobody puts to them." Nevertheless, there is promise in this new situation, too: "If, on the other hand, they do address themselves seriously to the historical questions for which the new age demands answers, the period might justly come to be known in historiography as the age of reinterpretation."

Although dated 1959, "The Age of Reinterpretation" sounds amazingly contemporary. Potter's assessment of Woodward—written in 1969—made this point as well. Referring to Woodward's conception of history "as a key which the past gives us for guidance in confronting the problems of the present," Potter explained that

the difficulty with this conception lies in the dilemma: can history retain its integrity as a rigorous and disciplined form of scholarly inquiry even while partaking of public and functional uses in our encounters with current issues? . . . The resolution can only be meaningful at the operative level, and it is here that Woodward has made one of his most distinctive contributions to historiography. . . . he has been remarkably successful in demonstrating that history can retain its basic scholarly validity even in a context of active presentism.[49]

Finally, in 1972, when Fritz Stern revised his helpful sampling of historical writings *(The Varieties of History: From Voltaire to the Present)*, Woodward's "Clio with Soul"—the cautionary Organization of American Historians presidential address in 1969 about the impact of black history on American historical writing—was the final selection. In his introduction Stern wrote that Woodward's essay

mirrors Woodward's own development and analyzes one of the fundamental problems that historians have had to face in this century: how to respond to the sudden and insistent demands of their own time—demands that may have arisen from a minority struggling to find its historic identity, from a new nation seeking to establish its legitimacy, or from a confused generation seeking its bearings. Few historians have stated the problem as clearly as Woodward, and few have succeeded as he has in making an authentic past speak to present needs.[50]

Responding to the urgent demands of today while applying authentic history to present-day needs—Woodward's dilemma is shared by many postwar American historians.

CHAPTER 14

Consensus: American Historical Writing in the 1950s

CHARLES BEARD'S DEATH in 1948 may be taken as a symbolic ending for the period of American historical writing dominated by the Progressive historians. Appropriately, that same year saw the publication of Richard Hofstadter's *The American Political Tradition and the Men Who Made It*. In retrospect, the book clearly helped establish a new dominant view, which came to be called neo-conservative, or "consensus," history.

Most perceptive readers of history know that a historian is merely a human being whose writing is affected by his or her time, place, and values. Robert Allen Skotheim performed a useful service by editing a book on this subject in 1969 entitled *The Historian and the Climate of Opinion*. By "climate of opinion" he meant "the fundamental assumptions and attitudes shared by significant elements of a population at a given time." He looked at three climates of opinion and the impact they had on American historical writing: the earlier decades of the 1900s, the period after World War II, and the 1960s.[1] Gene Wise, in *American Historical Explanations*, labeled the history written in these three stages as "Progressive, Counter-Progressive and New Left."

Clearly, there are problems with forcing any work in American history into a comfortable mold as either "conflict and change" history or "consensus and continuity" history. For example, if we think of Richard Hofstadter as the founder of a consensus school of American historical writing, we must acknowledge that it is a school from which he dissociated himself rather quickly. His work was far too sophisticated, complex, and open to change to be appropriately labeled in any simple way. In a footnote in *The Progressive Historians* in 1968 he wrote that "in discussing the so-called consensus school I am discussing a tendency with which my own work has often been associated. I suppose the first statement, however brief and inarticulate, of the consensus idea . . . was in the Introduction to my book *The American Political Tradition* (1948), and it is developed fragmentarily in other writings." Hofstadter concluded, however, "while I still find use for insights derived from consensus history, it no longer seems as satisfactory to me as it did ten or twenty years ago."[2]

"It may seem strange," English historian J. R. Pole once suggested, "that American historians should be moved to take sides over the very question of whether there are any sides to take."[3] Yet the idea of consensus and conflict became a central organizing concept for American historical writing, apparently more so than anyone ever intended.

John Higham was among the first to criticize the concept. In an article in *Commentary* in 1959 he charged that a "cult" of consensus had developed in our historical writing. He said that American historians in the 1950s were "carrying out a massive grading operation to smooth over America's social convulsions," and he concluded with a call for a renewed "appreciation of the crusading spirit, a responsiveness to indignation, a sense of injustice."[4] Higham continued his criticism in 1962 in the *American Historical Review:* "The conservative frame of reference is giving us a bland history in which conflict is muted, in which classic issues of social justice are underplayed, in which the elements of spontaneity, effervescence, and violence in American life get little sympathy or attention." It was time, he said, to move "beyond consensus."[5]

Also in 1962, J. Rogers Hollingsworth wrote critically of the consensus-continuity position in the *South Atlantic Quarterly,* and predicted that "it will not be long before historians ... again stress the variety, change, and conflict which have made American history so rich in human experience."[6] He was right, of course—the New Left, or radical American historians, began to do just that in response to their climate of opinion in the 1960s (civil rights, Vietnam, and so on), leading some to label them "neo-Progressives." Barton J. Bernstein published an edited collection of their writings in 1968. His introduction was specifically critical of consensus history and ended with a reference to Higham's article of 1962, saying that "we have, by necessity, moved beyond objective history to the realm of values. In this venture we are ... responding in a modest way to the call issued a few years ago to move 'beyond consensus.' "[7]

In the meantime, however, Higham had begun to have second thoughts. In his important book *History: The Development of Historical Studies in the United States* (published in 1965 with coauthors Leonard Krieger and Felix Gilbert), he moderated somewhat his earlier criticism of consensus histories. By 1969 he had come to feel that "the whole fuss about 'consensus' and 'conflict' has become stale and hackneyed, and the sooner it subsides the better." In 1970 he said of his "beyond consensus" article: "Writing at the height of the conservative reaction against progressive history, I feared it would go too far. It did go too far, and we are now in the throes of an impetuous reaction against that reaction."[8] The "impetuous reaction," of course, was the New Left, which dismayed Higham as much as the extremities of consensus.

Thus Richard Hofstadter, who started the consensus approach, ceased to find it satisfactory, and John Higham, who started the criticism of it, came to consider the whole debate counterproductive. Still, the consensus-conflict dichotomy clearly expressed a simple and fundamental truth, and it proved so helpful in organizing the massive body of American historical writing since World War II that it developed great staying power. Allen F. Davis and Harold D. Woodman compiled a two-volume anthology utilizing the approach—*Consensus and Conflict in Early American History* and *Consensus and Conflict in Modern American History*—that was successful enough to go through five editions between 1966 and 1980. The compilers acknowledged in the 1980 edition that "the lines that divide the conflict from the consensus historians are not so sharp as they once were, and many contemporary historians are drawing from both in their analyses of America's past" (indeed, the title was changed from *Conflict or Consensus* in 1966 to *Conflict and Consensus* in 1980). Davis and Woodman also acknowledged that conflict and consensus were by no means the only unifying themes available to organize their collection of differing interpretations. Still, they insisted correctly that "the choice has not been completely arbitrary in that these themes—conflict and consensus—expressed either explicitly or implicitly, may be found in virtually all major interpretations of our country's past."9

Granted that the concept can easily be carried too far, that not all American historical writing since World War II clearly fits into either "school," and that not all of American history clearly supports either school's approach, the idea still provides a helpful and meaningful organizational device to examine a major portion of that vast, complex body of work which constitutes post–World War II American historiography.

Richard Hofstadter

Richard Hofstadter's first book, *Social Darwinism in American Thought*, was published in 1944; the author was at the University of Maryland at the time and was only twenty-eight years old. "Although it was meant to be a reflective study rather than a tract for the times," he wrote in an introductory note to a revised edition, "it was naturally influenced by the political and moral controversy of the New Deal era." It was typical of Hofstadter to acknowledge that his work was influenced by the climate of opinion of the period in which he wrote. His was one of the great minds in the historical profession in this country, and, unlike many professional historians since the scientific revolution of the late nineteenth century, Hofstadter wrote well. From 1944, the year of his first book, to 1970, the year of his untimely death, there was never a period of more than four years without a major contribution from his pen.

Hofstadter was simultaneously attracted to intellectual history and political history; his work seemed to shuttle between the two and sometimes, at its finest, to fuse them. *Social Darwinism in American Thought* was essentially intellectual history, a description of the impact of Charles Darwin's scientific discoveries upon American ways of thinking outside scientific circles. "There was nothing in Darwinism," Hofstadter maintained, "that inevitably made it an apology for competition or force. [Pyotr Alekseyevich] Kropotkin's interpretation of Darwinism was as logical as [William Graham] Sumner's. [Lester Frank] Ward's rejection of biology as a source of social principles was no more unnatural than [Herbert] Spencer's assumption of a universal dynamic common to biology and society alike." In other words, "Darwinism had from the first this dual potentiality; intrinsically it was a neutral instrument, capable of supporting opposite ideologies." If this was so, then why did the "rugged-individual" version of Darwinism emerge in America? For Hofstadter the answer lay in the nature of the American environment. "American society saw its own image in the tooth-and-claw version of natural selection," he suggested, and "its dominant groups were therefore able to dramatize this version of competition as a thing good in itself."

If there was a weakness in Hofstadter's *Social Darwinism*, it was his failure to demonstrate convincingly the interaction between ideas and the changing social structure. Before Hofstadter had a chance to work out this problem, he joined the faculty of Columbia University and turned to political history. He published in 1948 his all-important book *The American Political Tradition and the Men Who Made It*. It is somewhat ironic that this book has been so often regarded as the beginning of a consensus school of American historical writing, for the author only once suggested that viewpoint, in his introduction, which apparently was almost an afterthought to the book. Hofstadter wrote in the introduction that he had become convinced "of the need for a reinterpretation of our political traditions which emphasizes the common climate of American opinion," the existence of which had been "much obscured by the tendency to place political conflict in the foreground." The struggles in American political history, he claimed, had always been "bounded by the horizons of property and enterprise.... However much at odds on specific issues, the major political traditions have shared a belief in the rights of property, the philosophy of economic individualism, the value of competition; they have accepted the economic virtues of capitalist culture as necessary qualities of man." The historian went on to say that the "sanctity of private property, the right of the individual to dispose of and invest it, the value of opportunity, and the natural evolution of self-interest and self-assertion, within broad legal limits, into a beneficent social order" have also been "staple tenets of the central faith in American political ideologies."

It is worth noting that Hofstadter referred here to "traditions" and "ideologies" in the plural, while the title of the book and most of the argument referred to a single tradition and a single ideology. The body of the book consists of a series of brief but brilliant political biographies of Americans from the Founding Fathers to Franklin D. Roosevelt. Hofstadter always knew how to turn a phrase, especially a critical one, and examples are easy to find. On Jefferson: No one of Jefferson's social status "could be quite the democrat Jefferson imagined himself." On Jackson: "A man like Jackson who had been on the conservative side of economic issues in Tennessee could become the leader of a national democratic movement without feeling guilty of any inconsistency." On Grover Cleveland: "A taxpayer's dream, the ideal bourgeois statesman for his time: out of heartfelt conviction he gave to the interests what many a lesser politician might have sold them for a price." Clearly, one of the advantages of Hofstadter's stance was that it enabled him to be critical of whomever he pleased without taking sides.

One noteworthy review of *The American Political Tradition* appeared in the *American Historical Review;* it was written by Arthur M. Schlesinger, Jr., whose important book *The Age of Jackson* (1945) had made the dominant position of Progressive history seem unassailable. Observing that "Mr. Hofstadter in his introduction happily resolves American political conflict into a shared belief 'in the rights of property, the philosophy of economic individualism, the value of competition,'" Schlesinger suggested that "one is almost tempted to ask why he did not add God, home, and mother, in which our political leaders doubtless also shared a belief." Schlesinger wrote perceptively of the forces influencing American historical writing in post–World War II America: "The crisis in the middle of the twentieth century may lead us in principle to talk broadly about the great unities of our past"; he added in a tone at once humorous and critical, "but they fortunately do not lead Mr. Hofstadter as a historian to confuse Franklin D. Roosevelt with Herbert Hoover." Despite his criticisms, Schlesinger knew that *The American Political Tradition* was "an important and refreshing work" and Hofstadter "a new talent of first-rate ability in the writing of American history."[10]

Hofstadter continued to demonstrate his ability; his next major work, *The Age of Reform: From Bryan to F. D. R.*, published in 1955, won him a Pulitzer Prize. Stanley Elkins and Eric McKitrick, who edited a collection of essays by former students of Hofstadter entitled

The Hofstadter Aegis: A Memorial (1974) and who wrote one essay therein, said that *The Age of Reform* "established Richard Hofstadter as a leading historian of his generation." To illustrate the importance of the book as an example for an emerging generation of historians, they also quoted Robert Wiebe: "To those of us who encountered *The Age of Reform* in graduate school, he, more than any other writer, framed the problems, explored the techniques, and established the model of literate inquiry that would condition our study of the American past."[11]

Hofstadter's subject matter this time was the period from 1890 to 1940 with special emphasis on Populism and Progressivism, including a final chapter contrasting the latter movement to the New Deal. It was Hofstadter's treatment of the Populists which became the most controversial material in his work. Much of what he said was not new, for he was by no means the first to point to the real grievances that led to Populism, nor to praise many of the movement's proposed remedies. Hofstadter wrote: "Populism was the first modern political movement of practical importance in the United States to insist that the federal government has some responsibility for the common weal; indeed, it was the first such movement to attack seriously the problems created by industrialism. . . . Most of the "radical" reforms in the Populist program proved in later years to be either harmless or useful." It was in his interpretation of Populist motivation that Hofstadter caused controversy: "Rank in society! That was close to the heart of the matter," he wrote, "for the farmer was beginning to realize acutely not merely that the best of the world's goods were to be had in the cities . . . but also that he was losing in status and respect." Thus Hofstadter introduced his concept of "status politics," as opposed to "interest politics," to explain Populism. He went on to be highly critical of the Populist movement. Arthur M. Schlesinger, Jr., explained in *Pastmasters:*

> Hofstadter appeared to suggest that the "reality" of Populism lay not in its program but in its rhetoric; in, moreover, precisely that side of its rhetoric which expressed the politics of nostalgia and conspiracy. "The utopia of the Populists was in the past, not the future." They "looked backward with longing to the lost agrarian Eden." They wanted to "restore the conditions prevailing before the development of industrialism and the commercialization of agriculture." Locked into a world of chimeras, they saw plots everywhere, pursued scapegoats, especially Jews and foreigners, and were a retrogressive force in American life. The longer Populism lasted, moreover, the worse it became. In our day the Populist tradition "has turned sour, become illiberal and ill-tempered." The process of "deconversion from reform to reaction" presumably led straight to McCarthyism.[12]

This view of Populism soon fell under serious criticism from such scholars as C. Vann Woodward, Norman Pollack, and Walter T. K. Nugent.

Hofstadter also used status politics to explain Progressivism, and though his interpretation has not been without its critics, it is generally conceded that his concept worked better here than with the Populists. The historian held that Progressives became such "not because of economic deprivations but primarily because they were victims of an upheaval in status." Progressivism was "led by men who suffered from the events of their time not through a shrinkage in their means but through the changed pattern in the distribution of deference and power. . . . They were expropriated, not so much economically as morally." Progressivism, then, "at its heart, was an effort to realize familiar and traditional ideals under novel circumstances." In Hofstadter's view the Progressives accepted the competitive order and wished to keep the functions of government minimal. Like the Populists they tried to hold on to some of the values of agrarian life, to save personal entrepreneurship and individual opportunity and the character type they engendered, and to maintain a homogeneous Yankee civilization."

It is interesting that Hofstadter has been criticized for *not* applying his concept of status politics to the New Deal. His brief treatment of that period is not the most important part of *The Age of Reform*, but it deserves mention. Hofstadter saw the New Deal as "a drastic new departure . . . different from anything that had yet happened in the United States." It differed from earlier reform movements in its problems, constituencies, objectives, intellectual temper, and moral tone. Alone among previous reform movements it had to meet the problems of economic collapse. It was more concerned with offering security to urban workers and ethnic minorities than with restoring opportunity to established American entrepreneurs. Finally, it did not share the moral indignation of earlier efforts at reform but placed its emphasis upon results, leading Hofstadter to call it "the new opportunism."

Hofstadter maintained an exceptionally active publication record. His work with C. DeWitt Hardy on a volume entitled *The Development and Scope of Higher Education in the United States* (1952) led to *The Development of Academic Freedom in the United States*, with Walter P. Metzger as coauthor, which was published in 1955. Also in 1955, *The Age of Reform* and a revised edition of *Social Darwinism in American Thought* appeared. This productivity continued with textbooks, anthologies, collections of documents, articles, and book reviews in great profusion. Among the more significant of these miscellaneous items were two books coedited with sociologist Seymour Martin Lipset, *Sociology and History: Methods* and *Turner and the Sociology of the Frontier*, both published in 1968, and one coedited with Michael Wallace, *American Violence: A Documentary History*, published in 1970.

Before his death in 1970 at the age of only fifty-four, Richard Hofstadter produced four additional major works: *Anti-Intellectualism in American Life* in 1963, *The Paranoid Style in American Politics and Other Essays* in 1965, *The Progressive Historians: Turner, Beard, Parrington* in 1968, and *The Idea of a Party System: The Rise of Legitimate Opposition in the United States, 1780–1840* in 1969. One additional volume, never completed, appeared after his death as *America at 1750: A Social Portrait.*

Anti-Intellectualism in American Life won Hofstadter another Pulitzer Prize, although it does not stand up as one of his best books. He acknowledged in the preface that it was a very personal work and wrote in the first chapter, "Although this book deals mainly with certain aspects of the remoter American past, it was conceived in response to the political and intellectual conditions of the 1950's." It was during that decade that the term "anti-intellectualism" became "a familiar part of our national vocabulary of self-recrimination and intramural abuse." Hofstadter was quite specific: "Primarily it was McCarthyism which aroused the fear that the critical mind was at a ruinous discount in this country." Hofstadter's procedure, then, according to Elkins and McKitrick, "was to run a line through American history in each of four general realms of endeavor — religion, politics, business, and education — and to see what conditions in each most made for anti-intellectualism." Elkins and McKitrick were clearly among Hofstadter's great admirers, but they freely acknowledged that *Anti-Intellectualism* was not "an unqualified success" and "should probably be counted as one of the less fortunate by-products [of McCarthyism], locked as it is in the very present-mindedness Hofstadter thought he was warning against." When Hofstadter described a great American heartland "filled with people who are often fundamentalist in religion, nativist in prejudice, isolationist in foreign policy, and conservative in economics" as a standing menace to intellectuals and intellectualism, he was, suggested Elkins and McKitrick, "victimized by the 'Progressive' fallacy which he himself, in other ways, had done so much to expose."[13]

Elkins and McKitrick felt that a "more salutary side of what McCarthyism did for Hofstadter's understanding" could be seen in *The Paranoid Style in American Politics,* published in 1965.[14] This volume was a collection of various essays, originally published between 1951 and 1965, all of which had as a central theme the politics of the irrational; that is, all the essays were concerned with political movements whose participants' behavior seemed out of proportion to the actual issues. Many, such as the Anti-Masons, the nativists of the 1840s and 1850s, the Populists, and the McCarthyites, showed an obsession with plots and conspiracies. Some, such as the jingoists who demanded war with Spain in 1898 and the Goldwaterites of 1964 (who seemed at times to want above all else to punish the liberal Republicans), were extravagantly pugnacious. It has already been noted that Hofstadter became discontented with the "consensus" label; it should also be emphasized that the term "consensus" does not always mean conservatism. Any historian who critically analyzes the conservative Republican presidential campaign of Barry Goldwater as an example of the "paranoid style" of American politics is hardly a conservative in most people's definition of the term—though it should also be noted that what Hofstadter did, in part, was to deny that Goldwater was a conservative. Admitting that questioning Goldwater's conservatism "may seem gratuitous," Hofstadter still insisted on doing so: "What is at stake, as Robert J. Donovan puts it, is whether the Republican party can learn to make 'a distinction between the conservatism represented by Senator Goldwater and his supporters and the conservatism that conserves.'" Hofstadter entitled his essay "Goldwater and Pseudo-Conservative Politics."

Hofstadter continued to make use of his concept of status politics here and explained it succinctly: "We have, at all times, two kinds of processes going on in inextricable connection with each other: *interest politics*, the clash of material aims and needs among various groups and blocs; and *status politics*, the clash of various projective rationalizations arising from status aspirations and other personal motives." In times of prosperity, Hofstadter held, status politics tends to dominate, whereas in depressions "politics is more clearly a matter of interests."

Hofstadter's next major book, *The Progressive Historians*, appeared in 1968. To the historiographer it is not only Hofstadter's most important book but one of the most important in the entire field of American historical writing. As Arthur M. Schlesinger, Jr., said in *Book World*, "it is a distinguished book about distinguished historians by a distinguished historian." As it has been utilized extensively to deal with the Progressive historians, not much more need be said of it here. Most of it, of course, was devoted to Frederick Jackson Turner, Charles A. Beard, and Vernon L. Parrington, but with an informative opening chapter, "Historical Writing Before Turner," and a closing one entitled "Conflict and Consensus in American History," it is very nearly a general history of American historical writing. It has not been at all unusual for historiography to be taken lightly by many historians. Schlesinger, for example, said in his essay on Hofstadter in *Pastmasters* that "Hofstadter's historiographical preoccupations have always somewhat stood between himself and historical research."[15] The implication is that the admittedly somewhat different kind of research that goes into historiography is somehow *qualitatively* different from other historical research, inferior to it, and perhaps not even really historical research. Gene Wise was among those who knew better. Praising (in *American*

Historical Explanations) Hofstadter's *The Progressive Historians* as "the richest study ever made of a school of American historians" and "a testimony to the possibilities of historiography in American historical scholarship," Wise concluded on this optimistic note: "After *The Progressive Historians*, it should be harder for members of the profession to dismiss historiography as not being 'real' scholarship."[16]

In 1969, Hofstadter returned to a more strictly political history once again with *The Idea of a Party System: The Rise of Legitimate Opposition in the United States, 1780–1840.* The book grew out of the Jefferson Memorial Lectures which Hofstadter had given at the University of California at Berkeley in the fall of 1966. The "primary paradox" of his inquiry, said Hofstadter, was that "Jefferson, the founder, or more accurately, co-founder, of the first modern popular party, had no use for political parties. This seeming inconsistency is but one aspect of a larger problem: the creators of the first American party system on both sides, Federalists and Republicans, were men who looked upon parties as sores on the body politic." In the Anglo-American world of the eighteenth century, Hofstadter correctly pointed out, political discussion "was pervaded by a kind of anti-party cant." Hofstadter's job, then, performed in a brilliant series of lectures, was to show how the two-party system of modern times emerged from that situation.

Even the experience of the Jeffersonian Republicans as an opposition "had not fully reconciled them to the necessity of an opposition," wrote Hofstadter. It was not until "the second generation of American political leaders—that is, among men who were in the main still children when the Federalist and Republican parties were founded"—that the modern idea of the political party and "a fully matured conception of the function of legitimate opposition" came into existence:

Where the Federalists and Republicans, still enchanted with eighteenth-century visions of political harmony, had schemed to devour, absorb, or annihilate each other, many Republicans raised on the one-party politics of the misnamed Era of Good Feelings, began to see clearly and consistently what such predecessors as Madison and Jefferson had seen only dimly and fitfully—the merits of the party organizations as a positive principle, and of two-party competition as an asset to the public interest.

New York's Albany Regency served as "archetypes of the new advocates of party," and Hofstadter chose to focus on Martin Van Buren, "an intelligent and seasoned exponent of the emerging partisan creed, and the first representative of the new generation and mentality to become President."

The Idea of a Party System was the last book that Richard Hofstadter completed. In the spring of 1969 he announced to his publisher his intention to devote roughly the next twenty years to writing a three-volume interpretative history of the United States from 1750 to the present, primarily a political history but with "whatever is necessary in the way of economic, cultural, and biographical background." As Elkins and McKitrick noted, Hofstadter's "guess of more than a dozen years before—that the historian who hoped somehow to count could not rest content with small things, that he would eventually feel called upon to deal with 'the great turning points in human experience'—had become a self-fullfilling prophecy." As they also suggested, "It may well have occurred to him that the most recent major effort in any way analogous to what he had in mind was still Charles and Mary Beard's *Rise of American Civilization*, which had made so singular an impression on him in his youth."[17] The existing body of his work suggests that a general interpretative history from Richard Hofstadter would have been an outstanding contribution indeed. He was able to devote only one year to the task, however, before his death in 1970. The fragment he had completed was published in 1971 as *America at 1750: A Social Portrait.*

America at 1750 is a good book but obviously far from being complete; it was only remotely suggestive of what his finished work might have been. Two excellent chapters were "Population and Immigration" and "The Middle-Class World." Two groups of chapters dealt with religion (especially the Great Awakening) and with white servitude and black slavery. Perhaps it was in the portions on religion that Hofstadter made his greatest contribution. To Elkins and McKitrick he was once more on "the threshold of what amounted to a new interpretative idea. This was the emerging conception, hitherto largely undeveloped by anyone, of the functions of religion in shaping political practice in provincial America."[18]

Daniel J. Boorstin and Louis Hartz

Although Richard Hofstadter is frequently regarded as the founder of the consensus school of American historical writing, Daniel J. Boorstin and Louis Hartz are generally considered its two primary proponents. Boorstin did give us a full interpretative history from the consensus perspective: its main title is *The Americans*, and its three volumes are entitled *The Colonial Experience* (1958), *The National Experience* (1965), and *The Democratic Experience* (1973). Boorstin not only saw consensus in the American past but celebrated it, and the labels "conservative" or "neoconservative" or "counter-Progressive" for the consensus school fit him more comfortably than they did any of the others in his field. *The Americans*, however, was not where he introduced his viewpoint;

that had come earlier with *The Genius of American Politics* in 1953, five years after Hofstadter's *American Political Tradition* and two years before Hartz's *Liberal Tradition in America.*

Boorstin wrote *The Genius of American Politics,* in the words of English historian J. R. Pole in *Pastmasters,* "during the period when the international crisis of the Cold War was compounded by the domestic crisis of McCarthyism, and part of the purpose was to give his countrymen some historical bearings by which they could help to steady themselves."[19] Although published in 1955 it was actually a revised collection of the Charles R. Walgreen Foundation Lectures delivered at the University of Chicago in 1952. Boorstin's doctoral degree was from Yale, and he had studied and taught in England and Italy before going to Chicago, and his travels had clearly had an impact on his thinking. Much has been written about Boorstin and his interpretation of American history, and he has often been misunderstood. *The Genius of American Politics* is probably the most important place to seek a grasp of his view of the American past and present.

Much of that view was spelled out succinctly in the introduction Boorstin supplied for the lectures when he committed them to print. "The genius of American democracy comes not from any special virtue of the American people but from the unprecedented opportunities of this continent and from a peculiar and unrepeatable combination of historical circumstances," he began. "These circumstances have given our institutions their character and their virtues." The same facts which explain these virtues, however, "explain also our inability to make a 'philosophy' of them." They explain "our lack of interest in political theory, and why we are doomed to failure in any attempt to sum up our way of life in slogans and dogmas." Therefore, they also explain "why we have nothing in the line of a theory that can be exported to other peoples of the world." The thesis of the book, Boorstin stated quite simply, is that "nothing could be more un-American than to urge other countries to imitate America." Boorstin found American democracy unique: "It possesses a 'genius' all its own." On a separate but clearly related point Boorstin first showed his positive response to the absence of conflict he perceived in the American past: "A pretty good rule-of-thumb for us in the United States is that our national well-being is in inverse proportion to the sharpness and extent of the theoretical differences between our political parties." The "genius" of American politics, Boorstin stated bluntly, "adds up to a warning that, if we rely on the 'philosophy of American democracy' as a weapon in the world-wide struggle, we are relying on a weapon which may prove to be a dud." This was so because "the peculiar strengths of American life have saved us from the European preoccupation with political dogmas and have left us inept and uninterested in political theory." Finally, Boorstin promised, "I shall try to show how American history has nourished in a very special way and to an extraordinary degree our feeling for that principle of social science which I shall later call the 'seamlessness' of culture." American geography and history have both led to "an unspoken assumption, and axiom, so basic to our thinking that we have hardly been aware of it at all," Boorstin concluded; specifically, it is

the axiom that institutions are not and should not be the grand creations of men toward large ends and outspoken values; rather they are organisms which grow out of the soil in which they are rooted and out of the tradition from which they have sprung. Our history has fitted us, even against our will, to understand the meaning of conservatism. We have become the exemplars of the continuity of history and of the fruits which come from cultivating institutions suited to a time and place, in continuity with the past.

There is little conflict and change in American history, Boorstin seemed to be saying, and much consensus and continuity—and that, he said, was good. In a series of essays (originally lectures) with such revealing titles as "How Belief in the Existence of an American Theory Has Made a Theory Superfluous," "The American Revolution: Revolution Without Dogma," and "The Civil War and the Spirit of Compromise," Boorstin elaborated upon this view. It is in the first of these that he introduced the concept of "givenness" that is so central to his work: "For the belief that an explicit political theory is superfluous precisely because we already somehow possess a satisfactory equivalent, I propose the name 'givenness.'" He defined it as "the belief that values in America are in some way or other automatically defined: *given* by certain facts of geography or history peculiar to us." This concept has three "faces," Boorstin suggested: "First is the notion that we have received our values as a gift from the *past;* that the earliest settlers or Founding Fathers equipped our nation at its birth with a perfect and complete political theory, adequate to all our future needs." The second notion is that "in America we receive values as a gift from the *present,* that our theory is always implicit in our institutions. This is the idea that the 'American Way of Life' harbors an 'American Way of Thought' which can do us for a political theory, even if we never make it explicit." Boorstin explained that "while according to the first axiom of 'givenness' our values are the gift of our history, according to the second they are the gift of our landscape." Finally, the third part of givenness is a belief which links the first two parts: "It is a belief in the continuity or homogeneity of our history. It is the quality of our experience which makes us see our national past as an uninterrupted continuum of similar events, so that our past merges indistinguishably into our present."

Boorstin noted in his final chapter that "we all know that people are prone to parade their weaknesses as if they were virtues." Some critics have accused him of doing just that when he went on to write, with apparent pride: "It is surely no accident that we have accomplished relatively little in the arts of painting, sculpture, chamber music, and chamber poetry. It is equally no accident that we have contributed so little in political philosophy."

Boorstin invited comparison with the other leading consensus theorist of the 1950s, Louis Hartz. The basic difference between Hartz and Boorstin is that Hartz did not necessarily like the consensus he observed in the American past; he seemed somehow less simplistic, more thoughtful than Boorstin. Hartz's major contribution in this field was *The Liberal Tradition in America,* published in 1955. His basic contention was that America had come into being after the age of feudalism; thus, lacking a feudal past, Americans did not have to contend with the established feudal structure that characterized the ancien régime in Europe—titled aristocracy, national church, national army, and so on. The United States was "born free" and did not require a radical social revolution to become a liberal society, because it already was one. The absence of a feudal heritage enabled the liberal-bourgeois ideas embodied in Lockean political principles to flourish almost unchallenged in America. "The ironic flaw in American liberalism," wrote Hartz (use of the word "flaw" is significant), "lies in the fact that we have never had a conservative tradition." What then of the "conservatives" in the American past about whom the Progressives had written? They had much more in common with their fellow American "liberals" than with their European counterparts, Hartz maintained; many of their presumed differences were essentially shadowboxing, for both agreed on a common body of liberal political principles. Certainly if measured in terms of a spectrum of thought that included European ideologies, the American conflicts took place well within the limits of a broad Lockean consensus.

The tone of Hartz's work is remarkably different from that of Boorstin's. The "basic ethical problem of a liberal society," Hartz maintained, was "not the danger of the majority which has been its conscious fear, but the danger of unanimity, which has slumbered unconsciously behind it: the 'tyranny of opinion' that Tocqueville saw unfolding as even the pathetic social distinctions of the Federalist era collapsed before his eyes." In recent times, continued Hartz, "this manifestation of irrational Lockianism, or of 'Americanism,' to use a favorite term of the American Legion, one of the best expounders of the national spirit that Whiggery discovered after the Civil War, has neither slumbered nor been unconscious. It has been very much awake in a red scare hysteria which no other nation in the West has really been able to understand."

Hartz, a historian more willing and able to see conflict than Boorstin, acknowledged that we must be careful not "to obscure or to minimize the nature of the internal conflicts which have characterized American political life." He went on to say, however, that "what we learn from the concept of a liberal society, lacking feudalism and therefore socialism and governed by an irrational Lockianism, is that the domestic struggles of such a society have all been projected with the setting of Western liberal alignments." Hartz's view of the Progressive historians is an interesting one. He fully acknowledged that "after all is said and done Beard somehow stays alive, and the reason for this is that, as in the case of Marx, you merely demonstrate your subservience to a thinker when you spend your time attempting to disprove him." Yet, for reasons of his own, Hartz was quite critical of Beard and other Progressives. He claimed that they "went back to the origins of American history, splitting into two warring camps, discovering a 'social revolution' in the eighteenth century, and in general making it impossible to understand the American liberal community." While their treatment of the Constitution may have lacked the piety of the "patriotic" historians, he said, "it was as 'American' as anything those historians developed. Indeed one might even argue that the others, by stressing a kind of happy national family, were a shade closer to the Lockian solidarity of the nation, which indeed was flourishing as never before in a commonly accepted 'Americanism.'" Finally, Hartz noted that the Progressive historians had "many comforts . . . which the liberal society analysis can never claim." For one thing, they "always had an American hero available to match any American villain they found, a Jefferson for every Hamilton. Which meant that in their demonology the nation never really sinned: only its inferior self did." The analyst of American liberalism, on the other hand, "is not in so happy a spot, for concentrating on unities as well as conflict, he is likely to discover on occasion a national villain, such as the tyrannical force of Lockian sentiment, whose treatment requires a new experience for the whole country rather than the insurgence of a part of it."

The Liberal Tradition in America was not without its critics. Perhaps the most vigorous was Stuart Gerry Brown, in *Ethics*. If Hartz's book was in part a product of the cold war environment, Brown's review of the book was even more clearly so. What Hartz showed, said Brown, was that

the factions of American life have had a tendency, gradual but relatively sure, to move toward, rather than away from, agreement with one another, so that such antidemocratic systems as fascism, state socialism, and communism have seemed more alien and have been unable to put down any roots in the United States. But to refer this grateful development to a growing unanimity of belief in the "liberal" economics of capitalist business enterprise and to assert that this *is* the American tradition is to distort our history and our principles and to leave us, as Hartz does, helpless before our Communist enemy.

Paraphrasing Hartz, Brown continued, "Because there was no feudalism, there was no revolution — only a war for independence to determine whether the Englishmen of America or the Englishmen of England should control our destinies." Brown argued that "this thesis is becoming a bit tiresome from frequent repetition in the literature of the 'new conservatism'" and suggested: "Fortunately for freedom, the American tradition is far richer and more various than Hartz would have us think, and whether we had feudalism or not, we *did* have a revolution. In that Revolution the rights of republican liberty were made available, for the first time in human history, to a whole people." Brown listed primogeniture, entail, quitrents, and property qualifications for voting as some of the vestiges of feudal institutions which were soon abolished as a result of the American Revolution. "It is precisely because our principles are revolutionary, whether we acknowledge them or not, that the Communists and all totalitarians fear us," according to Brown. Finally, he concluded vigorously, "To assert the 'non-revolutionary' character of America is no service to freemen of America or elsewhere in a time when tyranny threatens to engulf the human race, and it is bad scholarship and bad history. To revive conservatism in an age that calls for liberal experiment on a scale as yet unimagined is to commit a tragic political blunder."[20]

Eric F. Goldman was critical, too, in the *Political Science Quarterly* but was more balanced. Hartz's thesis of minimal conflict in the American past fits the twentieth century better than it fits earlier periods, he suggested. The best part of Goldman's review, however, was that in which he brilliantly summarized, even while in the midst of it, what was happening to historiography in post–World War II America: "Something important is astir in American political and historical writings," he began. "For a number of years the tendency had been to emphasize the economic and social conflicts in the past of the United States and to make them much the same as the European pattern. Since World War II, the trend has been to stress the uniqueness of the American tradition and to find that uniqueness in our relative lack of genuine ideological conflicts." After suggesting that one of the most interesting aspects of Hartz's book was the way it raised "the eternal question of historiography," Goldman concluded with two rhetorical questions: "Could it be that historians and political scientists of the 1930's frame of mind, thinking amid such strident ideological warfare, overemphasized the degree of cleavage in previous decades? Could it be that a later generation, thinking amid rampant middle-roadism, is overemphasizing the extent of agreement in the past?"[21]

Stuart Gerry Brown compared Boorstin and Hartz somewhat incorrectly when he said that the difference between *The Genius of American Politics* and *The Liberal Tradition in America* was "so slight as to involve no more than a matter of idiom." Richard L. Rapson, in *Major Interpretations of the American Past,* was one of many to be more perceptive than was Brown about the real differences. Much of Hartz's book dealt with "the liabilities of consensus," he wrote, while Boorstin *"celebrated* consensus and indicted ideological conflict." Rapson held that *The Liberal Tradition in America* was Hartz's only major contribution to consensus history; *The Genius of American Politics* was, on the other hand, only the beginning for Boorstin. *The Colonial Experience,* the first volume of Boorstin's trilogy *The Americans,* was the "high water mark of the consensus outlook," said Rapson. Bernard Bailyn correctly saw the relationship between Boorstin's *Genius* (1953) and *The Colonial Experience* (1958) when he described the latter in a review in the *New Republic* as "a 400-page footnote" to the former. Perhaps the only new element that Boorstin added, or at least newly emphasized, was Americans' practicality. He was more interested in practical American innovations in science, speech, the press, war, and so on, than in thought, political or otherwise—of which there was little anyway, in his view.[22] John Higham has been perhaps the most damning critic of Boorstin: he noted the "anti-intellectual bias" of *The Colonial Experience* and called *The Genius of American Politics* a "celebration of the mindlessness of American life."[23]

Much has been made of the comparison of Boorstin with Hartz; there is also at least one significant point of comparison between Boorstin and Hofstadter. Hofstadter showed a willingness, an ability—even an eagerness—to change and to develop his views; he ultimately rejected the consensus approach as too confining. Boorstin, on the other hand, has been consistent, continuing his approach through two more massive volumes of *The Americans* and other works. Bailyn criticized *The Colonial Experience* as "an extraordinary apologia for his [Boorstin's] disillusioned conservatism" and as "more a sensitive reaction to the unprecedented whisperings of our present political climate than . . . a result of the careful dissecting, ordering, and interpreting of knowledge." Seeking "in history proof of the necessity and immemorial rightness of his present political views," Boorstin "has sketched a colorful, occasionally brilliant, but lopsided image of the past." Essentially, Bailyn's criticisms ring true.

Another example of the presentism Bailyn found in *The Colonial Experience* is in Boorstin's *The Decline of Radicalism: Reflections on America Today* (1969). The title of the book is honest, seemingly admitting that the analysis contained therein is, as Marian J. Morton described it (in *The Terrors of Ideological Politics: Liberal Historians in a Conservative Mood*), "a-historical." The title of Boorstin's book was significant for other reasons. Morton suggested that it "sounds peculiar from a historian who has never admitted that radicalism existed in this country."[24] Some critics have even suggested that the title should have been "The Decline of Daniel J. Boorstin"—for in this insubstantial little collection of essays, loosely related at best, Boorstin seemed almost to be blindly lashing out at the forces of conflict and change in the 1960s that his comfortable consensus-and-continuity view of the American past could not allow him to understand. He could see Black Power, for example, only as "racism."

Boorstin caught himself in an even greater dilemma in his analysis of student radicals, for one of his major criticisms of these young people, whom he termed "the New Barbarians," was that they offered "no content, no ideology"—a strange criticism, indeed, for a historian who had previously glorified the early Americans for exactly the same deficiencies. It is rather rare for the *American Historical Review* to publish in article form a critique of the work of an individual historian, but such an article appeared on Boorstin in 1971. The author was John P. Diggins, who saw clearly Boorstin's problem. There is "cold irony here," Diggins suggested, for Boorstin was "now asking the militant young to do what he previously believed to be alien to the American character," namely "to give philosophical content to their thoughts, to go to the root of matters by posing questions of ultimate knowledge and value, to 'search for meaning'; in short, to become speculative theorists rather than mindless activists." Concluded Diggins, "The unpardonable sin of the New Left, it would seem, is that it learned all too well America's genius for dismissing all problems of ideology and philosophy as superfluous."[25]

Among those who had trouble understanding Boorstin's insecurity evinced in his *Decline of Radicalism* was M. J. Morton: "How this admittedly tiny fraction of Americans [Black Power advocates and student militants] could endanger the stability of a nation which had earlier survived a full-scale Revolution and a bloody Civil War is a mystery."[26] But then Boorstin and most of the other consensus historians had never really seen the Revolution as revolutionary, and they had never really explained the Civil War; rather, they had ignored it because it was the most difficult part of the American past to force into their mold.

An analysis of Daniel J. Boorstin should not end on a critical note, however. He did excellent work, before he became directly involved in the consensus controversy, in such books as *The Mysterious Science of the Law,* a study of Sir William Blackstone published in 1941, and *The Lost World of Thomas Jefferson,* published in 1948. Also, his "monumental paean to pragmatic American consensus"—as William H. Goetzmann called *The Americans*—surely ranks among the major sustained contributions to American historiography made by an individual or school of thought since World War II.[27] It is also one of the best examples available in American historical writing of a work which both influenced and was influenced by the climate of opinion of its time.

The New American Nation Series and Other Developments

The New American Nation Series, which began publication in 1954, was so called because it was intended to replace the old A. B. Hart series, The American Nation: A History. In between these two, however, there had been another multivolume series of considerable importance, although its goals were somewhat more limited. This was the thirteen-volume set edited by Arthur M. Schlesinger and Dixon Ryan Fox, significantly entitled A History of American Life, published between 1927 and 1943.

By the time the last of the American Nation volumes had come off the press, the series had acquired a slightly old-fashioned look in the eyes of younger students. The newer generation of historians, believing that politics had been overemphasized in historical writing, proclaimed as their purpose the recording of the cultural history of the American people, a subject which they thought had been ignored by previous historians. In the remarks of critical scholars there was the implicit conviction that social history was the real guardian of the values of the past, as well as a guide to future social progress, whereas political and military history seemed to celebrate man's idolatry of false gods— war and the state. There was, however, less novelty in these self-conscious proclamations than was supposed.

The importance of including more material on a people's activities than on politics and war in a historical narrative had long since been granted; John Bach McMaster had been a pioneer in social history as early as the 1880s. A vigorous proponent of the "new history" as a record of the culture of a people was Edward Eggleston, who had already attained fame as the author of *The Hoosier Schoolmaster.* He planned a series of volumes to constitute a history of American life— the sources and development of its ideas and habits. "It will be a work," he said, "designed to answer the questions 'How?' and 'Whence?' and 'Why?' " Unfortunately, Eggleston lived to finish only two volumes, *The Beginners of a Nation* (1896) and *The Transit of Civilization* (1901), which together covered less than half of the seventeenth century. Because his work was incomplete, his informative and well-written volumes are not as widely known as they should be. Even so, Eggleston, who was opposed to "drum and trumpet" history, had a strong influence on the younger generation of scholars; they saw in his work an excellent example of social history written with charm and coherence. He spelled out his approach in his presidential address before the American Historical Association in 1900.

It remained, however, for Schlesinger and Fox's History of American Life to move to the extreme position that politics could be almost entirely neglected in a narrative. A series of twelve volumes was projected (the thirteenth was added later); illustrations and bibliographies were important features of this publication. Herbert I. Priestley, in *The Coming of the White Man, 1492–1848,* made special reference to the French and Spanish settlements, noting particularly the existence of a rich Spanish culture long before the English colonies were established. Included in the last two chapters were the Dutch and the Swedes, the former receiving a realistic estimate of their legacy to posterity. Thomas J. Wertenbaker wrote the next volume, *The First Americans, 1604–1690,* followed by James Truslow Adams, who took the social history of the colonies to 1763 in *Provincial Society, 1690–1763.* Evarts B. Greene, who had spent many years studying the years of Revolution, wrote *The Revolutionary Generation, 1763–1790.* The succeeding period, through the Civil War, was covered in three volumes: John A. Krout and Dixon R. Fox wrote *The Completion of Independence, 1790–1830;* Carl Russell Fish, *The Rise of the Common Man, 1830–1850;* and Arthur C. Cole, *The Irrepressible Conflict, 1850–1865.* The next volumes, Allan Nevins's *Emergence of Modern America, 1865–1878* and Arthur M. Schlesinger's *Rise of the City, 1878–1898,* covered the period of economic and social reconstruction; Ida Tarbell's *Nationalizing of Business, 1878–1898* dealt specifically with economic development. Harold U. Faulkner's *Quest for Social Justice, 1898–1914* was filled with the successes and failures of the liberal movement and the abandonment of laissez-faire, while Preston W. Slosson's *Great Crusade and After, 1914–1928* continued the narrative to the date of publication. World War I and the postwar years, with their exhilaration and their disillusionment, comprised the theme of this volume, which contained many facts but was weak in interpretation. Dixon Wecter's *Age of the Great Depression, 1929–1941* was a supplement to the original twelve-volume set.

The defect of Slosson's volume on the years from 1914 to 1928 was a weakness shared by most of the books in A History of American Life—a dearth of comment on the meaning of the facts; too often the work had the appearance of a catalog. Because the historian may not be sure what the facts mean, he is not therefore absolved from some attempt at interpretation. On the other hand, it would have been possible to write each one of these volumes with a different set of facts, and thus, the ones selected do give a picture of what was happening in American society. The proper scope of social history is, of course, still a matter filled with controversial elements, as is the problem of relative emphasis. A History of American Life certainly deserves credit as a pioneer effort in social history. Its continuing value was recognized by the decision to reprint the entire series in 1971.

In 1972 publication began of the new, seven-volume series *The History of American Society*, edited by Jack P. Greene. This series placed itself firmly within the tradition of A History of American Life but was, of course, updated. It was to include volumes by such diverse but noted scholars as the Englishman J. R. Pole *(Foundations of American Independence, 1763–1815)* and the New Left historian Howard Zinn *(Postwar America, 1945–1971)*. Greene in his editor's foreword to each volume lamented that American historians lagged behind all other Western nations in the development of social history.

Henry Steele Commager and Richard B. Morris, both respected historians for works of their own, would deserve high praise if they had done nothing more than edit the New American Nation Series. It began publication in 1954 and has reached some forty volumes to date. Although the quality of individual volumes varies greatly, as with any such series, the overall standard is high enough to make the New American Nation the best-known and most respected project of its kind ever attempted in the United States and clearly one of the major events of post–World War II American historical writing. It is impossible to impose comfortably any label on the series as a whole. Many of its volumes, some earlier ones especially, are consensus-oriented, some are not, and for some this is simply not an issue. Many of the individual volumes are excellent and have achieved the status of classic works in their field, while others are notoriously weak and have already been almost forgotten. For a series so large, and spanning almost thirty years in composition, such diversities should not be surprising.

The first four volumes appeared in 1954, and each became a well-known standard: *The American Revolution, 1775–1783*, by John R. Alden; *The English People on the Eve of Colonization, 1603–1630*, by Wallace Notestein; *Woodrow Wilson and the Progressive Era, 1910–1917*, by Arthur S. Link; and *The Coming of the Revolution, 1763–1775*, by Laurence Henry Gipson. Other contributions that appeared in the

1950s include Foster Rhea Dulles's volume on the American rise to world power after the Spanish-American War, Louis B. Wright's on the cultural life of the colonies, George E. Mowry's on the era of Theodore Roosevelt, Glyndon G. Van Deusen's on the age of Jackson, and Harold U. Faulkner's on the 1890s.

The diversity of the series is well illustrated by two of the books on the American frontier. Ray Allen Billington, the highly respected disciple of Frederick Jackson Turner, contributed to the series *The Far Western Frontier, 1830–1860,* published in 1956. Billington (see chapter 12) told the story of those frontier years in a way that essentially confirmed the validity of Turner's views. His volume has been highly praised by historians of the American frontier.

By contrast, *The Rise of the West, 1754–1830,* published in 1965 by the relatively unknown Francis S. Philbrick, was a strange volume, indeed. Philbrick in his preface recalled his own days on the frontier and freely acknowledged that he made "no attempt . . . to tell the whole story of anything." Rather, he said, his book was "a commentary on the West's role in our history, and, to some extent, on traditional presentations of its story." Philbrick's polite language actually meant that his work was devastatingly critical of Frederick Jackson Turner, from the preface to the end of the book, which featured a special appendix (replacing the bibliographical essay that was normally an important part of each volume in the series) declaring that Turner's explanation of American history was "totally unacceptable." While there is room for criticism of Turner, Philbrick's diatribe seems excessive, especially considering that without Turner's pioneering efforts it probably would never have occurred to the editors of a multivolume history of the United States to include several books on the frontier. It is not surprising that Philbrick's volume was generally criticized by experts in the field.

Of the many works in the New American Nation Series that appeared in the 1960s, among the more notable were George Dangerfield's *Awakening of American Nationalism, 1815–1828,* John C. Miller's *Federalist Era, 1789–1801,* William E. Leuchtenburg's *Franklin D. Roosevelt and the New Deal, 1932–1940,* Clement Eaton's *Growth of Southern Civilization, 1790–1860,* John A. Garraty's *New Commonwealth, 1877–1890,* John D. Hicks's *Republican Ascendancy, 1921–1933,* Charles Gibson's *Spain in America,* and the only two-volume work in the series, A. Russell Buchanan's *The United States in World War II.*

The editors' introduction in each of the early volumes of the New American Nation included a description of the series as "a comprehensive, cooperative survey of the history of the area now embraced in the United States from the days of discovery to the mid-twentieth century."

In their introduction to Billington's volume, Commager and Morris noted that

since the publication . . . of the American Nation Series, over half a century ago, the scope of history has been immensely broadened, many new approaches explored, and some developed. . . . The time has now come for a judicious reappraisal of the new history, a cautious application of the new techniques of investigation and presentation, and a large-scale effort to achieve a synthesis of new findings with the familiar facts, and to present this whole in attractive literary form. To this task the New American Nation Series is dedicated.

Interestingly, in their later introductions Commager and Morris shortened the above to a single phrase describing the series as "a comprehensive and co-operative survey of the history of the area now embraced in the United States."

On occasion several years passed during which no new volumes were added to the series. Some critics believe there has also been a decline in the quality of the more recent volumes; perhaps, however, it is simply that the New American Nation was an idea more appropriate to the 1950s than to subsequent decades, or at least that the series should have ended at some reasonable point in time. Of the volumes published in the 1970s, *France in America,* (1972) by W. J. Eccles, has been one of the most severely criticized, while *The Impending Crisis, 1848–1861,* by the great David M. Potter, has been one of the most highly praised (the latter volume was completed after Potter's death in 1971 by Don E. Fehrenbacher and published in 1976). Other more recent titles have been *The Confederate Nation: A Southern Nation, 1861–1865* by Emory M. Thomas; two volumes on constitutional history (*The Development of the American Constitution, 1877–1917,* published in 1971 by Loren P. Beth, and *The Constitution in Crisis Times, 1918–1969,* by Paul L. Murphy, published in 1972); *Discovering America, 1700–1875,* by Henry Savage, Jr. (1980); *The Indian in America,* by Wilcomb E. Washburn (1975); *North America from Earliest Discovery to First Settlement: The Norse Voyages to 1612,* by David B. Quinn (1977); *Society and Culture in America, 1830–1860,* by Russel Blaine Nye (1974); and *The Transformation of American Foreign Relations, 1865–1900,* by Charles S. Campbell (1976).

Many developments in American historical writing in the 1950s illustrated the consensus trend more clearly than The New American Nation Series; already noted were the works of Hofstadter, Hartz, and Boorstin and the criticisms of Charles Beard's economic interpretation of the Constitution by Robert E. Brown and Forrest McDonald. In 1962, J. Rogers Hollingsworth published an article in the *South*

Atlantic Quarterly entitled "Consensus and Continuity in Recent American Historical Writing," which perceptively summarized and analyzed the historiography of the 1950s. He added the names of Benjamin F. Wright and Clinton Rossiter to those of Boorstin, Hartz, and Brown on the list of historians who viewed the American Revolution as nonrevolutionary; Wright even entitled his book on the subject *Consensus and Continuity, 1776–1787.* Hollingsworth deftly summarized much consensus writing on pre–Civil War America:

> . . . as part of this monolithic approach to American history, other writers tell us that prior to the adoption of the federal Constitution, American society was fundamentally equalitarian and middle class, not divided sharply along economic lines; that there was never the straightforward cleavage between Hamilton and Jefferson that has frequently been depicted; that the Jacksonians, being neither radicals nor innovators, were trying to maintain the values of a bygone age; and that both the North and the South during the two decades immediately preceding the Civil War were not nearly as distinct in outlook as they have generally been portrayed.

The influence of the new writing was equally evident for the post–Civil War period, noted Hollingsworth: "Thus, some of our better historians contend that Reconstruction can be meaningful only if viewed in terms of the totality of American history. Maintaining that the sectional approach to the study of Reconstruction has lost its vitality, they stress the similarities of patterns which are visible in North, South, and West." Studies of more recent periods in our history reveal even more clearly the historian's preoccupation with present-day values, according to Hollingsworth. Hofstadter's reinterpretation of the Populists and the Progressives in *The Age of Reform* is one outstanding example. Daniel Aaron, Arthur A. Ekirch, John Blum, and Arthur Link are cited as examples of writers who have stressed the conservative side of Progressivism. Link, on the other hand, also argued that Progressivism was far from dead in the 1920s, leading Hollingsworth to note correctly that "one characteristic of the continuity theme is that a reinterpretation of any one period affects all subsequent American history. Thus, as the twenties have become a decade of Progressivism, the New Deal has become more conservative." Henry Steele Commager once wrote that the New Deal "was no revolution, but rather the culmination of half a century of historical development" and even asserted that Franklin D. Roosevelt was "the greatest conservative since Alexander Hamilton."

"At the same time that the distinctions between periods have disappeared [continuity], historians have also played down the distinctions between groups [consensus]," Hollingsworth observed. Clearly, this was at least in part a reaction by the historian to the increasing homogeneity of American society. Although one can find such writing on almost any aspect of American history, said Hollingsworth, "the consensus thesis has been particularly important in reinterpreting regional, social, and intellectual history." As examples he cited the collection of essays entitled *The Southerner as American,* explained well enough by its title; the Englishman Henry Pelling's *American Labor,* which "stresses the similarity in the economic thinking of management and labor during much of the American past, and points out that both held views akin to a laissez-faire concept of economics"; and Sidney E. Mead's research in the field of religious history in which he argued that "the essentials of every sect have been held in common by all groups." In foreign affairs, Hollingsworth continued, Samuel Lubell and others are telling us that "to continue thinking in terms of a conflict between isolationists and internationalists is meaningless, that the concept of isolationism must be discarded as a myth." Finally, according to Hollingsworth, "in no type of historical writing are the themes of continuity and consensus so well combined as in recent American literary scholarship. The fashion is to discover in American literature a stable, unchanging tradition."

Hollingsworth was careful to point out that not all historical writing between 1945 and 1962 was consensus-and-continuity oriented. Among the important works in the period that were not so oriented were those of Allan Nevins and Bruce Catton on the Civil War period and of Arthur M. Schlesinger, Jr., on Andrew Jackson and Franklin D. Roosevelt. Hollingsworth was also perceptive about the approaching demise of consensus-and-continuity as the major approach to the interpretation of the American past. "As American historians continue to reflect the values and sentiments of their contemporary society," he wrote from the perspective of the early 1960s, "the themes of conflict and diversity will probably receive greater emphasis in historical writing during the sixties. Already, there is evidence that the tone of the 1960s will be substantially different from that of the Age of Eisenhower." Hollingsworth concluded somewhat prophetically, "Perhaps it will not be long before historians respond to this new temper and again stress the variety, change, and conflict which have made American history so rich in human experience."[28]

CHAPTER 15

Conflict: American Historical Writing in the 1960s

RICHARD HOFSTADTER may have helped start the consensus trend in American historiography with the introduction to his *American Political Tradition* in 1948, but unlike many other historians who came to fit into that mold he saw its problems and limitations and proceeded to move beyond it. In *The Progressive Historians* (published in 1968), Hofstadter noted that it was to Daniel J. Boorstin that "we owe such an extended use of consensus as an overarching explanatory principle that we can say that its limits have already been quite substantially explored." Two volumes of Boorstin's *Americans* had appeared at the time Hofstadter was writing. In them, said Hofstadter, Boorstin was most successful "chiefly as a social historian writing about selected aspects of our social life in which conflict is not uppermost. . . . Where he most typically fails is in dealing with the fundamental problems of American political culture with which he began." Warming to his critical task, Hofstadter observed that, as Boorstin's work had progressed, he had "turned his back on the basic problems of political conflict in our history, and often of social conflict as well." Boorstin did not even mention the bank war during Andrew Jackson's presidency, for example, but he did write about Frederic Tudor (the "Ice King," who discovered the utility and marketability of ice), granite quarrying, balloon-frame houses, the organization of the early factory, and the whole phenomenon which Boorstin liked to call "the Know-how Revolution." However, Hofstadter concluded firmly, "In following such concerns Boorstin has not resolved the problem of conflict, he has simply abandoned it."[1]

Hofstadter turned from Boorstin to Louis Hartz: "Hartz, loosely speaking, represents the intellectual wing of consensus history, Daniel Boorstin . . . represents its anti-intellectualist wing, and in this respect is perhaps more characteristically American." After quoting approvingly Hartz's observation in *The Liberal Tradition in America* that "the argument over whether we should 'stress' solidarity or conflict misleads us by advancing a false set of alternatives," Hofstadter wrote a powerful sentence—and an interesting one, indeed, for a historian frequently regarded as the founder of a consensus school: "Yet I think it is a valid comment on the limits of consensus history to insist that in one form or another conflict finally does remain, and ought to remain, somewhere near the center of our focus of attention."[2]

In conclusion, Hofstadter suggested "three major areas in which a history of the United States organized around the guiding idea of consensus breaks down." First, "it cannot do justice to the genuinely revolutionary aspects of the American Revolution." Second, "it is quite helpless and irrelevant on the Civil War and the issues related to it." Finally, "it disposes us to turn away from one of the most significant facts of American social life—the racial, ethnic, and religious conflict with which our history is saturated."[3]

One can attribute no element of the prophetic to these statements made by Hofstadter in 1968, as one perhaps can for those of J. Rogers Hollingsworth in 1962, but both suggested, to a great extent, one of the dominant strands of American historical writing in the 1960s. Called variously the New Left, the radical, or even the neo-Progressive historians, the persons writing this history were clearly responding in part to changes in their climate of opinion. Rather than consensus and continuity, they saw conflict and change around them—the assassination of John F. Kennedy and its aftermath, the black revolution, Vietnam, student radicalism, feminism, the ecology crusade—and thus they began to see more conflict in the American past as well. That was not all, however. Hofstadter, explaining the emergence of the consensus approach in post–World War II America, wrote that "the change in the historical mood was not simply a response to the new political environment":

Ideas have an inner dialectic of their own. The Progressive historians and the generation of historical specialists that worked under their inspiration had pushed polarized conflict as a principle of historical interpretation so far that one could go no further in that direction without risking self-caricature. The pendulum had to swing in the opposite direction: if we were to have any new insight into American history, it began to appear that we had to circumvent the emphasis on conflict and look at the American past from another angle.[4]

In the 1960s, for many, the pendulum swung again.

William Appleman Williams

William Appleman Williams is regarded by many as the founder—the "grand old man"—of the New Left. He was writing New Left views of American history long before anyone had even coined the term. He began as a diplomatic historian but broadened his field to become essentially a general interpreter of the meaning of the American past—

and present. Williams was born in Iowa, grew up there during the Depression, and was educated at the Naval Academy and at the University of Wisconsin. He served briefly in World War II and was active in the civil-rights movement very early, just after the war. Joseph M. Siracusa, in *New Left Diplomatic Histories and Historians*, succinctly blended all this into William's climate of opinion: "Thus, downtrodden farmers and their discontent with the vicissitudes of a free market-place economy, their noninterventionist tendencies and their class and anti-big-business consciousness, along with his military training and reaction to it, his view of war at first hand and an acute awareness of racial inequality and an effort to do something about it, contributed to the world outlook of William Appleman Williams."[5]

Siracusa acknowledged Williams as "the single most important influence on the New Left" historians, and provided a helpful brief summary of Williams's views:

A critical analysis of the ideas and presuppositions contained in Williams's published studies suggest that his principal contribution to the New Left diplomatic literature that emerged in the 1960's was the general thesis, in his words, that "empire is as American as apple pie." Through his frontier-expansionist theory of causation, which assumed that United States foreign policy derived rationally and logically (if routinely) from an inherently expansionist capitalist political economy, Williams revived and updated an earlier economic revisionism, subsumed and moved beyond the Realist critique of his own generation, and called for the reconstruction of American national life along democratic lines, economically self-sufficient and politically free from overseas entanglements. In so doing, Williams passed on to the new revisionism a basically ironic interpretation of American diplomatic history which attempted to show that as more and more America pursued peace and the expectation of prosperity through the construction of a stable, freely trading open door world, greater and greater became the illusion of long-term prosperity and less and less the chance of peace. A view of foreign policy that sought only to project its own image onto the world flew in the face of history and was doomed from the beginning. Williams passed to the new revisionists a presentist concept of history, a sense of urgency, and, most importantly, an apocalyptic vision of the failure to heed his warning.[6]

Given Siracusa's insight into what made Williams's views and his ability to synthesize those views even more conveniently than Williams himself has ever managed to do, it is strange and unfortunate that Siracusa was excessively and sometimes unfairly critical of Williams and other New Left diplomatic historians. Siracusa seemed to think that by noting the views of several traditional diplomatic historians who had responded critically to the New Left he had essentially demolished the radicals as important contributors to the understanding of America's past relationship with the rest of the world. The New Left was not so easily demolished, however, especially not Williams. He came to be so highly regarded by his colleagues for his contributions, even by many who clearly rejected most of his views, that he was elected president of the Organization of American Historians for 1980–81.

Williams described in detail his vision of the American past in some dozen books, beginning in 1952 with the publication of *American-Russian Relations, 1781–1947*. This first major work grew out of Williams's doctoral dissertation. Despite the title it dealt for the most part with the period from 1867 to 1939. Some of the broad outlines of Williams's overall view of the American diplomatic past were already clear. "The transfer of Alaska was indeed the great divide in the contour of American-Russian relations," he wrote. "For the United States it marked the final advance on the continent prior to a large-scale effort to penetrate the markets of Asia. . . . The financial and industrial powers of the United States soon came to dominate their domestic market and looked abroad for new economic opportunities." Williams concluded explicitly, "That moment—the overseas expansion of American economic forces—ultimately clashed with Russian activity along the Amur; and though their respective interests might conceivably have been fruitfully harmonized, the final result was bitter antagonism." As a result, "at no time a serious competitor in the markets of either China or Manchuria, Russia was nevertheless designated the principal enemy." Thus, owing largely to the expansionism inherent in the American system, the diplomatic atmosphere between America and Russia was poisoned at a very early date, long before the outbreak of the Bolshevik Revolution, which was, of course, the pivotal event in modern Russian-American relations.

Williams was devastatingly critical of the American response to the Bolshevik Revolution. America's policy, he said, was "based in part on the assumption that Lenin would miraculously disappear and that the Soviet government would—because it should—collapse." Blame, in Williams's view, went to both Secretary of State Robert Lansing and President Woodrow Wilson, but especially to Wilson, for he should have known better. "The essential tragedy of Wilson's failure," Williams wrote, "lies in the fact that he realized and acknowledged that the Soviets represented a desperate attempt on the part of the dispossessed to share the bounty of industrial civilization." Wilson "knew that they must be given access to that share if further resort to violence was to be forestalled," yet his "keen insight was first dimmed then ultimately beclouded by antagonism to the Soviets and the conscious desire to expand American influence abroad." Ultimately, then, Wilson's decision to cooperate with the Allied intervention in Russia to overthrow the Bolsheviks showed that he was concerned less about the

Russian people than about expanding American influence in China, Manchuria, and Siberia. Siracusa, again critical but perceptive, analyzed Williams's interpretation:

> From a somewhat different perspective, Williams's analysis of the official United States reaction to the Russian Revolution clearly revealed both the function of New Left diplomatic historiography, which sought to call into question the nature of American society by a critique of its external relations, and the inner workings of the author's mind. If it could be demonstrated "that the Soviets represented a desperate attempt on the part of the dispossessed to share the bounty of industrial civilization," then perhaps it also could be demonstrated that Washington's opposition to that goal was symptomatic of a political economy that similarly denied the realization of a better life to the dispossessed of America. Under these circumstances the failure of American diplomacy could become the failure of American society, the lesson being that until the latter was corrected the former would have little chance of succeeding. In this sense a critique of foreign relations became the back door to reform.[7]

Although Williams insisted that "to project this study [*American-Russian Relations*] beyond 1939 is a task impossible of execution," he did so anyway in a last chapter bearing the title "The Sophistry of Super-Realism." Though he was more tentative here than he had been in the earlier portions of the book, Williams gave a quite specific view of the origins of the Cold War:

> Thus the breakdown of the unity exemplified at Teheran occurred in a complex pattern. First came the wartime refusal to reach territorial settlements on the basis of Russia's 1941 proposals *before* the Red Army carried that frontier farther west. Then—once that opportunity had been lost—the failure to link resolution of the new problem with Russia's postwar economic needs, as revealed in her persistent demands for reparations in kind from Germany and Italy and her formal request for direct aid from the United States. In Asia, where the basic territorial commitments were made, the subsequent failure to validate them by facing the challenge of the Bolshevik Revolution in terms of China's *internal* development. Disintegration was speeded by Roosevelt's apparent inability to realize that delay served only to decrease the number of possible options at his disposal.
>
> For the President's on-again, off-again efforts to evade the relationship between military occupation and political influence only re-enforced Russia's lack of confidence in the West's objectives—particularly in Eastern Europe, the area of most immediate concern to Moscow. There remained, under the circumstances, but one way to secure Allied solidarity once Germany and Japan were defeated: use Russia's preoccupation with economic rehabilitation as the means to secure negotiated settlements. When this approach was abandoned—or, more exactly, ignored—the cold war was declared by default. For

without negotiation the highly prized freedom of action could be achieved only by force, a fact that was to be formalized in George Frost Kennan's policy of containment in 1947.

Williams's next book, *The Shaping of American Diplomacy: Readings and Documents in American Foreign Relations, 1750–1955,* was published in 1956 and, as the title suggests, was considerably different from *American-Russian Relations. The Shaping of American Diplomacy* was a massive, 1,130-page reader for use in courses in American diplomatic history. As its subtitle suggests, it was essentially an edited, rather than an original work, for Williams included both excerpts from the works of other historians and documents from the period being treated. For example, the chapter entitled "Markets, Crusades, and Colonies: The Crisis of 1898–1900" includes both Julius W. Pratt's article "American Business and the Spanish-American War" and Grover Cleveland's view of the Cuban crisis; both Fred Harvey Harrington's classic piece "The Anti-Imperialist Movement in the United States, 1898–1900" and Theodore Roosevelt's account of his efforts to bring about the war. Williams's guiding hand, however, is evident throughout: he provided the interpretative framework, selected the items to be included, and clearly explained his own views about them in his introductory comments. Through this book Williams has exercised an extensive influence on students of American foreign relations.

Williams published *The Tragedy of American Diplomacy* in 1959; many regard it as his most important work. The tragedy of American diplomacy, according to Williams, "is not that it is evil, but that it denies and subverts American ideas and ideals." The result, he continued, "is a most realistic failure, as well as an ideological and moral one; for in being unable to make the American system function satisfactorily without recourse to open door expansion (and by no means perfectly even then), American diplomacy suffers by comparison with its own claims and ideas as well as other approaches." The problem, he insisted, was the American weltanschauung, or world view—Williams is fond of the word—which held that "freedom and prosperity depend upon the continued expansion of its economic and ideological system through the policy of the open door." What America needed instead, Williams proposed, was "a radically different concept: Instead, it appears that America's political and economic well-being depend upon the rational and equitable use of its own human and material resources at home and in interdependent co-operation with *all* other peoples of the world." America, he concluded, "can neither take its place in nor make its contribution to the world community until it believes and demonstrates that it can sustain prosperity and democracy without recourse to open-door imperialism." A necessary first step to achieve that, in William's thinking, is evident in the title of his concluding chapter: "The Wisdom of an Open Door for Revolutions."

Clearly Williams was by now moving beyond diplomatic history as traditionally defined. His next book, *The Contours of American History*, was published in 1961 and thus was Williams's first book of the 1960s. In it he turned to a general interpretation of American history. Any perceptive reader of Williams's books up to this time would have noticed the influence of Charles A. Beard. In *Contours*, Williams was quite open about this: "It . . . seems appropriate, in view of all the bigoted and career-building attacks, acts of purification in the form of misrepresentation, and even smart-alec criticism by supposed aristocrats, to acknowledge formally my respect for and indebtedness to Charles Austin Beard." Williams suggested that the failure of the Pulitzer Prize Committee to find "either the intelligence or the courage" to honor Beard, even posthumously, "is one of the most illuminating aspects of our times. He was a man of rare intellectual capacity, courage, and humaneness." That Beard's analysis and interpretations differed from his own at many points was "irrelevant to the central issue," said Williams, concluding; "He was a great historian." Williams also acknowledged his indebtedness to Karl Marx, whose influence was made more explicit in a later work.

The preface to *Contours* was the well-known essay with the title— "History as a Way of Learning"—that Williams gave in 1973 to a collection of his previously published essays. As a way of learning, said Williams, history "begins by leaving the present; by going back into the heretofore, by beginning again. Only by grasping what we were is it possible to see how we changed, to understand the process and the nature of the modifications, and to gain some perspective on what we are." The study of history is not a matter of "staying in the present and looking back" but rather of "going back into the past and returning to the present with a wider and more intense consciousness of the restrictions of our former outlook." Thus we "return with a broader awareness of the alternatives open to us and armed with a sharper perceptiveness with which to make our choices." Finally, "In this manner it is possible to loosen the clutch of the dead hand of the past and transform it into a living tool for the present and the future."

The heart of *Contours* was a periodization of American history according to three dominant world views: "The Age of Mercantilism, 1740-1828," "The Age of Laissez-Nous Faire, 1819-1896," and "The Age of Corporation Capitalism, 1882-." In the conclusion, "History as a Way of Breaking the Chains of the Past," Williams made it clear that his own vision was a socialist one. In Eugene V. Debs, he suggested,

America had "produced a man who understood that expansion was a running away, the kind of escape that was destructive of the dignity of men." Williams continued:

> He also believed and committed his life to the proposition that Americans would one day prove mature and courageous enough to give it up as a child's game; that they would one day "put away childish things" and undertake the creation of a socialist commonwealth. Americans therefore do have a third choice to consider alongside that of an oligarchy and that of a class-conscious industrial gentry. They have the chance to create the first truly democratic socialism in the world.
>
> That opportunity is the only real frontier available to Americans in the second half of the 20th century. If they revealed and acted upon the kind of intelligence and morality and courage that it would take to explore and develop that frontier, then they would have finally broken the chains of their own past. Otherwise, they would ultimately fall victims of a nostalgia for their childhood.

Williams applied the emerging general pattern of his interpretation to several specific incidents and topics in several books. *America and the Middle East: Open Door Imperialism or Enlightened Leadership?* appeared in 1958; as the title may suggest, it is an edited volume in Rinehart's series Source Problems in World Civilization. *The United States, Cuba, and Castro: An Essay on the Dynamics of Revolution and the Dissolution of Empire* came out in 1962 and *Some Presidents: Wilson to Nixon* in 1972. The latter is a brief collection of essays originally published as reviews of books about twentieth-century presidents and their foreign policies. Williams also wrote the revealingly titled book *The Great Evasion: An Essay on the Contemporary Relevance of Karl Marx and on the Wisdom of Admitting the Heretic into the Dialogue About America's Future.* In 1964, when it was published, it seemed a timely demand for a new hearing for Marx, but it now seems one of Williams's most dated works because of the statistical information he used to explore such Marxian ideas as alienation, conflict between city and country, proletarianization, and the loss of community. Williams also edited the anthology *From Colony to Empire: Essays in the History of American Foreign Relations,* published in 1972. This collection of essays by historians displayed a stronger New Left slant than *The Shaping of American Diplomacy;* most of the chapters were written either by Williams himself or by such radical members of the "Wisconsin school of diplomatic history" as Walter LaFeber, Robert Freeman Smith, and Lloyd Gardner. In 1978, Williams also published a textbook, *Americans in a Changing World: A History of the United States in the Twentieth Century.*

Like the works of many other idea historians, Williams's books increasingly became efforts to say more effectively what he had already said. This tendency (as well as his proclivity for long titles) is evident in a book published in 1980, *Empire as a Way of Life: An Essay on the Causes and Character of America's Present Predicament, Along with a Few Thoughts About an Alternative.* Two more of Williams's books deserve special notice: *The Roots of the Modern American Empire: A Study of the Growth and Shaping of Social Consciousness in a Marketplace Society* and *America Confronts a Revolutionary World, 1776–1976.*

The Roots of the Modern American Empire (1969) was one of Williams's most substantial works. Its central argument was stated succinctly in this sentence, italicized, in the preface: "I came to see that the expansionist outlook that was entertained and acted upon by metropolitan American leaders during and after the 1890s was actually a crystallization in industrial form of an outlook that had been developed in agricultural terms by the agrarian majority of the country between 1860 and 1893." What followed was a massive and massively documented effort to prove that contention. The preface itself was a strange combination of interpretation, philosophy of history, acknowledgments, and autobiography. There had been a marked tendency, Williams noted, to overlook the primary importance of *expansion* in Frederick Jackson Turner's work and to think only in terms of *frontier.* Yet such important Americans as Brooks Adams, Theodore Roosevelt, and Woodrow Wilson had given serious attention to the expansionist theme in Turner's thesis. "Perhaps I owe my greatest obligation, however," said Williams, waxing autobiographical, "to the dirt farmers whom I have known as members of my family, or as close friends and teachers." Anyone, he continued, "who grew up in Iowa during the Depression learned very quickly (and well) about the deep and direct relationship between the fluctuations of the business cycle and the conditions of life for the farmer." Finally, "one learned early and at first hand how the farm was tied into the world marketplace." This kind of "export-dominated relationship with the world political economy" had admittedly elicited different responses from the American farmer at different times. In the years from 1903 to 1914 and from 1920 to 1939, for example—some of those few "delightful moments of history" when "the capitalist system has functioned with some meaningful approximation to the forecasts of its innovators and the promises of its advocates"—the American farmer "manifested a relaxed acceptance of the rest of the world and a willingness to live and let live. He revealed an understanding of the inherent, as well as the explicit, limits on any effort by the United States to control or change the rest of mankind." Williams could not view as positively one of the other responses:

But there have also been times when the farmer's export-dominated relationship with the world marketplace led him to develop and advocate a vigorously assertive and expansionist foreign policy, or to support such a policy formulated by others. And, since he actively and causally related his freedom in the marketplace with his personal political and social freedom, the farmer was strongly inclined to defend and justify such expansionism on the grounds that it extended the freedom of all men. Opening the foreigner's marketplace, he often argued, would open the foreigner's society for the foreigner. American farmers evolved and agitated just such a militantly expansionist foreign policy between 1860 and 1893, and continued to exert a pervasive influence on American thinking about foreign affairs throughout the twentieth century.

Then, in an open effort to establish "the relevance of history," Williams concluded that "American farmers, acting at a time when they composed the great majority of the nation's population, were crucial actors in developing an outlook that has carried our contemporary industrialized system to a major crisis in foreign affairs." If we could only "understand that history as a prelude to accepting it, and accept it as a prelude to changing those ideas and policies, then we nonagrarians who compose the great majority of today's America can give the other (largely agrarian) peoples of the world a chance to make their own history by acting on our own responsibility to make our own history." Concluded Williams, "If that be isolationism, then the time has come to make the most of it." The history of their own that Williams wanted Americans to make was, of course, socialism.

Williams reached the same conclusion in *America Confronts a Revolutionary World, 1776–1976,* published, appropriately, in the bicentennial year of the American Revolution, 1976. The conclusion was arrived at this time, however, by a very different route. Americans emerged from their revolution with a world view—the weltanschauung again—made up of five major elements, said Williams: an unqualified commitment to the right of revolutionary self-determination, an intense consciousness of being unique, a hyperactive sense of mission, a deep sense of aloneness (or isolation), and an awareness of internal differences and conflicts that threatened the sense of uniqueness. Superimposed over all of these, however, relating them to each other and holding them together, was expansion, which "lies at the center of the American *Weltanschauung.*" The problem, as Williams saw it, was that Americans, believing that they had wrought the perfect social, economic, and political structure, turned their backs on their own revolutionary tradition. *America Confronts a Revolutionary World,* therefore, as its title suggests, is an overview of American foreign (and sometimes domestic) policy, emphasizing America's failure to honor its Revolutionary heritage, especially the right of self-determination. Some of the revisions Williams made of historical figures' reputations certainly utilized this perspective. John Quincy Adams and Herbert Hoover, for example, became near-heroes, while Abraham Lincoln and Woodrow Wilson were rather severely criticized. For Williams to berate Wilson was, of course, nothing new, but what about Lincoln? It was the historian's interpretation here that led to much criticism of Williams—not only by Lincoln's admirers but by Civil War historians in general, and also by advocates of civil rights for blacks who believed that the support of the federal government had been crucial in bringing about some progress. Williams asserted, "Put simply, the cause of the Civil War was the refusal of Lincoln and other northerners to honor the revolutionary right of self-determination—the touchstone of the American Revolution." What then, about the slaves? Williams was aware of the problem. "It is important to assert and reassert the evil of slavery," he wrote, "but that will not enable one to wriggle off the hook. . . . It is the right and responsibility of Blacks—and any other people, including ourselves—to self-determine themselves. We save ourselves in the hope that we can then come together to create a community."

It was in his suggestions of methods creating that community in the present that Williams offered one of his most intriguing ideas. A hint was provided by his inclusion of the Articles of Confederation as an appendix. Williams was still talking about the need for socialism, but with the Articles of Confederation as a starting point. "I suggest that we embark upon a sustained effort to organize a social movement dedicated to replacing the American empire with a federation of regional communities," he wrote. "No euphemisms and no talk about reform. The objective is to create a federation of democratic Socialist communities." Williams continued:

> Hence we must move another step into the Past beyond Madison. Unlike Lincoln, we must seek to honor rather than to supersede our revolutionary forefathers. That means evoking and using the Past to create a Future that honors our primary commitment to self-determination. We must return therefore to the Articles of Confederation. That document offers us a base from which to begin our voyage into a human Future; a model of government grounded in the idea and the ideal of self-determined communities coming together as equals when and as it is necessary to combine forces to honor common values and realize common objectives.

Eugene D. Genovese

It is obvious that most American historians do not share William

Appleman Williams's socialist vision. It is equally obvious that most of them are not Marxists. It is, therefore, interesting to find in a 1981 issue of the *Journal of American History,* a publication of the Organization of American Historians, the names of Williams and Eugene D. Genovese (widely regarded as America's premier Marxist historian) listed as two of the three recent past presidents serving on the organization's executive board. Genovese, who teaches in the University of Rochester, has won the respect of the vast majority of professional historians because of the unmistakable quality of his work and because his Marxism is not obtrusive, dogmatic, or abrasive. He is, in short, an excellent historian who happens to be a Marxist. His field is southern history, especially that of racism and slavery; in addition, he has utilized the comparative approach both extensively and effectively. His major book to date is *Roll, Jordan, Roll: The World the Slaves Made,* published in 1974, but several other works also deserve notice, and *Roll, Jordan, Roll* makes more sense when seen as a part of the entire body of Genovese's work.

The Political Economy of Slavery, mostly a collection of articles, was published in 1965 and brought Genovese to the attention of the profession at large. Many readers had already noticed some of the articles published earlier in various journals. It is not surprising that students who do not know that Genovese is a Marxist can read *The Political Economy of Slavery* and still not know it. Marx is mentioned in only two places, one of them a footnote; but, more significantly, some of Genovese's most important insights and interpretations are not necessarily Marxist, or at least not immediately recognizable as such. "The South's greatest economic weakness was the low productivity of its labor force," he declared flatly. This weakness, he said, was the major factor in the "economic backwardness that condemned the slaveholding South to defeat" in the wartime years from 1861 to 1865, and it expressed itself in several ways. "Most significant was the carelessness and wastefulness of the slaves," Genovese insisted, for "bondage forced the Negro to give his labor grudgingly and badly, and his poor work habits retarded those social and economic advances that could have raised the general level of productivity." Less direct hindrances for the South were "limitations imposed on the free work force, on technological development, and on the division of labor." Genovese argued convincingly that "the attempts of reformers to improve methods of cultivation, diversify production, and raise more and better livestock" were all "undermined at the outset by a labor force without versatility or the possibility of increasing its productivity substantially." It is noteworthy that among the reasons Genovese stressed for the low productivity of slave labor was the slaves' diet, which "was well suited to guarantee the appearance of good health and to provide the fuel to keep him going in the fields, but . . . not sufficient to ensure either sound bodies or the stamina necessary for sustained labor." *The Political Economy of Slavery* is probably the best account of the intertwining of slavery with everything else in the southern lifestyle. Said Genovese of the slaveholders: "Slavery represented the cornerstone of their way of life, and life to them meant an honor and dignity associated with the power of command. When the slaveholders rose in insurrection, they knew what they were about: in the fullest sense, they were fighting for their lives."

In 1969, Genovese published his second major book, *The World the Slaveholders Made*, subtitled *Two Essays in Interpretation*. It was really two brief books in one. The first part, "The American Slave Systems in World Perspective," was the earliest indication of the deep interest in comparative history which Genovese subsequently developed. The second part, "The Logical Outcome of the Slaveholders' Philosophy," was a brilliant exposition and interpretation of the social thought of George Fitzhugh, the author of *Cannibals All! or, Slaves Without Masters* and one of the South's chief defenders of slavery. Fitzhugh's "great achievement," in Genovese's view, "lay in the negative insight that slavery as a system of society, not merely as an occasional or peripheral economic devise, was incompatible with capitalism and that the two could not long co-exist." Ultimately Fitzhugh failed, for although he properly explained and interpreted his world, he could not transcend it. "His failure reflected the failure of a class, its world, and its world view." "And," Genovese concluded broadly, "it exposed the limits of all modern reaction: The reconstruction and consolidation of an archaic world order being an impossibility, all attempts at a prebourgeois restoration can only end as the counter-revolution of the bourgeoisie itself."

Genovese soon developed a reputation for writing clever, humorous, and revealing introductions. In the one to *The World the Slaveholders Made* he suggested that one of his objectives was "to offer some suggestions for the development of the Marxian interpretation of history." The attempt to do this—characteristically made explicit in only one chapter and "left implicit throughout [the rest of] the book"—involved an effort "to transcend the narrowly economic notion of class and come to terms with the 'base-superstructure' problem that has plagued Marxism since its inception." Marxists, Genovese believed, "have tended to let themselves be suspended between the assertion of the primacy of 'material' forces and the necessity to recognize that ideas, once called into being and rooted in important social groups, have a life of their own." Genovese claimed that "the most important work being done [by Marxists] today is to be found in particular historical investigations, rather than in grand theoretical pronouncements," and his own works demonstrated his belief. He expressed his indebtedness to such English Marxists as Christopher Hill, Eric J. Hobsbawm, and E. P. Thompson.

The introductory material to Genovese's next book, *In Red and Black: Marxian Explorations in Southern and Afro-American History*, consisted of a long dedication and a short preface. He dedicated the book to seven "leftwing" faculty members in Sir George Williams University, in Montreal, for helping to restore "sanity to the remains of the miscalled and abortive 'New Left'" after the "high-water mark of campus frustration and confusion" of 1968 and 1969. This hints at the reason why Genovese clashed at times with other New Left historians such as Staughton Lynd. The preface to the book, like its title, showed that Genovese was being more open than usual about the Marxist orientation of his work. Like *The Political Economy of Slavery*, *In Red and Black* consisted of previously published essays; they represent, wrote Genovese, "an attempt to bring a Marxian viewpoint to the black experience without, I hope, imposing some external ideological position on it." Genovese, simultaneously displayed his sense of humor and addressed an important point when he wrote: "When . . . I am asked, in the fashion of our insane times, what right I, as a white man, have to write about black people, I am forced to reply in four-letter words." Accepting literally some of the arguments of the time, he suggested, "I have concluded that I am qualified to write only the history of Italian immigration—a subject I know nothing about."

Some of the more revealing segments of *In Red and Black* are those in which Genovese evaluates the work of other historians, including Stanley M. Elkins, Ulrich B. Phillips, David Potter, C. Vann Woodward, and Staughton Lynd, only the last of whom he treated harshly. The opening essay, "On Being a Socialist and a Historian," revealed the most about Genovese's approach. All historical writing, he insisted, "is unavoidably political intervention," but "ideologically motivated history is bad history and ultimately reactionary politics." Socialists, therefore, "do not advocate pure scholarship and value-free social science because we do not advocate the impossible. But we do insist that the inevitability of ideological bias does not free us from the responsibility to struggle for maximum objectivity." Socialists, Genovese admitted, are guilty of other "sins" as well. Smugness: "We really do believe that our political movement represents the hope of humanity and the cause of the exploited and oppressed of the world." Conceit: "We are so convinced we are right that we believe we have nothing whatever to fear from the truth about anything. . . . Our pretensions, therefore, lead us to the fantastic idea that all good (true, valid, competent) history serves our interest and that all poor (false, invalid, incompetent) history serves the interest of our enemies — or at least of someone other than ourselves." All of this led Genovese to a simple conclusion about the debate that was raging at the time over the proper role of the radical scholar: ". . . the 'role' of the socialist historian is to be a good historian; . . . the question of 'relevance' is irrelevant to anything of importance beyond the egos of those who prate about it; . . . the study of history, and in fact all humane learning, is the major responsibility of those intellectuals who would work for a better society."

"For radicals," argued Genovese, "the success of imperialism abroad remains inseparable from the success of imperialist-generated moral decay at home." Yet the "study of history can rarely be put to direct political use." This was only one of the points at which Genovese took issue with many other radical scholars. Elsewhere in the book he wrote in the same vein about their emphasis on the need to get away from elite history, to include the common people in the story of the past, to view history, in short, "from the bottom up." Genovese contended: "History written from the bottom up is neither more nor less than history written from the top down: It is not and cannot be good history." He continued:

> In short, an unbridgeable gulf separates socialist intellectuals from the "revolutionaries" who proclaim the arrival of the Day of Judgment and who demand relevance and their own style of engagement. They have nothing of importance in common with each other. No wonder, then, that those naive Establishment historians who lump them together as "radical historians" discover that these crazy radicals can never agree on anything. Precisely so. And for that reason it behooves the esteemed gentlemen of the Establishment to stop making fools of themselves, much as it behooves those on the left to put an end to the pretense that they are all part of something called "The Movement."

Because of this kind of approach Genovese has not been popular with many radicals, especially non-Marxists — no other "coherent radical interpretation of history" has arisen except Marxism, he insisted. His approach, however, may also help explain why his work has come to be so highly regarded by nonradicals.

"Socialists have generally been arrogant about their ostensibly superior intellectual qualities," Genovese admitted. This attitude was merely a part of the "greatest embarrassment" of socialist scholars, for "with the exception of William Appleman Williams, no socialist historian of the United States could be mentioned in the same breath with C. Vann

Woodward or Richard Hofstadter, . . . two of the outstanding men now under attack from the Left." "How strange," concluded Genovese appropriately, "that people who claim for themselves moral and intellectual superiority and a more scientific viewpoint than others possess do not do work anywhere near as good." Thus of his own work he wrote, "As part of a growing group of leftwing historians, I have tried in these essays and elsewhere to contribute, as best I can, to the development of a Marxian interpretation of history—specifically, Southern and Afro-American history." This interpretation constitutes a way "of seeing history as a process and of binding the past to the future," not as prediction "but in the sense of suggesting the contours both of that which is possible and of disasters to be avoided." Marxism "maintains that the root of the great qualitative leaps in social development are to be sought in the rise, development, and confrontation of social classes." Yet clearly not all important historical changes are the result of class conflict. "Our Marxism, therefore, is itself a process of labor, which binds us to nothing that cannot be verified or maintained as the most plausible explanation of the facts at our disposal."

Genovese has done a great deal of editing in his career. With Laura Foner he coedited a collection of essays, published in 1969, by such scholars as Frank Tannenbaum, Stanley M. Elkins, David Brion Davis, and Winthrop D. Jordan; it was entitled *Slavery in the New World: A Reader in Comparative History*. He coedited with Elinor Miller a book published in 1974, *Plantation, Town, and Country: Essays on the Local History of American Slave Society*. With Stanley L. Engerman—best known as the coauthor of the controversial quantified study of slavery entitled *Time on the Cross: The Economics of American Negro Slavery*—Genovese edited a collection of essays entitled *Race and Slavery in the Western Hemisphere: Quantitative Studies* (1975). In the words of its preface, *Race and Slavery* showed that "black history has become the leading arena in the effort to apply quantitative methods to historical research." This volume was one in a series entitled Quantitative Studies in History, sponsored by the History Advisory Committee of the Mathematical Social Science Board. Thus it may be said that *Race and Slavery* showed Genovese's involvement in two of the more important trends in American historical writing in the 1960s, black history and quantification. Genovese independently edited a two-volume work entitled *The Slave Economies* (1973). The first volume explored historical and theoretical perspectives, while the second brought together different approaches to slavery in the international economy. Finally, he edited and supplied the introduction for a book consisting of excerpts from the writings of Ulrich B. Phillips. Genovese had already made it clear in *The Political Economy of Slavery* that he considered Phillips's work on slavery "the best introduction despite his debilitating race prejudice."

In 1980, Genovese, with David Burner and Forrest McDonald, wrote *The American People*, a textbook for a college level course in American history. It appears that Burner did most of the writing; Genovese's contribution consisted primarily of a series of provocative debates with the conservative and strongly consensus-oriented McDonald on such topics as the American Revolutionary era and industrial capitalism. Genovese's book *From Rebellion to Revolution: Afro-American Slave Revolts in the Making of the Modern World*, published in 1979, was based on his Walter Lynwood Fleming lectures in southern history delivered in 1973 at Louisiana State University. "The history of slavery and of slave revolts in the Americas corresponds roughly to the transition from seigneurialism to capitalism," wrote Genovese in the preface. In this transition "nothing better testifies to the integral role of slavery"— in ideological as well as socioeconomic terms—"than the history of the slave revolts." Finally, "Nor can any other social movement better illuminate the rich and contradictory process whereby the slaves fashioned their own history within the contours of the dominant modes of production."

Genovese wrote in *From Rebellion to Revolution*, "I have proceeded on the assumption that the extraordinary scholarship of recent years has finally laid to rest the myth of slave docility and quiescence." Indeed, he added, "no enslaved people in world history rose in revolt so often or in such numbers or with so large a measure of success." Of course, he admitted that all this applied less to the slaves in the American South than to those in the Caribbean and South America, but, he said, the Americans too "made vital contributions to the history of revolt." It is ironic that in this book Genovese finds an occasion to agree with Herbert Aptheker, a leading figure of the "Old Left" who deserves much credit for pioneering the study of slave resistance with his *American Negro Slave Revolts* (1943). Although Genovese frequently disagreed with Aptheker, he wrote in *From Rebellion to Revolution*, "At bottom, I agree with Herbert Aptheker's blunt remark that the 'cause' of slave revolt was slavery."

Roll, Jordan, Roll, Genovese's major work, was published in 1974, with the significant subtitle *The World the Slaves Made*. Whether or not one accepts any part of Genovese's Marxist framework of analysis, *Roll, Jordan, Roll* must be ranked as one of the truly significant works on American slavery, along with those by Ulrich B. Phillips, Kenneth M. Stampp, and Stanley M. Elkins. Indeed, Stampp praised Genovese for dealing with slaves "as human beings and not as disembodied abstractions."[8] Genovese himself said of the whole body of his own work: "I started studying the masters and decided I could not understand much about them unless I studied the slaves closely. Once I started, they became an obsession." That obsession, fortunately, led to this book.

John Anthony Scott was excessively critical of *Roll, Jordan, Roll* in parts of his long review of the work in *Challenge,* but he recognized Genovese's contribution and provided this thoughtful general characterization:

The theory that plantation slavery was a benevolent system which existed to educate and protect its black dependents, and not to make money, received classic formulation fifty years ago in the work of the Georgia scholar, Ulrich B. Phillips. Genovese has achieved a fresh and original formulation of that theory which purges it of its racial bias and introduces the concept of an autonomous black community growing and developing within the four walls of the exploitative system.[9]

Genovese was not alone in attempting to view slavery at least in part from the perspective of the slave. He was not even the first, for in 1972, John Blassingame *(The Slave Community: Plantation Life in the Antebellum South)* and George P. Rawick *(From Sundown to Sunup: The Making of the Black Community)* had done so. Perhaps the central concept and contribution of Genovese was paternalism. In his preface he said that his "primary responsibility," as he saw it, was to "tell the story of slave life as carefully and accurately as possible." He added, "Many years of studying the astonishing effort of black people to live decently as human beings even in slavery had convinced me that no theoretical advance suggested in their experience could ever deserve as much attention as that demanded by their demonstration of the beauty and power of the human spirit under conditions of extreme oppression." The first chapter opened with a section entitled "On Paternalism," which ended with this revealing summary:

Thus, the slaves, by accepting a paternalistic ethos and legitimizing class rule, developed their most powerful defense against the dehumanization implicit in slavery. Southern paternalism may have reinforced racism as well as class exploitation, but it also unwittingly invited its victims to fashion their own interpretation of the social order it was intended to justify. And the slaves, drawing on a religion that was supposed to assure their compliance and docility, rejected the essence of slavery by projecting their own rights and value as human beings.

The rest of this massive and brilliant book is largely an elaboration of that paragraph.

"Paternalism and slavery merged into a single idea to the masters," said Genovese, noting that the slaves "proved much more astute in separating the two; they acted consciously and unconsciously to transform paternalism into a doctrine of protection of their own rights— a doctrine that represented the negation of the idea of slavery itself." Although Genovese repudiated Stanley M. Elkins's "Sambo" thesis and insisted that slaves found "ways to develop and assert their manhood and womanhood despite the dangerous compromises forced upon them," Genovese did acknowledge that paternalism left a debilitating legacy: "And the intersection of paternalism with racism worked a catastrophe, for it transformed elements of personal dependency into a sense of collective weakness." It was not, continued Genovese, "that the slaves did not act like men. Rather, it was that they could not grasp their collective strength as a people and act like political men." The black struggle on that front, Genovese concluded, has paralleled that of every other oppressed people and has not yet been won.

Genovese's framework of analysis led him to some penetrating insights on specific aspects of slavery. For example, on the traditional division between house servants and field hands, he said, "the deeper commitment of the house servants to a dependency relationship—their closer identification with their white folks which has always drawn so much comment—did not imply a commitment to slavery. The house servants knew their white folks too well to see them as ten feet tall." Genovese's view of the controversy over the black family was evident in his title for a section on that subject: "The Myth of the Absent Family." Taking issue with Aptheker, Genovese acknowledged that "the slaves of the Old South, unlike those of the Caribbean and Brazil, did not take up arms often enough or in large enough numbers to forge a revolutionary tradition." Genovese concluded that "the significance of the slave revolts in the United States lies neither in their frequency nor in their extent, but in their very existence as the ultimate manifestation of class war under the most unfavorable conditions." On the closely related subject of individual slaves who ran away, Genovese observed: "That they chose to leave as individuals may say no more than that they saw the futility of insurrection and the probable destruction of their people. They may, that is, have made the greatest contribution to the spirit of collective resistance that objective conditions made possible."

Religion plays a major role in Genovese's concept of paternalism; thus it is not surprising that he returned to it in the concluding section of *Roll, Jordan, Roll:*

The slaves' religion developed into the organizing center of their resistance within accommodation; it reflected the hegemony of the master class but also set firm limits to that hegemony. Not often or generally did it challenge the regime frontally. It rendered unto Caesar that which was Caesar's, but it also narrowed down considerably that which in fact was Caesar's. Black religion, understood as a critical world-view in the process of becoming—as something unfinished, often inconsistent, and in some respects even incoherent—emerged as the slaves' most formidable weapon for resisting slavery's moral and psychological aggression. . . .

However much the slaves, as Christians, felt the weight of sin, they resisted those perversions of doctrine which would have made them feel unworthy as a people before God. Their Christianity strengthened their ties to their "white folks" but also strengthened their love for each other and their pride in being black people. And it gave them a firm yardstick with which to measure the behavior of their masters, to judge them, and to find them wanting. The slaves transformed the promise of personal redemption, prefigured in the sign of Jonas, into a promise of deliverance as a people in this world as well as the next.

Staughton Lynd

Eugene Genovese's strident criticism of Staughton Lynd illustrates once again that the exercise of placing historians in schools of thought is somewhat arbitrary, for they are both generally regarded as two of the most significant contributors to the New Left or radical vision of American history. Genovese reviewed Lynd's two most important books, *Class Conflict, Slavery, and the United States Constitution: Ten Essays* (1967) and *Intellectual Origins of American Radicalism* (1968), for the *New York Review of Books;* it later formed a part of *In Red and Black* under the title "Staughton Lynd as Historian and Ideologue." Genovese's first point is made by the title: "Normally, it would be bad manners to confuse the two roles, but Lynd has argued forcefully that they ought not to be separated, and both books . . . are plainly meant to serve direct political ends." Genovese considered it "ironic that even historians who do not consider themselves Marxists are steadily building a genuine American version of Marxism by the very act of destroying the caricature to which they fell heir." *Class Conflict* he considered "by far the better of the two books," claiming that it came "close to replacing economic determinism with a sophisticated class analysis of historical change"; Genovese even said that the four essays in the first part of the book ("Class Conflict"), together with Lynd's other work on the Revolutionary period, "justify his reputation as a thoughtful scholar of early American history." In the second and third parts, however, where Lynd turned to slavery, Genovese thought that he lost his way: "His argument is finally no more than an indictment of the Founding Fathers for having failed to make a moral stand against slavery." In short, suggested Genovese, "Lynd moves from the economic determinist view of the first part of his book to a subjective and ahistorical one in the second. Unable to justify his moralistic condemnation of slavery according to his materialist theory, he asserts a moral absolutism that contradicts the theory itself."

In *Intellectual Origins*, however, said Genovese, Lynd "abandons all attempts at a materialistic interpretation." Yet the real problem, Genovese said, was that he also abandoned history: "The book is . . . not history at all . . . but a political testament with historical references added to establish a pedigree. . . . a travesty of history."

Genovese was far too harsh with Lynd, who deserves a chance to speak for himself. Lynd exhibited several of the most important traits of radical scholarship. He hoped to radicalize the profession by forcing historians to take a stand on the issues of the day, such as the war in Vietnam. He insisted that the individual historian was obligated to be an activist. Lynd himself lived out that belief in the civil-rights and antiwar movements; apparently this sort of attitude and activity contributed to his failure to receive tenure at Yale (even Genovese defended him there). He insisted on paying attention to groups that historically have been oppressed in this country, such as minorities and unskilled workers. In general, he insisted on viewing history "from the bottom up" (the phrase is most closely associated with Jesse Lemisch) rather than from the top down (that is, from the viewpoint of the common people rather than that of the elites). Finally, Lynd hoped to find in radicalisms of the past appropriate models for the present. It is this latter hope that is most important in a consideration of his *Intellectual Origins of American Radicalism*. "But let me put the baldest face on my intention," wrote Lynd in his preface:

> In one sense the concern of the following chapters is ahistorical. I am less interested in eighteenth-century radicalism than in twentieth-century radicalism. Accordingly, the process of historical causation—how certain ideas came into being, what influence they subsequently had—matters less to me than the fact that those ideas existed. I want to show, simply, that we are not the first to have found an inherited deterministic radicalism inhibiting, nor is ours the first attempt to make an opportunity of that dilemma. The characteristic concepts of the existential radicalism of today have a long and honorable history. Acquaintance with that history may help in sharpening intellectual tools for the work of tomorrow.

"Any critic of the American present must have profoundly mixed feelings about our country's past," Lynd asserted. "On the one hand, he will feel shame and distrust toward Founding Fathers who tolerated slavery, exterminated Indians, and blandly assumed that a good society must be based on private property." On the other hand, "he is likely to find himself articulating his own demands in the Revolutionary language of inalienable rights, a natural higher law, and the right to revolution." The preamble to the Declaration of Independence, said Lynd, was "the single most concentrated expression of the revolutionary intellectual tradition." Among the traditional radical affirmations that Lynd dealt with in *Intellectual Origins* were

that the proper foundation for government is a universal law of right and wrong self-evident to the intuitive common sense of every man; that freedom is a power of personal self-direction which no man can delegate to another; that the purpose of society is not the protection of property but fulfillment of the needs of living human beings; that good citizens have the right and duty, not only to overthrow incurably oppressive governments, but before that point is reached to break particular oppressive laws; and that we owe our ultimate allegiance, not to this or that nation, but to the whole family of man.

The tradition was both English and American, said Lynd. "Radical American 'praxis' (the word Marx used to describe practical-critical activity) derived from radical English theory." This Anglo-American tradition was linked in turn to Rousseau and to Marx. Lynd's way of organizing his look at this American radical tradition—which he thought contemporary radicals should find useful—was thematic in *Intellectual Origins:* "The Right of Revolution," "Truths Self-Evident," "Certain Inalienable Rights," "The Earth Belongs to the Living," "Cast Your Whole Vote," "My Country Is the World," and "Bicameralism from Below." Genovese notwithstanding, Lynd's look was ultimately quite effective and certainly made *Intellectual Origins* one of the more important books produced by a New Left historian.

Lynd's other books clearly reflect his interests. Parts of *Class Conflict, Slavery, and the United States Constitution* grew out of Lynd's master's thesis, *Anti-Federalism in Dutchess County, New York: A Study of Democracy and Class Conflict in the Revolutionary Era.* The thesis won an award as the best in American history at Columbia in 1961 and was published as a book the following year. In it (and in *Class Conflict*) Lynd asserted that "in Dutchess County, New York, the Revolution was indeed—in Becker's famous phrase—a struggle as to who should rule at home as well as a struggle for home rule" and that, despite some qualifications, "the Dutchess evidence on the whole confirms Beard and Becker rather than their critics." Lynd, however, did not blindly worship the Progressive historians; in one essay in *Class Conflict* he rather severely took to task both Turner and Beard for neglecting the Negro and slavery. Lynd also showed his interest in, and particular point of view on, black history in his editing of *Reconstruction,* a book of selected readings published in 1967. He carefully included excerpts from the works of scholars with differing points of view, including W. E. B. Du Bois, James Ford Rhodes, William A. Dunning, Howard K. Beale, Eric McKitrick, and Kenneth Stampp. When it was Lynd's turn to write, he said it was time to "end the debate about whether Northern policy was too soft or too hard." It was, he continued, "hard in the wrong way, or more precisely, in the wrong area of social life." The "fundamental error in Reconstruction policy," then, was that "it did not give the freedman land of his own." Without "the economic independence to resist political intimidation, manhood suffrage was inevitably artificial; supported by the presence of Union soldiers, it collapsed when they were withdrawn."

In 1966, Lynd published two books indicative of his antiwar views. One, with Thomas Hayden as coauthor, entitled *The Other Side*, was the notorious and controversial account of the trip to North Vietnam made by Lynd, Hayden, and American Communist historian Herbert Aptheker. The other book, a more scholarly one, was a collection entitled *Nonviolence in America: A Documentary History*. The editors of the series in which it appeared claimed that it was the "first collection of materials on the American tradition of nonviolence." It was indeed a broad and valuable collection, but it clearly had a point of view. For example, Lynd insisted that, despite the usual emphasis on Gandhi and Tolstoy as forerunners of contemporary nonviolence, America "has more often been the teacher than the student of the nonviolent idea." Furthermore, no doubt is left that Lynd is an advocate of nonviolence as well as a scholar thereof; again, the editors said that the book "beckons scholars to tread the paths he [Lynd] has opened, at the same time that it invites those who are dedicated to the goals of social justice and racial equality in a world at peace to clarify the means of reaching those goals." To combine scholarship with social action was a central concern of the New Left. Lynd included excerpts from works by members of the Society of Friends (Lynd's own religious affiliation), abolitionists, anarchists, trade unionists, civil-rights activists, and, of course, conscientious objectors from both of the world wars and Vietnam.

Three books published in 1973 bore Lynd's name; they represented some of the later aspects of his work. *Strategy and Program: Two Essays Toward a New American Socialism* was written jointly with New Left diplomatic historian Gar Alperovitz. The words "new" and "American" are significant qualifiers. Whereas socialism is a "long-term hope," in the words of the authors, "we mean to imply that the word must be conceived differently from the way it has often been understood in the past, or in other countries." They referred specifically to "the miscarriage of socialism in the Soviet Union" and claimed to "believe, contrary to well-established Cold War stereotypes, that public ownership and democracy are not irreconcilable."

The other two books that appeared in 1973 were labor history: *American Labor Radicalism: Testimonies and Interpretations*, which Lynd edited alone, and *Rank and File: Personal Histories by Working-Class Organizers*, which he edited with his wife, Alice. *Rank and File* consists essentially of interviews with radical labor organizers in the Chicago area steel industry in the 1930s (some of the interviewees were still active after World War II). "What unites these remarkable individuals," wrote the Lynds, "is that . . . they belong to a tradition of working-class democracy."

It is appropriate to allow Staughton Lynd the final word on his role as a historian. He contributed the selection on history to the important collection of essays by radical scholars from several different disciplines (English, economics, political science, philosophy, and so on) edited by Theodore Roszak and entitled *The Dissenting Academy* (1968). In Lynd's essay "Historical Past and Existential Present," he began by considering the word "profession": "The word itself suggests that a profession is not just something a person does but something he believes in doing." Belief continued to be important in Lynd's analysis, for he readily admitted that he entered the field of history in part because, "as one considerably alienated from America's present, I wanted to know if there were men in the American past in whom I could believe." Historians, Lynd suggested, "are not supposed to be influenced by their personal experiences, but I was, profoundly." He taught for three years at Spelman College, a Negro women's college in Atlanta, and became actively involved in the civil-rights movement. As a teacher he increasingly came to feel that the student should encounter history with the question, "What can I learn about how to live?" He came to be "more and more committed to the thesis that the professor of history should also be a historical protagonist, . . . someone called to *making* history as well as writing it."

Lynd suggested that a historian should perform two important tasks which he readily conceded were "presently unfamiliar." One was "the sensitive chronicling in depth of the important events of his own lifetime"; the other, "the projection of alternative futures on the basis of the richness of our past experience." He concluded that "what distinguishes the historian from other social scientists is not that he writes about the past but that he considers things in process of development." History and sociology "are not concerned with different objects; they are different ways of looking at the same object." Therefore, "the historian need not be embarrassed if he concerns himself more with the present and future than with the past." The historian should remember, however, that his "business with the future is not to predict but to envision, to say (as Howard Zinn has put it) not what *will* be but what *can* be. The past is ransacked, not for its own sake, but as a source of alternative models of what the future might become."

Howard Zinn

It is appropriate for Lynd to quote Howard Zinn, for in many ways their roles in New Left historiography have been similar. Zinn spent most of his academic career at Boston University, though he taught earlier, as did Lynd, at Spelman College. His books reveal his changing interests and involvements.

Zinn's first major work, published in 1958, was an admiring study of the congressional career, from 1917 to 1933, of the crusading reformer Fiorello LaGuardia, who, of course, is known best as the mayor of New York during the New Deal era. *New Deal Thought* (1966), edited by Zinn, was a follow-up to the LaGuardia study. Zinn carefully tried to include all points of view on the New Deal, including LaGuardia's, but his own point of view certainly came through. Although the New Deal's accomplishments, Zinn wrote, were "considerable," still, "when it was over, the fundamental problem remained—and still remains—unsolved: how to bring the blessings of immense natural wealth and staggering productive potential to every person in the land." Sounding much like Lynd, who insisted on looking at past radicalism primarily to find solutions to today's problems, Zinn said that his ultimately "harsh estimate of New Deal achievements derives from the belief that the historian discussing the past is always commenting—whether he realizes it or not—on the present; . . . It is for today, then, that we turn to the thinking of the New Deal period." Among other works, Zinn edited *The Pentagon Papers: Critical Essays* (1972, with Noam Chomsky) and *Justice in Everyday Life* (1974).

The Southern Mystique and *SNCC: The New Abolitionists,* both published in 1964, were excellent examples of the kind of chronicling in depth of one's own time that Lynd advocated. *The Southern Mystique* included extensive treatment of the mass demonstrations (in which Zinn participated) in Albany, Georgia, in 1961 and 1962. This portion of the book drew praise even from those who were critical of the whole. It was when Zinn argued that racial prejudice in the South was not instinctive but circumstantial, and therefore could be changed, that he drew criticism. He drew even more for insisting that the idea of southern exceptionalism was a myth. The South, he said, was a mirror, the essence of the nation, for it contained, "in concentrated and dangerous form, a set of characteristics which mark the country as a whole." Among those characteristics Zinn cited racism, violence, religious fundamentalism, nativism, hypocrisy in the elevation of women, suppression of class grievances, and poverty. SNCC, the Student Nonviolent Coordinating Committee, was one of the most important and radical organizations to emerge from the civil-rights movements in the 1960s. Zinn's book, as the title suggests, compared SNCC's members with those who fought against slavery before the Civil War. He wrote in praise of them: "For the first time in our history a major social movement, shaking the nation to its bones, is being led by youngsters. . . . All Americans owe them a debt for—if nothing else—releasing the idealism locked so long inside a nation that has not recently tasted the drama of a social upheaval. And for making us look on the young people of the country with a new respect."

Zinn next turned his attention to the war in Vietnam. The title of one book he published in 1967 is self-explanatory: *Vietnam: The Logic of Withdrawal.* In the same year he broadened his field with the publication of *Disobedience and Democracy: Nine Fallacies on Law and Order.* Zinn's starting point was the widely circulated essay by Supreme Court Justice Abe Fortas, *Concerning Dissent and Civil Disobedience.* "For the crisis of our time, the slow workings of American reform, the limitations on protest and disobedience and innovation set by liberals like Justice Fortas, are simply not adequate," according to Zinn. "We need devices . . . to resist the government's actions against the lives and liberties of its citizens; to pressure, even to shock the government into change; to organize people to replace the holders of power, as one round in the continuing cycle of political renewal which alone can prevent tyranny."

Among the specific fallacies that Zinn pointed to were "that the rule of law has an intrinsic value apart from moral ends"; "that the person who commits civil disobedience must accept his punishment as right"; "that our principles for behavior in civil disobedience are to be applied to individuals, but not to nations; to private parties in the United States, but not to the United States in the world"; and "that we, the citizenry, should behave as if we are the state and our interests are the same."

Zinn's two most important books appeared after the 1960s. *The Politics of History* was published in 1970, but most of the essays contained in it had appeared before. It is a ringing call for history to be relevant. It establishes some criteria for a radical history and, in a series of case studies, attempts to meet them. *A People's History of the United States* appeared in 1980; it can be viewed as essentially a New Left textbook in American history.

Zinn, appropriately, began *The Politics of History* by quoting Diderot on Voltaire: "Other historians relate facts to inform us of facts. You relate them to excite in our hearts an intense hatred of lying, ignorance, hypocrisy, superstition, tyranny; and the anger remains even after the memory of the facts has disappeared." Zinn's aim, as stated in his introduction, was "to stimulate a higher proportion of socially relevant, value-motivated, action-inducing historical work." In short, he argued "for the notion of the historian as actor." In the important essay "What Is Radical History?" Zinn said that his starting point was "the idea of writing history in such a way as to extend human sensibilities, not out of this book into other books, but into the ongoing conflict over how people shall live, and whether they shall live." He then discussed "five ways in which history can be useful"; in effect, five criteria for radical history. First, "We can intensify, expand, sharpen our perception of how bad things are, for the victims of the world." Second, "We can expose the pretensions of governments to either neutrality or beneficence." Third, "We can expose the ideology that pervades our culture—using 'ideology' in Mannheim's sense: rationale for the going order." Fourth, "We can recapture those few moments in the past which show the possibility of a better way of life than that which has dominated the earth thus far" (in discussing this point, Zinn sided with Lynd in the dispute between Genovese and Lynd over *Intellectual Origins of American Radicalism*). Finally, "We can show how good social movements can go wrong, how leaders can betray their followers, how rebels can become bureaucrats, how ideals can become frozen and reified."

All of this appeared in the first part of *The Politics of History*, entitled "Approaches." The second part, "Essays in American History," attempted to begin to meet those criteria in a series of brief, sometimes powerful essays organized under the topics class, race, and nationalism. The third and final part of the book, "Theory and Praxis" was a critique, sometimes devastating, of what historians do when they work in "philosophy of history." Much of the work in that area, Zinn argued, is "trivial, pretentious, tangential." Scholars in this field, whether they are historians or philosophers, "seem to have lost their way without realizing it because they have forgotten the humanistic goals of historical work. If they are not lost, it is because they are content to wander aimlessly so long as it is 'interesting' or in respectable company" (Zinn explained that he put "interesting" in quotation marks "because we have weakened the word by neglecting its denotation as some *interest* to be gained or lost, beyond mere curiosity"). Finally Zinn was very hard on the much-heralded book by John Higham and others, *History*, published in 1965; it was, he said, "an inadvertent summary of the formalism and academic detachment that mark much of American historiography today."

In 1980, Zinn's textbook *A People's History of the United States* appeared and immediately aroused controversy. Praise came from Luther Spoehr in the *Saturday Review:* "In the past decade, many historians have written history 'from the bottom up,' bringing to light the lives of the inarticulate and the downtrodden. Happily, Zinn compiles many of their findings." Even stronger praise came from James Levin in the *Library Journal:* "Zinn has written a brilliant and moving history of the American people from the point of view of those who have been exploited politically and economically and whose plight has been largely omitted from most histories. . . . the book is an excellent antidote to establishment history. . . . While the book is precise enough to please specialists, it should satisfy any adult reader. It will also make an excellent college text for basic history courses." Harvard's renowned Oscar Handlin, however, writing in the *American Scholar*, was explicitly nasty. Zinn's history was "deranged," a "fairy tale," and "anti-American."[10]

What was it about the book that led to such extremes of evaluation? Eric Foner provided a far more balanced and perceptive assessment in the *New York Times Book Review*: "Those accustomed to the texts of an earlier generation, in which the rise of American democracy and the growth of national power were the embodiment of Progress, may be startled by Professor Zinn's narrative. From the opening pages, an account of 'the European invasion of the Indian settlements in the Americas,' there is a reversal of perspective, a reshuffling of heroes and villains." The book, concluded Foner accurately, "bears the same relation to traditional texts as a photographic negative does to a print: the areas of darkness and light have been reversed." Foner suggested that not only would open-minded readers profit from Zinn's account but "historians may well view it as a step toward a coherent new version of American history."[11]

For the most part, however, Zinn should be allowed to speak for himself. "As for the title of this book," he wrote in the last chapter of *A People's History of the United States*, "it is not quite accurate; a 'people's history' promises more than any one person can fulfill, and it is the most difficult kind of history to recapture. I call it that anyway because, with all its limitations, it is a history disrespectful of governments and respectful of people's movements of resistance." As Zinn readily acknowledged, "That makes it a biased account, one that leans in a certain direction." To this he added, "I am not troubled by that, because the mountain of history books under which we all stand leans so heavily in the other direction—so tremblingly respectful of states

and statesmen and so disrespectful, by inattention, to people's movements—that we need some counterforce to avoid being crushed into
submission."

Clearly, one goal that Zinn hoped to accomplish by his approach
was to encourage the people to make their own history. "All the histories
of this country centered on the Founding Fathers and the Presidents,"
Zinn wrote, "weigh oppressively on the capacity of the ordinary citizen
to act. They suggest that in times of crisis we must look to someone
to save us: in the Revolutionary crisis, the Founding Fathers; in the
slavery crisis, Lincoln; in the Depression, Roosevelt; in the Vietnam-
Watergate crisis, Carter. And that between occasional crises everything
is all right, and it is sufficient for us to be restored to that normal
state." Traditional American history books, he continued, also teach us
that "the supreme act of citizenship is to choose among saviors, by going
into a voting booth every four years to choose between two white and
well-off Anglo-Saxon males of inoffensive personality and orthodox
opinions." The people should be allowed to a great extent to *tell* their
own history as well. As James Levin said of *A People's History,* "Seldom
have quotations been so effectively used; the stories of blacks, women,
Indians, and poor laborers of all nationalities are told in their own
words."[12] As Zinn explains further:

> . . . in that inevitable taking of sides which comes from selection and emphasis
> in history, I prefer to try to tell the story of the discovery of America from
> the viewpoint of the Arawaks, of the Constitution from the standpoint of the
> slaves, of Andrew Jackson as seen by the Cherokees, of the Civil War as seen
> by the New York Irish, of the Mexican war as seen by the deserting soldiers
> of Scott's army, of the rise of industrialism as seen by the young women in
> the Lowell textile mills, of the Spanish-American war as seen by the Cubans,
> the conquest of the Philippines as seen by black soldiers on Luzon, the Gilded
> Age as seen by southern farmers, the First World War as seen by socialists,
> the Second World War as seen by pacifists, the New Deal as seen by blacks
> in Harlem, the postwar American empire as seen by peons in Latin America.
> And so on, to the limited extent that any one person, however he or she
> strains, can "see" history from the standpoint of others.

All this makes for a very different textbook, indeed—and a much-
needed corrective.

Two New Left Anthologies—and Other Trends of the 1960s

If Zinn's *People's History of the United States* constitutes a New Left
textbook in American history, two anthologies, one edited by Barton J.
Bernstein—*Towards a New Past: Dissenting Essays in American History*

(1967)—and the other by Irwin Unger—*Beyond Liberalism: The New Left Views American History* (1971)—essentially constitute encyclopedias of the New Left's interpretation of our past.

Raymond A. Sokolov, writing in *Newsweek*, correctly labeled *Towards a New Past* "a collection of fierce attacks on established views of American history."[13] Bernstein in his introduction to the volume made it clear that, although the work of the Progressive historians had been flawed (especially in its failure to deal adequately with racism, slavery, and imperialism), still the young "left" scholars who contributed essays to *Towards a New Past* identified more with the Progressives than with the consensus historians of the 1950s. The label "New Left" was vague, Bernstein readily acknowledged, including Marxists, neo-Beardians, radicals, left-liberals, and so on. Jesse Lemisch's "The American Revolution Seen from the Bottom Up" opened the volume with a ringing call for breaking with the elitist orientation of so much of America's past historical writing. "The American Revolution can best be re-examined from a point of view which assumes that all men are created equal, and rational," said Lemisch, "and that since they can think and reason they can make their own history." These assumptions, Lemisch argued convincingly, "are nothing more nor less than the democratic credo." It was not just study of the American Revolution that could profit from this approach: "All of our history needs re-examination from this perspective. The history of the powerless, the inarticulate, the poor has not yet begun to be written because they have been treated no more fairly by historians than they have been treated by their contemporaries."

Staughton Lynd and Eugene Genovese are represented in this collection, as are Lloyd C. Gardner and Robert Freeman Smith, both from the "Wisconsin school" of diplomatic history, influenced by William Appleman Williams. Stephan Thernstrom, later to become in the view of many the central figure in the "new social history," contributed the essay "Urbanization, Migration, and Social Mobility in Late Nineteenth-Century America." Bernstein wrote on the New Deal, emphasizing that it was quite inadequate from a radical perspective. "The liberal reforms of the New Deal did not transform the American system," Bernstein insisted, but merely "conserved and protected American corporate capitalism, occasionally by absorbing parts of threatening programs."

Beyond Liberalism was different in several ways from *Towards a New Past*. It was larger and more comprehensive; it appeared later (in 1971), when the New Left had taken a more definite shape; and it was edited by Irwin Unger, who in 1967 had written an article in the *American Historical Review* criticizing the New Left, especially its "exaggerated present-mindedness." Unger wrote perceptively of the New Left, however, in his introduction. "How could so imperfect a nation have had so perfect a past?" was the question many on the left began to ask in the 1960s. "Already alienated from the American present, they have come to deplore much of the American past, to doubt the successes, and to focus on the compelling failures. Their outrage against the apologists for present America," Unger continued, "soon was transformed into anger against the apologists for past America," until finally, by 1970, "they were well on their way to constructing a version of American history that was influenced by their deep conviction of the country's recent failings." Unger correctly traced the beginnings of New Left history to Williams and his students at the University of Wisconsin.

Lemisch, Lynd, Genovese, Williams, Thernstrom, Gardner, Bernstein, and Zinn are all represented in *Beyond Liberalism*. Other essays include Gabriel Kolko's labeling the Progressive era from 1900 to 1916 the "triumph of conservatism"; Walter LaFeber's emphasizing the economic roots of American expansionism in the period from 1860 to 1898 in an excerpt from *The New Empire;* and David Horowitz's, pointing the accusatory finger at the United States for starting the Cold War in an excerpt from *The Free World Colossus*. The New Left's pioneering roles in black history and women's history were portrayed in essays by Robert L. Allen and Cellestine Ware, respectively. There is also a selection by Martin Duberman, "The Northern Response to Slavery," taken from the important proabolitionist anthology he edited in 1965 entitled *The Antislavery Vanguard*. Duberman, however, had subsequently departed from many other leftists, especially in his pessimism about what history had to say to the present. In an essay "On Becoming an Historian" (1969), which was reprinted in his book *The Uncompleted Past*, Duberman had made quite clear his disillusionment with a life devoted to history. "There cannot be a New History, in the sense our younger malcontents are calling for it—that is, a History researched, written and taught in such a way as to aid directly in the eradication of social ills," Duberman contended. Becoming quite personal, he added, "For those among the young, historians and otherwise, who are chiefly interested in changing the present, I can only say, speaking from my own experience, that they doom themselves to a bitter disappointment if they seek their guides to action in a study of the past." Although he had tried to make it otherwise, said Duberman, he had found that a life spent in the study of history had given him "very limited information or perspective with which to understand the central concerns of my own life and my own times." Apparently with Staughton Lynd's *Intellectual Origins of American Radicalism* in mind,

Duberman wrote, "It seems to me that *if* we are interested in finding out what produces radicals, we would learn far more by studying radicals today than by investigating the life histories of radicals in our past." Elsewhere he cautioned that "the chief lesson to be derived from a study of the past is that it holds no simple lesson—and the historian's main responsibility is to prevent anyone from claiming that it does."[14]

Perhaps it is appropriate to end consideration of the New Left on that cautionary note from one of its ablest voices and to mention other developments in American historical writing in the decade of the 1960s. Some consensus-oriented history, of course, continued to be written, and some important historical writing was not clearly oriented toward either a consensus or conflict perspective. Edward N. Saveth took on the extremely difficult task of summarizing the historiography of the 1960s; the results of his effort appeared in the yearbook for 1973 of the National Council for the Social Studies, entitled *The Reinterpretation of American History and Culture* (edited by William H. Cartwright and Richard L. Watson, Jr.). Saveth acknowledged that the New Left was one of the most important events of the decade, but he was too hostile and defensive to treat it very well. It was not, for example, a very helpful level of analysis to say that Staughton Lynd "would have a rather short life span in the Marxist paradises of Brezhnev and Mao." Saveth too, made a point but exaggerated it when he wrote that radicals did not dominate American historical writing in the decade: "Most historians are not radicals and this is a reflection of a certain amount of conservatism that has always characterized American historians and, more importantly, the profession's indifference to ideology and theory in history generally." The exaggeration was most evident when Saveth insisted that "there is ample indication that the 'consensus' school of historical writing which attracted so much attention in the fifties was not eclipsed during the sixties."[15] Quite simply, if one is thinking in terms of major trends, the consensus approach *was* eclipsed.

Saveth was somewhat more perceptive in treating other trends of the 1960s. The fate of liberalism as an ideology, he noted, was evident in two books by Arthur M. Schlesinger, Jr.; *The Politics of Hope* was published in 1962, but by the end of the decade it was *The Crisis of Confidence* (1969) that received Schlesinger's attention. Saveth also made rather effective use of some American Historical Association presidential addresses to illustrate developments in the profession. Carl Bridenbaugh, for example, president in 1962, complained about the inroads into the profession made by young, lower-middle-class, and foreign elements and about emotionalism and the search for relevance. His strongest attack was on "that Bitch-goddess, *Quantification.*" As Saveth noted, the historiography of the 1960s moved in exactly the directions to which Bridenbaugh was opposed. At the end of the decade Oscar Handlin—whose background included the very same elements of urbanism and foreignism to which Bridenbaugh objected—complained in a similar way about the inroads of quantification and relevance and also lamented the absence of a community of scholars in a profession grown outsize.[16]

There was a marked impact upon history by the social sciences in the 1960s, Saveth noted; there were both quantifiers and nonquantifiers among historians oriented in the social sciences. Saveth mentioned that there was much talk again of a "new" history, "this time centered in quantifiable data and quantitative techniques: 'new' political history; 'new' economic history; and 'new' social history. The focus—but not the exclusive focus—was upon group behavior with the group outline defined by the kind of variables that could be quantified or that lent themselves to statistical expression." The social science approach to history, Saveth insisted, was "essentially value neutral."[17]

Saveth also noted a "search for smaller and, presumably, more viable units of analysis," which he labeled "the microanalytic trend." This led first to attention to family history and then to psychohistory. Finally, one response to the complexity of the 1960s which Saveth saw was a revival of interest in the traditional staple: narrative history. His major example was Allan Nevins and his monumental eight-volume history of the Civil War era, *Ordeal of the Union.* Nevins began the work in 1947 and finally completed it in 1971. Saveth ended on a note of qualified optimism. Even with "all of the crises of the decade," he said, "amplified by the historian's fear that technology would destroy us and that his work would not live on in the psychic experience, there were fewer signs of crisis mentality among historians than were apparent in other fields of literary-cultural endeavor."[18]

CHAPTER 16

Complexity: American Historical Writing in the 1970s—and Beyond

ICHARD HOFSTADTER, as we have seen, was one of the most perceptive observers of the American historiographical scene. It is not surprising, then, that in *The Progressive Historian,* published in 1968, not long before his untimely death in 1970, he came up with the phrase that best characterizes American historical writing of the 1970s: "the rediscovery of complexity in American history." Hofstadter predicted, "As more and more historians become aware that conflict and consensus require each other and are bound up in a kind of dialectic of their own, the question whether we should stress one or the other may recede to a marginal place, and give way to other issues that are at stake."[1] Richard Kirkendall, executive secretary of the Organization of American Historians, made the same point about complexity, though in a different context, in the January, 1979, *OAH Newsletter:* "The profession has, looked at in terms of social composition, become much more complex, and its conception of history has moved in the same direction. No longer monopolized by white 'Anglo-Saxon' males, the profession no longer believes that historical study should focus only on political elites."[2] Certainly the call for papers for the 1980 meeting of the OAH in the same issue of the newsletter reinforced the point:

> The work of historians has broadened markedly in the last twenty years, with regard to the methods used, the groups of people considered, and the questions asked about their behavior, their work, their ideas, and the quality of their lives. Therefore, for the 1980 meeting, . . . the Program Committee intends to highlight this "New American History" by developing a series of core sessions that reflect the theme "To Study the People" (working class, immigrants, Afro-Americans, Native Americans, women, Chicanos, middle class, Marxists, elites, homosexuals, the aged, artists, intellectuals, and so forth).[3]

To state it simply, there is no easily discernible single dominant trend in American historical writing in the 1970s to compare with consensus in the 1950s and conflict in the 1960s (of course, not all historical writing in those decades fit those molds, either). The phenomenon usually known as the "new social history" perhaps is closest.

It is possible to lament this situation, as John Higham already seemed to be doing in 1970 when he said in *Writing American History* that "we have today no unifying theme which assigns a direction to American history and commands any wide acceptance among those who write it. Nothing in the current situation of the historian more seriously compromises his civic function and influence."[4] Lack of a unifying theme, however, is not necessarily negative; and, admittedly, the problem may be in part that we are too close to see; in 2001 it may be possible to say quite simply and confidently what was the dominant trend.

For now, it must suffice to look at black history and women's history—two areas that had their roots at least as far back as the 1960s but continued as major trends through the 1970s—the "new social history," and the assessment of contemporary historical writing in the United States edited by Michael Kammen, *The Past Before Us.*

John Hope Franklin and Black History

"A curious aspect of the 'new' social history," Laurence Veysey suggested, "is that it is almost never pursued as such. Instead, what is pursued is demographic history, urban history, the history of the family, of women, blacks, Chicanos, or native Americans, the history of radical social movements, the history of social mobility. *The* society, in its overall dimensions as an evolving structure, is hardly ever studied."[5]

Black history, of course, had been around for a long time before the civil-rights movement and the "black revolution" of the 1960s. These movements, however, helped give black history greater attention and respectability. Earl E. Thorpe, in a helpful survey published in 1971 entitled *Black Historians: A Critique*—based on his work of 1958 which bore the significantly different title *Negro Historians in the United States*—divided black American historiography into four major schools. The first group of historians, writing in the period from 1800 to 1896, Thorpe labeled the "beginning school" and characterized them as "justifiers of emancipation." The second, the "middle group," he called "builders of black studies"; they wrote between 1896 and 1930. The "modern laymen" constituted a third school which overlapped chronologically both the second and the fourth, the "new school" (those who have written black history since 1930). According to Thorpe, the four black historians of greatest stature were William Wells Brown and George Washington Williams in the nineteenth century and W. E. B. Du Bois and Carter G. Woodson in the twentieth.[6]

William Wells Brown was born a slave in Kentucky in 1814. He escaped when he was about twenty years of age and became a lecturer and writer; he soon joined the abolitionist movement. He is frequently credited with being the first American Negro to write a novel and a play. His first historical work, *St. Domingo: Its Revolution and Its Patriots*, published in 1855, was actually a reprint in pamphlet form of a speech Brown had given on the great black revolutionary leader Toussaint L'Ouverture. Brown's two important historical contributions were *The Black Man: His Antecedents, His Genius, and His Achievements*, published during the Civil War in 1863, and *The Rising Son; or, The Antecedents and Advancement of the Colored Race*, published in 1874.

The *Black Man* consisted primarily of laudatory biographical sketches of such prominent blacks as Alexandre Dumas, Nat Turner, and Frederick Douglass. It was very well received; both Lewis Tappan and Douglass praised it highly. Perhaps this praise, along with its publication in the year of the Emancipation Proclamation, helped account for its success. It became so popular that Thorpe referred to Brown as "probably the first Afro-American author to receive remuneration from his writings."[7]

The Rising Son was supposedly a general history of Afro-American beginnings. Although it was better organized and more comprehensive than *The Black Man*, it consisted largely of the same biographical sketches found in that volume. It may have been the best work of its kind available at the time, but it still left much to be desired; Thorpe called it "sermonistic," "uncritical," and "almost devoid of documentation."[8]

The timing of Brown's works places him, of course, in Thorpe's "beginning school." Writers of this school—who "wrote history only incidentally, not as a major interest"—attempted to "justify emancipation by showing that some members of their race had committed distinctive acts in the past, and that the numbers of such individuals could be multiplied many times by giving the race better opportunities," and "usually had no formal training in history or historical methodology, did superficial research, and documented poorly."[9] On this latter point one should note in all fairness that they were like the great majority of their white contemporaries.

George Washington Williams belongs in the beginner's group as well, yet his major historical work, *A History of the Negro Race in America from 1619 to 1880*, published in two volumes in 1883, represented a significant improvement over Brown's works, especially in terms of research and documentation. Slavery, according to Williams, was "the blackest curse that ever scourged the earth" and should have been abolished at the founding of the nation. "It was then and there," he wrote of the Constitutional Convention, "that the hydra of slavery struck its fangs into the Constitution; and, once inoculated with the poison of the monster, the government was only able to purify itself in the flames of a great civil war." Williams justified his omission of a thorough treatment of the Reconstruction era on the grounds that he was preparing a separate work on that period; unfortunately, that work never appeared.

A History of the Negro Race was well received; its success, along with Williams's own experiences in the Union army, encouraged him to write *A History of the Negro Troops in the War of the Rebellion, 1861–1865,* published in 1888. Although it was quite laudatory of the Negro soldier and written in a highly oratorical style, the work was heavily documented. Also, Williams's personal knowledge of much of what he wrote about enabled him at times to be quite vivid in his descriptions.

Though not as important as a historian as he was for other accomplishments, the great Booker T. Washington merits inclusion in Thorpe's "beginning school" because of his biography of Frederick Douglass (published in 1906) and his two-volume *Story of the Negro,* published in 1909. Washington was primarily a popularizer—his work was based on Williams and other secondary sources—but he did add more information than most on the social history of the Negro.

W. E. B. Du Bois stands out as one of the true great black scholars of all times; he was also, of course, a founder of the National Association for the Advancement of Colored People, and broke with Booker T. Washington over the degree of militancy necessary for blacks to achieve equality. Du Bois was born in Massachusetts in 1868 of black and French ancestry. He was always proud of his background and grew up largely unaware of prejudice against blacks. He first encountered racial hostility as a student at Fisk University, in Nashville, Tennessee, and there he developed his belligerent attitude toward the color bar which was a dominant motivating factor for the rest of his life. Du Bois received a master's degree at Harvard; studied for awhile in Berlin, where he was exposed to the new "scientific" history, and returned to Harvard to complete his doctoral degree in 1895. His first teaching position was at Wilberforce University, a Negro college in Ohio, but he quickly moved on to Atlanta University, where he spent many years. His growing radicalism on the race issue led him out of teaching into the founding of the NAACP; his conversion to Marxism, in turn, led him to give up that work as well. He dabbled in radical politics but eventually left the United States for Ghana, where he died in 1963.

Du Bois's first major book, *The Suppression of the African Slave-Trade to the United States of America, 1638–1870,* was published in 1896 as the first volume in a series called the Harvard Historical Studies. The book grew directly out of his master's thesis and doctoral dissertation. By traditional scholarly standards it was one of Du Bois's finest works; Vernon Loggins, in *The Negro Author,* said that it was "by far the greatest intellectual achievement which had by 1900 came from any American Negro."[10] Du Bois said that his purpose in the work was "to set forth the efforts made in the United States of America, from early colonial times to the present, to limit and suppress the trade in slaves between Africa and these shores."

The Philadelphia Negro: A Social Study appeared in 1899. Although, as its title suggests, it was more sociology than history, many consider it Du Bois's greatest work; Thorpe referred to it as "epochal" and "one of the first scientific sociological treatises to come from the pen of an American."[11] It has also stood the test of time surprisingly well.

In 1907, Du Bois collaborated on a volume with Booker T. Washington entitled *The Negro in the South.* It was revealing in at least two ways. First, it showed Du Bois's disdain for war in general and the American Civil War in particular, referring to the latter as "that disgraceful episode of civil strife when, leaving the arguments of men, the nation appealed to the last resorts of dogs, murdering and ravishing each other for four long shameful years." Second, Du Bois introduced the view of Reconstruction which he was to expand some thirty years later into *Black Reconstruction:*

Although the new voters . . . introduced in the South were crude and ignorant, and in many ways ill-fitted to rule, nevertheless in the fundamental postulates of American freedom and democracy they were sane and sound. Some of them were silly, some were ignorant, and some were venal, but they were not as silly as those who had fostered slavery in the South, nor as ignorant as those who were determined to perpetuate it, and the black voters of South Carolina never stole half as much as the white voters of Pennsylvania are stealing today.

In 1909, Du Bois published a biography of abolitionist John Brown in the American Crisis Biography series edited by Ellis Paxson Oberholtzer. Though frequently overlooked in Du Bois's extensive bibliography, the work was well written, ably documented, and generally moderate. "Today at last we know, John Brown was right," wrote Du Bois; he also praised Brown, suggesting that he "of all Americans has perhaps come nearest to touching the real souls of black folk."

Three of Du Bois's books were very closely related. *Black Folk Then and Now: An Essay in the History and Sociology of the Negro Race* (1939) was essentially based on *The Gift of Black Folk: The Negroes in the Making of America* (1924), which itself was similar to the book simply entitled *The Negro* (1915). All three were general studies of the Negro in American history, but the evolution of Du Bois's views can be traced through these works. *The Negro* was a popular study, written for inclusion in the Home University Library of Modern Knowledge. *The Gift of Black Folk* had as its thesis that "despite slavery, war and caste, and despite our present Negro problem, the American Negro is and has been a distinct asset to this country and has brought a contribution without which America could not have been; and that perhaps the essence of our so-called Negro problem is the failure to recognize this fact." Though Thorpe praised *Black Folk Then and Now* for its generally restrained and temperate tone, Du Bois wrote in that volume that "it seems clear today that the masses of men within and without civilization are depressed, ignorant and poor chiefly because they have never had a chance." Further, mankind can go on to far greater achievements "if mere political democracy is allowed to widen into industrial democracy and the democracy of culture and art. The possibility of this had long been foreseen and emphasized by the socialists, culminating in the magnificent and apostolic fervor of Karl Marx and the Communists." It was also in this volume that Du Bois wrote his oft-quoted sentence, "The problem of the twentieth century is the problem of the color line."

In 1910, Du Bois presented a paper, "Reconstruction and Its Benefits," at a meeting of the American Historical Association; Ulrich B. Phillips was among those who did not receive it very well. The paper became a part of *Black Reconstruction,* which Du Bois published in 1935, and it clearly revealed for the first time his conversion to economic determinism. Du Bois advanced the thesis that the former slaves were well on their way to creating a better society in the period after the Civil War when they were defeated by reactionary forces. In fact, he argued, there was a democratic movement in the North as well as in the South which was crushed by the combination of reactionary elements in both sections. Noting that historians had generally emphasized the evils of the Reconstruction period, thus missing the constructive achievements of those years, Du Bois vigorously redressed the balance. He claimed that because leading radicals—Thaddeus Stevens and Charles Sumner especially—were genuinely interested in the welfare of the Negro people, white historians had vilified them and purposely distorted history.

Du Bois's later works showed his broadening world view and his increasing identification with Africa. *Color and Democracy: Colonies and Peace,* for example, published in 1945, was intended to help shape the postwar world, and called for the granting of democracy to all peoples, especially those long subjected to European colonialism. *The World and Africa* (1947) was designed, in Du Bois's own words, "to remind readers of the crisis of civilization, of how critical a part Africa has played in human history, past and present, and how impossible it is to forget this and rightly explain the present plight of mankind." Du Bois used mostly secondary sources; "I have done in this book the sort of thing, at which every scholar shudders," he acknowledged. "With meager preparation and all too general background of learning, I have essayed a task, which, to be adequate and complete, should be based upon the research of a lifetime." *The World and Africa*, he suggested, was "not so much a history of the Negroid peoples as a statement of their integral role in human history from prehistoric to modern times."

Du Bois produced many other books, including five novels, the first volume of a projected multivolume series entitled *Encyclopedia of the Negro*, and the largely autobiographical *Dusk of Dawn: An Essay Toward an Autobiography of a Race Concept* (1940). Perhaps his best-known work was the collection of essays entitled *The Souls of Black Folk*, which appeared in 1903.

Clearly, though George Bancroft is generally credited with being the "father" of American history, there were many who wrote it before him. It is just so with the "father" of Negro history, Carter G. Woodson. Born in Virginia in 1875, to former slaves, Woodson completed his bachelor's and master's degrees at Chicago and his doctorate at Harvard, where he studied under Edward Channing among others. He taught briefly and served as a dean at both Harvard University and the West Virginia Institute but moved quickly on to his lifework. In 1915 he organized the Association for the Study of Negro Life and History; the next year he began publication of the *Journal of Negro History*. He subsequently organized Associated Publishers to handle the publication and sale of books on Negro history. In 1926 he founded Negro History Week. He began publication in 1937 of the popular *Negro History Bulletin*, intended primarily for use in the schools. All of this established Woodson as the father of Negro history. As Thorpe has written, Woodson's "greatest contribution to historiography lies not so much in his writings . . . but in the fact that he launched and popularized a successful movement."[12]

Still, Woodson's writings were not without significance. In 1914 he published *Education of the Negro Prior to 1861*, which was generally praised for its high level of scholarship. Unfortunately—and somewhat reminiscent of Du Bois—Woodson was not always precise in documentation in some of his later writings. His best-known book, *The Negro in Our History*, first published in 1922, was the most important text in the field until John Hope Franklin's *From Slavery to Freedom* was published in 1947. *The Negro in Our History* was very temperate and objective and, in Thorpe's words, "deserves a high place among the forces and events which have won general acceptance for the field of Negro history."[13] It went through many editions and was adapted for both elementary and high school use.

Among Woodson's other important writings were *The History of the Negro Church* (1921) and *The African Background Outlined* (1936). *The Negro Church* was important as a pioneer work in the field, despite its lack of documentation. *The African Background* was a widely used syllabus for the study of Afro-American history.

Although Thorpe did not use the term, he appropriately made Woodson sound almost like a precursor of the New Left's "from the bottom up" kind of history when he wrote that Woodson

was a strong believer in cultural history. No doubt he was influenced in this belief by the New History movement led by James Harvey Robinson, which was tending in this general direction. But it is highly probable that his desire for a greater consideration of the Negro underprivileged minority was a considerable factor in causing him to champion a history which included the story of the masses.[14]

Woodson complained that most written history was "that sort . . . which is merely the record of the successes and disappointments, the vices, the follies and the quarrels of those who engage in the contention for power." The "real makers of history," he claimed, had been "those servants of the truth who had labored to enlighten humanity, to lift it out of drudgery into comfort, out of darkness into light, and out of selfishness into altruism."

In a very real sense, it has taken John Hope Franklin to establish with finality the scholarly respectability of the field pioneered by Woodson. Franklin has become so widely respected that he must be regarded not just as one of the outstanding scholars in the field of black history, but as one of the preeminent members of the historical profession; it is not without significance that he was selected to write the foreword for the American Historical Association's *The Past Before Us: Contemporary Historical Writing in the United States* (1980; edited by Michael Kammen). Franklin has been the president of the American Historical Association, the Organization of American Historians, and the Southern Historical Association. Born in Oklahoma, he received his doctoral degree from Harvard and has spent most of his academic career at the University of Chicago. In 1943 a revised version of his dissertation, entitled *The Free Negro in North Carolina, 1790–1860*, was published; each of his subsequent books has made a major contribution.

Immediately upon its publication *The Free Negro in North Carolina* was accepted as a standard text, perhaps the definitive work in its field. The basic paradox for the free Negro, of course (in North Carolina and elsewhere in the antebellum South), was that he was not a slave, yet he never enjoyed the full benefits of citizenship. Although Franklin made it clear that North Carolina was more liberal in its treatment of free blacks than any other southern state, they were even there "an unwanted people" whose freedom was constantly in jeopardy. Franklin used a variety of sources such as county records, papers of the state legislature and supreme court, private diaries and letters, and newspapers to examine every aspect of Negro life in the state: population growth, legal status, and economic, social, eduational, and religious aspects.

The book for which Franklin has long been best known, *From Slavery to Freedom: A History of Negro Americans,* appeared in 1947 and has gone through some five editions. It immediately replaced Woodson's *The Negro in Our History* as the standard text in the field. Only Benjamin Quarles's *The Negro in the Making of America* (1964) and August Meier and Elliott M. Rudwick's *From Plantation to Ghetto: An Interpretive History of American Negroes* (1966) could be considered as serious rivals, but neither is as comprehensive as Franklin's or has shown Franklin's staying power. Each new edition of Franklin has also included one of the finest bibliographies on black history available at the date of its publication.

"In the present work I have undertaken to bring together the essential facts in the history of the American Negro from his ancient African beginnings down to the present time," wrote Franklin in the first edition of *From Slavery to Freedom.* Negro history, though clearly distinctive in some ways, was not separate, according to Franklin. "It has been necessary, therefore, to a considerable extent, to retell the story of the evolution of the people of the United States in order to place the Negro in his proper relationship and perspective." Franklin also attempted, usually successfully, to maintain "a discreet balance between recognizing the deeds of outstanding persons and depicting the fortunes of the great mass of Negroes." When "dominant personalities forged to the front and assumed roles of responsibility and leadership," Franklin recognized them. "But," he insisted vigorously, "the history of the Negro in America is essentially the story of the strivings of the nameless millions who have sought adjustment in a new and sometimes hostile world." Like Woodson, he was somewhat in anticipation of the history-from-the-bottom-up emphasis after the 1960s. The greatest challenge for Franklin, of course, as he made his subsequent revisions, was to incorporate the latest revolutionary developments for black Americans. He accomplished the task very well; one of the major marks of *From Slavery to Freedom* has always been its balance and objectivity.

Franklin has not always limited himself strictly to black history.

The image brought to mind by the title of his book *The Militant South, 1800-1861,* published in 1956, is an accurate one. As Franklin stated it, "This volume seeks to identify and describe those phases of life that won for the ante-bellum South the reputation of being a land of violence." Typically, however, Franklin was careful to be moderate: "This study implies at no point that all Southerners, or even almost all of them, were bellicose or militant." The coming of the Civil War, he said, is far easier to understand when one is aware of the many strands of the militant tradition in the South, including the fear of slaves, the Indian threat, the prevalence of dueling, the heightened devotion to Manifest Destiny, and the growth of military schools and local militia organizations. Finally, Franklin cautioned us not to assume that the South's tendency toward violent resolution of conflict died out with the Civil War.

Kenneth Stampp's *The Era of Reconstruction, 1865-1877* (published in 1965) and Franklin's *Reconstruction: After the Civil War* (published in 1961) are probably the two major general works on the period written from a revisionist perspective. That is to say, they rejected the old interpretation (identified with William A. Dunning and Claude G. Bowers) in which radical Republican Reconstruction was portrayed as a "bad thing" and the period characterized as an era in which ignorant former slaves, corrupt carpetbaggers, and unprincipled scalawags imposed a reign of terror, extravagance and corruption upon the South that was ended only by white organizations such as the Ku Klux Klan and by a revival of decent, moderate white opinion in the North. Instead, Franklin emphasized that there was no long military occupation of the South, that the Reconstruction governments there made significant positive accomplishments, and that Reconstruction ended because of illegal white violence and northern betrayal. As Stampp wrote, "If it was worth four years of civil war to save the Union, it was worth a few years of radical reconstruction to give the American Negro the ultimate promise of equal civil and political rights."[15]

Franklin's historical writing of the 1960s continued with *The Emancipation Proclamation,* published in 1963, the centennial year of the document. This was also the peak year of the civil-rights movement and the year in which W. E. B. Du Bois died. Historians had apparently dealt adequately with the Proclamation as a phase or aspect of the Civil War, but Franklin observed that "they have given scant attention to the evolution of the document in the mind of Lincoln, the circumstances and conditions that led to its writing, its impact on the course of the war at home and abroad, and its significance for later generations." Franklin, however, did so. "For the last hundred years the Emancipation Proclamation has maintained its place as one of America's truly important documents," he wrote. "Even when the principles it espoused were not universally endorsed and even when its beneficiaries were the special target of mistreatment of one kind or another, the Proclamation somehow retained its hold on the very people who saw its promises unfulfilled." It did this not because of the perfection of its goal, Franklin noted, for "at best it sought to save the Union by freeing *some* of the slaves." Nor did it do this because of the sublimity of its language, for "it had neither the felicity of the Declaration of Independence nor the simple grandeur of the Gettysburg address." Franklin concluded, "But in a very real sense it was another step toward the extension of the ideal of equality about which Jefferson had written."

His last published work in the 1960s was his edition of a collection of essays entitled *Color and Race* (1968). The volume grew out of the Copenhagen Conference on Race and Color, held in 1965, and included selections by such notables as C. Eric Lincoln, David Lowenthal, and Talcott Parsons. Franklin also edited several other volumes, including new editions of such classic works as Albion Tourgee's *A Fool's Errand* and Thomas Wentworth Higginson's *Army Life in a Black Regiment.* With coauthors John Caughey and Ernest May he wrote a textbook in American history, published in 1965, entitled *Land of the Free.* He also cooperated with the editors of Time-Life Books in the production of the *Illustrated History of Black Americans* in 1970.

By 1976, Franklin's prestige led to invitations to give both the Walter Lynwood Fleming Lectures in Southern History at Louisiana State University and the new Jefferson Lecture in the Humanities for the National Endowment for the Humanities; the former led to the significant volume *A Southern Odyssey: Travelers in the Antebellum North;* the latter, to the eminently readable summary *Racial Equality in America.*

Gerda Lerner and Women's History

"American historical writing, until very recently, has been the province of white males," wrote Donald V. Gawronski in *History: Meaning and Method* (1975), "and they have by and large written about a white male-oriented society." It is difficult to argue with his point. "The cultural milieu within which American historians have traditionally operated," Gawronski continued, "has precluded them from giving more than cursory attention to the roles, contributions, and achievements of two very large groups of people in American society: women (comprising approximately 51 percent of the population) and blacks (comprising approximately 11 percent of the population)." Thus, concluded Gawronski, "except for references to the women's suffrage movement or to the institution of slavery or to individual women and blacks who simply could not be ignored (e.g., Margaret Fuller and George Washington Carver), the works of women and blacks have generally been over-looked." The development of the historiography of these two neglected groups has begun, however, and was "made possible largely through the efforts of the civil rights and women's movements of the post-World War II decades." Gawronski accurately noted that "the fact that attention is now being directed to hitherto forgotten groups of Americans illustrates the idea of history as a dynamic process of rein-terpreting the past in light of the contemporary cultural milieu and the availability of new evidence."[16]

Concluding his treatment of Carter G. Woodson, Gawronski sug-gested that Woodson was "responsible for making black history viable both on scholarly and popular levels and for making possible the full development of black historiography." His contention that "American women, unfortunately, possessed no such counterpart in their historio-graphic development"[17] makes an important distinction between the two fields, but it may also be something of an exaggeration. Although the important works on women's history were few, far between, and generally inferior in the nineteenth century, there were some, and the early years of the twentieth century saw the dawning of a new era. Arthur Schlesinger's important *New Viewpoints in American History* (1922) included a chapter on "The Role of Women in American His-tory." Ernest Groves's *The American Woman: The Feminine Side of a Masculine Civilization* appeared in 1924 and, among other things, chided historians for not giving women their proper place in American history. Finally, and most important, there was the work of Mary R. Beard. She wrote several works with her husband, Charles A. Beard, in addition to engaging in important pioneering work in women's history and women's studies. Gerda Lerner, arguably the most important practi-tioner of women's history today, found inspiration in the endeavors of Beard. "In a very real sense," wrote Lerner in the autobiographical introduction to her important book *The Majority Finds Its Past: Placing Women in History*, "I consider Mary Beard, whom I never met, my principal mentor as a historian."

Lerner was born in Austria in 1920. She became a refugee after the Nazi takeover and went to America, where she married, reared two children, and worked at all sorts of "women's jobs." It was, she wrote, "as good an education as any for becoming a specialist in the history of women." She secured a bachelor's degree from the New School for Social Research at age forty-three and went on to earn master's and doctoral degrees from Columbia. After teaching in the New School, Long Island University, and Sarah Lawrence College for several years, she moved to the University of Wisconsin, where she introduced a new graduate program in American women's history. In acknowledgment of both her stature and that of her field, she was elected president of the Organization of American Historians in 1981.

The Majority Finds Its Past: Placing Women in History, published in 1979, is a collection of Lerner's pieces written over the years. In the introduction she suggested that the volume "represents not only the personal intellectual growth of an individual historian, but also stages in the growth of a new field"; basically, this is true. The very term "women's history," Lerner noted appropriately, "calls attention to the fact that something is missing from historical scholarship and it aims to document and reinterpret that which is missing." Seen in this light, women's history is simply "the history of women." But it is also far more than that. It is "a methodology, a stance, an angle of vision," even, most broadly, "both a world view and a compensatory strategy for offsetting the male bias of traditional history."

Lerner came to the study of history through her work on a biography of Sarah and Angelina Grimké, the famous sisters from South Carolina who became leaders of both the abolitionist and women's-rights movements in the nineteenth century. Because Lerner had formerly written fiction (short stories, novels, screenplays, and so on), she had in mind a fictionalized biography. Soon, however, she came up against her deficiencies as a historian. "I was seriously handicapped by my lack of academic training and my inadequate knowledge of American history," she said, and began the seven years of work culminating in the attainment of her doctorate.

The book on the Grimké sisters, which Lerner eventually published in 1969, was entitled *The Grimké Sisters from South Carolina: Rebels Against Slavery.* Lerner had clearly overcome any deficiencies she may have had as a historian. *The Grimké Sisters* is an excellent and important piece of work; it is engrossing from the opening scene (in which Angelina Grimké addresses the Massachusetts Legislature) to Lerner's final assessment:

The Grimké sisters' lives had spanned almost a century. Now they were gone. Slavery was ended, but the black man was far from free and equal. Women, considerably freer to educate and express themselves than they had been during the sisters' early years, were many decades away from even the limited achievement of their citizenship rights. Perhaps women would not quite, as Angelina had liked to say, "turn the country upside down," but they would stand upright, and no man—guardian, father or husband—would "keep his foot upon their neck." That, according to Sarah, was what the movement was all about and the work of the sisters had been part of it.

Sarah and Angelina Grimké had lived their faith, with stubbornness, courage and dedication—a faith in the freedom and dignity of man, regardless of race, regardless of sex.

The Woman in American History, Lerner's next book, published in 1971, was really intended as a textbook for use in high schools and junior colleges, but it stands as a very good survey indeed, and it is one of the earlier general histories of women in America. It did an excellent job of striking a balance between "the contributions of outstanding women" and "the ways in which ordinary women have contributed to the American quest for freedom, security, and abundance." Also it showed that Lerner already understood and was sympathetic toward the new women's movement. "What all new feminists have in common," she wrote, "is anger at the continuance of unequal economic status for women, determination to incorporate sexual equality into all the institutions of our society, and an awareness that the subordinate position of women in many areas of life adversely affects them psychologically and hinders their achievements."

Lerner next began working on a source book of primary documents on women's history for Bobbs-Merrill's American Heritage Series; she called it in her mind "Woman in the Making of the Nation" and planned chapters based on traditional political chronology. She was, however, diverted from that project for some time. First she worked with her husband on the film version of John Howard Griffin's best-selling novel *Black like Me*. While working on the film, and as she pursued her historical studies, she began to notice the absence of black women from history. In her antislavery research she had found many largely unused sources for the history of black women. "Now it seemed to me I would be making a contribution to the civil rights movement and to scholarship," Lerner wrote, "by continuing this line of research and publishing a source book for the history of black women." In 1972 she did publish such a work, *Black Women in White America: A Documentary History*. It is a massive and valuable collection of primary documents on literally every aspect of the lives of black women in the United States from slavery to civil rights, and it includes material on education, work, politics, and organizations. Lerner provided an excellent preface as well as brief introductions to each of the documents. Noting that both American blacks and women "have been denied their history," she concluded that black women, therefore, "have been doubly victimized by scholarly neglect and racist assumptions. Belonging as they do to two groups which have traditionally been treated as inferior by American society . . . they have been doubly invisible. Their records lie buried, unread, infrequently noticed and even more seldom interpreted." At the end of her effort to remedy that situation, Lerner concluded that "if there is one theme that can emerge from the documentary record here presented, it is the strength, racial pride and sense of community of black women."

Having completed her project on black women, Lerner returned to her work on the source book of primary documents on women's history. The shape of the work had changed considerably, however:

> I no longer believed that I should tell the history of women under the title "Women in the Making of the Nation." I no longer thought that a chapter organization by traditional periods was adequate. But what to substitute for it? The solution came, as so often happens, in a flash of insight—I found a new title, long before I knew how well it fitted my content. The title, "The Female Experience," gave me the clue for reorganizing my research. I gave up the old chapter plan and arranged the material according to female life stages (Childhood, Youth, Marriage and the Single State, etc.) and to stages of the growth of feminist consciousness.

This describes rather well the book that was published in 1977 under the title *The Female Experience: An American Documentary*. The editors of the series were correct in their claim that the book was "the richest collection of rare materials on these themes to be assembled in one volume." Once again Lerner's introduction to the documents made a major contribution in itself. What she had attempted to do in the volume, she wrote, was "to give a selective composite picture of the female past, assembled so as to tell a story and help the reader to share some of the experiences, concerns, fears, and hopes of American women." She concluded the introduction:

> The process of creating feminist consciousness and a theory of female emancipation is still underway. The challenges of present-day American women are grounded in past experience, in the buried and neglected female past. Women have always made history as much as men have, not "contributed" to it, only they did not know what they had made nor did they have the tools for interpreting their own experience. What is new at this time is that women are now fully claiming their past and shaping the tools by which to interpret it. To this endeavor, it is hoped, this volume will make a modest contribution.

In other words, as Lerner said in *The Majority Finds Its Past*, "historical analysis of women has progressed, from compensatory and contribution history, to the new social history, and, most recently, women-oriented history."

In addition to these books Lerner contributed an excellent pamphlet published by the American Historical Association entitled *Teaching Women's History* (1981) and edited an extensive *Bibliography in the His-*

tory of American Women (third revised edition, 1978). Eric Foner wrote in the *History Book Club Review* that women's history is one of the most rapidly growing and conceptually innovative areas of American history; Gerda Lerner's work is a major contribution to that field.

Carl Degler, of Stanford University, also contributed to the history of women in America and related that topic to another important and relatively new one in his book *At Odds: Women and the Family in America from the Revolution to the Present* (1980). He also wrote an essay on "Women and the Family" for *The Past Before Us*. While family history is largely a European innovation, Degler noted, women's history is almost entirely American in its origins. While Degler acknowledged that "sexuality is to women's oppression what color has been to black oppression" and that "the study and understanding of the past is advanced by women's participation in the writing of history" because "they perceive important connections in the past that male historians tend to overlook," he was cautious in his assessment of the status of women's history and family history in relation to the mainstream of American history. Women's history, he noted, has moved ahead far more successfully than family history, but, ironically, the same reason that helps explain this also helps account for "the slowness with which it has been integrated into history in general," that is, "the strongly ideological or presentist origin of the field." Neither women's history nor family history will be integrated into American general history, Degler suggested, especially in the sense of inclusion in textbooks, until Americans' sense of the past has changed:

Especially is this true of women's history, since the conventional past was not only conceived (invented?) by men but includes, almost by definition, only those activities in which men have been engaged, while ignoring almost entirely the historical activities of women. That the definition of history ought to include women is no longer debatable; that doubt has been removed by recent scholarship in the field and by the recognition that if we are to understand the past from which all of us have emerged, we must know how women helped to shape it. The challenge is now to rethink our conception of the past we teach and write about so that women and the family are integrally included.[18]

Stephan Thernstrom and The New Social History

If it requires rethinking our conception of the past to incorporate women properly, it is even more true of the broad spectrum of groups and topics included under the rubric of the "new social history." While it may be true, as Laurence Vesey suggested, that the new social history has tended to deal with specific groups (women, blacks) and topics (the family, the city) but seldom with the society as a whole, Stephan Thernstrom's work has come close; at least it has raised implications for dealing with society as a whole.

Thernstrom himself, however, would be the first to acknowledge the pioneering efforts in the field by Harvard's Oscar Handlin. In a History Book Club review of Handlin's *A Restless People: Americans in Rebellion, 1770–1787* (written with his wife, Lilian Handlin) Gordon S. Wood described Handlin as "the dean of American social historians," who for more than four decades "has been writing about all aspects of American history, from the seventeenth-century to the present, from childrearing to immigration. Long before the history of the 'inarticulate' became fashionable, Handlin was delving into the lives of ordinary people."[19]

Handlin's two best-known works are *Boston's Immigrants, 1790–1865: A Study in Acculturation* (1941) and *The Uprooted* (1951), which won a Pulitzer Prize; he also was involved, along with Arthur M. Schlesinger, Sr., Arthur M. Schlesinger, Jr., Samuel Eliot Morison, Frederick Merk, and Paul H. Buck, in editing the indispensable *Harvard Guide to American History* (1954). In 1979, Handlin produced an end-of-the-decade collection of essays, entitled *Truth in History*, which among other things greatly lamented the disarray he perceived in the state of the discipline. Handlin's brand of social history is thus quite different from a great deal of the newer work in the field. Of the Handlins' *A Restless People* Wood wrote:

Although the social history of common people is popular these days, the Handlins' approach to this kind of history will be regarded by some as old-fashioned. There are no charts or graphs here, no Guttman scales or Lorenz curves. To be sure, there are measurement and social science theories, but they are behind the scenes, part of the scholarly scaffolding taken down and put out of sight for the presentation of the work.

Another difference, perhaps more important because it involves a basic point of view, is made clear by recalling the interesting connection between the new social history and the New Left's insistence on viewing history not only "from the bottom up" but also critically. Said Wood: "The Handlins also have a different conception of America from that expressed recently by other historians." They "reveal no shame or guilt in recounting America's history. They do not deplore and lament past American treatment of Indians, black Africans, or women." The reason, Wood concluded, that the Handlins "do not wallow in America's collective guilt is because they have never succumbed to a belief in America's collective innocence, which is really the other side of the same myth."[20]

Social historian Stephan Thernstrom, who earned his doctoral degree under Handlin at Harvard in 1962, was sometimes associated with the New Left in the early phases of his work. His essay on social mobility taken from his first book, *Poverty and Progress: Social Mobility in a Nineteenth-Century City* (1964), appeared in Irwin Unger's collection *Beyond Liberalism: The New Left Views American History* (1971). Thernstrom's results, noted Unger, did "not support the exaggerated conservative view of mobility in 19th century America." Many radicals came to regard social mobility studies in general as conservative, however.

Radical history and the new social history do indeed have an interesting relationship to each other. As James Neuchterlein wrote in *Commentary* in October, 1980, "Whatever its ideological implications, the new social history was most notably radical in its manner of defining what history as a field was all about." The new history, Neuchterlein went on to explain, "turned scholars' attention away from their traditional preoccupations—political, institutional, and intellectual developments as determined by the most visible and prominent elements in society—toward a new emphasis on the aggregate everyday experiences of life by ordinary people."[21] Laurence Veysey ably summarized the "canons" of the new social history in his article in *Reviews in American History:*

. . . that history should be viewed in terms of the processes affecting the great majority of people alive at any given time, with special attention to the anonymously downtrodden, those whose standard of living and prestige are the lowest . . . , and that the historian should be intensely skeptical of literary sources of evidence, always the product of a small elite, instead making use of whatever bare quantitative data exist to assure that one's conclusions are truly representative of the social aggregate being discussed.[22]

Although Neuchterlein was insistent on the affinity between the New Left and the new social history, he did acknowledge that "the new social history is less a conceptual monolith than was the New Left."[23] Stephan Thernstrom is most appropriately thought of as a leading proponent of the new social history.

The city studied in Thernstrom's *Poverty and Progress: Social Mobility in a Nineteenth-Century City* was Newburyport, Massachusetts. The subject was rather limited; the title tells all: social mobility in one city in Massachusetts in the nineteenth century. Like the best social histories, however—indeed, like the best of all histories—*Poverty and Progress* carefully placed its subject in the broader context, especially in a concluding chapter entitled "Newburyport and the Larger Society."

Thernstrom began by acknowledging his indebtedness to Handlin, referring to his teacher's "pioneering scholarship in American social history." In his introduction Thernstrom noted that no other nation has talked so much of social mobility as the United States; but, he asked, Is this a myth? Does the idea of America as a unique land of opportunity for the common man square with historical reality? "One of the most glaring gaps in our knowledge of nineteenth century America," Thernstrom observed, "is the absence of reliable information about the social mobility of its population, particularly at the lower and middle levels of society." One problem, of course, was source material for writing that kind of history; the written documents historians had traditionally required for their research do not exist for such a subject. Fortunately, however, Thernstrom noted, there is one source of information about the economic and social situation of ordinary, unorganized laborers: original manuscript schedules of the United States Census:

Starting in 1850, when a new method of census-taking was initiated, manuscript census schedules provide the historian with a primitive social survey of the entire population of a community; occupation, place of birth, property holdings, literacy, and other useful information about every inhabitant is listed. These skeletal facts, supplemented by data from contemporary newspapers and other sources, made it possible to fix the social position of the unskilled laboring families of Newburyport at decade intervals, and to measure how much social mobility they experienced in the period 1850–1880.

Thernstrom carefully acknowledged earlier historians who had pioneered in the use of these materials, including Handlin in *Boston's Immigrants* and F. L. Owsley in *Plain Folk of the Old South* (1949). Neither of these, however, had traced specific individuals from one census to the next. The only work closely comparable to his, Thernstrom thought, was Merle E. Curti's *The Making of an American Community: A Case Study of Democracy in a Frontier County*, a history of Trempealeau County, Wisconsin, published in 1959.

An important limitation to this kind of history is that sources for it exist, or at least can be used, only for the period from 1850 to 1880 (many of the 1890 records were destroyed by fire). The censuses before 1850 aimed at little more than a simple enumeration of the population, and those for the twentieth century are closed to the public except for their aggregate data so that it is impossible to trace individuals over time. New social historians, however, have learned to supplement the census data with an impressive array of additional sources, including city and county directories, state censuses, local birth and death records, tax and assessment lists, parish and school records, cemetery lists, and voter registration records.

Using primarily these available census materials, Thernstrom wrote an excellent book, one that is understandable even to the reader not well versed in the new methods of quantification and that does indeed reveal much about the larger American society, past and present. A reviewer for the *American Historical Review* said that "Mr. Thernstrom admirably succeeds in bringing the American dream of economic success down to the objective ground of census schedules, local directories, and tax assessors' lists."[24] Thernstrom cautiously noted that "chances to rise from the very bottom of the social ladder in the United States have not declined visibly since the nineteenth century; they seem, in fact, to have increased moderately in recent decades." Even more cautiously, however, he concluded that "this is not to say that opportunities are boundless in present-day America," for they "are neither boundless nor are they equal." Indeed, "tens of millions of Americans still live in a milieu which thwarts the development of their full human potentialities. . . . In the United States today the climb upward from the bottom rungs of the social ladder is not often rapid or easy, but *it never was*, if the experiences of the working class families of nineteenth century Newburyport are at all representative." Not only was upward mobility slow and difficult but "few of these men and few of their children rose very far." Thernstrom concluded:

If a more realistic evaluation of the past thus provides a less lurid perspective on the tendencies of the present, it need inspire no complacency. The romantic nostalgia which has led many Americans to believe that opportunity is "noticeably shrinking" is surely not the only basis for dissatisfaction with the status quo. The petty success stories enacted in nineteenth century Newburyport still occur daily. Whether the presence of opportunity of this kind is a sufficient test of the good society, however, may be doubted.

Thernstrom's next book *Nineteenth-Century Cities*, was coedited with Richard Sennett and appeared in 1969. The subtitle, *Essays in the New Urban History*, is indicative of an important trend of the time but also raises serious questions about labels. There was not only a new urban history but a new economic history, even a new political history — and, of course, broadest and most important of all, a new social history. In the midst of all this it should not be forgotten that in the earliest years of the twentieth century James Harvey Robinson called for a "new history," and what he meant by it was in many ways closely related to the various "new" histories mentioned above.

Nineteenth-Century Cities was a valuable collection. It grew out of a conference at Yale in 1968 on the nineteenth-century industrial city. Its four parts were "Urban Class and Mobility Patterns," "Urban Residential Patterns," "Urban Elites and Political Control," and "Urban

Families," showing well the major concerns of the new urban history. Several of the major names in the field were represented; in addition to the editors, Herbert G. Gutman, Michael B. Katz, and Leo F. Schnore were included. Thernstrom's contribution (in the section on class and mobility, of course) was entitled "Immigrants and WASPs: Ethnic Differences in Occupational Mobility in Boston, 1890–1940," and it became a part of his next major book.

The Other Bostonians: Poverty and Progress in the American Metropolis, 1880–1970 appeared in 1973. A reviewer for the *New York Times Book Review* said that it was "the best piece of quantitative history yet published" and that it was "destined to be a highly influential book."[25] Thernstrom had by now become the editor of the important Harvard Studies in Urban History series, of which the book is a part. *The Other Bostonians* is a study of the common people of Boston from 1880 to the present. Thernstrom used the methods of quantification which he had refined even further than in his Newburyport study. Once again, as in the earlier study, the phrase "poverty and progress" is in the title (in this case, the subtitle). Once again Thernstrom carefully ended on a general note: "The Boston Case and the American Pattern." He wrote that the "patterns of mobility that existed in Boston were not peculiar to that city, but rather were products of forces that operated in much the same way throughout American society in the nineteenth and twentieth centuries." Thernstrom again acknowledged Handlin, this time as one of several people who read the entire manuscript. Indeed, one of the most productive approaches to *The Other Bostonians* is to compare it with Handlin's *Boston's Immigrants*, in part to show the differences between the "new" social history and the "old."

Handlin's book is primarily a narrative; it uses statistics, but only occasionally and to establish facts. Handlin was more interested in providing comprehensive summaries of motives and social patterns; for example: "Boston [in 1845] was a comfortable and well-to-do city in which the people managed to lead contented and healthy lives." Handlin was not at all hesitant to quote an elite literary figure such as Ralph Waldo Emerson to show "the fundamental ideas and basic assumptions permeating the social and economic structure of the society."

Thernstrom's *The Other Bostonians*, on the other hand, is essentially a discussion of statistical tables—how they were arrived at and what they mean. The book is an argument from beginning to end. Thernstrom listed specific questions he wanted to answer: "Who came to Boston, and who remained there and settled in? . . . Did the immigrants who flocked to the New World cluster in ghetto neighborhoods from which escape was rarely possible? . . . Did patterns of migration and social mobility change drastically in the course of urbanization?" He proceeded to accumulate the statistics in an attempt to answer those questions.

Laurence Veysey, who also engaged in a comparison of these two books, closed with the thoughtful observation that "Thernstrom's version of the 'new' social history is far less tuned to conflict than narrative social history such as Oscar Handlin's." Veysey acknowledged that this is ironic, since Handlin explicitly disliked ethnic conflict and painted, for example, a rosy view of prospects for blacks in Boston, while Thernstrom emphasized the bleakness of their opportunities in life. Concludes Veysey: "Though claiming to arise out of a concern for the history of nonelite masses, quantitative history like Thernstrom's has little in common with leftist-inspired history, which is conflict-oriented or at the very least tied to questions of power and domination and is usually antiquantitative in its approach to evidence."[26] To the extent that this latter point is true, it raises some doubt about James Neuchterlein's insistence on the close relationship between the New Left and the new social history. The problem may be resolved by viewing the New Left as essentially an ideological trend and the new social history as essentially a methodological one. Sometimes they have overlapped; probably more often they have not.

In 1980, Thernstrom edited (with Handlin as consulting editor) the massive and important reference work, the *Harvard Encyclopedia of American Ethnic Groups,* one of the finest products of what Gerald N. Grob and George Athan Billias (in *Interpretations of American History*) called the "ethnocultural approach" to American history.[27]

Grob and Billias saw the emergence of the new social history as the result of three major forces: (1) the French *annales* school, led by Lucien Febvre and Marc Bloch, which took a broad interdisciplinary approach to what some called historical sociology; (2) the proliferation of work by social and behavioral scientists after World War II on such topics as race relations, family problems, social and geographical mobility, crime, and educational and economic opportunities; and (3) the increased use of the computer and new quantitative techniques which made it possible to analyze historical evidence from heretofore unusable sources, such as manuscript census schedules.[28]

Grob and Billias also suggested that the new social history, itself a part of the fragmentation of the discipline in recent years, has fragmented further, especially into a "new" economic, political, and urban history. The new economic history has specialized in using historical data to test hypotheses derived from economic theories; one of their main interests has been to describe and explain the patterns of America's economic growth. The new political historians have been especially influenced by the behavioral approach of political science. By engaging in quantitative analyses of voting behavior, roll-call analyses of legislatures, shifts in public opinion on political issues, and so on, they have moved political history closer to social history by attempting to elucidate the social bases of political behavior. The new urban history has been interested in such diverse topics as urbanization, suburbs, neighborhoods, educational systems, and city political bosses and machines.[29] In studying these topics, urban historians have made use not only of new methods but new sources and interdisciplinary approaches as well. Bruce Stave's book *The Making of Urban History: Historiography Through Oral History* (1979) is a helpful and unique introduction to this field through interviews with several of its leading practitioners; thus, it is also an interesting exercise in oral history. Among those interviewed are Blake McKelvey, Bayrd Still, Constance McLaughlin Green, Richard C. Wade, Sam Bass Warner, Jr., Eric E. Lampard, Samuel P. Hays, and, of course, Handlin and Thernstrom.

The new social history not only deals with demography, family history, and community studies but also is concerned with such previously neglected groups as the poor, the unemployed, the sick, the infirm, the handicapped, the insane, the aged, criminals, and juvenile delinquents. Finally, Grob and Billias appropriately remind us that not all history in recent years has been of the "new social" variety. They suggest four specific approaches to the discipline which have continued along more traditional lines: (1) the "neo-Progressive" (including the New Left); (2) the new intellectual history, influenced by Perry Miller and others, which has placed more emphasis on analyzing ideas than on describing them (and which is quite different in orientation from the Progressives, either old or new, because of their emphasis on ideas as primary determinants in history); (3) comparative history; and (4) "the organizational school of scholars," who, said Grob and Billias, "regarded the rise of bureaucratic structures in society and the acceleration of professionalization as the most significant influences shaping American life since the closing of the frontier in the 1890s" and who "emphasized that the behavior of individuals might be better understood when seen within an organizational context."[30]

The Past Before Us

Most of the trends delineated by Grob and Billias, and quite a few others as well, are dealt with in the book edited by Michael Kammen for the American Historical Association, *The Past Before Us: Contemporary Historical Writing in the United States* (1980). *The Past Before Us* is one of those periodic state-of-the-art volumes which appear from time to time. Whether or not it lives up to its billing as a "searching assessment of the major advances in historical methods as well as in historical knowledge during the 1970s" and as a "comprehensive overview of the work being done by historians in the United States today" is open for discussion. The reviewer for the *History Teacher*, for example, thought that "what *The Past Before Us* does *not* do is provide an easily comprehensible overview of what professional historians have been doing in the last ten years." The reviewer acknowledged that this was in part because the writing of academic history in the United States has become too diverse to permit any tidy generalizations. The same reviewer may have been excessively critical, however, when he wrote, "Indeed, the overall picture which emerges here is one of confusion—hundreds of historians going about their esoteric business with little or no regard for what fellow practitioners in other disciplines might be doing."[31] *The Past Before Us* consists of essays prepared for presentation on the occasion of the Fifteenth International Congress of Historical Sciences, held in Bucharest, Romania, in August, 1980. One can quibble about what was included and what was not, and one can point out that some selections are clearly better than others, but no collection can escape that response. As a whole, it is a good assessment of American historiography at the beginning of the 1980s.

John Hope Franklin, president of the American Historical Association at the time, supplied a brief foreword. The introduction, "The Historian's Vocation and the State of the Discipline in the United States," written by editor Michael Kammen, of Cornell University, is thoughtful and ultimately optimistic ("Clio's current health is robust"). Kammen noted three major developments: a shift from descriptive to analytical history, the proliferation of methodological innovations, and the changing relationship of the new social history to other subdisciplines. Simultaneously with those developments, the degree of change within the profession during the 1970s was affected by the deaths of such outstanding historians as Richard Hofstadter (1970), Allan Nevins (1971), David M. Potter (1971), Samuel Flagg Bemis (1973), Roy F. Nichols (1973), Constance McLaughlin Green (1975), and Samuel Eliot Morison (1976).

The Past Before Us is divided into three parts. The first, "Units of Time and Areas of Study," while it is interesting and important, need not concern us here, for it deals with the work of American historians in non-American fields of history. Of the two parts on American history, the first, "Expanding Fields of Inquiry," involves content; the other, "Modes of Gathering and Assessing Historical Materials," involves method. "Expanding Fields of Inquiry" includes essays by Peter A. Stearns on social history; Allan G. Bogue, on the new political history; David Brody, on labor history; Kathleen Neils Conzen, on community studies and urban and local history; Jay Saunders Redding, on black history; Carl N. Degler, on women and the family; Robert Darnton, on intellectual and cultural history; and Charles S. Maier, on diplomatic history.

Brody carefully noted the impact of the new social history on labor history; the concern, he said, has come to be with the lives of all working people, not just with the organized labor movement. Conzen freely acknowledged that academic historians are relative latecomers to the field of local history, which has its own long and honorable history in the popular realm. Redding's "The Negro in American History: As Scholar, As Subject" is unfortunately one of the weaker essays in *The Past Before Us*. Redding's judgments are sometimes extreme, and he seems strangely out of touch with the field. Perhaps it would have been better if one of the outstanding young scholars from the 1960s or 1970s had written on this subject; there are many, for Redding's claim is basically valid that "Afro-American history is no longer perceived as adjunctive, but as central to American history." Darnton, of course, was concerned with the "crisis" of intellectual history perceived by many as the new social history has come to dominate American historical writing but he noted that the importance of intellectual history has actually fluctuated very little over the years, and he found cause for optimism about the survival and even the growth of the field. American diplomatic history, dealt with here by Maier as a part of the broader historiography of international relations, has been another traditional field somewhat crowded out in recent years; it cannot, Maier acknowledged in something of an understatement, "be counted among the pioneering fields of the discipline in the 1970's." But the quality of work done in the field has improved, Maier insisted, and he, too, ended on an optimistic note.

Methodological innovations have been many and important during the last decade or so in American historical writing and have had much to do with the changing fortunes of some of the subfields of history. The final part of *The Past Before Us*, "Modes of Gathering and Assessing Historical Materials," deals with oral history (Herbert T. Hoover), psychohistory (Peter Loewenberg), quantitative history (J. Morgan Kousser), comparative history (George M. Fredrickson), and the teaching of history (Hazel Whitman Hertzberg).

The thoughtful essay by Loewenberg on psychohistory acknowledges William L. Langer's important presidential address for the American Historical Association in 1957 as central to the origins of the approach and Erik H. Erickson's theories as central to its continuation. While Loewenberg saw great potential in the psychohistorical approach, he also recognized that "the historical profession has, on the whole, been wary of, if not antagonistic to, the use of psychoanalytic perceptions in historical research and interpretation." Clearly, though, he was not as critical as the revealingly titled book published in 1980 by David E. Stannard, *Shrinking History: On Freud and the Failure of Psychohistory.* Nor would Loewenberg be likely to share Laurence Veysey's sentiment: "Psychohistory strikes me more as a curiously delayed spin-off from the climate of the 1950's, when Freud was so much in vogue, than as a major new direction in historical writing."[32] Despite its continued and perhaps inevitably controversial nature, the psycho-historical approach has spawned such journals as the *Psychohistory Review* and the *Journal of Psychohistory* (formerly the *History of Childhood Quarterly*), and continues as a not insignificant subfield within the discipline of history. Among the better introductions to it are *Explorations in Psychohistory* (1974), edited by Robert Jay Lifton, which includes essays by Erikson himself, Bruce Mazlish, and Kenneth Keniston and the helpful introductory essay "On Psychohistory" by Lifton; *History and Psychoanalysis: An Inquiry into the Possibilities and Limits of Psychohistory*, by Saul Friedlander, originally published in French in 1975; and *Our Selves/Our Past: Psychological Approaches to American History* (1981), edited by Robert J. Brugger, which includes essays by such standard writers in the field as Lifton and Mazlish but also by such mainstream historians as Winthrop D. Jordan (on Jefferson) and Stanley M. Elkins (on slavery).

The comparative approach has not become as important as many thought it would when C. Vann Woodward edited *The Comparative Approach to American History* in 1968. Of course, "All history that aims at explanation or interpretation involves some type of explicit or implicit comparison," as George M. Frederickson—who won an award from the Organization of American Historians for his *White Supremacy: A Comparative Study in American and South African History* (1981)—reminds us. "The body of work that qualifies as comparative history in the strict sense" Frederickson continued, "is characterized both by its relative sparseness and by its fragmentation." Comparative history "does not really exist yet as an established field within history or even as a well-defined method of studying history." The subjects that have stimulated the greatest amount of comparative history among American historians, Frederickson noted, are those that grew out of the hope that something new about American history can be learned by comparing it with an analogous phenomenon in another society; therefore, comparative history includes frontier history, the history of slavery and race relations, and the history of women and sex roles.

There are many who would dispute Michael Kammen's claim that

"Clio's current health is robust" and the conclusion on the dust jacket of *The Past Before Us* that the survey therein reveals "a healthy and richly diverse profession in a period of astonishing intellectual growth." At least in terms of the amount and overall quality of historical writing being done today, perhaps those claims are indeed valid. The only great need seems to be for a historian who can incorporate all the recent diverse analytical contributions into a broad narrative pattern. Bernard Bailyn, in his presidential address before the American Historical Association in December, 1981, saw this as "the great challenge of modern historical scholarship." Large areas of our history, Bailyn noted, "have become shapeless, and scholarship is heavily concentrated on unconnected technical problems." While we will always have and need the technical and analytical works, the *critical* need, Bailyn said, "is to bring order into large areas of history and thus to reintroduce history in a sophisticated form to a wider reading public, through synthetic works, narrative in structure, on major themes, works that explain some significant part of the story of how the present world came to be the way it is."[33]

John Higham, long a perceptive observer of American historical writing, has noted that "Americans have been writing their own history with uninterrupted enthusiasm since it began. In sheer bulk the product equals or surpasses the historical literature on any other modern nation."[34] This is true, but it is not only in bulk that American historiography compares well with that of other nations. Timothy Paul Donovan, in an excellent volume published in 1973, entitled *Historical Thought in America: Postwar Patterns,* attempted to describe the "Perfect Historian." Among the many necessary qualities he delineated are: a balance between the unattainable ideal of objectivity and the healthy kind of subjectivity "which spurns the bitterness of partisanship while yet embracing the passion of involvement," intuition, imagination, literary artistry, humility, integrity.[35] Now, clearly, even more than in colonial America when the writing of American history began, it is extremely difficult to be even a good historian, much less a "perfect" one. That so many have succeeded so well and that some of the best have even risen above the limitations of nationalism make the story recounted in this volume a remarkable one.

Notes

CHAPTER 1

1. D. R. Fox, *Herbert Levi Osgood* (New York, 1924), pp. 13-15.
2. M. Thórdarson, *The Vinland Voyages*, trans. T. J. Walters (New York, 1930), pp. 56, 57, n. 64.
3. J. F. Jameson, ed, *The Northmen, Columbus, and Cabot*, in *Original Narratives of Early American History* (New York, 1906), pp. 25, 26, 53.
4. G. M. Gathorne-Hardy, *The Norse Discoverers of America: The Wineland Sagas* (Oxford, 1920), part 2; E. Reman, *The Norse Discoveries and Explorations in America* (New York, 1949). F. J. Pohl, *The Lost Discovery: Uncovering the Track of the Vikings in America* (New York, 1952), says that Vinland was on Cape Cod.
5. J. B. Thacher, *Christopher Columbus* (3 vols., New York, 1903-1904), 1:62-63.
6. F. A. MacNutt, *De Orbe Novo: The Eight Decades of Peter Martyr D'Anghera* (New York, 1912).
7. MacNutt, *Bartolomé de las Casas* (New York, 1909); L. Hanke, *Bartolomé de las Casas* (The Hague, 1951), chap. 2.
8. Washington Irving, *The History of the Life and Voyages of Christopher Columbus* (3 vols., New York, 1850), 3:429.
9. H. Harrisse, *Bibliotheca Americana Vetustissima* (New York, 1866), p. 457. See also F. T. McCann, *English Discovery of America to 1585* (New York, 1952), for the origins of the "New World" concept in England.
10. G. B. Parks, *Richard Hakluyt and the English Voyages* (New York, 1928), p. 23; McCann, *English Discovery*, chap. 7. Elizabeth Baer, in *Essays Honoring Lawrence C. Wroth* (Portland, Maine, 1951), emphasizes the influence of Martyr on Eden.
11. Parks, *Richard Hakluyt*, p. 2.
12. *North American Review* 29 (October, 1829): 432. See, in addition to Parks's biography of Hakluyt, the spirited essay by Walter Raleigh in his *Early English Voyages* (Glasgow, 1910); see also B. Penrose, *Travel and Discovery in the Renaissance, 1420-1620* (Cambridge, Mass., 1952), chap. 17.

CHAPTER 2

1. Cotton Mather, *Magnalia Christi Americana* (2 vols., Hartford, Conn., 1855), 2:581.
2. B. J. Loewenberg, *American History in American Thought: Christopher Columbus to Henry Adams* (New York, 1972), p. 84.
3. A. T. Vaughan, *American Genesis: Captain John Smith and the Founding of Virginia* (Boston, 1975), p. viii.
4. E. F. Bradford, "Conscious Art in Bradford's *History of Plimoth Plantation,*" *New England Quarterly* 1 (April, 1928): 133-57.

5. J. F. Jameson, ed., *Johnson's Wonder-working Providence*, in *Original Narratives* (New York, 1910), p. 10.

6. *Dictionary of American Biography*, 10:95.

7. Hubbard's history was printed in *Massachusetts Historical Society Collections*, 2d ser., 5–6 (1848).

8. S. G. Drake, *Early History of New England...* (Boston, 1864), p. 238.

9. Charles Orr, ed., *History of the Pequot War* (Cleveland, Ohio, 1897), contains four contemporary accounts.

10. M. C. Tyler, *A History of American Literature*, (New York, 1879), 2:74.

11. "The Diary of Cotton Mather," *Massachusetts Historical Society Collections*, 7th ser., 7, pt. 1 (1911): 445.

12. V. L. Parrington, *Main Currents in American Thought* (New York, 1927), 1:109.

13. See also interesting remarks on Mather in *North American Review* 6 (January, 1818): 255–72.

14. Peter Gay, *A Loss of Mastery: Puritan Historians in Colonial America* (Berkeley, Calif., 1966), p. 87.

15. Ibid., p. 25.

CHAPTER 3

1. J. Higham, L. Krieger, and F. Gilbert, *History* (Englewood Cliffs, N.J., 1965), p. 3.

2. C. K. Shipton, "Provincial Literary Leaven," *New England Quarterly* 9 (June, 1936).

3. I have used the second edition, which lacks many of the sharp comments on politics contained in the original. See L. B. Wright's edition of Beverley's *The History and Present State of Virginia* (Chapel Hill, N.C., 1947).

4. Loewenberg, *American History in American Thought*, p. 117.

5. W. Douglass, *A Summary Historical and Political... of the British Settlements in North America* (Boston, 1752), 1:202, 362.

6. *Dictionary of National Biography*, 14:1009.

7. Ibid., p. 1010.

8. Ibid., p. 1012.

9. L. C. Wroth, *An American Bookshelf, 1775* (Philadelphia, 1934), p. 92. See article on Colden's history in *Historical Magazine* 9 (January, 1865): 9–13, probably written by the editor, J. G. Shea.

10. "Cadwallader Colden Papers," *New York Historical Society Collections* 9 (1935): 283–355, 359–434.

11. *Rhode Island Historical Society Collections*, 4 (1838): 178.

12. *Massachusetts Historical Society Collections*, 6th ser., 4 (1891): 489–91; see W. H. Whitmore, "Life and Labors of Thomas Prince," *North American Review*, 91 (October, 1860): 354–75.

13. A useful index to Stith's history was published by M. P. Robinson in *Virginia State Library Bulletin* 5 no. 1 (1912).

14. A valuable bibliographical essay on Stith's history is in *Southern Literary Messenger*, 37 (September, 1863): 554.

15. Smith and William Livingston published a digest of the laws of New York in two volumes (1752–1762).

16. See Colden's letters on Smith's history, 1759–60, *New York Historical Society Collections* 8 (1868): 181–235.

17. *Monthly Review* (October, 1755), quoted in Wroth, *American Bookshelf*, pp. 88–89. An important work, reflecting an imperial point of view, was Edmund Burke's *An*

Account of the European Settlements in America (2 vols., London, 1757); within twenty years, six editions appeared. For colonial historians, see also Jarvis M. Morse, *American Beginnings* (Washington, D.C., 1952).

CHAPTER 4

1. Letter from A. Wibird to Belknap, April 14, 1779, *Massachusetts Historical Society Collections*, 6th ser., 4 (1891): 139.
2. Stiles, *Diary*, February 11, 1770.
3. *New England Historical and Genealogical Register* 26 (1872): 159-64, 230-33, especially May 7, 1764.
4. The manuscript of Stiles's "History" is in the Yale University Library.
5. W. G. McLoughlin. *Isaac Backus and the American Pietistic Tradition* (Boston, 1967), p. 192.
6. A. Hovey, *A Memoir of. . . the Rev. Isaac Backus* (Boston, 1858).
7. *New York Post-Boy*, May 5, 1755.
8. S. Briggs, *The Essays . . . of Nathaniel Ames, Father and Son, . . . from Their Almanacks* (Cleveland, Ohio, 1891), 269-70, 381-83.
9. Fothergill, Portfolio 38 (86), September 10, 1766 (Friends House, London).
10. Cf. L. N. Richardson, *A History of Early American Magazines, 1741-1789* (New York, 1931).
11. H. T. Colbourn, *The Lamp of Experience: Whig History and the Intellectual Origins of the American Revolution* (Chapel Hill, N.C., 1965), pp. 192-93.
12. *Massachusetts Historical Society Collections*, 5th ser., 3 (1877): 258; May 16, 1791.
13. Ibid., 6th ser., 4 (1891): p. 151; September 13, 1779; see also Hazard MSS, Library of Congress, Washington, D.C.
14. A. O. Hansen, *Liberalism and American Education in the Eighteenth Century* (New York, 1926), pp. 56-57, 99.
15. Ibid., p. 153.
16. William Smith, *Common Place Book*, New York Public Library, New York City.
17. John Adams, *The Works of John Adams*, ed. C. F. Adams (10 vols., Boston, 1850-56), 5:491-96.
18. B. Trumbull, *A General History of the United States of America* (Boston, 1810), Preface.
19. Bancroft *Transcripts*, January 7, 1766, New York Public Library.
20. B. Bailyn, *The Ordeal of Thomas Hutchinson* (Cambridge, Mass., 1974), pp. 384-85.
21. L. S. Mayo, *American Antiquarian Society Proceedings*, October, 1931; Hutchinson's second volume benefited from friendly criticisms of the first.
22. J. K. Hosmer, *Life of Hutchinson* (Boston, 1896), pp. 85-86.
23. *American Historical Review* 2 (October, 1896): 163-70.
24. T. Hutchinson, *The History of the Colony and Province of Massachusetts Bay*, ed. L. S. Mayo (3 vols., Cambridge, Mass., 1936).
25. J. E. Illick III, "Robert Proud and *The History of Pennsylvania*," in L. H. Leder, ed., *The Colonial Legacy* (New York, 1971-73), 1:177.
26. *Massachusetts Historical Society Collections*, 6th ser., 4 (1891): 568-69; March 13, 1794.
27. Herbert Baxter Adams, *Life and Writings of Jared Sparks*, (2 vols., Boston, 1893), 2: 383-84; see G. A. Cockroft, *The Public Life of George Chalmers* (New York, 1939), pp. 57-63.
28. "Letters of William Gordon," *Massachusetts Historical Society Proceedings* 63 (1931): 309-613.

29. O. G. Libby, "A Critical Examination of Gordon's *History of the American Revolution,*" *American Historical Association Annual Report for the Year 1899* 1 (1900): 365-83.

30. Loewenberg, *American History in American Thought,* p. 186.

31. D. D. Van Tassel, *Recording America's Past: An Interpretation of the Development of Historical Studies in America, 1607-1884* (Chicago, 1960), p. 40.

32. J. S. Bassett, *The Middle Group of American Historians* (New York, 1917), p. 28.

33. *Massachusetts Historical Society Collections,* 5th ser., 2 (1877): 293-98; January 13, 1784.

34. Ibid., vol. 3 (1877): 198; October 22, 1789.

35. Bassett, *The Middle Group of American Historians,* pp. 40-41.

36. L. S. Mayo, "Jeremy Belknap and Ebenezer Hazard, 1782-1784," *New England Quarterly* 2 (April, 1929): 183-98.

37. J. B. Marcou, *Life of Jeremy Belknap* (New York, 1847), p. 214, letters of May 12, 1779.

38. *Massachusetts Historical Society Collections,* 5th ser., 3 (1877): 157, 165, 244-45; ibid., 6th ser., 4 (1891): 446-48; August 26, 1788.

39. S. A. Eliot, "Jeremy Belknap," *Massachusetts Historical Society Proceedings* 66 (1942): 102-103.

40. W. C. Lane, "Letters of Christoph D. Ebeling," *American Antiquarian Society Proceedings* 35, pt. 2 (October, 1925): 306; letter to Rev. William Bentley, September 16, 1798.

41. J. Daniell, "Jeremy Belknap and the *History of New Hampshire,*" in Leder, ed., *Colonial Legacy,* 3-4:241.

42. *Massachusetts Historical Society Collections,* 6th ser., 4 (1891): 473; January 5, 1791.

43. *A Memoir of Miss Hannah Adams, Written by Herself* (1832), p. 22.

44. *Massachusetts Historical Society Collections,* 72 (1917); August 14, 1777; ibid., 73 (1925); October 24, 1782; March 25, 1790.

45. Ibid., 5th ser., 4 (1878): 432; August 8, 1807.

46. Ibid., pp. 463, 489-90.

47. W. R. Smith, "Mercy Otis Warren's Radical View of the American Revolution," in Leder, ed., *The Colonial Legacy,* 2:224.

48. *North American Review* 46 (April, 1838): 477-79.

49. W. B. Sprague, *The Life of Jedidiah Morse* (New York, 1874), p. 193.

50. Ibid., pp. 205.

51. *Massachusetts Historical Society Collections,* 5th ser., 3 (1877): 361, January 14, 1796.

52. A. J. Beveridge, *The Life of John Marshall* (4 vols., New York, 1916-19), vol. 3, chap. 5.

53. *Monthly Anthology* 5 (1808): 261.

54. See E. Channing, *History of the United States* (6 vols., New York, 1905-25), 2:310.

55. *Monthly Anthology* 5 (1808): 261.

56. J. B. McMaster, *History of the People of the United States* (8 vols., New York, 1883-1913), 5:294; Beveridge, *Marshall,* 3:267.

57. Adams, *Jared Sparks,* 2:37.

58. Beveridge, *Marshall,* 3:265.

59. W. A. Foran, "John Marshall as a Historian," *American Historical Review* (October, 1937): 51-64.

60. D. R. Gilbert, "John Marshall and the Development of a National History," in Leder, ed., *Colonial Legacy,* 3-4:197.

61. L. C. Wroth, *Parson Weems* (Baltimore, 1911).

62. W. A. Bryan, *George Washington in American Literature 1775–1865* (New York, 1952), pp. 14, 15.

CHAPTER 5

1. Adams, *Works*, 10:62, August 31, 1813; ibid., p. 37, April 14, 1813.

2. Ibid., 10:475–76, December 15, 1778.

3. Ibid., p. 17, January, 1814.

4. Adams, *Jared Sparks*, 2:49; ibid., 1:499.

5. Adams, *Works*, 10:274, January, 1818; ibid., February 13, 1818.

6. Ibid., p. 17, July 30, 1815; ibid., pp. 176, 180, November 20, 26, 1815.

7. P. Wilstach, *Correspondence of John Adams and Thomas Jefferson, 1812–1826* (Indianapolis, 1925), p. 114, August 10, 1815; ibid., pp. 159–60, May 5, 1817; ibid., p. 161, May 17, 1818.

8. James Madison, *The Writings of James Madison*, ed. G. Hunt (9 vols., New York, 1900–10) 9:128, March 19, 1823.

9. Adams, *Works*, 10:230, passim, especially letter of November 16, 1816.

10. *North American Review* 6 (January, 1818): 257.

11. W. C. Ford, ed., *Statesman and Friend* (Boston, 1927), p. 137, August 17, 1817.

12. G. Ticknor, *Life, Letters and Journals of George Ticknor*, ed. G. S. Hillard (2 vols., Boston, 1876), 1:338; R. M. Dorson, ed., *America Rebels: Narratives of the Patriots* (New York, 1953).

13. M. D. Peterson, "The Jefferson Image, 1829," *American Quarterly Review* 3, no. 3 (Fall, 1951): 204–20.

14. Thomas Jefferson, *The Writings of Thomas Jefferson*, ed. P. L. Ford (10 vols., New York, 1892–99), 10:191, August 17, 1821.

15. Wilstach, *Correspondence of Adams and Jefferson*, p. 195, March 25, 1826.

16. Adams, *Works*, 10:177, November 20, 1815.

17. *North American Review*, 46 (April, 1838): 476.

18. Ibid., 23 (October, 1826): 276–92.

19. Hillard Ticknor, *Life of George Ticknor*, pp. 1, 72.

20. Bancroft, in *North American Review* 46 (April, 1838): 486.

21. Force Papers, vol. 21, January 4, 1847, Library of Congress; Bassett, *The Middle Group of American Historians*, chap. 5; *Historical Magazine* 9, no. 11 (November, 1865): 337.

22. *North American Review* 20 (October, 1829): 432 n.1.

23. Adams, *Jared Sparks*, 2:522 n. 1; see L. W. Dunlap, *American Historical Societies, 1790–1860* (Madison, Wis., 1944).

24. A. E. Ticknor, *The Life of Joseph Green Cogswell* (Cambridge, Mass., 1874), chaps. 21–26.

25. *Historical Magazine* 1, no. 2 (February, 1857): 33–34. See Alex Ladenson, "Herman Ernst Ludewig, 1809–1856," *Library Quarterly* (April, 1944).

26. Philip Hone, *Diary*, ed. B. Tuckerman (2 vols., New York, 1889), 2:236–37; E. A. Duyckinck and G. L. Duyckinck, *Cyclopedia of American Literature* (2 vols., New York, 1856), 2:595.

27. *Historical Magazine* 4, no. 10 (October, 1860): 314–15.

28. R. Wolcott, *Correspondence of William Hickling Prescott* (New York, 1925), October 19, 1840.

29. W. H. Prescott, *Biographical and Critical Miscellanies* (New York, 1845), pp. 308–10.

30. Adams, *Jared Sparks*, 2:192 n. 1.

31. Quoted in F. L. Mott, *The History of American Magazines, 1741-1850* (New York, 1930), pp. 178, 399.

32. *Historical Magazine,* 6, no. 2 (February, 1862): 41.

33. *North American Review,* 20 (October, 1829): 429-41.

34. Lane, "Letters of C. D. Ebeling," *American Antiquarian Society Proceedings* 35, pt. 2 (October, 1925): 310, 413. See also E. E. Doll, "American History as Interpreted by German Historians from 1770 to 1815," *American Philosophical Society Transactions,* n.s., 38, pt. 5 (1949).

35. *Massachusetts Historical Society Collections,* 2d ser., 8 (1826): 270-75; ibid., 6th ser., 4 (1891).

36. *Analectic Magazine* 5 (May, 1815): 385; see Adams's discussion in *Works,* 10: 171-72; J. D. Fiore, "Carlo Botta, *Italica* 28, no. 3 (September, 1951): 155-71.

37. Adams, *Jared Sparks,* 2:93.

38. James Madison, *Letters and Other Writings of James Madison* (4 vols., Philadelphia, 1865), 3:177, July 3, 1820; also ibid., pp. 203-204, January, 1821.

39. *Historical Magazine,* n.s., 1, no. 2 (February, 1867): 102-105.

40. Adams, *Jared Sparks,* 1:554; ibid., 2:217.

CHAPTER 6

1. Adams, *Jared Sparks,* 1:509.

2. Ibid., 2:117.

3. Ibid., 2:278.

4. Ibid., pp. 189, 193.

5. F. Wharton, *The Revolutionary Diplomatic Correspondence of the United States* (6 vols., Washington, D.C., 1889), vol. 1, Preface.

6. Adams, *Jared Sparks,* 2:292-93 n. 1, February 1, 1841.

7. W. R. Dean, in *Historical Magazine,* 10, no. 5 (May, 1866): 146-56.

8. Adams, *Jared Sparks,* 2:419.

9. Loewenberg, *American History in American Thought,* p. 221.

10. In addition to Adams, *Jared Sparks,* see Bassett, "Jared Sparks," in *Middle Group of American Historians;* M. A. De Wolfe Howe, *Life and Letters of George Bancroft* (2 vols., New York, 1908); and Wolcott, *Correspondence of Prescott.*

11. Loewenberg, *American History in American Thought,* p. 238.

12. Cf. Voltaire's phrase, "The history of great events in the world is scarcely more than a history of crimes."

13. Bancroft, *Life and Letters of George Bancroft,* 1:205-206.

14. W. H. Prescott, *Biographical and Critical Miscellanies,* 337.

15. Adams, *Jared Sparks,* 1:494.

16. See J. B. Black, *The Art of History* (London, 1926).

17. *The Necessity, the Reality, and the Promise of the Progress of the Human Race,* an address to the New York Historical Society, 1854.

18. Bancroft, *Life and Letters of George Bancroft,* 2:183.

19. Cf. E. F. Goldman, "Democratic Bifocalism," in George Boas, ed., *Romanticism in America* (Baltimore, Md., 1940), pp 1-11.

20. S. G. Fisher, "Legendary and Myth-making Process in Histories of the American Revolution," *American Philosophical Society Proceedings,* 51 (1912): 69.

21. *Harvard Graduates Magazine,* 16 (June, 1908): 652; Howe, *Life and Letters of George Bancroft;* Bassett, *The Middle Group of American Historians;* N. H. Dawes and F. T. Nichols, "Revaluing George Bancroft," *New England Quarterly,* 6 (June, 1933): 278-93; J. F. Jameson, *The History of Historical Writing in America* (Boston, 1891);

R. B. Nye, *George Bancroft* (New York, 1945).

22. G. N. Grob and G. A. Billias, eds., *Interpretations of American History: Patterns and Perspectives*, 4th ed. (New York, 1982), 1:5.

23. E. R. Hoar, *Massachusetts Historical Society Proceedings* 18 (1881): 422-23; Palfrey, "A Discourse," *Massachusetts Historical Society Collections*, 3d ser., 9 (1846): 165-88; Adams, "The Sifted Grain and the Grain Sifters," *American Historical Review* 6, no. 2 (January, 1901): 221.

24. D. D. Van Tassel, *Recording America's Past: An Interpretation of the Development of Historical Studies in America, 1607-1884* (Chicago, 1960), p. 126.

25. *Despotism in America* . . . (1854), pp. 13-14. In this work it is worth noting that Hildreth was very friendly to Jefferson as a democrat but hostile to him as a plantation owner with slaves.

26. See essay on Hildreth in Theodore Parker, *The American Scholar* (Boston, 1907).

27. Loewenberg, *American History in American Thought*, p. 269.

28. A. H. Kelly, "Richard Hildreth," in W. T. Hutchinson, ed., *The Marcus W. Jernegan Essays in American Historiography* (Chicago, 1937), p. 41.

29. A. M. Schlesinger, Jr., "The Problem of Richard Hildreth," *New England Quarterly* 13, no. 2 (June, 1940):223-45; D. E. Emerson, "Richard Hildreth," *Johns Hopkins University Studies in Historical and Political Science*, 64th ser., no. 2 (1946); M. M. Pingel, *An American Utilitarian: Richard Hildreth as a Philosopher* (New York, 1948).

30. E. M. Coulter, "What the South Has Done About Its History," *Journal of Southern History* 2, no. 1 (February, 1936): 5.

31. See *Southern Literary Messenger* 1, no. 1 (August, 1834).

32. For historical writing in this period see R. L. Rusk, *The Literature of the Middle Western Frontier* (2 vols., New York, 1925), 1:242-49.

33. *Southern Literary Messenger* 1, no. 8 (April, 1835): 408-20.

34. L. C. Helderman, "A Social Scientist of the Old South," *Journal of Southern History* (May, 1936).

35. "Gayarré Memorial Number," Louisiana *Historical Society Publications* 3, pt. 4 (March, 1906); *Louisiana Historical Quarterly* 12, no. 1 (January, 1929): 5-32, contains Gayarré autobiography and bibliography; letters of Gayarré to E. A. Duyckinck, New Orleans, January 23, 1867, *Louisiana Historical Quarterly* 33, no. 2 (April, 1950): 237.

36. Washington Irving, *The Life and Letters of Washington Irving*, ed. P. M. Irving, 2:254.

37. Ibid., pp. 424-25, December 18, 1829.

38. Adams, *Jared Sparks*, 2:508-509.

39. S. T. Williams, *The Life of Washington Irving* (2 vols., New York, 1935), vol. 1, chap. 13 vol. 2, pp. 227-31, 296-308.

CHAPTER 7

1. W. R. Taylor, "Francis Parkman," in M. Cunliffe and R. W. Winks, eds., *Pastmasters: Some Essays on American Historians* (New York, 1969), pp. 4, 19.

2. H. H. Peckham, *Pontiac and the Indian Uprising* (Princeton, N.J., 1947), checks Parkman on several points and is friendlier to the Indians.

3. D. C. Seitz, *Letters from Parkman to E. G. Squier* (Cedar Rapids, Iowa, 1911), p. 45, October 24, 1867.

4. "Letters of Francis Parkman to Pierre Margry," *Smith College Studies in History* 8, nos. 3-4 (1923): 165, December 15, 1875.

5. H. D. Sedgwick, *Francis Parkman* (Boston, 1904); C. H. Farnham, *Life of Parkman* (Boston, 1900); of many centennial appreciations see Joseph Schafer, *Missis-*

sippi Valley Historical Review 10, no. 4 (March, 1924): 351–64; W. L. Schramm, *Francis Parkman* (New York, 1937); Mason Wade, *Francis Parkman: Heroic Historian* (New York, 1942); O. A. Pease, *Parkman's History* (New Haven, Conn., 1953).

6. Taylor, "Francis Parkman," pp. 37–38.

CHAPTER 8

1. G. N. Grob and G. A. Billias, eds., *Interpretations of American History: Patterns and Perspectives,* 4th ed. (New York, 1982), 1:6.

2. B. L. Pierce, *Public Opinion and the Teaching of History* (New York, 1926), chap. 2; R. E. Thursfield, ed., *The Study and Teaching of American History* (Seventeenth Yearbook of the National Council for the Social Studies, 1946), chap. 2, by W. H. Cartwright.

3. F. Weber, *Beiträge zur Charakteristik der älteren geschichtschreiber über Spanish-Amerika* . . . .(Leipzig, 1911), pp. 22–27. See J. C. Brevoort, "Spanish-American Documents Printed or Inedited," *Magazine of American History* 3, pt. 1 (1879): 175–78, showing the vigorous effect on scholarship of the publication of these documents.

4. P. Margry, *Découvertes et établissements des Francais dans l'ouest et dans le sud de l'Amérique Septentrionale, 1641–1754* (1876–86). For Shea's work see the Rev. John P. Cadden, *The Historiography of the American Catholic Church* (Washington, D.C., 1944), chap. 2.

5. H. Harrisse, *The Late S. L. M. Barlow* (New York, 1889), p. 11.

6. José T. Medina, the great bibliographer and historian, said that Harrisse was the real founder of the modern school of historians of the era of discovery and exploration; *Bibliotheca Hispano-Americana, 1493–1810* (Santiago, Chile, 1898–1907), 6:cxvii.

7. For biographical details see A. Growoll, *Henry Harrisse* (New York, 1899); H. Cordier, in *Bulletin du Bibliophile et du Bibliothécaire* (1910): 489–505; letters to Ildebrando Rossi, in *Bibliofilia* 28 (1927): 258–67; autobiographical letter to Barlow, 1884, MS in New York Public Library; R. G. Adams, *Three Americanists* . . . (Philadelphia, 1939); J. A. Borome, ed., "Interview of Justin Winsor with Harrisse, 1891," *Hispanic American Historical Review,* August, 1952.

8. *Historical Magazine* 10, no. 5 (May, 1866): 166–67.

9. Trescot Papers, Library of Congress, August, 1870.

10. MS letters, Century Collection, New York Public Library.

11. Carl Schurz, *Speeches, Correspondence and Political Papers of Carl Schurz,* ed. F. Bancroft, (6 vols., New York, 1913), 3:113–15, November 27, December 3, 1874.

12. *The Life of Peter Van Schaack* (New York, 1842), by his son, H. C. Van Schaack, was called "the first attempt to present to the public of the United States a justificatory memoir of one of the Tories in the Revolution." See C. F. Adams, *North American Review* 55 (July, 1842): 99.

13. C. B. Robson, "Papers of Francis Lieber," *Huntington Library Bulletin, no. 3 (February, 1933): 147; see also Frank Freidel, Francis Lieber* (Baton Rouge, La., 1947).

14. Henry Adams, *A Cycle of Adams Letters,* ed. W. C. Ford (2 vols., Boston, 1920), 1:196, November 21, 1862.

15. Elizabeth Lecky, *A Memoir of William E. H. Lecky by His Wife* (London, 1909), pp. 51–52.

16. For the early influence of Comte in America, see R. L. Hawkins, *Auguste Comte and the United States, 1816–1853* (Cambridge, Mass., 1936).

17. H. T. Buckle, *History of Civilization in England,* 1833 ed. (2 vols., New York), 1:5n.

18. Adams, *A Cycle of Adams Letters,* 1:253, 281.

19. John Weiss, *Life and Correspondence of Theodore Parker* (2 vols., Boston, 1864), 1:467ff.; H. M. Jones, *Life of Moses Coit Tyler* (Ann Arbor, Mich., 1933), p. 141.

20. Draper, a professor of chemistry in New York University, was the author of *A History of the Intellectual Development of Europe* (New York, 1863), which had wide influence because of its evolutionary approach to history; see Donald Fleming, *John William Draper and the Religion of Science* (Philadelphia, 1950), chap. 8.

21. H. B. Adams, "Seminary Libraries and University Extension," *Johns Hopkins University Studies in History and Political Science* 5, no. 11 (1887): 445.

22. Ibid., p. 451.

23. J. F. Rhodes, "John Richard Green," in *Historical Essays* (New York, 1909).

24. Quoted in Sidney Ratner, "Evolution and the Rise of Scientific Spirit in America," *Philosophy of Science* 3, no. 1 (January, 1936): 113.

25. C. F. Adams, "Historians and Historical Societies," *Massachusetts Historical Society Proceedings*, 2d ser., 13 (1900): 89-90.

26. J. Higham, L. Kreiger, and F. Gilbert *History* (Englewood Cliffs, N.J., 1965), p. 99.

27. Ticknor, *Life of George Ticknor*, 1:73n.

28. Lane, "Letters of C. D. Ebeling," *American Antiquarian Society Proceedings* 35, pt. 2 (October, 1925), to Joseph McKean, June 11, 1817.

29. Ticknor, *Life of George Ticknor*, 2:422, May 17, 1859.

30. E. de Laboulaye published a three-volume history of the United States (1862-66); K. Neumann also published one in three volumes in 1866.

31. "The Johns Hopkins Anniversary," *Dial* 32, no. 377 (March 1, 1902): 144.

32. *Herbert Baxter Adams: Tributes of Friends*, p. 45; see also W. Stull Holt, ed., *Historical Scholarship in the United States, 1876-1901, as Revealed in the Correspondence of Herbert B. Adams* (Baltimore, Md., 1938).

33. F. N. Thorpe, "The Study of History in American Colleges and Universities," *U.S. Bureau of Education Circular of Information*, no. 2 (1887): 252.

34. C. F. Adams, *Massachusetts Historical Society Proceedings*, 2d ser., 13 (1900): 89-115.

35. *American Historical Review* 41, no. 1 (October, 1935): 81.

36. Henry Adams, *A Letter to American Teachers of History* (Baltimore, Md., 1910).

37. C. A. Beard and A. Vagts, "Currents of Thought in Historiography," *American Historical Review* 42, no. 3 (April, 1937): 460-83; W. S. Holt, "The Idea of Scientific History in America," *Journal of the History of Ideas* 1, no. 3 (June, 1940): 352-62.

38. H. E. Barnes, *The New History and the Social Studies* (New York, 1925), pp. 36, 198-203.

39. Becker, *Everyman His Own Historian* (New York, 1935), pp. 170-72.

40. Becker, "Some Aspects of the Influence of Social Problems and Ideas upon the Study and Writing of History," *American Journal of Sociology* 18, no. 5 (March, 1913): 641-75.

CHAPTER 9

1. William Jordy, *Henry Adams: Scientific Historian* (New Haven, Conn., 1952), p. 22; H. D. Cater, *Henry Adams and His Friends* (Boston, 1947), p. 126; Max I. Baym, *The French Education of Henry Adams* (New York, 1951).

2. Quoted in R. F. Nichols, "The Dynamic Interpretation of History," *New England Quarterly* 8, no. 2 (June, 1935): 163-78, November 17, 1896.

3. Adams, *Letters of Henry Adams*, June 30, 1876; S. Mitchell, "Henry Adams and His Students," *Massachusetts Historical Society Proceedings* 66 (1942): 294-312; Ernest Samuels, *The Young Henry Adams* (Cambridge, Mass., 1948), chap. 7.

4. L. Swift, "A Course in History at Harvard College in the Seventies," *Massa-*

chusetts Historical Society Proceedings 52 (1919): 73.

5. Cater, *Henry Adams*, p. 81.

6. Ibid., p. 125, Adams to S. J. Tilden, January 24, 1883; the work was prepared with financial assistance from the Gallatin family.

7. Adams, *Letters of Henry Adams*, September 3, 1882.

8. Ibid., May 13, July 9, 1880; July 15, 1888.

9. Ibid., May 15, 1876.

10. B. J. Loewenberg, *American History in American Thought*, p. 529.

11. R. Reinitz, *Irony and Consciousness: American Historiography and Reinhold Neibuhr's Vision* (Lewisburg, Pa., 1980), pp. 74–75.

12. Adams, *Letters of Henry Adams*, May 21, 1881.

13. Ibid., to John Hay, September 3, 1882; Cater, *Henry Adams*, p. 126.

14. Quoted in Jordy, *Henry Adams: Scientific Historian*, p. 57.

15. Cater, *Henry Adams*, p. 480, October 6, 1899.

16. H. S. Commager, "Henry Adams," in Hutchinson, ed., *Jernegan Essays*, pp. 195, 197.

17. Ibid., pp. 198, 191, 193 (italics added).

18. Ibid., p. 192.

19. Ibid., p. 199.

20. Irving Brant, "James Madison and His Times," *American Historical Review* 57, no. 4 (July, 1952): 853–70.

21. Adams, *Letters of Henry Adams*, January 27, 1869.

22. Ibid., January 2, February 6, 1891.

23. Loewenberg, *American History in American Thought*, 545.

CHAPTER 10

1. Edward A. Freeman, *Life and Letters of Edward A. Freeman* (New York, 1895), 2:242.

2. J. W. Pratt, "The Ideology of American Expansion," *Essays in Honor of William E. Dodd* (Chicago, 1935); see also Edwin Mims, Jr., *American History and Immigration* (Bronxville, N.Y., 1950), chap. 2.

3. A. H. Kelly, "Richard Hildreth," in Hutchinson, ed., *Jernegan Essays*, p. 42.

4. In the 1890s, von Holst opposed American expansionist tendencies; E. F. Goldman, "Hermann E. von Holst," *Mississippi Valley Historical Review* 23, no. 4 (March, 1937): 515.

5. C. R. Wilson, "Hermann Eduard von Holst," in Hutchinson, ed., *Jernegan Essays*, pp. 60–83.

6. Schouler, "The Spirit of Historical Research," *American Historical Association Papers*, 4, pt. 3 (July, 1890): 98–99.

7. For autobiography, see Schouler, *Historical Briefs* (New York, 1896); L. E. Ellis, "James Schouler," in Hutchinson, ed., *Jernegan Essays*, pp. 84–101.

8. W. R. Shepherd, in H. W. Odum, ed., *American Masters of Social Science* (New York, 1927).

9. J. W. Burgess, *Reminiscences of an American Scholar* (New York, 1934), p. 131.

10. Ibid., p. 289.

11. Letter to R. U. Johnson, October 22, 1908, Century Collection, New York Public Library.

12. F. M. Anderson, "Letters of James Ford Rhodes to Edward L. Pierce," *American Historical Review* 36, no. 4 (July, 1931): 778–85.

13. J. R. Lynch, "Some Historical Errors of James Ford Rhodes," *Journal of Negro*

History 2, no. 4 (October, 1917); 345-68.

14. L. B. Shippee, "Rhodes's *History of the United States,*" *Mississippi Valley Historical Review* 8, nos. 1-2 (June, September, 1921): 133-48.

15. Cf. N. W. Stephenson, "Mr. Rhodes as Historian," *Yale Review* 10, no. 4 (July, 1921): 860-65.

16. Howe, *James Ford Rhodes;* Rhodes, *Historical Essays* (New York, 1909); R. C. Miller, "James Ford Rhodes," in Hutchinson, ed., *Jernegan Essays,* pp. 171-90.

17. Loewenberg, *American History in American Thought;* p. 460.

18. Ibid., p. 464.

19. C. M. Andrews, "These Forty Years," *American Historical Review* 30 (January, 1925): 234.

20. R. L. Schuyler, *Political Science Quarterly* 33, no. 3 (September, 1918): 433; John Fiske, *Life and Letters of John Fiske* ed. J. S. Clark (Boston, 1917); J. B. Sanders, "John Fiske," in Hutchinson, ed., *Jernegan Essays,* pp. 144-70; Henry Steele Commanger, "John Fiske: An Interpretation," *Massachusetts Historical Society Proceedings* 66 (1942): 332-45.

21. Loewenberg, *American History in American Thought,* p. 465.

22. Woodrow Wilson, "On the Writing of History," *Century Magazine* 50 (September, 1895): 791.

23. Ibid., pp. 788-93.

24. Letter to Ellen Axson, 1883, in Woodrow Wilson, *Woodrow Wilson; Life and Letters,* ed. R. S. Baker (8 vols., New York, 1927-35) 1:211, 214.

25. Woodrow Wilson, "The Proper Perspective of American History," *Forum* 19 (1895): 544-53.

26. M. L. Daniel, "Woodrow Wilson: Historian," *Mississippi Valley Historical Review* 21, no. 3 (December, 1934): 361-74 (an essay by Wilson, "The Truth of History"); L. M. Sears, "Woodrow Wilson," in Hutchinson, ed., *Jernegan Essays,* 102-21; Wilson, *Woodrow Wilson: Life and Letters,* vols. 1-5.

27. E. P. Cheyney, *American Historical Review* 37, no. 4 (July, 1932): 826.

28. Cf. Thomas B. Macaulay in his *History of England:* "It will be my endeavor to relate the history of the people as well as the history of the government; to trace the progress of useful and ornamental arts, . . . the rise of religious sects, . . . the changes of literary taste, . . . to portray the manners of successive generations, and not to pass by . . . even the revolutions which have taken place in dress, furniture, repasts and public amusements."

29. E. P. Oberholtzer, "John Bach McMaster," *Pennsylvania Magazine of History and Biography* 57, no. 1 (January, 1933): 25.

30. W. T. Hutchinson, "John Bach McMaster," in Hutchinson, ed., *Jernegan Essays,* pp. 122-43; C. R. Fish, review of McMaster, *Mississippi Valley Historical Review* 1, no. 1 (June, 1914): 31-43; A. B. Hart, "The Writing of American History," *Current History* 33, no. 6 (March, 1931): 858-61; E. F. Goldman, *John Bach McMaster: American Historian* (Philadelphia, 1943).

31. Oberholtzer, "John Bach McMaster," p. 19.

32. J. A. Borome, "The Life and Letters of Justin Winsor" (Master's thesis, Columbia University, 1950), pp. 404-37.

33. Edward Channing, "Justin Winsor," *American Historical Review* 3, no. 2 (January, 1898): 197-202.

34. Loewenberg, *American History in American Thought,* p. 456.

35. Samuel Eliot Morison, "Edward Channing," *Massachusetts Historical Society Proceedings* 64 (1932): 250-84.

36. L. W. Labaree strongly qualified this estimate of colonial governors in his

Royal Government in America (New Haven, Conn., 1930).

CHAPTER 11

1. Lecky, *A Memoir of W. E. H. Lecky,* pp. 185-86, A. D. White to Lecky, July 30, 1890.
2. Jones, *Moses Coit Tyler,* p. 111.
3. "The Study of History in American Colleges and Universities," *U.S. Bureau of Education Circular of Information,* no. 2 (1887): 156.
4. Jones, *Moses Coit Tyler,* p. 141.
5. For Tyler's diary see J. T. Austen, *Moses Coit Tyler* (New York, 1911).
6. G. M. Trevelyan, *Sir George Otto Trevelyan: A Memoir by His Son* (London, 1932).
7. For Doyle's critical approach to the Revolution, see an essay on Trevelyan in Doyle, *Essays on Various Subjects* (London, 1911).
8. C. M. Andrews, "American Colonial History, 1690-1750," *American Historical Association Annual Report for the Year 1898* (1899): 50.
9. D. R. Fox, *Herbert Levi Osgood* (New York, 1924); H. F. Coppock, "Herbert Levi Osgood," *Mississippi Valley Historical Review* 19, no. 3 (December, 1932): 394-413; E. C. O. Beatty, "Herbert Levi Osgood," in Hutchinson, ed., *Jernegan Essays,* pp. 271-93.
10. See Curtis Nettels, "Markets in the Colonial System," *New England Quarterly* 6, no. 3 (September, 1933): 491-512.
11. *George Louis Beer: A Tribute to His Life and Work* (New York, 1924); G. A. Cockroft, "George Louis Beer," in H. Ausubel et al., eds., *Some Modern Historians of Britain: Essays in Honor of Robert Livingston Schuyler* (New York, 1951).
12. Andrews, "American Colonial History," p. 50.
13. C. M. Andrews, "Materials in British Archives for American Colonial History," *American Historical Review* 10, no. 2 (January, 1905): 325.
14. C. M. Andrews, "The American Revolution: An Interpretation," *American Historical Review* 31, no. 2 (January, 1926): 221.
15. L. H. Gipson, "Charles M. Andrews and the Reorientation of the Study of American History," *Pennsylvania Magazine of History and Biography* 59, no. 3 (July, 1935): 209-22; some interesting biographical details are included in Andrews's "Historic Doubts Regarding Early Massachusetts History," *Colonial Society of Massachusetts Transactions* 28 (1935): 280-94; see essay by A. S. Eisenstadt in Ausubel et al., eds., *Some Modern Historians of Britain.*
16. See Harper, "Mercantilism and the American Revolution," *Canadian Historical Review* 23, no. 1 (March, 1942): 1-15, and Harper's essay in R. B. Morris, ed., *The Revolutionary Era: Studies Inscribed to Evarts Boutell Greene* (New York, 1939).
17. See L. B. Namier, *England in the Age of the American Revolution* (London, 1930).
18. S. J. Buck, "Clarence Walworth Alvord, Historian," *Mississippi Valley Historical Review* 15, no. 3 (1928-29): 309-20; Marion Dargan, Jr., "Clarence Walworth Alvord," in Hutchinson, ed., *Jernegan Essays,* pp. 323-38.
19. W. W. Abbott, "The Colonies to 1763," in W. H. Cartwright and R. L. Watson, Jr., eds., *The Reinterpretation of American History and Culture* (Washington, D.C., 1973), pp. 249-50.
20. R. A. Billington, ed., *The Reinterpretation of Early American History: Essays in Honor of John Edward Pomfret* (San Marino, Calif., 1966), p. 185.
21. C. Rossiter, *The Annals of the American Academy for Political and Social Science* 299 (May, 1955): 156.

22. L. H. Gipson, "The Imperial Approach to Early American History," in Billington, ed., *Reinterpretation of Early American History*, pp. 185-99.

CHAPTER 12

1. R. L. Rapson, ed., *Major Interpretations of the American Past* (New York, 1971), p. 38.
2. G. N. Grob and G. A. Billias, eds., *Interpretation of American History: Patterns and Perspectives*, 4th ed. (New York, 1982), 1:7.
3. G. Wise, *American Historical Explanations: A Strategy for Grounded Inquiry*, 2d. ed. (Minneapolis, Minn., 1980), p. 216.
4. C. Crowe, "The Emergence of Progressive History," *Journal of the History of Ideas* 27 (January-March, 1966): 112.
5. Grob and Billias, eds., *Interpretation of American History*, 1:8; Richard Hofstadter, *The Progressive Historians: Turner, Beard, Parrington* (New York, 1968), p. 438.
6. Wise, *American Historical Explanations*, p. 215; Hofstadter, *Progressive Historians*, p. xii.
7. H. C. Nixon, "Precursors of Turner in the Interpretation of the American Frontier," *South Atlantic Quarterly* 28, no. 1 (January, 1929): 83-90.
8. Letter to C. L. Skinner, March 15, 1922, in *Wisconsin Magazine of History* 19, no. 1 (September, 1935): 91-103.
9. Carl Becker, "Frederick Jackson Turner," in H. W. Odum, ed., *American Masters of Social Science*, pp. 281-82; Avery Craven, "Frederick Jackson Turner," in Hutchinson, ed., *Jernegan Essays*, pp. 252-70.
10. Frederick Jackson Turner, "The Character and Influence of the Indian Trade in Wisconsin," *Johns Hopkins University Studies in Historical and Political Science* 9, nos. 11-12 (Baltimore, Md., 1891): 74-75.
11. Turner, Letter to C. L. Skinner.
12. Turner, "The Significance of the Frontier in American History," reprinted in *The Frontier in American History* (New York, 1920).
13. See Turner's collected essays in *The Significance of Sections in American History* (New York, 1932); Fulmer Mood, "The Origin, Evolution, and Application of the Sectional Concept, 1750-1900," in M. Jensen, ed., *Regionalism in America* (Madison, Wis., 1951).
14. Max Farrand, "F. J. Turner at the Huntington Library," *Huntington Library Bulletin*, no. 3 (February, 1933): 157-64.
15. W. R. Jacobs, J. W. Caughey, and J. B. Frantz, *Turner, Bolton, and Webb: Three Historians of the American Frontier* (Seattle, Wash., 1979), vi, 14.
16. Ibid., pp. 10, 33; Hofstadter, *Progressive Historians*, p. 114.
17. H. R. Lamar, "Frederick Jackson Turner," in Cunliffe and Winks, eds., *Pastmasters*, pp. 74-109. Billington's *Land of Savagery* has been reissued in paperback (Norman, Okla., 1985).
18. R. A. Billington, *The American Frontier* (Washington, D.C., 1965), p. 4.
19. Billington, *America's Frontier Heritage* (New York, 1966), p. 235.
20. Billington, ed., *The Frontier Thesis: Valid Interpretation of American History?* (New York, 1966), p. 100.
21. Hofstadter, *Progressive Historians*, p. 104.
22. Ibid., pp. 48, 71-73.
23. Ibid., pp. 92, 163-64.
24. R. E. Brown, *Charles Beard and the Constitution* (Princeton, N.J., 1956), p. 200.
25. *Social Science Quarterly* 57 (June, 1976): 229.

26. Hofstadter, *Progressive Historians*, p. 223.

27. F. McDonald, "Charles A. Beard," in Cunliffe and Winks, eds., *Pastmasters*, p. 117.

28. Hofstadter, *Progressive Historians*, p. 224.

29. Ibid., p. 225.

30. S. Lynd, *Class Conflict, Slavery, and the United States Constitution* (Indianapolis, Ind., 1967), pp. 3-21.

31. Hofstadter, *Progressive Historians*, p. 292.

32. Ibid., pp. 298-99.

33. See J. E. Wisan, *The Cuban Crisis as Reflected in the New York Press, 1895-1898* (New York, 1934).

34. Hofstadter, *Progressive Historians*, pp. 285-92.

35. C. A. Beard, "Written History as an Act of Faith," *American Historical Review* 39 (January, 1934): 219-29.

36. Hofstadter, *Progressive Historians*, pp. 305-306.

37. Samuel Eliot Morison, "Faith of a Historian," *American Historical Review* 56 (January, 1951): 261-75.

38. Ibid., p. 266.

39. Ibid.

40. Hofstadter, *Progressive Historians*, pp. 318, 341.

41. Morison, "Faith of a Historian," p. 267.

42. Hofstadter, *Progressive Historians*, pp. 334-35.

43. R. G. Collingwood, *The Idea of History* (London, 1946), p. 28.

44. C. M. Destler, "Some Observations on Contemporary Historical Theory," *American Historical Review* 55 no. 3 (April, 1950): 503-29.

45. R. L. Schuyler, "Man's Greatest Illusion," *American Philosophical Society Proceedings* 92, no. 1 (1948): 46-51.

46. Hofstadter, *Progressive Historians*, p. 344.

47. Ibid., p. 345.

48. Ibid., p. 352.

49. Ibid., p. 349.

50. Ibid., p. 352; R. H. Gabriel, "Vernon Louis Parrington," in Cunliffe and Winks, eds., *Pastmasters*.

51. Hofstadter, *Progressive Historians*, p. 375.

52. Ibid., p. 354.

53. W. T. Utter, "Vernon Louis Parrington," in Hutchinson, ed., *Jernegan Essays*, pp. 394-408; E. F. Goldman, *Rendezvous with Destiny* (New York, 1952), pp. 37-38, 106 and n.

54. Hofstadter, *Progressive Historians*, pp. xvi-xvii.

CHAPTER 13

1. Quoted by J. W. Caughey, "Hubert Howe Bancroft, Historian of Western America," *American Historical Review* 50, no. 3 (April, 1945): 468.

2. Hubert Howe Bancroft, *The Works of Hubert Howe Bancroft* (39 vols., San Francisco, 1882-90), vol. 39, *Literary Industries*, p. 197.

3. H. H. Bancroft, "Methods of Writing History," *Retrospection, Political and Personal* (New York, 1912), p. 328.

4. W. A. Morris, "The Origin and Authorship of the Bancroft Pacific States Publications: A History of a History," *Oregon Historical Society Quarterly* 4 (March-December, 1903): 287-364.

5. Bancroft, *The Works of Hubert Howe Bancroft*, 38:84-85.

6. J. W. Caughey, *Hubert Howe Bancroft: Historian of the West* (Berkeley, Calif., 1946).

7. R. G. Thwaites, *Jesuit Relations* (73 vols., Cleveland, Ohio, 1896-1901), vol. 72, Preface.

8. Frederick Jackson Turner, *Reuben Gold Thwaites, Memorial Address* (Madison, Wis., 1914); C. W. Alvord on Thwaites, in *Mississippi Valley Historical Association Proceedings for the Year 1913-14* 7 (1914): 321-33.

9. Roosevelt to Lodge, June 7, 1886.

10. The Roosevelt-Lodge letters are in *Selections from the Correspondence of Henry Cabot Lodge and Theodore Roosevelt, 1884-1918* (2 vols., New York, 1925), vol. 1, August 12, 1888; December 23, 1895; December 26, 1912; H. J. Thornton, "Theodore Roosevelt," in Hutchinson, ed., *Jernegan Essays*, pp. 227-51; R. C. Miller, "Theodore Roosevelt, Historian," in J. L. Cate and E. N. Anderson, eds., *Medieval and Historiographical Essays in Honor of James Westfall Thompson* (Chicago, 1938).

11. J. W. Caughey, "Herbert Eugene Bolton," in Jacobs, Caughey, and Frantz, eds., *Turner, Bolton, and Webb*, pp. 44-46.

12. J. F. Bannon, ed., *Bolton and the Spanish Borderlands* (Norman, Okla., 1964), pp. 17, 3-4.

13. J. B. Frantz, "Foreword," in N. S. Furman, *Walter Prescott Webb: His Life and Impact* (Albuquerque, N. Mex., 1976), p. xi.

14. K. R. Philp and E. West, eds., *Essays on Walter Prescott Webb* (Austin, 1976), pp. xvii-xxi.

15. Jacobs, Caughey, and Frantz, eds., *Turner, Bolton, and Webb*, pp. viii.

16. Ibid., pp. 75-83.

17. See the sharp criticism of Webb's book in Fred A. Shannon, *An Appraisal of Walter Prescott Webb's "The Great Plains," Critiques of Research in the Social Sciences*, vol. 3 (New York, 1940); see also J. W. Caughey's comment on the *Critique* in *Mississippi Valley Historical Review* 27, no. 3 (December, 1940): 442-44.

18. Jacobs, Caughey, and Frantz, eds., *Turner, Bolton, and Webb*, p. 82.

19. Walter Prescott Webb, "History as High Adventure," *American Historical Review* 64 (January, 1959): 273-74.

20. Quoted in Rapson, ed., *Major Interpretations of the American Past*, pp. 141, 138.

21. J. B. Frantz, "Walter Prescott Webb and the South," in Philp and West, eds., *Essays on Walter Prescott Webb*, p. 11.

22. Quoted in Jacobs, Caughey, and Frantz, eds., *Turner, Bolton, and Webb*, p. 93.

23. Ibid., p. vi.

24. See W. B. Weeden, *The Social Law of Labor* (Boston, 1882).

25. Some stimulating remarks are found in C. M. Andrews, "Historic Doubts Regarding Early Massachusetts History," *Colonial Society of Massachusetts Transactions* 28 (1935): 280-94.

26. Adams, *A Cycle of Adams Letters*, 1:10.

27. Wilstach, ed., *Correspondence of John Adams and Thomas Jefferson*, p. 68, July 18, 1813.

28. See Charles Francis Adams, *Autobiography* (Boston, 1916).

29. James Truslow Adams, "Is History Science?" in *The Tempo of Modern Life* (New York, 1931), p. 205.

30. In opposition, see C. K. Shipton, "A Plea for Puritanism," *American Historical Review* 40, no. 3 (April, 1935): 460-67.

31. J. T. Adams, *The Tempo of Modern Life*, p. 212.

32. R. Middlekauf, "Perry Miller," in Cunliffe and Winks, eds., *Pastmasters*, p. 183.

33. Ibid., pp. 183-84.

34. Ibid., p. 172.

35. R. Reinitz, *Irony and Consciousness: American Historiography and Reinhold Niebuhr's Vision* (Lewisburg, Pa., 1980), p. 191.

36. Middlekauf, "Perry Miller," 186.

37. E. S. Morgan, "The Historians of Early New England," in Billington, ed., *The Reinterpretation of Early American History*, p. 54.

38. W. P. Trent, "Historical Studies in the South," *American Historical Association Papers*, vol. 4, pt. 4 (October, 1890): 57-65; D. S. Freeman, *The South to Posterity* (New York, 1939).

39. See Woodrow Wilson, *Division and Reunion* (New York, 1893), esp. pp. 106ff.

40. For an analysis of Brown's work, see Wesley F. Craven, *Dissolution of the Virginia Company* (New York, 1932), pp. 12-21.

41. *American Historical Review* 18, no. 3 (April, 1913): 522-36; a number of these studies have since been undertaken and published.

42. D. Brogan, "David M. Potter," in Cunliffe and Winks, eds., *Pastmasters*, p. 316.

43. Quoted in Rapson, ed., *Major Interpretations of the American Past*, p. 156.

44. David M. Potter, *History and American Society: Essays of David M. Potter*, ed., D. E. Fehrenbacher (New York, 1973), p. v.

45. Brogan, "David M. Potter," in Cunliffe and Winks, eds., *Pastmasters*, pp. 317, 319.

46. D. M. Potter, "C. Vann Woodward," in Cunliffe and Winks, eds., *Pastmasters*, p. 383.

47. Ibid., pp. 377, 407.

48. Ibid., p. 388.

49. Ibid., pp. 406, 407.

50. F. Stern, ed., *The Varieties of History: From Voltaire to the Present* (New York, 1972), p. 474.

CHAPTER 14

1. R. A. Skotheim, ed., *The Historian and the Climate of Opinion* (Reading, Mass., 1969), p. 1.

2. Hofstadter, *The Progressive Historians*, p. 444.

3. Quoted in ibid., p. 450.

4. John Higham, "The Cult of the 'American Consensus': Homogenizing Our History," *Commentary* 27 (February, 1959): 93-101.

5. John Higham, "Beyond Consensus: The Historian as Moral Critic," *American Historical Review* 67, (April, 1962): 609-25.

6. J. Rogers Hollingsworth, "Consensus and Continuity in Recent American Historical Writing, *South Atlantic Quarterly* 61 (Winter, 1962): 50.

7. B. Bernstein, ed., *Towards a New Past: Dissenting Essays in American History* (New York, 1968), p. xiii.

8. J. Higham, *Writing American History: Essays on Modern Scholarship* (Bloomington, Ind., 1970), p. 138.

9. A. F. Davis and H. D. Woodman, eds., *Conflict and Consensus in Early American History*, 5th ed. (Lexington, Mass., 1980), pp. xxvi, xxiii.

10. Quoted in Rapson, ed., *Major Interpretations of the American Past*, pp. 104-106.

11. S. Elkins and E. McKitrick, eds., *The Hofstadter Aegis: A Memorial* (New York, 1974), p. 314.

12. Arthur M. Schlesinger, Jr., "Richard Hofstadter," in Cunliffe and Winks, eds., *Pastmasters*, p. 302.

13. Elkins and McKitrick, *Hofstadter Aegis*, pp. 334-36.

14. Ibid., p. 337.

15. Schlesinger, "Hofstadter," p. 284.

16. G. Wise, *American Historical Explanations: A Strategy for Grounded Inquiry*, 2d ed. (Minneapolis, Minn., 1980), p. 216.

17. Elkins and McKitrick, *Hofstadter Aegis*, p. 362.

18. Ibid., p. 365.

19. J. R. Pole, "Daniel J. Boorstin," in Cunliffe and Winks, eds., *Pastmasters*, p. 221.

20. Quoted in Rapson, ed., *Major Interpretations of the American Past*, pp. 171-73.

21. Ibid., pp. 173-75.

22. Ibid., pp. 171-72, 158, 178, 189.

23. Quoted in Rapson, ed., *Major Interpretations of the American Past*, pp. 203, 201.

24. M. J. Morton, *The Terrors of Ideological Politics: Liberal Historians in a Conservative Mood* (Cleveland, Ohio, 1972), pp. 134-35.

25. J. P. Diggins, "Consciousness and Ideology in American History: the Burden of Daniel J. Boorstin," *American Historical Review* 76 (February, 1971): 99-118.

26. Morton, *The Terrors of Ideological Politics*, p. 135.

27. W. H. Goetzmann, "Time's American Adventures: American Historians and Their Writing since 1776," *Social Science Quarterly* 57 (June, 1976): 31.

28. Hollingsworth, "Consensus and Continuity," pp. 40-50.

CHAPTER 15

1. Hofstadter, *The Progressive Historians*, pp. 457-58.

2. Ibid., pp. 448, 458.

3. Ibid., p. 459.

4. Ibid., p. 439.

5. J. M. Siracusa, *New Left Diplomatic Histories and Historians: The American Revisionists* (Port Washington, NY, 1973), pp. 26-27.

6. Ibid., pp. 48-49.

7. Ibid., pp. 37-38.

8. Quoted on dust jacket.

9. *Challenge* 18 (May-June, 1975): 71.

10. *American Scholar* 49 (Autumn, 1980): 546.

11. *New York Times Book Review*, March 2, 1980, p. 10.

12. *Library Journal* 105 (January 1, 1980): 101.

13. *Newsweek* 71 (April 22, 1968): 100.

14. M. Duberman, *The Uncompleted Past* (New York, 1969), pp. 356, 353, 79.

15. E. N. Saveth, "A Decade of American Historiography: The 1960's," in Cartwright and Watson, eds., *The Reinterpretation of American History and Culture*, pp. 20-21.

16. Ibid., pp. 21-23.

17. Ibid., pp. 25-26.

18. Ibid., pp. 27, 29-30.

CHAPTER 16

1. Hofstadter, *The Progressive Historians*, pp. 442, 463.

2. *Organization of American Historians Newsletter* 6 (January, 1979): 6.

3. Ibid., p. 4.

4. John Higham, *Writing American History: Essays on Modern Scholarship* (Bloomington, Ind., 1970), p. 173.

5. L. Veysey, "The 'New' Social History in the Context of American Historical

Writing," *Reviews in American History* 7 (March, 1979): 5.

6. E. E. Thorpe, *Black Historians: A Critique* (New York, 1971).

7. Ibid., pp. 40–41.

8. Ibid., p. 41.

9. Ibid., pp. 29–30.

10. V. Loggins, *The Negro Author: His Development in America* (New York, 1931), p. 282.

11. Thorpe, *Black Historians*, pp. 75, 86.

12. Ibid., p. 132.

13. Ibid., p. 119.

14. Ibid., pp. 130–31.

15. K. M. Stampp, *The Era of Reconstruction, 1865–1877* (New York, 1965), p. 215.

16. Donald V. Gawronski, *History: Meaning and Method*, 3d ed. (Glenview, Ill., 1975), pp. 93–94.

17. Ibid., p. 99.

18. C. N. Degler, "Women and the Family," in M. Kammen, ed., *The Past Before Us: Contemporary Historical Writing in the United States* (Ithaca, N.Y., 1980), pp. 308–26.

19. "Another New Selection from the History Book Club," History Book Club announcement (Stamford, Conn., May, 1982), p. 1.

20. Ibid.

21. J. Neuchterlein, "Radical Historians," *Commentary*, 70 (October, 1980): 59.

22. Veysey, "The 'New' Social History," pp. 4–5.

23. Neuchterlein, "Radical Historians," p. 59.

24. *American Historical Review* 70 (April, 1965): 900–901.

25. *New York Times Book Review*, December 16, 1973, pp. 5, 23.

26. Veysey, "The 'New' Social History," p. 7.

27. Grob and Billias, eds., *Interpretations of American History*, 1:21.

28. Ibid., pp. 19–20.

29. Ibid., pp. 20–21.

30. Ibid., p. 22.

31. *History Teacher* 14 (November, 1980): 144–45.

32. Veysey, "The 'New' Social History," p. 10.

33. B. Bailyn, "The Challenge of Modern Historiography," *American Historical Review* 87 (February, 1982): 1–24.

34. Higham, *Writing American History*, p. 106.

35. Timothy Paul Donovan, *Historical Thought in America: Postwar Patterns* (Norman, Okla., 1973), pp. 112–30.

Bibliography

BOOKS ON THE WRITING OF AMERICAN HISTORY

Adams, Herbert Baxter. *Historical Scholarship in the United States, 1876–1901.* Baltimore, Md.: Johns Hopkins University Press, 1971.

———. *Life and Writings of Jared Sparks.* 2 vols. Boston: Houghton Mifflin, 1893.

Adams, Ramon F. *Burs Under the Saddle: A Second Look at Books and Histories of the West.* Norman: University of Oklahoma Press, 1964.

———. *More Burs Under the Saddle: 200 Books and Histories of the West.* Norman: University of Oklahoma Press, 1979.

Anderson, Thornton. *Brooks Adams: Constructive Conservative.* Ithaca, N.Y.: Cornell University Press, 1951.

Anthony, Katherine Susan. *First Lady of the Revolution: The Life of Mercy Otis Warren.* Garden City, N.Y.: Doubleday, 1958.

Ausubel, Herman. *Historians and Their Craft: A Study of the Presidential Addresses to the American Historical Association, 1884–1945.* New York: Columbia University Press, 1952.

Aydelotte, William O. *Quantification in History.* London: Addison-Wesley, 1971.

Bailyn, Bernard. *The Ordeal of Thomas Hutchinson.* Cambridge, Mass: Harvard University Press, Belknap Press, 1974.

Bannon, John Francis. *Herbert Eugene Bolton: The Historian and the Man, 1870–1953.* Tucson: University of Arizona Press, 1978.

———, ed. *Bolton and the Spanish Borderlands.* Norman: University of Oklahoma Press, 1964.

Barnes, Harry E. *A History of Historical Writing.* 2d rev. ed. New York: Dover, 1962.

———. *Psychology and History.* New York: Century, 1925.

Barraclough, Geoffrey. *Main Trends in History.* New York: Holmes and Meier, 1979.

Barzun, Jacques. *Clio and the Doctors: Psycho-History, Quanto-History, and History.* Chicago: University of Chicago Press, 1974.

Bass, Herbert J., ed. *The State of American History.* Chicago: Quadrangle Books, 1970.

Bassett, John S. *The Middle Group of American Historians.* New York: Macmillan, 1917.

Baym, Max Isaac. *The French Education of Henry Adams.* New York: Columbia University Press, 1951.

Beale, Howard K., ed. *Charles A. Beard: An Appraisal.* Lexington: University of Kentucky Press, 1954.

Beard, Mary R. *The Making of Charles A. Beard: An Interpretation.* New York: Exposition Press, 1955.

Beatty, R. C. *William Byrd of Westover.* Boston: Houghton Mifflin, 1932.

Becker, Carl L. *Detachment and the Writing of History.* Ithaca, N.Y.: Cornell University Press, 1958.

———. *Everyman His Own Historian: Essays on History and Politics.* New York: Appleton-Century-Crofts, 1972.

Bellot, H. Hale. *American History and American Historians.* Norman: University of Oklahoma Press, 1952.

Bennett, James D. *Frederick Jackson Turner.* New York: Twayne, 1975.

Benson, Lee. *Toward the Scientific Study of History: Selected Essays.* New York: J. B. Lippincott, 1972.

———. *Turner and Beard: American Historical Writing Reconsidered.* Glencoe, Ill.: Free Press, 1960.

Beringause, Arthur P. *Brooks Adams: A Biography.* New York: Alfred A. Knopf, 1955.

Beringer, Richard E. *Historical Analysis: Contemporary Approaches to Clio's Craft.* New York: John Wiley and Sons, 1978.

Berkhofer, Robert F. *A Behavioral Approach to Historical Analysis.* Glencoe, Ill.: Free Press, 1968.

Berman, Milton. *John Fiske: The Evolution of a Popularizer.* Cambridge, Mass.: Harvard University Press, 1961.

Bernstein, Barton J., ed. *Towards a New Past: Dissenting Essays in American History.* New York: Vintage, 1968.

Beveridge, A. J. *The Life of John Marshall.* 4 vols. New York: Houghton Mifflin, 1916–19.

Billias, George Athan, and Gerald N. Grob, eds. *American History: Retrospect and Prospect.* New York: Free Press, 1971.

Billington, Ray Allen. *The American Frontier.* 2d ed. Washington, D.C.: American Historical Association, 1965.

———. *Frederick Jackson Turner: Historian, Scholar, Teacher.* New York: Oxford University Press, 1973.

———. *The Genesis of the Frontier Thesis: A Study in Historical Creativity.* San Marino, Calif.: Huntington Library, 1971.

———, ed. *Frontier and Section: Selected Essays of Frederick Jackson Turner.* Englewood Cliffs, N.J.: Prentice-Hall, 1961.

———, ed. *The Frontier Thesis: Valid Interpretation of American History?* New York: Holt, Rinehart and Winston, 1966.

———, ed. *The Reinterpretation of Early American History: Essays in Honor of John Edwin Pomfret.* San Marino, Calif.: Huntington Library, 1966.

Borning, Bernard C. *The Political and Social Thought of Charles A. Beard.* Seattle: University of Washington Press, 1962.

Brown, Alice. *Mercy Warren.* New York: Scribner's, 1903.

Brugger, Robert J., ed. *Our Selves/Our Past: Psychological Approaches to American History.* Baltimore, Md.: Johns Hopkins University Press, 1981.

Burgess, John W. *Reminiscences of an American Scholar.* New York: Columbia University Press, 1934.

Burnette, O. Lawrence, Jr. *Wisconsin Witness to Frederick Jackson Turner.* Madison: State Historical Society of Wisconsin, 1961.

Butterfield, Herbert. *George III and the Historians.* New York: Macmillan, 1959.

———. *The Whig Interpretation of History.* New York: W. W. Norton, 1965.

Callcott, George H. *History in the United States, 1800–1860.* Baltimore, Md.: Johns Hopkins University Press, 1969.

Canary, Robert H. *George Bancroft.* New York: Twayne, 1974.

Carter, Harvey L. *Far Western Frontiers.* Washington, D.C.: American Historical Association, 1972.

Cartwright, William H., and Richard L. Watson, Jr., eds. *Interpreting and Teaching American History.* Washington, D.C.: National Council for the Social Studies, 1961.

———, and ———, eds. *The Reinterpretation of American History and Culture.* Washington, D.C.: National Council for the Social Studies, 1973.

Cater, Harold Dean. *Henry Adams and His Friends.* Boston: Houghton Mifflin, 1947.

Caughey, J. W. *Hubert Howe Bancroft: Historian of the West.* Berkeley: University of California Press, 1946.

Cave, Alfred A. *Jacksonian Democracy and the Historians.* Gainesville: University of Florida Press, 1964.

Cockroft, Grace Amelia. *The Public Life of George Chalmers.* New York: Columbia University Press, 1939.

Cohen, Lester H. *The Revolutionary Historians: Contemporary Narratives of the American Revolution.* Ithaca, N.Y.: Cornell University Press, 1980.

Cohen, Warren I. *The American Revisionists.* Chicago: University of Chicago Press, 1966.

Colbourn, H. Trevor. *The Lamp of Experience: Whig History and the Intellectual Origins of the American Revolution.* Chapel Hill: University of North Carolina Press, 1965.

Collingwood, R. G. *The Idea of History.* London: Oxford University Press, 1946.

Commager, Henry Steele. *The Search for a Usable Past and Other Essays in Historiography.* New York: Alfred A. Knopf, 1967.

Conkin, Paul K., and Roland N. Stromberg. *The Heritage and Challenge of History.* New York: Dodd, Mead, 1971.

Cooke, Jacob E. *Frederic Bancroft: Historian.* Norman: University of Oklahoma Press, 1957.

Cruden, Robert. *James Ford Rhodes: The Man, the Historian, and His Work.* Cleveland, Ohio: Press of Western Reserve University, 1961.

Cunliffe, Marcus, and Robin W. Winks, eds. *Pastmasters: Some Essays on American Historians* New York: Harper and Row, 1969.

Dallek, Robert. *William E. Dodd: Democrat and Diplomat.* New York: Oxford University Press, 1968.

Davis, Allen F., and Harold D. Woodman, eds. *Conflict and Consensus in Early American History.* 5th ed. Lexington, Mass.: D. C. Heath, 1980.

———— and ————, eds. *Conflict and Consensus in Modern American History.* 5th ed. Lexington, Mass.: D. C. Heath, 1980.

Donovan, Timothy Paul. *Henry Adams and Brooks Adams: The Education of Two American Historians.* Norman: University of Oklahoma Press, 1961.

————. *Historical Thought in America: Postwar Patterns.* Norman: University of Oklahoma Press, 1973.

Doughty, Howard. *Francis Parkman.* New York: Macmillan, 1962.

Duberman, Martin. *The Uncompleted Past.* New York: Random House, 1969.

Dunning, William A. *Truth in History and Other Essays.* New York: Columbia University Press, 1937.

Dusinberre, William. *Henry Adams: The Myth of Failure.* Charlottesville: University Press of Virginia, 1980.

Eisenstadt, A. S. *Charles McLean Andrews: A Study in American Historical Writing.* New York: Columbia University Press, 1965.

Elkins, Stanley, and Eric McKitrick, eds. *The Hofstadter Aegis: A Memorial.* New York: Alfred A. Knopf, 1974.

Emerson, Donald E. *Richard Hildreth.* Baltimore, Md.: Johns Hopkins University Press, 1946.

Farnham, Charles Haight. *A Life of Francis Parkman.* Boston: Little, Brown, 1900.

Fehrenbacher, Don E., ed. *History and American Society: Essays of David M. Potter.* London: Oxford University Press, 1973.

Feis, Herbert, et al. *The Historian and the Diplomat: The Role of History and Historians in American Foreign Policy.* Edited by Francis L. Loewenheim. New York: Harper and Row, 1967.

Fischer, David Hackett. *Historians' Fallacies: Toward a Logic of Historical Thought.* New York: Harper and Row, 1970.

Fitzgerald, Frances. *America Revised.* Boston: Little, Brown, 1979.

Fitzsimons, Matthew A., Alfred G. Pundt, and Charles G. Nowell, eds. *The Development of Historiography.* Harrisburg, Pa.: Stackpole, 1955.

Flower, Milton E. *James Parton: The Father of Modern Biography.* Durham, N.C.: Duke University Press, 1951.

Ford, Worthington C., ed. *Letters of Henry Adams.* 2 vols. Boston: Houghton Mifflin, 1930.

Fox, Dixon Ryan. *Herbert Levi Osgood.* New York: Columbia University Press, 1924.

Friedlander, Saul. *History and Psychoanalysis: An Inquiry into the Possibilities and Limits of Psychohistory.* New York: Holmes and Meier, 1978.

Furman, Necah Stewart. *Walter Prescott Webb: His Life and Impact.* Albuquerque: University of New Mexico Press, 1976.

Gale, Robert L. *Francis Parkman.* New York: Twayne, 1973.

Gardiner, C. Harvey. *William Hickling Prescott: A Biography.* Austin: University of Texas Press, 1969.

————, ed. *The Papers of William Hickling Prescott.* Urbana: University of Illinois Press, 1964.

Garraty, John A. *Interpreting American History: Conversations with Historians.* 2 vols. New York: Macmillan, 1970.

Gatell, Frank Otto. *John Gorham Palfrey and the New England Conscience.* Cambridge, Mass.: Harvard University Press, 1963.

———, and Allen Weinstein, eds. *American Themes: Essays in Historiography.* New York: Oxford University Press, 1968.

Gawronski, Donald V. *History: Meaning and Method.* Glenville, Ill.: Scott, Foresman, 1975.

Gay, Peter. *A Loss of Mastery: Puritan Historians in Colonial America.* Berkeley: University of California Press, 1966.

———, and Victor G. Wexler, eds. *Historians at Work.* 4 vols. New York: Harper and Row, 1972-75.

Gilbert, Felix, and Stephen R. Graubard, eds. *Historical Studies Today.* New York: W. W. Norton, 1972.

Goldman, Eric F. *John Bach McMaster, American Historian.* Philadelphia: University of Pennsylvania Press, 1943.

———, ed. *Historiography and Urbanization.* Baltimore, Md.: Johns Hopkins University Press, 1941.

Gooch, G. P. *History and Historians in the Nineteenth Century.* Boston: Beacon Press, 1959.

Gottschalk, Louis, ed. *Generalization in the Writing of History: A Report of the Committee on Historical Analysis of the Social Science Research Council.* Chicago: University of Chicago Press, 1963.

Grob, Gerald N., and George Athan Billias, eds. *Interpretations of American History: Patterns and Perspectives.* 4th ed. 2 vols. New York: Free Press, 1982.

Guberman, J. *The Life of John Lothrop Motley.* The Hague: Nijhoff, 1973.

Guy, Francis Shaw. *Edmund Bailey O'Callaghan: A Study in American Historiography.* Washington, D.C.: Catholic University of America Press, 1934.

Haines, Gerald K., and J. Samuel Walker, eds. *American Foreign Relations: A Historiographical Review.* Westport, Conn.: Greenwood Press, 1981.

Handlin, Oscar. *Truth in History.* Cambridge: Belknap Press of Harvard University Press, 1979.

———, Arthur M. Schlesinger, Samuel Eliot Morison, Frederick Merk, Arthur M. Schlesinger, Jr., and Paul Herman Buck. *Harvard Guide to American History.* New York: Atheneum, 1967.

Harbert, Earl N. *The Force So Much Closer Home: Henry Adams and the Adams Family.* New York: New York University Press, 1977.

Herbst, Jurgen. *The German Historical School in American Scholarship: A Study in the Transfer of Culture.* Ithaca, N.Y.: Cornell University Press, 1965.

Herskowitz, Herbert, and Bernard Marlin. *A Guide to Reading in American History: The Unit Approach.* New York: New American Library, 1966.

Hexter, J. H. *Doing History.* Bloomington: Indiana University Press, 1971.

Higham, John. *History: Professional Scholarship in America.* New York: Harper and Row, 1965.

———, *Writing American History: Essays on Modern Scholarship.* Bloomington: Indiana University Press, 1970.

———, ed. *The Reconstruction of American History.* New York: Humanities Press, 1962.

————, and Paul Conkin, eds. *New Directions in American Intellectual History.* Baltimore, Md.: Johns Hopkins University Press, 1979.

————, Leonard Krieger, and Felix Gilbert. *History.* Englewood Cliffs, N.J.: Prentice-Hall, 1965.

Historical Scholarship in America: Needs and Opportunities. New York: American Historical Association, 1932.

Hofstadter, Richard. *The Progressive Historians: Turner, Beard, Parrington.* New York: Alfred A. Knopf, 1968.

Holt, W. Stull. *Historical Scholarship in the United States, 1876–1901, as Revealed in the Correspondence of Herbert B. Adams.* Baltimore, Md.: Johns Hopkins University Press, 1938.

————. *Historical Scholarship in the United States and Other Essays.* Edited by Lawrence Gelfand and Robert A. Skotheim. Seattle: University of Washington Press, 1967.

Hosmer, James K. *The Life of Thomas Hutchinson.* Boston: Houghton Mifflin, 1896.

Howe, M. A. DeWolfe. *James Ford Rhodes, American Historian.* New York: Appleton, 1920.

————. *Life and Letters of George Bancroft.* 2 vols. New York: Scribner's, 1908.

Hutchinson, William T., ed. *The Marcus W. Jernegan Essays in American Historiography.* Chicago: University of Chicago Press, 1937.

Iggers, George G., and Harold T. Parker, eds. *International Handbook of Historical Studies: Contemporary Research and Theory.* Westport, Conn. Greenwood Press, 1979.

Jacobs, Wilbur R. *The Historical World of Frederick Jackson Turner.* New Haven, Conn.: Yale University Press, 1968.

————, ed. *Frederick Jackson Turner's Legacy.* San Marino, Calif.: Huntington Library, 1965.

————, ed. *Letters of Francis Parkman.* 2 vols. Norman: University of Oklahoma Press, 1960.

————, John W. Caughey, and Joe B. Frantz. *Turner, Bolton, and Webb: Three Historians of the American Frontier.* Seattle: University of Washington Press, 1965.

Jameson, J. Franklin. *The History of Historical Writing in America.* Boston: Houghton Mifflin, 1891.

Jones, Howard. *The Life of Moses Coit Tyler.* Ann Arbor: University of Michigan Press, 1933.

Jordy, William H. *Henry Adams: Scientific Historian.* New Haven, Conn.: Yale University Press, 1952.

Joyce, Davis D. *Edward Channing and the Great Work.* The Hague: Nijhoff, 1974.

————. *History and Historians: Some Essays.* Washington, D. C.: University Press of America, 1983.

Karlman, Roland. *Evidencing Historical Classifications: In British and American Historiography, 1930–1970.* Atlantic Highlands, N.J.: Humanities Press, 1976.

Keys, Alice Mapelsden. *Cadwallader Colden: A Representative Eighteenth Century Official.* New York: Macmillan, 1906.

Landes, David S., and Charles Tilly, eds. *History as Social Science.* Englewood Cliffs, N.J.: Prentice-Hall, 1971.

Laquer, Walter, and George L. Mosse, eds. *The New History: Trends in Historical Research and Writing Since World War II.* New York: Harper and Row, 1966.

Leder, Lawrence H., ed. *The Colonial Legacy.* 4 vols. New York: Harper and Row, 1971-73.

Levenson, J. C. *The Mind and Art of Henry Adams.* Boston: Houghton Mifflin, 1957.

Levin, David. *History as Romantic Art: Bancroft, Prescott, Motley, and Parkman.* Stanford, Calif.: Stanford University Press, 1959.

Lichtman, Allan J., and Valerie French. *Historians and the Living Past.* Arlington Heights, Ill.: AHM, 1978.

Lifton, Robert Jay, ed. *Explorations in Psychohistory.* New York: Simon and Schuster, 1974.

Link, Arthur S., and Rembert W. Patrick, eds. *Writing Southern History: Essays in Historiography in Honor of Fletcher M. Green.* Baton Rouge: Louisiana State University Press, 1965.

Lipset, Seymour M., and Richard Hofstadter, eds. *Sociology and History.* New York: Basic Books, 1968.

Loewenberg, Bert James. *American History in American Thought: Christopher Columbus to Henry Adams.* New York: Simon and Schuster, 1972.

Lord, Clifford L., ed. *Keepers of the Past.* Chapel Hill: University of North Carolina Press, 1965.

Lottinville, Savoie. *The Rhetoric of History.* Norman: University of Oklahoma Press, 1976.

McLoughlin, William G. *Isaac Backus and the American Pietistic Tradition.* Boston: Little, Brown, 1967.

Maddox, Robert James, *The New Left and the Origins of the Cold War.* Princeton, N.J.: Princeton University Press, 1973.

Malin, J. C. *Essays on Historiography.* Lawrence, Kans.: The Author, 1953.

Marcou, Jane B. *Life of Jeremy Belknap.* New York: Harper and Brothers, 1847.

Middlekauff, Robert. *The Mathers: Three Generations of Puritan Intellectuals, 1596-1728.* New York: Oxford University Press, 1971.

Morison, Samuel Eliot. *By Land and By Sea: Essays and Addresses.* New York: Alfred A. Knopf, 1953.

Morton, Marian J. *The Terrors of Ideological Politics: Liberal Historians in a Conservative Mood.* Cleveland, Ohio: Press of Case Western Reserve University, 1972.

Murdock, Kenneth Ballard. *Increase Mather, the Foremost American Puritan.* Cambridge, Mass.: Harvard University Press, 1925.

Murray, James G. *Henry Adams.* New York: Twayne, 1974.

Nevins, Allan. *Allan Nevins on History.* New York: Scribner's, 1975.

———. *The Gateway to History.* Rev. ed. New York: Doubleday, 1962.

Noble, David W. *Historians Against History: The Frontier Thesis and the National Covenant in American Historical Writing Since 1830.* Minneapolis: University of Minnesota Press, 1965.

Norton, Aloysius A. *Theodore Roosevelt.* New York: Twayne, 1980.

Nye, Russell B. *George Bancroft.* New York: Twayne, 1964.

———. *George Bancroft: Brahmin Rebel.* New York: Alfred A. Knopf, 1944.

Odum, Howard W., ed. *American Masters of Social Science; An Approach to the Study of the Social Sciences Through a Neglected Field of Biography.* New York: Henry Holt, 1927.

Parks, George B. *Richard Hakluyt and the English Voyages.* New York: American Geographical Society, 1928.

Pease, Otis A. *Parkman's History: The Historian as a Literary Artist.* New Haven, Conn.: Yale University Press, 1953.

Perkins, Dexter, and John Snell. *The Education of Historians in the United States.* New York: McGraw-Hill, 1961.

Perry, Thomas Sargeant. *John Fiske.* Boston: Small, Maynard, 1906.

Philp, Kenneth R., and Elliott West, eds. *Essays on Walter Prescott Webb.* Austin: University of Texas Press, 1976.

Potter, David Morris. *The Lincoln Theme and American National Historiography.* Oxford: Clarendon Press, 1948.

Pressly, Thomas J. *Americans Interpret Their Civil War.* Princeton, N.J.: Princeton University Press, 1954.

Prisco, Salvatore, III. *An Introduction to Psychohistory: Theories and Case Studies.* Lanham, Md.: University Press of America, 1980.

Randel, W. P. *Edward Eggleston.* New York: King's Crown Press, 1946.

Rapson, Richard L., ed. *Major Interpretations of the American Past.* New York: Appleton-Century-Crofts, 1971.

Reinitz, Richard. *Irony and Consciousness: American Historiography and Reinhold Niebuhr's Vision.* Lewisburg, Pa.: Bucknell University Press, 1980.

Robinson, Donald W., ed. *As Others See Us: International Views of American History.* New York: Houghton Mifflin, 1969.

Rockwood, Raymond O., ed. *Carl Becker's Heavenly City Revisited.* Ithaca, N.Y.: Cornell University Press, 1958.

Rowney, Don K., and James Q. Graham, eds. *Quantitative History: Selected Readings.* Homewood, Ill.: Dorsey Press, 1968.

Rundell, Walter, Jr. *In Pursuit of American History: Research and Training in the United States.* Norman: University of Oklahoma Press, 1970.

———. *Walter Prescott Webb.* Austin, Texas: Steck-Vaughn, 1971.

Samuels, Ernest. *Henry Adams: The Major Phase.* Cambridge, Mass.: Harvard University Press, 1964.

———. *Henry Adams: The Middle Years.* Cambridge, Mass.: Harvard University Press, 1958.

———. *The Young Henry Adams.* Cambridge, Mass.: Harvard University Press, 1948.

Sanders, Jennings. *Historical Interpretations and American Historianship.* Yellow Springs, Ohio: Antioch Press, 1966.

Saveth, Edward N. *American Historians and European Immigrants, 1875–1925.* New York: Columbia University Press, 1948.

———, ed. *American History and the Social Sciences.* New York: Free Press, 1965.

Schlesinger, Arthur M. *In Retrospect: The History of a Historian.* New York: Harcourt, Brace and World, 1963.

Schramm, Wilbur Lang. *Francis Parkman, 1823–1893.* New York: American Books, 1938.

Sedgwick, Henry Dwight. *Francis Parkman.* Boston: Houghton Mifflin, 1904.

Shafer, Boyd, et al. *Historical Study in the West.* New York: Appleton-Century-Crofts, 1968.

Shaffer, Arthur H. *The Politics of History: Writing the History of the American Revolution, 1783–1815.* Chicago: Precedent, 1975.

Sheehan, Donald H., and Harold C. Syrett, eds. *Essays in American Historiography: Papers Presented in Honor of Allan Nevins.* New York: Columbia University Press, 1960.

Shi, David E. *Matthew Josephson, Bourgeois Bohemian.* New Haven, Conn.: Yale University Press, 1981.

Shorter, Edward. *The Historian and the Computer: A Practical Guide.* Englewood Cliffs, N.J.: Prentice-Hall, 1971.

Shotwell, James Thomson. *The History of History.* New York: Columbia University Press, 1939.

Siracusa, Joseph M. *New Left Diplomatic Histories and Historians: The American Revisionists.* Port Washington, N.Y.: Kennikat Press, 1973.

Skotheim, Robert Allen. *American Intellectual Histories and Historians.* Princeton, N.J.: Princeton University Press, 1966.

———, ed. *The Historian and the Climate of Opinion.* London: Addison-Wesley, 1969.

Smith, Bradford. *Bradford of Plymouth.* Philadelphia: Lippincott, 1951.

Smith, C. W. *Carl Becker: On History and the Climate of Opinion.* Ithaca, N.Y.: Cornell University Press, 1956.

Smith, William Raymond. *History as Argument: Three Patriot Historians of the American Revolution.* The Hague: Mouton, 1966.

Snyder, Phil L., ed. *Detachment and the Writing of History: Essays and Letters of Carl L. Becker.* Ithaca, N.Y.: Cornell University Press, 1958.

Sprague, William Buell. *The Life of Jedidiah Morse.* New York: A. D. F. Randolph, 1874.

Stannard, David E. *Shrinking History: On Freud and the Failure of Psychohistory.* New York: Oxford University Press, 1980.

Stave, Bruce M. *The Making of Urban History: Historiography Through Oral History.* Beverly Hills, Calif.: Sage, 1977.

Stephens, Lester D., ed. *Historiography: A Bibliography.* Metuchen, N.J.: Scarecrow Press, 1975.

Stephenson, Wendell H. *Southern History in the Making: Pioneer Historians of the South.* Baton Rouge: Louisiana State University Press, 1964.

Stern, Fritz, ed. *Varieties of History.* New York: Meridian, 1965.

Sternsher, Bernard. *Consensus, Conflict, and American History.* Bloomington: Indiana University Press, 1975.

Stevenson, Elizabeth. *Henry Adams.* New York: Macmillan, 1955.

Strout, Cushing. *The Pragmatic Revolt in American History: Carl Becker and*

Charles Beard. New Haven, Conn.: Yale University Press, 1958.

Swierenga, Robert P., ed. *Quantification in American History: Theory and Research.* New York: Atheneum, 1970.

Taylor, George Rogers, ed. *The Turner Thesis: Concerning the Role of the Frontier in American History.* 3d ed. Lexington, Mass.: D. C. Heath, 1972.

Thompson, J. W. *A History of Historical Writing.* 2 vols. New York: Macmillan, 1942.

Thorpe, Earl E. *Black Historians.* New York: William Morrow, 1971.

Unger, Irwin, ed. *Beyond Liberalism: The New Left Views American History.* Toronto: Xerox College Publishing, 1971.

Van Tassel, David D. *Recording America's Past: An Interpretation of the Development of Historical Studies in America, 1607–1884.* Chicago: University of Chicago Press, 1960.

Vaughan, Alden T. *American Genesis: Captain John Smith and the Founding of Virginia.* Boston: Little, Brown, 1975.

Vitzthum, Richard C. *The American Compromise: Theme and Method in the Histories of Bancroft, Parkman, and Adams.* Norman: University of Oklahoma Press, 1974.

Wade, Mason. *Francis Parkman, Heroic Historian.* New York: Viking, 1942.

Wilkins, Burleigh Taylor. *Carl Becker: A Biographical Study in American Intellectual History.* Cambridge, Mass.: MIT Press, 1961.

Williams, William Appleman. *History as a Way of Learning.* New York: New Viewpoints, 1973.

Wiltz, John E. *Books in American History: A Basic List for High Schools.* Bloomington: Indiana University Press, 1964.

Winks, Robin W., ed. *The Historian as Detective.* New York: Harper and Row, 1968.

Wise, Gene. *American Historical Explanations: A Strategy for Grounded Inquiry.* 2d ed., rev. Minneapolis: University of Minnesota Press, 1980.

Wish, Harvey. *The American Historian: A Social-Intellectual History of the Writing of the American Past.* New York: Oxford University Press, 1960.

———, ed. *American Historians: A Selection.* New York: Oxford University Press, 1962.

Wolcott, Roger, ed. *The Correspondence of William Hickling Prescott, 1833–1847.* Boston: Houghton Mifflin, 1925.

Woodward, C. Vann, ed. *A Comparative Approach to American History.* New York: Basic Books, 1968.

Wroth, Lawrence Counsalman. *Parson Weems: A Biographical and Critical Study.* Baltimore, Md.: Eichelberger, 1911.

Zinn, Howard. *The Politics of History.* Boston: Beacon Press, 1970.

Index

Note: Italicized page numbers refer to principal discussions of individuals or topics.